ENGINE CODE MANAUL
TOTAL SERVICE SERIES

Senior Vice President	Ronald A. Hoxter
Publisher & Editor-In-Chief	Kerry A. Freeman, S.A.E.
Executive Editors	Dean F. Morgantini, S.A.E., W. Calvin Settle, Jr., S.A.E.
Managing Editor	Nick D'Andrea
Special Products Manager	Kenneth Grabowski, A.S.E., S.A.E.
Senior Editors	Jacques Gordon, Michael L. Grady, Debra McCall, Kevin M. G. Maher, Richard J. Rivele, S.A.E., Richard T. Smith, Jim Taylor, Ron Webb
Project Managers	Martin J. Gunther, Will Kessler, A.S.E., Richard Schwartz, Paul Shanahan
Production Manager	Andrea Steiger
Product Systems Manager	Robert Maxey
Director of Manufacturing	Mike D'Imperio

CHILTON BOOK COMPANY

Manufactured in USA

© 1995 Chilton Book Company
Chilton Way, Radnor, PA 19089
ISBN 0-8019-8851-9
Library of Congress Catalog Card No. 95-83511
2345678901 6543210987

SAFETY NOTICE

Proper service and repair procedures are vital to the safe, reliable operation of all motor vehicles, as well as the personal safety of those performing repairs. This manual outlines procedures for servicing and repairing vehicles using safe, effective methods. The procedures contain many NOTES, CAUTIONS, and WARNINGS which should be followed along with standard procedures to eliminate the possibility of personal injury or improper service which could damage the vehicle or compromise its safety.

It is important to note that the repair procedures and techniques, tools and parts for servicing motor vehicles, as well as the skill and experience of the individual performing the work vary widely. It is not possible to anticipate all of the conceivable ways or conditions under which vehicles may be serviced, or to provide cautions as to all of the possible hazards that may result. Standard and accepted safety precautions and equipment should be used when handling toxic or flammable fluids, and safety goggles or other protection should be used during cutting, grinding, chiseling, prying, or any other process that can cause material removal or projectiles.

Some procedures require the use of tools specially designed for a specific purpose. Before substituting another tool or procedure, you must be completely satisfied that neither your personal safety, nor the performance of the vehicle will be endangered.

Although information in this manual is based on industry sources and is complete as possible at the time of publication, the possibility exists that some car manufacturers made later changes which could not be included here. While striving for total accuracy, Chilton Book Company cannot assume responsibility for any errors, changes or omissions that may occur in the compilation of this data.

PART NUMBERS

Part numbers listed in this reference are not recommendation by Chilton for any product by brand name. They are references that can be used with interchange manuals and aftermarket supplier catalogs to locate each brand supplier's discrete part number.

SPECIAL TOOLS

Special tools are recommended by the vehicle manufacturer to perform their specific job. Use has been kept to a minimum, but where absolutely necessary, they are referred to in the text by the part number of the tool manufacturer. These tools can be purchased, under the appropriate part number, from your local dealer or regional distributor, or an equivalent tool can be purchased locally from a tool supplier or parts outlet. Before substituting any tool for the one recommended, read the SAFETY NOTICE at the top of this page.

ACKNOWLEDGMENTS

Portions of materials contained herein have been reprinted with the permission of the General Motors Corporation, Service Technology Group.

1 How to Use This Manual

2 Basic Maintenance and Troubleshooting

3 Automotive Tools and Equipment

4 Air Pollution and Automotive Emissions

5 Basic Fuel and Emission Operation

6 Domestic Vehicle Self-Diagnostic Systems

7 Import Vehicle Self-Diagnostic Systems

8 Component Service Procedures

9 Warranty Information

10 Glossary

INTRODUCTION

Servicing later-model vehicles, which are equipped with many electronic and computer controlled devices, may seem intimidating to the do-it-yourselfer, but this shouldn't be the case.

Vehicles have evolved greatly since the middle 1970's, when breakerless ignition systems were first introduced. All sorts of control devices have been added to vehicles for the main purpose of lowering emissions. This is accomplished principally by maintaining precise control of the air/fuel mixture that is supplied to the engine.

Many electronic and mechanical components are involved in electronic fuel mixture control. These components include, computer(s), sensors, and actuators. These electronic engine control devices were introduced to help reduce exhaust emissions. The benefit we have received from today's technology is that engines provide more horsepower, run smoother and produce less exhaust emissions, all while using less fuel than the vehicles produced in earlier years. Some control systems even have the ability to automatically adjust for wear and driver habits.

Additionally, the self-diagnostic features built into the system can aid you in your repair work by providing Diagnostic Trouble Codes (DTCs). The Diagnostic Trouble Codes will help you to locate faulty component(s) or system(s).

Computer controlled vehicles can be serviced by the do-it-yourselfer. This manual will show you how easily it can be done by following logical step by step procedures. If vehicle-specific tools, manuals or information is needed, it will be explained in the procedure provided. Useful information on tools, safety procedures, and preventive maintenance is included in this manual.

The following descriptions of each chapter will help familiarize you with the contents of this book.

BASIC MAINTENANCE AND TROUBLESHOOTING

Chapter Two will provide you with information on general vehicle maintenance procedures and troubleshooting. There is also information about basic electricity and testing. We will explain how you can perform may of the tasks needed to keep your car in top running condition, such as oil changes, cooling system maintenance, ignition system service and other preventive maintenance.

Performing these maintenance procedures will also contribute to the proper operation of the electronic engine control system. As an example, a low coolant condition, or dirty coolant could cause a code related to the coolant temperature sensor to be set. If the coolant level is low, the sensor may read an air temperature since the coolant is not contacting the sensor. Dirty coolant may result in an abnormal vehicle operating temperature. The out-of-range readings, resulting trouble code(s), and time spent looking for the cause of the problem could all be avoided by proper vehicle maintenance. Other items, such as loose drive belts, dirty oil, or worn spark plugs can have a large effect on the computer's decisions regarding idle quality and overall engine performance.

If the task is difficult or requires any specific tools or repair manuals, it will be explained in the text. Useful information about spark plug heat ranges, oil viscosity and other automotive parts and products is included. Proper servicing and safety are covered in detail.

The information on basic electricity and testing will help you understand and test circuits and electrical components on your vehicle. The following subjects are covered in great detail:

- Basic Tune-up Procedures
- Charging System Service
- Engine Won't Start
- Fluids and Lubricants
- Fundamentals of Electricity
- Safe Vehicle Servicing Tips
- Serial Number Identification
- Starting System Service

AUTOMOTIVE TOOLS AND EQUIPMENT

Chapter Three focuses on automotive tools and equipment, from the basics to special diagnostic tools. The importance of tool quality is discussed, along with guidelines for planning your tool purchases.

Many useful illustrations are provided, as well as information pertaining to the function of many tools and the proper use of each.

The specific topics are:
- Basic Automotive Tools
- Electronic Testing Equipment
- Special Diagnostic Tools
- What Tools Do I Need?

AIR POLLUTION AND AUTOMOTIVE EMISSIONS

Chapter Four examines the different types of pollution that exist, and what the pollutants are. The effects of pollution and exhaust emissions are also discussed.

Automotive pollution and the composition of exhaust gases are specifically explained. The pollutants are described, as well as their reaction with other components in the exhaust gas, and their reaction with other environmental gases and sunlight. Crankcase and evaporative emissions are also described.

Some vehicles have indicator lamps which illuminate when emission system service intervals are reached. Typically, the lamp will come on at each 30,000 or 60,000 mile interval, indicating the need for an oxygen sensor replacement, or

Exhaust Gas Recirculation (EGR) system service. Oil change reminder lamps are also found on some vehicles.

These indicators need to be reset manually after the needed service is performed, so we have included a useful instruction guide for the reset procedures.

The following topics are addressed:
- Air Pollution
- Emission Controls
- Emission Testing
- Exhaust Emissions
- Emission Reminder Light Reset Procedures

BASIC OPERATION OF FUEL AND EMISSION COMPONENTS

Chapter Five will provide you with an overview of how computer-controlled fuel and emission systems and their individual components operate. This information will also help you understand how the different systems interact with each other, and can be very useful for performing effective troubleshooting.

Throttle Body Injection (TBI) and Multi-port Fuel Injection (MFI) system operation are described. The Feedback Carburetor (FBC) system used on earlier vehicles is also explained. An overview of each system is given, then the

individual components described in detail. Keep in mind that not every component will be found on every vehicle. The location of the individual components is provided. There are many illustrations to aid you in identifying these various components.

The main sections of the chapter are:
- Introduction
- Fuel Injection Systems
- Feedback Carburetor Systems

VEHICLE SELF-DIAGNOSTICS

Chapter Six and Chapter Seven contain Diagnostic Trouble Codes (DTCs) for domestic and imported vehicles. Automotive manufacturers have developed on-board computers to control engines, transmissions and many other components. These on-board computers, with dozens of sensors and actuators, have become almost impossible to test without the help of electronic test equipment.

One of these electronic test devices has become the on-board computer itself. The Powertrain Control Modules (PCM), sometimes called the Electronic Control Module (ECM), used on today's vehicles has a built in self testing system. This self test ability is called self-diagnosis. The self-diagnosis system will test many or all of the sensors and controlled devices for proper function. When a malfunction is detected, this system will store a code in memory that's related to that specific circuit. The computer can later be accessed to obtain fault codes recorded in memory using the procedures for Reading Codes. This helps narrow down what area to begin testing.

Keep in mind that fault codes do indicate the presence of a failure, but often don't identify the failed component directly. For example, you might retrieve a trouble code for the coolant temperature sensor. Before you get out your test equipment, check the coolant level in the vehicle, the condition of the radiator cap, and the thermostat. Any of these items could cause a code to be set; remember that the sensor only reports on the conditions it 'sees,' it is your job to determine where the fault *truly* lies. The benefits of performing checks like these are that time and money are often saved.

The procedures to access and clear codes are outlined. If a special tool is needed to access or clear codes, it will be

stated in the text. At the end of each manufacturer's section, the Diagnostic Trouble Codes (DTC)s are listed.

The domestic manufacturers covered are:
- Chrysler Corporation
- Ford Motor Company
- General Motors Corporation

The import manufacturers covered are:
- Acura
- Audi
- Daihatsu
- Honda
- Hyundai
- Infiniti
- Isuzu
- Jaguar
- Lexus
- Mazda
- Mitsubishi
- Nissan
- Peugeot
- Porsche
- Saab
- Subaru
- Suzuki
- Toyota
- Volkswagen
- Volvo
- Yugo

COMPONENT SERVICE

Chapter Eight contains information concerning the testing, replacement, and adjustment of the fuel and emission related components. Every component is listed the index alphabetically for easy reference. Once you have narrowed down the cause of the vehicle's problem, this chapter will enable you to perform the needed tests. Appropriate notes, warnings, and cautions are provided in the text. Ignition, fuel, and emission components are included.

Clearly written procedures will guide you through removal and installation, and adjustment instructions are given, if they are applicable.

A full list of the covered components may be found in the Chapter Eight Table of Contents. The following list includes some of the major components covered in the chapter:
- Coolant Temperature Sensor
- Crankshaft Sensor
- EGR Solenoid Valve
- EGR Valve
- Intake Air Temperature (IAT) Sensor
- Knock Sensor
- Manifold Absolute Pressure (MAP) Sensor
- Oxygen Sensor
- Positive Crankcase Ventilation (PCV) Valve
- Throttle Position (TP) Sensor
- Throttle Positioner Diaphragm
- Vacuum Switching Valve

WARRANTY INFORMATION

Chapter Nine provides information about vehicle warranties. The different types of coverage are described, along with information that can help you to maintain your warranty coverage. Emission system coverage is explained. Suggestions are given which may help you to resolve a warranty dispute, should one arise. The subject of replacing lost warranty information is addressed.

Here is the complete list of covered topics:
- Anti-Corrosion Coverage
- Basic Coverage
- Emission System Coverage
- General Information
- Obtaining Information
- Powertrain Coverage
- Safety Restraint Coverage
- Warranty Disputes

GLOSSARY

Chapter Ten is a glossary of automotive words, terminology, and abbreviations. In keeping with the subject material of this manual, many of the definitions pertain to emission, fuel, and ignition systems. A large portion of the definitions are universal, but we have also included many manufacturer-specific terms which will be useful to the do-it-yourselfer. Some basic electrical definitions are included.

Generally, you will find any definitions you need within the text when a word, term, or abbreviation is first used. If you need to refresh your memory later, simply look in the glossary to save time. Using the glossary on its own, as a learning tool, can help you enhance your automotive knowledge without even opening the hood of your vehicle.

Chapter Ten's heading is:
- Abbreviations and Definitions

2

BASIC MAINTENANCE AND TROUBLESHOOTING

WHERE DO I START?

Logical Diagnostic Procedures

Diagnosis of a driveability problem requires attention to detail and following the diagnostic procedures in the correct order. Resist the temptation to begin extensive testing before completing the preliminary diagnostic steps. The preliminary or visual inspection must be completed in detail before diagnosis begins. In many cases this will shorten diagnostic time and often cure the problem without the need for involved electronic testing.

There are two basic ways to check your vehicle engine for electronic problems. These are by symptom diagnosis and by the on-board computer self-diagnostic system. The first place to start is always the preliminary inspection. Intermittent problems are the most difficult to locate. If the problem is not present at the time you are testing you may not be able to locate the fault.

PRELIMINARY INSPECTION

▶ See Figures 1, 2, 3, 4 and 4

The visual inspection of all components is possibly the most critical step of diagnosis. A detailed examination of connectors, wiring and vacuum hoses can often lead to a repair without further diagnosis. Also, take into consideration if the vehicle has been serviced recently. Sometimes things get reconnected in the wrong place, or not at all. A careful inspector will check the undersides of hoses as well as the integrity of hard-to-reach hoses blocked by the air cleaner or other components. Correct routing for vacuum hoses can be obtained from your specific vehicle service manual, 'Chilton Total Car Care Manual', or Vehicle Emission Control Information (VECI) label in the engine compartment of the vehicle. Wiring should be checked carefully for any sign of strain, burning, crimping or terminals pulled out from a connector.

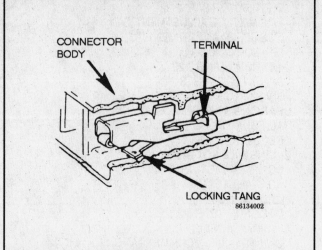

Fig. 2 Check the individual terminals and wiring connectors for damage

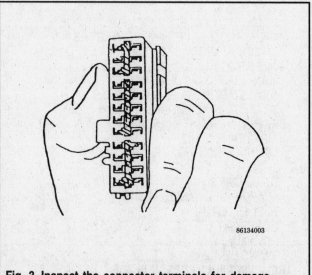

Fig. 3 Inspect the connector terminals for damage

Checking connectors at components or in harnesses is required; usually, pushing them together will reveal a loose fit. Also, check electrical connectors for corroded, bent, damaged, improperly seated pins, and bad wire crimps to terminals. Pay particular attention to ground circuits, making sure they are not loose or corroded. Remember to inspect connectors and hose fittings at components not mounted on the engine, such as the evaporative canister or relays mounted on the fender aprons. Any component or wiring in the vicinity of a fluid leak or spillage should be given extra attention during inspection.

Additionally, inspect maintenance items such as belt condition and tension, battery charge and condition and the radiator cap carefully. Any of these very simple items may affect the system enough to set a fault code.

Fig. 1 Perform underhood inspection of all wiring and hoses

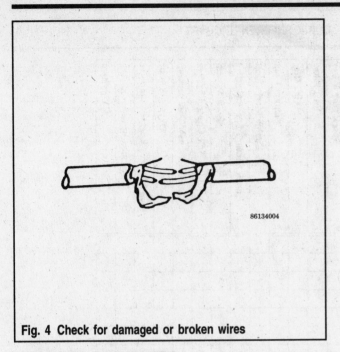

86134004

Fig. 4 Check for damaged or broken wires

DIAGNOSIS BY SYMPTOM

Before the advent of the self-diagnostic system, diagnosis by symptom was the only method for investigation of an automotive problem. An attempt was made to solve problems by reviewing the symptoms and performing tests on suspected components until a defective component was located. The problem was then corrected and the vehicle checked for any other problems. This method is still used frequently today when a driveability complaint is made, but no code is set in the electronic control unit's memory.

When diagnosing by symptom the first step is to find out if the problem really exists. This may sound like a waste of time but you must be able to recreate the problem before you begin testing. This is called an 'operational check'. Each operational check will give either a positive or negative answer (symptom). A positive answer is found when the check gives a positive result (the horn blows when you press the horn button). A negative answer is found when the check gives a negative result (the radio does not play when you turn the knob on). After performing several operational checks, a pattern may develop. This pattern is used in the next step of diagnosis to determine related symptoms.

In order to determine related symptoms, perform operational checks on circuits related to the problem circuit (the radio does not work and the dash lights do not go on). These checks can be made without the use of any test equipment. Simply follow the wires in the wiring harness or, if available, obtain a copy of your vehicle's specific wiring diagram. If you see that the radio and the dash lights are on the same circuit, first check the radio to see if it works. Then check the dash lights. If the neither the radio or dash lights work, this tells you that there is a problem in that circuit. Perform additional operational checks on that circuit and compile a list of symptoms.

When analyzing your answers, a defect will always lie between a check which gave a positive answer and one which gave a negative answer. Look at your list of symptoms and try to determine probable areas to test. If you get negative answers on related circuits, then maybe the problem is at the common junction. After you have determined what the symptoms are and where you are going to look for defects, develop a plan for isolating the trouble. Ask a knowledgable automotive person which components frequently fail on your vehicle. Also notice which parts or components are easiest to reach and how can you accomplish the most by doing the least amount of checks.

A common way of diagnosis is to use the split-in-half technique. Each test that is made essentially splits the trouble area in half. By performing this technique several times the area where a problem is located becomes smaller and smaller until the problem can be isolated in a single wire or component. This area is most commonly between the two closest check points that produced a negative answer and a positive answer.

After the problem is located, perform the repair procedure. This may involve replacing a component, repairing a component or damaged wire, or making an adjustment.

➡**Never assume a component is defective until you have thoroughly tested it.**

The final step is to make sure the complaint is corrected. Remember, the symptoms that you uncover may lead to several problems that require separate repairs. Repeat the diagnosis and test procedures again and again until all negative symptoms are corrected.

DIAGNOSIS BY THE STORED TROUBLE CODE

When a fault code is detected, it appears as a flash of the CHECK ENGINE light on the instrument panel. This indicates that an abnormal signal in the system has been recognized by the ECM.

When diagnosing by code, the first step is to read any fault codes from the ECM. These codes will identify the area to perform more in-depth testing. After the fault codes have been read, proceed to test each of the components and component circuits indicated. Continue performing individual component tests until the failed component is located. Remember, fault codes do indicate the presence of a failure, but they do not identify the failed component directly.

DIAGNOSIS BY SYMPTOM — QUICK REFERENCE CHART

	Throttle Position Sensor	Coolant Temperature Sensor	MAP or MAF sensor	Air Temperature Sensor	Ignition Coil	Distributor	Spark Plug Wires	Fuel Filter	Air Filter	Vacuum Leak	Engine Mechanical	Knock Sensor / Spark Control	EGR System	Idle Control System	Camshaft sensor/Dist. pick-up	Oxygen Sensor	Ignition Module / Engine Computer	Torque Converter Clutch	PCV System
No Start	u	u	u		•	•		•		u	•			•	•		•		
Hard Start	•	•	•		•	•	•												u
Hesitation	•		•		•	•	•	•		•			•						
Stalling	•				•	•	•	•		•	•			•				•	u
Poor Idle	•				•	•	•			•				•	•				•
Dieseling								•				•		•					
Engine Lamp ON	•	•	•	•								•	•		•	•	•		
Knocks or Pings							•					•	•				•	•	•
High Hydrocarbons	u	u	u		•	•	•	u	•	u	•			u		•			
Black Smoke	u	•	•	•				•								•			
Blue Smoke											•								
Poor Fuel Mileage	•	•	•	•	•	•	•		•	•			•			•		•	u
Lack of Power	•	•	•	•	•	•	•	•	•	•								•	u
Back fires		•			•	•	•		•	•	•							•	u
Runs Poor Cold	•			•	•	•	•	•	•	•		u	•			•		u	u
Runs Poor Hot	•	•	•	•	•	•	•	•		•	•		•		u	•	•	u	u
High speed surging			•	•						•								•	u

u: Although possible it is unlikely this component is at fault. A totally open or shorted circuit, or severe component fault may cause this condition.

8736MW01

SAFE VEHICLE SERVICING TIPS

It is virtually impossible to anticipate all of the hazards involved with automotive service, but care and common sense should prevent most accidents.

The rules of safety for mechanics range from 'don't smoke around gasoline' to 'use the proper tool for the job.' The trick to avoiding injuries is to develop safe work habits and take every possible precaution.

Do's

• Do keep a fire extinguisher and first aid kit handy.
• Do wear safety glasses or safety goggles when cutting, drilling, grinding or prying. If you wear glasses for the sake of vision, wear safety goggles over your regular glasses.
• Do shield your eyes whenever you work around the battery. Batteries contain sulfuric acid. In case of contact with the eyes or skin, flush the area with water or a mixture of water and baking soda, then get medical attention immediately.

• Do use safety stands for any under-vehicle service. Jacks are for raising vehicles; jackstands are for making sure the vehicle stays raised until you want it to come down. Whenever the vehicle is raised, block the wheels remaining on the ground and set the parking brake.
• Do use adequate ventilation when working with chemicals. Asbestos dust from some worn brake linings can cause cancer.
• Do disconnect the negative battery cable when working on the vehicle.
• Do follow manufacturer's directions whenever working with potentially hazardous materials. Both brake fluid and most types of antifreeze are poisonous if taken internally.
• Do properly maintain your tools. Loose hammerheads, mushroomed punches and chisels, frayed or poorly grounded electrical cords, excessively worn screwdrivers, spread wrenches (open end), cracked sockets, slipping ratchets, or faulty droplight sockets can cause accidents.

- Do use the proper size and type of tool for the job.
- Do, when possible, pull on a wrench handle rather than push on it, and adjust your stance to prevent a fall.
- Do be sure that adjustable wrenches are tight on the nut or bolt and pulled so the force is on the fixed jaw.
- Do select a wrench or socket that fits the nut or bolt. The wrench or socket should sit straight, not cocked.
- Do strike squarely with a hammer. Avoid glancing blows.
- Do set the parking brake and block the wheels if work requires that the engine be running.

Don'ts

- Don't run an engine in a garage or anywhere else without proper ventilation — EVER! Carbon monoxide is poisonous and it is absorbed by the body faster than oxygen. It takes a long time to leave the human body, and you can build a deadly supply of it in your system by simply breathing in a little every day. You may not realize you are slowly poisoning yourself. Always use power vents, windows, fans or open the garage.
- Don't work around moving parts while wearing loose clothing. Short sleeves are much safer than long, loose sleeves.

Hard-toed shoes with neoprene soles protect your toes and give a better grip on slippery surfaces. Jewelry such as watches, fancy belt buckles, beads, or body adornment of any kind is not safe while working around a vehicle. Long hair should be hidden under a hat or cap.

- Don't use pockets for toolboxes. A fall or bump can drive a screwdriver deep into you body. Even a wiping cloth hanging from the back pocket can wrap around a spinning shaft or fan.
- Don't smoke around gasoline, solvent or any flammable material.
- Don't smoke around the battery. When the battery is being charged, it gives off explosive hydrogen gas.
- Don't use gasoline to wash your hands. There are excellent soaps available. Gasoline contains compounds which are hazardous to your health and it removes natural oils from the skin so that bone dry hands will suck up oil and grease.
- Don't service the air conditioning system unless you are equipped with the necessary tools and training. The refrigerant is extremely cold, and when exposed to the air, will instantly freeze any surface it comes in contact with, including your eyes. Keep refrigerant away from open flames; poisonous gas will be produced if refrigerant burns.

SERIAL NUMBER IDENTIFICATION

Vehicle Identification Number

▶ See Figures 5, 6, 7 and 8

The Vehicle Identification Number (VIN) is the number that will perhaps tell you just about every thing you need to know concerning your vehicle. The VIN number is somewhat like a Social Security Number in an automotive sense. The VIN is a standardized 17 digit number. Each digit of this number has a specific meaning or designation. Example: the 8th digit designates the engine code, the 10th digit designates the model year of the vehicle etc. The vehicle serial number is stamped on a plate fastened to the driver's side door pillar.

This number is usually located on the one of the fender aprons in the engine compartment (behind the wheel arch).

All models have the vehicle identification number stamped on a plate attached to the left side of the instrument panel. The plate is visible through the windshield.

The vehicle identification (model variation codes) may be interpreted as follows:

Using a Nissan vehicle as an illustration, look at the VIN number (JN6H D2 1S*MW 000001), all models use a four letter prefix followed by the model designation (D21), then a four letter suffix (five on 1991 and later models), as shown in the illustration.

The serial number on all models is the new 17-digit format. The first three digits are the World Manufacturer Identification number. The next five digits are the Vehicle Description Sec-

tion (same as the series identification number). The remaining nine digits are the production numbers.

➡For specific identification of your vehicle see the Vehicle Identification Label on the vehicle you are working with. If the vehicle has be altered in some way or the engine or transmission has been changed the VIN may not coincide with the change that has been made. It a case like this, look for the serial number on the component to be sure the correct ordering of parts are made. For a complete explanation of the Vehicle Identification Number of your specific vehicle, consult your 'Chilton Total Car Care Manual'.

Fig. 5 Vehicle Identification Number — visible through the windshield

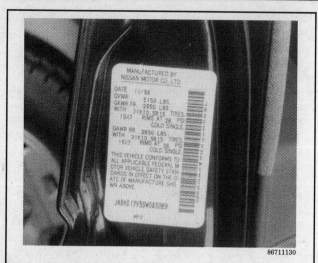

Fig. 6 Manufacturer's label located in the door pillar area — note that the build date of vehicle is at the top

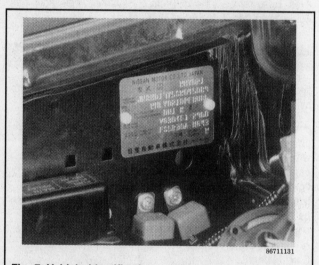

Fig. 7 Vehicle identification number is on the firewall-mounted label in the engine compartment

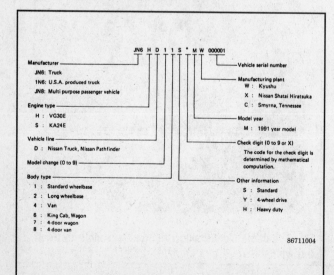

Fig. 8 Vehicle Identification Number (VIN) translation

Engine Serial Number

▶ **See Figure 9**

The engine serial number consists of an engine series identification number followed by a six-digit production number. The number may be found in various places, depending upon the particular engine. Observe the following examples:

• Z24i Engine — the serial number is stamped on the left side of the cylinder block, below the No. 3 and No. 4 spark plugs.

• KA24E Engine — the serial number is stamped on the left side of the cylinder block, below the No. 2 and No. 3 spark plugs.

• VG30i and VG30E Engines — the serial number is stamped on the cylinder block, below the rear of the right side cylinder head.

➡ **The illustrations given here are for a Nissan. For specific information on the vehicle you are working with, consult your 'Chilton Total Car Care Manual'.**

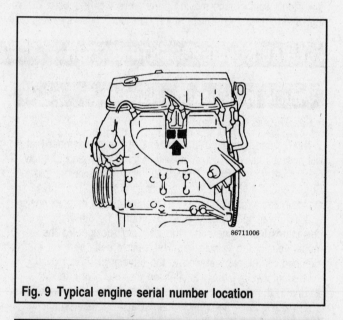

Fig. 9 Typical engine serial number location

Transmission Serial Number

▶ **See Figure 10**

The transmission serial number is stamped on the front upper face of the transmission case on manual transmissions, or on the right side of the transmission case on automatic transmissions.

➡ **The illustrations given here are for a Nissan. For specific information on the vehicle you are working with, consult your 'Chilton Total Car Care Manual'.**

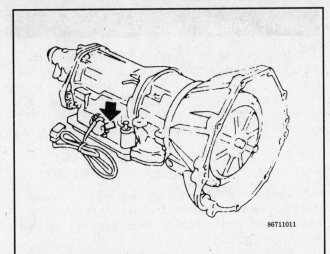

Fig. 10 Typical automatic transmission serial number location

Transfer Case Serial Number

▶ See Figure 11

The transfer case serial number is stamped on the front upper face of the transfer case.

➡ **The illustrations given here are a generalization and may not apply to your vehicle. For specific information on the vehicle you are working with, consult your 'Chilton Total Car Care Manual'.**

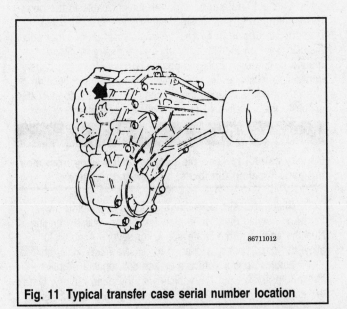

Fig. 11 Typical transfer case serial number location

Vehicle Emissions Control Information (VECI) label

▶ See Figure 12

The Vehicle Emissions Control Information (VECI) label provides a wealth of information pertaining to the engine's Emission Control System. First, it identifies the engine's Cubic Inch Displacement (CID) and size in Liter(s). It provides information for tune-up, such as spark plug gap, ignition timing, idle/mixture and valve lash specifications. In some cases, it will provide a specific adjustment procedure as required. Some labels will also incorporate the vacuum routing of your engine's emission control system. Although the VECI label is very helpful to the person working on the vehicle, it should not be used as the main source for repair information. However, if there have not been any alterations to the engine and the Manual and sticker do not agree, use the Vehicle Emissions Control Information (VECI) sticker information, as it often reflects changes made during the production run.

Always check your 'Chilton Total Car Care Manual' for more detailed information concerning the vehicle you are working with. Always keep in mind that the vehicle you are working with may have had an engine change. If this is the case, you will have to identify the year and engine code you have in the vehicle. If the vehicle is missing the Emission Control Information label, a new one can be ordered from your local dealer.

The Vehicle Emissions Control Information (VECI) label is usually located in the engine compartment. On some vehicles it will be found directly under the hood. Others may have it on the strut tower or radiator support.

Fig. 12 Vehicle Emission Control Information (VECI) label located in the engine compartment

JUMP STARTING

Jump Starting a Dead Battery

▶ See Figure 13

Whenever a vehicle must be jump started, precautions must be followed in order to prevent the possibility of personal injury. Remember that batteries contain a small amount of explosive hydrogen gas which is a by-product of battery charging. Sparks should always be avoided when working around batteries, especially when attaching jumper cables. To minimize the possibility of accidental sparks, follow the procedure carefully.

✳✳WARNING

NEVER hook the batteries up in a series circuit or the entire electrical system will go up in smoke, especially the starter!

Vehicles equipped with a diesel engine utilize two 12 volt batteries, one on either side of the engine compartment. The batteries are connected in a parallel circuit (positive terminal to positive terminal, negative terminal to negative terminal). Hooking the batteries up in parallel circuit increases battery cranking power without increasing total battery voltage output. Output remains at 12 volts. On the other hand, hooking two 12 volt batteries up in a series circuit (positive terminal to negative terminal, positive terminal to negative terminal) increases total battery output to 24 volts (12 volts plus 12 volts).

Jump Starting Precautions

1. Be sure that both batteries are of the same voltage. All vehicles covered by this manual and most vehicles on the road today utilize a 12 volt charging system.
2. Be sure that both batteries are of the same polarity (have the same grounded terminal; in most cases NEGATIVE).
3. Be sure that the vehicles are not touching or a short circuit could occur.
4. On serviceable batteries, be sure the vent cap holes are not obstructed.
5. Do not smoke or allow sparks anywhere near the batteries.
6. In cold weather, make sure the battery electrolyte is not frozen. This can occur more readily in a battery that has been in a state of discharge.
7. Do not allow electrolyte to contact your skin or clothing.

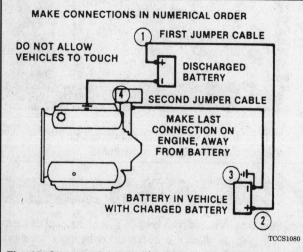

MAKE CONNECTIONS IN NUMERICAL ORDER

① FIRST JUMPER CABLE

DO NOT ALLOW VEHICLES TO TOUCH

DISCHARGED BATTERY

SECOND JUMPER CABLE

MAKE LAST CONNECTION ON ENGINE, AWAY FROM BATTERY

BATTERY IN VEHICLE WITH CHARGED BATTERY

TCCS1080

Fig. 13 Connect the jumper cables to the batteries and engine in the order shown

Jump Starting Procedure

1. Make sure that the voltages of the 2 batteries are the same. Most batteries and charging systems are of the 12 volt variety.
2. Pull the jumping vehicle (with the good battery) into a position so the jumper cables can reach the dead battery and that vehicle's engine. Make sure that the vehicles do NOT touch.
3. Place the transmissions of both vehicles in NEUTRAL or PARK, as applicable, then firmly set their parking brakes.

➡**If necessary for safety reasons, both vehicle's hazard lights may be operated throughout the entire procedure without significantly increasing the difficulty of jump starting the dead battery.**

4. Turn all lights and accessories **OFF** on both vehicles. Make sure the ignition switches on both vehicles are turned to the **OFF** position.
5. Cover the battery cell caps with a rag, but do not cover the terminals.
6. Make sure the terminals on both batteries are clean and free of corrosion or proper electrical connection will be impeded. If necessary, clean the battery terminals before proceeding.
7. Identify the positive (+) and negative (-) terminals on both batteries.
8. Connect the first jumper cable to the positive (+) terminal of the dead battery, then connect the other end of that cable to the positive (+) terminal of the booster (good) battery.
9. Connect one end of the other jumper cable to the negative (-) terminal of the booster battery and the other cable clamp to an engine bolt head, alternator bracket or other solid, metallic point on the dead battery's engine. Try to pick a ground on the engine that is positioned away from the battery, in order to minimize the possibility of the 2 clamps touching should one loosen during the procedure. DO NOT connect this clamp to the negative (-) terminal of the bad battery.

✳✳CAUTION

Be very careful to keep the jumper cables away from moving parts (cooling fan, belts, etc.) on both engines.

10. Check to make sure that the cables are routed away from any moving parts, then start the donor vehicle's engine. Run the engine at moderate speed for several minutes to allow the dead battery a chance to receive some initial charge.
11. With the donor vehicle's engine still running slightly above idle, try to start the vehicle with the dead battery. Crank the engine for no more than 10 seconds at a time and let the starter cool for at least 20 seconds between tries. If the vehicle does not start within 3 tries, it is likely that something else is also wrong.
12. Once the vehicle is started, allow it to run at idle for a few seconds to make sure that it is properly operating.
13. Turn on the headlights, heater blower and, if equipped, the rear defroster of both vehicles in order to reduce the severity of voltage spikes and subsequent risk of damage to the vehicles' electrical systems when the cables are disconnected.

14. Carefully disconnect the cables in the reverse order of connection. Start with the negative cable that is attached to the engine ground, then the negative cable on the donor battery. Disconnect the positive cable from the donor battery, then disconnect the positive cable from the formerly dead battery. Be careful when disconnecting the cables from the positive terminals not to allow the alligator clips to touch any metal on either vehicle or a short circuit and sparks will occur.

CHARGING SYSTEM

Alternator

▶ **See Figure 14**

The alternator converts the mechanical energy supplied by the drive belt into electrical energy by a process of electromagnetic induction. When the ignition switch is turned **ON**, current flows from the battery through the charging system light (or ammeter) to the voltage regulator, and finally to the alternator. When the engine is started, the drive belt turns the rotating field (rotor) in the stationary windings (stator), inducing alternating current. This alternating current is converted into usable direct current by the diode rectifier. Most of this current is used to charge the battery and to supply power for the vehicle's electrical accessories. A small part of this current is returned to the field windings of the alternator, enabling it to increase its power output. When the current in the field windings reaches a predetermined level, the voltage regulator grounds the circuit preventing any further increase. The cycle is continued so that the voltage supply remains constant.

All models use a 12-volt alternator. Amperage ratings vary according to the year and model. All models have an electronic, nonadjustable regulator, integral with the alternator.

ALTERNATOR PRECAUTIONS

To prevent damage to the alternator and regulator, the following precautionary measures must be taken when working with the electrical system:

- Never reverse the battery connections. Always visually check the battery polarity before any connections are made, to ensure that all connections correspond to the vehicle's battery ground polarity.
- Booster batteries must be connected properly. Make sure the positive cable of the booster battery is connected to the positive terminal of the battery which is getting the boost.
- Disconnect the battery cables before using a fast charger; the charger has a tendency to force current through the diodes in the opposite direction for which they were designed.
- Never use a fast charger as a booster for starting the vehicle.
- Never disconnect the voltage regulator while the engine is running, unless as noted for testing purposes.
- Do not ground the alternator output terminal.
- Do not operate the alternator on an open circuit with the field energized.
- Do not attempt to polarize the alternator.
- Disconnect the battery cables and remove the alternator before using an electric arc welder on the vehicle.
- Protect the alternator from excessive moisture. If the engine is to be steam cleaned, cover or remove the alternator.

REMOVAL & INSTALLATION

The procedure below is just a general procedure; consult your 'Chilton Total Care Care Manual' for specific procedure's concerning the vehicle you are working with.

➡**On some models, the alternator is mounted very low on the engine. On these models, it may be necessary to remove the gravel shield and work from beneath the vehicle in order to gain access to the alternator.**

1. Disconnect the negative battery cable.
2. On vehicles where the alternator can only be accessed from underneath the vehicle, raise the vehicle and support it safely with jackstands. Make sure the jackstands are at proper locations.
3. Remove the alternator pivot bolt. Push the alternator inward and remove the drive belt.
4. Pull back the rubber boots and disconnect the wiring from the back of the alternator.
5. Remove the alternator mounting bolt, then withdraw the alternator from its bracket.

To install:

6. Position the alternator in its mounting bracket, then lightly tighten the mounting and adjusting bolts.
7. Connect the electrical leads at the rear of the alternator, and return rubber boots to the proper position.
8. Adjust the belt tension.
9. Connect the negative battery cable.
10. Start the engine and perform a charging system voltage test to insure the charging system is putting out adequately.

You can make a basic check to see if the charging system is charging by using a voltmeter. Connect the voltmeter to the battery, battery voltage is approximately 12.6 volts. Start the engine and observe the voltmeter reading, it should read between 13.2-14 volts. If it remains at 12.6 volts the system is not charging. If this is the case, consult your 'Chilton Total Car Care Manual'.

Regulator

Regulators may be located internally to the the alternator or externally mounted on the firewall or inner fender panel depending on the vehicle. If faulty, it must be replaced; there are no adjustments which can be made.

REMOVAL & INSTALLATION

Internal Regulator

The electronic regulator is located inside the alternator. On some alternators the regulator is a simple bolt-on procedure, others may be soldered to the brush assembly. With a little

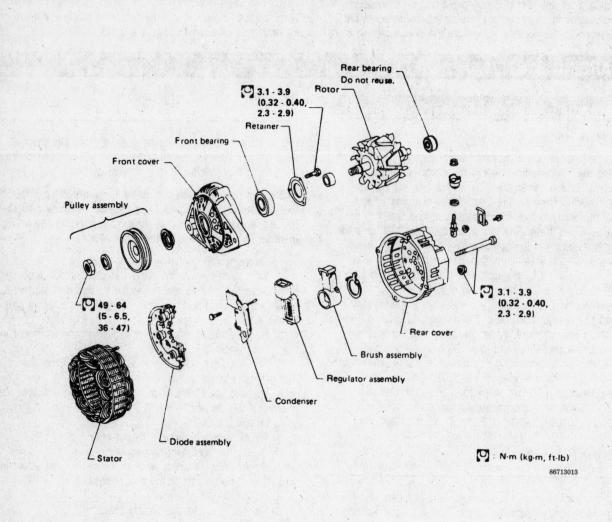

Fig. 14 Exploded view of a typical alternator assembly

knowledge of soldering you should be able to accomplish the job. The following procedure is for a regulator that is soldered to the brush assembly. For specific instructions on the vehicle you are working with, consult your 'Chilton Total Car Care Manual'. The regulator is non-adjustable, and must be replaced together with the brush assembly, if faulty.

1. Remove the alternator.
2. Remove the thru-bolts and separate the front cover from the stator housing.
3. Unsolder the wire connecting the diode plate to the brush at the brush terminal.
4. Remove the bolt retaining the diode plate to the rear cover.
5. Remove the nut securing the battery terminal bolt.
6. Lift the stator slightly, together with the diode plate, to gain access to the diode plate screw. Remove the screw.
7. Separate the stator and diode, then remove the brush and regulator assembly.
8. On assembly, apply soldering heat sparingly, carrying out the operation as quickly as possible, to avoid damage to the transistors and diodes. Before assembling the alternator

halves, bend a piece of wire into an L-shape and slip it through the rear cover, next to the brushes. Use the wire to hold the brushes in a retracted position until the case halves are assembled. Remove the wire carefully, to prevent damage to the slip rings.

9. Install the alternator.
10. Start the engine and perform a charging system voltage test to insure charging system is putting out adequately.

You can make a basic check to see if the charging system is charging by using a voltmeter. Connect the voltmeter to the battery, battery voltage is approximately 12.6 volts. Start the engine and observe the voltmeter reading, it should read between 13.2-14 volts. If it remains at 12.6 volts the system is not charging. If this is the case, consult your 'Chilton Total Car Care Manual'.

External Regulator

Depending on the vehicle, the external regulator may be mounted on the firewall or inner fender panel. These regulators are much simpler to replace.

1. Disconnect the negative battery cable.

2. Locate the regulator.

3. Disconnect the harness connector from the regulator.

4. Remove the bolts holding the regulator to its mounting base and remove the regulator.

To install:

5. Install the regulator to the mounting base and secure it in place with the mounting screws.

6. Apply a coating of dielectric grease on the harness electrical connectors and connect.

7. Connect the negative battery cable.

8. Start the engine a perform a charging system voltage test to insure charging system is putting out adequately.

You can make a basic check to see if the charging system is charging by using a voltmeter. Connect the voltmeter to the battery, battery voltage is approximately 12.6 volts. Start the engine and observe the voltmeter reading, it should read between 13.2-14 volts. If it remains at 12.6 volts the system is not charging. If this is the case, consult your 'Chilton Total Car Care Manual'.

ADJUSTMENT

Voltage regulators on modern vehicles are not adjustable, most are electronic or even computer controlled.

STARTING SYSTEM

Starter

REMOVAL & INSTALLATION

▶ **See Figures 15, 16, 17, 18, 19 and 20**

The procedure below is just a general procedure, consult your 'Chilton Total Care Care Manual' for specific procedure concerning the vehicle you are working with.

1. Disconnect the negative battery cable at the battery, then disconnect the positive battery cable at the starter.

2. On vehicles where the starter can only be accessed from underneath the vehicle, observe the following caution:

❊❊CAUTION

Raise the vehicle a support it safely with suitable jackstands. Be sure to position the jackstands at proper frame locations.

3. On some 4wd vehicles it may be necessary to perform the following procedure:

    a. Remove the front gravel shield.

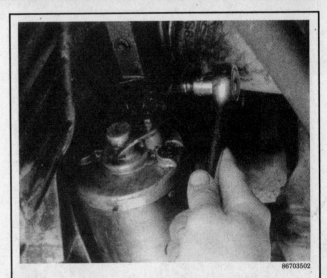

Fig. 16 Remove the starter bracket, if equipped

    b. Detach the oil pressure switch connector.

    c. Drain the engine oil and remove the oil filter.

❊❊CAUTION

The EPA warns that prolonged contact with used engine oil may cause a number of skin disorders, including cancer! You should make every effort to minimize your exposure to used engine oil. Protective gloves should be worn when changing the oil. Wash your hands and any other exposed skin areas as soon as possible after exposure to used engine oil. Soap and water, or waterless hand cleaner should be used.

    d. Remove the exhaust manifold heat insulator.

    e. Remove the fuel tube retainer bolt.

4. On some vehicles it may be necessary to perform the following procedure:

    a. Remove the front right wheel.

    b. Remove the front gravel shield.

    c. Remove the exhaust manifold heat insulator.

    d. Remove the exhaust manifold.

    e. Detach the oil pressure switch connector.

5. Unfasten the remaining electrical connections at the starter solenoid.

Fig. 15 Disconnect the cable attached the starter

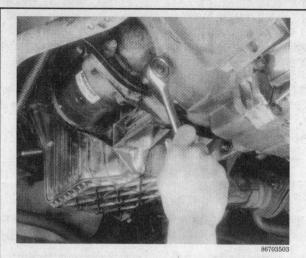

Fig. 17 Loosen the holding the nose bracket, if equipped

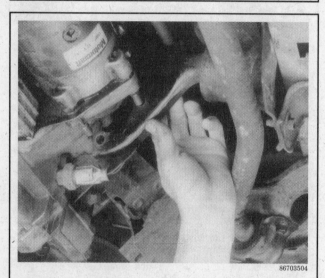

Fig. 18 Remove the nose bracket, if equipped

Fig. 19 Remove the bolts holding the starter in place

Fig. 20 Remove the the starter from the engine

6. Remove the two nuts holding the starter to the bell housing, then pull the starter toward the front of the vehicle and out.

To install:

7. Insert the starter into the bell housing, being sure that the starter drive is not jammed against the flywheel.

8. Tighten the attaching nuts and secure all electrical connections to the starter assembly.

9. Install all remaining components in reverse order of removal.

10. Reconnect the battery cables. If applicable, refill and check the oil level. Check the starter assembly for proper operation.

OVERHAUL

▶ See Figure 21

The procedure below is just a general procedure, consult your 'Chilton Total Care Care Manual' for specific procedure concerning the vehicle you are working with.

Solenoid Replacement

1. Remove the starter.

2. Unscrew the two solenoid switch (magnetic switch) retaining screws.

3. Remove the solenoid. In order to unhook the solenoid from the starter drive lever, lift it up at the same time that you are pulling it out of the starter housing.

4. Installation is in the reverse order of removal. Make sure that the solenoid switch is properly engaged with the drive lever before tightening the mounting screws.

Brush Replacement

NON-REDUCTION GEAR TYPE

1. Remove the starter.

2. Remove the solenoid (magnetic switch).

3. Unfasten the two end frame cap mounting bolts and remove the end frame cap.

4. Remove the O-ring and lock plate from the armature shaft groove, then slide the shims off the shaft.

5. Unfasten the two long housing screws (at the front of the starter) and carefully pull off the end plate.

6. Using a screwdriver, separate the brushes from the brush holder.

7. Slide the brush holder off of the armature shaft.

8. Crush the old brushes off of the copper braid and file away any remaining solder.

9. Fit the new brushes to the braid and spread the braid slightly.

➡ **Use a soldering iron of at least 250 watts.**

10. Using a light-grade solder, solder the brush to the braid. Grip the copper braid with flat pliers to prevent the solder from flowing down its length.

11. File off any extra solder and then repeat the procedure for the remaining three brushes.

12. Installation is in the reverse order of removal.

➡ **When installing the brush holder, make sure that the brushes line up properly.**

REDUCTION GEAR TYPE

1. Remove the starter and the solenoid.

2. Remove the through-bolts and the rear cover. The rear cover can be pried off with a small pry tool, but be careful not to damage the O-ring.

3. Separate the starter housing, armature, and brush holder from the center housing. They can be removed as an assembly.

4. Remove the positive side brush from its holder. The positive brush is insulated from the brush holder, and its lead wire is connected to the field coil.

5. Carefully lift the negative brush from the commutator and remove it from the holder.

6. Installation is in the reverse order of removal.

Starter Drive Replacement

NON-REDUCTION GEAR TYPE

1. With the starter motor removed from the vehicle, separate the solenoid from the starter.

2. Remove the two through-bolts and separate the gear case from the yoke housing.

3. Remove the pinion stopper clip and the pinion stopper.

4. Slide the starter drive off the armature shaft.

5. Install the starter drive and reassemble the starter in the reverse order of removal.

REDUCTION GEAR TYPE

1. Remove the starter.

2. Unfasten the solenoid and the shift lever.

3. Remove the bolts securing the center housing to the front cover and separate the parts.

4. Remove the gears and starter drive.

5. Installation is in the reverse order of removal.

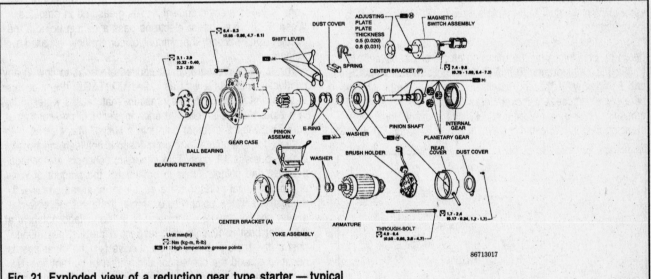

Fig. 21 Exploded view of a reduction gear type starter — typical

FUNDAMENTALS OF ELECTRICITY

▶ **See Figures 22 and 23**

A good understanding of basic electrical theory and how circuits work is necessary to successfully perform the service and testing outlined in this manual. Therefore, this section should be read before attempting any diagnosis and repair.

All matter is made up of tiny particles called molecules. Each molecule is made up of two or more atoms. Atoms may be divided into even smaller particles called protons, neutrons and electrons. These particles are the same in all matter and differences in materials (hard or soft, conductive or non-conductive) occur only because of the number and arrangement of these particles. In other words, the protons, neutrons and electrons in a drop of water are the same as those in an ounce of lead, there are just more of them (arranged differently) in a lead molecule than in a water molecule. Protons and neutrons packed together form the nucleus of the atom, while electrons orbit around the nucleus much the same way as the planets of the solar system orbit around the sun.

The proton is a small positive natural charge of electricity, while the neutron has no electrical charge. The electron carries a negative charge equal to the positive charge of the proton. Every electrically neutral atom contains the same number of protons and electrons, the exact number of which determines the element. The only difference between a conductor and an insulator is that a conductor possesses free electrons in large quantities, while an insulator has only a few. An element must have very few free electrons to be a good insulator and vice-versa. When we speak of electricity, we're talking about these free electrons.

In a conductor, the movement of the free electrons is hindered by collisions with the adjoining atoms of the element (matter). This hindrance to movement is called **RESISTANCE** and it varies with different materials and temperatures. As temperature increases, the movement of the free electrons increases, causing more frequent collisions and therefore increasing resistance to the movement of the electrons. The

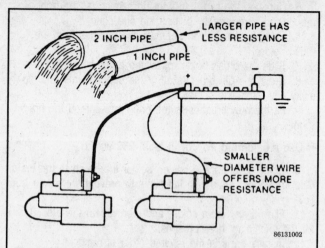

Fig. 23 Electrical resistance can be compared to water flow through a pipe. The smaller the wire (pipe), the more resistance the flow of electrons (water)

number of collisions (resistance) also increases with the number of electrons flowing (current). Current is defined as the movement of electrons through a conductor such as a wire. In a conductor (such as copper) electrons can be caused to leave their atoms and move to other atoms. This flow is continuous in that every time an atom gives up an electron, it collects another one to take its place. This movement of electrons is called electric current and is measured in amperes. When 6.28 billion, billion electrons pass a certain point in the circuit in one second, the amount of current flow is called 1 ampere.

The force or pressure which causes electrons to flow in any conductor (such as a wire) is called **VOLTAGE**. It is measured in volts and is similar to the pressure that causes water to flow in a pipe. Voltage is the difference in electrical pressure measured between 2 different points in a circuit. In a 12 volt system, for example, the force measured between the two battery posts is 12 volts. Two important concepts are voltage potential and polarity. Voltage potential is the amount of voltage or electrical pressure at a certain point in the circuit with respect to another point. For example, if the voltage potential at one post of the 12 volt battery is 0, the voltage potential at the other post is 12 volts with respect to the first post. One post of the battery is said to be positive (+); the other post is negative (-) and the conventional direction of current flow is from positive to negative in an electrical circuit. It should be noted that the electron flow in the wire is opposite the current flow. In other words, when the circuit is energized, the current flows from positive to negative, but the electrons actually move from negative to positive. The voltage or pressure needed to produce a current flow in a circuit must be greater than the resistance present in the circuit. In other words, if the voltage drop across the resistance is greater than or equal to the voltage input, the voltage potential will be zero — no voltage will flow through the circuit. Resistance to the flow of electrons is measured in ohms. One volt will cause 1 ampere to flow through a resistance of 1 ohm.

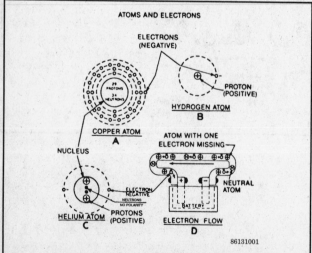

Fig. 22 Typical atoms of Copper (A), Hydrogen (B) and Helium (C). Electron flow in a battery circuit

Units Of Electrical Measurement

▶ **See Figure 24**

There are 3 fundamental characteristics of a direct-current electrical circuit: volts, amperes and ohms.

VOLTAGE in a circuit controls the intensity with which the loads in the circuit operate. The brightness of a lamp, the heat of an electrical defroster, the speed of a motor are all directly proportional to the voltage, if the resistance in the circuit and/or mechanical load on electric motors remains constant. Voltage available from the battery is constant (normally 12 volts), but as it operates the various loads in the circuit, voltage decreases (drops).

AMPERE is the unit of measurement of current in an electrical circuit. One ampere is the quantity of current that will flow through a resistance of 1 ohm at a pressure of 1 volt. The amount of current that flows in a circuit is controlled by the voltage and the resistance in the circuit. Current flow is directly proportional to resistance. Thus, as voltage is increased or decreased, current is increased or decreased accordingly. Current is decreased as resistance is increased. However, current is also increased as resistance is decreased. With little or no resistance in a circuit, current is high.

OHM is the unit of measurement of resistance, represented by the Greek letter Omega (Ω). One ohm is the resistance of a conductor through which a current of one ampere will flow at a pressure of one volt. Electrical resistance can be measured on an instrument called an ohmmeter. The loads (electrical devices) are the primary resistances in a circuit. Loads such as lamps, solenoids and electric heaters have a resistance that is essentially fixed; at a normal fixed voltage, they will draw a fixed current. Motors, on the other hand, do not have a fixed resistance. Increasing the mechanical load on a motor (such as might be caused by a misadjusted track in a power window system) will decrease the motor speed. The drop in motor rpm has the effect of reducing the internal resistance of the motor because the current draw of the motor varies directly with the mechanical load on the motor, although its actual resistance is unchanged. Thus, as the motor load increases, the current draw of the motor increases, and may increase up to the point where the motor stalls (cannot move the mechanical load).

Circuits are designed with the total resistance of the circuit taken into account. Troubles can arise when unwanted resistances enter into a circuit. If corrosion, dirt, grease, or any other contaminant occurs in places like switches, connectors and grounds, or if loose connections occur, resistances will develop in these areas. These resistances act like additional loads in the circuit and cause problems.

OHM'S LAW

Ohm's law is a statement of the relationship between the 3 fundamental characteristics of an electrical circuit. These rules apply to direct current (DC) only.

Ohm's law provides a means to make an accurate circuit analysis without actually seeing the circuit. If, for example, one wanted to check the condition of the rotor winding in a alternator whose specifications indicate that the field (rotor) current draw is normally 2.5 amperes at 12 volts, simply connect the rotor to a 12 volt battery and measure the current with an ammeter. If it measures about 2.5 amperes, the rotor winding can be assumed good.

An ohmmeter can be used to test components that have been removed from the vehicle in much the same manner as an ammeter. Since the voltage and the current of the rotor windings used as an earlier example are known, the resistance can be calculated using Ohms law. The formula would be ohms equals volts divided by amperes.

If the rotor resistance measures about 4.8 ohms when checked with an ohmmeter, the winding can be assumed good. By plugging in different specifications, additional circuit information can be determined such as current draw, etc.

$$I = \frac{E}{R} \quad \text{or} \quad \text{AMPERES} = \frac{\text{VOLTS}}{\text{OHMS}}$$

$$R = \frac{E}{I} \quad \text{or} \quad \text{OHMS} = \frac{\text{VOLTS}}{\text{AMPERES}}$$

$$E = I \times R \quad \text{or} \quad \text{VOLTS} = \text{AMPERES} \times \text{OHMS}$$

86131003

Fig. 24 Ohms Law is the basis for all electrical measurement. By simply plugging in two values, the third can be calculated using this formula

Electrical Circuits

▶ **See Figures 25, 26, 27, 28, 29, 30, 31, 32, 33 and 34**

An electrical circuit must start from a source of electrical supply and return to that source through a continuous path. Circuits are designed to handle a certain maximum current flow. The maximum allowable current flow is designed higher than the normal current requirements of all the loads in the circuit. Wire size, connections, insulation, etc., are designed to prevent undesirable voltage drop, overheating of conductors, arcing of contacts and other adverse effects. If the safe maximum current flow level is exceeded, damage to the circuit components will result; it is this condition that circuit protection devices are designed to prevent.

Protection devices are fuses, fusible links or circuit breakers designed to open or break the circuit quickly whenever an overload, such as a short circuit, occurs. By opening the circuit quickly, the circuit protection device prevents damage to the wiring, battery and other circuit components. Fuses and fusible links are designed to carry a preset maximum amount of current and to melt when that maximum is exceeded, while circuit breakers merely break the connection and may be manually reset. The maximum amperage rating of each fuse is marked on the fuse body and all contain a see-through portion that shows the break in the fuse element when blown. Fusible link maximum amperage rating is indicated by gauge or thickness

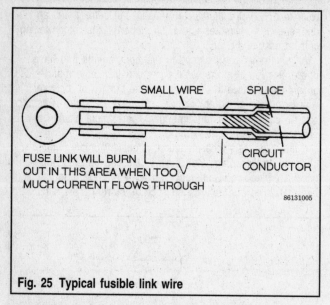

Fig. 25 Typical fusible link wire

of the wire. Never replace a blown fuse or fusible link with one of a higher amperage rating.

❋❋CAUTION

Resistance wires, like fusible links, are also spliced into conductors in some areas. Do not make the mistake of replacing a fusible link with a resistance wire. Resistance wires are longer than fusible links and are stamped 'RESISTOR-DO NOT CUT OR SPLICE.'

Circuit breakers consist of 2 strips of metal which have different coefficients of expansion. As an overload or current flows through the bimetallic strip, the high-expansion metal will elongate due to heat and break the contact. With the circuit open, the bimetal strip cools and shrinks, drawing the strip down until contact is re-established and current flows once again. In actual operation, the contact is broken very quickly if the overload is continuous and the circuit will be repeatedly broken and remade until the source of the overload is corrected.

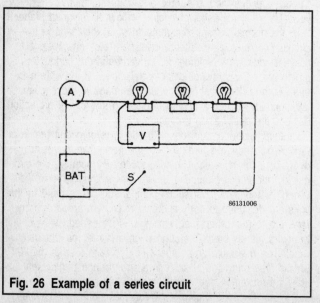

Fig. 26 Example of a series circuit

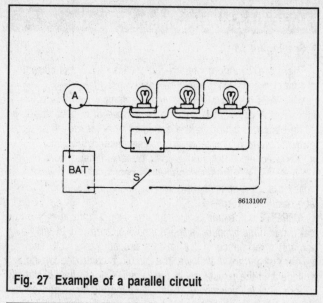

Fig. 27 Example of a parallel circuit

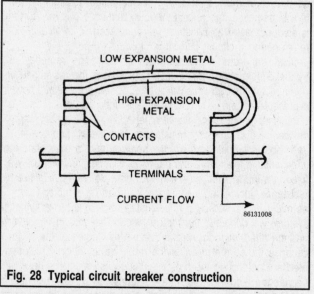

Fig. 28 Typical circuit breaker construction

The self-resetting type of circuit breaker is the one most generally used in automotive electrical systems. On manually reset circuit breakers, a button will pop up on the circuit breaker case. This button must be pushed in to reset the circuit breaker and restore power to the circuit. Always repair the source of the overload before resetting a circuit breaker or replacing a fuse or fusible link. When searching for overloads, keep in mind that the circuit protection devices protect only against overloads between the protection device and ground.

There are 2 basic types of circuit; Series and Parallel. In a series circuit, all of the elements are connected in chain fashion with the same amount of current passing through each element or load. No matter where an ammeter is connected in a series circuit, it will always read the same. The most important fact to remember about a series circuit is that the sum of the voltages across each element equals the source voltage. The total resistance of a series circuit is equal to the sum of the individual resistances within each element of the circuit. Using ohms law, one can determine the voltage drop across each element in the circuit. If the total resistance and source voltage is known, the amount of current can be calculated. Once the amount of current (amperes) is known, values can be substituted in the Ohms law formula to calculate the voltage drop across each individual element in the series circuit. The individual voltage drops must add up to the same value as the source voltage.

A parallel circuit, unlike a series circuit, contains 2 or more branches, each branch a separate path independent of the others. The total current draw from the voltage source is the sum of all the currents drawn by each branch. Each branch of a parallel circuit can be analyzed separately. The individual branches can be either simple circuits, series circuits or combinations of series-parallel circuits. Ohms law applies to parallel circuits just as it applies to series circuits, by considering each branch independently of the others. The most important thing to remember is that the voltage across each branch is the same as the source voltage. The current in any branch is that voltage divided by the resistance of the branch. A practical method of determining the resistance of a parallel circuit is to divide the product of the 2 resistances by the sum of 2 resis-

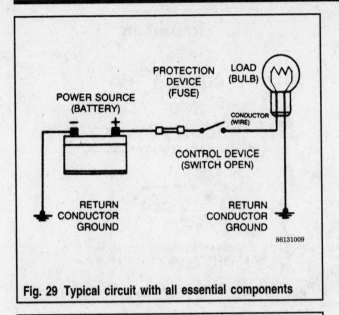

Fig. 29 Typical circuit with all essential components

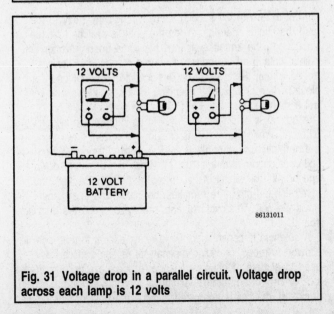

Fig. 30 Example of a series-parallel circuit

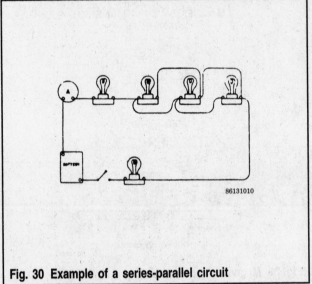

Fig. 31 Voltage drop in a parallel circuit. Voltage drop across each lamp is 12 volts

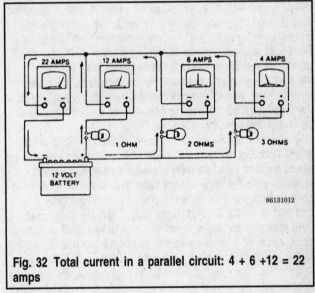

Fig. 32 Total current in a parallel circuit: 4 + 6 +12 = 22 amps

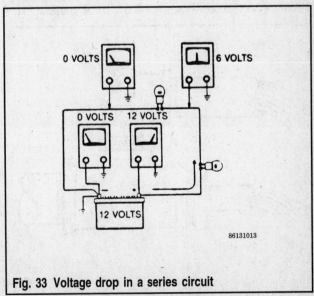

Fig. 33 Voltage drop in a series circuit

tances at a time. Amperes through a parallel circuit is the sum of the amperes through the separate branches. Voltage across a parallel circuit is the same as the voltage across each branch.

By measuring the voltage drops the resistance of each element within the circuit is being measured. The greater the voltage drop, the greater the resistance. Voltage drop measurements are a common way of checking circuit resistances in automotive electrical systems. When part of a circuit develops excessive resistance (due to a bad connection) the element will show a higher than normal voltage drop. Normally, automotive wiring is selected to limit voltage drops to a few tenths of a volt. In parallel circuits, the total resistance is less than the sum of the individual resistances; because the current has 2 paths to take, the total resistance is lower.

Magnetism and Electromagnets

▶ See Figures 35, 36 and 37

Electricity and magnetism are very closely associated because when electric current passes through a wire, a magnetic field is created around the wire. When a wire carrying electric current is wound into a coil, a magnetic field with North and South poles is created just like in a bar magnet. If an iron core is placed within the coil, the magnetic field becomes stronger because iron conducts magnetic lines much easier than air. This arrangement is called an electromagnet and is the basic principle behind the operation of such components as relays, buzzers and solenoids.

A relay is basically just a remote-controlled switch that uses a small amount of current to control the flow of a large amount of current. The simplest relay contains an electromagnetic coil in series with a voltage source (battery) and a switch. A movable armature made of some magnetic material pivots at one end and is held a small distance away from the electromagnet by a spring or the spring steel of the armature itself. A contact point, made of a good conductor, is attached to the free end of the armature with another contact point a small distance away. When the relay is switched on (energized), the magnetic field created by the current flow attracts the armature, bending it until the contact points meet, closing a circuit and allowing

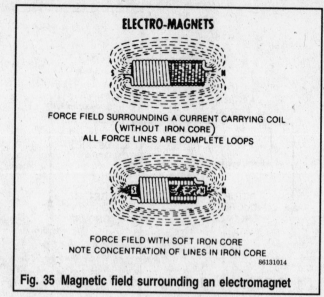

ELECTRO-MAGNETS

FORCE FIELD SURROUNDING A CURRENT CARRYING COIL
(WITHOUT IRON CORE)
ALL FORCE LINES ARE COMPLETE LOOPS

FORCE FIELD WITH SOFT IRON CORE
NOTE CONCENTRATION OF LINES IN IRON CORE
86131014

Fig. 35 Magnetic field surrounding an electromagnet

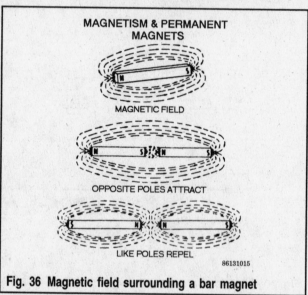

MAGNETISM & PERMANENT MAGNETS

MAGNETIC FIELD

OPPOSITE POLES ATTRACT

LIKE POLES REPEL
86131015

Fig. 36 Magnetic field surrounding a bar magnet

current to flow in the second circuit through the relay to the load the circuit operates. When the relay is switched off (de-energized), the armature springs back and opens the contact points, cutting off the current flow in the secondary, or controlled, circuit. Relays can be designed to be either open or closed when energized, depending on the type of circuit control a manufacturer requires.

A buzzer is similar to a relay, but its internal connections are different. When the switch is closed, the current flows through the normally closed contacts and energizes the coil. When the coil core becomes magnetized, it bends the armature down and breaks the circuit. As soon as the circuit is broken, the spring-loaded armature remakes the circuit and again energizes the coil. This cycle repeats rapidly to cause the buzzing sound.

A solenoid is constructed like a relay, except that its core is allowed to move, providing mechanical motion that can be used to actuate mechanical linkage to operate a door or trunk lock or control any other mechanical function. When the switch is closed, the coil is energized and the movable core is drawn

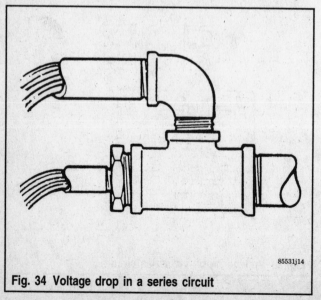

85531j14

Fig. 34 Voltage drop in a series circuit

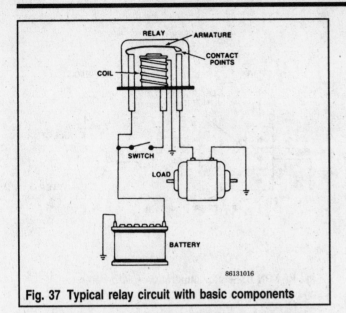

Fig. 37 Typical relay circuit with basic components

into the coil. When the switch is opened, the coil is de-energized and spring pressure returns the core to its original position.

Basic Solid State

The term 'solid state' refers to devices utilizing transistors, diodes and other components which are made from materials known as semiconductors. A semiconductor is a material that is neither a good insulator nor a good conductor; principally silicon and germanium. The semiconductor material is specially treated to give it certain qualities that enhance its function, therefore becoming either P-type (positive) or N-type (negative) material. Most semiconductors are constructed of silicon and can be designed to function either as an insulator or conductor.

DIODES

▶ **See Figures 38 and 39**

The simplest semiconductor function is that of the diode or rectifier (the 2 terms mean the same thing). A diode will pass current in one direction only, like a one-way valve, because it has low resistance in one direction and high resistance on the other. Whether the diode conducts or not depends on the polarity of the voltage applied to it. A diode has 2 electrodes, an anode and a cathode. When the anode receives positive (+) voltage and the cathode receives negative (-) voltage, current can flow easily through the diode. When the voltage is reversed, the diode becomes non-conducting and only allows a very slight amount of current to flow in the circuit. Because the semiconductor is not a perfect insulator, a small amount of reverse current leakage will occur, but the amount is usually too small to consider. The application of voltage to maintain the current flow described is called 'forward bias.'

A light-emitting diode (LED) is made of a particular type of crystal that glows when current is passed through it. LED's are used in display faces of many digital or electronic instrument clusters. LED's are usually arranged to display numbers (digital

readout), but can be used to illuminate a variety of electronic graphic displays.

Like any other electrical device, diodes have certain ratings that must be observed and should not be exceeded. The forward current rating (or bias) indicates how much current can safely pass through the diode without causing damage or destroying it. Forward current rating is usually given in either amperes or milliamperes. The voltage drop across a diode remains constant regardless of the current flowing through it. Small diodes designed to carry low amounts of current need no special provision for dissipating the heat generated in any electrical device, but large current carrying diodes are usually mounted on heat sinks to keep the internal temperature from rising to the point where the silicon will melt and destroy the diode. When diodes are operated in a high ambient temperature environment, they must be de-rated to prevent failure.

Another diode specification is its peak inverse voltage rating. This value is the maximum amount of voltage the diode can safely handle when operating in the blocking mode. This value can be anywhere from 50-1000 volts, depending on the diode.

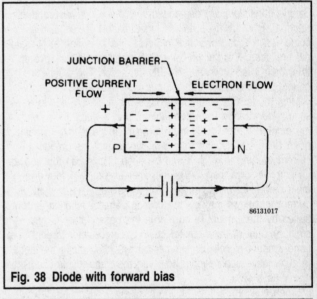

Fig. 38 Diode with forward bias

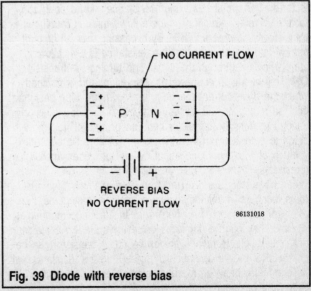

Fig. 39 Diode with reverse bias

If voltage amount is exceeded, it will damage the diode just as too much forward current will. Most semiconductor failures are caused by excessive voltage or internal heat.

One can test a diode with a small battery and a lamp with the same voltage rating. With this arrangement one can find a bad diode and determine the polarity of a good one. A diode can fail and cause either a short or open circuit, but in either case it fails to function as a diode. Testing is simply a matter of connecting the test bulb first in one direction and then the other and making sure that current flows in one direction only. If the diode is shorted, the test bulb will remain on no matter how the light is connected.

TRANSISTORS

▶ **See Figures 40, 41, 42, 43, 44, 45 and 46**

The transistor is an electrical device used to control voltage within a circuit. A transistor can be considered a 'controllable diode' in that, in addition to passing or blocking current, the transistor can control the amount of current passing through it. Simple transistors are composed of 3 pieces of semiconductor material, P and N type, joined together and enclosed in a container. If 2 sections of P material and 1 section of N material are used, it is known as a PNP transistor; if the reverse is true, then it is known as an NPN transistor. The 2 types cannot be interchanged.

Most modern transistors are made from silicon (earlier transistors were made from germanium) and contain 3 elements; the emitter, the collector and the base. In addition to passing or blocking current, the transistor can control the amount of current passing through it and because of this can function as an amplifier or a switch. The collector and emitter form the main current-carrying circuit of the transistor. The amount of current that flows through the collector-emitter junction is controlled by the amount of current in the base circuit. Only a small amount of base-emitter current is necessary to control a large amount of collector-emitter current (the amplifier effect). In automotive applications, however, the transistor is used primarily as a switch.

When no current flows in the base-emitter junction, the collector-emitter circuit has a high resistance, like to open contacts of a relay. Almost no current flows through the circuit and transistor is considered **OFF**. By bypassing a small amount of current into the base circuit, the resistance is low, allowing current to flow through the circuit and turning the transistor **ON**. This condition is known as 'saturation' and is reached when the base current reaches the maximum value designed into the transistor that allows current to flow. Depending on various factors, the transistor can turn on and off (go from cutoff to saturation) in less than one millionth of a second.

Much of what was said about ratings for diodes applies to transistors, since they are constructed of the same materials. When transistors are required to handle relatively high currents, such as in voltage regulators or ignition systems, they are generally mounted on heat sinks in the same manner as diodes. They can be damaged or destroyed in the same manner if their voltage ratings are exceeded. A transistor can be checked for proper operation by measuring the resistance with an ohmmeter between the base-emitter terminals and then between the base-collector terminals. The forward resistance

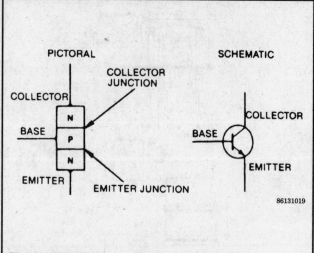

Fig. 40 NPN transistor illustration (pictorial and schematic)

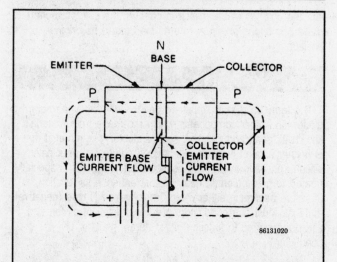

Fig. 41 PNP transistor with base switch closed (base emitter and collector emitter current (flow)

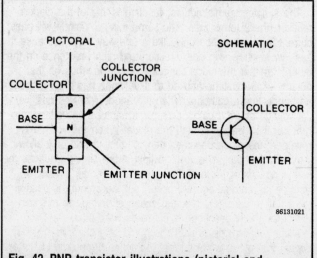

Fig. 42 PNP transistor illustrations (pictorial and schematic)

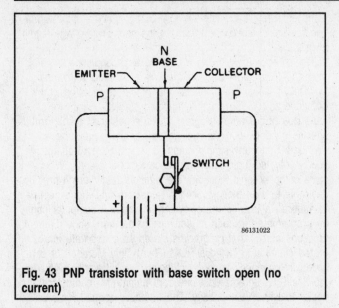

Fig. 43 PNP transistor with base switch open (no current)

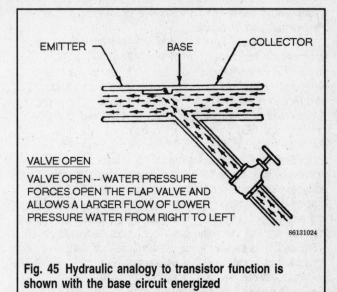

VALVE OPEN

VALVE OPEN -- WATER PRESSURE FORCES OPEN THE FLAP VALVE AND ALLOWS A LARGER FLOW OF LOWER PRESSURE WATER FROM RIGHT TO LEFT

Fig. 45 Hydraulic analogy to transistor function is shown with the base circuit energized

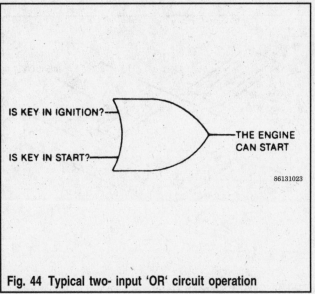

Fig. 44 Typical two- input 'OR' circuit operation

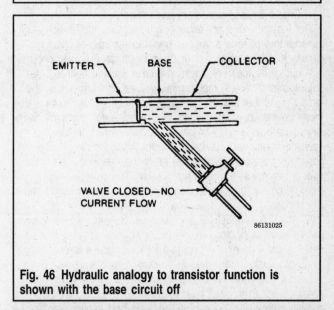

VALVE CLOSED—NO CURRENT FLOW

Fig. 46 Hydraulic analogy to transistor function is shown with the base circuit off

should be small, while the reverse resistance should be large. Compare the readings with those from a known good transistor. As a final check, measure the forward and reverse resistance between the collector and emitter terminals.

INTEGRATED CIRCUITS

The integrated circuit (IC) is an extremely sophisticated solid state device that consists of a silicone wafer (or chip) which has been doped, insulated and etched many times so that it contains an entire electrical circuit with transistors, diodes, conductors and capacitors miniaturized within each tiny chip. Integrated circuits are often referred to as 'computers on a chip' and are largely responsible for the current boom in electronic control technology.

Microprocessors, Computers and Logic Systems

▶ **See Figures 47, 48, 49, 50, 51, 52 and 53**

Mechanical or electromechanical control devices lack the precision necessary to meet the requirements of modern control standards. They do not have the ability to respond to a variety of input conditions common to antilock brakes, climate control and electronic suspension operation. To meet these requirements, manufacturers have gone to solid state logic systems and microprocessors to control the basic functions of suspension, brake and temperature control, as well as other systems and accessories.

One of the more vital roles of microprocessor-based systems is their ability to perform logic functions and make decisions. Logic designers use a shorthand notation to indicate whether a voltage is present in a circuit (the number 1) or not present (the number 0). Their systems are designed to respond in different ways depending on the output signal (or the lack of it) from various control devices.

There are 3 basic logic functions or 'gates' used to construct a microprocessor control system: the AND gate, the OR gate or the NOT gate. Stated simply, the AND gate works when voltage is present in 2 or more circuits which then energize a third (A and B energize C). The OR gate works when voltage is present at either circuit A or circuit B which then energizes circuit C. The NOT function is performed by a solid state device called an 'inverter' which reverses the input from a circuit so that, if voltage is going in, no voltage comes out and vice versa. With these three basic building blocks, a logic designer can create complex systems easily. In actual use, a logic or decision making system may employ many logic gates and receive inputs from a number of sources (sensors), but for the most part, all utilize the basic logic gates discussed above.

Stripped to its bare essentials, a computerized decision-making system is made up of 3 subsystems:
- Input devices (sensors or switches)
- Logic circuits (computer control unit)
- Output devices (actuators or controls)

The input devices are usually nothing more than switches or sensors that provide a voltage signal to the control unit logic circuits that is read as a 1 or 0 (on or off) by the logic circuits. The output devices are anything from a warning light to solenoid-operated valves, motors, linkage, etc. In most cases, the logic circuits themselves lack sufficient output power to operate these devices directly. Instead, they operate some intermediate device such as a relay or power transistor which in turn operates the appropriate device or control. Many problems diagnosed as computer failures are really the result of a malfunctioning intermediate device like a relay. This must be kept in mind whenever troubleshooting any microprocessor-based control system.

As computer capacity is improved by the manufacturers, so does sensor technology. A few years ago, the on-board computer would receive a message from an engine sensor in a 'go or no-go' form; for example the coolant temperature would either be above or below 150°F. Today's systems allow the same sensor to to pass progressively more voltage as the engine warms up. The engine computer now knows exactly

what temperature the coolant is at all times. With this information the the computer can react to the changing voltage signal from the sensor instantly and control other engine functions based on engine warm-up or over heating conditions.

The logic systems discussed above are called 'hardware' systems, because they consist only of the physical electronic components (gates, resistors, transistors, etc.). Hardware systems do not contain a program and are designed to perform specific or 'dedicated' functions which cannot readily be changed. For many simple automotive control requirements, such dedicated logic systems are perfectly adequate. When more complex logic functions are required, or where it may be desirable to alter these functions (e.g. from one model vehicle to another) a true computer system is used. A computer can be programmed through its software to perform many different functions and, if that program is stored on a separate integrated circuit chip called a ROM (Read Only Memory), it can be easily changed simply by plugging in a different ROM with the desired program. Most on-board automotive computers are designed with this capability. The on-board computer method

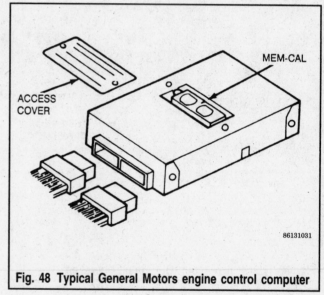

Fig. 48 Typical General Motors engine control computer

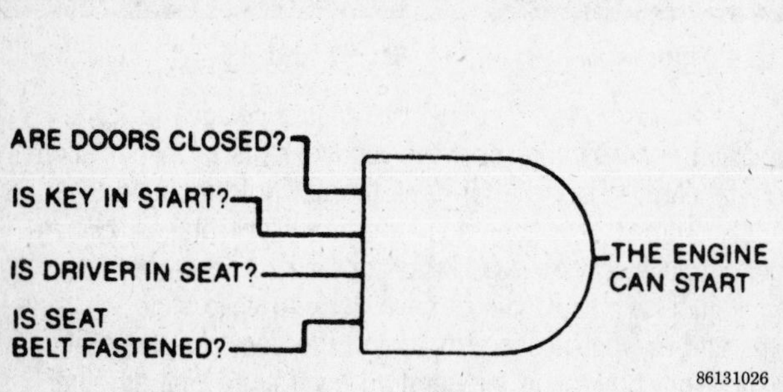

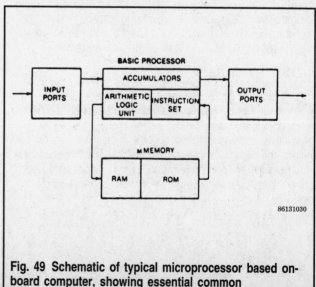

Fig. 47 Multiple inputs 'AND' operation in a typical automotive starting circuit

Fig. 49 Schematic of typical microprocessor based on-board computer, showing essential common

of engine control offers the manufacturer a flexible method of responding to data from a variety of input devices and of controlling an equally large variety of output controls. The computer response can be changed quickly and easily by simply modifying its software program.

The microprocessor is the heart of the microcomputer. It is the thinking part of the computer system through which all the data from the various sensors passes. Within the microprocessor, data is acted upon, compared, manipulated or stored for future use. A microprocessor is not necessarily a microcomputer, but the differences between the 2 are becoming very minor. Originally, a microprocessor was a major part of a microcomputer, but nowadays microprocessors are being called 'single-chip microcomputers'. They contain all the essential elements to make them behave as a computer, including the most important ingredient-the program.

All computers require a program. In a general purpose computer, the program can be easily changed to allow different tasks to be performed. In a 'dedicated' computer, such as most on-board automotive computers, the program isn't quite so easily altered. These automotive computers are designed to perform one or several specific tasks, such as maintaining the passenger compartment temperature at a specific, predetermined level. A program is what makes a computer smart; without a program a computer can do absolutely nothing. The term 'software' refers to the computer's program that makes the hardware preform the function needed.

The software program is simply a listing in sequential order of the steps or commands necessary to make a computer perform the desired task. Before the computer can do anything at all, the program must be fed into it by one of several possible methods. A computer can never be 'smarter' than the person programming it, but it is a lot faster. Although it cannot perform any calculation or operation that the programmer himself cannot perform, its processing time is measured in millionths of a second.

Because a computer is limited to performing only those operations (instructions) programmed into its memory, the program must be broken down into a large number of very simple steps. Two different programmers can come up with 2 different programs, since there is usually more than one way to perform any task or solve a problem. In any computer, however, there is only so much memory space available, so an overly long or inefficient program may not fit into the memory. In addition to performing arithmetic functions (such as with a trip computer), a computer can also store data, look up data in a table and perform the logic functions previously discussed. A Random Access Memory (RAM) allows the computer to store bits of data temporarily while waiting to be acted upon by the program. It may also be used to store output data that is to be sent to an output device. Whatever data is stored in a RAM is lost when power is removed from the system by turning **OFF** the ignition key, for example.

Computers have another type of memory called a Read Only Memory (ROM) which is permanent. This memory is not lost when the power is removed from the system. Most programs for automotive computers are stored on a ROM memory chip. Data is usually in the form of a look-up table that saves computing time and program steps. For example, a computer designed to control the amount of distributor advance can have this information stored in a table. The information that determines distributor advance (engine rpm, manifold vacuum and

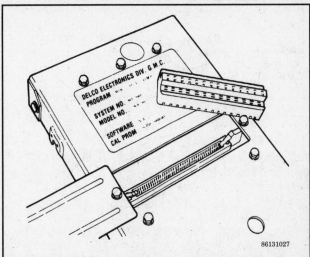

Fig. 50 Electronic control module with Mem-Cal, used in General Motors vehicles

temperature) is coded to produce the correct amount of distributor advance over a wide range of engine operating conditions. Instead of the computer computing the required advance, it simply looks it up in a pre-programmed table. However, not all electronic control functions can be handled in this manner; some must be computed. On an antilock brake system, for example, the computer must measure the rotation of each separate wheel and then calculate how much brake pressure to apply in order to prevent one wheel from locking up and causing a loss of control.

There are several ways of programming a ROM, but once programmed the ROM cannot be changed. If the ROM is made on the same chip that contains the microprocessor, the whole computer must be altered if a program change is needed. For this reason, a ROM is usually placed on a separate chip. Another type of memory is the Programmable Read Only Memory (PROM) that has the program 'burned in' with the appropriate programming machine. Like the ROM, once a PROM has been programmed, it cannot be changed. The advantage of the PROM is that it can be produced in small quantities economically, since it is manufactured with a blank

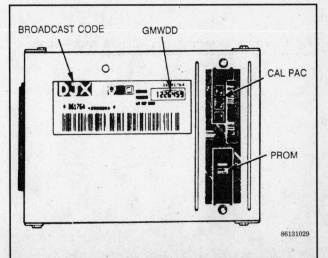

Fig. 51 Identification of a General Motors powertrain control module (PCM)

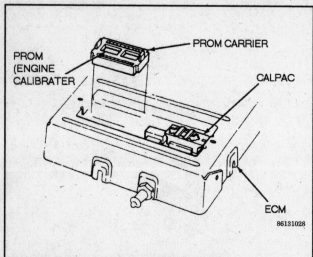

Fig. 52 Electronic control module with PROM and CALPAK, used in General Motors vehicles

memory. Program changes for various vehicles can be made readily. There is still another type of memory called an EPROM (Erasable PROM) which can be erased and programmed many times. EPROM's are used only in research and development work, not on production vehicles.

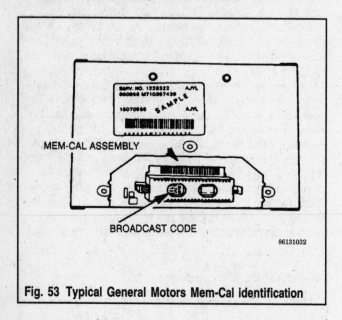

Fig. 53 Typical General Motors Mem-Cal identification

General Motors refers to the engine controlling computer as an Electronic Control Module (ECM). The ECM contains the PROM necessary for all engine functions, it also contains a device called a CalPak. This allows the fuel delivery function should other parts of the ECM become damaged. It has an access door in the ECM, like the PROM has. There is a third type control module used in some ECMs called a Mem-Cal. The Mem-Cal contains the function of PROM, CalPak and Electronic Spark Control (EST) module. Like the PROM, it contains the calibrations needed for a specific vehicle, as well as the back-up fuel control circuitry required if the rest of the ECM should become damaged and the spark control. An ECM containing a PROM and CalPak can be identified by the 2 connector harnesses, while the ECM containing the Mem-Cal has 3 connector harnesses attached to it.

Engines coupled to electronically controlled transmissions employ a Powertrain Control Module (PCM) to oversee both engine and transmission operation. This unit may be referred to as the PCM, the ECM/PCM or the PCM/TCM (Transmission Control Module). The integrated functions of engine and transmission control allow accurate gear selection and improved fuel economy.

For engine diagnostics, the PCM may be considered identical to an ECM system, although the combined unit will display additional codes relating to transmission function and components.

➡**When the term Powertrain Control Module (PCM) is used in this manual it will refer to the engine control computer regardless that it may be a Powertrain Control Module (PCM) or Electronic Control Module (ECM).**

BASIC TUNE-UP PROCEDURES

▶ **See Figure 54**

In order to extract the best performance and economy from your engine, it is essential that it be properly tuned at regular intervals. A regular tune-up/inspection will keep the engine running smoothly and will prevent the annoying minor breakdowns and poor performance associated with an untuned engine.

A complete tune-up/inspection should generally be performed every 30,000 miles (48,000 km) or 24 months, whichever comes first. This interval should be halved (as a general rule of thumb) if the vehicle is operated under severe conditions, such as trailer towing, prolonged idling, continual stop and start driving, or if starting or running problems are noticed. It is assumed that the routine maintenance has been kept up, as this will have a decided effect on the results of a tune-up.

Some 1994 and newer vehicles are specified to go up to 100,000 miles between engine tune-ups, you can always refer the owners guide or a Maintenance Interval Chart found in a 'Chilton Total Car Care Manual'. A tune-up/inspection for all models should consists of the following items

- Inspect the drive belts.
- If necessary, check and adjust valve clearance.
- Clean the air filter housing and replacing the air filter element.
- If equipped, replace the PCV filter and Pulsed secondary air injection filter.
- Inspect or replace the fuel filter assembly.
- Inspect all fuel and vapor lines.
- Check or replace the distributor cap, rotor and ignition wires.
- Replace the spark plugs and make all necessary engine adjustments.
- Always refer to the Maintenance Interval Chart for additional service information.

➡**If the tune-up specifications on the Vehicle Emission Control Information sticker in the engine compartment of your vehicle disagree with the Tune-Up Specifications in** the repair manual, the figures on the sticker must be used. The sticker often reflects changes made during the production run.

Spark Plugs

➡**The platinum type spark plug is not recommended by all manufacturers. If the vehicle has an aftermarket type platinum plug installed, these plugs are usually marked and are not to be cleaned or regapped.**

Spark plugs ignite the air and fuel mixture in the cylinder as the piston reaches the top of the compression stroke. The controlled explosion that results forces the piston down, turning the crankshaft and the rest of the drive train.

The average life of a spark plug is about 30,000 miles (48,000 km). This is, however, dependent on a number of factors: the mechanical condition of the engine, the type of fuel, the driving conditions and the driver.

When you remove the spark plugs, check their condition. Plugs are a good indicator of engine condition. A small deposit of light tan or gray material on a spark plug that has been used for any period of time is to be considered normal. Any other color, or abnormal amounts of deposit, indicates that there may be something wrong in the engine.

When a spark plug is functioning normally or, more accurately, when the plug is installed in an engine that is functioning properly, the plugs can be taken out, cleaned, regapped, and reinstalled in the engine without causing the engine any harm.

When, and if, a plug fouls and begins to misfire, you will have to investigate, correct the cause of the fouling, and either clean or replace the plug. There are several reasons why a spark plug will foul and you can learn which is at fault by just looking at the plug.

There are many spark plugs suitable for use in your engine and are offered in a number of different heat ranges. The amount of heat which the plug absorbs is determined by the length of the lower insulator. The longer the insulator the hotter the plug will operate; the shorter the insulator, the cooler it will operate. A spark plug that absorbs (or retains) little heat and remains too cool will accumulate deposits of lead, oil, and carbon, because it is not hot enough to burn them off. This leads to fouling and consequent misfiring. A spark plug that absorbs too much heat will have no deposits, but the electrodes will burn away quickly and, in some cases, pre-ignition may result. Pre-ignition occurs when the spark plug tips get so hot that they ignite the air/fuel mixture before the actual spark fires. This premature ignition will usually cause a pinging sound under conditions of low speed and heavy load. In severe cases, the heat may become high enough to start the air/fuel mixture burning throughout the combustion chamber rather than just to the front of the plug. In this case, the resultant explosion could be strong enough to damage pistons, rings, and valves.

In most cases the factory recommended heat range is correct; it is chosen to perform well under a wide range of operating conditions. However, if most of your driving is long distance, high speed travel, you may want to install a spark plug

Fig. 54 Because of the tangle of underhood wiring, ALWAYS tag/note wire locations before removal

86712038

one step colder than standard. If most of your driving is of the short trip variety, when the engine may not always reach operating temperature, a hotter plug may help burn off the deposits normally accumulated under those conditions.

REMOVAL

▶ **See Figures 55, 56, 57, 58, 59, 60, 61 and 62**

➡**Some engines use two spark plugs per cylinder, be sure to replace them all.**

1. Disconnect the negative battery cable.

➡**Always keep track of the spark plug cable routing and plug wire bracket locations.**

2. Number the spark plug wires so that you won't cross them when they are reconnected.
3. Remove the wire from the end of the spark plug by grasping the rubber boot. If the boot sticks to the plug, remove

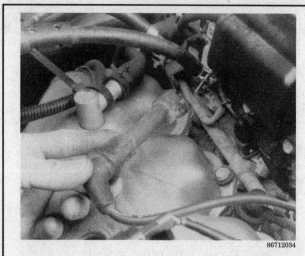

Fig. 57 Mark and remove the spark plug wires one at a time to avoid a mix-up

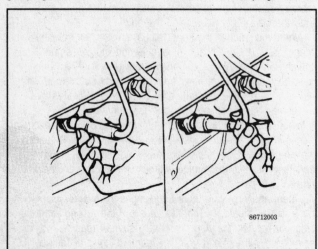

Fig. 55 Twist and pull on the rubber boot to remove the spark plug wires; NEVER pull on the wire itself

Fig. 58 Carefully unthread the spark plug from the cylinder head using the proper tools

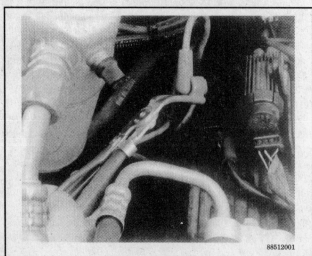

Fig. 56 Using this special tool to remove the spark plug wire makes the job easier; NEVER pull on the wire itself

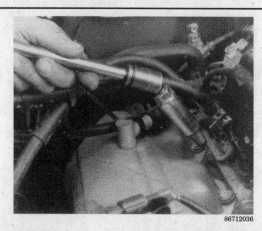

Fig. 59 In this case, a universal joint made plug removal easier — be careful when using a universal joint on a spark plug, a shear force may be applied if the tool is not properly supported

GAP BRIDGED

IDENTIFIED BY DEPOSIT BUILD-UP CLOSING GAP BETWEEN ELECTRODES.

CAUSED BY OIL OR CARBON FOULING, REPLACE PLUG, OR, IF DEPOSITS ARE NOT EXCESSIVE THE PLUG CAN BE CLEANED.

OIL FOULED

IDENTIFIED BY WET BLACK DEPOSITS ON THE INSULATOR SHELL BORE ELECTRODES.

CAUSED BY EXCESSIVE OIL ENTERING COMBUSTION CHAMBER THROUGH WORN RINGS AND PISTONS, EXCESSIVE CLEARANCE BETWEEN VALVE GUIDES AND STEMS, OR WORN OR LOOSE BEARINGS. CORRECT OIL PROBLEM. REPLACE THE PLUG.

CARBON FOULED

IDENTIFIED BY BLACK, DRY FLUFFY CARBON DEPOSITS ON INSULATOR TIPS, EXPOSED SHELL SURFACES AND ELECTRODES.

CAUSED BY TOO COLD A PLUG, WEAK IGNITION, DIRTY AIR CLEANER, DEFECTIVE FUEL PUMP, TOO RICH A FUEL MIXTURE, IMPROPERLY OPERATING HEAT RISER OR EXCESSIVE IDLING. CAN BE CLEANED.

NORMAL

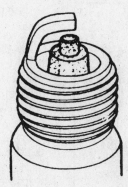

IDENTIFIED BY LIGHT TAN OR GRAY DEPOSITS ON THE FIRING TIP.

PRE-IGNITION

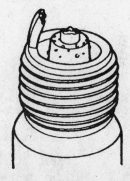

IDENTIFIED BY MELTED ELECTRODES AND POSSIBLY BLISTERED INSULATOR. METALIC DEPOSITS ON INSULATOR INDICATE ENGINE DAMAGE.

CAUSED BY WRONG TYPE OF FUEL, INCORRECT IGNITION TIMING OR ADVANCE, TOO HOT A PLUG, BURNT VALVES OR ENGINE OVERHEATING. REPLACE THE PLUG.

OVERHEATING

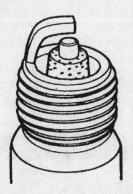

IDENTIFIED BY A WHITE OR LIGHT GRAY INSULATOR WITH SMALL BLACK OR GRAY BROWN SPOTS AND WITH BLUISH-BURNT APPEARANCE OF ELECTRODES.

CAUSED BY ENGINE OVER-HEATING, WRONG TYPE OF FUEL, LOOSE SPARK PLUGS, TOO HOT A PLUG, LOW FUEL PUMP PRESSURE OR INCORRECT IGNITION TIMING. REPLACE THE PLUG.

FUSED SPOT DEPOSIT

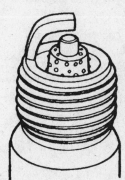

IDENTIFIED BY MELTED OR SPOTTY DEPOSITS RESEMBLING BUBBLES OR BLISTERS.

CAUSED BY SUDDEN ACCELERATION. CAN BE CLEANED IF NOT EXCESSIVE. OTHERWISE REPLACE PLUG.

TCCS2002

Fig. 60 Inspect the spark plug to determine engine running conditions

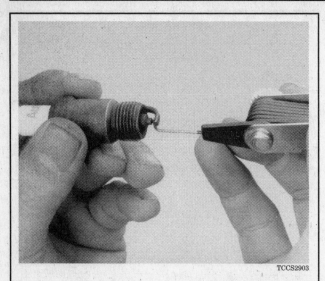

TCCS2903

Fig. 61 Check the spark plugs with a wire feeler gauge

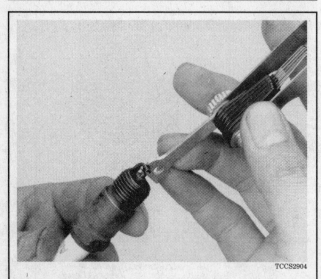

TCCS2904

Fig. 62 Bend the side electrode to adjust the gap

it by twisting and pulling at the same time. DO NOT pull wire itself or you will damage the core.

4. Use a spark plug socket to loosen all of the plugs about two turns.

➡**Remove the spark plugs when the engine is cold, if possible, to prevent damage to the threads. If removal of the plugs is difficult, apply a few drops of penetrating oil or silicone spray to the area around the base of the plug, and allow it a few minutes to work.**

5. If compressed air is available, apply it to the area around the spark plug holes. Otherwise, use a rag or a brush to clean the area. Be careful not to allow any foreign material to drop into the spark plug holes.

6. Remove the plugs by unscrewing them the rest of the way from the engine.

INSPECTION

Check the plugs for deposits and wear. If they are not going to be replaced, clean the plugs thoroughly. Remember that any kind of deposit will decrease the efficiency of the plug. Plugs can be cleaned on a spark plug cleaning machine, which can sometimes be found in service stations, or you can do an acceptable job of cleaning with a stiff brush. If the plugs are cleaned, the electrodes must be filed flat. Use an ignition points file, not an emery board or the like, which will leave deposits. The electrodes must be filed perfectly flat with sharp edges; rounded edges reduce the spark plug voltage by as much as 50%.

Check spark plug gap before installation. The ground electrode (the L-shaped one connected to the body of the plug) must be parallel to the center electrode and the specified size wire gauge (please refer to the Tune-Up Specifications chart for details) must pass between the electrodes with a slight drag.

➡**NEVER adjust the gap on a used platinum type spark plug.**

Always check the gap on new plugs as they are not always set correctly at the factory. Do not use a flat feeler gauge when measuring the gap on a used plug, because the reading may be inaccurate. A wire type gapping tool is the best way to check the gap. Wire gapping tools usually have a bending tool attached. Use that to adjust the side electrode until the proper distance is obtained. Absolutely never attempt to bend the center electrode. Also, be careful not to bend the side electrode too far or too often as it may weaken and break off within the engine, requiring removal of the cylinder head to retrieve it.

INSTALLATION

1. Lubricate the threads of the spark plugs with a drop of oil. Install the plugs and tighten them by hand first. Take care not to cross-thread them.

2. Tighten the spark plugs with a plug socket. Do not apply the same amount of force you would use for a bolt; just snug them in. If a torque wrench is available, tighten to specific specifications for the vehicle you are working with. Consult your 'Chilton Total Car Care Manual.'

3. Install the wires on their respective plugs. Make sure the wires are firmly connected. You will be able to feel them click into place. Check the spark plug cable routing and always make sure the plug wires are in the correct plug wire bracket.

4. Connect the negative battery cable.

Spark Plug Wires

CHECKING & REPLACEMENT

◗ **See Figures 63 and 64**

At every tune-up/inspection, visually inspect the spark plug cables for burns cuts, or breaks in the insulation. Check the

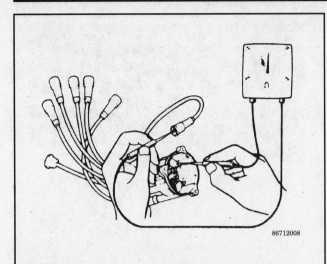

Fig. 63 Checking plug wire resistance through the distributor cap with an ohmmeter

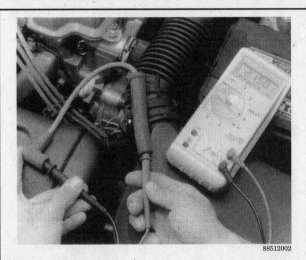

Fig. 64 Checking individual plug wire resistance with an digital ohmmeter

boots and the nipples on the distributor cap and coil. Replace any damaged wiring.

Every 50,000 miles (80,000 Km) or 60 months, the resistance of the wires should be checked with an ohmmeter. Wires with excessive resistance will cause misfiring, and may make the engine difficult to start in damp weather.

To check resistance, remove the distributor cap, leaving the wires attached. Connect one lead of an ohmmeter to an electrode within the cap; connect the other lead to the corresponding spark plug terminal (remove it from the plug for this test). Replace any wire which shows a resistance over 30,000 ohms. Test the high tension lead from the coil by connecting the ohmmeter between the center contact in the distributor cap and either of the primary terminals of the coil. If resistance is more than 25,000 ohms, remove the cable from the coil and check the resistance of the cable alone. Anything over 15,000 ohms is cause for replacement. It should be remembered that resistance is also a function of length; the longer the cable, the greater the resistance. Thus, if the cables on your vehicle are longer than the factory originals, resistance will be higher, and quite possibly outside these limits.

➡**The resistance reading given above is just a general specification, consult to your 'Chilton Total Car Care Manual' for specific specifications on your vehicle.**

When installing new cables, replace them one at a time to avoid mix-ups. Start by replacing the longest one first. Install the boot firmly over the spark plug. Route the wire over the same path as the original. Insert the nipple firmly into the tower on the cap or the coil. Check the spark plug cable routing and always make sure the plug wires are in the correct plug wire bracket.

Ignition Timing

▶ **See Figures 65, 66, 67 and 68**

Ignition timing is the measurement in degrees of crankshaft rotation of the instant the spark plug fires, in relation to the location of the piston (while the piston is on its compression stroke).

Although no periodic service is necessary, ignition timing can be adjusted by loosening the distributor locking device and turning the distributor in the engine.

Ideally, the air/fuel mixture in the cylinder will be ignited (by the spark plug) and just begin its rapid expansion as the piston passes top dead center (TDC) of the compression stroke. If this happens, the piston will be beginning the power stroke just as the compressed (by the movement of the piston) air/fuel mixture starts to expand. The expansion of the air/fuel mixture will then force the piston down on the power stroke and turn the crankshaft.

It takes a fraction of a second for the spark from the plug to completely ignite the mixture in the cylinder. Because of this, the spark plug must fire before the piston reaches TDC, if the mixture is to be completely ignited as the piston passes TDC. This measurement is given in degrees (of crankshaft rotation) Before the piston reaches Top Dead Center (BTDC). For example: if the ignition timing setting for your engine is seven (7°) BTDC, this means that the spark plug must fire at a time when the piston for that cylinder is 7° before top dead center of its compression stroke. However, this only holds true while your engine is at idle speed.

As you accelerate from idle, the speed of your engine, in revolutions per minute (rpm), increases. The increase in rpm means that the pistons are now traveling up and down much faster. Because of this, the spark plugs will have to fire even sooner if the mixture is to be completely ignited as the piston passes TDC. To accomplish this, the ECU unit incorporates means to advance the timing of the spark as engine speed increases.

If ignition timing is set too far advanced (too far BTDC), the ignition and expansion of the air/fuel mixture in the cylinder will try to force the piston down the cylinder while it is still traveling upward. This causes engine 'ping', a sound which resembles marbles being dropped into an empty tin can. If the ignition timing is too far retarded (after, or ATDC), the piston will have already started down on the power stroke when the air/fuel mixture ignites and expands. This will cause the piston to be forced down only a portion of its travel, resulting in poor engine performance and lack of power.

Fig. 65 Checking and adjusting the ignition timing to specifications

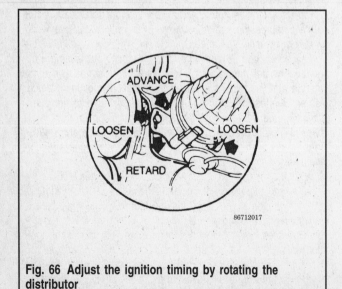

Fig. 66 Adjust the ignition timing by rotating the distributor

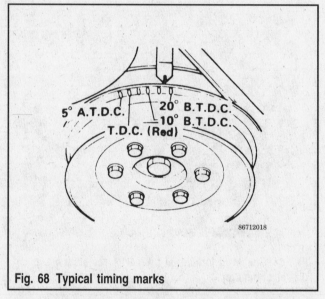

Fig. 67 Timing marks on a 6 cylinder engine — note the fan was removed for a better view

Fig. 68 Typical timing marks

Ignition timing adjustment is checked with a timing light. This instrument is connected to the Number One (No. 1) spark plug of the engine. The timing light flashes every time an electrical current is sent from the distributor, through the No. 1 spark plug wire, to the spark plug. The crankshaft pulley and the front cover of the engine are marked with a timing pointer and a timing scale. When the timing pointer is aligned with the **0** mark on the timing scale, the piston for the No. 1 cylinder is at TDC of its compression stroke. With the engine running, and the timing light aimed at the timing pointer/scale, the flashes from the timing light will allow you to check the ignition timing. The timing light flashes every time the spark plug in the No. 1 cylinder of the engine fires. Since the flash from the timing light makes the crankshaft pulley seem stationary for a moment you will be able to read the exact position of the piston in the No. 1 cylinder on the timing scale.

There are three basic types of timing lights available. The first is a simple neon bulb with two wire connections (one for the spark plug and one for the plug wire, connecting the light in series). This type of light is quite dim, and must be held closely to the marks to be seen, but it is inexpensive. The second type of light operates from the battery. Two alligator clips connect to the battery terminals, while a third wire connects to the spark plug with an adapter. This type of light is more expensive, but the xenon bulb provides a nice bright flash which can even be seen in sunlight. The third type replaces the battery source with 110 volt house current. Some timing lights have other functions built into them, such as dwell meters, tachometers, or remote starting switches. These are convenient, in that they reduce the tangle of wires under the hood, but may duplicate the functions of tools you already have.

For most vehicles, it is best to use a timing light with an inductive pickup. This pickup simply clamps onto the No. 1 plug wire, eliminating the adapter. It is not susceptible to crossfiring or false triggering, which may occur with a conventional light, due to the greater voltages produced by electronic ignition.

INSPECTION AND ADJUSTMENT

Idle Mixture Adjustment

Most vehicles today use a rather complex electronic fuel injection system which is regulated by a series of temperature, altitude (for California) and air flow sensors which feed information into an Electronic Control Unit (ECU). The control unit then relays an electronic signal to the injector nozzle(s), which allow(s) a predetermined amount of fuel into the combustion chamber. In this way all mixture control adjustments are regulated by the ECU, therefore on these vehicles no manual adjustments are necessary or possible.

➡For specific information consult your 'Chilton Total Car Care Manual' that applies to the vehicle you are working with.

Idle Speed Adjustment

▶ **See Figures 69 and 70**

Because of ECU control used on many vehicles today, no periodic service adjustments are necessary. If however the vehicle you are working with requires adjustment or an idle check, a general procedure is shown below. Consult your 'Chilton Total Car Care Manual' for the specific vehicle you are working with. ALSO, always refer to the instructions or specifications found on the Vehicle Emission Control Information (VECI) label found underhood for additional or updated information which is applicable to your particular vehicle.

❊❊CAUTION

For manual transmission models, set parking brake and check idle speed in N position. For automatic transmission equipped models, shifted into D for idle speed checks. When in Drive, the parking brake must be fully applied with both front and rear wheels chocked.

1. Turn **OFF** the: headlights, heater blower, air conditioning, and rear window defogger. If the vehicle has power steering,

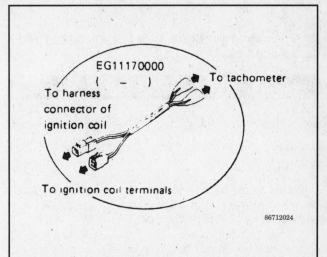

Fig. 69 Some vehicles require a special harness for the tachometer connection to check idle speed

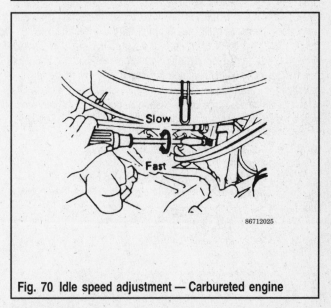

Fig. 70 Idle speed adjustment — Carbureted engine

make sure the wheels are in the straight ahead position. The ignition timing must be correct to get an effective idle speed adjustment. Connect a tachometer (a special adapter harness may be needed) according to the instrument manufacturer's directions.

2. Start the engine and warm the engine so it reaches normal operating temperature. The water temperature indicator should be in the middle of the gauge.

❊❊CAUTION

NEVER run the engine in a closed garage. Always make sure there is proper ventilation to prevent carbon monoxide poisoning.

3. Run engine at 2000 rpm for about 2 minutes under no load.

4. Race the engine to 2000-3000 rpm a few times under no load and then allow it to return to idle speed.

5. Apply the parking brake securely. If equipped with an automatic, put the transmission into **D**.

6. Adjust the idle speed by turning the idle speed adjusting screw.

7. Turn the engine **OFF** and remove the tachometer. Road test for proper operation.

Distributor Cap

CHECKING & REPLACEMENT

▶ See Figure 71

Disconnect the negative battery cable. Individually disconnect each ignition wire (one at a time) from the distributor cap and inspect the cap towers for corrosion build-up. Note, do not remove all of the spark plug wires from the cap, do this removing one wire, inspect the tower and wire contact then plug it back in. This will avoid getting the wires mixed up and out of the correct firing order. If all towers and spark plug wire contacts look good, make sure each wire is securely plug in its correct tower. Unfasten the retaining clips or unscrew the caps retaining screws and lift the cap off with the wires still attached. Inspect the underside of the distributor cap for cracks or carbon streaking between the contacts. Inspect the contacts for corrosion or wear. Replace the cap if any of the signs exists.

Some times water or condensation under the distributor cap will cause electrical current to short out between the contacts of the distributor cap or even wet ignition wires. If you have ever gone through a deep puddle of water and the engine stalls, chances are the ignition wires have become wet or the under the distributor cap. In this case it is possible to get the engine started by using a dry cloth and thoroughly drying the under side of the cap and the wires as best you can.

Distributor

REMOVAL

The procedure given below is a generalization and may not apply to the vehicle you are working with. Be sure to consult your 'Chilton Total Car Care Manual' for the vehicle your are working on.

1. Disconnect the negative battery cable.

2. Unfasten the retaining clips (only remove the coil wire if necessary) and lift the distributor cap straight off. It will be easier to install the distributor if the spark plug wiring is left connected to the cap. If the plug wires must be removed from the cap, mark their positions to aid in installation.

3. Remove the dust cover and mark the position of the rotor relative to the distributor body; then mark the position of the distributor body relative to the engine block.

4. Detach the harness assembly connector.

5. Remove the pinch-bolt and lift the distributor straight out, away from the engine. The rotor and body are marked so that they can be returned to the position from which they were removed. Do not turn or disturb the engine (unless absolutely necessary) after the distributor assembly has been removed.

INSTALLATION

Timing Not Disturbed
▶ See Figures 72, 73, 74, 75 and 77

1. Insert the distributor in the block and align ALL matchmarks made during removal.

2. Engage the distributor driven gear with the distributor drive.

3. Install the distributor clamp and secure it with the pinch-bolt.

4. Install the distributor cap and fasten the harness electrical connector.

5. If necessary, install the spark plug wires and coil wire.

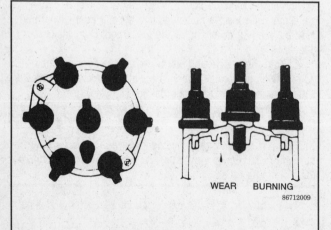

Fig. 71 Check under the distributor cap for cracks; check the cable ends for wear

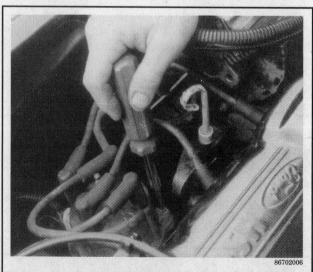

Fig. 72 Unscrew the distributor cap retaining screws

Fig. 73 Place the distributor cap and wires aside

Fig. 76 Remove the distributor retaining bolt

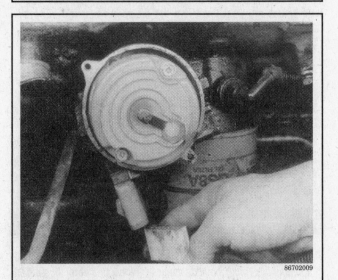

Fig. 74 Unplug the distributor harness connector

Fig. 77 Carefully remove the distributor

Fig. 75 Paint alignment marks on both the rotor cap and engine block

6. Start the engine. Check the timing and adjust it if necessary.

Timing Disturbed

▶ **See Figures 78 and 79**

This procedure gives you a basic and simple way to install the distributor correctly if the engine was cranked while the distributor was out of the engine. Another reason this procedure may be helpful is if when the distributor was removed from the engine it was not marked for installation position as mentioned in the above procedure. However, for specific instructions on the vehicle you are working with, consult your 'Chilton Total Car Care Manual'.

1. It is necessary to place the No. 1 cylinder in the firing position to correctly install the distributor. To locate this position, the ignition timing marks on the crankshaft front pulley can be used.

2. Remove the No. 1 cylinder spark plug. Turn the crankshaft until the piston in the No. 1 cylinder is moving up on the compression stroke. This can be determined by placing your

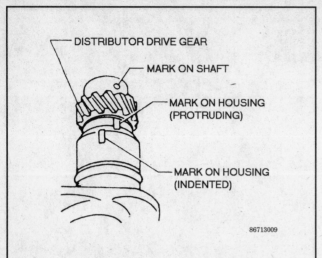

Fig. 78 Align the mark on the housing with the mark on the shaft

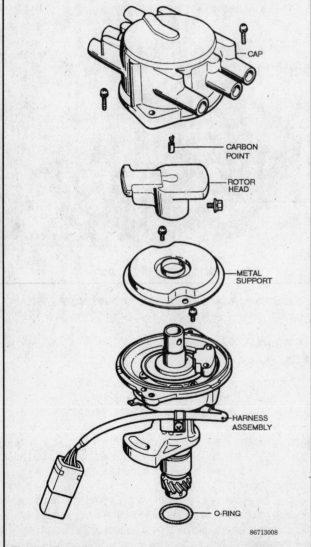

Fig. 79 Exploded view of the distributor assembly — typical 6 cylinder engine

thumb over the spark plug hole and feeling the air being forced out of the cylinder. Stop turning the crankshaft when the timing marks indicate **TDC** or **0**.

3. Oil the distributor housing lightly where the distributor bears on the cylinder block.

4. Install the distributor so that the rotor, which is mounted on the shaft, points toward the No. 1 spark plug terminal tower position when the cap is installed. Of course, you won't be able to see the direction in which the rotor is pointing if the cap is installed, so lay the cap on the top of the distributor and make a mark on the side of the distributor housing just below the No. 1 spark plug terminal. Make sure that the rotor points toward that mark when you install the distributor.

➡Some engines may have an alignment mark on the distributor shaft which should be aligned with the protruding mark on the distributor housing.

5. When the distributor shaft has reached the bottom of the hole, gently move the rotor back and forth slightly until the driving lug on the end of the shaft enters the slots cut in the end of the oil pump shaft and the distributor assembly slides down into place.

6. Fasten the distributor hold-down bolt.

7. Install the spark plug into the No. 1 spark plug hole.

8. Install the distributor cap and engage the harness electrical connector.

9. If necessary, attach the spark plug wires and coil wire.

10. Start the engine. Check the timing and adjust it if necessary.

As you can see, there are many variations depending on which vehicle your are working with. For specific procedures on the vehicle you are working on, consult your 'Chilton Total Car Care Manual'.

Ignition Coil

▶ See Figures 80, 81 and 82

Ignition coils may be externally mounted or internally located within the distributor. The procedure given below is a basic procedure for an externally mounted ignition coil. For specific

Fig. 80 Remove the coil assembly mounting bolts

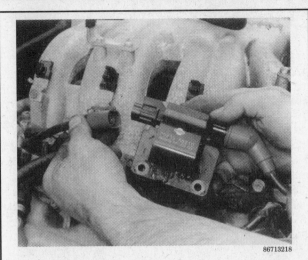

Fig. 81 Disconnect the electrical connection from the coil assembly

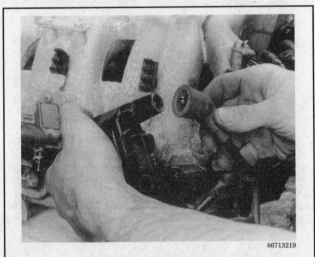

Fig. 82 Remove the coil ignition wire from the coil assembly

procedures on your vehicle, consult your 'Chilton Total Car Care Manual'.

REMOVAL & INSTALLATION

The procedure below is just a general procedure, consult your 'Chilton Total Care Care Manual' for specific procedure concerning the vehicle you are working with.

1. Disconnect the negative battery cable.
2. Remove the two mounting bolts and lift off the ignition coil.
3. Tag and disconnect all electrical leads at the coil.
4. Disconnect the coil high tension lead and remove the coil from the engine.

To install:

5. Connect all electrical leads to the coil as tagged.
6. Plug the high tension coil wire into the coil tower.
7. Install the coil in position and tighten the mounting bolts.
8. Connect the negative battery cable.

Engine Will Not Start

The procedure below is just a general procedure, consult your 'Chilton Total Care Care Manual' for specific procedure concerning the vehicle you are working with.

No Start Testing

1. Connect a voltmeter across the battery terminals. If battery voltage is not at least 12 volts, charge and test the battery before proceeding.
2. Turn the key to the **START** position and observe the voltmeter. If the engine turned over and battery voltage remained above 9.6 volts, go to next step. If the engine failed to crank and/or voltage was below 9.6 volts, proceed as follows:

   a. If the instrument panel lights dim, load test the battery, check the battery terminals and cables, test the starter motor and verify the engine turns.

   b. If the instrument panel lights do not dim, check the battery terminal connections, the ignition switch/wiring and the starter.

3. Using a spark tester, check for spark at two or more spark plugs. If okay go to next step, if not okay, perform No Spark Testing.
4. Cycle the ignition switch on and off, several times, while listening for fuel pump operation. If fuel pump operates, proceed to next step. If fuel pump does not operate begin testing of the fuel pump circuit.
5. Verify adequate fuel in the tank, then connect a fuel pressure gauge and check fuel pressure. If fuel pressure is within specifications, proceed to next step, if not okay continue on checking the fuel pump and supply system.
6. Disconnect the fuel injector connector and connect a noid light to the wiring harness. Crank the engine, while watch-

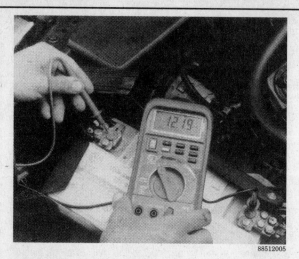

Fig. 83 Battery voltage should remain over 9.6 volts, while the engine is cranking

2. Check for spark from the ignition coil wire. If spark does not exist go to next step, if spark is okay, check distributor cap, rotor and ignition wires.

3. Check the ignition coil wire with an ohmmeter. Resistance should not exceed 1000 ohms per inch of cable. If wire resistance exceeds specification, replace the wire and retest. If wire is okay, proceed to the next step.

4. Connect a test light to the negative side of the ignition coil. Turn the key to the **ON** position and observe the test light. If the light remains brightly lit, proceed to the next step. If the light did not light, or glowed dim, check the ignition switch and power supply circuit.

5. Observe the light while cranking the engine. If the light was flashing during cranking, check the ignition coil. If the light did not flash, verify the distributor rotates smoothly, then test the ignition module, pick-up coil or hall effect switch.

ing the light. Perform this test on at least two injectors before proceeding. If the light does not flash, go to the next step. If the light flashes, check the engine valve timing and overall mechanical condition of the engine. If okay, items such as; poor fuel quality, faulty injectors and computer controlled devices should be checked. Although these items are less likely, a shorted TPS or faulty coolant temperature sensor, are possibilities.

7. Check and verify the Malfunction Indicator Lamp (MIL) is operating properly. If the light does not operate, check the ECM and related wiring. If the MIL lamp is operational, check the injector wiring and circuitry.

No Spark Testing

1. Check for spark at two or more spark plugs. If spark does not exist go to next step, if spark is okay, check spark plugs, fuel system and engine mechanical condition.

Fig. 84 Testing the ignition coil resistance

RELIEVING FUEL PRESSURE

The procedure is a generic procedure for most fuel injected vehicles. Carbureted vehicles may not use an electric fuel pump. Carbureted systems are lower pressure. For specific procedures on your vehicle, consult your 'Chilton Total Car Care Manual'.

1. Disable the fuel pump by one of the following methods:
   - Remove the fuel pump fuse.
   - Remove the fuel pump relay.
   - Locate and disconnect the fuel pump wiring.

➡When removing the fuel pump fuse or relay to disable the fuel pump, it is important to make certain that the fuel injectors are not part of this circuit. If the injectors do not operate the residual fuel system pressure will not be relieved.

2. Start the engine and operate it until it stalls. Once the engine has stalled, crank the starter for an additional 10 seconds.

3. Place a rag over the connection in which you intend to disconnect and carefully separate the connections. Use the rag to absorb any remaining fuel.

PREVENTIVE MAINTENANCE

Air Cleaner

The air cleaner element should be replaced at the recommended maintenance intervals. If your vehicle is operated under severely dusty conditions or severe operating conditions, more frequent changes will certainly be necessary. Inspect the element at least twice a year. Early spring and early fall are good times for an inspection. Remove the element and check for any perforations or tears in the filter. Check the cleaner housing for signs of dirt or dust that may have leaked through the filter element or in through the snorkel tube. Position a droplight on one side of the element and look through the filter at the light. If no glow of light can be seen through the element material, replace the filter. If holes in the filter element are apparent, or signs of dirt seepage through the filter are evident, replace the filter.

REMOVAL & INSTALLATION

◆ See Figures 85, 86, 87 and 88

Air cleaners come a wide selection of shapes and sizes. Most common are either round or rectangular. In any event, air filter element replacement is usually pretty simple.

If your vehicle is equipped with a round type air cleaner, it probably has one or two wing nuts and/or some clips holding the air cleaner lid in place. Just remove the wing nuts and unclip the retaining clips. Lift the lid off and remove the element.

If your vehicle is equipped with a rectangular type air cleaner, unclip the retaining clips and lift off the air cleaner lid. remove the element from the assembly. Some these units may not be as easily accessible and may require removing a hose or two, but all in all it's pretty simple to do.

Air Cleaner Assembly (Housing)

1. Disconnect all hoses, ducts and vacuum tubes from the air cleaner assembly, after tagging them for easy identification.

2. Remove the top cover wing nuts and grommet (if so equipped). Most models also utilize four to five side clips to further secure the top of the assembly. Simply pull the wire tab and release the clip. On most 1990 and later vehicles, air cleaners are secured solely by means of clips (air box-to-cleaner housing). Remove the cover and lift out the filter element.

3. Remove any side mount brackets and/or retaining bolts, then lift off the air cleaner assembly.

4. Clean or replace the filter element as detailed previously. Wipe clean all surfaces of the air cleaner housing and cover. Check the condition of the mounting gasket and replace if it appears worn or broken.

5. Reposition the air cleaner assembly, then install the mounting bracket and/or bolts.

6. Reposition the filter element in the case and install the cover being careful not to overtighten the wingnut(s). On

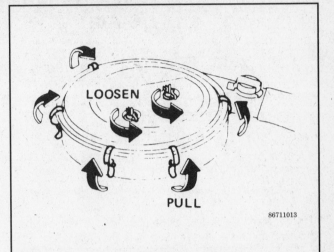

Fig. 85 Removing the air cleaner filter element — round type

Fig. 86 Removing the air cleaner filter element — rectangular

round-style cleaners, be certain that the arrows on the cover lid and the snorkel match up properly.

➡Filter elements on many engines have a TOP and BOTTOM side; be sure they are inserted correctly.

7. Reconnect all hoses, ductwork and vacuum lines.

➡Never operate the engine without the air filter element in place.

Air Cleaner Element
◆ See Figures 89, 90, 91, 92 and 93

The air cleaner element can be replaced by removing the wingnut(s) and/or side clips, then removing the top cover as previously detailed.

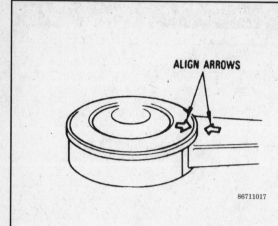

Fig. 87 Many air cleaner assemblies have arrows on the housing and lid — always make sure they align

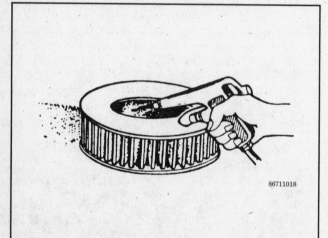

Fig. 88 The air filter element may be cleaned with low pressure compressed air

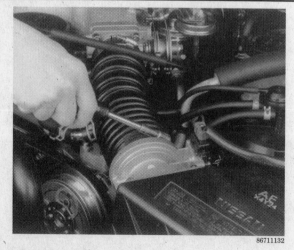

Fig. 89 Loosen the air intake hose clamp before removing the filter element

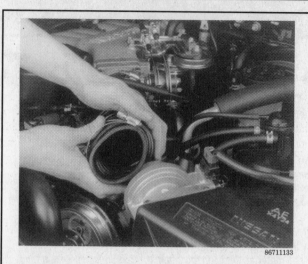

Fig. 90 Disconnect the air intake hose, being careful not to lose the retaining clamp

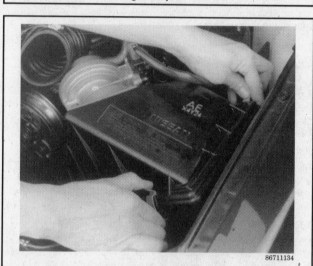

Fig. 91 Unfasten the side retaining clamps so that the air filter housing can be opened

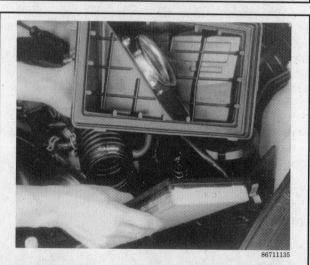

Fig. 92 Remove the air filter element from the air filter housing

Fig. 93 View of the air filter element. Make sure that the element is installed in the housing properly before fastening the side clamps

Crankcase Ventilation Filter

▶ **See Figure 94**

Certain models may also utilize an air cleaner-mounted crankcase ventilation filter. If so, it should also be cleaned or replaced at the same time as the regular air filter element. To replace the filter, remove the air cleaner top cover and pull the filter from its housing on the side of the air cleaner assembly. Push a new filter into the housing and reinstall the cover. If the filter and plastic holder need replacement, remove the clip mounting the feeder tube to the air cleaner housing, then remove the assembly from the air cleaner.

Fuel Filter

REMOVAL & INSTALLATION

▶ **See Figures 95, 96 and 97**

✳✳CAUTION

NEVER SMOKE WHEN WORKING AROUND OR NEAR GASOLINE! MAKE SURE THAT THERE IS NO ACTIVE IGNITION SOURCE NEAR YOUR WORK AREA!

✳✳WARNING

Never attempt to remove the fuel filter without first relieving the fuel system pressure!

The procedure below is just a general procedure, consult your 'Chilton Total Care Care Manual' for specific procedure concerning the vehicle you are working with.

1. Release the fuel pressure from the fuel line as follows:
   a. Remove the fuel pump fuse at the fuse box.
   b. Start the engine.
   c. After the engine stalls, crank the engine two or three times to make sure that the fuel pressure is released.
   d. Turn the ignition switch **OFF** and reinstall the fuel pump fuse.
2. Loosen the hose clamps at the fuel inlet and outlet lines. Wrap a shop towel or absorbent rag around the filter, then slide each line off the filter nipples.
3. Remove the fuel filter and old hose clamps.

To install:

4. Place new hose clamps on the fuel inlet and outlet lines.
5. Connect the fuel filter, being careful to observe the correct direction of flow, then tighten the hose clamps.
6. Start the engine and check for fuel leaks.

➡**Always use a high pressure-type fuel filter assembly. Do not use a synthetic resinous fuel filter.**

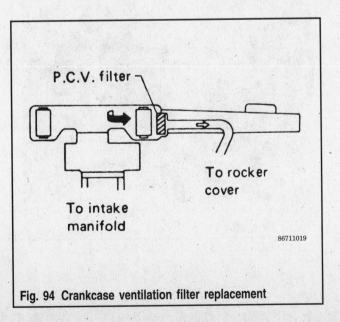

Fig. 94 Crankcase ventilation filter replacement

Fig. 95 Remove the fuel pump fuse when releasing the fuel pressure — the fuse's location may vary in the box

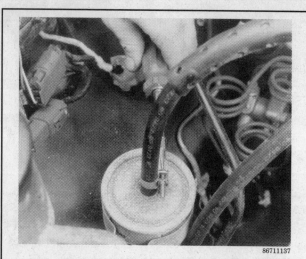

Fig. 96 Remove the fuel line hose clamp after releasing the fuel pressure

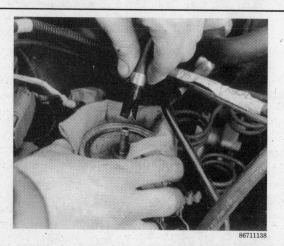

Fig. 97 When removing the fuel line from the fuel filter, have a shop towel in position to catch any fuel that may spill from the filter

PCV Valve

▶ **See Figures 98 and 99**

The PCV valve regulates crankcase ventilation during various engine operating conditions. At high vacuum (idle speed and partial load range) it will open slightly, and at low vacuum (full throttle) it will open fully. This causes vapor to be removed from the crankcase by the engine vacuum and then be sucked into the combustion chamber where it is burned.

➡**The PCV system will not function properly unless the oil filler cap is tightly sealed. Check the gasket on the cap and be certain it is not leaking. Replace the cap and/or gasket, if necessary, to ensure proper sealing.**

TESTING

▶ **See Figure 100**

1. Check the ventilation hoses and lines for leaks or clogging. Clean or replace as necessary.
2. With the engine running at idle, locate the PCV valve in the cylinder head cover or intake manifold and remove the ventilation hose from the valve; a strong hissing sound should be heard as air passes through the valve.
3. With the engine still idling, place your finger over the valve; a strong vacuum should be felt.
4. If the PCV valve failed either of the preceding two checks (and the ventilation hose is not clogged or broken), the valve will require replacement.

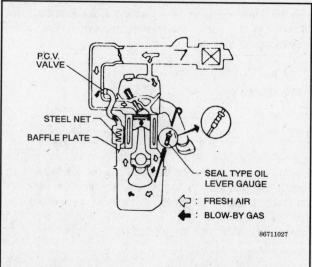

Fig. 98 PCV valve location — typical 4 cylinder engine

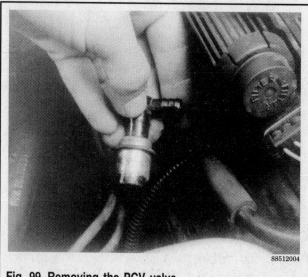

Fig. 99 Removing the PCV valve

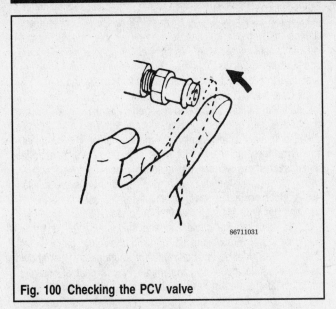

86711031

Fig. 100 Checking the PCV valve

REMOVAL & INSTALLATION

1. If not already done, detach the ventilation hose from the PCV valve.
2. Remove the PCV valve. If its base is threaded, unscrew the valve; otherwise, simply pull the valve from its retaining grommet.

To install:

3. Depending on the type of valve, either screw in the replacement PCV valve or push it into its retaining grommet.
4. Slide the ventilation hose onto the end of the PCV valve.

➡**For further information on the PCV system, consult your 'Chilton Total Car Care Manual'.**

Air Induction Valve Filter

REMOVAL & INSTALLATION

Regular maintenance for this component includes a check of the drive belt tension and replacement of the air pump air filter at the specified interval. The air filter case is located in the left front of the engine compartment on most models. To replace the air filter, simply unscrew the wing nut(s) securing the cover to the case, withdraw the old filter, install the new one, and reinstall the case. If your vehicle is equipped with and Air Induction system, refer to your 'Chilton Total Car Care Manual' for your specific servicing.

Battery

➡**On a maintenance-free sealed battery, a built-in hydrometer or 'eye' is used for checking the fluid level and specific gravity readings. If your battery is equipped with an eye, use it for checking the condition of the battery by observing the color of the eye. A green colored eye indi-**

cates good condition and a dark colored eye indicates the need for service. Replacement batteries could be either the sealed (maintenance-free) or non-sealed type.

FLUID LEVEL (EXCEPT MAINTENANCE-FREE SEALED BATTERIES)

▶ **See Figure 101**

Check the battery electrolyte level at least once a month, or more often in hot weather or during periods of extended operation. The level can be checked through the case on translucent polypropylene batteries; the cell caps must be removed on other models. The electrolyte level in each cell should be kept filled to the bottom of the split ring inside, or to the line marked on the outside of the case.

If the level is low, add only distilled water, or colorless, odorless drinking water, through the opening until the level is correct. Each cell is completely separate from the others, so each must be checked and filled individually.

If water is added in freezing weather, the vehicle should be driven several miles to allow the water to mix with the electrolyte. Otherwise, the battery could freeze.

SPECIFIC GRAVITY (EXCEPT MAINTENANCE-FREE BATTERIES)

▶ **See Figures 102 and 103**

➡**On a maintenance-free sealed battery, a built-in eye is used for checking the specific gravity readings. Refer to the battery case for further instructions.**

At least once a year, check the specific gravity of the battery. It should be 1.26-1.28 at room temperature.

The specific gravity can be checked with the use of a hydrometer, an inexpensive instrument available from many sources, including auto parts stores. The hydrometer has a squeeze bulb at one end and a nozzle at the other. Battery electrolyte is sucked into the hydrometer until the float is lifted from its seat. The specific gravity is then read by noting the

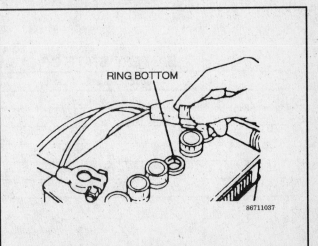

RING BOTTOM

86711037

Fig. 101 Fill each battery cell to the bottom of the split ring with distilled water

position of the float. Generally, if after charging, the specific gravity of any two cells varies more than 50 points (0.50), the battery is bad and should be replaced.

It is not possible to check the specific gravity in this manner on sealed (maintenance-free) batteries. Instead, the indicator built into the top of the case must be relied on to display any signs of battery deterioration. On most batteries if the indicator is a light color, the battery can be assumed to be OK. If the indicator is a dark color, the specific gravity is low, and the battery should be charged or replaced. There should be specific notations on the battery you are working with as to what color the indicator will be depending on the batteries state of charge.

CABLES AND CLAMPS

▶ **See Figures 104, 105, 106 and 107**

Once a year, the battery terminals and the cable clamps should be checked and cleaned, if necessary. Make sure that

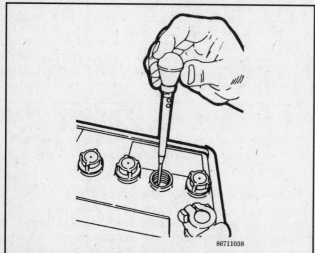

Fig. 102 The specific gravity of the battery can be checked with a simple float-type hydrometer

the ignition switch is turned to the **OFF** position. Loosen the clamps and remove the cables, negative cable first. On batteries with posts on top, the use of a puller specially made for this purpose is recommended. These are inexpensive, and available in most auto parts stores. Side terminal battery cables are secured with a bolt.

Clean the cable clamps and the battery terminal with a wire brush, until all corrosion, grease, etc., is removed and the metal is shiny. It is especially important to clean the inside of the clamp thoroughly, since a small deposit of foreign material or oxidation there will prevent a sound electrical connection and inhibit either starting or charging. Special tools are available for cleaning these parts, one type for top post batteries and another type for side terminal batteries.

Before installing the cables, loosen the battery hold-down clamp or strap, remove the battery and check the battery tray. Clear it of any debris, and check it for soundness. Rust should be wire brushed away, and the metal given a coat of anti-rust paint. Install the battery and tighten the hold-down clamp or strap securely, but be careful not to overtighten, as doing so may crack the battery case.

After the clamps and terminals are clean, reinstall the cables, negative cable last; do not hammer on the clamps to install. Tighten the clamps securely, but do not distort them. Give the clamps and terminals a thin external coat of grease after installation, to retard corrosion.

Check the cables at the same time that the terminals are cleaned. If the cable insulation is cracked or broken, or if the ends are frayed, the cable should be replaced with a new cable of the same length and gauge.

✳✳CAUTION

Keep flame or sparks away from the battery; it gives off explosive hydrogen gas! Battery electrolyte contains sulfuric acid! If you should splash any on your skin or in your eyes, flush the affected area with plenty of clear water. If it lands in your eyes, get medical help immediately!

BATTERY STATE OF CHARGE AT ROOM TEMPERATURE

Specific Gravity Reading	Charged Condition
1.260–1.280	Fully Charged
1.230–1.250	3/4 Charged
1.200–1.220	1/2 Charged
1.170–1.190	1/4 Charged
1.140–1.160	Almost no Charge
1.110–1.130	No Charge

Fig. 103 Battery state of charge at room temperature — Generalized Specifications

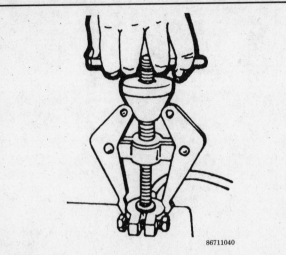

Fig. 104 Special pullers are available to remove cable clamps

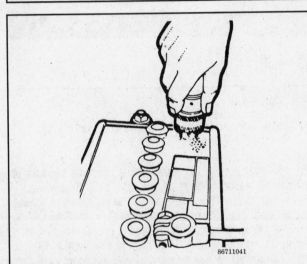

Fig. 105 Clean the battery posts with a wire brush or the special tool shown

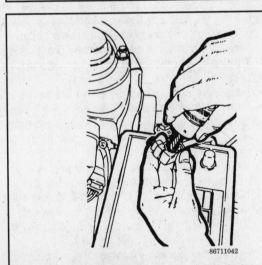

Fig. 106 Clean the inside of the clamps with a wire brush or the special tool

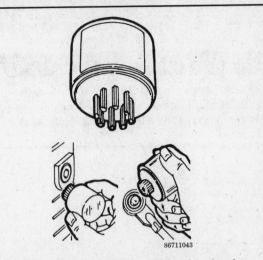

Fig. 107 Special tools are also available for cleaning the posts and clamps of side terminal batteries

REPLACEMENT

When it becomes necessary to replace the battery, be sure to select a new battery with a cold cranking power rating equal to or greater than the battery originally installed. Deterioration, embrittlement and just plain aging of the battery cables, starter motor and associated wires makes the battery's job all the more difficult in successive years. The slow increase in electrical resistance over time makes it prudent to install a new battery with a greater capacity than the old.

REMOVAL

1. Make sure The ignition switch is turned **OFF**.
2. Disconnect the negative battery cable from the terminal, then disconnect the positive cable. Special pullers are available to remove the clamps.

➡**To avoid sparks, always disconnect the negative cable first and reconnect it last.**

3. Unscrew and remove the battery hold-down clamp.
4. Remove the battery, being careful not to spill any of the acid.

➡**Spilled acid can be neutralized with a baking soda and water solution. If you somehow get acid into your eyes, flush it out with lots of clean water and get to a doctor as quickly as possible.**

To install:
5. Clean the battery posts thoroughly.
6. Clean the cable clamps using the special tools or a wire brush, both inside and out.
7. Install the battery, then fasten the hold-down clamp.

8. Connect the positive and then the negative cable. Do not hammer them into place. Coat the terminals with grease to prevent corrosion.

❋❋CAUTION

Make absolutely sure that the battery is connected properly before you turn on the ignition switch. Reversed polarity can burn out the alternator and regulator in a matter of seconds.

Fig. 110 Place the tool over the terminals and twist to clean the post

Drive Belts

INSPECTION

▶ **See Figure 111**

Check the condition of the drive belts, and check the belt tension at least every 30,000 miles (48,000 km) or every 24 months.

Periodic inspection of the drive belts is important because of the following reasons; first of all, the drive belts drive various components such as the engine water pump, alternator, power steering pump and emission pump, etc.

Two of the components mention above play a vital part in keeping the engine running. They are the alternator and water pump. To give you a little example of how important drive belt inspection is picture this; suppose the alternator belt were to break due to wear or cracking, the alternator would be completely disabled and the battery would eventually go dead.

In case a like this you just may find yourself sitting on the side of the road seeking someone to give you a jump to get started. Not to mention, a possible tow job, battery charge and replacement of that drive belt that could have been detected during the inspection.

The water pump drive belt could cause even more severe complications, how about an excessively overheated engine. This could result in a very expensive engine repair, like a head gasket replacement, etc. So be sure to keep a good maintenance check on the drive belts.

1. Inspect the belts for signs of glazing or cracking. A glazed belt will be perfectly smooth from slippage, while a good belt will have a slight texture of fabric visible. Cracks will generally start at the inner edge of the belt and run outward. Replace the belt at the first sign of cracking or if the glazing is severe.

2. By placing your thumb midway between the two pulleys, it should be possible to depress the belt 1/4-1/2 in. (6-13mm). If any of the belts can be depressed more than this, or cannot be depressed this much, adjust the tension. Inadequate tension

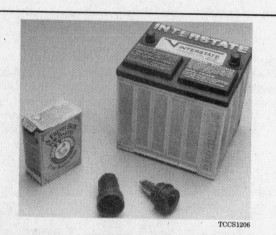

Fig. 108 Battery maintenance may be accomplished with household items (such as baking soda to neutralize spilled acid) or with special tools such as this post and terminal cleaner

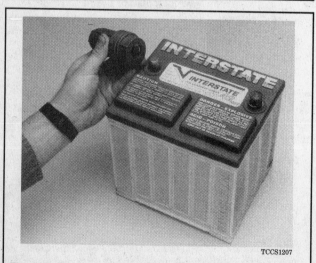

Fig. 109 The underside of this special battery tool has a wire brush to clean post terminals

will result in slippage or wear, while excessive tension will damage pulley bearings and cause belts to fray and crack.

3. It's not a bad idea to replace all drive belts at 60,000 miles (96,000 km) or 48 months, regardless of their condition.

ADJUSTMENT

▶ See Figure 112

Pivot Type Adjustment

This type of belt tension adjustment is commonly used in most vehicles today. This is a general procedure, consult your 'Chilton Total Care Care Manual' for specific adjustment and tension specifications for the vehicle you are working with.

1. Loosen the pivot and mounting bolts on the alternator.
2. Using a wooden hammer handle or broomstick (or even your hand if you're strong enough), move the alternator one way or the other until the tension is within acceptable limits.

➡**Never use a screwdriver or any other metal device, such as a pry bar, as a lever when adjusting the alternator belt tension!**

3. Tighten the mounting bolts securely. If a new belt has been installed, always recheck the tension after a few hundred miles of driving.

Tension Bolt Type Adjustment

▶ See Figures 113, 114 and 115

Some belt tensions are adjusted by means of a tension adjusting bolt. This method of adjustment may use an idler pulley or the component being moved may slide on a bracket to increase or decrease belt tension. The procedure given below is is a general procedure, consult your 'Chilton Total Care Care Manual' for specific adjustment and tension specifications for the vehicle you are working with.

1. Loosen the pivot bolt, then turn the adjusting bolt until proper tension is achieved.
2. Tighten the mounting bolts securely. If a new belt has been installed, always recheck the tension after a few hundred miles of driving.

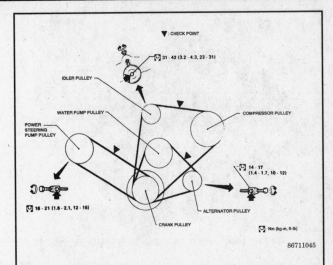

Fig. 112 Drive belt tension inspection and adjustment points — typical

Fig. 113 On some vehicles it is easier to access a component from underneath the vehicle

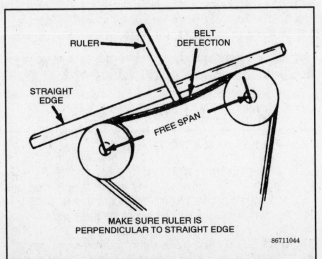

Fig. 111 Measuring belt deflection with a straightedge and ruler

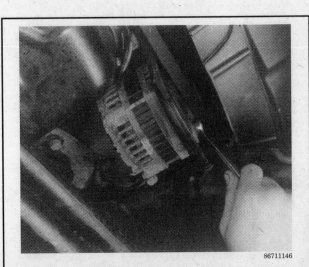

Fig. 114 Loosen the alternator pivot bolt with a box wrench or a ratchet and socket

Fig. 115 Use the adjusting bolt to vary tension on the belt

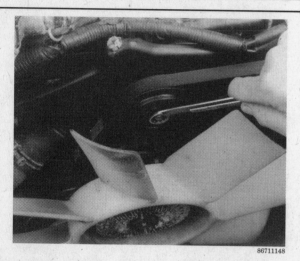

Fig. 116 Loosen the locknut on the idler pulley before adjusting the belt

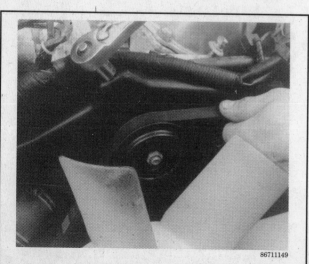

Fig. 117 Turn the adjusting bolt until the correct belt tension is achieved

Tensioner Type Adjustment

This type of belt tension adjustment is very commonly used in most vehicles today. Usually a serpentine type drive belt is used with the the tensioner type adjustment. The serpentine belt is one large single belt that wraps around each component's pulley. It will usually drive 3-4 components at the same time. Example: the alternator, water pump, air pump and power steering pump may be driven from this one belt. The procedure below is just a general procedure, consult your 'Chilton Total Care Care Manual' for specific adjustment and tension specifications for the vehicle you are working with.

1. Loosen the tensioner's pivot bolt.

2. Usually the tensioner will have a large nut where by you can use a wrench to relieve the tension from the belt. Moving against the tension of the tensioner will relieve the tension on the the belt. Allowing the tension of the tensioner to release will increase the tension on the belt within acceptable limits.

3. Tighten the pivot bolt securely. If a new belt has been installed, always recheck the tension after a few hundred miles of driving.

Timing Belt

INSPECTION

The timing belt is a bit more involved and a more critical service procedure. Although you can service the timing belt, remember that the correct procedures must be followed exactly. Be sure to have the correct repair manual for the vehicle. If you can enlist the aid of someone who is experienced with timing belt replacement, it would be helpful.

➡**Do not bend or twist the timing belt. If the timing belt breaks while driving, or the crankshaft and/or camshaft are turned separately after the timing belt is removed, valves may strike the piston heads, causing engine damage. Make sure the timing belt and tensioner are clean and free from oil and water.**

As a average rule, replace the timing belt at 60,000 miles (96,000 km). These are just generalizations, always consult your 'Chilton Total Care Care Manual' for specific adjustment and tension specifications for the vehicle you are working with.

Evaporative Canister

SERVICING

▶ **See Figures 118, 119, 120, 121 and 122**

Check the evaporation control system, if so equipped, every 15,000 miles (24,000 km) or every 12 months. Check the fuel and vapor lines/hoses for proper connections, correct routing, and condition. Replace damaged or deteriorated parts as necessary.

To check the operation of the carbon canister purge control valve, disconnect the rubber hose between the canister control valve and the T-fitting at the T-fitting. Apply vacuum to the hose leading to the control valve. The vacuum condition should be maintained indefinitely. If the control valve leaks, remove the top cover of the valve and check for a dislocated or cracked diaphragm. If the diaphragm is damaged, a repair kit containing a new diaphragm, retainer, and spring is available and should be installed.

The carbon canister has a replaceable air filter in the bottom of the canister. The filter element should be checked once a year or every 15,000 miles (24,000 km); more frequently if the vehicle is operated in dusty areas. Replace the filter by pulling it out of the bottom of the canister and installing a new one.

Hoses

INSPECTION

Inspect the condition of the radiator hoses, heater hoses and clamps periodically. Early spring and late fall are often good times to perform this, as well as other routine maintenance.

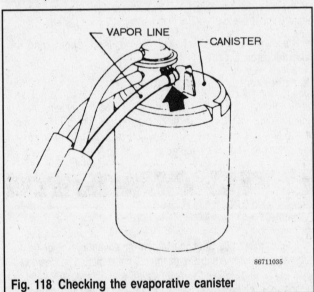

Fig. 118 Checking the evaporative canister

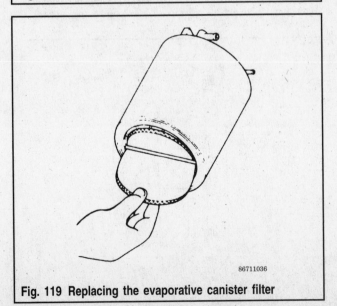

Fig. 119 Replacing the evaporative canister filter

Fig. 120 Remove the lines to the evaporative canister assembly before removing the canister

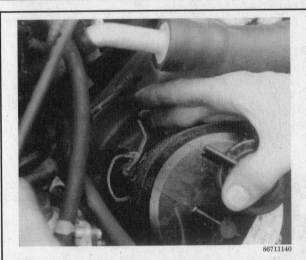

Fig. 121 Unfasten the evaporative canister assembly retaining clamp

Fig. 122 Remove the evaporative canister assembly from the vehicle

Make sure the engine and cooling system are cold. Visually inspect for cracked, rotted or collapsed hoses, and replace as necessary. Run your hand along the length of the hose. If a weak or swollen spot is noted when squeezing the hose wall, replace the hose.

REPLACEMENT

1. Drain the coolant into a suitable container (if the coolant is to be reused).

❋❋CAUTION

When draining the coolant, keep in mind that cats and dogs are attracted by ethylene glycol antifreeze, and are quite likely to drink any that is left in an uncovered container or in puddles on the ground. This will prove fatal in sufficient quantity. Always drain the coolant into a sealable container. Coolant should be reused unless it is contaminated or several years old.

2. Loosen the hose clamps at each end of the hose that requires replacement.
3. Twist, pull and slide the hose off the radiator, water pump, thermostat housing or heater connection.
4. Clean the hose mounting connections. Inspect the hose clamps and replace any which are rusted or worn.
5. Position the hose clamps on the new hose.

6. Coat the connection surfaces with a water resistant sealer or equivalent and slide the hose into position. Make sure the hose clamps are located beyond the raised bead of the connector (if equipped) and centered in the clamping area of the connection.
7. Tighten the clamps evenly. Do not overtighten.
8. Refill the cooling system.
9. Start the engine and allow it to reach normal operating temperature. Check for coolant leaks, then top off the coolant level as necessary.

ADDITIONAL PREVENTIVE MAINTENANCE CHECKS

Antifreeze

In order to prevent heater core freeze-up during A/C operation, it is necessary to maintain permanent-type antifreeze protection of +15°F (-9°C) or lower. A reading of -15°F (-26°C) is ideal since this protection also supplies sufficient corrosion inhibitors for the protection of the engine cooling system.

➡**The same antifreeze should not be used longer than the manufacturer specifies.**

Radiator Cap

For efficient operation of the vehicle's cooling system, the radiator cap should have a holding pressure which meets manufacturer's specifications. A cap which fails to hold the specified pressure should be replaced.

FLUIDS AND LUBRICANTS

Fluid Disposal

Used fluids such as engine oil, transmission fluid, antifreeze and brake fluid are hazardous wastes and must be disposed of properly. Before draining any fluids, consult with the local authorities; in many areas, waste oil, antifreeze, etc. are being accepted as a part of recycling programs. A number of service stations and auto parts stores are also accepting waste fluids for recycling.

Be sure of the recycling center's policies before draining any fluids, as many will not accept different fluids that have been mixed together, such as oil and antifreeze.

Oil and Fuel Recommendations

ENGINE OIL

▸ **See Figures 123, 124 and 125**

The SAE (Society of Automotive Engineers) grade number indicates the viscosity of the engine oil (its resistance to flow at a given temperature). The lower the SAE grade number, the lighter the oil. For example, the mono-grade oils begin with SAE 5 weight, which is a thin, light oil, and continue in viscosity up to SAE 80 or 90 weight, which are heavy gear lubricants. These oils are also known as 'straight weight,' meaning

they are of a single viscosity, and do not vary with engine temperature.

Multi-viscosity oils offer the important advantage of being adaptable to temperature extremes. These oils have designations such as 10W-40, 20W-50, etc. For example, 10W-40 means that in winter (the 'W' in the designation) the oil acts like a thin 10 weight oil, allowing the engine to spin easily

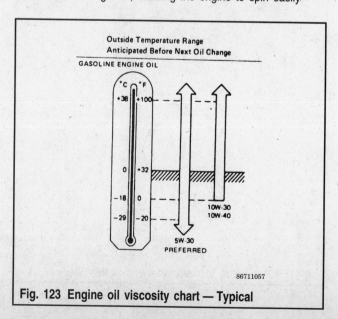

Fig. 123 Engine oil viscosity chart — Typical

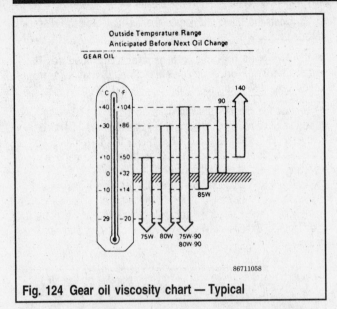

Fig. 124 Gear oil viscosity chart — Typical

when cold and offering rapid lubrication. Once the engine has warmed up, however, the oil acts like a straight 40 weight, maintaining good lubrication and protection for the engine's internal components. A 20W-50 oil would therefore be slightly heavier than, and not as ideal, in cold weather as the 10W-40, but would offer better protection at higher rpm and temperatures because, when warm, it acts like a 50 weight oil. Whichever oil viscosity you choose when changing the oil and filter, you are anticipating the temperatures your engine will be operating in until the oil is changed again. Refer to the oil viscosity chart that applies to your specific vehicle for oil recommendations according to temperature.

The API (American Petroleum Institute) designation indicates the classification of engine oil used under certain given operating conditions. Only oils designated for use 'Service SG' should be used. Oils of the SG type perform a variety of functions inside the engine in addition to the basic function as a lubricant. Through a balanced system of metallic detergents and polymeric dispersants, the oil prevents the formation of high and low temperature deposits, and also keeps sludge and dirt particles in suspension. Acids, particularly sulfuric acid, as well as other by-products of combustion, are neutralized. Both the SAE grade number and the API designation can be found on the oil container.

Synthetic Oil

There are many excellent synthetic and fuel-efficient oils currently available that can provide better gas mileage, longer service life and, in some cases, better engine protection. These benefits do not come without a few hitches, however, the main one being the price of synthetic oils, which is three or four times the price per quart of conventional oil.

Synthetic oil is not for every vehicle and every type of driving, so you should consider your engine's condition and your type of driving. Also, check your vehicle's warranty conditions regarding the use of synthetic oils.

Brand new engines and older, high mileage engines are not good candidates for synthetic oil. The synthetic oils are so slippery that they can prevent the proper break-in of new engines; most manufacturers recommend that you wait until the engine is properly broken in (3000 miles) before using synthetic oil. Older engines with wear have a different problem with synthetics: they 'use' (consume during operation) more oil as they age. Slippery synthetic oils get past these worn parts easily. If your engine is using conventional oil, it will use synthetics much faster. Also, if your vehicle is leaking oil past old seals, you'll have a much greater leak problem with synthetics.

Consider your type of driving. If most of your accumulated mileage is high speed, highway type driving, the more expensive synthetic oils may be a benefit. Extended highway driving gives the engine a chance to warm up, accumulating fewer acids in the oil, and putting less stress on the engine over the long run. Under these conditions, the oil change interval can be extended (as long as your oil filter can last the extended life of the oil) up to the advertised mileage claims of the synthetics. Vehicles with synthetic oils may show increased fuel economy in highway driving, due to less internal friction. However, many automotive experts agree that 50,000 miles (80,000 km) is too long to keep any oil in your engine.

Vehicles used under harsher circumstances, such as stop-and-go, city type driving, short trips, or extended idling, should

RECOMMENDED LUBRICANTS

Component	Lubricant
Engine oil	API SG
Coolant	Ethylene Glycol-based Antifreeze
Manual Transmission	API GL-4, SAE 75W-90
Automatic Transmission	ATF DEXRON®
Transfer Case	1989: API GL-4, SAE 75W-90
	1990-95: ATF DEXRON®
Differentials	API GL-5, SAE 80W-90
Limited Slip	Nissan-approved LSD
Master Cylinder	DOT 3, SAE J1703
Power Steering	ATF DEXRON®
Manual Steering	API GL-4, SAE 90W
Multi-Purpose Grease	NLGI #2
Free-Running Hub	Nissan-approved grease

Fig. 125 Example of a Recommended lubricants chart

be serviced more frequently. For the engines in these vehicles, the much greater cost of synthetic or fuel-efficient oils may not be worth the investment. Internal wear increases much quicker on these vehicles, causing greater oil consumption and leakage.

➡**The mixing of conventional and synthetic oils is possible but not recommended. Non-detergent or straight mineral oils must never be used in the engine.**

FUEL

It is important to use fuel of the proper octane rating in your vehicle. Octane rating is based on the quantity of anti-knock compounds added to the fuel, and also reflects the speed at which the gas will burn. The lower the octane rating, the faster it burns. The higher the octane, the slower the fuel will burn, and the greater the percentage of compounds in the fuel to prevent spark ping (knock), detonation and preignition (dieseling).

As the temperature of the engine increases, the air/fuel mixture exhibits a tendency to ignite before the spark plug is fired. If fuel of an octane rating too low for the engine is used, this will allow combustion to occur before the piston has completed its compression stroke, thereby creating a very high pressure very rapidly.

Fuel of the proper octane rating, for the compression ratio and ignition timing of your vehicle, will slow the combustion process sufficiently to allow the spark plug enough time to ignite the mixture completely and smoothly. The use of super-premium fuel is no substitution for a properly tuned and maintained engine.

Light spark knock may be noticed when accelerating or driving up hills. The slight knocking may be considered normal (with 87 octane) because the maximum fuel economy is obtained under condition of occasional light spark knock. Gasoline with an octane rating higher than 87 may be used, but it is not necessary (in most cases) for proper operation.

➡**Your engine's fuel requirement can change with time, mainly due to carbon buildup, which changes the compression ratio. If your engine pings, knocks or runs on, switch to a higher grade of fuel. Sometimes just changing brands may cure the problem.**

OIL LEVEL CHECK

▶ **See Figures 126, 127, 128 and 129**

Every time you stop for fuel, check the engine oil as follows:
1. Park the vehicle on level ground.

➡**Although it is best for the engine to be at operating temperature, checking the oil immediately after stopping will lead to a false reading. Wait a few minutes after turning off the engine to allow the oil to drain back into the crankcase.**

2. Open the hood and locate the dipstick. Pull the dipstick from its tube, wipe it clean and reinsert it.

➡**Keep in mind that this is a generalized procedure. The actual markings on your vehicle's dipstick may vary from those described here.**

3. Pull the dipstick out again, and holding it horizontally, read the oil level. The oil should be between the **H** and **L** marks on the dipstick. If the oil is below the **L** mark, add oil of the proper viscosity and classification through the capped opening on top of the cylinder head cover.

4. Insert the dipstick and check the oil level again after adding any oil. Be careful not to overfill the crankcase. Approximately one quart of oil will raise the level from the **L** mark to the **H** mark. Excess oil will generally be consumed at an accelerated rate.

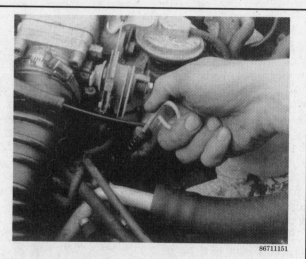

86711151

Fig. 126 The oil dipstick in the engine compartment may be painted yellow on newer models

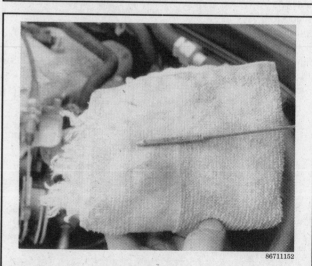

86711152

Fig. 127 Check the oil dipstick for the correct level of engine oil — never overfill the engine oil

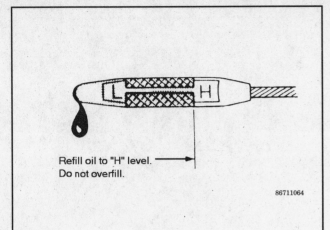

Refill oil to "H" level.
Do not overfill.

86711064

Fig. 128 The engine oil level should be maintained between the L and H marks

86711153

Fig. 129 If the engine oil level is low, add engine oil, but do not overfill

OIL AND FILTER CHANGE

▶ **See Figures 130, 131, 132 and 133**

➡**It may be a good idea to look under the vehicle, before starting any service procedure, to familiarize yourself with the necessary components and locations.**

The oil should be changed at least every 7500 miles (12,000 km) or every 6 months. Some manufacturers recommend changing the oil filter with every other oil change; we suggest that the filter be changed with **every** oil change. There is approximately 1 quart of dirty oil remaining in the old oil filter if it is not changed! A few dollars more every year seems a small price to pay for extended engine life — so change the filter every time you change the oil!

❊❊CAUTION

Prolonged and repeated skin contact with used engine oil, with no effort to remove the oil, may be harmful. Always follow these simple precautions when handling used motor oil.

- Avoid prolonged skin contract with used motor oil
- Remove oil from skin by washing thoroughly with soap and water, or waterless hand cleaner. Do not use gasoline, thinners or other solvents
- Avoid prolonged skin contact with oil-soaked clothing

The mileage figures given are sample recommended intervals assuming normal driving and conditions. If your vehicle is being used under dusty, polluted or off-road conditions, change the oil and filter more frequently than specified. The same goes for vehicles driven in stop-and-go traffic or only for short distances. Always drain the oil after the engine has been running long enough to bring it to normal operating temperature. Hot oil will flow easier and more contaminants will be removed along with the oil than if it were drained cold. To change the oil and filter:

❊❊CAUTION

The EPA warns that prolonged contact with used engine oil may cause a number of skin disorders, including cancer! You should make every effort to minimize your exposure to used engine oil. Protective gloves should be worn when changing the oil. Wash your hands and any other exposed skin areas as soon as possible after exposure to used engine oil. Soap and water, or waterless hand cleaner should be used.

1. Run the engine until it reaches normal operating temperature.
2. Jack up the front of the vehicle and support it on safety stands.
3. Slide a drain pan of at least 6 quarts capacity under the oil pan.
4. Loosen the drain plug. Turn the plug out by hand. By keeping inward pressure on the plug as you unscrew it, oil won't escape past the threads, and you can remove it without being burned by hot oil.

❊❊CAUTION

The oil will be HOT! Be careful when removing the plug, so that you don't take a bath in hot engine oil.

5. Allow the oil to drain completely. Clean and inspect the drain plug and oil pan sealing surface. If the plug is equipped with a removable gasket, also clean and inspect it.
6. Using a new plug gasket, if necessary, install the drain plug and tighten to correct specifications. Don't overtighten the

plug; otherwise, you'll be buying a new pan or a replacement plug for stripped threads.

➡**Always consult your 'Chilton Total Car Care Manual' for specific service and specifications on the vehicle you are working with.**

7. Some engines will require the use of a oil filter strap wrench to remove the oil filter. Others may require a cap-type filter removal tool. Keep in mind that the filter is holding about one quart of dirty, hot oil.

➡**If the oil filter cannot be loosened by conventional methods, punch a hole through both sides near the mounting base of the filter and insert a punch, then turn to loosen the oil filter. After the oil filter is loosened, remove it from the engine with an oil filter wrench or equivalent.**

8. Empty the old filter into the drain pan and properly dispose of the filter.

Fig. 132 Lubricate the gasket on the new filter with clean engine oil. A dry gasket may not make as good a seal, and could allow the filter to leak

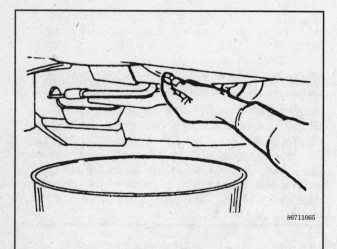

Fig. 130 By keeping inward pressure on the drain plug as you unscrew it, oil won't escape past the threads

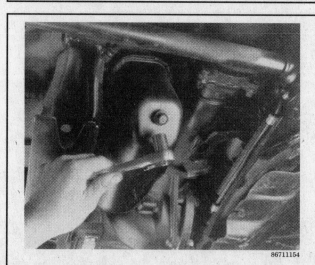

Fig. 133 Removing the oil drain plug — do not over torque this drain plug upon installation

9. Using a clean rag, wipe off the filter adapter on the engine block. Be sure that the rag doesn't leave any lint which could clog an oil passage.

10. Coat the rubber gasket on the filter with fresh oil. Spin it onto the engine by hand; when the gasket touches the adapter surface, give it another 1/2-3/4 turn. Do not overtighten, or you'll distort the gasket and it will leak.

11. Refill the engine with the correct amount of fresh oil. See the Capacities Chart in your 'Chilton Total Car Care Manual'.

12. Check the oil level on the dipstick. It is normal for the level to be a bit above the full mark. Start the engine and allow it to idle for a few minutes.

➡**Do not run the engine above idle speed until it has built up oil pressure, as indicated when the oil light goes out.**

13. Shut off the engine and allow the oil to drain into the crankcase for a few minutes, then check the oil level. Check around the filter and drain plug for any leaks and correct as necessary.

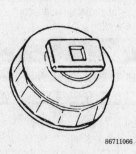

Fig. 131 On some models, a cap-type oil filter removal tool works best

Power Steering Pump

▶ See Figures 134, 135, 136 and 137

Check the power steering fluid level every 6 months or 6000 miles (9600 km).

1. Park the vehicle on a level surface. Run the engine until normal operating temperature is reached.

2. Turn the steering all the way to the left and then all the way to the right several times. Center the steering wheel and shut off the engine.

3. Open the hood and check the power steering reservoir fluid level.

4. Remove the filler cap and wipe the attached dipstick clean.

5. Reinsert the dipstick and tighten the cap. Remove the dipstick and note the fluid level indicated on the dipstick.

6. The level should be at any point below the upper hash mark, but not below the lower hash mark (in the HOT or COLD ranges).

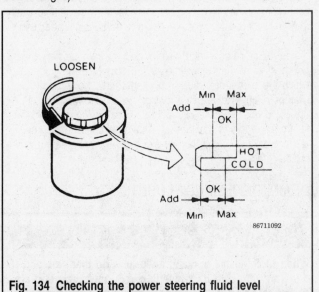

Fig. 134 Checking the power steering fluid level

Fig. 135 Remove the power steering cap to check the fluid level

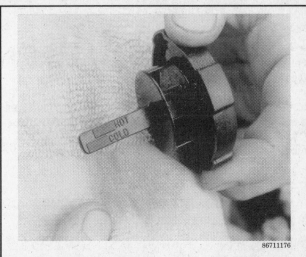

Fig. 136 View of the power steering cap dipstick — note the hot and cold marks

Fig. 137 Adding power steering fluid — use a funnel to avoid spills

7. Add fluid as necessary, but do not overfill.

Cooling System

FLUID RECOMMENDATIONS

When additional coolant is required to maintain the proper level, always add a mixture of aluminum-compatible antifreeze/coolant and water. Typically, a 50/50 mixture of antifreeze and water is recommended (even for vehicles which are not exposed to cold winter temperatures), since this mixture also imparts the necessary corrosion inhibition. A greater concentration of antifreeze may be used, but the coolant mixture's level of protection actually lessens if too much antifreeze is used. Unless you are simply topping off the cooling system, straight antifreeze should never be added without some water. For additional information on determining the optimum concentration for your vehicle, refer to the antifreeze manufacturer's labeling.

➡️Although most manufacturers recommend ethylene glycol-based antifreeze (which has long been the prevalent type on the market), other types (such as propylene glycol) may also be suitable for use in your vehicle. Be sure to thoroughly read the alternative product's labeling to ensure compatibility before switching to a different formula. Check vehicle manufacturer's recommendations to be sure.

FLUID LEVEL CHECK

▶ **See Figures 138, 139, 140, 141, 142 and 143**

Dealing with the cooling system can be a tricky matter unless the proper precautions are observed. It is best to check the coolant level in the radiator when the engine is cold. This is done by checking the expansion tank. If coolant is visible

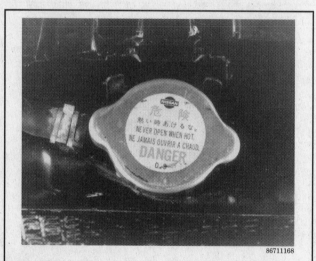

Fig. 138 View of the radiator cap installed — never open when the engine is hot!

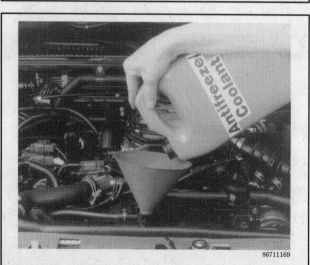

Fig. 139 Add engine coolant to the radiator with a funnel to avoid spills

above the **MIN** mark on the tank, the level is satisfactory. Always be certain that the filler caps on both the radiator and the reservoir are tightly closed.

In the event that the coolant level must be checked when the engine is warm or on engines without an expansion tank, place a thick rag over the radiator cap, then slowly turn the cap counterclockwise until it reaches the first detent. Allow all the hot steam to escape. This will allow the pressure in the system to drop gradually, preventing an explosion of hot coolant. When the hissing noise stops, remove the cap the rest of the way.

It's a good idea to check the coolant every time that you stop for fuel. If the coolant level is low, add equal amounts of suitable antifreeze and clean water. Fill the expansion tank to the **MAX** level. On models without an expansion tank, add coolant through the radiator filler neck.

➡️Never add cold coolant to a hot engine unless the engine is running, to avoid cracking the engine block.

Avoid using water that is known to have a high alkaline content or is very hard, except in emergency situations. Drain and flush the cooling system as soon as possible after using such water.

The radiator hoses and clamps and the radiator cap should be checked at the same time as the coolant level. Hoses which are brittle, cracked, or swollen should be replaced. Clamps should be checked for tightness (screwdriver-tight only)! Do not allow the clamp to cut into the hose or crush the fitting. The radiator cap gasket should be checked for any tears, cracks, swelling, or any signs of incorrect seating in the radiator neck.

DRAIN, REFILL AND FLUSH

✴✴CAUTION

When draining the coolant, keep in mind that cats and dogs are attracted by ethylene glycol antifreeze, and are quite likely to drink any that is left in an uncovered container or in puddles on the ground. This will prove fatal in sufficient quantity. Always drain the coolant into a sealable container. Coolant should be reused unless it is contaminated or two years old.

Complete draining and refilling of the cooling system at least once every two years will remove accumulated rust, scale and other deposits.

➡️Use a good quality antifreeze with water pump lubricants, rust inhibitors and other corrosion inhibitors along with acid neutralizers.

1. Drain the existing coolant as follows: Position suitable drain pans beneath the radiator and engine block. Open the radiator petcock and engine drain plug(s); there may be 1 or 2 drain plugs on the engine block depending on the type of engine. Another method of draining coolant is to disconnect the bottom radiator hose at the radiator outlet.

➡️If it is rusted or difficult to open, spray the radiator petcock with some penetrating lubricant.

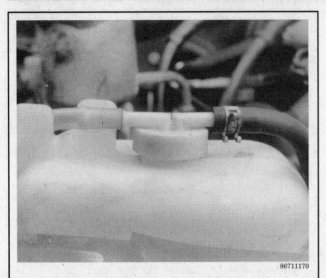

Fig. 140 View of the coolant expansion tank

Fig. 141 Remove the cap on the coolant expansion tank and add coolant to the proper level

Fig. 142 Fluid level marks on the coolant recovery tank

Fig. 143 Add engine coolant to the expansion tank with a funnel to avoid spills

2. Set the heater temperature controls to the full HOT position.

3. Close the petcock and tighten the drain plug(s) to correct specifications or reconnect the lower hose. Open the air relief plug, if so equipped, then fill the system with water.

4. Add a can of quality radiator flush. Be sure the flush is safe to use in engines having aluminum components.

5. Idle the engine until the upper radiator hose gets hot. Race it 2 or 3 times, then shut it **OFF**. Let the engine cool down.

6. Drain the system again.

7. Repeat this process until the drained water is clear and free of scale.

8. Close the petcock and drain plug(s) or, if applicable, connect the radiator hose.

9. If equipped with a coolant recovery system, flush the reservoir with water and leave empty.

➡**Always open the air relief plug before filling the cooling system, in order to bleed the trapped air. Only when the cooling system is bled properly can the correct amount of coolant be added to the system.**

10. Determine the capacity of your cooling system. (See your Chilton 'Total Car Care Manual'.) Add the appropriate ratio of quality aluminum-compatible antifreeze and water (normally a 50/50 mix) to provide the desired protection. With the air relief plug open, add the coolant mixture through the radiator filler neck until full, then close the bleeder plug and radiator cap.

11. Using the same concentration of clean antifreeze and water, fill the expansion tank to the **MAX** line, then cap the tank.

SYSTEM INSPECTION

Most permanent antifreeze/coolants have a colored dye added which makes the solution an excellent leak detector. When servicing the cooling system, check for leakage at:
- All hoses and hose connections
- Radiator seams, radiator core, and radiator draincock
- All engine block and cylinder head freeze (core) plugs, and drain plugs
- Edges of all cooling system gaskets (head gaskets, thermostat gasket)
- Transmission fluid cooler
- Heating system components
- Water pump

In addition, check the engine oil dipstick for signs of coolant in the oil; also, check the coolant in the radiator for signs of oil. Investigate and correct any indication of coolant leakage.

Check the Radiator Cap

▶ See Figure 144

While you are checking the coolant level, check the radiator cap for a worn or cracked gasket. If the cap doesn't seal properly, fluid will be lost and the engine will overheat. A worn cap should be replaced with a new one. The radiator cap must maintain pressure when the engine is running, or the cooling system will 'boil over'. The radiator cap also has a 2-way valve design to allow coolant to be drawn into the radiator from the coolant overflow tank. If this valve is not functioning properly, the vacuum cause in the system as the engine cools down can collapse and damage the hoses.

Clean Radiator of Debris

▶ See Figure 145

Periodically clean any debris such as leaves, paper, insects, etc., from the radiator fins. Pick the large pieces off by hand. The smaller pieces can be washed away with water pressure from a hose.

Carefully straighten any bent radiator fins with a pair of needlenose pliers. Be careful, the fins are very soft. Don't wiggle the fins back and forth too much. Straighten them once and try not to move them again.

CHECKING SYSTEM PROTECTION

▶ See Figure 146

A 50/50 mix of antifreeze/coolant concentrate and water will usually provide the necessary protection. Freeze protection may be checked by using a cooling system hydrometer. Inexpensive hydrometers (floating ball types) may be obtained from a local department store (automotive section) or an auto supply store. Follow the directions packaged with the coolant hydrometer when checking protection.

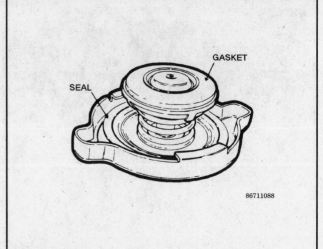

Fig. 144 Check the radiator cap seal and gasket condition

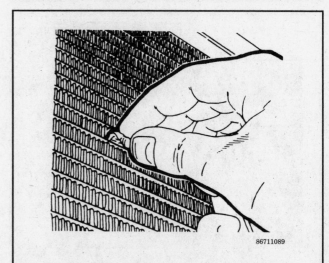

Fig. 145 Clean the radiator fins of any debris which impedes air flow

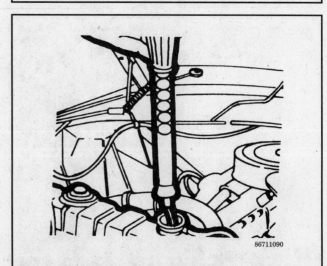

Fig. 146 The freeze protection rating can be checked with an antifreeze tester

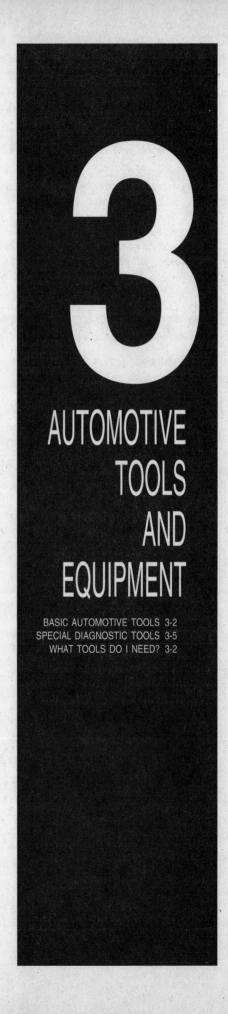

3

AUTOMOTIVE TOOLS AND EQUIPMENT

WHAT TOOLS DO I NEED?

Analyze Yours Needs

Nearly everybody needs some tools, whether they are fixing a kitchen sink, or overhauling the engine in the family car. As far as car repairs go, pliers and a can of oil won't to get you very far down the path of do-it-yourself service. But, you don't have to equip your garage like the local service station either. Somewhere between these two extremes is a level that suits the average do-it-yourselfer. Just where that point is depends on your ability and your interest. The strategy is to match your tools and equipment to the tasks you would like to tackle.

First, sort things out in a orderly manner. Think about your repair work in three levels: Basic, average and advanced,. Before you purchase any tools, sit down and determine level of expertise, job you need to accomplish and cost. Knowing what repairs you can or want to do is the most important step. Obviously, if all your intend to do is change the oil and spark plugs you don't need many tools. If you plan some fairly extensive repair work, you are going to end up with a pretty complete collection of tool. Many expensive tools can be rented from automotive parts jobbers or tool rental centers. This allows many of us to do special repairs on an occasional basis.

Basic Automotive Tools

▶ **See Figures 1, 2, 3, 4, 5, 6, 7, 8, 9, 10, 11, 12 and 13**

Naturally, without the proper tools it is impossible to properly service your vehicle. It would be impossible to catalog each tool that you would need to perform every operation in this book. It would also be unwise for the amateur to rush out and buy an expensive set of tools on the theory that one or more may be needed at sometime.

The best approach is to proceed slowly, gathering together a good quality set of those tools that are used most frequently. Don't be misled by the low cost of bargain tools. It is far better to spend a little more for better quality. Forged wrenches, 6-point sockets and fine tooth ratchets are by far preferable to their less expensive counterparts. As any good mechanic can tell you, there are few worse experiences than trying to work on a truck with bad tools. Your monetary savings will be far outweighed by frustration and mangled knuckles.

Certain tools, plus a basic ability to handle them, are required to get started. A basic tool set and a torque wrench, are good for a start. Begin accumulating those tools that are used most frequently (tools associated with routine maintenance/tune-up and engine repair). In addition to the normal

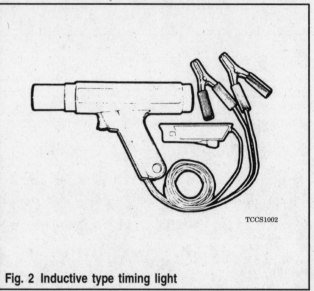

Fig. 2 Inductive type timing light

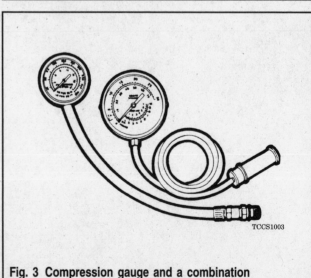

Fig. 3 Compression gauge and a combination vacuum/fuel pressure test gauge

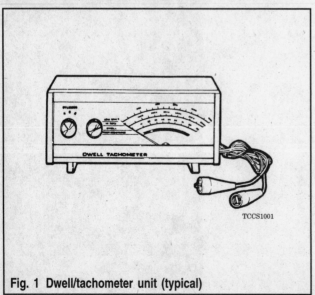

Fig. 1 Dwell/tachometer unit (typical)

assortment of screwdrivers and pliers, you should have the following tools for routine maintenance:

- Metric wrenches, sockets and combination open end/box end wrenches in sizes from 3-19mm, and a spark plug socket (⅝ inch or 16mm). If possible, buy various length socket drive extensions. One break in this department is that the metric sockets available in the U.S. will fit SAE ratchet handles and extensions you may already have (¼ in., ⅜ in., and ½ in. drive).
- Jackstands for support.
- Oil filter wrench.
- Oil filler spout or funnel.
- Grease gun for chassis lubrication.
- Hydrometer or battery tester for checking the battery.
- A low flat pan for draining oil.
- Lots of rags for wiping up the inevitable mess.

In addition to the above items, there are several others that are not absolutely necessary, but handy to have around. These include oil-dry, a transmission fluid funnel and the usual supply of lubricants and fluids, although these can be purchased as needed. This is a basic list for routine maintenance, but only your personal needs and desires can accurately determine your list of tools.

The second list of tools is for tune-ups. While these tools are slightly more sophisticated, they need not be outrageously expensive. There are several inexpensive tach/dwell meters on the market that are every bit as good for the average mechanic as a costly professional model. Just be sure that it goes to at least 1200-1500 rpm on the tach scale and that it works on 4 and 6-cylinder engines. A basic list of tune-up equipment could include:

- Tach/dwell meter.
- Spark plug wrench.
- Timing light (a DC light that works from the truck's battery is best).
- Wire spark plug gauge/adjusting tools.

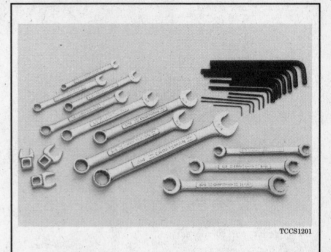

Fig. 5 In addition to ratchets, a good set of wrenches and hex keys will be necessary

Here again, be guided by your own needs. In addition to these basic tools, there are several other tools and gauges you may find useful. These include:

- A compression gauge. The screw-in type is slower to use, but eliminates the possibility of a faulty reading due to escaping pressure.
- A manifold vacuum gauge.
- A test light.
- An DVOM digital volt-ohmmeter. This meter allows direct testing of electrical components and grounds.

As a final note, you will probably find a torque wrench necessary for most work. The beam type models are perfectly adequate, although the newer click (breakaway) type are more precise, and you don't have to crane your neck to see a torque reading in awkward situations. The breakaway torque wrenches are more expensive and should be recalibrated periodically.

Correct tighten of bolts is an extremely important item on today's automobiles. The torque specification for each fastener will be given in the procedure whenever a specific torque value is required. An example of torque specifications are

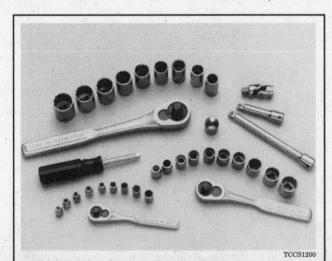

Fig. 4 All but the most basic procedure will require an assortment of ratchets and sockets

Fig. 6 A hydraulic floor jack and a set of jackstands are essential for lifting and supporting the vehicle

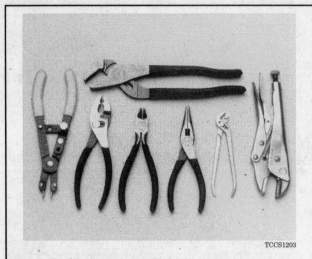

Fig. 7 An assortment of pliers will be handy, especially for old rusted parts and stripped bolt heads

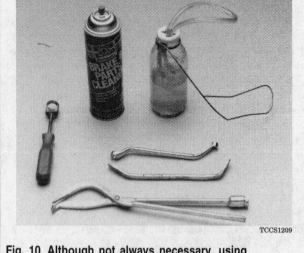

Fig. 10 Although not always necessary, using specialized brake tools will save time

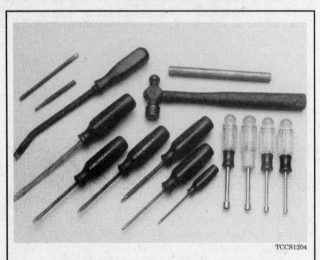

Fig. 8 Various screwdrivers, a hammer, chisels and prybars are necessary to have in your toolbox

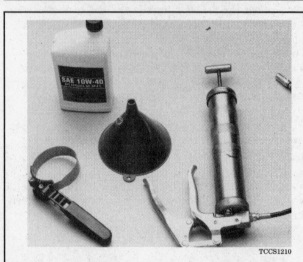

Fig. 11 A few inexpensive lubrication tools will make regular service easier

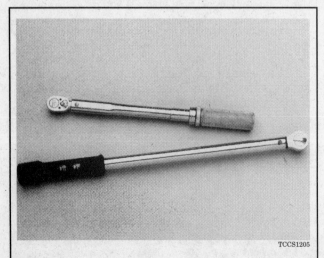

Fig. 9 Many repairs will require the use of a torque wrench to assure the components are properly fastened

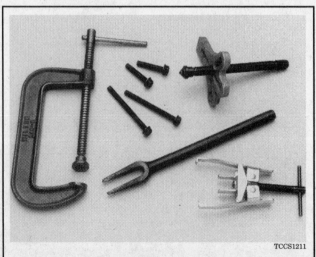

Fig. 12 Various pullers, clamps and separator tools are needed for the repair of many components

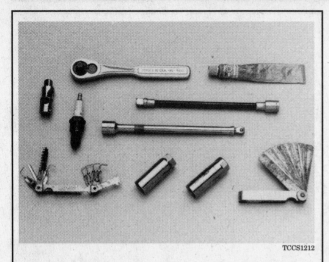

TCCS1212

Fig. 13 A variety of tools and gauges are needed for spark plug service

given, these values are only a guide, based upon fastener size:

Bolts marked 6T
6mm bolt/nut: 5-7 ft. lbs. (7-10 Nm)
8mm bolt/nut: 12-17 ft. lbs. (16-23 Nm)
10mm bolt/nut: 23-34 ft. lbs. (31-46 Nm)
12mm bolt/nut: 41-59 ft. lbs. (56-80 Nm)
14mm bolt/nut: 56-76 ft. lbs. (76-103 Nm)

Bolts marked 8T
6mm bolt/nut: 6-9 ft. lbs. (8-12 Nm)
8mm bolt/nut: 13-20 ft. lbs. (18-27 Nm)
10mm bolt/nut: 27-40 ft. lbs. (37-54 Nm)
12mm bolt/nut: 46-69 ft. lbs. (62-94 Nm)
14mm bolt/nut: 75-101 ft. lbs. (102-137 Nm)

➡ **Refer to your specific Chilton Total Car Care repair manual for exact removal, installation and tightening instructions when replacing components.**

Special Tools

Normally, special factory tools are avoided for repair procedures, since these many not be readily available for the do-it-yourself mechanic. When it is possible to perform the job with more commonly available tools, it will be pointed out, but occasionally, a special tool was designed to perform a specific function and should be used. Before substituting another tool, you should be convinced that neither your safety nor the performance of the vehicle will be compromised.

Some special tools are available commercially from major tool manufacturers. Others can be purchased from your dealer or from Kent-Moore Corporation, 29784 Little Mack, Roseville, Michigan 48066-2298. In Canada, contact Kent-Moore of Canada, Ltd., 2395 Cawthra Mississauga, Ontario, Canada L5A 3P2.

SPECIAL DIAGNOSTIC TOOLS

Frequent references to specific test equipment will be found in the text and in the diagnostic charts. This usually refers to scan tools used to communicate with electronic control units or special electronic testers. Among other features, scan tools combine many standard testers into a single device for quick and accurate circuit diagnosis. For many tests, a multimeter, test light, or other general test equipment can be substituted but the technician must be aware of the risk involved. The general test equipment may not be capable of safely testing the system or may generate incomplete or inaccurate test results. Some tests require activating system components and often this can only be done with scan tools or other special equipment.

Most test equipment is available through aftermarket tool manufacturers, but some can only be obtained through the vehicle manufacturer. Care should be taken that all test equipment being used is designed to diagnose that particular system accurately without damaging control modules or other components.

➡**When using special test equipment, the manufacturer's instructions provided with the tester should be read and clearly understood before attempting any test procedures.**

Electrical Test Tools

ORGANIZED TROUBLESHOOTING

When diagnosing a specific problem, there are certain troubleshooting techniques that are standard:

1. Establish when the problem occurs. Does the problem appear only under certain conditions? Were there any noises, odors, or other unusual symptoms? Make notes on any symptoms found, including warning lights and trouble codes, if applicable.

2. Isolate the problem area. To do this, make some simple tests and observations; then eliminate the systems that are working properly. Check for obvious problems such as broken wires, split or disconnected vacuum hoses. Always check the obvious before assuming something complicated is the cause. Be suspicious of fuses, switches and connectors; wiring itself rarely fails.

3. Test for problems systematically to determine the cause once the problem area is isolated. Are all the components functioning properly? Is there power going to electrical switches and motors? Is there vacuum at vacuum switches and/or actuators? Doing careful, systematic checks will often turn up most causes on the first inspection without wasting time checking components that have little or no relationship to the problem.

4. Test all repairs after the work is done to make sure that the problem is fixed. Some causes can be traced to more than 1 component, so a careful verification of repair work is impor-

tant to pick up additional malfunctions that may cause a problem to reappear or a different problem to arise. A blown fuse, for example, is a simple problem that may require more than another fuse to repair.

The diagnostic tree charts are designed to help solve problems by leading the user through closely defined conditions and tests. Only the most likely components, vacuum and electrical circuits are checked for proper operation when troubleshooting a particular malfunction. By using the diagnostic trees to eliminate those systems and components which normally will not cause the condition described, a problem can be isolated within 1 or more systems or circuits without wasting time on unnecessary testing.

Experience has shown that most problems tend to be the result of a fairly simple and obvious cause, such as loose or corroded connectors; making careful inspection of components during testing is essential to quick and accurate troubleshooting. Frequent references to special test equipment will be found in the text and in the diagnosis charts. These devices or a compatible equivalent are necessary to perform some of the more complicated test procedures listed. Testers are available from a variety of aftermarket sources as well as from the vehicle manufacturer. Care should be taken that any test equipment being used is designed to diagnose that particular system accurately without damaging the computer control modules or components being tested.

➡**Pinpointing the exact cause of trouble in an electrical system can sometimes be accomplished only by the use of special test equipment. In addition to the information covered in this section, the manufacturer's instructions booklet provided with the tester should be read and clearly understood before attempting any test procedures.**

Testers and Equipment

JUMPER WIRES

▶ **See Figures 14, 15 and 16**

Jumper wires are simple, yet extremely valuable, pieces of test equipment. Jumper wires are merely wires that are used to bypass sections of a circuit. The simplest type of jumper wire is a length of multi-strand wire with an alligator clip at each end. Jumper wires are usually fabricated from lengths of standard automotive wire and whatever type of connector (alligator clip, spade connector or pin connector) is required for the vehicle being tested. Some jumper wires are made with 3 or more terminals coming from a common splice for special-purpose testing. In cramped, hard-to-reach areas it is advisable to have insulated boots over the jumper wire terminals in order to prevent accidental grounding and possible system damage.

Jumper wires are used primarily to locate open electrical circuits, on either the ground (-) side of the circuit or on the hot (+) side. If an electrical component fails to operate, connect the jumper wire between the component and a good ground. If the component operates only with the jumper installed, the ground circuit is open. If the ground circuit is good, but the component does not operate, the circuit between the

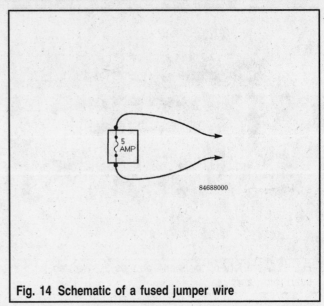

Fig. 14 Schematic of a fused jumper wire

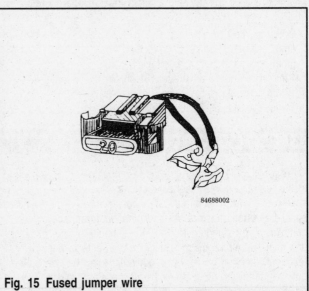

Fig. 15 Fused jumper wire

power feed and component is open. Sometimes a fused jumper wire is connected directly from the battery to the hot terminal of the component, but first make sure the component uses 12 volts in operation.

By inserting an in-line fuse between a set of test leads, a fused jumper wire is created. A fused jumper wire can be used for bypassing open circuits. Use a 5 amp fuse to provide circuit protection.

➡**Never use jumpers made from wire that is of lighter gauge (smaller diameter) than used in the circuit under test. If the jumper wire is too small, it may overheat and possibly melt. Never use jumpers to bypass high-resistance loads (such as motors) in a circuit. Bypassing resistances, in effect, creates a short circuit which may cause damage and fire. Never use a jumper for anything other than temporary bypassing of components in a circuit, damage or fire could result.**

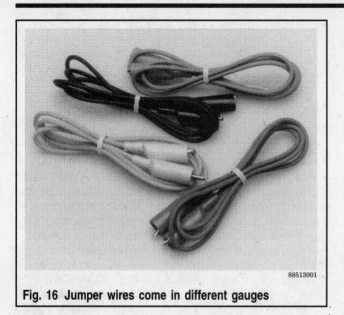

Fig. 16 Jumper wires come in different gauges

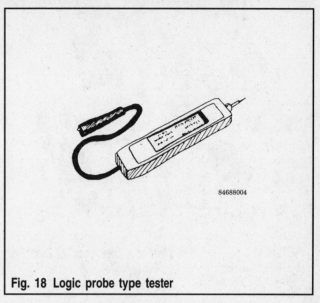

Fig. 18 Logic probe type tester

TEST LIGHTS

12 Volt Test Light
▶ See Figures 17, 18, 19, 20, 21, 22 and 23

The 12 volt test light is used to check circuits and components while electrical current is flowing through them. It is used for voltage and ground tests. Twelve volt test lights come in different styles, but all have 3 main parts; a ground clip, a probe and a light.

➡Avoid piercing the insulation of any wire. While most probes are designed to pierce insulation, this can lead to corrosion or broken conductors within the wire. Trace the wire to a terminal that can be probed before piercing the insulation.

The most commonly used 12 volt test lights have pick-type probes. To use a 12 volt test light, connect the ground clip to a good ground and probe wherever necessary with the pick.

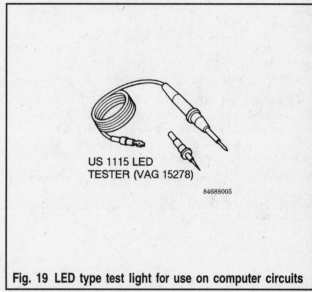

US 1115 LED TESTER (VAG 15278)

Fig. 19 LED type test light for use on computer circuits

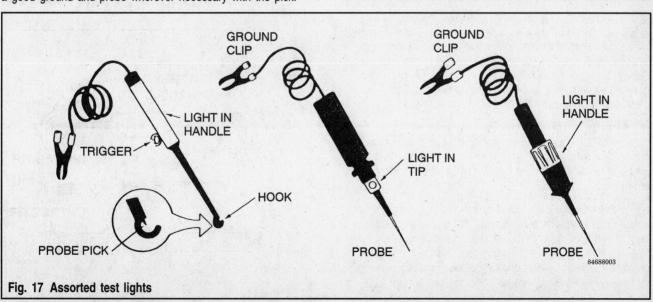

Fig. 17 Assorted test lights

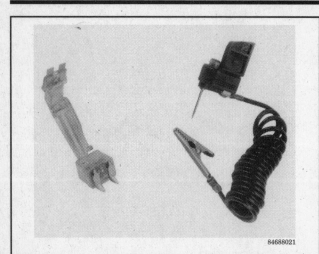

Fig. 20 The device on the left is a fuse checker and the test light on the right is a LED type for use on computer circuits

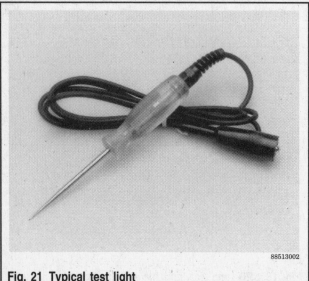

Fig. 21 Typical test light

The wrap-around light is handy in hard to reach areas or where it is difficult to support a wire to push a probe pick into it. To use the wrap around light, hook the wire to be probed with the hook and pull the trigger. A small pick will be forced through the wire insulation into the wire core. Only use this type of test light as a last resort and do not use it on SRS or computer data lines.

➡Never use a pick-type test light to probe wiring on computer controlled systems unless specifically instructed to do so. Any wire insulation that is pierced by the test light probe should be taped and sealed with silicone after testing.

The test light does not detect specific voltage amounts; it only detects that voltage is present. It is advisable before using the test light to touch its terminals across the battery posts to make sure the light is operating properly. Do not attempt to determine voltage by how brightly the tester glows; use a voltmeter if an exact reading is needed.

Use of a LED type test light is recommended for computer controlled circuits. A standard incandescent bulb test light can load the circuit causing a high current to flow and damage the components. An LED type test light will not load the circuit and is safer to use in a computer controlled circuit.

Self-Powered Test Light

The self-powered test light usually contains a 1.5 volt pen-light battery. One type is similar in design to the 12 volt test light. This type has both the battery and the light in the handle and pick-type probe tip. The second type has the light toward the open tip, so that the light illuminates the contact point. The self-powered test light is a dual-purpose piece of equipment. It can be used to test for either open or short circuits when power is isolated from the circuit (continuity test). A powered test light should never be used on any computer controlled system or component unless specifically instructed to do so.

The 1.5 volt battery in the test light does not provide much current. A weak battery may not provide enough power to illuminate the test light even when a complete circuit is made (especially if there are high resistances in the circuit). Always make sure that the test battery is strong. To check the battery, briefly touch the ground clip to the probe; if the light glows brightly, the battery is strong enough for testing. Never use a self-powered test light to perform checks for opens or shorts when power is applied to the electrical system under test. The 12 volt vehicle power will quickly burn out the 1.5 volt light bulb in the test light.

VOLTMETER

A voltmeter is used to measure voltage at any point in a circuit, or to measure the voltage drop across any part of a circuit. Voltmeters usually have various scales on the meter dial and a selector switch to allow the selection of different test ranges. The voltmeter has a positive and a negative lead. To avoid damage to the meter, connect the negative lead, usually black, to the negative (-) side of circuit or to ground. Connect the positive lead, usually red, to the positive (+) or power side of the circuit.

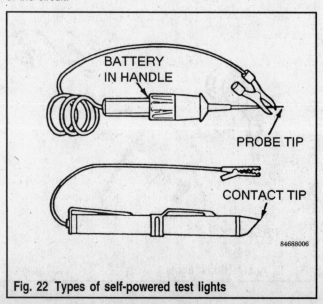

Fig. 22 Types of self-powered test lights

Fig. 23 This computer circuit testing kit includes LED test lights that are safe for use on electronic circuits.

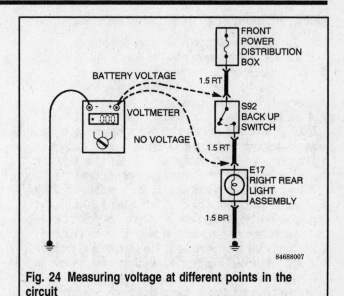

Fig. 24 Measuring voltage at different points in the circuit

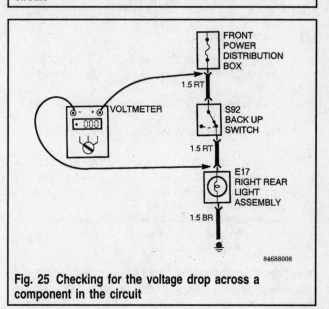

Fig. 25 Checking for the voltage drop across a component in the circuit

A voltmeter can be connected either in parallel or in series with a circuit and has a very high resistance to current flow. When connected in parallel, only a small amount of current will flow through the voltmeter current path; the rest will flow through the normal current path and the circuit will work normally. When the voltmeter is connected in series with a circuit, only a small amount of current can flow through the circuit. The circuit will not work properly, but the voltmeter reading will show if the circuit is complete or not.

Available Voltage Measurement
▶ See Figures 24 and 25

Set the voltmeter selector switch to the 20V position and connect the meter negative lead to the negative post of the battery and connect the positive meter lead to the positive post of the battery. Read the voltage on the meter or digital display. A well-charged battery should register over 12 volts. If the meter reads below 11.5 volts, the battery power may be insufficient to operate the electrical system properly. This test determines voltage available from the battery and should be the first step in any electrical trouble diagnosis procedure. Many electrical problems, especially on computer controlled systems, can be caused by a low state of charge in the battery. Excessive corrosion at the battery cable terminals can cause a poor contact that will prevent proper charging and full battery current flow.

Nominal battery voltage is 12 volts but, when fully charged, should be about 13.2 volts. When the battery is supplying current to 1 or more circuits it is said to be under load. When everything is **OFF** the electrical system is under a no-load condition. A fully charged battery showing about 12.5 volts at no load may drop to 12 volts under medium load and will drop even lower under heavy load. If the battery is partially discharged, the voltage decrease under heavy load may be excessive, even though the battery shows 12 volts or more at no load. For this reason, it is important that the battery be fully charged during all testing procedures to avoid errors in diagnosis and incorrect test results.

Voltage Drop

When current flows through a resistance, the voltage beyond the resistance is reduced. The larger the current, the greater the voltage reduction. When the circuit is off, there is no voltage drop because there is no current. All points in the circuit which are connected to the power source are at the same voltage as the power source. In a long circuit with many connectors, a series of small, unwanted voltage drops due to corrosion at the connectors can add up to a total loss of voltage which impairs the operation of the loads in the circuit.

INDIRECT COMPUTATION OF VOLTAGE DROPS

1. Set the voltmeter selector switch to the 20 volt position.
2. Connect the meter negative lead to a good ground.
3. Probe all resistances in the circuit with the positive meter lead.
4. Operate the circuit in all modes and observe the voltage readings.

DIRECT MEASUREMENT OF VOLTAGE DROPS

1. Set the voltmeter switch to the 20 volt position.
2. Connect the voltmeter negative lead to the ground side of the resistance load to be measured.
3. Connect the positive lead to the positive side of the resistance or load to be measured.
4. Read the voltage drop directly on the 20 volt scale.

Too high a voltage indicates too high a resistance. If, for example, a blower motor runs too slowly, there may be too high a resistance in the resistor pack. By taking voltage drop readings in all parts of the circuit, the problem can be isolated. Too low a voltage drop indicates too low a resistance. If, for example, a blower motor runs too fast in the **MED** and/or **LOW** position, the problem can be isolated to the resistor pack by taking voltage drop readings in all parts of the circuit to locate a possibly shorted resistor. The maximum allowable voltage drop under load is critical, especially if there is more than one high resistance problem in a circuit; all voltage drops are cumulative. A small drop is normal due to the resistance of the conductors.

High Resistance Testing

1. Set the voltmeter selector switch to the 2 volt position.
2. Connect the voltmeter positive lead to the positive post of the battery.
3. Turn **ON** the headlights and heater blower to provide a load.
4. Probe various points in the circuit with the negative voltmeter lead.
5. Read the voltage drop. Some average maximum allowable voltage drops are:

> Fuse panel — 0.7 volts
> Ignition switch — 0.5 volts
> Headlight switch — 0.7 volts
> Ignition coil (+) — 0.5 volts
> Any other load — 0.5-1.3 volts

➡**Voltage drops are all measured while a load is operating; without current flow, there will be no voltage drop.**

OHMMETER

▶ **See Figures 26 and 27**

The ohmmeter is designed to read resistance (ohms) in a circuit or component. Although there are several different styles of ohmmeters, all will usually have a selector switch which permits the measurement of different ranges of resistance. Usually the selector switch allows the multiplication of the meter reading by 10, 100, 1000, 10,000, etc. A calibration knob allows the meter to be set at zero for accurate measurement. Since all ohmmeters are powered by an internal battery (usually 9 volts), the ohmmeter can be used as a self-powered test light. When the ohmmeter is connected, current from the ohmmeter flows through the circuit or component being tested. Since the ohmmeter's internal resistance and voltage are

known values, the amount of current flow through the meter depends on the resistance of the circuit or component being tested.

The ohmmeter can be used to perform continuity tests for opens or shorts and to read actual resistance in a circuit. It should be noted that the ohmmeter is used to check the resistance of a component or wire while there is no voltage applied to the circuit. Current flow from an outside voltage source (such as the vehicle battery) can damage the ohmmeter, so the circuit or component should be isolated from the vehicle electrical system before any testing is done. Since the ohmmeter uses its own voltage source, either lead can be connected to any test point.

➡**When checking diodes or other solid state components, the ohmmeter leads can only be connected one way in order to measure current flow in a single direction. Make sure the positive (+) and negative (-) terminal connections are as described in the test procedures to verify the one-way diode operation.**

When using the meter for continuity checks, do not be concerned with the actual resistance readings. Zero resistance, or any resistance reading, indicates continuity in the circuit. Infinite resistance indicates an open in the circuit. A high resistance reading where there should be none indicates a problem in the circuit. Checks for short circuits are made in the same manner as checks for open circuits except that the circuit must be isolated from both power and normal ground. Infinite resistance indicates no continuity to ground, while zero resistance indicates a dead short to ground.

Resistance Measurement

The batteries in an ohmmeter may be affected by temperature and will weaken with age. The ohmmeter must be calibrated or 'zeroed" before taking measurements. To zero the meter, place the selector switch in its lowest range and touch

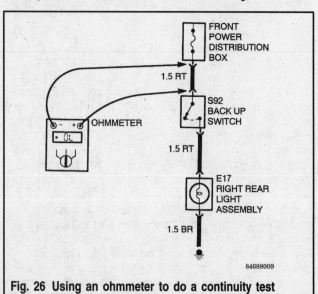

Fig. 26 Using an ohmmeter to do a continuity test

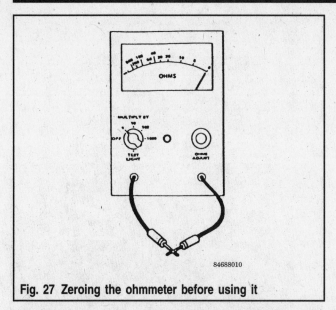

Fig. 27 Zeroing the ohmmeter before using it

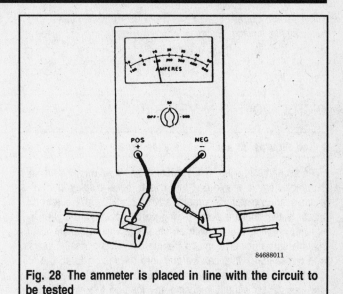

Fig. 28 The ammeter is placed in line with the circuit to be tested

the 2 leads together. Turn the calibration knob until the meter needle is exactly on zero.

➡All analog (needle) type ohmmeters must be zeroed before use, but some digital ohmmeter models are automatically calibrated when the switch is turned ON. Self-calibrating digital ohmmeters do not have an adjusting knob, but it's a good idea to check for a zero readout before use by touching the leads together. All computer controlled systems require the use of a digital ohmmeter with at least 10 megohms impedance for testing. Before any test procedures are attempted, make sure the ohmmeter used is compatible with the electrical system, or damage to the on-board computer could result.

To measure resistance, first isolate the circuit from the vehicle power source by disconnecting the battery cables or the harness connector. Make sure the key is OFF when disconnecting any components or the battery. Where necessary, also isolate at least one side of the circuit to be checked to avoid reading parallel resistances. Parallel circuit resistances will always give a lower reading than the actual resistance of either of the branches. When measuring the resistance of parallel circuits, the total resistance will always be lower than the smallest resistance in the circuit. Connect the meter leads to both sides of the circuit (wire or component) and read the actual measured ohms on the meter scale. Make sure the selector switch is set to the proper ohm scale for the circuit being tested to avoid misreading the ohmmeter test value.

➡Never use an ohmmeter with power applied to the circuit. Like the self-powered test light, the ohmmeter is designed to operate on its own power supply. The normal 12 volt automotive system could damage the meter.

AMMETERS

▶ See Figures 28 and 29

An ammeter measures the amount of current flowing through a circuit in units called amperes or amps. Amperes are units of electron flow which indicate how fast the electrons are flowing

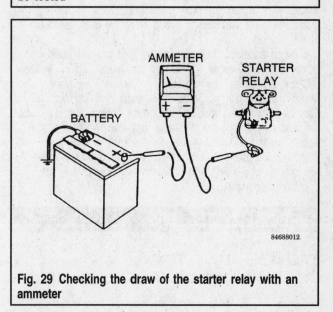

Fig. 29 Checking the draw of the starter relay with an ammeter

through the circuit. Since Ohm's Law dictates that current flow in a circuit is equal to the circuit voltage divided by the total circuit resistance, increasing voltage also increases the current level (amps). Likewise, any decrease in resistance will increase the amount of amps in a circuit. At normal operating voltage, most circuits have a characteristic amount of amperes, called 'current draw" which can be measured using an ammeter. By referring to a specified current draw rating, measuring the amperes, and comparing the 2 values, one can determine what is happening within the circuit to aid in diagnosis. An open circuit, for example, will not allow any current to flow so the ammeter reading will be zero. More current flows through a heavily loaded circuit or when the charging system is operating.

An ammeter is always connected in series with the circuit being tested. All of the current that normally flows through the circuit must also flow through the ammeter; if there is any other path for the current to follow, the ammeter reading will not be accurate. The ammeter itself has very little resistance to current flow and therefore will not affect the circuit, but it will measure current draw only when the circuit is closed and electricity is flowing. Excessive current draw can blow fuses and/or drain the battery; a reduced current draw can cause motors to run slowly, lights to dim and other components to operate improperly.

DIGITAL VOLT-OHM METER (DVOM)

▶ **See Figures 30 and 31**

As its name implies, this tool combines a voltmeter and an ohmmeter into a single unit that has a digital display instead of a scale and pointer. The major advantage of a fully electronic meter is that there are no moving parts that require power to operate. Analog meters with an ultra light weight needle still require some power to move the needle. This limits the range and the features that can be built into the meter. Even the most basic DVOM can read a much greater range of voltage and resistance without imposing any load on the circuit being tested. It is usually the only equipment suitable for testing computer controlled circuits and is often the only test equipment needed.

Several additional features can be built into the same unit, such as circuitry for testing diodes and measuring AC voltage, AC and DC current, temperature, duty cycle, frequency, pulse width, dwell, and rpm. Some of the more sophisticated units also have storage capability, bar graph display, automatic shut-off, and can display the difference between two readings. A top-of-the-line DVOM designed for automotive testing is probably the most useful and cost effective diagnostic tool available. Be sure to buy a unit with a high impedance, usually 10 megohms or higher.

SPECIALITY TESTERS

FREQUENCY PROCESSOR

Some older DVOMs are not equipped to read frequency. There is at least one unit on the market that converts fre-

Fig. 30 Different styles of multimeters allow you a choice of meter functions

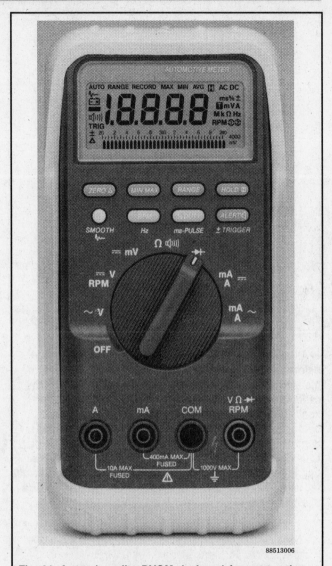

Fig. 31 A good quality DVOM designed for automotive testing is the most useful diagnostic tool available.

quency signals to a millivolt signal that any DVOM can read. It is a simple box with input and output jacks and a 'wake-up' circuit that automatically turns the unit on when needed. Its range of 10-5000 Hz makes it useful for checking rpm sensors, mass air flow sensors, Hall effect sensors and more. Instructions provided with the processor show how to interpret the readings.

BREAK-OUT BOX

▶ **See Figure 32**

The electronic break-out box (BOB) is used to tap into the wiring of a control unit. The main connector to the electronic control unit is connected to the break-out box and another wire harness is connected from the box to the control unit. The break-out box then allows the technician to access each circuit while it is operating without piercing the wire or causing damage to the connectors. All testing with the DVOM can be done safely at these terminals, eliminating the risk of damage due to

Fig. 32 A break-out box makes it possible to tee into control unit circuits.

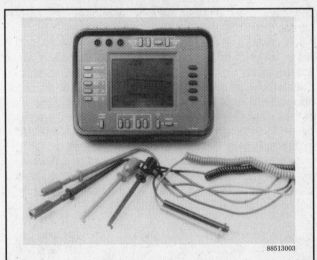

Fig. 33 An Oscilloscope shown with related testing probes

backprobing at the control unit. Many times a break-out box is the only way to test a control unit function.

An intelligent break-out box (IBOB) connects to the vehicle diagnostic connector and has connector ports for a scan tool and/or a computer. On earlier electronic control units that do not generate a data stream, an IBOB will collect input/output data while the engine is running and present it to a scan tool or PC. Additionally, some manufacturers provide plastic overlays for the break-out box. This allows the box to be used on a variety of models; different overlays identify the changes in wire use or labeling. With the proper cable adaptors, an IBOB can be used with any engine, body or ABS control unit on any vehicle.

OSCILLOSCOPE

▶ See Figures 33, 34 and 35

An oscilloscope is a voltmeter that presents a graphic picture of the voltage reading over time. Unlike a DVOM, it can show a voltage that exists for only a fraction of a second or occurs only at a specific time. Ignition oscilloscopes have been around for many years, but the latest generation of service bay oscilloscopes are more like those found in electronics labs. They can read voltages as small as one millivolt and can show a spike that occurs for as little as 10 nanoseconds (1 ns = of a second). Both the voltage and time scales are adjustable, so the same tool can be used to measure the fast, high voltage signal of the secondary ignition system and slow stable signals such as a temperature sensor. Another major feature of all oscilloscopes is an extremely high input impedance, meaning the oscilloscope imposes negligible current draw on the circuit being measured that might influence that measurement. Many times an oscilloscope is the only tool that can be used to measure low voltage, frequency, or duty cycle signals.

Like a timing light, an oscilloscope must be triggered. The trigger can be internal (automatic) or can come from an external source. On a multi-channel oscilloscope, displaying the external trigger signal can show the timing of two events. For example, by taking the trigger from a suspected faulty fuel

injector, it is possible to see the oxygen sensor signal only at the time of that injection event. The voltage level required to trigger the oscilloscope can also be adjusted, providing a simple method to look for low level or intermittent faults that may not set a code.

A digital oscilloscope converts the analog input signal to a digital form. A digital signal can be stored and played back by itself or along with another trace. Some units can also display the signal as numbers, min/max values, change value and average value. If the oscilloscope is equipped with a computer port, the digitized traces and other data can also be downloaded to save and/or print out. There is computer software available to aid organization and analysis of wave forms.

With its extremely fast sampling rate and graphic display, an oscilloscope can easily show a malfunction that occurs too fast for a voltmeter to show. For example, by adjusting the time sweep of the oscilloscope to show the full up-and-down stroke of a throttle position sensor, an intermittent fault in the signal can be clearly shown. A voltmeter may also detect the fault but cannot change the display fast enough to show the resistance spike. A storage oscilloscope with min/max value capa-

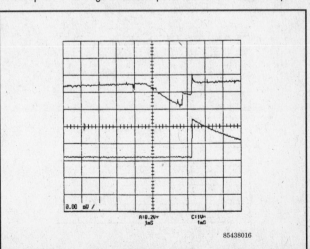

Fig. 34 The oxygen sensor trace (top) shows a delayed cross-over coinciding with an injector pulse (bottom trace).

bility can locate intermittent faults that even other oscilloscopes cannot.

Any oscilloscope used for automotive testing must be designed for use with automobiles. Standard lab oscilloscopes are usually not able to cope with the relatively harsh automotive electronic environment. Automotive oscilloscopes are available in a variety of types with a variety of features. Some are portable hand held models that operate on batteries or vehicle power. Even though they are small, the newest portable units include multi-trace and storage capabilities and are rugged enough to be used under the hood or on road tests. Larger more powerful models mounted in a console are often part of a top-of-the-line engine analyzer package. Most of the major diagnostic tool manufacturers produce at least one oscilloscope model.

As vehicles become more sophisticated and electronic controls become more powerful, an oscilloscope is fast becoming a necessary diagnostic tool. When the technician becomes proficient with an oscilloscope, many other diagnostic tools become unnecessary.

SCAN TOOL

▶ **See Figures 36, ?, 37 and 38**

This is the generic name for portable diagnostic equipment that communicates directly with an electronic control unit. The major vehicle manufacturers each have their own scan tool that is used by dealership technicians, such as Nissan's Consult and Honda's PGM Tester. Some of these are available through the dealer parts network or are sold outside the network under another name. Others such as Volkswagen's VAG 1551 are available only to authorized dealerships.

Scan tools are used to read and erase trouble codes stored in the control unit memory and to provide a direct data transfer link with the control unit's On Board Diagnostic (OBD) system. Reading the control unit memory through the scan tool is more complete than reading codes with the flashing light on the instrument panel. Some information is only available through the scan tool, such as the number of engine starts since the fault first appeared. Data transfer provides a real time display

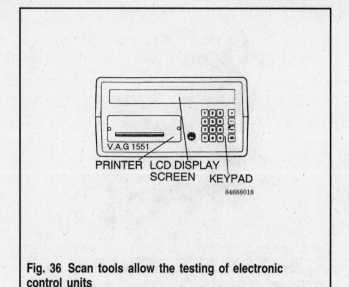

Fig. 36 Scan tools allow the testing of electronic control units

Fig. 37 Aftermarket scan tool with a program module installed

of control unit input/output signals. Data such as the oxygen sensor reading or idle control motor duty cycle can be displayed while the engine is running. The scan tool can also be used as a volt/ohmmeter to check selected circuits without disconnecting them.

Some scan tools are designed to simulate sensor inputs to test the sensor circuit, the control unit and the output device. On many vehicles, the scan tool can communicate with every control unit on the vehicle through a single diagnostic connector. Some of the more advanced scan tools are equipped with a data memory to store test data during a road test. The test data is down loaded into a PC through an RS232 computer port, greatly increasing the processing power and expanding the amount of memory and information available.

Aftermarket scan tools require adaptors to match the different vehicle diagnostic connectors. A cartridge that plugs into the scan tool contains software needed for communicating with the different control units. The software is the tool's real power and is continuously evolving to enhance its capabilities. As the tool manufacturer's data base has grown, software now in-

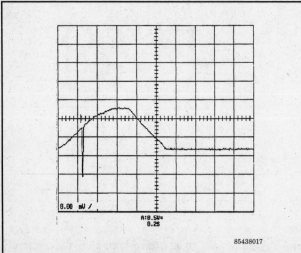

Fig. 35 An intermittent fault in the throttle position sensor shows clearly on the scope trace.

cludes VIN-specific information that addresses some of the most common trouble codes and driveability problems that don't always generate codes. Tests are menu-driven and many of the specifications are included right there in the program. Depending on the vehicle and the amount of computer control used, systems which may be viewed or investigated with a scan tool include:

1. Engine controllers/ECUs
2. Fuel/ignition systems
3. Electronic transmission control
4. Charging system
5. Suspension control functions
6. Anti-Lock brake system.
7. Passive restraint system
8. Anti-theft system
9. Climate Control Systems

Body electrical systems including power locks, entertainment systems, sunroofs, and defoggers.

Aftermarket scan tools work well with most vehicles, but no scan tool can be used on all models and all are limited in their ability to communicate with European models. The Federal On-Board Diagnostic (OBD) specification requires all vehicles to have the same diagnostic connector and diagnostic trouble codes and to use the same data transfer language. This makes it possible to use a single scan tool to communicate with all engine control units from all manufacturers. Some manufacturers began production of OBD vehicles for the 1994 model year and all new vehicles must comply by the 1998 model year. As vehicle control units and scan tools become more powerful, data acquisition and test capabilities will also improve dramatically with each new generation of control unit and scan tool software.

EXHAUST GAS ANALYZERS

Exhaust gas analysis has long been an extremely valuable and versatile diagnostic tool. It can be used to troubleshoot fuel and ignition systems, locate vacuum leaks or EGR malfunctions, even diagnose mechanical problems such as worn

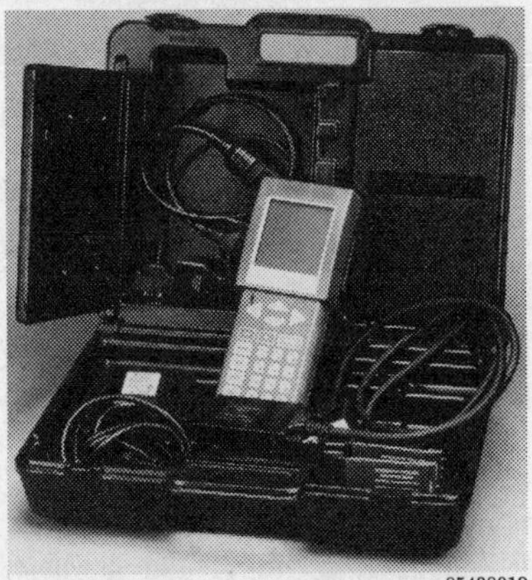

85438019

Fig. 38 This type scan tool, used by dealer technicians, is available outside the dealer network and can scan all OBD II-spec vehicles. This one includes a built-in oscilloscope.

valve guides. On most vehicles, it is the only way to accurately check air/fuel mixture.

The federal government regulates three exhaust gas components: hydrocarbons (HC), carbon monoxide (CO), and oxides of nitrogen (NOx). HC and CO are relatively easy to measure and have long been tested in states that require emissions inspections. Measuring carbon dioxide (CO_2) and oxygen (O_2) are also valuable diagnostic aids but NOx cannot be accurately measured at idle or no-load conditions. However as states enact tighter Inspection and Maintenance programs, service bay NOx analyzers and test procedures are being developed. For complete diagnostic and certification testing, a five-gas analyzer is required.

Most gas analyzers include a single tailpipe sample probe, sample pump and filtration system and a detector cell for each of the gasses being measured. Most stand-alone four-gas analyzers used for emissions inspections are equipped with a small microprocessor that includes testing and calibration programs, a self diagnostic program and a built-in printer. Other units are designed as part of a complete diagnostic station and are connected to a PC based computer, printer and monitor screen. There is at least one portable four-gas analyzer that is used along with the same manufacturer's scan tool. The scan tool's software guides the user through test procedures based on the gas and sensor readings.

There is also a series of small, hand-held oxygen and CO monitors available that do not require a sample pump and filter system. The measuring cell is built into the tailpipe probe and the monitor is battery operated. Since there is only a wire between the probe and the monitor, these units can easily be used on a road test. They are also equipped with a memory that can record three minutes of test data. The CO monitor can be particularly useful for routine air/fuel adjustments. Each unit is available with its own display, with voltage outputs to use a DVOM display, or with computer ports and PC based software that includes test procedures.

All gas analyzers must be calibrated at least once per day. Industry standard calibration gasses are usually available through parts stores or tool outlets.

ENGINE ANALYZERS

A large, fully-equipped engine analyzer usually includes an oscilloscope, exhaust gas analyzer, vacuum and pressure sensors, a timing light and probe, electrical measuring equipment, and a computer. With a variety of electrical connections and a tail pipe probe, this analyzer can check the primary and secondary ignition systems, fuel injection controls and injectors, EGR systems, engine vacuum and compression, and the starting and charging systems. The computer can be used to read the engine control unit's data stream through the vehicle diagnostic connector. Even on earlier vehicles with no sensors or data stream, an engine analyzer is still a powerful diagnostic tool.

The computer is the real power behind an engine analyzer. The computer's ability to determine the ignition pulse at cylinder number one can be used to index all other engine events to particular cylinders. For example, the analyzer can measure the starter current needed to move each piston to TDC, indicating the relative compression of each cylinder. The analyzer can also display spark plug firing voltage and duration on the oscilloscope. A spark plug that requires more voltage with less duration could indicate a faulty injector. The analyzer can detect and clearly show all the differences between cylinders. The computer can help the technician diagnose the data, determine the necessary repairs and even provide a print-out to present a clear explanation to the vehicle owner.

These analyzers are a major investment and are well supported by the manufacturer. They are frequently updated with a computer floppy disc that includes new vehicle information and test procedures. Some machines include CD-ROM equipment to read service manuals that are available on disc. They may also include a modem to communicate with the manufacturer or other computers via telephone. As vehicles and other shop equipment become more sophisticated, it should be possible to keep a computer based engine analyzer up to date and useful almost indefinitely.

Specific Test Equipment

There are many special diagnostic tools for testing individual components or systems, such as a Hall effect sensor, idle air control motor, fuel injectors, secondary ignition systems, and others. Most are designed for use on as many vehicles as possible. Some are designed to test parts or systems on specific vehicles, such as the ABS tester for all Mitsubishi vehicles. Generally these devices allow the technician to quickly test components or sub-systems without going through a long diagnostic procedure. However there is a risk of incorrect diagnosis. These tools can only be dependable if the technician is familiar with their use and understands what the test results really mean. A simple vacuum leak or loose connection may produce the same test result as a faulty component.

LEAK DETECTORS

▶ See Figure 39

A battery powered, hand-held vacuum leak detector uses a microphone and amplifier that detects noise in the ultrasonic range. Air moving through a vacuum leak will generate sound waves in the 40 kHz range, well above the range of human hearing. The detector will sound a beeper when a leak is found. Because of the high frequency sensed by the detector, it is not generally affected by normal engine or shop noises.

Leak detectors for air conditioning systems have a vacuum pump and probe to draw an air sample into the detecting cell. The cell detects halogen gas that is common to all air conditioning refrigerants. Most are capable of indicating the type of freon in the system, as well as the rate of leakage. There are battery powered hand-held models and larger AC powered units suitable for mounting on an air conditioning service cart. The newest models are capable of detecting R134a and the sensitivity can be adjusted for possible background interference.

A combustible gas leak detector reacts to hydrocarbons present in fuels, exhaust gases, coolants, and lubricants. Models with adjustable sensitivity are typically used to look for fuel vapor leaks, head gasket leaks, and to measure the amount of exhaust leaking into the interior of a vehicle. With some imagination, this can be an extremely useful tool.

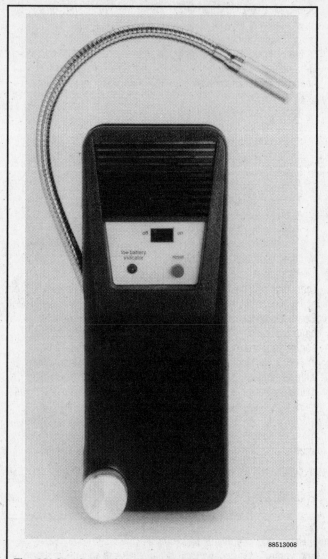

88513008

Fig. 39 An ultrasonic vacuum leak detector is unaffected by engine or shop noise.

PYROMETER

A pyrometer measures a wide range of temperatures with a probe that only needs to touch the item being measured. As a general diagnostic tool, a hand held pyrometer can quickly locate hot or cold spots in a cooling system, a seized brake caliper, a dry bearing, test heater and A/C performance or even find a weak cylinder by measuring exhaust manifold runner temperatures. Most pyrometers are available with special probes for penetration and for measuring tire temperatures. There are even optical infrared non-contact pyrometers that measure temperature by the heat emission of a surface. This is useful as the surface to be measured does not have to actually touched with a probe. They can be calibrated quickly, have a very wide temperature range and can usually be switched to display Fahrenheit or Celsius degrees. With a little imagination, this can be an extremely useful tool.

IDLE AIR CONTROL TESTER

This is a kit used to isolate and test idle air control solenoids, motors, and signals. Some are made for use with a specific system, others include adaptors for use with many different vehicles. The device can activate solenoid valves and control motors to test the full range of motion with the engine not running. It can also be used to control idle speed for timing adjustment or other engine tests. Some can also check the control unit output signal to the idle air control motor. These functions can also be accomplished with scan tools but this tester can be faster and easier to use for some tests.

FUEL INJECTOR TESTER

▶ **See Figure 40**

This device can quickly check the coil resistance and current draw of an electric fuel injector while it is under load. Each injector is tested individually and the results are reported on a DVOM or oscilloscope. This information makes it possible to electronically check injector balance and detect intermittent faults. When used with equipment that measures fuel pressure and injection quantity, every function of the fuel system can be tested.

OXYGEN SENSOR TESTER

This kit usually includes a propane enrichment control valve, special connectors and test instructions, and the hose and fittings needed for connecting the valve to an intake manifold. The kit allows the technician to control air/fuel mixture and check the oxygen sensor response time. When the oxygen sensor is disconnected, forcing the control unit into open loop, sensor output voltage or resistance can be read with a DVOM. The instructions also include procedures for testing the control unit's response to the oxygen sensor signal.

SENSOR SIMULATOR

This device is used to take a sensor 'out of the loop' and simulate its input signals to the control unit. It can simulate every type of voltage, resistance, and frequency signal one at a time to test the control unit's response to the input. The simulator can also measure any sensor output signal by back-probing the sensor connector. In addition to displaying the reading directly, some units can also output the reading to an oscilloscope, scan tool, or other diagnostic equipment.

POWER STEERING TESTER

▶ **See Figure 41**

A power steering tester can quickly confirm that the hydraulic system is functioning properly and indicate excess loads on the system due to mechanical malfunction in the suspension or steering linkage. The mechanical tester consists of a gauge, a heavy duty hose, and adapters for various models. Newer testers use an electronic pressure transducer that converts the pressure to an electrical signal. This allows the technician to road test variable effort power steering systems with a DVOM.

ELECTRONIC SIGHTGLASS

This device, used for troubleshooting air conditioning systems, includes two transducers and a battery operated meter. The transducers attach to the outside of the metal air conditioning lines without disconnecting the lines. While the A/C system is operating, the device ultrasonically detects bubbles in the refrigerant and uses an LED display to simulate a sightglass, allowing the technician to actually 'see' the bubbles in the system. The transducers can be fitted to any metal line at almost any point in the system, making it possible to test expansion valves and capillary tubes, or find other undesired restrictions.

88513009

Fig. 40 A fuel injector tester measures voltage drop while the injector is being activated.

85438023

Fig. 41 A power steering system testing gauge can quickly isolate hydraulic or linkage problems.

ANTI-LOCK BRAKE TESTER

▶ **See Figure 42**

Anti-lock brake system control units are equipped with a self-diagnostic program that checks the system at engine start-up and de-activates the system if a fault is detected. Most control units also store diagnostic trouble codes. An ABS tester is basically a scan tool used to read and erase trouble codes and to provide a data link with the ABS control unit. The data link allows the tester to check sensor inputs and activate each solenoid and control valve to test the output system.

The testers for some of the early anti-lock braking systems are usually available only to dealers and function only with that manufacturer's vehicles. The aftermarket scan tool makers have developed the necessary adapters and software cartridges so that most scan tools used to communicate with engine control units can also be used on ABS control units. Unfortunately there are major differences in ABS designs and no scan tool is able to communicate with all ABS control units.

The most complete ABS test equipment is a software package, connector and interface pod that establishes a data link between the control unit and a PC-based computer in an engine analyzer or alignment station. This software uses the power of the computer to completely check the control unit and 'bench test' every component of the system in about one minute. It is suitable for use with every anti-lock braking system on the market and the software can be updated as required to keep the system current.

Even without a scan tool, all of the system's sensors, solenoids, and actuators can still be individually checked with a DVOM and an oscilloscope. The trouble codes and other control unit functions can only be accessed with the correct scan tool or tester.

PASSIVE RESTRAINT TESTER

▶ **See Figure 43**

While there are some differences, the air bag system in most vehicles operates basically the same way. This has made

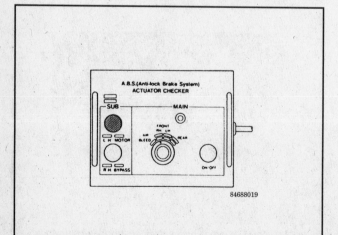

Fig. 42 An ABS checker allows the testing of the anti-lock system

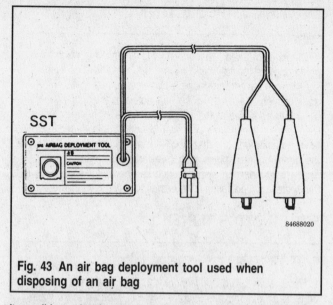

Fig. 43 An air bag deployment tool used when disposing of an air bag

it possible to develop a unit that will test the circuits while they are fully connected and operating. It uses LEDs to read out circuit continuity, power supply, switch state and output device state. On some scan tools, such as the Nissan CONSULT or Subaru Select Monitor, a software cartridge gives the tool the ability to test the passive restraint system.

✳✳CAUTION

If not familiar with disarming procedures and air bag system operation, do not attempt air bag system service. The air bag system must be disabled for some vehicle tests and before removing the steering wheel or dashboard air bag module. Failure to follow air bag safety procedures could result in accidental deployment and serious or fatal injury.

The air bag must function in an extremely short period of time after the crash sensor switches have closed. Most air bag systems include their own power supply. The squib that fires the gas generator charge must operate at low power levels to assure it will still fire if vehicle power is lost in the accident. This makes an air bag module quite sensitive to even small currents like static electricity. Even with such a 'hair trigger', it is not difficult to test the system or handle an air bag module safely.

Air Bag Service Precautions

✳✳CAUTION

An air bag is an explosive device. Before beginning any air bag system service, disconnect and isolate the negative battery cable and backup power supply. Follow the procedures for disarming the air bag system exactly. Do not use any type of computer memory saver device. Do not use any self powered test equipment or test lights until the system is properly disabled. Failure to follow these precautions could result in accidental deployment of the air bag and possible serious or fatal injury.

- Disconnect and isolate the battery cable and any backup power supply when servicing the air bag system.
- Do not use a memory saver.
- When re-activating an air bag system, connect the power last and make sure no one is in the vehicle.
- Do not attempt to measure the resistance across the air bag module connectors with any type of ohmmeter. The ohmmeter battery can fire the air bag module.
- When working on air bag components in the passenger compartment, try to work away from where an air bag would deploy. Accidental deployment of the air bag against a body that is not in the proper position could result in severe or fatal injury.
- A removed air bag module must be placed away from sources of heat, sparks, or electricity, including static electricity.
- A removed air bag module must be placed with the cover pad facing up, so that accidental deployment will not launch the module into the air. Also be sure to carry the module with the cover pad facing away from the body.
- When the air bag module is removed, place it away from loose objects that would be thrown in the event of accidental deployment.
- When removing a steering column with the steering wheel attached, pay attention to where the air bag is aimed. Never stand the column on the face of the steering wheel. Lock the column to avoid damage to the clockspring.
- When handling an air bag which has been deployed, there may be a powdery residue which, though mostly talc, may irritate skin, eyes, and breathing passages. Wear gloves, glasses, and a dust mask while wrapping the deployed air bag in a plastic bag for disposal.
- Sensor positioning is critical for proper system operation. If the sensor is in an area of vehicle damage, replace the sensor whether or not the air bag deployed. The proper torquing of the sensor retainers is critical.
- Any part of the air bag system found to be faulty must be replaced. No part can be repaired, not even the wiring.
- All diagnostic work is to be done with the air bag module(s) removed. Air bag simulators are available and can be installed for a full functional test of the control unit.

Mechanical Test Equipment

VACUUM GAUGE

▶ **See Figure 44**

Intake manifold vacuum is used to operate various systems and devices on all cars. To correctly diagnose and solve problems in vacuum control systems, a vacuum source is necessary for testing. In some cases, vacuum can be taken from the intake manifold when the engine is running, but vacuum is normally provided by a hand vacuum pump.

Most gauges are graduated in inches of Mercury (in. Hg), although a device called a manometer reads vacuum in inches of water (in. H_2O). The vacuum reading usually varies between 18 and 22 in. Hg at sea level. To test engine vacuum, the vacuum gauge must be connected to a source of manifold vacuum. Many engines have a plug in the intake manifold which can be removed and replaced with an adapter fitting. Connect the vacuum gauge to the fitting with a suitable rubber hose or, if no manifold plug is available, connect the vacuum gauge to any device using manifold vacuum, such as EGR valves, etc. The vacuum gauge can be used to determine the amount of vacuum reaching a component.

HAND VACUUM PUMP

Small, hand-held vacuum pumps come in a variety of designs and provide a source of vacuum for testing components without the engine operating. Most have a built-in vacuum gauge and allow a component to be tested without removing it from the vehicle. Operate the pump lever or plunger, applying the correct amount of vacuum required for the test. The level of vacuum in inches of Mercury (in. Hg) is indicated on the pump gauge. For some testing, an additional vacuum gauge may be necessary.

COMPRESSION GAUGE

A compression gauge measures the amount of pressure in pounds per square inch (psi) that a cylinder is producing. Some gauges have a hose that screws into the spark plug hole while others have a tapered rubber tip which is held by hand in the spark plug hole. Engine compression depends on the sealing ability of the rings, valves, head gasket and spark plug gaskets. If any of these parts are not sealing properly, compression will be lost and the power output of the engine will be reduced. The compression in each cylinder should be measured and the variation between cylinders should be noted. The engine should be cranked through 5 or 6 compression strokes while warm, with all plugs removed, ignition disabled and throttle valves wide open.

FUEL PRESSURE GAUGE

A fuel pressure gauge is required to test the operation of the fuel delivery and injection systems. Some systems also need a 3-way valve to check the fuel pressure in various modes of operation. Gauges may require special adapters for making fuel connections. Always observe the cautions outlined in the fuel system service section of your repair manual when working around any pressurized fuel system.

USING A VACUUM GAUGE

White needle = steady needle   *Dark needle = drifting needle*

The vacuum gauge is one of the most useful and easy-to-use diagnostic tools. It is inexpensive, easy to hook up, and provides valuable information about the condition of your engine.

Indication: Normal engine in good condition

Gauge reading: Steady, from 17–22 in./Hg.

Indication: Sticking valve or ignition miss

Gauge reading: Needle fluctuates from 15–20 in./Hg. at idle

Indication: Late ignition or valve timing, low compression, stuck throttle valve, leaking carburetor or manifold gasket.

Gauge reading: Low (15–20 in./Hg.) but steady

Indication: Improper carburetor adjustment, or minor intake leak at carburetor or manifold

NOTE: Bad fuel injector O-rings may also cause this reading.

Gauge reading: Drifting needle

Indication: Weak valve springs, worn valve stem guides, or leaky cylinder head gasket (vibrating excessively at all speeds).

NOTE: A plugged catalytic converter may also cause this reading.

Gauge reading: Needle fluctuates as engine speed increases

Indication: Burnt valve or improper valve clearance. The needle will drop when the defective valve operates.

Gauge reading: Steady needle, but drops regularly

Indication: Choked muffler or obstruction in system. Speed up the engine. Choked muffler will exhibit a slow drop of vacuum to zero.

Gauge reading: Gradual drop in reading at idle

Indication: Worn valve guides

Gauge reading: Needle vibrates excessively at idle, but steadies as engine speed increases

88513010

Fig. 44 A vacuum tool is a good gauge for diagnosing the general condition of an engine

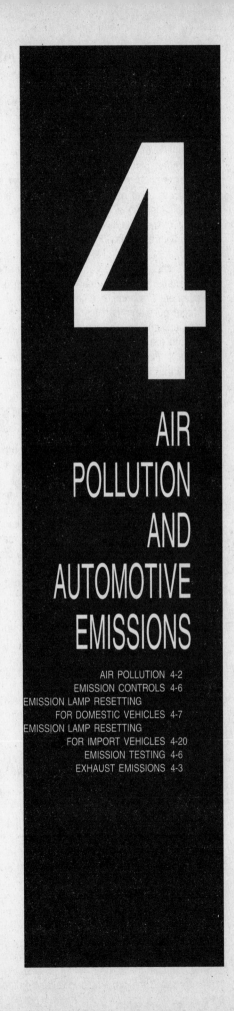

4

AIR POLLUTION AND AUTOMOTIVE EMISSIONS

AIR POLLUTION

The earth's atmosphere, at or near sea level, consists approximately of 78 percent nitrogen, 21 percent oxygen and 1 percent other gases. If it were possible to remain in this state, 100 percent clean air would result. However, many varied causes allow other gases and particulates to mix with the clean air, causing the air to become unclean or polluted.

Certain of these pollutants are visible while others are invisible, with each having the capability of causing distress to the eyes, ears, throat, skin and respiratory system. Should these pollutants become concentrated in a specific area and under certain conditions, death could result due to the displacement or chemical change of the oxygen content in the air. These pollutants can also cause great damage to the environment and to the many man made objects that are exposed to the elements.

To better understand the causes of air pollution, the pollutants can be categorized into 3 separate types, natural, industrial and automotive.

Natural Pollutants

Natural pollution has been present on earth since before man appeared and continues to be a factor when discussing air pollution, although it causes only a small percentage of the overall pollution problem existing in our country today. It is the direct result of decaying organic matter, wind born smoke and particulates from such natural events as plain and forest fires (ignited by heat or lightning), volcanic ash, sand and dust which can spread over a large area of the countryside.

Such a phenomenon of natural pollution has been recently seen in the form of volcanic eruptions, with the resulting plume of smoke, steam and volcanic ash blotting out the sun's rays as it spreads and rises higher into the atmosphere. As it travels into the atmosphere the upper air currents catch and carry the smoke and ash, while condensing the steam back into water vapor. As the water vapor, smoke and ash traveled on their journey, the smoke dissipates into the atmosphere while the ash and moisture settle back to earth in a trail hundreds of miles long. In some cases, lives are lost and millions of dollars of property damage result. Ironically, man can only stand by and watch it happen.

Industrial Pollution

Industrial pollution is caused primarily by industrial processes, the burning of coal, oil and natural gas, which in turn produce smoke and fumes. Because the burning fuels contain large amounts of sulfur, the principal ingredients of smoke and fumes are sulfur dioxide and particulate matter. This type of pollutant occurs most severely during still, damp and cool weather, such as at night. Even in its less severe form, this pollutant is not confined to just cities. Because of air movements, the pollutants move for miles over the surrounding countryside, leaving in its path a barren and unhealthy environment for all living things.

Working with Federal, State and Local mandated regulations and by carefully monitoring the emissions, big business has greatly reduced the amount of pollutant emitted from its industrial sources, striving to obtain an acceptable level. Because of the mandated industrial emission clean up, many land areas and streams in and around the cities that were formerly barren of vegetation and life, have now begun to move back in the direction of nature's intended balance.

Automotive Pollutants

The third major source of air pollution is automotive emissions. The emissions from the internal combustion engine were not an appreciable problem years ago because of the small number of registered vehicles and the nation's small highway system. However, during the early 1950's, the trend of the American people was to move from the cities to the surrounding suburbs. This caused an immediate problem in transportation because the majority of suburbs were not afforded mass transit conveniences. This lack of transportation created an attractive market for the automobile manufacturers, which resulted in a dramatic increase in the number of vehicles produced and sold, along with a marked increase in highway construction between cities and the suburbs. Multi-vehicle families emerged with a growing emphasis placed on an individual vehicle per family member. As the increase in vehicle ownership and usage occurred, so did pollutant levels in and around the cities, as suburbanites drove daily to their businesses and employment, returning at the end of the day to their homes in the suburbs.

It was noted that a fog and smoke type haze was being formed and at times, remained in suspension over the cities, taking time to dissipate. At first this 'smog', derived from the words 'smoke' and 'fog', was thought to result from industrial pollution but it was determined that automobile emissions shared the blame. It was discovered that when normal automobile emissions were exposed to sunlight for a period of time, complex chemical reactions would take place.

It is now known that smog is a photo chemical layer which develops when certain oxides of nitrogen (NOx) and unburned hydrocarbons (HC) from automobile emissions are exposed to sunlight. Pollution was more severe when smog would become stagnant over an area in which a warm layer of air settled over the top of the cooler air mass, trapping and holding the cooler mass at ground level. The trapped cooler air would keep the emissions from being dispersed and diluted through normal air flows. This type of air stagnation was given the name 'Temperature Inversion'.

Temperature Inversion

In normal weather situations, the surface air is warmed by heat radiating from the earth's surface and the sun's rays and will rise upward, into the atmosphere. Upon rising it will cool through a convection type heat exchange with the cooler upper air. As warm air rises, the surface pollutants are carried upward and dissipated into the atmosphere.

When a temperature inversion occurs, we find the higher air is no longer cooler but warmer than the surface air, causing the cooler surface air to become trapped. This warm air blanket can extend from above ground level to a few hundred or even a few thousand feet into the air. As the surface air is trapped, so are the pollutants, causing a severe smog condition. Should this stagnant air mass extend to a few thousand feet high, enough air movement with the inversion takes place to allow the smog layer to rise above ground level but the pollutants still cannot dissipate. This inversion can remain for days over an area, with the smog level only rising or lowering from ground level to a few hundred feet high. Meanwhile, the pollutant levels increase, causing eye irritation, respiratory problems, reduced visibility, plant damage and in some cases, disease.

This inversion phenomenon was first noted in the Los Angeles, California area. The city lies in terrain resembling a basin and with certain weather conditions, a cold air mass is held in the basin while a warmer air mass covers it like a lid.

Because this type of condition was first documented as prevalent in the Los Angeles area, this type of trapped pollution was named 'Los Angeles Smog', although it occurs in other areas where a large concentration of automobiles are used and the air remains stagnant for any length of time.

Gasoline Engine Pollutants

Consider the internal combustion engine as a machine in which raw materials must be placed so a finished product comes out. As in any machine operation, a certain amount of wasted material is formed. When we relate this to the internal combustion engine, we find that through the input of air and fuel, we obtain power during the combustion process to drive the vehicle. The by-product or waste of this power is, in part, heat and exhaust gases with which we must dispose.

EXHAUST EMISSIONS

Composition Of The Exhaust Gases

The exhaust gases emitted into the atmosphere are a combination of burned and unburned fuel. To understand the exhaust emission and its composition, we must review some basic chemistry.

When the air/fuel mixture is introduced into the engine, we are mixing air, composed of nitrogen (78 percent), oxygen (21 percent) and other gases (1 percent) with the fuel, which is 100 percent hydrocarbons (HC), in a semi-controlled ratio. As the combustion process is accomplished, power is produced to move the vehicle while the heat of combustion is transferred to the cooling system. The exhaust gases are then composed of nitrogen, a diatomic gas (N_2), the same as was introduced in the engine, carbon dioxide (CO_2), the same gas that is used in beverage carbonation and water vapor (H_2O). The nitrogen (N_2), for the most part passes through the engine unchanged, while the oxygen (O_2) reacts (burns) with the hydrocarbons (HC) and produces the carbon dioxide (CO_2) and the water vapors (H_2O). If this chemical process would be the only process to take place, the exhaust emissions would be harmless. However, during the combustion process, other compounds are formed which are considered dangerous. These pollutants are carbon monoxide (CO), hydrocarbons (HC), oxides of nitrogen (NOx) oxides of sulfur (SOx) and engine particulates.

Heat Transfer

The heat from the combustion process can rise to over 4,000°F (2,204°C). The dissipation of this heat is controlled by a ram air effect, the use of cooling fans to cause air flow and having a liquid coolant solution surrounding the combustion area to transfer the heat of combustion through the cylinder walls and into the coolant. The coolant is then directed to a thin-finned, multi-tubed radiator, from which the excess heat is transferred to the atmosphere by 1 of the 3 heat transfer methods, conduction, convection or radiation.

The cooling of the combustion area is an important part in the control of exhaust emissions. To understand the behavior of the combustion and transfer of its heat, consider the air/fuel charge. It is ignited and the flame front burns progressively across the combustion chamber until the burning charge reaches the cylinder walls. Some of the fuel in contact with the walls is not hot enough to burn, thereby snuffing out or quenching the combustion process. This leaves unburned fuel in the combustion chamber. This unburned fuel is then forced out of the cylinder and into the exhaust system, along with the exhaust gases.

Many attempts have been made to minimize the amount of unburned fuel in the combustion chambers due to the snuffing out or quenching, by increasing the coolant temperature and lessening the contact area of the coolant around the combustion area. Design limitations within the combustion chambers prevent the complete burning of the air/fuel charge, so a certain amount of the unburned fuel is still expelled into the exhaust system, regardless of modifications to the engine.

HYDROCARBONS

Hydrocarbons (HC) are essentially fuel which was not burned during the combustion process or which has escaped into the atmosphere through fuel evaporation. The main sources of incomplete combustion are rich air/fuel mixtures, low engine temperatures and improper spark timing. The main sources of hydrocarbon emission through fuel evaporation on most cars used to be the vehicle's fuel tank and carburetor bowl.

To reduce combustion hydrocarbon emission, engine modifications were made to minimize dead space and surface area in the combustion chamber. In addition the air/fuel mixture was made more lean through the improved control which feedback carburetion and fuel injection offers and by the addition of external controls to aid in further combustion of the hydrocarbons outside the engine. Two such methods were the addition of an air injection system, to inject fresh air into the exhaust manifolds and the installation of a catalytic converter, a unit that is able to burn traces of hydrocarbons without affecting the internal combustion process or fuel economy. The vehicles covered in this manual may utilize either, both or none of these methods, depending on the year and model.

To control hydrocarbon emissions through fuel evaporation, modifications were made to the fuel tank to allow storage of the fuel vapors during periods of engine shut-down.

Modifications were also made to the air intake system so that at specific times during engine operation, these vapors may be purged and burned by blending them with the air/fuel mixture.

CARBON MONOXIDE

Carbon monoxide is formed when not enough oxygen is present during the combustion process to convert carbon (C) to carbon dioxide (CO_2). An increase in the carbon monoxide (CO) emission is normally accompanied by an increase in the hydrocarbon (HC) emission because of the lack of oxygen to completely burn all of the fuel mixture.

Carbon monoxide (CO) also increases the rate at which the photo chemical smog is formed by speeding up the conversion of nitric oxide (NO) to nitrogen dioxide (NO_2). To accomplish this, carbon monoxide (CO) combines with oxygen (O_2) and nitric oxide (NO) to produce carbon dioxide (CO_2) and nitrogen dioxide (NO_2). ($CO + O_2 + NO = CO_2 + NO_2$).

The dangers of carbon monoxide, which is an odorless and colorless toxic gas are many. When carbon monoxide is inhaled into the lungs and passed into the blood stream, oxygen is replaced by the carbon monoxide in the red blood cells, causing a reduction in the amount of oxygen being supplied to the many parts of the body. This lack of oxygen causes headaches, lack of coordination, reduced mental alertness and should the carbon monoxide concentration be high enough, death could result.

NITROGEN

Normally, nitrogen is an inert gas. When heated to approximately 2,500°F (1,371°C) through the combustion process, this gas becomes active and causes an increase in the nitric oxide (NOx) emission.

Oxides of nitrogen (NOx) are composed of approximately 97-98 percent nitric oxide (NO). Nitric oxide is a colorless gas but when it is passed into the atmosphere, it combines with oxygen and forms nitrogen dioxide (NO_2). The nitrogen dioxide then combines with chemically active hydrocarbons (HC) and when in the presence of sunlight, causes the formation of photo chemical smog.

OZONE

To further complicate matters, some of the nitrogen dioxide (NO_2) is broken apart by the sunlight to form nitric oxide and oxygen. (NO_2 + sunlight = NO + O). This single atom of oxygen then combines with diatomic (meaning 2 atoms) oxygen (O_2) to form ozone (O_3). Ozone is one of the smells associated with smog. It has a pungent and offensive odor, irritates the eyes and lung tissues, affects the growth of plant life and causes rapid deterioration of rubber products. Ozone can be formed by sunlight as well as electrical discharge into the air.

The most common discharge area on the automobile engine is the secondary ignition electrical system, especially when inferior quality spark plug cables are used. As the surge of high voltage is routed through the secondary cable, the circuit builds up an electrical field around the wire, acting upon the oxygen in the surrounding air to form the ozone. The faint glow along the cable with the engine running that may be visible on a dark night, is called the 'corona discharge'. It is the result of the electrical field passing from a high along the cable, to a low in the surrounding air, which forms the ozone gas. The combination of corona and ozone has been a major cause of cable deterioration. Recently, different and better quality insulating materials have lengthened the life of the electrical cables.

Although ozone at ground level can be harmful, ozone is beneficial to the earth's inhabitants. By having a concentrated ozone layer called the 'ozonosphere', between 10 and 20 miles (16-32km) up in the atmosphere, much of the ultra violet radiation from the sun's rays are absorbed and screened. If this ozone layer were not present, much of the earth's surface would be burned, dried and unfit for human life.

There is much discussion concerning the ozone layer and its density. A feeling exists that this protective layer of ozone is slowly diminishing and corrective action must be directed to this problem. Much experimentation is presently being conducted to determine if a problem exists and if so, the short and long term effects of the problem and how it can be remedied.

OXIDES OF SULFUR

Oxides of sulfur (SOx) were initially ignored in the exhaust system emissions, since the sulfur content of gasoline as a fuel is less than $1/10$ of 1 percent. Because of this small amount, it was felt that it contributed very little to the overall pollution problem. However, because of the difficulty in solving the sulfur emissions in industrial pollutions and the introduction of catalytic converter to the automobile exhaust systems, a change was mandated. The automobile exhaust system, when equipped with a catalytic converter, changes the sulfur dioxide (SO_2) into the sulfur trioxide (SO_3).

When this combines with water vapors (H_2O), a sulfuric acid mist (H_2SO_4) is formed and is a very difficult pollutant to handle since it is extremely corrosive. This sulfuric acid mist that is formed, is the same mist that rises from the vents of an automobile battery when an active chemical reaction takes place within the battery cells.

When a large concentration of vehicles equipped with catalytic converters are operating in an area, this acid mist will rise and be distributed over a large ground area causing land, plant, crop, paints and building damage.

PARTICULATE MATTER

A certain amount of particulate matter is present in the burning of any fuel, with carbon constituting the largest percentage of the particulates. In gasoline, the remaining particulates are the burned remains of the various other compounds used in its manufacture. When a gasoline engine is in good internal condition, the particulate emissions are low but as the engine wears internally, the particulate emissions increase. By visually inspecting the tail pipe emissions, a determination can be made as to where an engine defect may exist. An engine with light gray or blue smoke emitting from the tail pipe normally indicates an increase in the oil consumption through burning due to internal engine wear. Black smoke would indicate a defective fuel delivery system, causing the engine to operate in a rich mode. Regardless of the color of the smoke, the internal part of the engine or the fuel delivery system should be repaired to prevent excess particulate emissions.

Diesel and turbine engines emit a darkened plume of smoke from the exhaust system because of the type of fuel used. Emission control regulations are mandated for this type of emission and more stringent measures are being used to prevent excess emission of the particulate matter. Electronic components are being introduced to control the injection of the fuel at precisely the proper time of piston travel, to achieve the optimum in fuel ignition and fuel usage. Other particulate after-burning components are being tested to achieve a cleaner emission.

Good grades of engine lubricating oils should be used, which meet the manufacturers specification. Cut-rate oils can contribute to the particulate emission problem because of their low flash or ignition temperature point. Such oils burn prematurely during the combustion process causing emissions of particulate matter.

The cooling system is an important factor in the reduction of particulate matter. With the cooling system operating at a temperature specified by the manufacturer, the optimum of combustion will occur. The cooling system must be maintained in the same manner as the engine oiling system, as each system is required to perform properly in order for the engine to operate efficiently for a long time.

Other Automobile Emission Sources

Before emission controls were mandated on the internal combustion engines, other sources of engine pollutants were discovered, along with the exhaust emission. It was determined the engine combustion exhaust produced 60 percent of the total emission pollutants, fuel evaporation from the fuel tank and carburetor vents produced 20 percent, with the another 20 percent being produced through the crankcase as a by-product of the combustion process.

CRANKCASE EMISSIONS

Crankcase emissions are made up of water, acids, unburned fuel, oil fumes and particulates. The emissions are classified as hydrocarbons (HC) and are formed by the small amount of unburned, compressed air/fuel mixture entering the crankcase from the combustion area during the compression and power strokes, between the cylinder walls and piston rings. The head of the compression and combustion help to form the remaining crankcase emissions.

Since the first engines, crankcase emissions were allowed into the atmosphere through a road draft tube, mounted on the lower side of the engine block. Fresh air came in through an open oil filler cap or breather. The air passed through the crankcase mixing with blow-by gases. The motion of the vehicle and the air blowing past the open end of the road draft tube caused a low pressure area at the end of the tube.

Crankcase emissions were simply drawn out of the road draft tube into the air.

To control the crankcase emission, the road draft tube was deleted. A hose and/or tubing was routed from the crankcase to the intake manifold so the blow-by emission could be burned with the air/fuel mixture. However, it was found that intake manifold vacuum, used to draw the crankcase emissions into the manifold, would vary in strength at the wrong time and not allow the proper emission flow. A regulating type valve was needed to control the flow of air through the crankcase.

Testing, showed the removal of the blow-by gases from the crankcase as quickly as possible, was most important to the longevity of the engine. Should large accumulations of blow-by gases remain and condense, dilution of the engine oil would occur to form water, soots, resins, acids and lead salts, resulting in the formation of sludge and varnishes. This condensation of the blow-by gases occur more frequently on vehicles used in numerous starting and stopping conditions, excessive idling and when the engine is not allowed to attain normal operating temperature through short runs.

FUEL EVAPORATIVE EMISSIONS

Gasoline fuel is a major source of pollution, before and after it is burned in the automobile engine. From the time the fuel is refined, stored, pumped and transported, again stored until it is pumped into the fuel tank of the vehicle, the gasoline gives off unburned hydrocarbons (HC) into the atmosphere. Through redesigning of the storage areas and venting systems, the pollution factor was diminished, but not eliminated, from the refinery standpoint. However, the automobile still remained the primary source of vaporized, unburned hydrocarbon (HC) emissions.

Fuel pumped from an underground storage tank is cool but when exposed to a warmer ambient temperature, will expand. Before controls were mandated, an owner would fill the fuel tank with fuel from an underground storage tank and park the vehicle for some time in warm area, such as a parking lot. As the fuel would warm, it would expand and should no provisions or area be provided for the expansion, the fuel would spill out the filler neck and onto the ground, causing hydrocarbon (HC) pollution and creating a severe fire hazard. To correct this condition, the vehicle manufacturers added overflow plumbing and/or gasoline tanks with built in expansion areas or domes.

However, this did not control the fuel vapor emission from the fuel tank. It was determined that most of the fuel evaporation occurred when the vehicle was stationary and the engine not operating. Most vehicles carry 5-25 gallons (19-95 liters) of gasoline. Should a large concentration of vehicles be parked in one area, such as a large parking lot, excessive fuel vapor emissions would take place, increasing as the temperature increases.

To prevent the vapor emission from escaping into the atmosphere, the fuel system is designed to trap the fuel vapors while the vehicle is stationary, by sealing the fuel system from the atmosphere. A storage system is used to collect and hold the fuel vapors from the carburetor and the fuel tank when the engine is not operating. When the engine is started, the storage system is then purged of the fuel vapors, which are drawn into the engine and burned with the air/fuel mixture.

EMISSION CONTROLS

Due to varying state, federal, and provincial regulations, specific emission control equipment may vary by area of sale. The U.S. emission equipment is divided into two categories: California and Federal. In this section, the term 'California' applies only to cars originally built to be sold in California. Some California emissions equipment are not shared with equipment installed on cars built to be sold in the other states. Models built to be sold in Canada also have specific emissions equipment, although in many cases the Federal and Canadian equipment are the same.

Both carbureted and fuel injected cars require an assortment of systems and devices to control emissions. Newer cars rely more heavily on computer (ECM) management of many of the engine controls. This eliminates many of the vacuum hoses and linkages around the engine. Remember that not every component is found on every car.

EMISSION TESTING

In addition to mandating that vehicles must be equipped with emission controls, the law may also require that vehicles in certain areas be tested to ensure that they remain within specified limits for emissions.

This type of testing began long after emission controls were being installed, but it was discovered that some areas still had growing pollution problems. Part of the reason for this was that some vehicles had been poorly maintained, or had emission control devices altered or removed.

Early forms of testing generally involved running the vehicle at idle, or some other steady speed, and inserting the probe of the emissions analyzer into the tailpipe in order to obtain the readings. Exhaust gases such as hydrocarbons (HC) and carbon monoxide (CO) were typically measured, either as parts per million (PPM) or as a percentage of exhaust gas content. Certain information, such as the Vehicle Identification Number (VIN), vehicle type, vehicle or engine year, number of cylinders, technician number and inspection station number would have to be entered into the machine, in order to promote accurate and honest testing.

After the testing was completed, there was generally a printout of the results, including a Pass/Fail message. Even though this type of testing criteria goes back to the California Bureau of Automotive Repair (BAR) standard of 1979, (known as BAR 80), it is still used in some areas, with whatever variations are required by individual states or localities.

The newest testing program is referred to as IM240. The abbreviation stands for Inspection/Maintenance 240 Seconds.

Some states require this type of emissions testing. It was mandated to begin on January 1, 1995. There have been delays in some cases, and earlier program starting dates in some locations.

There are two types of IM240 tests, Basic and Enhanced. Factors such as population and pollution levels in a given area are used to determine which test will be utilized. Major metropolitan areas would be more apt to require the Enhanced test, while lightly populated rural areas may not use any type of IM240 testing at all.

The Basic test is similar to some current IM programs. The Enhanced test, which takes 240 seconds to perform, is designed to provide a more accurate picture of a vehicle's emissions during an actual operating cycle, not just at idle. This is done by testing the vehicle on a chassis dynamometer. Emissions are constantly monitored as the vehicle idles, accelerates, cruises at two different road speeds, and decelerates.

In areas using IM240, testing will be performed on 1968 and later model passenger cars and light trucks.

The following exhaust by-products are measured:
- Hydrocarbons (HC)
- Carbon Monoxide (CO)
- Carbon Dioxide (CO_2)
- Nitrogen Oxides (NOx)

The exhaust gas is more thoroughly checked for pollutants than it was with pre-IM240 testing methods. The measurements are made in grams per mile for these tests.

The following tests may be performed, depending on the model year of the vehicle:
- Evaporative Performance Test
- Evaporative System Integrity Test

The Evaporative Performance Test checks that the fuel vapors stored in the purge canister are being delivered to the engine for combustion at an acceptable rate.

The Evaporative System Integrity Test is a pressure test of all items in the fuel system, including the fuel cap, which control fuel vapors. Any loss of pressure greater than the standards permit will cause the vehicle to fail the test. Furthermore, if the pressure does not release when the fuel cap is removed, the vehicle will fail the test.

If you reside in an area where you will need to have the Enhanced Test performed on your vehicle, there are a few things you can check before you go to the test station which will expedite the testing procedure. All tires must be in good condition, with no cords or steel belts showing through the tread. The tire pressure should be at the correct level, or it will have to be adjusted before the test can be done. No space saver spare tires may be mounted on the vehicle.

Additionally, no vehicle with an exhaust leak will be permitted to test, and any vehicle which is in an overheated condition must be back at normal operating temperature before the test can be performed. Switch accessories **OFF**, when possible, before turning the vehicle over to the technician.

Should the vehicle require repair(s) to pass the test, keep in mind that basic items such as a clogged air filter or Positive Crankcase Ventilation (PCV) valve may cause an emission test failure. Therefore, it is good practice to perform preventive maintenance before taking the vehicle for the test. Preventive maintenance is discussed in Chapter Two of this book. In addition to servicing items that may need attention, be sure to perform a visual inspection for anything that might cause poor running or increased emissions, such as loose connections or vacuum hoses.

EMISSION LAMP RESETTING FOR DOMESTIC VEHICLES

AMERICAN MOTORS

Emission Maintenance Reminder

1980-81 Models

The models are equipped with an emission maintenance reminder light on the instrument panel which will be illuminated every 30,000 miles. If the reminder light is illuminated, it indicates the oxygen sensor must be inspected. If faulty, the oxygen sensor must be replaced. The reminder light is reset as follows:

1. Locate the switch between the upper and lower speedometer cable next to the firewall in the engine compartment.
2. Slide the rubber boot up and using a suitable tool, turn the reset screw clockwise 1/4 turn until the detent resets within the switch.

1982-84 Except Alliance and Encore

The emission maintenance light will illuminate after 1000 hours of engine operation to indicate required service for the oxygen sensor. After performing the required service, the emission maintenance E-cell timer must be replaced by removing the printed circuit board from its enclosure and inserting a replacement timer. The timer is located in the passenger compartment, within the wire harness leading to the ECM.

1987-88 Eagle Station Wagon

The vehicle is equipped with an emission light timer that will start flashing the oxygen (O_2) sensor service light at approximately 82,500 miles. At this time the oxygen (O_2) sensor and timer should be replaced. The timer is located under the dash panel to the right of the steering column. Remove the timer mounting screws and disconnect the wiring. Install the timer in its original location.

CHRYSLER CORPORATION

Emission Maintenance Reminder

1980 Passenger Cars

The vehicles are equipped with a mileage counter that activates an emission reminder light at intervals of 12,000/15,000/30,000 and/or 52,000 miles. There are 2 types of reset used, mechanical and electrical. If the vehicle is equipped with a mechanical reset, use the reset procedure as noted for the 1980-81 American Motor vehicles.

The electronic type uses a 9 volt battery which supplies power to the electronic counter to prevent memory loss when the vehicle battery is disconnected. To reset the electronic type, proceed as follows:

➡ **The vehicle battery must be connected during resetting procedure to prevent power loss to memory.**

Locate the green, red or tan plastic case behind the instrument panel in the lower left cluster area. Slide the case from the bracket and slide the cover open. Remove the 9 volt battery and insert a small rod into the hole switch to close the contacts. Replace the battery with a new 9 volt alkaline type. Close the case and slide the switch back into the bracket.

1981-95 Passenger Cars

As of 1981 Chrysler no longer used resets in passenger cars, however the reset is still being used in some trucks and vans.

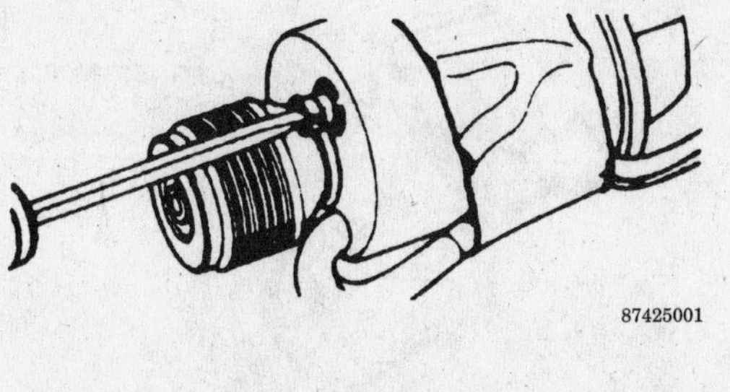

87425001

Fig. 1 Resetting the mechanical maintenance reminder light — American Motors and Chrysler Corp.

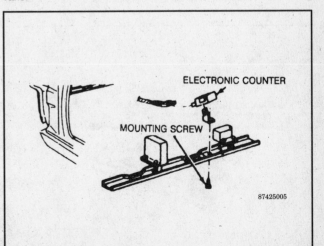

ELECTRONIC COUNTER

MOUNTING SCREW

87425005

Fig. 2 Resetting the electronic maintenance reminder light — Chrysler Corp.

1988-92 Eagle Premier and Monaco

The Premier is equipped with a Vehicle Maintenance Monitor (VMM), with a **SERVICE** light incorporated into this monitor. The **SERVICE** light will illuminate at 7500 miles (12,000 kms) intervals to indicate that regular service and maintenance procedures are due. After the required service has been performed, press the **RESET** button on the dash below the VMM display window until the sound of a beep is heard. When the beep is heard, the VMM will then clear the display (service light).

1980-82 Light Trucks and Vans

The EGR maintenance reminder system is a mileage counting system. An instrument cluster light will come on when the vehicle reaches its first 30,000 miles and then subsequently every 30,000 miles thereafter.

Locate the green, red or tan plastic case behind the instrument panel in the lower left cluster area. Slide the case from the bracket and slide the cover open. Remove the 9 volt battery and insert a small rod into the hole switch to close the contacts. Replace the battery with a new 9 volt alkaline type. Close the case and slide the switch back into the bracket.

1983-87 Light Trucks and Vans

The maintenance reminder system is a mileage counting system. An instrument panel light will come on between 12,000 and 30,000 miles on some models and 52,500, 82,500 and 105,000 miles on other models. The purpose of the system is a reminder that emission maintenance service must be performed as soon as possible. It is not intended to indicate a warning or a state of emergency exists which must be corrected to insure safe vehicle operation.

The system consists of 2 major elements, mileage counting contacts in the speedometer and an electronic digital module attached to the brake pedal support under the instrument panel.

After necessary pulses are stored, the output transistors activate and turn on the emission maintenance reminder light. The circuit immediately returns to zero mileage condition and starts to count and accumulate pulses until the necessary mileages are again stored and the reset process is repeated.

The light will remain lit until the module is reset by inserting a small thin rod into the hole in the module case closing a switch which turns off the light. The 9 volt battery must be removed before resetting the light switch and a new battery must be installed after resetting the maintenance light.

➡ **The vehicle battery must be connected during resetting procedure to prevent power loss to memory.**

The electronic module is housed in a beige, green, white or red colored plastic case. The case is usually mounted on a bracket on or near the steering column support, below the headlight switch on the back side of the instrument panel. It can be removed by sliding it from the bracket.

➡ **There is no test procedure for the system and any attempt to test it will result in damage to the system components.**

1988-89 Light Trucks and Vans

The system is designed to act as a reminder that scheduled vehicle emission maintenance service should be performed. It is not intended to indicate a warning that a state of emergency exists which must be corrected to insure safe vehicle operation. The components covered by the system include the EGR system, PCV valve, oxygen sensor, delay valves, vacuum controlled orifice, fuel tank vapor and bi-level purge valves.

The maintenance required system is based on a time measuring module which uses ignition **ON** time to calculate the maintenance intervals. When the predetermined time intervals have elapsed, the **MAINT REQD** light in the instrument panel will illuminated. The light will remain illuminated until the module is reset by insert a small blade or rod into the module to depress the reset switch which will then turn off the light. On the Dakota, the module is located on a bracket below the headlight switch, on the rear of the instrument panel. On 1988-89 FWD vans, is usually located in the instrument cluster behind the fuel gauge on the standard cluster or behind the tachometer on the optional cluster. On 1980-87 light trucks and 1988 Vans it is usually located on the brake pedal support. On

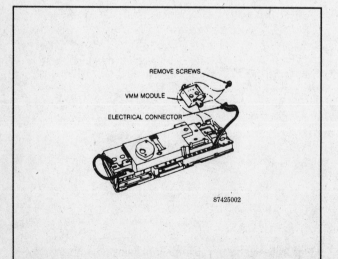

Fig. 3 Vehicle Maintenance Monitor (VMM) location — Premier

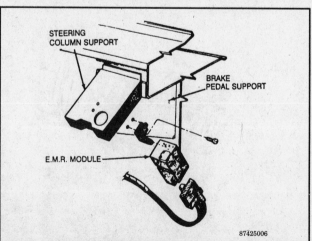

Fig. 4 Typical emission maintenance reminder module location is on brake pedal support — 1988 RWD vans shown

most other models the module is located behind the right side of the instrument panel, next to the glove box.

➡ **There is no test procedure for the system. Any attempt to test it will result in damage to the system components.**

1990-93 Light Trucks and Vans

The system is designed to act as a reminder that scheduled vehicle emission maintenance should be performed. It is not intended to indicate a warning that a state of emergency exists which must be corrected to insure safe vehicle operation. Some 1990 vehicles may use 1989 module design.

➡ **To reset the emission maintenance light, it is necessary to use the Chrysler Digital Read Out Box II Tester (DRB-II) tool C-4805 or equivalent.**

1. Connect the Chrysler DRB-II Tester C-4805 or equivalent to the vehicle as directed by the manufacturers instructions.

2. Turn the tester selector switch to the **EMR MEMORY CHECK**. The tester display should read **EMR MEMORY CHECK ARE YOU SURE?**. Press the **YES** key on the tester.

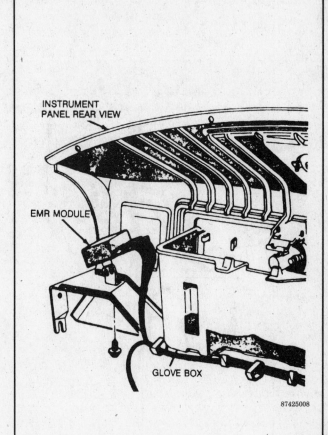

Fig. 6 Behind the glovebox is a typical emission maintenance module location — 1988 RWD truck shown

3. The tester should next display the following message; **IS INSTRUMENT PANEL MILEAGE BETWEEN 9953 AND 10051?**. If the odometer mileage on the vehicle is within the specified mileage, press the **YES** key on the tester.

4. The tester should now display, **EMR MEMORY CHECK TEST COMPLETE**. The EMR light is now reset. If the speedometer mileage is not within specifications, go on to Step 5.

5. Press the **NO** key on the tester. The tester will then display **DO YOU WANT TO CORRECT EMR MILEAGE?**. Press the **YES** key on the tester.

6. The tester should now display **ENTER MILEAGE SHOWN ON INSTRUMENT PANEL USE ENTER TO KEY TO END**.

7. Enter the mileage shown on the speedometer. Do not enter the tenths. Press the **ENTER** key on the tester. The tester will now ask for verification of the entry.

8. If the mileage entered was correct, the tester will display **EMR MEMORY CHECK TEST COMPLETE**. The vehicle must now be driven approximately 8-10 miles for the mileage reset to take place.

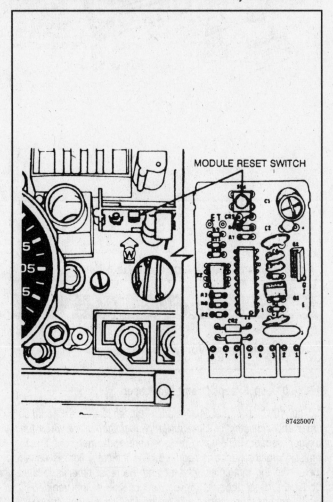

Fig. 5 Emission maintenance module location — 1988 FWD vans shown

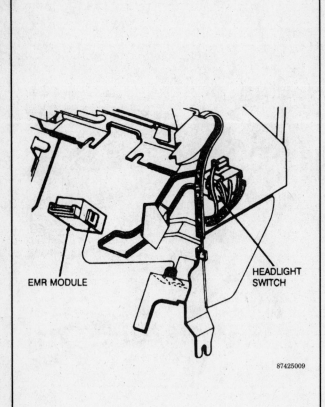

Fig. 7 Emission maintenance module location — 1988 Dakota

1994-95 Light Trucks and Vans

As of 1994 Chrysler no longer used resets in Light Trucks and Vans.

Check Engine Light

The **CHECK ENGINE** light will light upon a fault. The fault code will be stored in the ECU. Once the source of the problem has been rectified the light should extinguish itself and the Logic Module will cancel the fault code in the ECU after 20-40 ignition key cycles.

Fig. 8 Chrysler DRB-II — digital readout box

CHRYSLER JEEP DIVISION

Emission Maintenance Reminder

1988-90 Jeep Except Grand Wagoneer

Until 1993 on some Jeep models the emission maintenance timer and indicator light are used to alert the owner when the oxygen sensor, PCV valve replacement and other scheduled emission maintenance is required. The indicator light is usually located in the instrument cluster and the reset timer is located under the dash panel at the passenger side of the vehicle.

The reset timer is operated by the ignition system. It activates (flashes) the indicator light when the vehicle mileage reaches the scheduled maintenance interval of 82,500 miles. The life cycle coincides with the emission maintenance interval of 82,500 miles. The timer cannot be reset and must be replaced or disconnected after reaching the mileage interval.

➡**The oxygen sensor and timer are independent. If the timer should fail prematurely, the oxygen sensor must be replaced along with the timer; this is important in preserving the correct sensor replacement interval and ensuring proper engine performance.**

REMOVAL AND INSTALLATION

1988-90 Cherokee, Comanche and Wagoneer

The emission maintenance timer used on some model until 1993 is mounted on the dash panel to the right of the steering column.

1. Disconnect the negative battery cable.
2. On models with cruise control, remove the cruise control module attaching screws and remove the module.
3. Remove the screws attaching the maintenance emission timer to the dash bracket and remove the timer from the bracket.
4. Disconnect the timer electrical wires and remove the timer from the vehicle.
5. Installation is the reverse order of the removal procedure.

1989-90 Wrangler

1. Disconnect the negative battery cable.
2. Disconnect the timer electrical wire harness. Remove the screws attaching the maintenance emission timer to the dash bracket and remove the timer from the bracket.
3. Installation is the reverse order of the removal procedure.

1991-93 Vehicles

Vehicles equipped with the Emission Maintenance Reminder (EMR) or Service Reminder Indicator (SRI), the Maintenance Required (MAIN REQ) light will illuminate when the vehicle mileage reaches the scheduled maintenance interval of 82,500 miles. The life cycle coincides with the emission maintenance interval of 82,500 miles. At this time, the oxygen sensor should be replaced and the EGR and PCV systems checked. After all maintenance is performed, the indicator light must be reset for the next interval. Reset the light as follows.

➡**To reset the emission maintenance light, it is necessary to use the Chrysler Digital Read Out Box II Tester (DRB-II) tool C-4805 or equivalent.**

1. Connect the DRB II, or an equivalent scan tool, to the diagnostic connector. Turn the ignition switch **ON**.
2. Enter the SELECT SYSTEMS menu of the scan tool. Select the appropriate engine and accessories.
3. Select FUEL AND IGNITION. Select ADJUSTMENTS.
4. Select RESET EMR light. Turn the ignition switch **OFF** and disconnect the scan tool.

1994-95 Vehicles

As of 1994, resets are no longer used in Jeep vehicles.

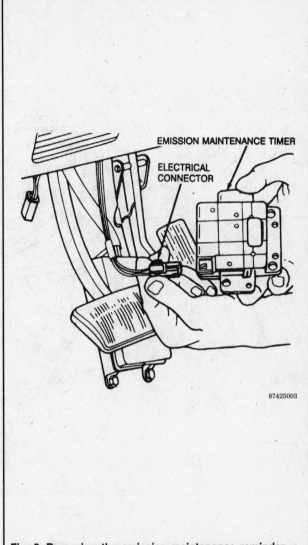

EMISSION MAINTENANCE TIMER
ELECTRICAL CONNECTOR

87425003

Fig. 9 Removing the emission maintenance reminder timer — Cherokee, Comanche and Wagoneer

Check Engine Light

The **CHECK ENGINE** light will light upon a fault. The fault code will be stored in the ECU. Once the source of the problem has been rectified the light should extinguish itself.

FORD MOTOR COMPANY

Service Interval Reminder Light

1985-93 Passenger Cars

➡**The 1980-1984 passenger cars did not use an emission maintenance reminder light. Beginning in 1985, a SERVICE interval reminder light was used on some vehicles.**

Approximately every 5000 or 7500 miles, (depending on engine application) the word **SERVICE** will appear on the electronic display for the first 1.5 miles to remind the driver that it

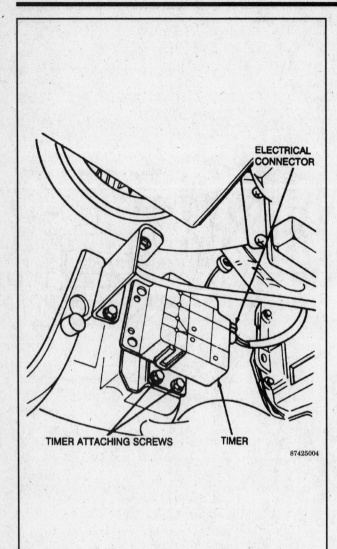

ELECTRICAL CONNECTOR

TIMER ATTACHING SCREWS   **TIMER**

87425004

Fig. 10 Removing the emission maintenance reminder timer — Wrangler

is time for the regular vehicle service interval maintenance (i.e. oil change).

To reset the service interval reminder light for another interval on all models except the Continental, Sable/Taurus, Probe and Mark VIII, use this procedure. With the engine running, press the **TRIP** and **TRIP RESET** buttons at the same time. Hold the buttons down until 3 beeps are heard to verify that the service reminder has been reset.

On the Continental, with the engine running, press the **SYSTEM CHECK** and **TRIP RESET** buttons. Hold the buttons down until the **SERVICE** light disappears from the display and 3 audible beeps are heard to verify that the service reminder has been reset.

On the Sable/Taurus, with the engine running, press the **ODO SEL** and **TRIP RESET** buttons. Hold the buttons down until the **SERVICE** light disappears from the display and 3 audible beeps are heard to verify that the service reminder has been reset.

On the 1989-93 Probe, with the engine running, press and hold the **SERVICE RESET** button located on the speed alarm keyboard. Hold the button until the **SERVICE** light disappears

from the display and 3 audible beeps are heard to verify that the service reminder has been reset.

➡ On 1989-93 Probes not equipped with the speed alarm keyboard, locate the ³⁄₁₆ in. hole in the overhead console. Use a small rod or other tool to depress the reset button located behind the hole.

On the Mark VIII, press the **OIL CHANGE RESET** button and hold it down for 5 seconds. The **CHANGE OIL SOON** or **OIL CHANGE REQUIRED** message will disappear after the 5 second interval.

1994-95 Passenger Cars

The Service Interval Reminder light is used only in the Continental. All other models no longer use it.

During the SYSTEM CHECK sequence, the SERVICE symbol comes on and displays the miles (kilometers) to go before the next normal service is due. After service is complete, reset the service interval reminder as follows:
1. Press the SYSTEM CHECK button.
2. Press the RESET button.
3. Press the SYSTEM CHECK and the RESET button at the same time. The display now shows 7,200 miles (11, 580 km) and the mileage counts down from here.

The 1994-95 Mark VIII continues to use the **CHANGE OIL SOON** or **OIL CHANGE REQUIRED** light. When oil life left is between five percent and zero percent, the **CHANGE OIL SOON** will be displayed on the message center. When oil life reach zero percent, the **OIL CHANGE REQUIRED** message will be displayed.

The message center indicator will indicate the percent of oil life left during System Check. This percentage is based on the drivers driving history and the time since the last oil change. In order to ensure oil life left indications, the driver should only perform the OIL CHANGE RESET procedure after every oil change. Reset the system by pressing the **OIL CHANGE RESET** switch and hold for 5 seconds. After a successful reset the Message Center will display oil life indicators. The **CHANGE OIL SOON** or **OIL CHANGE REQUIRED** message will disappear after the 5 second interval.

Vehicle Maintenance Monitor

1989-93 Thunderbird and Cougar

The Vehicle Maintenance Monitor (VMM) warns the driver of low oil, low radiator coolant, low fuel and low washer fluid conditions and indicates when to change engine oil. The system consists of an electronic module with a display, a coolant level sensor, a washer fluid level sensor, a combination oil level and temperature sensor, a fuel sender, a tachometer and a rheostat.

The module lights all segments of the display for 1 second, blanks them for 1 second and then goes to normal operation whenever the ignition key switches to the **RUN** position. The oil change display turns off after 15 minutes if the engine is not running. This alerts the user that the VMM module is not getting a tachometer signal.

The module is located in the top center of the instrument panel directly above the radio, retained by 2 spring clips, 1 at each side. A reset switch access hole is located on the left front of the module. The module is not removed to be reset.

The low fuel, low radiator coolant and low washer fluid indications are the result of input from various sensors. Correcting the fluid level will cause the light to go out. The oil change indicator is different. The green bar under the **OK** on the oil change display is lit for 0-89 percent of the oil change cycle. The word **SOON** under the word **CHANGE** is lit for 90-99 percent of the cycle. The word **NOW** is lit for 100-115 percent of the oil change cycle and flashes every 18 minutes for 17 seconds after 115 percent of the oil change cycle.

The oil change display will turn OFF after 15 minutes if the VMM receives no tachometer signal. This is a diagnostic precaution that could be caused by an intermittent connection or by the engine not being on.

The VMM monitors oil temperature and engine tachometer signals to measure quality of oil and indicate when engine oil should be changed.

The VMM has a self-diagnosis test built into the module that can be performed with the module in the vehicle and the engine running. This test determines whether the module is getting and processing the signals necessary to function correctly. The self-test mode will test the module's response to engine rpm, oil temperature, fluid levels and engine and Electronic Instrument Cluster (EIC) wiring harness strap inputs.

Enter the test by starting the vehicle and within 16 seconds from engine start, press the reset switch and hold continuously for 4 seconds. The entire display will flash when the reset switch is pressed. If the reset switch is released within 4 seconds, the display will stop flashing and normal operation will continue. Do not run the engine faster than 6100 rpm. If only the oil change display flashes then the tach input signal to the module is missing. The self diagnostics test cannot be entered until this signal is provided. Each reset switch press and release advances the module to the next test. Turn the ignition switch to **OFF** to terminate the self diagnostics test.

As soon as diagnostics is entered, the module is in the Tach Input Test mode and the display lights up segments **OK, CHANGE, NOW, SOON** and **GREEN BAR** is sequence, proportional to the number of tach pulses measured (engine rpm). The faster the engine rpm, the faster the sequence lights.

When the Reset switch is pressed and released, the display advances to to the Oil Temperature Test. The **OIL** nomenclature is lit and the oil temperature will be indicated in the following manner:

If the oil temperature is cold, display will be: Green Bar, Oil

If the oil temperature is cool, display will be: Green Bar, Soon, Oil

If the oil temperature is normal, display will be: Green Bar, Soon, Now, Oil

If the oil temperature is warm, display will be: Green Bar, Soon, Now, Low Radiator, Oil

If the oil temperature is hot, display will be: Green Bar, Soon, Now, Low Radiator, Radiator, Oil

The VMM oil change indicator must be reset every time the vehicle's oil is changed. The oil change indicator must be reset even if the vehicle's oil is changed before the VMM has indicated an oil change is necessary. The reset procedure is necessary to keep the information in the oil change indicator updated whenever the oil is changed. If the reset procedure is not done, the VMM will indicate an oil change prematurely.

After the oil is changed, manually reset the VMM oil change indicator by using the following procedure:

1. Turn the ignition switch to **RUN**.

2. Within 15 seconds of turning the ignition to **RUN**, reset the VMM by inserting a straightened paper clip or similar tool through the reset hole in the face of the VMM. Press firmly.

3. Note that it is not possible to feel the reset switch operating because it has no perceptible movement when it is pushed.

4. The oil change message window will begin to flash when the switch has been activated.

➡**If the reset procedure is not done within 15 seconds, the procedure must be redone starting from Step 1 above. If NOW is flashing, do not wait for it to stop before pushing the reset switch to initiate the oil change reset.**

5. Continue to depress the reset switch until the oil change display stops flashing, which will take about 4 seconds.

➡**If the reset switch is released before the oil change display stops flashing, the reset procedure must be redone starting from Step 1 above.**

1994-95 Thunderbird and Cougar

As of 1994 the Vehicle Maintenance Monitor (VMM) is no longer used.

1985-93 Light and Medium Duty Trucks

All 1985-93 Federal light and medium duty trucks are equipped with an emission maintenance reminder light. Prior to 1985, none were used.

The Emission Maintenance Warning (EMW) module operates a light that is located on the instrument panel. For 1985-87 models, the light will display the word **EMISSIONS**. For 1988-93 model year vehicles, the light will display the words **CHECK ENGINE**. When the light is lit, it is indicating that the 60,000 mile emission maintenance should be performed. After the maintenance is performed, the EMW module must be reset to zero time.

The system actually measures accumulated vehicle ignition key on-time and is designed to continuously close an electrical circuit to the amber lens after 2000 hours of vehicle operation. Assuming an average vehicle speed of 30 mph, the 2000 hours equates to approximately 60,000 miles of vehicle operation. Actual vehicle mileage intervals will vary considerably as individual driving habits vary.

Every time the ignition switch is turned **ON**, the warning light will glow for approximately 2-5 seconds as a bulb check and to verify the system is operating properly. When approximately 60,000 miles has been reached, the warning light will be illuminated continuously to indicate that service is required. After the required maintenance is performed, the Emission Maintenance Warning (EMW) sensor must be reset for another 60,000 mile interval. The sensor locations are as follows:

1. Aerostar — The EMW is located under the dash panel on a bracket below the EEC computer.

2. Bronco — The EMW is located under the dash panel on a bracket below the EEC computer.

3. Bronco II and Ranger — The EMW is located above the right front corner of the glove box.

4. Light and Medium Duty Trucks — The EMW is located under the dash panel, adjacent to the EEC power relay.

The emission maintenance reminder warning light timer may be reset either before or after the time-out period has been exceeded. The procedure is the same for either condition. The procedures to reset the emission maintenance reminder warning light are as follows:

5. Turn the ignition switch to the **OFF** position.

6. Lightly push a small rod (shank end of a No. 2 or $7/32$ inch drill bit) through the 0.200 in. diameter hole, with the covering sticker labeled **RESET** and lightly push down on the button and hold.

7. Still pressing the small rod down into the reset hole, turn the ignition switch to the **RUN** position. The **EMW** light will then light and should remain illuminated for as long as the small rod is pressed down in the reset hole. Continue to hold the small rod down for approximately 5 seconds.

8. Remove the small rod. The **EMW** light should go out within approximately 5-10 seconds, indicating a reset has occurred. (If the light does not go out, begin at Step 1 again). Turn the ignition switch to the **OFF** position and go to the next Step.

9. Turn the ignition switch to the **RUN** position. The **EMW** light will light for approximately 2-5 seconds and will then go out. This verifies that a proper reset of the module has been accomplished. If the light should remain on, then the proper reset has not occurred and the reset procedure should be repeated. Turn the ignition switch to the **OFF** position when the reset has been completed.

➡**Some models use a non-resettable control unit. When reset is required, replace it with a resettable type.**

1994-95 Light and Medium Duty Trucks

No reset procedure is required. The TCIL and other warning lights turn **OFF** automatically when the fault is corrected.

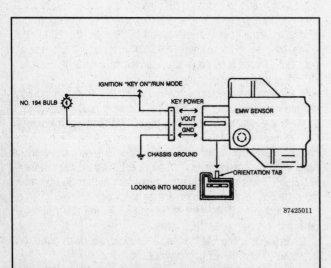

Fig. 11 EMW module emission maintenance light system schematic — Ford Motor Company

Check Engine Light

Resetting Light after clearing codes — EEC-IV

Vehicles not using and EMW module have the **CHECK ENGINE** light controlled by the EEC-IV processor.

1. Once the source of the trouble codes has been repaired or replaced, the codes must be cleared to prevent the **CHECK ENGINE** light from lighting again.

2. While reading the codes with an analog VOM, disconnect the jumper wire between the Self-Test Input (STI) and the Signal Return Pin of the Self-Test connector.

3. If the codes were read using a STAR tester releasing the center button to the **UP** position will clear the codes.

Resetting Light after clearing codes — EEC-V

The Malfunction Indicator Lamp (MIL) is a light in the dash that reads CHECK ENGINE. The MIL is intended to alert the driver of certain malfunctions in the EEC-V system. The light will stay ON for at least 10 seconds then stay ON as long as the fault causing it is present. The light will reset if there are no faults after 3 consecutive drive cycles. If the MIL flashes quickly, the MIL circuit should be checked for proper operation or the engine for severe misfire.

Resetting Light after clearing codes — EEC (NON-NAAO) Management System

The CHECK ENGINE light (MIL) is used to inform the driver of possible engine malfunctions and emission system failure. The light is controlled by the PCM. The PCM monitors engine, ignition and emission related components and signals the driver, through the CHECK ENGINE light, when the engine is running improperly or emissions are unsatisfactory. If the CHECK ENGINE light illuminates during vehicle operation, the cause of the fault or malfunction must be determined and corrected. After the problem area is repaired, the CHECK ENGINE light can be turned OFF by disconnecting the negative battery cable for at least 10 seconds.

GENERAL MOTORS

Emission Maintenance Reminder

Most 1980 GM vehicles used an emission maintenance warning system in the form of a plastic flag that would appear in the speedometer face, normally over the odometer, thus indicating the need for servicing the oxygen sensor and emission system. The flag would appear at 30,000 miles on all models except the Cadillac, which would appear at 15,000 miles. The flag is reset by using the following procedure:

All 1980 except Cadillac

1. Disconnect the negative battery cable. Remove the instrument panel trim plate.

2. Remove the instrument cluster lens.

3. Using a suitable tool, apply a small downward pressure on the plastic notches in the flag stem until the flag resets in its original position.

4. The should be an alignment mark that will appear in the left center of the odometer window when the flag is properly reset.

5. Installation of the removed components, is the reverse of the removal procedure.

1980 Cadillac

1. Disconnect the negative battery cable. Remove the lower steering column cover.

2. The sensor reset cable is located to the left of the speedometer cluster. Pull on the sensor reset cable lightly with approximately 2 lbs. of force.

3. After the sensor flag is reset, reinstall the lower steering column cover. Reinstall the negative battery cable.

Oxygen Sensor Maintenance Light

1984-86 Sprint

The Sprint models are equipped with an oxygen sensor light that will illuminate and flash every 30,000 miles. The light indicates that the emission system and components should be checked for proper operation and the oxygen sensor should be replaced. After the sensor has been replaced and the emission system checked, reset the maintenance light as follows:

1. To reset the emission reminder light, the cancellation switch must be used. The switch is mounted on the right side of the pull down fuse panel which is located on the left side of the steering column, on the lower dash panel.

2. Press the cancel switch to the **OFF** position and start the engine to be sure the light has been reset.

Service Interval Reminder Light

1986-90 Pontiac 6000 and 1989-90 Bonneville

The **SERVICE REMINDER** section of the Driver Information Center (DIC) display shows how many miles remain until service is needed. When the **RESET** button is pressed twice, the

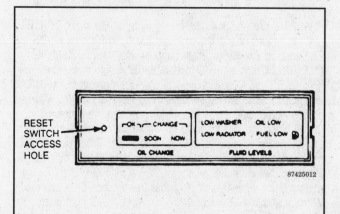

RESET SWITCH ACCESS HOLE

87425012

Fig. 12 Resetting the emission reminder flag — General Motors Corporation

type of service and the number of miles remaining until that service is needed, will be displayed. Each time the **RESET** button is pressed, another type of service and the miles remaining for it will be displayed.

With the ignition switch in the **RUN**, **BULB TEST** or **START** positions, voltage is applied from the ECM fuse through the pink/black wire to the Electronic Control Module (ECM). As the vehicle is driven, the speed sensor sends electrical pulses to the ECM. The ECM sends a signal to the speed signal input of the DIC module. The DIC module converts the pulses into miles. The module subtracts the miles traveled from the distance remaining for each item of the service reminder.

When the miles remaining for a service approaches zero, that service will be displayed on the DIC display. All 4 types of service can be shown at the same time.

Service Reminder Reset

To reset the service light, it will be necessary to subtract the mileage from the service interval light that is illuminated. The miles remaining for a certain type of service can be decreased by holding the **RESET** button, the miles remaining will be decreased in steps of 500 miles, every 5 seconds. In the first step, the miles will decrease to a multiple of 500. For example, 2880 miles will decrease to 2500 miles. If the **RESET** button is held in and the miles remaining reach zero, the DIS display will show the service interval for the service selected. The service intervals are as follows:

1. Change Oil — 7500 miles.
2. Oil Filter Change — 7500 miles.
3. Next Filter Change — 15,000 miles.
4. Rotate Tires — 7500 miles.
5. Next Tire Rotation — 15,000 miles.
6. Tune Up — 30,000 miles.

If the **RESET** button is still held down, the miles will decrease in steps of 500 miles from the service interval. When the **RESET** button is released, the mile display shown will be the new distance until the service should be performed.

When a service distance reaches zero, the service reminder item will be displayed. If the service interval is reset within 10 miles, the display will go out immediately. If more than 10 miles passes before the service interval is reset, the item will remain displayed for another 10 miles after being reset before going out.

➡ **On some models, it may be necessary to depress the SYSTEM RECALL button in order to display the service interval light on the driver information center, in order to be able to decrease the mileage from it so as to reset the interval light.**

1991-93 Pontiac Bonneville

The Driver Information Center lights up for a few seconds when the ignition is turned to **ON**. To see the entire DIC, press and release the DIC button to the right of the display. The system is divided into 4 main systems: Function Monitor, Lamp Check, Security and Service Reminder. These systems monitor the following:

1. FUNCTION MONITOR:
   a. Checks windshield washer fluid. Message comes ON when fluid is less than 40 percent full.

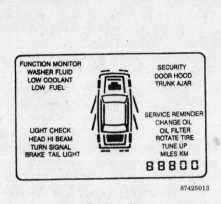

Fig. 13 Driver Information Center (DIC) display — General Motors Corporation

b. Checks engine coolant level. Message comes ON when coolant level has fallen to about half full.

c. Checks fuel level. Message comes ON when approximately 2½ gallons of fuel remain.

2. LAMP CHECK:

a. Checks headlights, turn signal, brake lights and taillights.

b. Message comes ON if a problem exists at 1 of the lights. The problem area is indicated on the vehicle outline shown on the DIC. Note that if a burned out bulb is replaced, the warning light will stay on until the bulb is energized or turned on.

3. SECURITY:

a. Checks if doors are fully closed. The problem area is indicated on the vehicle outline shown on the DIC.

b. Checks if hood or trunk isn't fully closed.

4. SERVICE REMINDER:

a. Lets vehicle operator know when to have the following service work done: Change engine oil, change oil filter, rotate tires and have engine tune-up.

b. The figures at the bottom of the DIC show the number of miles remaining before the work should be done.

To use the service reminder, the vehicle owner must first decide which service item to check. For example, if the owner wants to know when to next rotate the tires, push and hold the DIC button until the **SERVICE REMINDER** light comes ON. Then push and release the DIC button until **ROTATE TIRES** appears. The number at the bottom then shows how many miles there are to go before the tires should be rotated.

To reset the service reminder, push the DIC until the service item desired appears and do not release the button. In 5-10 seconds the display will start to count down, 500 miles at a time. When the display reads the distance the vehicle owner wishes to set, release the button. Note that sometimes a service reminder display will stay ON even though it has been reset, but the reminder should go OFF after the vehicle has been driven about 10 miles.

1994-95 Pontiac Bonneville and Buick LeSabre

As of 1994 the Service Reminder is no longer used in these vehicles.

1989-91 Eldorado and Seville

1. Press the **ENG DATA** button until the oil life index is displayed on the Driver's Information Center.

2. Press **ENG DATA** and **RANGE** buttons at the same time until the oil life index resets to 100 and hold for 5 seconds.

1992-93 ELDORADO AND SEVILLE

1. Press the **INFORMATION** button until the oil life index is displayed.

2. Press **STORE/RECALL** until the oil life index resets to 100 and hold for 5 seconds.

1991-93 Deville, Fleetwood and Sixty Special

1. Press **RANGE** and **FUEL USED** buttons at the same time to display oil life index.

2. Press **RANGE** and **RESET** buttons at the same time until the **CHANGE OIL SOON** light flashes and hold for 5 seconds. The oil life index will not remain displayed.

1993-95 Fleetwood (Rear Wheel Drive)

After changing engine oil, reset the engine oil life indicator whether the 'CHANGE OIL' warning/indicator lamp came on or not.

Reset the engine oil life monitor as follows:

1. Turn ignition switch to 'ON' position, but don't start engine.

2. Depress accelerator pedal to wide open throttle (WOT) position and release it three times within five seconds.

3. If 'CHANGE OIL' warning/indicator lamp blinks twice, then goes out, system has been reset.

If 'CHANGE OIL' warning/indicator lamp does not reset, turn ignition switch to 'OFF' and repeat procedure.

1989-93 Allante

1. Press the **RANGE** button until the oil life index is displayed.

2. Press **AVE SPEED** and **RANGE** buttons at the same time until the oil life index resets to 100 and hold for 5 seconds.

1994-95 DeVille, DeVille Concours, Eldorado and Seville

Vehicles are equipped with an engine oil life index (EOLI) feature as part of the Driver Information Center display (DIC). Engine oil life is displayed through engine data as the 'OIL LIFE INDEX' and as a 'CHANGE ENGINE OIL' message. The 'OIL LIFE INDEX' is displayed following a number between 0 and 100. This is the percentage of oil life REMAINING based on driving conditions, engine oil temperature, and mileage driven since the last time the oil life indicator was reset. When the oil life index reaches 10% or less a 'CHANGE OIL SOON' message will appear as a reminder to schedule an oil change. When the oil life index reaches 0, the 'CHANGE ENGINE OIL' message will appear indicating that the oil should be changed within the next 200 miles (320 km). After the oil has been changed, display the 'OIL LIFE INDEX' message by pressing the 'INFORMATION' button several times. Press and hold the 'RESET' button until the display shows '100'. This will reset the oil life index. The 'CHANGE ENGINE OIL' message will remain off until the next oil change is needed. The percentage of oil life remaining may be checked at any time by pressing the 'INFORMATION' button several times until the 'OIL LIFE INDEX' appears.

1994 Chevrolet Caprice

After changing engine oil, reset the engine oil life indicator whether the 'CHANGE OIL' warning/indicator lamp came on or not.

Reset the engine oil life monitor as follows:

1. Remove the instrument panel fuse box cover.
2. Turn the ignition switch to the **ON** position but do not start the engine.
3. Press and hold the OIL RESET button for 5 seconds. The CHANGE OIL light should go out. The system has been reset.

If 'CHANGE OIL' warning/indicator lamp does not reset, turn ignition switch to 'OFF' and repeat procedure.

1995 Chevrolet Caprice, Impala SS

After changing engine oil, reset the engine oil life indicator whether the 'CHANGE OIL' warning/indicator lamp came on or not.

Reset the engine oil life monitor as follows:

1. Turn ignition switch to 'ON' position, but don't start engine.
2. Depress accelerator pedal to wide open throttle (WOT) position and release it three times within five seconds.
3. If 'CHANGE OIL' warning/indicator lamp blinks twice, then goes out, system has been reset.

If 'CHANGE OIL' warning/indicator lamp does not reset, turn ignition switch to 'OFF' and repeat procedure.

1990-91 Corvette

The **CHANGE OIL** monitor light is on the left side of the instrument cluster.

When changing oil, reset the engine oil life monitor whether the **CHANGE OIL** light came on or not. Reset the monitor as follows:

1. Turn the key to the **ON** position but do not start the engine.
2. Press the **ENG MET** button on the trip monitor and release. Press the button again within 5 seconds.
3. Within 5 seconds of pressing the button the second time, press and hold the **RANGE** button on the trip monitor. The **CHANGE OIL** light will flash.
4. Hold the **RANGE** button until the **CHANGE OIL** light stops flashing and extinguishes. The monitor is reset at this point. Repeat this procedure if the light does not go out.

1992-95 Corvette

1. Turn the key to the **ON** position but do not start the engine.
2. Press the **ENG MET** button on the trip monitor and release. Press the button again within 5 seconds.
3. Within 5 seconds of pressing the button the second time, press and hold the **GAUGES** button on the trip monitor. The **CHANGE OIL** light will flash.
4. Hold the **GAUGES** button until the **CHANGE OIL** light stops flashing and extinguishes. The monitor is reset at this point. Repeat this procedure if the light does not go out.

1991-93 Buick Park Avenue

An optional system illuminates **CHANGE OIL SOON** when the system determines the oil life has degraded to the point where the engine oil must be changed. This light is lit for 3 seconds as a bulb check before the engine is started. If an oil change is required, it will stay ON for 60 seconds each time the engine is started.

After changing the engine oil, the system should be reset. The reset button is inside a hole under the passenger's side of the instrument panel, near the door. With the ignition in the **RUN** position, but the engine not started, use a pencil to push the reset button, holding it in for at least 5 seconds but not more than 60 seconds. After 5 seconds, the **CHANGE OIL SOON** light will flash 4 times. This indicates that the Oil Life Monitor System has acknowledged the reset.

1994-95 Buick Park Avenue

After the engine oil has been changed, the Engine Oil Monitor must be reset. The reset button is located in the glove box. Reset as follows:

With the ignition key in the RUN position, push the reset button, hold it in for at least 5 seconds but not more than 60 seconds. The CHANGE OIL SOON light will flash 4 times and then go off. This indicates that the Oil Life Monitor System has been reset.

1995 Buick Roadmaster

After changing engine oil, reset the engine oil life indicator whether the 'CHANGE OIL' warning/indicator lamp came on or not.

Reset the engine oil life monitor as follows:

1. Turn ignition switch to 'ON' position, but don't start engine.
2. Depress accelerator pedal to wide open throttle (WOT) position and release it three times within five seconds.
3. If 'CHANGE OIL' warning/indicator lamp blinks twice, then goes out, system has been reset.

If 'CHANGE OIL' warning/indicator lamp does not reset, turn ignition switch to 'OFF' and repeat procedure.

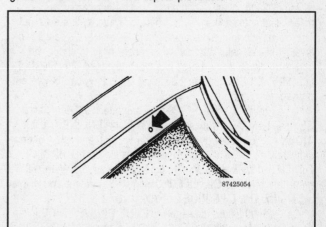

87425054

Fig. 14 The reset button is inside this hole, which is under the passenger side of the instrument panel, near the door — 1991-93 Park Avenue

1994-95 Buick Riviera

After the engine oil has been changed, display the oil life index on the Drivers Information Center (DIC), then hold the **RESET** button for 5 seconds. When a DIC message of **RESET** is displayed and the oil life index equals 100 percent, the reset is complete.

1989-93 Oldsmobile

Vehicles equipped with an **ENGINE OIL LIFE INDEX** display as a part of the **DRIVER INFORMATION SYSTEM (DIS)**, have a display that will show when to change the engine oil.

The oil change interval is determined by the driver information system and will usually fall at or between the 2 recommended alternative intervals of 3000 miles and 7500 miles, but it could be shorter than 3000 miles under some severe driving conditions. The driver information system will also signal the need for an oil change at 7500 miles or one year passed since the last oil change. If the driver information system does not indicate the need for an oil change after 7500 miles or one year or if the **ENGINE OIL LIFE INDEX** display fails to appear, the oil should be changed and the driver information system serviced.

When the **ENGINE OIL LIFE INDEX** reaches 10 percent or less, the **CHANGE OIL** light display will function as a reserve trip odometer (indicating the distance to an oil change). Until the **ENGINE OIL LIFE INDEX** reset is performed, the driver information system will display the distance to the oil change and sound a beep when the ignition switch is turned to the **ACCESSORY** or **RUN** position the first time each day.

When the distance to the next oil change reaches 0, the driver information system will display the **CHANGE OIL NOW** light. Until an **ENGINE OIL LIFE INDEX** reset is performed, the driver information system will display the **CHANGE OIL NOW** light and sound a beep when the ignition switch is turned to the **ACCESSORY** or **RUN** position at the beginning of each day.

The driver information system will not detect dusty conditions or engine malfunctions which may affect the engine oil. If driving in severe conditions exists, be sure to change the engine oil every 3000 miles or 3 months which ever comes first, unless instructed otherwise by the driver information system. The driver information center does not measure the engine oil level. It still remains the owner's responsibility to check the engine oil level. After the oil has been changed, the **ENGINE OIL LIFE INDEX** light must be reset. Resetting can be accomplished as follows:

1. All models, except 1989-92 Toronado, 1992-93 Ninety Eight and 1991-93 Cutlass Supreme — the **ENGINE OIL LIFE INDEX** can be reset by pressing the **RESET** and **OIL** buttons simultaneously for at least 5 seconds while on the **ENGINE OIL LIFE INDEX** display. The driver information system will reset the **ENGINE OIL LIFE INDEX** to 100 percent and display a **ENGINE OIL LIFE INDEX** of 100 percent.

2. 1989-90 Toronado — the **ENGINE OIL LIFE INDEX** can be reset by pressing the **ENGINE DATA** and **GAUGES** buttons on the instrument panel console simultaneously for at least 5 seconds (as if as to enter the diagnostic mode) during this time the **CHANGE OIL** message will remain off until the next oil change is needed. Be sure to hold the **ENGINE DATA** and **GAUGES** buttons simultaneously until the **ENGINE OIL LIFE INDEX 100** message appears.

3. 1991-92 Toronado — Press the **ENG DATA** button to select the oil life display. Then hold the **RESET/ENTER** button for at least 5 seconds. The oil life will be reset to 100 percent.

4. 1992-93 Ninety Eight — Press the **OIL** button to display the oil message and then press the **RESET** button for at least 5 seconds. The oil life monitor will be reset to 100 percent.

5. 1991-93 Cutlass Supreme — Press the **OIL** button to display the oil message and then press the **OIL** and **RESET** buttons at the same time for at least 5 seconds. The oil life monitor will be reset to 100 percent.

➡ The Engine Oil Life Index is stored on a non-volatile memory chip and will not require resetting by disconnecting the battery cables and/or fuse.

1994-95 Oldsmobile

1994-95 vehicles that are equipped with a Drivers Information Center and have an Oil life index, will require the Oil Life indicator to be reset after each oil change.

Press the **SEL** to select **OIL**. Press **SEL** if necessary to display the oil life. The display will show a reading of the estimated oil life left. Example: **OIL LIFE 85%** . When the remaining oil life is 9% or less, the display will show **CHANGE OIL SOON**. Then the vehicle is started tone will sound an the **CHANGE OIL SOON** message will display each time the vehicle is started.

When the oil life is zero, la tone will sound and the display will show, **CHANGE OIL NOW**. Then when the vehicle is started a tone will sound and the **CHANGE OIL NOW** message will display each time the vehicle is started. Reset the Oil Life Display as follows:

1. Acknowledge all diagnostic messages in the Drivers Information Center by pressing **RESET**.

2. Press the **SEL** button on the left to select **OIL** . Press **SEL** button on the right if necessary to display oil life.

3. Press and hold the **RESET** button for about 5 seconds. Once the oil life index has been reset, a **RESET** message will be displayed and then oil life will change to 100% .

Be careful not reset the oil life accidentally at any time other than when the oil has just been changed. It can not be reset accurately until the next oil change.

1994-95 Oldsmobile Aurora

After the engine oil has been changed, display the oil life index on the Drivers Information Center (DIC), then hold the **RESET** button for 5 seconds. When a DIC message of **RESET** is displayed and the oil life index equals 100 percent, the reset is complete.

Transmission Fluid Change Reset

1994-95 DeVille, Concours, Eldorado and Seville

All Cadillacs with 4.6L Northstar engines and 4T80-E transaxles are equipped with a transaxle fluid change indicator. A 'CHANGE TRANS FLUID' message will display on the Information Center when the Powertrain Control Module monitors actual operating conditions and displays a change trans fluid message based on calculations based on those conditions or 100,000 miles (160,000 km.) Change fluid by removing lower pan and side cover drain plug.

Change both the transmission fluid and the filter every 15,000 miles (25,000 km) if the vehicle is mainly driven under one or more of these conditions:

• In heavy city traffic where outside temperature regularly reached 90°F (32°C) or higher.
  • On highly or mountain terrain.
  • Frequent trailer pulling.
  • Used for delivery service.
  • If the vehicle is not used under any of these conditions, change both the fluid and filter (or service the screen) every 100,000 miles (160,000 km). Reset the light as follows:

When the 'CHANGE TRANS FLUID' message appears, change the fluid in both the pan and side cover. Reset the indicator as follows:

Turn the key 'ON' with the engine stopped. Press and hold the 'OFF' and 'REAR DEFOG' buttons on the climate control simultaneously until the 'TRANS FLUID RESET' message appears in the Information Center (between 5 and 20 seconds) The system is now reset.

Check Engine Light

The **CHECK ENGINE** light will light to indicate a fault in the engine control system. Once the fault code has been retrieved from the ECM memory and the problem rectified, the fault code should be cleared from the memory. This can be done by removing power to the ECM by disconnecting the ECM harness from the positive battery pigtail or by removing the ECM fuse. Either way the ignition switch must be in the **OFF**

position and the power removed for a minimum of 10 seconds. Once power has been restored the vehicle should be driven at part throttle with medium acceleration to allow the ECM to readjust itself. A change in performance may be noted initially, but the performance should return to normal as the ECM relearns its operating parameters.

SATURN

Service Engine Soon Light

The **SERVICE ENGINE SOON** light will light to indicate a fault in the engine control system. Removing power from the Powertrain Control Module (PCM) will clear codes from the General Information portion of the PCM memory. Flags and codes stored in the malfunction history however, will remain in the PCM memory even if power is disconnected. The data in malfunction history can only be read or cleared using a Saturn scan tool.

To clear the code and reset the **SERVICE ENGINE SOON** light, follow the steps below:

1. Turn the ignition switch **ON** and jumper terminals A and B of the ALDL together 3 times in 5 seconds. The **SERVICE ENGINE SOON** light should stop flashing and any Codes should be cleared.

2. If all faults have been repaired, cycling the ignition switch 50 times will automatically clear General Information of fault Codes.

EMISSION LAMP RESETTING FOR IMPORT VEHICLES

ACURA

Scheduled Service Due

1988-90 Legend Sedan

The 1988-90 Legend Sedan is equipped with a **SCHEDULED SERVICE DUE** warning light. The maintenance light will illuminate every 7500 miles to indicate that an oil and filter change is needed. However, if a shorter oil change interval is desired, there are 7 different intervals to choose, from 7500 to 1500 miles. To choose a new interval, push the **SERVICE RESET** button and the **ARROW** button for approximately 3 seconds, then push the **ARROW** button until the interval desired appears. Then push the **SET** button. After completing the necessary maintenance service, the maintenance light must be reset.

In order to reset the maintenance light, the **SERVICE RESET** button must be depressed. With the ignition switch in the **ON** position, hold the reset button in for at least 3 seconds. To verify that the reset is complete, turn the ignition switch **OFF** and **ON**, the light should not come on.

1987-90 Legend Coupe

The 1987-90 Legend Coupe is equipped with a **SCHEDULED SERVICE DUE** warning light. The maintenance light will illuminate every 7500 miles to indicate that scheduled maintenance is needed. To reset the light after performing the maintenance, hold the button in for a period of 5 seconds.

The 1987-90 Legend Coupe is also equipped with a **OIL/FILTER CHANGE DUE** warning light. The warning light will illuminate every 7500 miles. However, if a shorter oil change interval is desired, there are 7 different intervals to choose, from 7500 to 1500 miles. To choose a new interval, push the **SERVICE RESET** button and the **ARROW** button for approximately 3 seconds, then push the **ARROW** button until the interval desired appears. Then push the **SET** button. After completing the necessary maintenance service, the maintenance light must be reset.

To verify that the reset is complete, turn the ignition switch **OFF** and **ON**, the light should not come on.

Maintenance Required Indicator

1991-95 Legend Sedan, Coupe and Vigor

The Maintenance Reminder indicator reminds you when it is time for scheduled maintenance. When it is near 7,500 miles (12,000 km) since the last maintenance, the indicator will turn yellow. If you exceed 7,500 miles (12,000 km), the indicator will turn red. The indicator can be reset by inserting the ignition key or other similar object into the slot below the indicator. This will extinguish the indicator for the next 7500 miles.

1994-95 Integra

The maintenance required indicator reminds you that it is time for scheduled maintenance. For the first 6,000 miles (9,600 km) after the maintenance Required Indicator is reset, it will come on for 2 seconds when you turn the ignition **ON** (II).

Between 6,000 miles (9,600 km) and 7,500 miles (12,000 km) this indicator will light for two seconds when you first turn the ignition **ON** (II), and then flash for ten seconds. If you exceed 7,500 miles (12,000 km) without having the scheduled maintenance performed, this indicator will remain on as a constant reminder.

Reset the indicator by pressing the reset button. This button is located on the bottom of the dashboard to the right of the steering column.

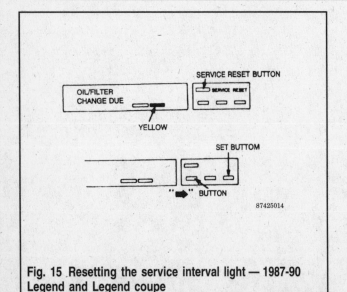

Fig. 15 Resetting the service interval light — 1987-90 Legend and Legend coupe

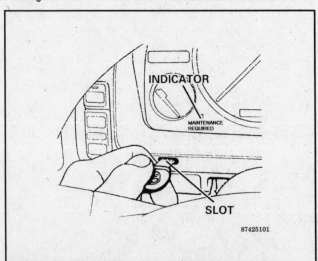

Fig. 16 Resetting the Maintenance Required Indicator — 1991-95 Legend Sedan, Coupe and Vigor

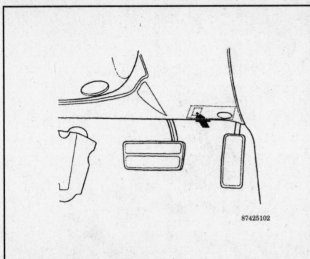

Fig. 17 Resetting the Maintenance Required Indicator — 1991-95 Acura Integra

Check Engine Light

The **CHECK ENGINE** light will illuminate when a trouble code develops. The light will be extinguished when the ignition switch is turned **OFF** and as long as the trouble code does not develop again the light will remain OFF when the ignition switch is turned **ON**. This does not hold true for the LED on the ECU. The LED will continue to illuminate until the trouble code is cleared from the ECU.

To clear the codes on the 1988-90 Integra remove the HAZARD fuse at the positive battery terminal for a minimum of 10 seconds. On the 1991-95 Integra remove the BACK UP fuse from the underhood relay box for a minimum of 10 seconds. On the 1988-90 Legend remove the ALTERNATOR SENSE fuse from the underhood relay box for a minimum of 10 seconds. On the 1991-95 Legend sedan, Legend Coupe and Vigor remove the No. 15 (7.5A) fuse from the underdash relay box for a minimum of 10 seconds. On the 1991-94 NSX remove the CLOCK fuse from the main relay box for a minimum of 10 seconds.

Once power has been restored, the vehicle should be driven at part throttle with medium acceleration to allow the ECU to go through a relearning procedure and adjust itself. A change in performance may be noted initially, but the performance should return to normal as the ECU relearns its operating parameters.

ALFA ROMEO

Oxygen Sensor Maintenance Reminder Light

A maintenance reminder light used on all of the Alfa Romeo models. The light will illuminate every 30,000 miles on the Graduate, Quadrifoglio and the Spider equipped with the 2.0L engine. The light will illuminate every 60,000 miles on the GTV-6 models equipped with the 2.5L engine. The reminder light is used as a preventive maintenance indicator in regards to the emission system and the oxygen sensor used on that vehicle. After the light has come on, the oxygen sensor replaced and the emission maintenance has been done, reset the light as follows:

Graduate, Quadrifoglio and Spider With 2.0L Engine

1. Locate the mileage counter that is located on the left side of the engine compartment.
2. To remove the plastic cover on the mileage counter, drill through the shank of the cover retaining screws and remove the cover.
3. Rotate the reset button and depress it to reset the reminder light. Reinstall the cover by using new retaining screws.

Gtv-6 With 2.5L Engine

1. On the GTV-6 models equipped with the 2.5L engine, it will be necessary to remove the ECU cover panel and the lower right side parcel shelf.
2. Locate the mileage counter usually located under the right side of the dash. Depress the white reset button to reset the reminder light. Turn the ignition switch to the **ON** position to be sure the light has been reset.

164 Series

The wear of the front brake pads and the level and temperature of the engine coolant are continuously monitored by an electronic control unit that in case of malfunction alerts the driver by turning on the appropriate warning light on the instrument panel.

Severe wear of the front brake pads causes opening of the contacts of the brake pad sensors. This breaks the continuity through pins **9B** and **10B** of the control unit. Replacement of the brake pads and their sensors will turn the warning light off.

The engine coolant level sensor contacts open when the engine coolant level drops below the minimum mark. This breaks the continuity of pin **4B** of the control unit to ground. Once the level has been restored the light will go out.

Check Engine Light

The **CHECK ENGINE** light will light upon a fault. The fault code will be stored in the ECU. Once the source of the problem has been rectified the light should extinguish itself.

AUDI

EGR Warning Light

Some models use an EGR maintenance light that will come on every 15,000 miles of operation. This indicates the need to inspect the EGR system and make any repairs as necessary. After the EGR system has been inspected and is found in proper working condition, push the EGR reset button located on the mileage counter that is attached to the speedometer cable, located in the engine cowl area.

Oxygen Sensor Maintenance Light

Most models are equipped with an oxygen sensor light that will illuminate every 30,000 miles (60,000 miles on some 1989-93 100/200). The light indicates that the emission system and components should be checked for proper operation and the oxygen sensor should be replaced. Once the sensor has been replaced and the emission system checked, reset the maintenance light as follows:

1980-83 4000, 5000 and 5000S

The oxygen sensor light is reset by pushing a white reset button on the in-line mileage counter. The in-line mileage counter on the 4000 models is attached to the speedometer cable, located in the engine cowl area.

The in-line mileage counter on the 5000 models, is mounted under the dash panel, to the left of the steering column, near the pedal assembly. It is recommended to remove the driver's side lower dash cover to reveal the in-line mileage counter. It may be possible to reach the reset button without removing the lower dash cover by using an appropriate bent rod. Whichever procedure is used, the white reset button must be depressed to reset the maintenance reminder light.

1984-88 4000, 5000 and 5000S

1. To reset the counter, disconnect the negative battery cable and remove the upper and lower instrument cluster cover screws.

2. Pull the cluster cover towards the steering wheel and lift the upper instrument cluster cover of the cluster. On some models, it may be necessary to remove the instrument cluster to gain access to the switch. If so, remove the cluster as follows:

a. Disconnect the speedometer cable at the transmission and the instrument panel cluster.

➡**Use care when removing the speedometer from the instrument panel. The panel cluster and parts are very fragile.**

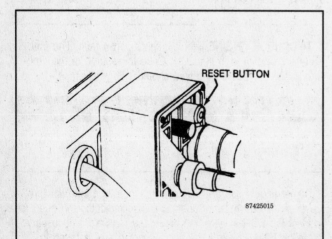

Fig. 18 In-line mileage counter and reset mechanism — Audi

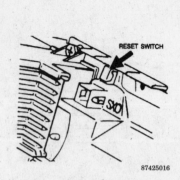

Fig. 19 Location of the reset button incorporated into the instrument panel — Audi

b. Disconnect electrical connectors from the cluster and remove the cluster. It may be to the technician's advantage to remove the steering wheel, allowing more room to work on the cluster.

3. At the top left center of the cluster, there should be the initials **OXS** imprinted on the cluster panel.

4. Locate the plastic breakaway box near the **OXS** initials and using a suitable tool, pull the box away from the cluster panel.

5. Insert a suitable tool into the **OXS** opening and push the cancel switch over to the opposite side in order to reset the reminder light.

1984-88 5000 Turbo and 1989-93 100/200 Turbo Models

The in-line mileage counter is used and is located under the rear seat. After checking the emission system and replacing the oxygen sensor, reset the reminder light as follows:

1. Push the rear seat cushion toward the rear of the vehicle, then lift the front of the seat cushion to release the cushion retainers.

2. Place the seat cushions out of the way. The counter is usually located on the left side of the vehicle.

3. Depress the button marked **OXS** and turn the ignition switch to the **ON** position.

4. Turn the ignition switch to the **OFF** position and then **ON** and **OFF** again to be sure the reminder light is reset and does not illuminate any longer.

1988-90 Except V8 Quattro

1. With the LED tester still connected and the codes retrieved, turn the ignition switch **OFF**.

2. Install a spare fuse into the top of the fuel pump relay.

3. Turn the ignition switch **ON**. The LED tester must light.

4. Remove the fuse after approximately 4 seconds. The LED tester must go **OFF** and then begin flashing fault Code 0000.

5. Install the fuse again for approximately 10 seconds and then remove. The LED tester should light and stay on. The memory is erased at this point.

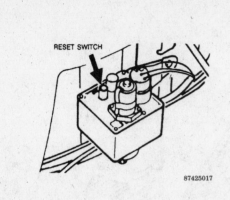

Fig. 20 Location of the mileage counter and reset mechanism located under the rear seat — Audi

1991-93 80, 90, 100 and 200 1990-93 V8 Quattro

1. Once the codes have been retrieved from the memory and the LED tester is still connected, check that Code 0000 has been displayed.

2. Join the test leads that are connected to terminals **1** and **2** of the diagnosis test point. Keep connected for approximately 4 seconds and then disconnect.

3. The codes have been erased when no additional codes are flashed on the LED tester.

Check Engine Light

When a temporary fault occurs, the **CHECK ENGINE** light illuminates until the ignition is switched **OFF**. When the ignition switch is switched **ON** again the light will be extinguished provided that the fault does not occur again or the defect was repaired and the vehicle is driven a minimum of 5 minutes. If a permanent fault occurs the fault will be stored in the ECU and will remain until it is cleared manually.

BMW

EGR Maintenance Reminder Light

1978 733i

Models equipped with an EGR sensor light, will illuminate every 25,000 miles. The light indicates its time to service the EGR system. When the light comes on, clean and inspect the system, including replacing gaskets under the thermal reactor.

To reset the light, remove lower trim panel from the center of the instrument panel and press the reset button marked 'EGR'.

Oxygen Sensor Maintenance Light

Most models are equipped with an oxygen sensor light that will illuminate every 30,000 miles (25,000 miles on the 528i models). The light indicates the emission system and components should be checked for proper operation and the oxygen sensor should be replaced. After the oxygen sensor has been replaced and the emission system checked, reset the maintenance light as follows:

1980-83 Models

The BMW 528E and 633 CSi models do not use a reset switch. On these models, it is necessary to remove the instrument panel and remove the bulb used to illuminate the oxygen sensor light.

1. Locate the in-line mileage counter which is usually placed above the left frame rail, near the transmission.

2. Locate the white reset button on the in-line mileage counter and depress the button to reset the maintenance reminder light.

➡**Due to the location of the in-line mileage counter, it is exposed road dirt and moisture. Therefore, when pushing the reset button, be sure to get it to click or the reminder light will remain illuminated. If the switch will not cancel out the reminder light, it must be replaced.**

1983-1995 Models

Most of the models were not equipped with an oxygen sensor reset. When the oxygen sensor light is illuminated at the designated mileage, it will be necessary to to remove the instrument panel and remove the bulb used to illuminate the oxygen sensor light. However there are some models (starting in late 1985) that are equipped with a reset button attached to the light control assembly that is usually located near the pedal assembly. If the vehicle is equipped with a reset button, after the oxygen sensor has been serviced, push the button to reset the maintenance reminder light.

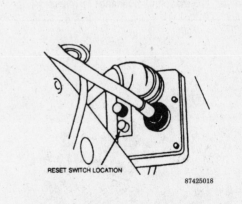

Fig. 21 In-line mileage counter and reset mechanism — 1980-83 BMW models

Service Interval Reminder Lights

The on-board computer is used to evaluate mileage, average engine speed, engine and coolant temperatures, as well as other computer input factors that determine maintenance intervals. There are 5 green, 1 yellow and 1 red **LED** used to remind the driver of oil changes and other maintenance services.

The green LEDs will be illuminated when the ignition is in the **ON** position and the engine is not running. There will not be as many green LEDs illuminated when maintenance time gets closer. A yellow LED that is illuminated when the engine is running, will indicate maintenance is now due. The red LED will be illuminated when the service interval has been exceeded by approximately 1000 miles.

There is a service interval reset tool manufactured by the Assenmacher Tool Company tool 62-1-100. The tool is used to reset BMW 6 cylinder models from 1983 and the 4 cylinder models from 1984. With the aid of an additional adapter, the tool can also be used on the 1988-93 models. There is also a means to reset the interval lights without the use of the special reset tool. Both reset procedures are as follows:

RESET

With Reset Tool

1. Locate the diagnostic connector near the thermostat housing.
2. Plug the special reset tool into the diagnostic connector and place the ignition switch in the **ON** position.
3. Depress the reset button on the tool until all 5 green **LEDs** are illuminated, showing that the reset has occurred.

Without Reset Tool

➡This is not a factory authorized procedure; if the wrong diagnostic connector terminal is used, it may result in internal control unit (computer) damage.

4. Turn off all the electrical accessories. Locate the diagnostic connector near the thermostat housing.
5. Turn the ignition switch to the **ON** position and using a volt/ohmmeter (10 megohm impedance is recommended) check

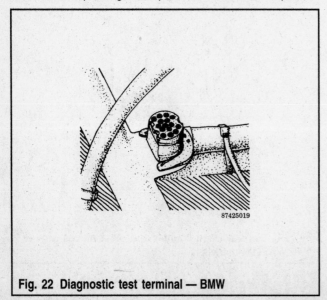

Fig. 22 Diagnostic test terminal — BMW

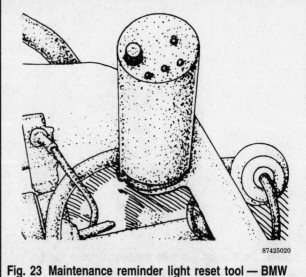

87425020

Fig. 23 Maintenance reminder light reset tool — BMW

to see if there is 5 volts present at the No. 7 (blue/white wire) terminal of the diagnostic connector.

6. Using a non-self powered test light, connect the negative lead to a good ground and the positive lead to the No. 7 (blue/white wire) terminal of the diagnostic connector.
7. Turn the ignition switch to the **ON** position. Ground the terminal through the volt/ohmmeter for 12 seconds. All 5 green **LEDs** should be illuminated, showing that the reset has occurred.

➡There is also a means to make a self made version of the reset tool. The version is made by soldering a small momentary contact switch to 2 ten foot lengths of 20 gauge standard wire. Install the switch into a small canister (such as a film canister). Solder 2 small probe connectors to the opposite ends of the wire. To use the tool, plug it into the proper diagnostic connector terminal (No. 7 blue/white wire) and use it just as the real reset tool is used. It must be noted that this is not a factory authorized procedure and if the wrong diagnostic connector terminal is used, it may result in internal control unit (computer) damage.

Check Engine Light

1988-95 Models

Except 750iL and 850i

The fault codes are cleared after the problem has been rectified and the engine has been started 5-10 times.

750iL and 850i

Codes can be cleared using the BMW tester cancel code command, if the BMW tester is available. The best way to cancel codes without the tester is to reactivate code sequence with the ignition switch **ON**. While flashing Code x000 is being displayed, close the full load switch for 10 seconds. Disconnecting the DME control wiring harness will also clear the codes. Do not disconnect the battery in attempt to clear the codes as this may not completely clear the codes and all the chassis functions with a memory feature will be cleared necessitating reprogramming.

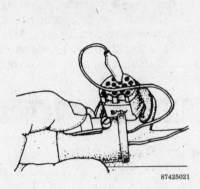

Fig. 24 Equivalent version of the maintenance reminder light reset tool — BMW

CHRYSLER IMPORT

EGR And Oxygen Sensor Light

The Mitsubishi car line imported under the Chrysler name-plate, does not use a maintenance warning light but some of the light trucks and van/wagons do use a maintenance warning light. The warning light will illuminate at approximately 50,000 miles for the EGR system and 80,000 miles for the oxygen sensor system. The light is used as a reminder to inspect the EGR emission systems. It is also used as a reminder to check and replace the oxygen sensor. After completing the necessary emission service, the maintenance light can be reset as follows:

1. On some models, the reset switch is located on the back of the instrument cluster near the speedometer junction. After the switch is located, slide the switch knob to the other side to reset the maintenance warning light.

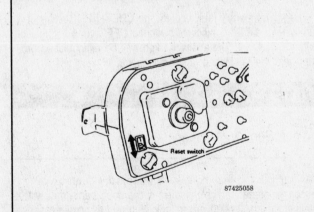

Fig. 25 EGR maintenance reset switch — 1986-88 Vista shown

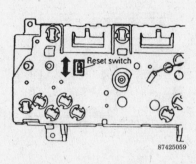

Fig. 26 EGR maintenance reset switch — 1989 Vista shown

Fig. 27 Using the reset switch on the front of the combination meter to reset the EGR warning system — Ram 50 shown

2. On the other models, the reset switch is located on the lower right hand corner of the instrument cluster, behind the instrument cluster face panel. After the switch is located, slide the switch knob to the other side to reset the maintenance warning light.

Remove the warning indicator bulb from the instrument cluster after the vehicle has reached the following mileage points. Colt Wagon and Colt Vista at 150,000 miles and 120,000 miles for Ram 50, Raider Van and Wagon.

Check Engine Light

The CHECK ENGINE light will indicate a fault with the engine management system. If the the problem is repaired or if the problem ceases to occur the light will extinguish but the fault will remain in the ECM memory.

To clear the memorized codes from the ECM remove power to the ECM for approximately 15 seconds with the ignition switch **OFF**. This can be accomplished by either disconnecting

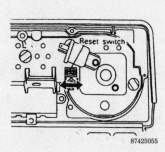

Fig. 28 Use the reset switch at the rear of the combination meter to switch off the warning light — 1988 Raider shown

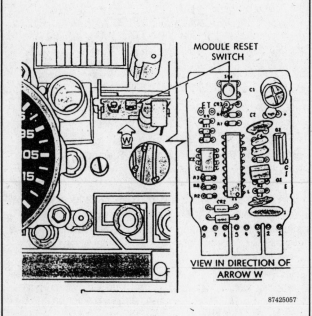

Fig. 29 Maintenance required reset switch — 1988 Caravan shown

the negative battery cable or by removing the ECM fuse, if equipped. If the battery cable is removed, the memories for any accessories that require constant power, such as a clock or radio station memory, will need to be reset. After resetting the ECM, drive the vehicle at medium speeds and accelerations to allow the ECM to memorize the necessary operating parameters for proper operation.

DAIHATSU

Oxygen Sensor Maintenance Light

An oxygen sensor maintenance light is used on the Daihatsu Rocky. A switch is geared to the odometer, tripping at 80,000 miles, turning on a red **O2S** light in the lower left corner of the instrument cluster. The factory recommends oxygen sensor replacement at 80,000 miles. At this time the maintenance reminder light bulb is to be permanently removed. Use the following procedure:

1. Disconnect the battery negative cable and remove the steering wheel assembly.
2. Remove the lower instrument panel trim panel by removing the 6 screws.
3. Remove the upper instrument panel trim panel by removing the 4 screws.
4. Remove the instrument panel cluster trim panel by removing the 4 screws.
5. Remove the oxygen sensor indicator bulb and discard it.

To assemble:

➡**When installing the screws, do not overtighten screws to prevent cracking plastic parts.**

6. Install the instrument panel cluster trim panel.
7. Install the upper then lower instrument panel trim panel. Then install the steering wheel assembly. Reconnect battery negative cable.

Check Engine Light

When a temporary fault occurs, the **CHECK ENGINE** light illuminates until the ignition is switched **OFF**. When the ignition switch is switched **ON** again the light will be extinguished provided that the fault does not occur again.

FIAT

Oxygen Sensor Maintenance Light

All fuel injected Fiat models are equipped with an oxygen sensor maintenance light, located in the dash panel that will illuminate every 30,000 miles, indicating that the oxygen sensor must be replaced. After the sensor has been replaced and the emission system checked, reset the maintenance light as follows:

1. The reset switch is located in the following positions:

a. On the Brava, the switch is located behind the left side of the dash panel.

b. On the Strada, the switch is located under the center of the dash panel in between the glove box and the radio.

c. On the Spider 2000, the switch is located under the left side of the dash panel, above the accelerator pedal between the radio and glove box.

d. On the X19 (Bertone), the switch is located behind the right side of the center console.

2. In order to reset the reminder switch, the switch retainer wire must be cut and the retainer screw removed.

3. Insert a suitable tool through the housing and press the contact switch so as to reset the reminder light.

4. After the switch has been pressed, check that the light has gone out. Install retainer screw and wire.

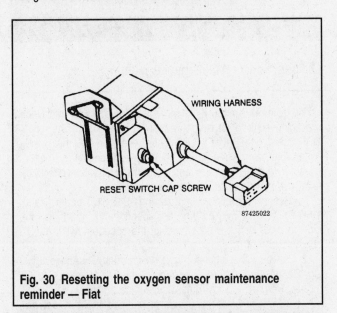

Fig. 30 Resetting the oxygen sensor maintenance reminder — Fiat

GEO

Malfunction Indicator Lamp

1989-93 Prizm and Storm

The Prizm is equipped with a malfunction indicator lamp. The malfunction indicator lamp illuminates as **CHECK ENGINE**. To reset the light after a malfunction is repaired, it is necessary to disconnect the ECM power. To do this, remove the ECM fuse, or disconnect the ECM power connector, located under the dash for a period of at least 30 seconds.

1989-93 Tracker

Federal/49 State vehicles are equipped with an emission reminder light system that will illuminate every 50,000 miles for the PCV and EGR systems, 80,000 miles for the oxygen sensor and 100,000 miles for the charcoal canister service. The light indicates the emission system and components should be checked for proper operation and the oxygen sensor should be replaced.

1. To reset the emission reminder light, a 3 wire cancellation switch must be used. The switch is located on the main wire harness behind the instrument cluster or behind the access panel below the steering column.

2. To reset, after locating the switch, push the cancel switch knob left or right to the opposite position until the **CHECK ENGINE** light goes out with the engine running in order to reset the emission light. Start the engine to be sure the light is out and has been reset.

1994-95 Prizm, Metro and Tracker

All models are equipped with a malfunction indicator lamp. The malfunction indicator lamp illuminates as **CHECK ENGINE**. If the malfunction goes away or is repaired, the light will go out but a corresponding Diagnostic Trouble Code (DTC) will remain in the ECM memory.

HONDA

Service Interval Flags

1982-85 Vehicles

Some 1982-85 Honda models use oil change service interval flags that will appear below the odometer every 7500 miles. To reset the flags, insert the ignition key into each slot below the indicator flags, at the lower right corner of the instrument panel, until the reminder flags turn from red back to green.

Maintenance Required Indicator

1991-95 Vehicles

Vehicles equipped with a Maintenance Reminder indicator will indicate it is time for scheduled maintenance. When it is near 7,500 miles (12,000 km) since the last maintenance, the indicator will turn yellow. If you exceed 7,500 miles (12,000 km), the indicator will turn red. The indicator can be reset by inserting the ignition key or other similar object into the slot below the indicator. This will extinguish the indicator for the next 7500 miles.

Oxygen Sensor Life Indicator light

The Passport DX model is equipped with and Oxygen Sensor Life Indicator light. The oxygen sensor must be replaced after 90,000 miles of vehicle operation. When the odometer reading reaches 90,000 miles, the oxygen sensor life indicator light (O2) will illuminate to remind the driver to change the oxygen sensor.

After replacing the oxygen sensor, the oxygen sensor life indicator light must be reset to remind the driver to replace the oxygen sensor after the next 90,000 miles. The reset screw is located in the back of the instrument cluster. Perform the reset procedure as follows:

1. Remove the Instrument panel cluster assembly.

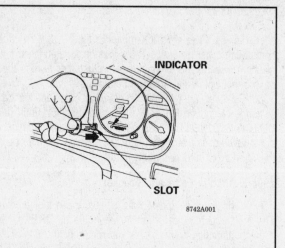

Fig. 31 Resetting the Maintenance Required Indicator — 1994-95 Honda Accord shown

2. Remove the masking tape from hole B.
3. Remove the screw from hole A and install it to hole B.
4. Apply new masking tape to hole A.

➡**The above procedure assumes that the oxygen sensor is being replaced for the first time (after 90,000 miles). For subsequent reset procedure (at next 90,000 miles), hole positions will be the opposite of the above procedure.**

Check Engine Light

The CHECK ENGINE light will indicate a problem with the engine management system. If the the problem is repaired or if the problem ceases to occur the light will extinguish with the next ignition switch cycle. Although the dash cluster CHECK ENGINE light will extinguish, the LED on the ECU will continue to flash. To reset the ECU pull the fuse that supplies power to the ECU for 10 seconds with the ignition **OFF**. The 1988-89 Accord and the 1988-93 Prelude use the CLOCK fuse to reset

the ECU. The 1990-93 Accord use the BACK UP fuse in the underhood relay box to reset the ECU and the 1988-93 Civic, CRX and delSol use the HAZARD fuse.

HYUNDAI

Check Engine Light

The CHECK ENGINE light will indicate a fault with the engine management system. If the the problem is repaired or if the problem ceases to occur the light will extinguish but the fault will remain in the ECU memory. To reset the ECU disconnect the negative battery cable for a minimum of 15 seconds and reconnect. Road test the vehicle at medium speeds and accelerations to allow the ECU to memorize the operating parameters required for proper operation.

ISUZU

Oxygen Sensor Maintenance Light

The 1988-95 Amigo, Pick-Up, Trooper II, Trooper and Rodeo are equipped with an oxygen sensor maintenance light, located in the dash panel, that will illuminate every 90,000 miles, indicating that the oxygen sensor must be replaced. After the sensor has been replaced and the emission system checked, reset the maintenance light as follows:
1. Reset the reminder light on the 1988-91 Trooper II and 1990-91 Trooper by removing the speedometer and then sliding the reset switch on the back of the speedometer to the opposite end of its slot.
2. To reset the reminder light on the 1988-95 Amigo, Pick-Up, Rodeo and 1992-95 Trooper, proceed as follows:
   a. Remove the instrument cluster assembly.
   b. Working on the backside of the instrument cluster, remove the masking tape over hole **B** in the instrument cluster.

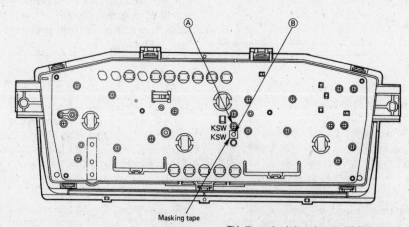

This illustration is based on the V6-3.2L model.

Fig. 32 Resetting the Oxygen Sensor Life Indicator — 1994-95 Honda Passport DX

c. Remove the screw from hole **A** of the instrument cluster and place that screw in hole **B** of the instrument cluster.

d. After switching the screw from hole **A** to hole **B**, be sure to place a piece of masking tape over hole **A** of the instrument cluster.

➡At the next 90,000 mile interval the screw hole positions will be the opposite of the previous replacement.

Check Engine Light

The CHECK ENGINE light will indicate a fault with the engine management system. If the the problem is repaired or if the problem ceases to occur, the light will extinguish but the fault will remain in the ECM memory. To clear the memorized codes from the ECM, remove power to the ECM for approximately 30 seconds. This can be accomplished by either disconnecting the negative battery cable or by removing the ECM fuse, if equipped. If the battery cable is removed, the memo-

ries for any accessories that require constant power, such as a clock or radio station memory, will need to be reset. After resetting the ECM, drive the vehicle at medium speeds and accelerations to allow the ECM to memorize the necessary operating parameters for proper operation.

JAGUAR

Catalytic Converter and EGR Light

The Catalytic Converter/EGR warning light will illuminate at the 25, 000 mile mark as a reminder for service. The mileage mechanism is inline with the speedometer cable. It is a mechanical reduction device and incorporates a magnetic operated reed switch.

The reminder switch may be reset by inserting a special reset key into the reset switch. Turn the key clockwise to '0'. The reset switch is accessible through the glow box.

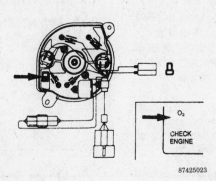

Fig. 33 Resetting the oxygen sensor reminder light switch located in back of the speedometer — 1988-91 Trooper II and 1990-91 Trooper — Isuzu

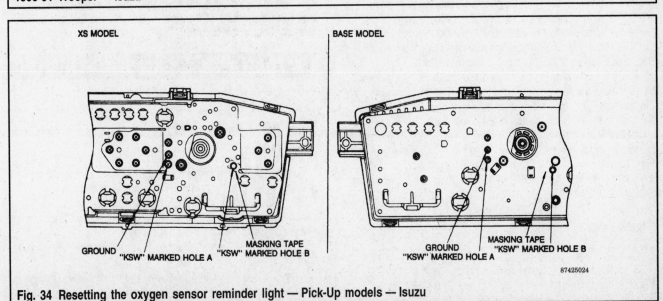

Fig. 34 Resetting the oxygen sensor reminder light — Pick-Up models — Isuzu

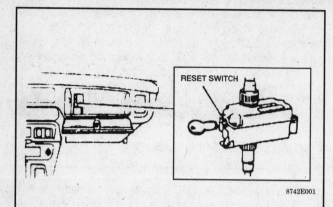

Fig. 35 Resetting the maintenance mileage counter for the catalytic converter and EGR reminder lights — Jaguar

Oxygen Sensor Maintenance Light

All fuel injected Jaguar models are equipped with an oxygen sensor maintenance light, located in the dash panel, that will illuminate every 30,000 miles, indicating that the oxygen sensor must be replaced. After the sensor has been replaced and the emission system checked, reset the maintenance light as follows:

1. The reset switch will be located in the following position:
   a. The 1980-83 XJ6 has the maintenance reminder reset mileage counter located on the right side of the engine, in front of the firewall in the engine compartment.

➡**On some of the 1980-83 models, the maintenance reminder reset mileage counter may be hidden on either side of the engine or behind the glove box.**

   b. The 1983-93 XJ6 and XJS models use a motorized maintenance reminder reset mileage counter, which is located inside the trunk compartment behind the trim panel.
2. Reset the mileage counter on the 1980-83 models by using the special key No. BLT-5007 or using 2 small pins to turn the reset disc on the mileage counter. Start the engine and check to see if the light has been turned off.
3. Reset the mileage counter on the 1983-93 XJ6 models by removing the trim panel at the head of the trunk to uncover the mileage counter. With the ignition switch in the **ON** position, depress the white button to reset the light.
4. Reset the mileage counter on the 1983-93 XJS models, by removing the trim panel from the left rear quarter panel in front of the wheel well to uncover the mileage counter. With the ignition switch in the **ON** position, depress the white button to reset the light.

Check Engine Light

As of 1986 some vehicles were equipped with a CHECK ENGINE light. By 1988 all vehicles were. The CHECK ENGINE light will illuminate if the ECM detects a fault with the engine management system. If the the problem is repaired or if the problem ceases to occur, the light will extinguish but the fault will remain in the ECM memory.

Maintenance Reminder Light

Vehicles equipped with Maintenance Indicator Reminder light (MIL), will illuminate indicating its time for a service interval or there is a problem in the engine management system. After service is completed, reset the maintenance light as follows.

1987-89 Range Rover

1. Locate the green or tan box below the steering column.
2. Peel back the sticker labeled 'Maintenance Light' or 'Maintenance Reminder Sticker'. Use a small paper clip or other suitable tool and press in on the reset button.
3. The light is now reset. Start the engine to ensure the light is out.

1991-95 Range Rover

1. Locate the green or tan box under the passenger seat.
2. Peel off the sticker 'Maintenance Light' or 'Maintenance Reminder Sticker'. Use small paper clip or other suitable tool and press in on the reset button.
3. The light is now reset. Start the engine to ensure the light is out.

Check Engine Light

As of 1995 the Maintenance Reminder Light is no longer used in Land Rover vehicles. However all vehicles from 1987-95 equipped with a CHECK ENGINE light, will illuminate should a fault in the engine management system occur. If the the problem is repaired or if the problem ceases to occur, the light will extinguish but the fault will remain in the ECU memory. After the cause of the fault has been rectified, the ECU memory should be cleared.

Timing Belt Warning Light

Diesel Pick-ups

Early model diesel pick-ups were equipped with a timing belt warning light. The light would illuminate at approximately 60,000 miles to indicate that a new timing belt should be installed. After the belt had been inspected or replaced, the warning light should be reset as follows:

1. Locate the 3 wires used to reset the timing belt warning light.
   a. Black wire located near the intermittent wiper control relay.
   b. Black wire with a white tracer located near the intermittent wiper control relay.

c. Black wire with a yellow tracer located near the intermittent wiper control relay.

➡ **The intermittent wiper control relay is located under the left side of the instrument panel.**

2. Remove the single black wire from the connector of the black wire with the white tracer.

3. Plug the single black wire into the connector of the black wire with the yellow tracer.

➡ **Whichever connector the single black wire was connected to originally, it must be removed and reconnected to the opposite connector from which it was removed, in order to reset the light.**

EGR Warning Light

1986 B2000 Federal Pick-ups
1986-87 B2200 and B2600

The EGR warning light illuminates at the first 60,000 miles to inform the operator that the emission components should be replaced and/or inspected. The suggested replacement components are the oxygen sensor, EGR control valve along with the hose and tube. The suggested inspected components are the PCV system and the ignition timing. The light can be reset as follows:

1. Locate above the left side kick panel, the single terminal green wire that is connected to a single terminal black wire.

2. In order to reset the warning light, disconnect the black wire from the green wire and leave it disconnected. Be sure to tape the disconnected wire to prevent shorting.

➡ **The connectors are sometimes located on the rear of the combination meter.**

Check Engine Light

All 1988-95 vehicles equipped with a CHECK ENGINE light with the exception as noted below, the CHECK ENGINE light will flash indicating a fault with the engine management system. If the the problem is repaired or if the problem ceases to occur the light will extinguish but the fault will remain in the ECM memory. The vehicles specified below require a maintenance reset.

1988-93 Pick-up

The Pick-Up models, in addition to displaying computer system malfunction codes (codes used on California models only), the **CHECK** light on the B2200 and B2600 Pick-Ups will act as an emission maintenance warning light. The **CHECK** engine warning light will come on at 60,000 miles for the EGR system and 80,000 miles for the oxygen sensor system. Once the emission system has been checked and/or the oxygen sensor replaced, reset the warning light as follows:

1. To reset warning light it will be necessary to locate the brown wire with the white tracer, the black wire and the green wires, which are usually under the left side of instrument panel taped to the wiring harness, above the fuse/relay block.

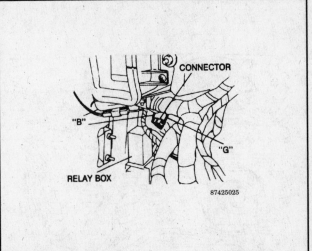

Fig. 36 Reset connector location — 1986 B2000 Pick-Ups — Mazda

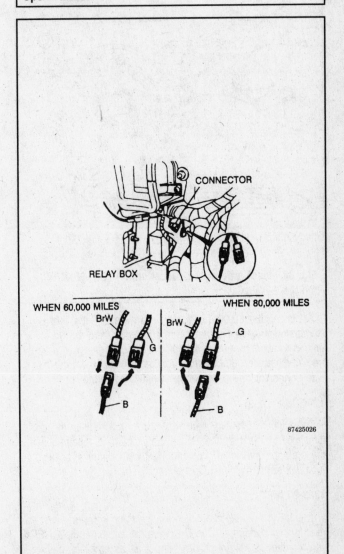

Fig. 37 Reset connector location — 1988-93 Pick-Ups, early 626 models similar — Mazda

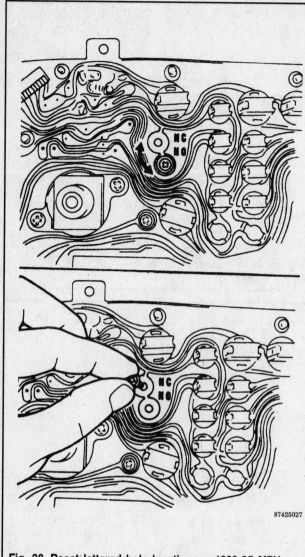

Fig. 38 Reset lettered hole locations — 1989-95 MPV models — Mazda

2. When the 60,000 mile interval arrives and the light is illuminated, unplug the black wire connector from the brown and white wire connector and plug it into the green wire connector. When the 80,000 mile interval arrives, return the black wire connector to the brown and white wire connector.

1994-95 Pick-up

The CHECK ENGINE light will indicate a fault with the engine management system. If the the problem is repaired or if the problem ceases to occur the light will extinguish but the fault will remain in the ECU memory.

1989-95 MPV

The MPV models, in addition to displaying computer system malfunction codes used on California models only, the **CHECK** light on the instrument cluster will act as an emission maintenance warning light. The **CHECK** engine warning light will

come on at 80,000 miles for the oxygen sensor system maintenance. After the emission system has been checked and the oxygen sensor replaced, reset the warning light as follows:

1. Disconnect the negative battery cable. Remove the instrument panel cluster assembly.

2. Locate the lettered reset holes **NO** and **NC** on the rear of the instrument cluster.

3. Remove the screw from the **NO** lettered reset hole and install it into the **NC** lettered hole. After an additional 80,000 miles, return the screw to the original lettered hole.

MERCEDES-BENZ

Catalytic Converter Warning Light

Vehicles equipped with a Catalytic Converter light will illuminate every 37, 000 miles as a reminder to service the Catalytic Converter. After the converter has been serviced, the light must be reset. Locate the mileage counter inline with the speedometer cable and press the button marked CAT.

Oxygen Sensor Warning Light

1980-85 Models

The models are equipped with an oxygen sensor maintenance warning light that works in junction with the mileage reset counter. The warning light will illuminate when the mileage counter reaches approximately 30,000 miles. The warning light is used as a reminder to check the emission system and to replace the oxygen sensor. After the emission system maintenance has been completed, the mileage counter must be reset. To reset the mileage counter, use the following procedure:

1. On the 280 series vehicles, the mileage counter is usually located in-line with the speedometer cable, under instrument panel. Disconnect the wiring plug from counter and leave it disconnected. No reset switch is provided.

2. To reset the counter on all other series, the instrument cluster must be partially removed. Insert a suitable hooked tool between the right side of cluster and the dash panel.

3. Turn the hook to engage the cluster and pull the cluster out of the spring retaining clips.

4. Remove the bulb from the lower corner of the instrument cluster. Press the instrument cluster back into position. There is no reset switch provided.

1986-89 Models

The oxygen sensor light is used as a malfunction indicator for the oxygen sensor circuit. A mileage counter is not used and there is no reset procedure required. Servicing and repairing the oxygen sensor circuit should turn light off. Removing and discarding the oxygen sensor warning light bulb from the warning light in the instrument cluster, will not resolve the emission system problems and may lead to other problems as well.

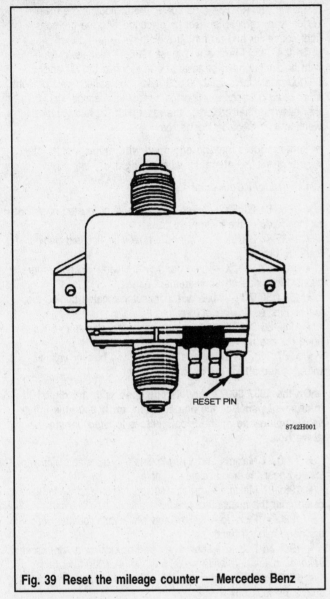

Fig. 39 Reset the mileage counter — Mercedes Benz

Check Engine Light

1990-95 Models

The CHECK ENGINE light illuminates to indicate a fault in the engine management system. Once the cause of the fault has been rectified and the codes have been pulled from the ECU memory, the fault codes must be erased. The codes must be erased one at a time as they are read from memory. After the LED blinks the code wait 2 seconds and press the button on the diagnostic connector or the impulse display counter for 6 seconds. The LED will blink once to signal that the code has been erased.

MITSUBISHI

EGR and Oxygen Sensor Light

1983-95 Light Truck, Vans and Wagons

The Mitsubishi car line does not use a maintenance warning light but some of the light trucks, van and wagons do use a maintenance warning light. The warning light will illuminate at approximately 50,000 miles for the EGR system and 80,000 miles for the oxygen sensor system. On the trucks, including the Montero, the light is used as a reminder to inspect the EGR emission systems. On the van and wagon models, the light is used as a reminder to check and replace the oxygen sensor. After completing the necessary emission service, the maintenance light can be reset as follows:

On some models, the reset switch is located on the back of the instrument cluster near the speedometer junction. After the switch is located, slide the switch knob to the other side to reset the maintenance warning light. On the other models, the reset switch is located on the lower right hand corner of the instrument cluster, behind the instrument cluster face panel. After the switch is located, slide the switch knob to the other side to reset the maintenance warning light.

➡**After 100, 000 miles, the warning lights bulbs should be removed.**

Check Engine Light

The CHECK ENGINE light will indicate a fault with the engine management system. If the the problem is repaired or if the problem ceases to occur, the light will extinguish but the fault will remain in the ECM memory.

To clear the memorized codes from the ECM, remove power to the ECM for approximately 15 seconds with the ignition switch **OFF**. This can be accomplished by either disconnecting the negative battery cable or by removing the ECM fuse, if equipped. If the battery cable is removed, the memories for

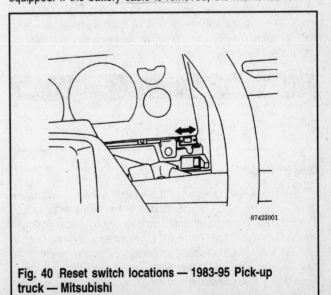

Fig. 40 Reset switch locations — 1983-95 Pick-up truck — Mitsubishi

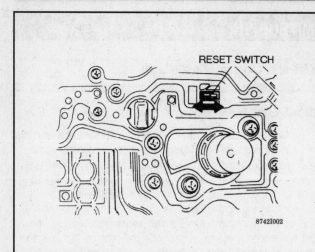

Fig. 41 Reset switch locations — 1983-1993 Montero and Van/Wagon — Mitsubishi

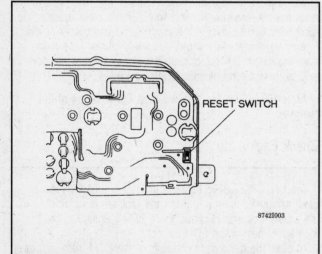

Fig. 42 Reset switch locations — 1994-95 Montero and Vans — Mitsubishi

any accessories that require constant power, such as a clock or radio station memory, will need to be reset. After resetting the ECM, drive the vehicle at medium speeds and accelerations to allow the ECM to memorize the necessary operating parameters for proper operation.

NISSAN/DATSUN

Oxygen Sensor Light

1980-87 Models

The models are equipped with a oxygen sensor maintenance reminder warning light that is located in the instrument cluster. The light will illuminate at approximately 30,000 miles. At this time, the oxygen sensor should be inspected and/or replaced and the entire emission system should be inspected. After the oxygen sensor and emission system have been serviced and repaired as necessary, the maintenance warning light must be

reset. On the 1980-84 (and some 1985) models, the maintenance warning light is reset by disconnecting the the sensor light connector and no further maintenance is required.

On the 1985 Maxima and most 1986-87 models, a warning light hold relay must be located and reset at 30,000 and 60,000 mile intervals. At 90,000 miles, the sensor warning light is disabled by disconnecting the sensor light connector. Use the following chart to locate the reset warning relay and/or warning light electrical connectors.

➡**Some models may be equipped with either means of resetting the maintenance warning light.**

Warning Light Connector Locations:

- 1980-84 200SX — green and white wire, located under the far right side of the instrument panel.
- 1985-87 200SX — pink and purple wire, located behind the fuse box
- 1982-83 280ZX — green and yellow wire, located under the far right side of the instrument panel.
- 1984 300ZX — white wire connector, located behind the left hand side kick panel.
- 1985-86 300ZX — white wire connector, located above the hood release handle.
- 1987 300ZX — gray and red, gray and blue or yellow wire, located above the hood release handle.

➡**On the 1987 300ZX models equipped with the digital instrument panel or the analog dash, at 30,000 mile intervals, unplug one of the 3 connectors located behind the glove box.**

- 1980-84 Maxima and 810 Maxima — yellow and blue wire, located near the hood release handle
- 1985-87 Maxima — green and red, green and white, located near the hood release handle.
- 1980-84 Pick-Up — yellow and white wire, located near the hood release handle.
- 1983-86 Pulsar — light green and black with a light green tracer or black and white wires, located near the fuse box
- 1987 Pulsar — red and black, red and blue wires, located above the fuse box.

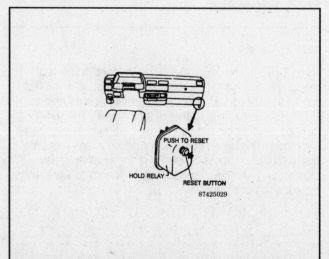

Fig. 43 Resetting the oxygen sensor warning light relay — 1985 Pulsar and Sentra — Nissan

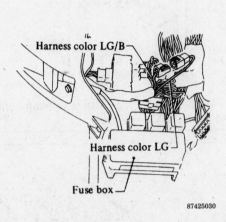

Harness color LG/B

Harness color LG

Fuse box

87425030

Fig. 44 Disconnecting the oxygen sensor warning light connector — 1983-86 Pulsar and Sentra — Nissan

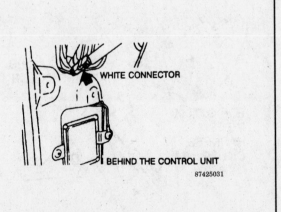

WHITE CONNECTOR

BEHIND THE CONTROL UNIT

87425031

Fig. 45 Disconnecting the oxygen sensor warning light connector — 1984-87 Stanza — Nissan

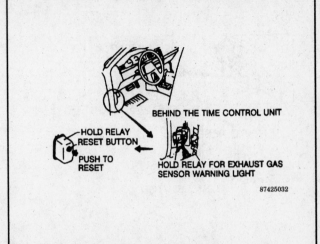

BEHIND THE TIME CONTROL UNIT

HOLD RELAY RESET BUTTON

PUSH TO RESET

HOLD RELAY FOR EXHAUST GAS SENSOR WARNING LIGHT

87425032

Fig. 46 Resetting the oxygen sensor warning light relay — 1985-86 Maxima — Nissan

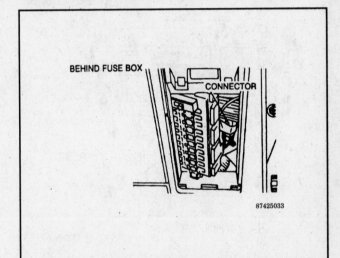

BEHIND FUSE BOX

CONNECTOR

87425033

Fig. 47 Disconnecting the oxygen sensor warning light connector — 1985-87 200SX — Nissan

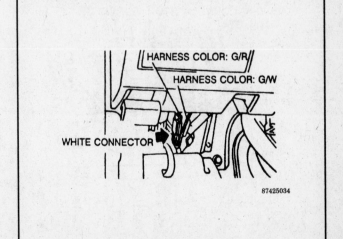

HARNESS COLOR: G/R

HARNESS COLOR: G/W

WHITE CONNECTOR

87425034

Fig. 48 Disconnecting the oxygen sensor warning light connector — 1987 Maxima — Nissan

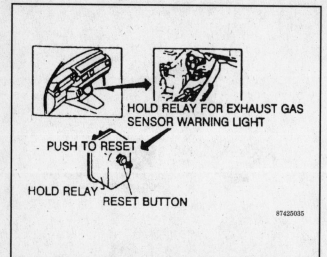

HOLD RELAY FOR EXHAUST GAS SENSOR WARNING LIGHT

PUSH TO RESET

HOLD RELAY

RESET BUTTON

87425035

Fig. 49 Resetting the oxygen sensor warning light relay — 1985-87 200SX — Nissan

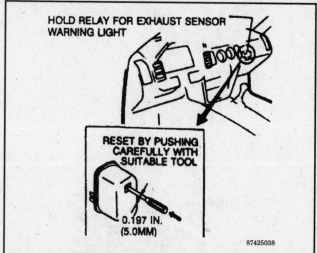

HOLD RELAY FOR EXHAUST SENSOR WARNING LIGHT

RESET BY PUSHING CAREFULLY WITH SUITABLE TOOL

0.197 IN. (5.0MM)

87425038

Fig. 52 Resetting the oxygen sensor warning light relay — 1986-87 300ZX — Nissan

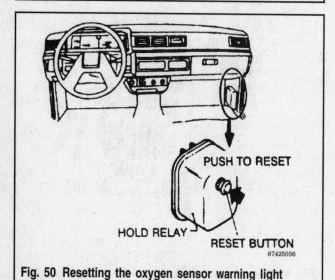

PUSH TO RESET

HOLD RELAY

RESET BUTTON

87425036

Fig. 50 Resetting the oxygen sensor warning light relay — 1986-87 Stanza — Nissan

HARNESS COLOR: YW

87425039

Fig. 53 Disconnecting the oxygen sensor warning light connector — Pick-Up with California emissions — Nissan

WHITE CONNECTOR HARNESS COLOR: BY/R, GY/L

87425037

Fig. 51 Disconnecting the oxygen sensor warning light connector — 1985-87 300ZX — Nissan

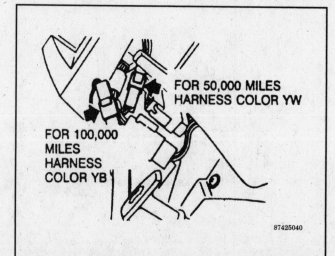

FOR 50,000 MILES HARNESS COLOR YW

FOR 100,000 MILES HARNESS COLOR YB

87425040

Fig. 54 Disconnecting the oxygen sensor warning light connector — Pick-Up with Federal emissions — Nissan

• 1982-83 Sentra — green and yellow or green and black wires, located above the fuse box.

• 1984 Sentra — light green and black with a light green tracker wires, located near the hood release handle.

• 1985-86 Sentra — light green and black wires, located above the fuse box.

• 1987 Sentra — red and black, red and blue wires, located above the fuse box.

• 1984-86 Stanza — yellow and red or yellow and green wires, located behind the left side kick panel.

• 1987 Stanza — green and brown wires, located above the fuse box.

• 1986-87 Stanza Wagon — red and yellow or red and blue wires, located behind the instrument panel.

Warning Light Relay Locations:

1. 1985-87 200SX — the reset relay is located under the center of the instrument panel behind the console. At 90,000 miles, disconnect the pink wire from the purple wire located behind the fuse box.

2. 1986-87 300ZX — the reset relay is located near the glove box. At 90,000 miles, disconnect the white connector with the gray/red wires and gray/blue wires located above the hood release handle.

➡On the 1987 300ZX models equipped with the digital instrument panel or the analog dash, at 30,000 mile intervals, unplug one of the 3 connectors located behind the glove box.

3. 1985-86 Maxima — the reset relay is located behind the left kick panel. At 90,000 miles, disconnect the green/red wire from the green/white wire located near the hood release handle.

4. 1987 Maxima — the reset relay is located behind the right kick panel. At 90,000 miles, disconnect the green/red wire from the green/white wire located near the hood release handle.

5. 1986 Pick-Up California — the reset relay is located behind the right kick panel. At 90,000 miles, disconnect the connector with the yellow/white wire located above the hood release handle.

6. 1986 Pulsar — the reset relay is located behind the right kick panel. At 90,000 miles, disconnect the connector with the red/black wire and red/blue wire located above the fuse box.

7. 1987 Pulsar — the reset relay is located behind the left kick panel. At 90,000 miles, disconnect the connector with the red/black wire and red/blue wire located above the fuse box.

8. 1985-86 Sentra — the reset relay is located behind the right kick panel. At 90,000 miles, disconnect the connector with the light green and black wire located near the hood release handle.

9. 1987 Sentra — the reset relay is located behind the right kick panel. At 90,000 miles, disconnect the connector with the red/black wire and red/blue wire located above the fuse box.

10. 1986-87 Stanza — the reset relay is located behind the right kick panel. At 90,000 miles, disconnect the white connector on the inside of the left kick panel on the 1986 models. On the 1987 models, disconnect the connector with the green and brown wire located above the fuse box.

11. 1986-87 Stanza Wagon — the reset relay is located under the right side passenger seat. At 90,000 miles, discon-

nect the red wire from the yellow wire or the red wire from the red/blue wire located behind the instrument panel.

1988-95 Models

After 1987 maintenance resets where no longer used. The CHECK ENGINE light will come on indicating a malfunction and a trouble code will be stored in the ECU memory. The light will extinguish when the problem is corrected.

Check Engine Light

As of 1986, some models used the CHECK ENGINE light, which will illuminate when a fault occurs with the engine management system. By 1988 all models used it. The fault code will be memorized by the ECU for recall at a later time. If the fault does not occur again, the memory of that fault will be automatically erased after 50 ignition switch cycles. If the memory is to be erased manually before the 50 cycles, turning the ignition switch **OFF** during the diagnosis mode of memory recall will erase the memory.

PEUGEOT

EGR Warning Light

All 1980 604 models are equipped with an **EGR** warning light. The light will illuminate approximately 12,500 mile intervals as determined by a in-line mileage counter. When the light illuminates, it will be necessary to perform maintenance on the EGR system. After completing the necessary maintenance on the EGR system, it will be necessary to reset the mileage counter in order to reset the warning light. The mileage counter can be reset as follows:

1. In order to reset the mileage counter, it will be necessary to unbolt the mileage counter from the inside of the left front wheelwell. Pull down the mileage counter without disconnecting the speedometer cables.

2. Remove the outer and inner covers from the mileage counter and turn the reset button counterclockwise until reaching a stopping point. This will reset the counter to zero.

3. Be sure the warning light is out. Replace the covers and reinstall the mileage counter.

EGR and Oxygen Sensor Light

1981-85 505 Models

Vehicles equipped with a EGR light will illuminate every 12,000 mile interval indicating the EGR system needs servicing. After the service is completed, the mileage counter must be reset. Same as applies to the oxygen sensor light.

All the 505 models equipped with gasoline engines have an oxygen sensor warning light. The warning light will illuminate at approximately 30,000 mile intervals. When the warning light is illuminated, it is an indication that the oxygen sensor must be replaced and that the mileage counter must be reset. By resetting the mileage counter the warning light will be turned off. The mileage counter can be reset as follows:

1. The mileage counter is located below the brake master cylinder. In order to gain access to the reset button, the white plastic cover must be removed and then unscrew the reset plug.

2. After the reset plug has been removed, use a suitable small punch or rod to press the reset button. Be sure the warning light is out, then replace the reset plug and cover.

1986-92 Models

After 1986 maintenance resets where no longer used. The CHECK ENGINE light will come on indicating a malfunction and a trouble code will be stored in the ECU memory. The light will extinguish when the problem is corrected.

Check Engine Light

To erase the fault memory after the CHECK ENGINE light has indicated a fault and the fault has been corrected, call up the fault codes using the appropriate tester until Code 11 appears with the ignition switch in the **RUN** position. Press the tester button until 00 is displayed. The codes will be reset at this point.

PORSCHE

Oxygen Sensor Warning Light

All models are equipped with an oxygen sensor circuit. All models, except the 928S with the LH Jetronic system, the 944S and the 968 models, are equipped with an **OXS** light that will illuminate at approximately 30,000 mile intervals as a reminder to replace the oxygen sensor. The 928S with the LH

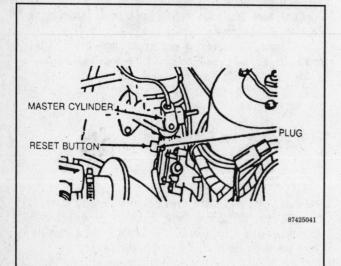

87425041

Fig. 55 Resetting the mileage counter — Peugeot

Jetronic system, the 944S and the 968 models do not use a warning light system. It should be noted that even though these models do not use the system, it is recommended that oxygen sensor be replaced every 60,000 miles. On all other models, after replacing the oxygen sensor and checking the emission systems, reset the warning lights as follows.

➡**The 1980-83 911 models also used an EGR maintenance reminder warning light system. The light is reset in the same manner as the OXS light.**

1. On the 911 and early 930S models, the **EGR** and **OXS** reset buttons were both mounted behind the speedometer. Disconnect the negative battery cable and remove the speedometer.

➡**On the 1980-83 911 and early 930S models, the speedometer head is held in place by a ribbed rubber collar. Use caution and gently pry the speedometer head loose in order to gain access to the reset buttons. On the later models, the reset button is visible through the speedometer mounting hole.**

2. Use a suitable piece of wire or rod to press the white reset button. Push the reset button all the way in against its stop. Reconnect the battery cable and check that the warning light is out.

➡**The procedure also applies to the early 930S models.**

3. On the 924 models, after replacing oxygen sensor and with the vehicle still raised and supported safely, located the mileage counter which is usually located on the left engine mount.

➡**On the 1980-82 924S turbo models, the mileage counter is located on the engine compartment side of the left strut tower. It may be necessary to follow the speedometer cable from the firewall downward, to be able to locate the mileage counter.**

4. Use a suitable piece of wire or metal rod to push in the reset button. Be sure to push the button in all the way to its stop. Make sure the **OXS** light is out. Lower the vehicle.

5. On the 928 and 928S models with the CIS system, the mileage counter is usually located at the right of the passenger seat floor panel under a trim plate between the seat and the step plate.

6. Remove the mileage counter cover retaining screw and the cover. Press the reset button in all the way in against its stop. Make sure the warning light is out.

Check Engine Light

As of 1989 some vehicles were equipped with a CHECK ENGINE light that will indicate a fault with the engine emission system. If the the problem is repaired or if the problem ceases to occur, the light will extinguish but the fault will remain in the ECU memory. After the cause of the fault has been rectified, the ECU memory should be cleared.

RENAULT

Oxygen Sensor Warning Light

The Renault 18is and Fuego models, are equipped with a mileage counter and have a dash mounted warning light that will illuminate at approximately 30,000 mile intervals as a reminder to replace the oxygen sensor. After replacing the oxygen sensor and performing any other emission system maintenance, reset the warning light, by resetting the mileage counter as follows:

1. Locate the mileage counter which is located near the firewall and in-line with the speedometer cable. Cut the retaining wires and remove the cover by disengaging the retaining clips.

2. Turn the reset button a ¼ turn counterclockwise toward the **0** mark to reset the mileage counter. Make sure the warning light is out. Replace the cover and secure it with new wires.

SAAB

Oxygen Sensor Warning Light

Some Saab models, except the 1985-87 turbo models, are equipped with a mileage counter and have a dash mounted **EXS** (EXH on some models) warning light that will illuminate at approximately 30,000 mile intervals as a reminder to replace the oxygen sensor. It should be noted that even though the 1985-87 turbo models do not use the system, it is recommended that oxygen sensor be replaced every 60,000 miles. After replacing the oxygen sensor and performing any other emission system maintenance, reset the warning light, by resetting the mileage counter as follows:

1. Locate the mileage counter which is located under the instrument panel to the left of the steering column, next to the flasher relay.

➡**Even though the mileage counter is hard to see, there should be no problem in reaching under the instrument panel and locating the mileage counter by feeling it out by hand. It is also possible to reach the mileage counter by reaching under the knee panel or going through the left defrost outlet duct.**

2. After the mileage counter has been located, push in the reset button, located on the mileage counter and make sure the warning light has gone out.

Service Warning Light

1994-95 900

The 900 series uses an information center called the Saab Information Display (SID). The TIME FOR SERVICE light will illuminate in the Saab Information Display (SID) when it is time for scheduled service. Reset the light after service is completed as follows.

Press and hold the CLEAR button for at least 8 seconds until TIME FOR SERVICE appears on the display and an audible signal is heard. After 21 starts of the engine the TIME FOR SERVICE reminder will be cancelled.

Check Engine Light

As of 1987 the 9000S was the only vehicle equipped with a CHECK ENGINE light. 1988-95 vehicles are all equipped with this system.

The CHECK ENGINE light will illuminate when a fault is sensed in the engine management system. The fault will be memorized by the ECU for recall later. Once the fault has been recalled and the cause of the fault repaired, the memory

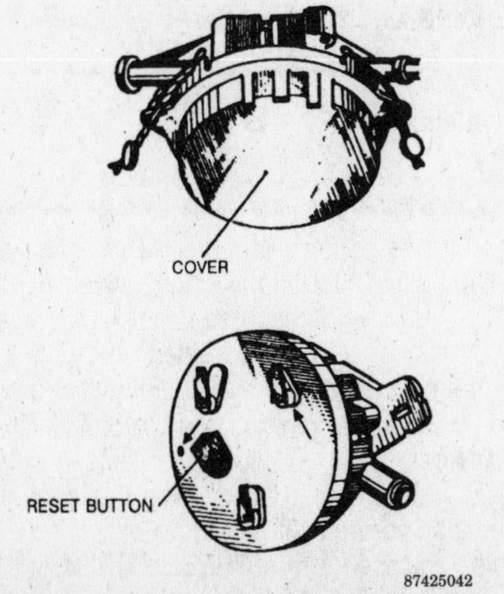

Fig. 56 Resetting the mileage counter — Renault

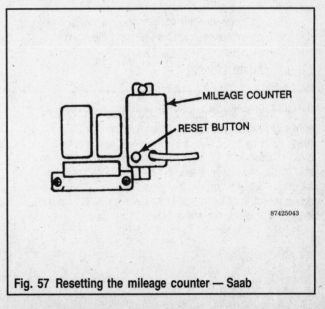

MILEAGE COUNTER

RESET BUTTON

87425043

Fig. 57 Resetting the mileage counter — Saab

should be erased. With the jumper switch in position to recall the fault codes and with fault codes already recalled, switch the jumper on for approximately 2.5 seconds. The CHECK ENGINE light will flash 3 times quickly and then switch the jumper off. The codes will be erased at this point.

STERLING

Check Engine Light

The CHECK ENGINE light will illuminate when a fault is sensed in the engine management system. The fault will be memorized by the ECU for recall later. Once the fault has been recalled and the cause of the fault repaired, the memory should be erased. To erase the memory, turn the ignition switch to **OFF** and pull the alternator fuse from the engine compartment fuse box for approximately 30 seconds. The ECU will be reset after this is done.

SUBARU

EGR Warning Light

The 1981-87 models are equipped with an **EGR** warning light located in the instrument cluster that will illuminate at approximately 30,000-50,000 miles. When the **EGR** light is lit, it is indicating that the EGR system should be checked and with the possibility of an EGR valve replacement.

It should be noted that the 1985-87 Turbocharged California models do not use a warning light system. After the EGR system has been checked and all necessary maintenance performed, reset the warning light as follows:

1. Remove the left cover under the instrument panel. Pull down the warning light connectors from behind the fuse panel.
2. Locate the single pin blue connector that is connected to another single pin blue connector. Near the blue connectors is a single green connector that is not connected to any wire terminal.
3. Unplug the connector from the blue connector and plug it into the green connector. This will reset the warning light.

Check Engine Light

The CHECK ENGINE light will illuminate when a fault is sensed in the engine management system. The fault will be memorized by the ECU for recall later. Once the fault has been recalled and the cause of the fault repaired, the memory should be erased. To erase the memory, turn the ignition switch to **ON** and connect the Read Memory Connector leads and connect the Test Mode Connector leads. With both connectors connected the memory will be cleared.

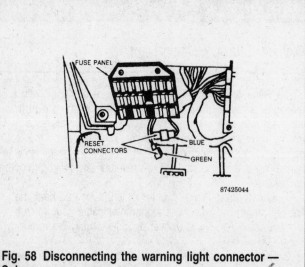

Fig. 58 Disconnecting the warning light connector — Subaru

SUZUKI

Oxygen Sensor Warning Light

1985-87 Samurai

The Samurai models are equipped with a **SENSOR** light that will flash at 60,000 mile intervals. The light will only flash when the engine is at operating temperature and running at 1500-2000 RPM. The flashing **SENSOR** light indicates that the ECM is in good condition and that the oxygen sensor should be checked and replaced as necessary. After the oxygen sensor has been replaced and the emission systems checked, reset the light as follows:

1. The warning light cancel switch is attached to the steering column support bracket. After the cancel switch is located, turn the cancel switch to the opposite position.
2. Start the engine and drive vehicle to be sure the light does not flash any longer.

Check Engine Light

1986-95 Models

As of 1988 the 02S sensor light was no longer used in the Samurai. The CHECK ENGINE light will flash continuously on Samurai and will remain **ON** in the Sidekick. This will occur at 50,000, 80,000 and 100, 000 mile mark, indicating it is time for service. When servicing is has been completed, reset the light by turning off the cancel switch, located under the instrument cluster, for 1988 Samurai and all Federal vehicles only.

On 1986-95 California vehicles, the CHECK ENGINE light will come **ON** only when a fault code is sensed in the engine management system. When the problem has been corrected, clear the codes and the light should go out.

All vehicles equipped with a CHECK ENGINE will illuminate when a fault is sensed in the engine management system. The fault will be memorized by the ECU for recall later. Once the fault has been recalled and the cause of the fault repaired, the

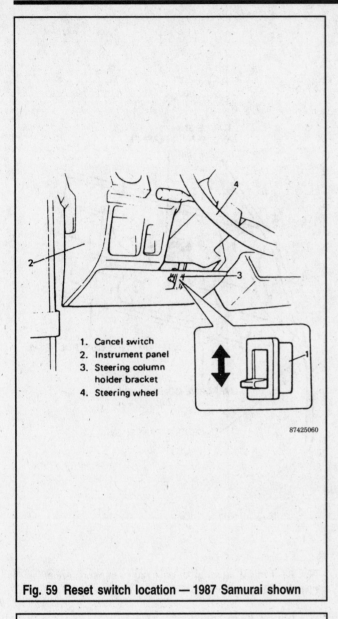

1. Cancel switch
2. Instrument panel
3. Steering column holder bracket
4. Steering wheel

87425060

Fig. 59 Reset switch location — 1987 Samurai shown

SENSOR

87425061

Fig. 60 Sensor lamp — 1987 Samurai shown

memory should be erased. Disconnect the negative battery cable for 60 seconds or more. Reconnect the cable and start the engine. Allow the engine to reach operating temperature and ground the diagnostic switch. Check for a Code 12 and disconnect the diagnostic switch. The codes will be reset at this point.

TOYOTA

Oxygen Sensor Warning Light

The 1980 Celica, Supra and Cressida models and all the 1981 models with gasoline engines, except Starlet, are equipped with an oxygen sensor. The vehicles are all equipped with a mileage counter that activates a warning light in the instrument cluster at approximately 30,000 miles. When the warning light is illuminated it is an indication that the oxygen sensor must be serviced at this time. After the oxygen sensor and emission systems have been serviced and repaired as required, reset the warning light as follows:

1. All models except the Supra, Land Cruiser and 1980 Celica models: In order to reset the warning light, remove the white cancel switch from top of the left kick panel. It should be noted that the cancel switch has been known to be taped to the main instrument panel wiring harness under the left side of the instrument panel. After the cancel switch has been located, open the switch cover and move the switch slide to the opposite position.

2. On the 1980 Celica, to reset the warning light, remove the black box which is usually located on the top of the bracket above the brake pedal. After the cancel switch has been located, open the switch cover and move the switch slide to the opposite position. It should be noted that some of the Celica models have the cancel switches positioned at the top of the left side kick panel.

3. On the Supra models, it is necessary to remove the small panel next to the steering column in order to gain access to the cancel switch. After the cancel switch has been located, open the switch cover and move the switch slide to the opposite position. It should be noted that some Cressida models have their cancel switch located in this position also.

4. On the Land Cruiser models, the cancel switch is located under the hood in the engine compartment near the firewall. After the cancel switch has been located, open the switch cover and move the switch slide to the opposite position.

Timing Belt Warning Light

Diesel Pick-Ups

Toyota diesel Pick-Ups have a maintenance reminder light that is located in the instrument cluster that will illuminate every 50,000 miles (60,000 miles on the 1982-83 models). When the light is illuminated, it is indicating that the timing belt should be replaced. After belt has been replaced, reset the warning light by removing the rubber grommet from the speedometer bezel and pressing the reset switch.

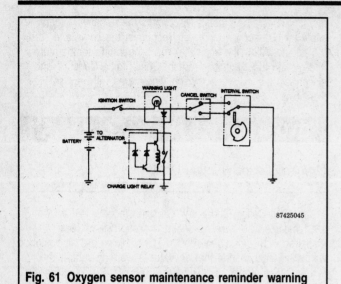

Fig. 61 Oxygen sensor maintenance reminder warning light wiring schematic — Toyota

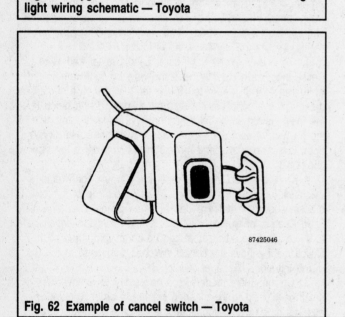

Fig. 62 Example of cancel switch — Toyota

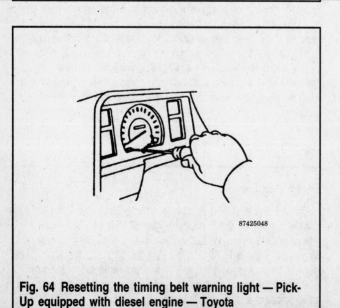

Fig. 64 Resetting the timing belt warning light — Pick-Up equipped with diesel engine — Toyota

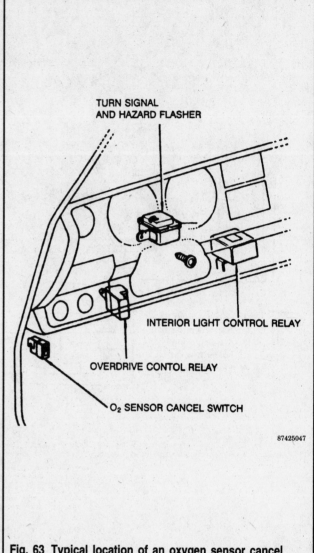

Fig. 63 Typical location of an oxygen sensor cancel switch — Toyota

Oil Change Reminder Light

1991-93 Previa

The Previa van is equipped with an oil change reminder light that will illuminate at the factory specified oil change intervals. To reset the light after the oil change has been completed, remove the cover from the reset knob on the instrument panel and insert a thin object, such as a pen, into the opening. Press the reset knob and the light should extinguish.

Check Engine Light

The CHECK ENGINE light will indicate a fault with the engine management system. If the the problem is repaired or if the problem ceases to occur, the light will extinguish but the fault will remain in the ECM memory.

To clear the memorized codes from the ECM, remove power to the ECM for approximately 30 seconds with the ignition

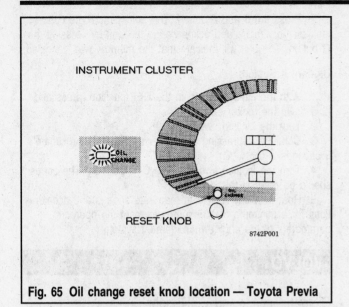

Fig. 65 Oil change reset knob location — Toyota Previa

switch **OFF**. This can be accomplished by either disconnecting the negative battery cable or by removing the ECM fuse, if equipped. If equipped with the fuse for the ECM, it will be marked **EFI**. If the battery cable is removed, the memories for any accessories that require constant power, such as a clock or radio station memory, will need to be reset. After resetting the ECM, drive the vehicle at medium speeds and accelerations to allow the ECM to memorize the necessary operating parameters for proper operation.

TRIUMPH/MG

Oxygen Sensor Warning Light

All fuel injected models are equipped with an oxygen sensor. The models also are equipped with a mileage counter and have a dash mounted warning light that will illuminate at approximately every 30,000 mile intervals as a reminder to replace the oxygen sensor. After the oxygen sensor has been replaced, reset the warning light as follows:

1. Locate the mileage counter which is in the engine compartment near the left inner fender panel, in-line with the speedometer cable.

2. After the mileage counter is located, reset the counter by using special key (BLT-5007) supplied in the kit with a new sensor, to turn the reset switch to the opposite position.

3. The mileage counter can also be reset by using 2 small pins that will fit into the reset key holes.

VOLKSWAGEN

EGR And Oxygen Sensor Lights

On some models there is an EGR warning light that is located in the instrument cluster. The system also uses a mileage counter. When the mileage counter reaches 15,000 miles, it will illuminate the EGR warning light. This will indicate that

the EGR and emission system should be checked for proper operation.

An oxygen sensor (OXS) warning light is located in the instrument cluster on all models. The system also uses a mileage counter. When the mileage counter reaches 30,000 miles, it will illuminate the OXS warning light. This will indicate that the oxygen sensor should be replaced. After the systems have been properly serviced, the maintenance lights can be reset has follows:

1. On Rabbit and Pick-Up models, remove the instrument panel cover trim plate. Locate the mileage counter release arms at the opening of the top left corner of speedometer housing.

2. Pull the release arms to reset the mileage counter. The left arm is used to reset the EGR warning light and the right arm is used to reset the oxygen sensor warning light.

3. On Vanagon models, locate the mileage counter below the driver's floorpanel, next to the spare tire carrier, in-line with the speedometer cable. One of the reset buttons may be covered by a small plug.

4. Remove the plug and using a suitable rod, depress the reset button. Be sure the warning light is out.

5. On all other models, locate the mileage counter which is located under the hood near the firewall, in-line with the speedometer cable. It is best to follow the speedometer cable from the transmission upwards to the firewall, to be able to locate the mileage counter easier.

6. Once the mileage counter is found it is a simple matter of pushing in the black reset button marked **EGR** or the white reset button marked **OXS** located on the mileage counter.

Check Engine Light

1987-88 only a few Volkswagens were equipped with a CHECK ENGINE light. 1989-95 are were equipped. The CHECK ENGINE light will indicate a fault with the engine management system. If the the problem is repaired or if the problem ceases to occur, the light will extinguish but the fault will remain in the ECU memory. After the cause of the fault has been rectified, the ECU memory should be cleared.

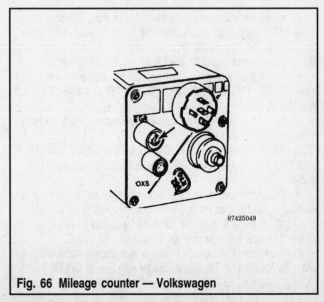

Fig. 66 Mileage counter — Volkswagen

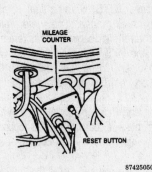

Fig. 67 Locating and resetting the in-line mileage counter — Volkswagen

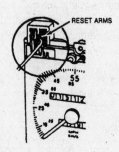

Fig. 68 Pulling down the mileage counter reset levers to reset the warning light — Volkswagen

CIS-E Montronic System

1. All communications with the ECU is done through the VAG 1551 diagnostic tester with the ignition switch **ON**. After the elimination of possible fault codes, re-input and acknowledge the address word 01 for ENGINE ELECTRONICS.

2. Press the right arrow button and the following will appear: RAPID DATA TRANSMISSION HELP and INPUT ADDRESS WORD XX

3. Press the **0** and **2** buttons to address the fault code memory recall function.

4. When the display, RAPID DATA TRANSMISSION HELP and 02 FAULT MEMORY RECALL appears, press the **Q** button.

5. Either the number of faults in memory will appear or a message saying that no faults were found will appear. Press the right arrow button to list all faults or in the case of no faults, prepare the memory for clearing.

6. Press the right arrow button again and the unit will display: RAPID DATA TRANSMISSION HELP and SELECT FUNCTION XX.

7. Press the **0** and **5** button. The unit will indicate cancel fault memory mode and acknowledge the unit by pressing the **Q** button. The unit will indicate that the memory was canceled.

Digifant II System

1. With the ignition switch in the **OFF** position, press and hold down the rocker switch.

2. Turn the ignition switch **ON**.

3. Continue depressing the rocker switch for approximately 5 seconds.

4. Turn the ignition switch to the **OFF** position. The codes should be reset at this point.

5. Road test the vehicle at moderate speeds and accelerations for a minimum of 10 minutes to reset the operating parameters of the engine management system.

VOLVO

Oxygen Sensor and EGR Light

1. On 1976-80 models equipped with an EGR warning light in the dash will illuminate at the 15,000 and 30,000 mile mark as a reminder to service the EGR system. To reset warning light, locate mileage counter in-line with speedometer cable. Remove the cover. Press the reset button. Ensure the reminder light is out.

2. On 1980-85 models and 1986 760 GLE models, equipped with an oxygen sensor system, a warning light in the dash will illuminate every 30,000 miles as a reminder to replace the oxygen sensor.

3. To reset warning light on 1980-84 models, locate mileage counter in-line with speedometer cable. Press the reset button. Ensure the reminder light is out.

4. On 1985 models and 1986 760 GLE models, locate mileage counter unit under the dash by following wires or small cable from the back of the speedometer to the unit. Remove retaining screw and switch cover. Press reset button. Ensure reminder light is out. Install switch cover.

5. On 1986 models (except 760 GLE) and 1987-89 models, there is no warning light used for oxygen sensor service intervals.

Service Interval Reminder Light

On some 1987-94 Volvo models, an oil service interval reminder light is located on the instrument cluster and will illuminate at 5000 mile intervals. The light will continue to illuminate for 2 minutes after each engine start or until the counter is reset. After completing the necessary service, reset the mileage counter as follows:

1987-90 740, 1987 760 and 780

1. To reset the mileage counter, remove the instrument cluster.

2. Locate the button behind the right center of the instrument cluster and press it in too reset the counter. Verify the light is out.

3. Reinstall the instrument cluster.

Fig. 69 Resetting the in-line mileage counter — 1980-86 Volvo

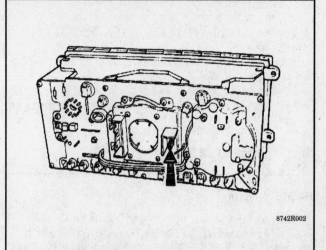

Fig. 71 Press upward on lever at rear of instrument cluster — 1989-92 Volvo 240 shown

1988-94 240

1. To reset the mileage counter, remove the instrument cluster.

2. Locate the button behind the right center of the instrument cluster and press the lever upward too reset the counter. Verify the light is out.

3. Reinstall the instrument cluster.

1988-91 760
1991-95 740, 940 and 960

1. To reset the mileage counter, remove the rubber plug located between the speedometer and the clock.

2. Remove the rubber plug and depress the reset button, using a small, suitable rod.

3. Verify the service indicator light is out and replace the rubber plug.

1992-94 850

1. Connect the Volvo diagnostic tester or equivalent to the information output connection.

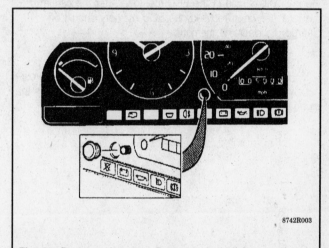

Fig. 72 Depress the reset button located between the speedometer and clock — 1988-91 760, 1991-94 740, 940 and 960 Volvo

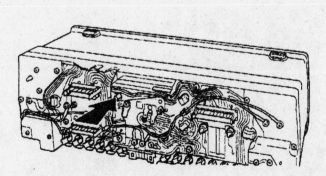

Fig. 70 Location of the mileage counter reset button — 1987-90 740, 1987 760 and 780 Volvo

2. Select position 7 on the diagnostic unit A.

3. Depress the button 4 times to enter test mode 4.

4. When the LED light stays lit, enter 1. The LED light may flicker or blink.

5. Once the LED light stays steadily lit, enter 5. Again the light may flicker or blink.

6. When the LED light stays steadily lit again, enter 1. The LED will flash several times and the service reminder lamp will go out.

Check Engine Light

1990-95 Vehicles

1990 was the first year Volvo began use of the CHECK ENGINE light, however the Service Reminder light is still in use today. The CHECK ENGINE light will indicate a fault with the engine management system. If the the problem is repaired or if the problem ceases to occur, the light will extinguish but the fault will remain in the ECU memory. After the cause of the fault has been rectified, the ECU memory should be cleared. To clear the memory:

1. Turn the ignition switch to the **ON** position.

2. Read the fault codes again.

3. Press and hold the diagnostic socket button for approximately 5 seconds. Release the button and after 3 seconds the diode should light.

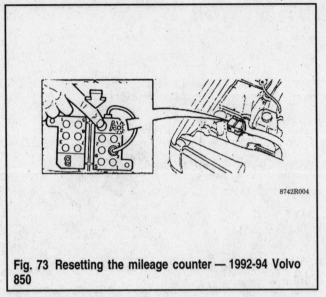

8742R004

Fig. 73 Resetting the mileage counter — 1992-94 Volvo 850

4. While the diode is lit, press the button again for approximately 5 seconds. Release the button and the diode should go out. The memory is cleared at this point.

5. To insure that the memory has been cleared, press the button again for 1 second (no longer than 3 seconds). The diode should flash 1-1-1 indicating that the engine management system is operating properly.

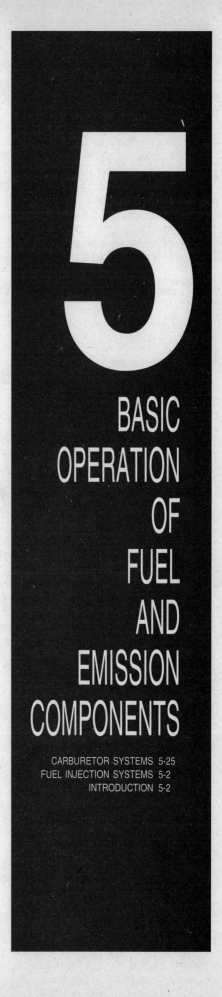

5

BASIC OPERATION OF FUEL AND EMISSION COMPONENTS

INTRODUCTION

There are 3 basic fuel control systems used on most manufacturer's vehicles. The feedback carburetor vehicles use a system some times referred to as a Computer Command Control (CCC) System on or more commonly referred to as the Feedback Carburetor System (FBC). The other two systems are fuel injection systems. The first system is called Throttle Body Injection (TBI). This system uses an injector built into the throttle body, which appears very much like a carburetor when you look under the hood. The second system is Multi-Port Injected (MPI) System. The MPI system has a throttle body mounted in the air stream with an injector mounted on the intake manifold at each intake valve. There is one injector for each cylinder.

➡**When the term Powertrain Control Module (PCM) is used in this manual it will refer to the engine control computer regardless that it may be a Powertrain Control Module (PCM), Electronic Control Assembly (ECS), Electronic Control Module (ECM) or any similar term used by different manufacturers.**

FUEL INJECTION SYSTEMS

There are 2 basic fuel injection systems; Throttle Body Injection (TBI) and Multi-Port Injection (MPI).

Throttle Body Injection

♦ **See Figures 1, 2 and 3**

The Throttle Body Injection (TBI) system provides a means of fuel distribution for controlling exhaust emissions within legislated limits. The TBI system, by precisely controlling the air/fuel mixture under all operating conditions, provides as near as possible complete combustion.

The TBI assembly is centrally located on the intake manifold where air and fuel are distributed through a single bore in the throttle body, similar to a carbureted engine. Air for combustion is controlled by a single throttle valve which is connected to the accelerator pedal linkage by a throttle shaft and lever assembly.

All fuel injection and ignition functions are controlled by the Powertrain Control Module (PCM). The PCM accepts inputs from various sensors and switches, calculates the optimum air/fuel mixture and operates the various output devices to provide peak performance within specific emissions limits. The PCM will attempt to maintain the air/fuel mixture of 14.7:1 in order to optimize catalytic converter operation. If a system failure occurs that is not serious enough to stop the engine, the PCM will illuminate the SERVICE ENGINE SOON light and operate the engine in a backup or fail-safe mode. In the backup mode the PCM delivers fuel according to inputs from the Manifold Absolute Pressure (MAP) sensor and the Coolant Temperature Sensor (CTS). Other operating modes in the PCM program are described later.

Fuel is supplied to the engine from a pump mounted in the fuel tank. The fuel pump module includes the gauge/sending unit, which can be replaced separately. Otherwise, the module must be replaced as an assembly. The pump is operated through a relay. A check valve in the tank unit maintains pressure in the system for a period of time after the engine is stopped in order to aid hot starting. The fuel tank must be removed to remove the pump module.

Other system components include a pressure regulator, an Idle Air Control (IAC) valve, a Throttle Position Sensor (TPS), Air Temperature Sensor (ATS), Coolant Temperature Sensor (CTS), a power steering pressure switch and an oxygen sensor. The fuel injector is a solenoid valve that the PCM pulses on and off many times per second to promote proper fuel atomization. The pulse width determines how long the injector is ON each cycle and this regulates the amount of fuel supplied to the engine.

The system pressure regulator is part of the throttle body. Intake manifold pressure is supplied to the regulator diaphragm, making system pressure partly dependent on engine load. The idle air control valve is a 2 coil stepper motor that controls the amount of air allowed to bypass the throttle plate. With this valve the PCM can closely control idle speed even when the engine is cold or when there is a high engine load at idle.

Fig. 1 Throttle body and related components — Chevrolet 4.3L TBI engine shown

THROTTLE BODY INJECTION OPERATING MODES

Starting Mode

When the ignition switch is first turned **ON**, the fuel pump relay is energized by the PCM for 2 seconds to build system pressure. When the crankshaft position signal tells the PCM that the engine is turning over or cranking, the pump will run continuously. In the start mode, the PCM checks the MAP sensor, TPS and CTS to determine the best air/fuel ratio for

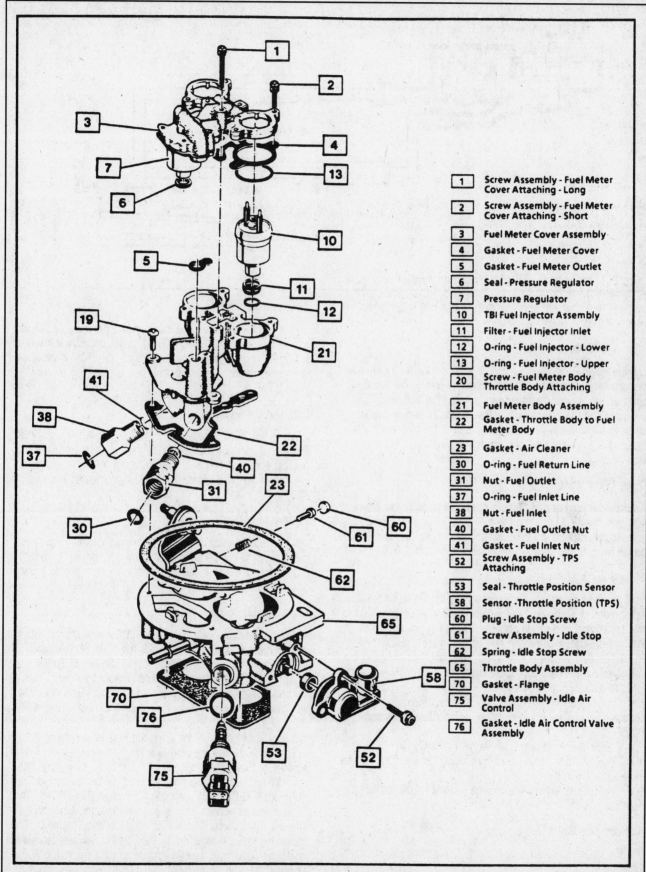

1	Screw Assembly - Fuel Meter Cover Attaching - Long
2	Screw Assembly - Fuel Meter Cover Attaching - Short
3	Fuel Meter Cover Assembly
4	Gasket - Fuel Meter Cover
5	Gasket - Fuel Meter Outlet
6	Seal - Pressure Regulator
7	Pressure Regulator
10	TBI Fuel Injector Assembly
11	Filter - Fuel Injector Inlet
12	O-ring - Fuel Injector - Lower
13	O-ring - Fuel Injector - Upper
20	Screw - Fuel Meter Body Throttle Body Attaching
21	Fuel Meter Body Assembly
22	Gasket - Throttle Body to Fuel Meter Body
23	Gasket - Air Cleaner
30	O-ring - Fuel Return Line
31	Nut - Fuel Outlet
37	O-ring - Fuel Inlet Line
38	Nut - Fuel Inlet
40	Gasket - Fuel Outlet Nut
41	Gasket - Fuel Inlet Nut
52	Screw Assembly - TPS Attaching
53	Seal - Throttle Position Sensor
58	Sensor - Throttle Position (TPS)
60	Plug - Idle Stop Screw
61	Screw Assembly - Idle Stop
62	Spring - Idle Stop Screw
65	Throttle Body Assembly
70	Gasket - Flange
75	Valve Assembly - Idle Air Control
76	Gasket - Idle Air Control Valve Assembly

0012D023

Fig. 2 Typical throttle body fuel injection unit — General Motor Design shown

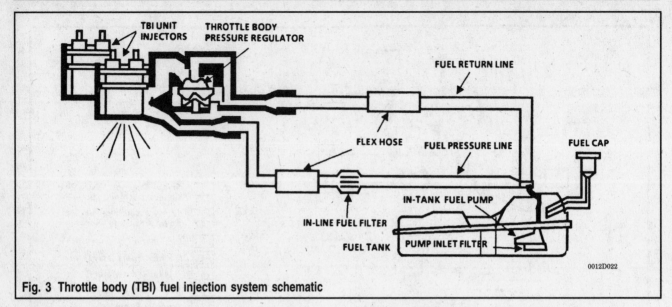

Fig. 3 Throttle body (TBI) fuel injection system schematic

starting. Ratios could range from 1.5:1 at -33°F (-36°C), to 14.6:1 at 201°F (94°C).

Clear Flood Mode

If the engine becomes flooded, it can be cleared by opening the accelerator to the full throttle position. When the throttle is open all the way and engine rpm is less than 400, the PCM will close the fuel injector while the engine is turning over in order to clear the engine of excess fuel. If throttle position is reduced below about 75 percent, the PCM will return to the start mode.

Open Loop Mode

When the engine first starts and engine speed rises above 400 rpm, the PCM operates in the Open Loop mode until specific parameters are met. Fuel requirements are calculated based on information from the MAP sensor and CTS.

Closed Loop Mode

When the correct parameters are met, the PCM will use O_2 sensor output and adjust the air/fuel mixture in order to maintain a narrow band of exhaust gas oxygen concentration. When the PCM is correcting and adjusting fuel mixture based on the oxygen sensor signal along with the other sensors, this is known as feedback air/fuel ratio control. The PCM will shift into Closed Loop mode when:

• Oxygen sensor output voltage is varies, indicating that the sensor has warmed up to operating temperature, minimum 600°F (318°C)
• Coolant temperature is above 68°F (20°C)
• The PCM has received an rpm signal greater than 400 for more than 1 minute
• On 1992-93 vehicles, a change in throttle position is detected

Acceleration Mode

If the throttle position is and manifold pressure is quickly increased, the PCM will provide extra fuel for smooth acceleration.

Deceleration Mode

As the throttle closes and the manifold pressure decreases, fuel flow is reduced by the PCM. If both conditions remain for a specific number of engine revolutions, the PCM decides fuel flow is not needed and stops the flow by shutting off the injector.

Fuel Cut-Off Mode

When the PCM is receiving a Vehicle Speed Sensor (VSS) signal and rpm goes above 6750, the injectors are shut off to prevent engine overspeed. The PCM will also shut off the injectors if the VSS signal is 0 and engine speed reaches 4000 rpm.

Battery Low Mode

If the PCM detects a low battery, it will increase injector pulse width to compensate for the low voltage and provide proper fuel delivery. It will also increase idle speed to increase alternator output.

Field Service Mode

When terminals A and B of the ALDL are jumpered with the engine running, the PCM will enter the Field Service Mode. If the engine is running in Open Loop Mode, the SERVICE ENGINE SOON light will flash quickly, about 2½ times per second. When the engine is in Closed Loop Mode, the light will flash only about once per second. If the light stays OFF most of the time in Close Loop, the engine is running lean. If the light is ON most of the time, the engine is running rich.

Throttle body fuel injection is a fuel metering system with the amount of fuel delivered by the throttle body injector(s) determined by an electronic signal supplied by the Electronic Control Module (ECM) or Powertrain Control Module (PCM). The PCM monitors various engine and vehicle conditions to calculate the fuel delivery time (pulse width) of the injector(s). The fuel pulse may be modified by the PCM to account for special operating conditions, such as cranking, cold starting, altitude, acceleration, and deceleration.

Multi-Port Fuel Injection

▶ **See Figure 4**

The Multi-Port Fuel Injection (MPI) system is controlled by the Powertrain Control Module (PCM) which monitors engine operations and generates output signals to provide the correct air/fuel mixture, ignition timing and engine idle speed control. Primary input to the control unit is provided by an oxygen sensor, coolant temperature sensor, detonation sensor, mass air flow sensor and throttle position sensor. The PCM also receives information concerning engine rpm, road speed, transmission gear position, power steering and air conditioning.

The PCM contains memories for the basic discharge duration at various engine speeds and manifold pressures. The basic discharge duration, after being read out from the memory, is further modified by signals sent from various sensors to obtain the final injector duration. The PCM also controls the basic ignition timing based on engine load, engine rpm, vehicle speed and coolant temperature.

If the PCM notes the loss or change out-of-range of a sensor signal, the computer will ignore the faulty signal and substitute a fixed value in its place. This value may not necessarily be correct for the immediate driving situation, but will allow the engine to operate. For example, many PCM decisions are based on the engine coolant temperature. Should the coolant temperature sensor signal be lost just after a cold start, the PCM will substitute the default value. This substitution value is based on an engine at normal temperature so vehicle performance will be affected until fully warmed up.

The PCM also tests itself while operating. If an abnormality occurs within the PCM, the system switches to a back-up circuit independent of the computing system. This system substitutes fixed values for all inputs and controls the injectors accordingly. Vehicle performance is usually reduced to minimal driveability. The back up function serves as a lifeboat to prevent the vehicle from being stranded in the event of PCM failure. When a abnormality occurs, the PCM lights the engine warning light and stores a failure code in its memory. The fault code can be retrieved during diagnosis.

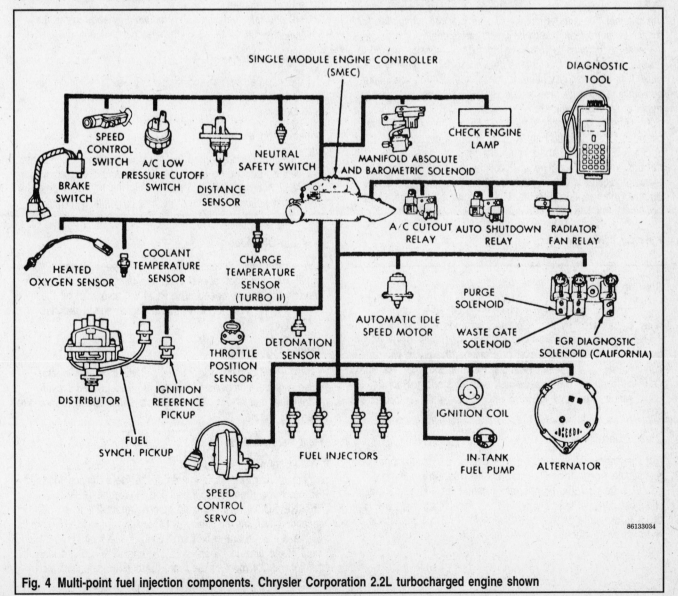

Fig. 4 Multi-point fuel injection components. Chrysler Corporation 2.2L turbocharged engine shown

86133034

Fuel is supplied to the engine from a pump mounted in the fuel tank. It is a positive displacement roller vane pump. The impeller serves as a vapor separator and pre-charges the high pressure assembly. A pressure regulator maintains a specific fuel pressure in the fuel line to the injectors and the excess fuel is fed back to the tank. A fuel accumulator is used to dampen the hydraulic line hammer in the system created when all injectors open simultaneously.The fuel pump module includes the gauge/sending unit, which can be replaced separately. Otherwise, the module must be replaced as an assembly. The pump is operated through a relay. A check valve in the tank unit maintains pressure in the system for a period of time after the engine is stopped to aid hot starting. The fuel tank must be removed to remove the pump module.

The injectors are located at each intake port, rather than the single injector found on the earlier throttle body system. The injectors are mounted on a fuel rail and are activated by a signal from the Powertrain Control Module. The injector is a solenoid-operated valve which remains open depending on the width of the electronic pulses (length of the signal) from the PCM; the longer the open time, the more fuel is injected. In this manner, the air/fuel mixture can be precisely controlled for maximum performance with minimum emissions.

On some engines, a Mass Air Flow (MAF) sensor is used to measure the mass of air that is drawn into the engine cylinders. It is located just ahead of the throttle body in the intake system and consists of a heated film which measures the mass of air, rather than just the volume.

The throttle body incorporates an Idle Air Control (IAC) that provides for a bypass channel through which air can flow. It consists of an orifice and pintle which is controlled by the PCM through a step motor. The IAC provides air flow for idle and allows additional air during cold start until the engine reaches operating temperature. As the engine temperature rises, the opening through which air passes is slowly closed.

OPERATING MODES

Starting Mode

When the ignition switch is first turned **ON**, the fuel pump relay is energized by the PCM for 2 seconds to build system pressure. When the crankshaft position signal tells the PCM that the engine is turning over or cranking, the pump will run continuously. In the start mode, the PCM checks the TPS and CTS to determine the best air/fuel ratio for starting. Ratios could range from 0.8:1 at -40°F (-40°C), to 14.6:1 at 220°F (104°C).

Clear Flood Mode

If the engine becomes flooded, it can be cleared by opening the accelerator to the full throttle position. When the throttle is open all the way and engine rpm is less than 400, the PCM will close the fuel injectors while the engine is turning over in order to clear the engine of excess fuel. If throttle position is reduced below about 75 percent, the PCM will return to the start mode.

Open Loop Mode

When the engine first starts and engine speed rises above 400 rpm, the PCM operates in the Open Loop mode until specific parameters are met. Fuel requirements are calculated based on information from the MAP sensor and CTS.

Closed Loop Mode

When the correct parameters are met, the PCM will use O_2 sensor output and adjust the air/fuel mixture in order to maintain a narrow band of exhaust gas oxygen concentration. When the PCM is correcting and adjusting fuel mixture based on the oxygen sensor signal along with the other sensors, this is known as feedback air/fuel ratio control.

The PCM will shift into Closed Loop mode when:

Oxygen sensor output voltage is varies, indicating that the sensor has warmed up to operating temperature, minimum 600°F (318°C)

Coolant temperature is above 68°F (20°C)

The PCM has received an rpm signal greater than 400 for more than 1 minute

1992 and later vehicles, also require a change in throttle position.

Acceleration Mode

If the throttle position and manifold pressure is quickly increased, the PCM will provide extra fuel for smooth acceleration.

Deceleration Mode

As the throttle closes and the manifold pressure decreases, fuel flow is reduced by the PCM. If both conditions remain for a specific number of engine revolutions, the PCM decides fuel flow is not needed and stops the flow by shutting off the injectors.

Fuel Cut-Off Mode

When the PCM is receiving a Vehicle Speed Sensor (VSS) signal and rpm goes above 6750, the injectors are shut off to prevent engine overspeed. The PCM will also shut off the injectors if the VSS signal is 0 and engine speed reaches 4000 rpm.

Battery Low Mode

If the PCM detects a low battery, it will increase injector pulse width to compensate for the low voltage and provide proper fuel delivery. It will also increase idle speed to increase alternator output.

Field Service Mode

When terminals A and B of the ALDL are jumpered with the engine running, the PCM will enter the Field Service Mode. If the engine is running in Open Loop Mode, the SERVICE ENGINE SOON light will flash quickly, about 2½ times per second. When the engine is in Closed Loop Mode, the light will flash only about once per second. If the light stays OFF most of the time in Close Loop, the engine is running lean. If the light is ON most of the time, the engine is running rich.

Computer Monitored Components

▶ **See Figure 5**

A variety of sensors provide information to the PCM regarding engine operating characteristics. These sensors and their functions are described below. Note that not every sensor described is used with every engine application.

➡**When the term Powertrain Control Module (PCM) is used in this manual it will refer to the engine control computer regardless that it may be a Powertrain Control Module (PCM), Electronic Control Assembly (ECS), Electronic Control Module (ECM) or any similar term used by different manufacturers.**

AIR CONDITIONING PRESSURE SENSOR

The air conditioning (A/C) pressure sensor or air conditioner signal request, provides a signal to the Powertrain Control Module (PCM) which indicates either A/C operation or varying A/C refrigerant pressure. The PCM uses this input to determine the A/C compressor load on the engine to help control the idle speed with the IAC valve.

BAROMETRIC PRESSURE (BAP) SENSOR

▶ **See Figure 6**

The barometric pressure sensor is used to compensate for altitude variations. From this signal, the PCM modifies the air/fuel ratio, spark timing, idle speed, and EGR flow. The barometric sensor is a design that produces a frequency based on atmospheric pressure (altitude).

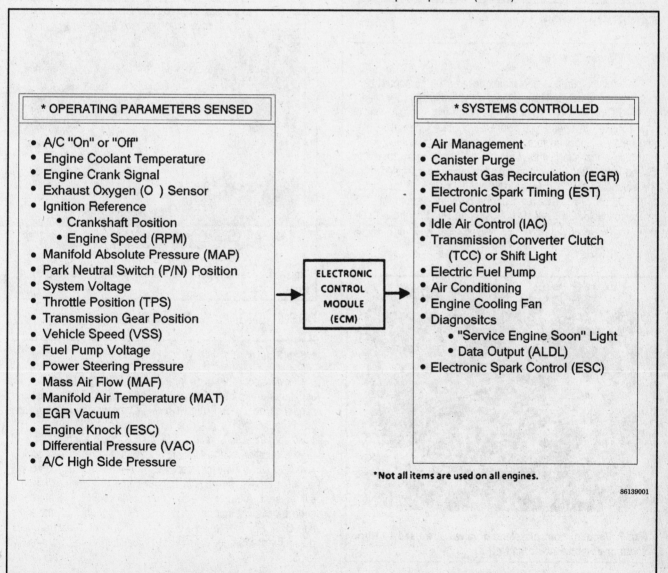

* OPERATING PARAMETERS SENSED

- A/C "On" or "Off"
- Engine Coolant Temperature
- Engine Crank Signal
- Exhaust Oxygen (O) Sensor
- Ignition Reference
  - Crankshaft Position
  - Engine Speed (RPM)
- Manifold Absolute Pressure (MAP)
- Park Neutral Switch (P/N) Position
- System Voltage
- Throttle Position (TPS)
- Transmission Gear Position
- Vehicle Speed (VSS)
- Fuel Pump Voltage
- Power Steering Pressure
- Mass Air Flow (MAF)
- Manifold Air Temperature (MAT)
- EGR Vacuum
- Engine Knock (ESC)
- Differential Pressure (VAC)
- A/C High Side Pressure

ELECTRONIC CONTROL MODULE (ECM)

* SYSTEMS CONTROLLED

- Air Management
- Canister Purge
- Exhaust Gas Recirculation (EGR)
- Electronic Spark Timing (EST)
- Fuel Control
- Idle Air Control (IAC)
- Transmission Converter Clutch (TCC) or Shift Light
- Electric Fuel Pump
- Air Conditioning
- Engine Cooling Fan
- Diagnositcs
  - "Service Engine Soon" Light
  - Data Output (ALDL)
- Electronic Spark Control (ESC)

*Not all items are used on all engines.

86139001

Fig. 5 Typical engine control system parameters

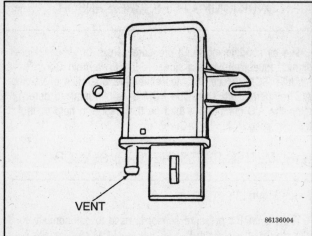

Fig. 6 Barometric pressure sensor doesn't use the vacuum connection. MAP and BARO sensor look alike on most vehicles

CANISTER PURGE

▶ See Figures 7, 8 and 9

The canister purge is sometimes called a purge control or cutoff solenoid valve. This solenoid valve, which is controlled by the PCM controls vacuum to the purge valve in the charcoal canister. In open loop, before a specified time has expired and below a specified rpm, the solenoid valve is energized and blocks vacuum to the purge valve. When the system is in closed loop, after a specified time and above a specified rpm, the solenoid valve is de-energized and vacuum can be applied to the purge valve. This releases the collected vapors into the intake manifold. On systems not using an PCM controlled solenoid, a Thermo Vacuum Valve (TVV) is used to control purge.

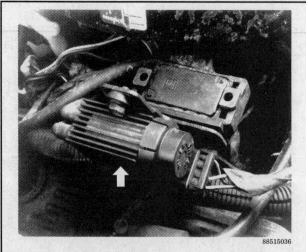

Fig. 7 Vacuum control solenoid valves are used to turn vacuum component on and off

Fig. 8 Frequency valve use in the Evaporative emission control system — Volkswagen with Motronic fuel injection shown

Fig. 9 Typical Evaporative Canister is located near the front fenders

CHECK ENGINE WARNING LAMP

▶ See Figure 10

The dashboard warning lamp will be lit by the PCM for 2 seconds during the initial ignition ON sequence. After this test sequence has ended, the PCM will illuminate the lamp anytime an electrical fault is noted within the system.

When a fault is detected, the dash warning lamp will stay on for the duration of the ignition ON cycle. Once the ignition is switched OFF, then recycled, the dashboard warning lamp will not light unless the original fault or some other (newer) fault is still present. Although the lamp does not re-light, the stored code for the original fault will remain in memory with the ignition OFF. For this reason, diagnosis should be based on the presence of fault codes, not the illumination of the warning lamp.

Fig. 10 Check engine lamp is always found in the intrument panel

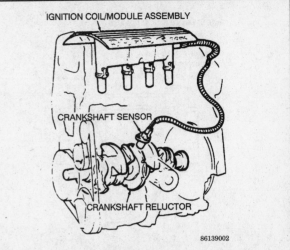

Fig. 11 Typical crankshaft sensor used on the General Motors 2.3L Quad-Four engine

COLD START VALVE

This valve is used in the CIS-E and CIS Motronic systems. The cold start valve injects extra fuel into the intake manifold during cold starts. The cold start valve is controlled by the PCM. Operation of the valve is determined by the coolant temperature, to prevent excess fuel from being injected. The cold start valve is located on the back of the intake manifold.

CRANKSHAFT SENSOR

▶ **See Figures 11 and 12**

The crankshaft sensor is sometimes called an engine position sensor, TDC sensor or cylinder sensor. Some systems use a magnetic crankshaft sensor, mounted remotely from the ignition module, which protrudes into the block within approximately 0.050 in. (0.127mm) of the crankshaft reluctor. The reluctor is a special wheel cast into the crankshaft with 7 slots machined into it, 6 of which are equally spaced. A seventh slot is spaced approximately 10 degrees from one of the other slots and serves to generate a SYNC PULSE signal. As the reluctor rotates as part of the crankshaft, the slots change the magnetic field of the sensor, creating an induced voltage pulse.

Based on the crank sensor pulses, the ignition module sends 2X reference signals to the PCM which are used to indicate crankshaft position and engine speed. The ignition module continues to send these reference pulses to the PCM at a rate of 1 per each 180 degrees of the crankshaft rotation. This signal is called the 2X reference because it occurs 2 times per crankshaft revolution.

The ignition also sends a second, 1X reference signal to the PCM which occurs at the same time as the SYNC PULSE from the crankshaft sensor. This signal is called the 1X reference because it occurs 1 time per crankshaft revolution. The 1X reference and the 2X reference signals are necessary for the PCM to determine when to activate the fuel injectors.

By comparing the time between pulses, the ignition module can recognize the pulse representing the seventh slot (sync

Fig. 12 Typical crankshaft sensor used in on the General Motors V6 or V8 engines

pulse) which starts the calculation of the ignition coil sequencing. The second crank pulse following the SYNC PULSE signals the ignition module to fire the No. 2-3 ignition coil and the fifth crank pulse signals the module to fire the No. 1-4 ignition coil.

DIFFERENTIAL PRESSURE REGULATOR

▶ **See Figure 13**

This regulator is used in the CIS-E and CIS Motronic systems only. The differential pressure regulator controls the fuel flow in the lower chamber of the fuel distributor. This helps to determine the fuel mixture. The regulator designates 0 milliamps (mA) as a reference point. When the vehicle is at normal operating temperature and all engine controls are operating properly, the regulator operates with current from the PCM between +10 mA (rich) to -10 mA (lean) ranges.

When the starter is operated, current to the differential pressure regulator is increased to enrich the fuel mixture. This will

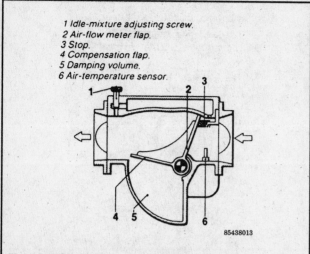

1 Idle-mixture adjusting screw.
2 Air-flow meter flap.
3 Stop.
4 Compensation flap.
5 Damping volume.
6 Air-temperature sensor.

85438013

Fig. 13 CIS injection air flow sensor is used to control fuel mixture and pressure regulation

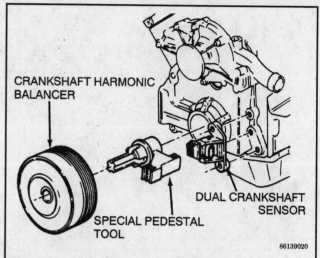

CRANKSHAFT HARMONIC BALANCER

DUAL CRANKSHAFT SENSOR

SPECIAL PEDESTAL TOOL

86139020

Fig. 14 Some engines use a Dual Crank sensor, in place of camshaft and crankshaft sensors

occur whenever the engine is started, and the amount of increase will be regulated by the coolant temperature. When the temperature is extremely cold, the current can be as high as 140 mA.

During cold acceleration, current can raise to approximately 6 mA to enrich the fuel mixture. Enrichment is determined by the engine speed and signals from the temperature sensor.

During full load operation, the full throttle switch closes, sending a signal to the PCM. The PCM sends a signal approximately 3 mA greater than the signal that is currently present. This signal will vary, depending on the engine speed and altitude.

When the vehicle is decelerated, fuel to the injectors is shut-off by reversing the current to -50 mA to -60 mA. The engine speed, at which this reversing will occur, is regulated by the coolant temperature. Current will also be reversed when engine speed reaches 6600 rpm. The differential pressure regulator is attached to the fuel distributor.

DUAL CRANK SENSOR/COMBINATION SENSOR

♦ See Figure 14

The dual crank sensor is usually mounted on a pedestal at the front of the engine near the harmonic balancer. The sensor consists of 2 Hall Effect switches, which depend on 2 metal interrupter rings mounted on the balancer to activate them. Windows in the interrupters activate the hall effect switches as they provide a patch for the magnetic field between the switches transducers and magnets. When one of the hall effect switches is activated, it grounds the signal line to the control module, pulling that signal line's (Sync Pulse or Crank) applied voltage low, which is interpreted as a signal.

Because of the way the signal is created by the dual crank sensor, the signal circuit is always either at a high or low voltage (square wave signal). Three crank signal pulses and one SYNC PULSE are created during each crankshaft revolution. The crank signal is used by the control module to create a reference signal which is also a square wave signal similar to the crank signal. The reference signal is used to calculate the engine rpm and crankshaft position by the PCM. The SYNC PULSE is used by the control module to begin the ignition coil firing sequence. Both the crank sensor and the SYNC PULSE signals must be received by the ignition module for the engine to start. A misadjusted sensor or bent interrupter ring could cause rubbing of the sensor resulting in potential driveability problems, such as rough idle, poor performance, or a nor start condition.

➡**Failure to have the correct clearance will damage the crankshaft sensor.**

The dual crank sensor is not adjustable for ignition timing but positioning of the interrupter ring is very important. A dual crank sensor that is damaged, due to mispositioning or a bent interrupter ring, can result in a hesitation, sag stumble or dieseling condition.

To determine if the dual crank sensor could be at fault, a special scanning tool will be necessary along with the testing charts in your vehicle service manual. If the engine rpm, using a special scan tool while driving the vehicle, shows an erratic display this indicates that a proper reference pulse has not been received by the PCM, which may be the result of a malfunctioning dual crank sensor.

EGR CONTROL SOLENOID VALVE (EGR CSV)

When EGR function is necessary to provide control of NOx emissions, the PCM grounds the control solenoid valve. The solenoid allows regulated vacuum to pass to the EGR, thus precisely controlling EGR function.

EXHAUST GAS RECIRCULATION (EGR) VALVE

▶ **See Figures 16, 17, 18, 19, 20 and 15**

All models are equipped with this system, which consists of a metering valve, a vacuum line to the carburetor or intake manifold, and cast-in exhaust passages in the intake manifold. The EGR valve is controlled by vacuum, which opens and closes in response to the vacuum signals to admit exhaust gases into the air/fuel mixture. The exhaust gases lower peak combustion temperatures, reducing the formation of NOx. The valve is closed at idle and wide open throttle, but is open between the two extreme positions.

There are actually four types of EGR systems: Ported, Positive Back-Pressure, Negative Backpressure and Digital. The principle of all the systems are the same; the only difference is in the method used to control how the EGR valve opens.

Too much EGR flow at idle, cruise or during cold operation may result in the engine stalling after cold start, the engine stalling at idle after deceleration, vehicle surge during cruise and rough idle. If the EGR valve is always open, the vehicle may not idle. Too little or no EGR flow allows combustion temperatures to rise, which could result in spark knock (detonation), engine overheating and/or emission test failure.

A thermal vacuum switch (TVS) or vacuum control solenoid may sometimes be used in combination with the EGR valve. The TVS will close off vacuum during cold operation. A vacuum control solenoid uses Pulse Width Modulation (PWM) to turn the solenoid ON and OFF numerous times a second and varies the amount of ON time (pulse width) to vary the amount of ported vacuum supplied the EGR valve.

Some manufacturers use an identification system to help with what type of EGR valve is used.
- Positive backpressure EGR valves will have a 'P' stamped on the top side of the valve below the date built
- Negative backpressure EGR valves will have a 'N' stamped on the top side of the valve below the date built
- Port EGR valves have no identification stamped below the date built

Basic service and testing an EGR valve is as follows:

1. Check to see if the EGR valve diaphragm moves freely. Use your finger to reach up under the valve and push on the diaphragm. If it doesn't move freely, the valve should be replaced. The use of a mirror will aid the inspection process.

❊❊CAUTION

If the engine is hot, wear a glove to protect your hand.

2. Install a vacuum gauge into the vacuum line between the EGR valve and the vacuum source. Start the engine and allow it to reach operating temperature.
3. With the car in either **P** or **N**, increase the engine speed until at least 5 in. Hg is showing on the gauge.
4. Remove the vacuum hose from the EGR valve. The diaphragm should move downward (valve closed). The engine speed should increase.
5. Install the vacuum hose and watch for the EGR valve to open (diaphragm moving upward). The engine speed should decrease to its former level, indicating exhaust recirculation.
6. If the diaphragm doesn't move, check engine vacuum; it should be at least 5 in. Hg with the throttle open and engine running.
7. Check to see that the engine is at normal operating temperature.
8. Check for vacuum at the EGR hose. If no vacuum is present, check the hose for leaks, breaks, kinks, improper connections, etc., and replace as necessary.
9. If the diaphragm moves, but the engine speed doesn't change, check the EGR passages in the intake manifold for blockage.

Ported Valve

In the ported system, the amount of exhaust gas admitted into the intake manifold depends on a ported vacuum signal. A ported vacuum signal is one taken from the carburetor above the throttle plates; thus, the vacuum signal (amount of vacuum) is dependent on how far the throttle plates are opened. When the throttle is closed (idle or deceleration) there is no vacuum signal. Thus, the EGR valve is closed, and no exhaust gas enters the intake manifold. As the throttle is opened, a vacuum

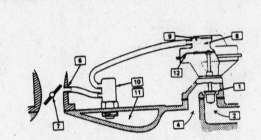

1. EGR valve
2. Exhaust gas
4. Intake flow
6. Vacuum port
7. Throttle valve
8. Vacuum chamber
9. Valve return spring
10. Thermal vacuum switch
11. Coolant
12. Diaphragm

85344025

Fig. 15 Thermostatic Vacuum Switch (TVS) controlled EGR system

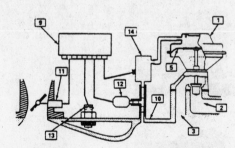

1. EGR valve
2. Exhaust gas
3. Intake air
5. Diaphragm
9. Electronic control module
10. Manifold vacuum
12. Manifold pressure sensor
13. Coolant temperature sensor
14. EGR control solenoid

85344026

Fig. 16 Solenoid controlled EGR system

is produced, which opens the EGR valve, admitting exhaust gas into the intake manifold.

Positive Backpressure Valve

This valve operates the same as the ported, except, it has an internal air bleed that acts as a vacuum regulator. The bleed valve controls the amount of vacuum inside the vacuum chamber during operation. When the valve receives sufficient exhaust backpressure through the hollow shaft, it closes the bleed; at this point the EGR valve opens.

➡This valve will not open, with vacuum applied to it, while the engine is idling or stopped.

Negative Backpressure Valve

This valve is similar to the positive backpressure type, except, the bleed valve spring is moved from above the diaphragm to below it. The bleed valve is normally closed.

At certain manifold pressures, the EGR valve will open. When the manifold vacuum combines with the negative ex-

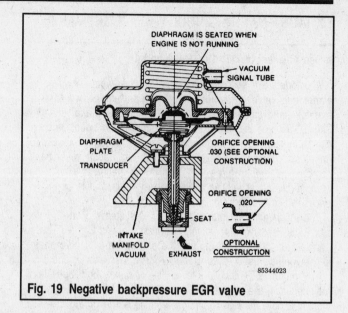

Fig. 19 Negative backpressure EGR valve

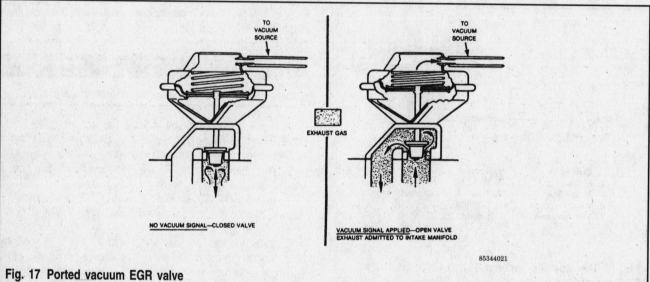

Fig. 17 Ported vacuum EGR valve

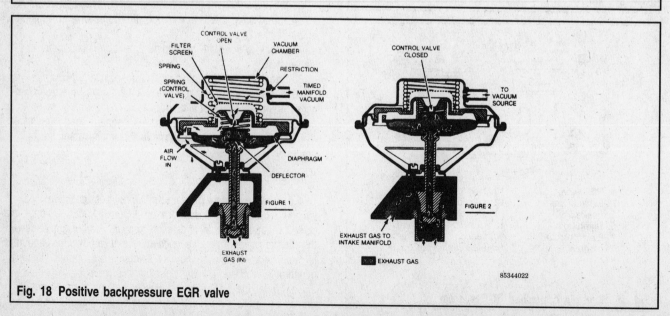

Fig. 18 Positive backpressure EGR valve

haust backpressure, the bleed hole opens and the EGR valve closes.

➡**This valve will open when vacuum is applied and the engine is not running.**

Digital EGR Valve

The digital EGR valve is designed to control the flow of EGR independent of intake manifold vacuum. The valve controls EGR flow through 3 solenoid-opened orifices, which increase in size, to produce 7 possible combinations. When a solenoid is energized, the armature with attached shaft and swivel pintle, is lifted, opening the orifice.

The digital EGR valve is opened by the ECM 'quad-driver' (QDR), grounding each solenoid circuit individually. The flow of EGR is regulated by the ECM which uses information from the Coolant Temperature Sensor (CTS), Throttle Position Sensor (TPS) and the Manifold Absolute Pressure (MAP) sensor to determine the appropriate rate of flow for a particular engine operating condition.

EGR VALVE POSITION (EVP) SENSOR

▶ **See Figures 21 and 22**

The EGR valve position sensor, sometimes known as an EGR valve lift sensor, is mounted on EGR valve. It signals the computer of EGR opening so that it may subtract EGR flow from total air flow into the manifold. In this way, EGR flow is excluded from air flow information used to determine mixture requirements.

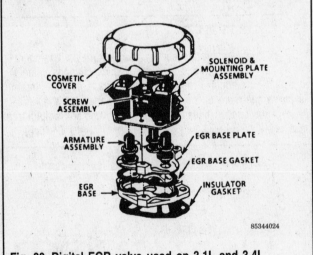

Fig. 20 Digital EGR valve used on 3.1L and 3.4L engines

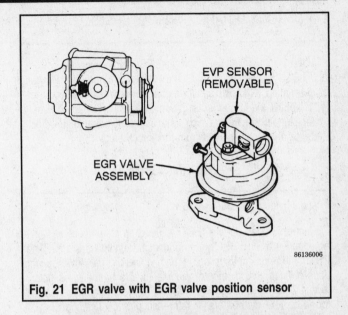

Fig. 21 EGR valve with EGR valve position sensor

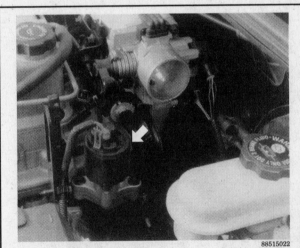

Fig. 22 EGR valve with position sensor mounted on top — Saturn with 1.9L MFI engine shown

ELECTRIC LOAD DETECTOR (ELD)

The Electric Load Detector is usually located in the underhood fuse and relay box. It detects the present of moderate to large electrical current in the system and sends a signal to the PCM.

The PCM will control the idle speed to compensate for the additional load of headlights, rear defroster, heater fan or similar heavy electrical loads.

ELECTRONIC SPARK CONTROL (ESC)

When engines are equipped with ESC in conjunction with EST, ESC is used to reduce spark advance under conditions of detonation. A knock sensor signals a separate ESC controller to retard the timing when it senses knock. The ESC controller signals the PCM which reduces spark advance until no more signals are received from the knock sensor.

ELECTRONIC SPARK TIMING (EST)

▶ See Figures 23, 24 and 25

Electronic spark timing (EST) is used on all engines equipped with HEI distributors and direct ignition systems. The EST distributor contains no vacuum or centrifugal advance and uses a 7-terminal distributor module. It also has 4 wires going to a 4-terminal connector in addition to the connectors normally found on HEI distributors. A reference pulse, indicating both

Fig. 25 View of a Coil pack — Saturn with 1.9L MFI engine shown) inputs

engine rpm and crankshaft position, is sent to the PCM. The PCM determines the proper spark advance for the engine operating conditions and sends an EST pulse to the distributor or coil pack on DIS Systems.

The EST system is designed to optimize spark timing for better control of exhaust emissions and for fuel economy improvements. The PCM monitors information from various engine sensors, computes the desired spark timing and changes the timing accordingly. A backup spark advance system is incorporated in the module in case of EST failure.

ENGINE COOLANT TEMPERATURE SENSOR

▶ See Figures 26 and 27

The coolant temperature sensor, also known as a temperature switch, is a thermistor (a resistor which changes value based on temperature) mounted in the engine coolant stream. As the temperature of the engine coolant changes, the resistance of the coolant sensor changes. Low coolant temperature produces a high resistance (100,000 ohms at -40°C/-40°F),

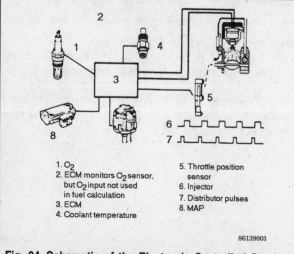

Fig. 23 Electronic Controlled Spark Timing Module — 4.3L Chevrolet engine shown

1. O₂
2. ECM monitors O₂ sensor, but O₂ input not used in fuel calculation
3. ECM
4. Coolant temperature
5. Throttle position sensor
6. Injector
7. Distributor pulses
8. MAP

Fig. 24 Schematic of the Electronic Controlled Spark Timing (EST) inputs

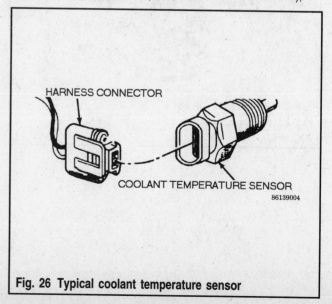

HARNESS CONNECTOR

COOLANT TEMPERATURE SENSOR

Fig. 26 Typical coolant temperature sensor

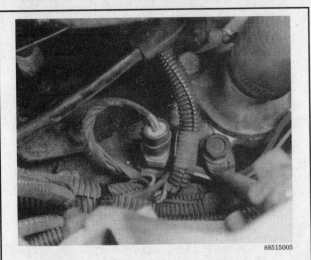

Fig. 27 Engine Coolant Temperature (ECT) sensor — Chevrolet with 4.3L TBI engine shown

while high temperature causes low resistance (70 ohms at 130°C/266°F).

The PCM supplies a 5 volt signal to the coolant sensor and measures the voltage that returns. By measuring the voltage change, the PCM determines the engine coolant temperature. The voltage will be high when the engine is cold and low when the engine is hot. This information is used to control fuel management, IAC, spark timing, EGR, canister purge and other engine operating conditions.

A failure in the coolant sensor circuit should set a code. These codes indicate a failure in the coolant temperature sensor circuit, indicating an open, shorted or out of range condition. Once the fault code is set, the PCM will use a default value for engine coolant temperature.

EXHAUST GAS TEMPERATURE SENSOR

The exhaust gas temperature sensor, which is found on California models, monitors exhaust gas temperature and transmits a signal to the PCM. The temperature sensing unit employs a thermistor which is sensitive to the change in temperature. Electric resistance of the thermistor decreases in response to the temperature rise.

FUEL INJECTOR(S)

▶ See Figures 28, 29 and 30

The fuel injector(s) is an electric solenoid driven by the PCM. The PCM, based on sensor inputs, determines when and how long the fuel injector(s) should operate. When an electric current is supplied to the injector, a spring loaded ball is lifted from it's seat. This allows fuel to flow through 6 spray orifices and deflects off the sharp edge of the injector nozzle. This action causes the fuel to form a 45 degree cone shaped spray pattern before entering the air stream in the throttle body.

Fuel is supplied to the injector constantly at a regulated pressure (about 14.5 psi on throttle body injected engines

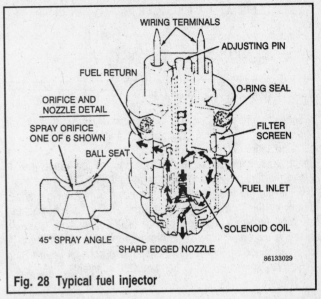

Fig. 28 Typical fuel injector

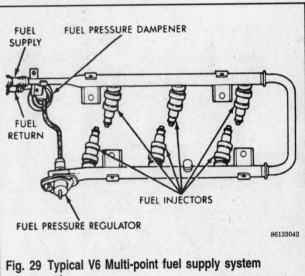

Fig. 29 Typical V6 Multi-point fuel supply system components

Fig. 30 View of the fuel injectors used in Throttle body fuel injection — Chevrolet with 4.3L TBI engine shown

higher on MPI systems) the unused fuel is returned to the fuel tank.

FUEL PRESSURE REGULATOR

▶ **See Figures 31, 32, 33 and 34**

The pressure regulator is a mechanical device located downstream of the fuel injector. Its function is to maintain a constant pressure across the fuel injector tip. The regulator uses a spring loaded rubber diaphragm to uncover a fuel return port. When the fuel pump becomes operational, fuel flows past the injector into the regulator, and is restricted from flowing any further by the blocked return port. When fuel pressure reaches the predetermined setting, it pushes on the diaphragm, compressing the spring, and uncovers the fuel return port. The diaphragm and spring will constantly move from an open to closed position to keep the fuel pressure constant.

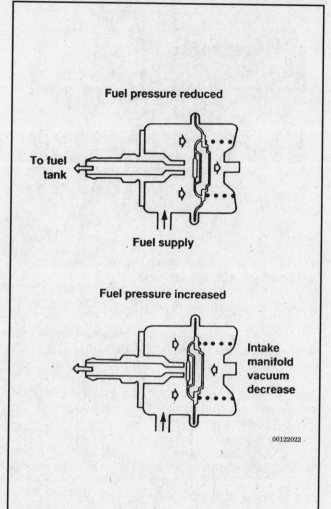

Fuel pressure reduced

To fuel tank

Fuel supply

Fuel pressure increased

Intake manifold vacuum decrease

00122022

Fig. 33 The Differential Pressure Regulator varies the fuel flow back to the fuel tank in response to manifold vacuum. The lower the vacuum, the less fuel flows back to the fuel tank, increasing the injection pressure

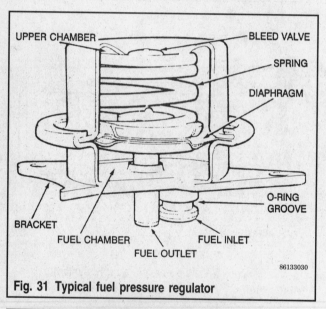

UPPER CHAMBER
BLEED VALVE
SPRING
DIAPHRAGM
O-RING GROOVE
BRACKET
FUEL CHAMBER
FUEL OUTLET
FUEL INLET

86133030

Fig. 31 Typical fuel pressure regulator

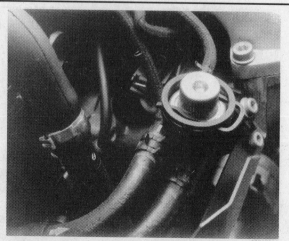

88515008

Fig. 32 Fuel pressure regulator used in a Saturn with 1.9L MFI engine shown

88515031

Fig. 34 Location of the fuel pressure regulator on a Chevrolet 4.3L TBI engine

IDLE AIR CONTROL (IAC)

▶ **See Figures 35 and 36**

The purpose of the Idle Air Control (IAC) or Electronic Air Control Valve system is to control engine idle speed while preventing stalls due to changes in engine load. Fuel injected engines use the IAC assembly, mounted on the throttle body, to control bypass air around the throttle plate. By extending or retracting a conical valve, a controlled amount of air can move around the throttle plate. If rpm is too low, more air is diverted around the throttle plate to increase rpm.

During idle, the proper position of the IAC valve is calculated by the ECM based on battery voltage, coolant temperature, engine load, and engine rpm. If the rpm drops below a specified rate, the throttle plate is closed. The ECM will then calculate a new valve position.

IDLE SPEED CONTROL (ISC)

▶ **See Figure 37**

The idle speed control or stepper motor does just what its name implies-it controls the idle. The ISC is used to maintain low engine speeds while at the same time preventing stalling due to engine load changes. The system consists of a motor assembly mounted on the carburetor which moves the throttle lever so as to open or close the throttle blades.

The whole operation is controlled by the ECM. The ECM monitors engine load to determine the proper idle speed. To prevent stalling, it monitors the air conditioning compressor switch, the transmission, the park/neutral switch and the ISC throttle switch. The ECM processes all this information and

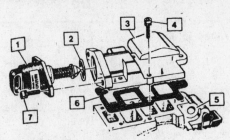

1. Idle air control (IAC) valve assembly
2. Idle air control valve O-ring
3. Idle air/vacuum signal housing assembly
4. Idle air/vacuum signal assembly screw
5. Throttle body assembly
6. Idle air/vacuum signal assembly gasket
7. Idle air control valve screw

85344064

Fig. 36 Some IAC valves are retained by screws, like the GM MFI system

88515032

Fig. 37 Idle speed on the Saturn is control by an IAC valve

then uses it to control the ISC motor which in turn will vary the idle speed as necessary.

IGNITION IGNITER

The more common name for an Igniter is an Ignition Control Module. This device is a small computer module that controls the firing of the igntion coil or coils. Although part of the ignition system, the igniter is triggered by a signal from the PCM. The timing of the spark, including advance, is handled by the engine controller.

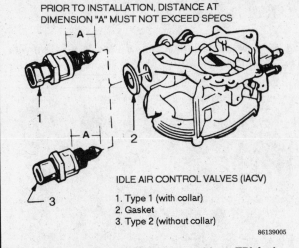

PRIOR TO INSTALLATION, DISTANCE AT DIMENSION "A" MUST NOT EXCEED SPECS

IDLE AIR CONTROL VALVES (IACV)

1. Type 1 (with collar)
2. Gasket
3. Type 2 (without collar)

86139005

Fig. 35 Typical idle air control assembly — TBI fuel injection

INTAKE AIR TEMPERATURE (TA) SENSOR

▶ **See Figures 38 and 39**

This device, also known as a Manifold Air Temperature Sensor (MAT) is a thermistor and is placed in the intake manifold. It acts much like the water temperature sensor but with a reduced thermal capacity for for quicker response. The injector duration determined by the PCM is altered for different operating conditions by the signals sent from this sensor.

KNOCK (DETONATION) SENSOR

▶ **See Figures 40 and 41**

This sensor is a piezoelectric sensor is usually located near the back of the engine. It generates electrical impulses which are directly proportional to the frequency of the knock which is detected. A buffer then sorts these signals and eliminates all

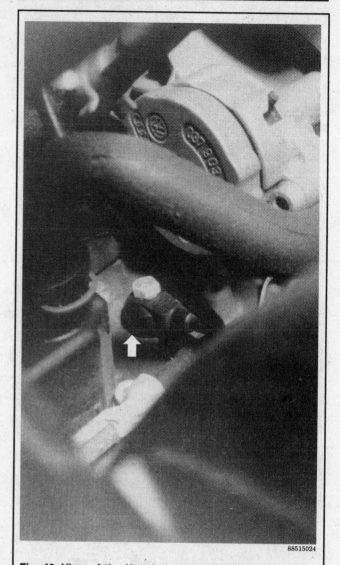

88515024

Fig. 40 View of the Knock sensor used in a Saturn with 1.9L MFI engine shown

88515003

Fig. 38 Intake Air Temperature (IAT) sensor used in a Saturn with 1.9L MFI engine shown

88515020

Fig. 39 Intake Air Temperature (IAT) sensor used in a Volkswagen with Motronic fuel injection shown

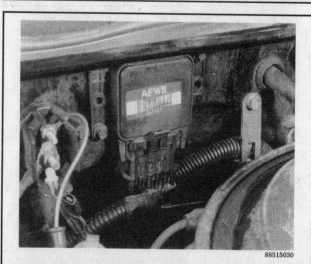

88515030

Fig. 41 Many manufacturers have a control module that is used for spark timing to control knock

except for those frequency range of detonation. This information is passed the PCM, so that the ignition timing advance can be retarded until the detonation stops.

MAIN RELAY

▶ See Figure 42

Although part of the main relay is energized by the ignition switch, the PCM controls ground to another part of the relay. When the PCM receives information that the the ignition switch is **ON** and a either a cranking or engine rpm signal is present, the PCM closes the relay circuit for the fuel pump system.

MANIFOLD ABSOLUTE PRESSURE (MAP) SENSOR

▶ See Figures 43, 44 and 45

The Manifold Absolute Pressure (MAP) sensor or Atmospheric Pressure Sensor, measures the changes in the intake manifold pressure which result from engine load and speed changes. The pressure measured by the MAP sensor is the difference between barometric pressure (outside air) and manifold pressure (vacuum). A closed throttle engine coastdown would produce a relatively low MAP value (approximately 20-35 kPa), while wide-open throttle would produce a high value (100 kPa). This high value is produced when the pressure inside the manifold is the same as outside the manifold, and 100% of outside air (or 100 kPa) is being measured. This MAP output is the opposite of what you would measure on a vacuum gauge. The use of this sensor also allows the PCM to adjust automatically for different altitude.

There are 2 basic types of MAP sensors. The major difference between the two is the Piezoresitive (PRT) design (used on most vehicles except Ford) provides a dc voltage proportional to pressure. The Silicon Capacitive Absolute Pressure (SCAP) design provides a variable frequency. The PCM sends a 5 volt reference signal to the MAP sensor. As the MAP changes, the electrical resistance or frequency of the sensor

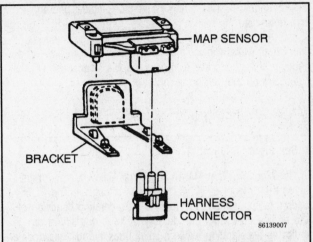

Fig. 43 The vacuum solenoid shown here has the Manifold Absolute Pressure (MAP) sensor mounted behind the bracket

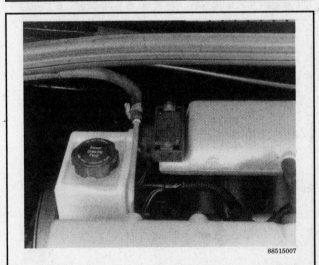

Fig. 44 Manifold Absolute Pressure (MAP) sensor used in a Saturn with 1.9L MFI engine shown

Fig. 42 Main relay is usually located in the main relay box or on a fenderwell

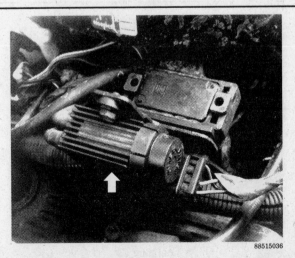

Fig. 45 MAP sensors are usually located on the firewall, or on or near the air cleaner

also changes. By monitoring the sensor output signal the PCM can determine the manifold pressure. On a typical PRT design, the higher pressure, lower vacuum (high voltage) requires more fuel, while a lower pressure, higher vacuum (low voltage) requires less fuel. The PCM uses the MAP sensor to control fuel delivery and ignition timing.

MASS AIR FLOW (MAF) SENSOR

▶ **See Figures 46 and 47**

The Mass Air Flow (MAF) sensor or Airflow Meter, measures the amount of air which passes through it. The PCM uses this information to determine the operating condition of the engine, to control fuel delivery. A large quantity of air indicates acceleration, while a small quantity indicates deceleration or idle. Many General Motors and European type MAF sensors function on a hot wire principle. A wire is heated to a certain temperature. The amount of voltage necessary to keep the wire at that temperature with air flowing over it is used to

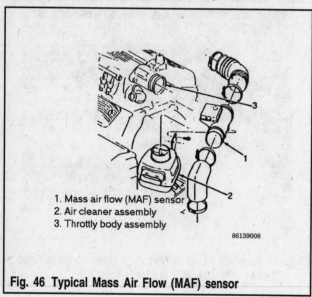

1. Mass air flow (MAF) sensor
2. Air cleaner assembly
3. Throttly body assembly

86139008

Fig. 46 Typical Mass Air Flow (MAF) sensor

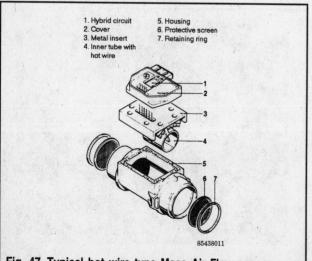

1. Hybrid circuit
2. Cover
3. Metal insert
4. Inner tube with hot wire
5. Housing
6. Protective screen
7. Retaining ring

85438011

Fig. 47 Typical hot wire type Mass Air Flow sensor components

calculate airflow. Some import manufacturers use a mechanical door system where a door is pushed by the incoming air. The wider the door is open, the larger the amount of air flow.

OIL PRESSURE SWITCH

The oil pressure switch is usually mounted on the back of the engine, just below the intake manifold. Some vehicles use the oil pressure switch as a parallel power supply, with the fuel pump relay and will provide voltage to the fuel pump, after approximately 4 psi (28 kPa) of oil pressure is reached. This switch will also help prevent engine seizure by shutting off the power to the fuel pump and causing the engine to stop when the oil pressure is lower than 4 psi.

OXYGEN SENSOR

▶ **See Figures 48, 49, 50 and 51**

The exhaust oxygen sensor is mounted in the exhaust system where it can monitor the oxygen content of the exhaust gas stream. The oxygen content in the exhaust reacts with the oxygen sensor to produce a voltage output. This voltage ranges from approximately 100 millivolts (high oxygen — lean mixture) to 900 millivolts (low oxygen — rich mixture).

By monitoring the voltage output of the oxygen sensor, the PCM will determine what fuel mixture command to give to the injector (lean mixture — low voltage — rich command, rich mixture — high voltage — lean command).

Remember that oxygen sensor indicates to the PCM what is happening in the exhaust. It does not cause things to happen. It is a type of gauge: high oxygen content = lean mixture; low oxygen content = rich mixture. The PCM adjust fuel to keep the system working.

The oxygen sensor, if open will store a DTC (Diagnostic Trouble Code). A constant low voltage in the sensor circuit should set a code as well as a constant high voltage in the circuit. DTC will also be set as a result of fuel system problems, like a leaking injector.

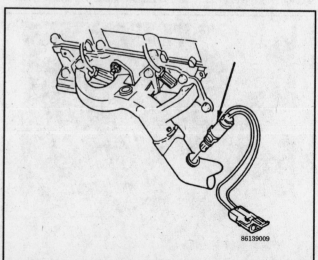

86139009

Fig. 48 The oxygen sensor is mounted in the exhaust manifold

Fig. 49 The Oxygen sensor on this Saturn 1.9L MFI engine is difficult to locate

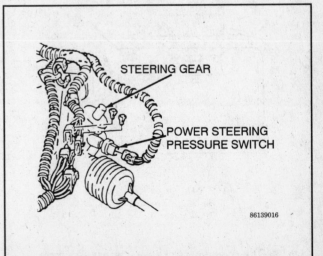

Fig. 51 Removing the Oxygen Sensor from the exhaust manifold

PARK/NEUTRAL SWITCH

This switch indicates to the PCM when the transmission is in **P** or **N**. the information is used by the PCM for control on the torque converter clutch, EGR, and the idle air control valve operation.

➡**Vehicle should not be driven with the park/neutral switch disconnected as idle quality may be affected in park or neutral and a DTC for the VSS may be set.**

POWER STEERING PRESSURE SWITCH

▶ **See Figure 52**

The power steering pressure switch is used so that the power steering oil pressure pump load will not effect the engine idle. Turning the steering wheel increase the power steering oil pressure and pump load on the engine. The power steering pressure switch will close before the load can cause

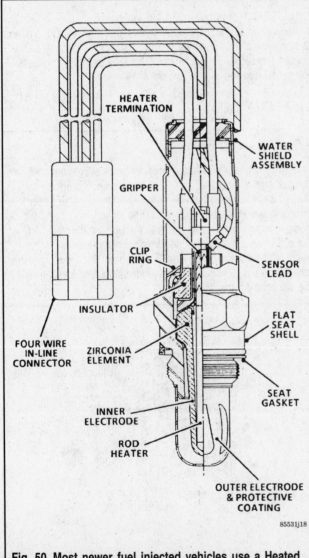

HEATER TERMINATION

WATER SHIELD ASSEMBLY

GRIPPER

CLIP RING

SENSOR LEAD

INSULATOR

FOUR WIRE IN-LINE CONNECTOR

ZIRCONIA ELEMENT

FLAT SEAT SHELL

SEAT GASKET

INNER ELECTRODE

ROD HEATER

OUTER ELECTRODE & PROTECTIVE COATING

Fig. 50 Most newer fuel injected vehicles use a Heated Oxygen for quick feedback response

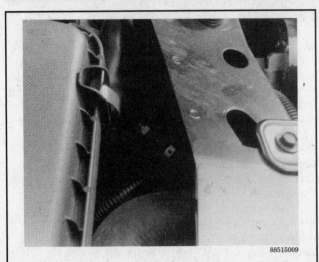

STEERING GEAR

POWER STEERING PRESSURE SWITCH

Fig. 52 Typical power steering pressure switch at the pump or supply pressure hose

an idle problem. The PCM will also turn the A/C clutch off when high power steering pressure is detected.

PRESSURE REGULATOR CUT-OFF SOLENOID VALVE

Primarily used on Asian vehicles, this valve is activated by the PCM during hot restarts if the intake air and/or coolant temperature are above preset limits. When energized, the valve cuts off vacuum to the fuel pressure regulator for 60-80 seconds, allowing the pressure to build within the fuel rail. This reduces the occurrence of fuel boiling and improves hot-restart characteristics.

PROM

▶ **See Figure 53**

The PCM consists of 3 parts; a Controller (the PCM without a PROM), a Calibrator called a PROM (Programmable Read Only Memory) and/or a Cal-Pak. The PROM is used on General Motors fuel systems. Other manufacturers use a computer chip like the PROM, but most are not replaceable like the General Motors PROM.

To allow 1 model of the PCM to be used for many different vehicles, a computer chip called a Calibrator (or PROM) is used. The PROM is located inside the PCM and has information on the vehicle's weight, engine, transmission, axle ratio and other components.

While one PCM part number can be used by many different vehicles, a PROM is very specific and must be used for the right vehicle. A replacement PCM comes without a PROM. The PROM from the old PCM must be carefully removed and installed in the new PCM.

SECONDARY THROTTLE SENSOR

The secondary throttle sensor is used on vehicles with traction control. It responds to the movement of the throttle motor, which is controlled by the Traction Control Module (TCM). This sensor is a type of potentiometer that transforms the secondary valve position into output voltage, and emits the voltage signal to the TCM. In addition, the sensor detects the opening and closing speed and position of the secondary throttle valve and feeds the voltage signal to the TCM.

When the secondary throttle valve opening becomes smaller than the ordinary throttle valve opening due to TCS operation, then, and only then, the signal from the secondary throttle valve is used for engine control in place of the signal from the ordinary throttle sensor. The signal of the secondary throttle valve first enters the TCM, from where it is sent to the PCM.

STARTER SIGNAL

The **START** position on the ignition switch causes a signal to be sent to the PCM. During cranking, the PCM will increase the amount of fuel injected into the manifold according to the engine temperature. The amount of fuel injected is gradually reduced when the starter switch is released.

THROTTLE BODY

▶ **See Figures 54, 55 and 56**

The TBI throttle body assembly replaces a conventional carburetor and is mounted on top of the intake manifold. The throttle body houses the fuel injector(s), pressure regulator, throttle position sensor, automatic idle speed motor and throttle body temperature sensor. Air flow through the throttle body is controlled by a cable operated throttle blade located in the base of the throttle body. The throttle body itself provides the chamber for metering atomizing and distributing fuel throughout the air entering the engine.

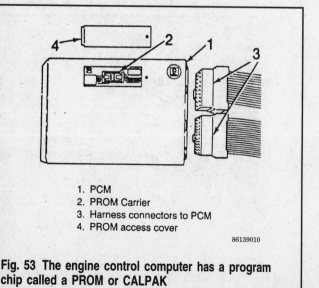

1. PCM
2. PROM Carrier
3. Harness connectors to PCM
4. PROM access cover

86139010

Fig. 53 The engine control computer has a program chip called a PROM or CALPAK

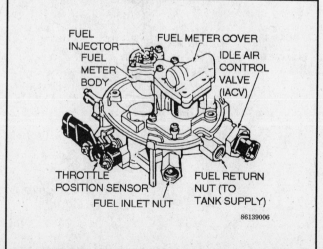

86139006

Fig. 54 Throttle body mounted components — typical TBI fuel system shown

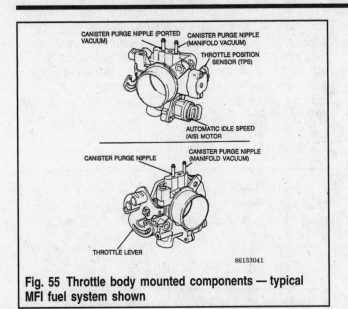

Fig. 55 Throttle body mounted components — typical MFI fuel system shown

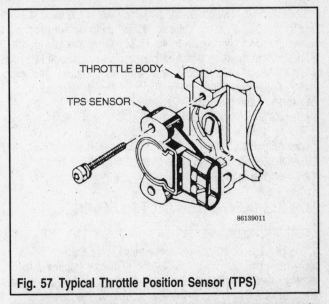

Fig. 57 Typical Throttle Position Sensor (TPS)

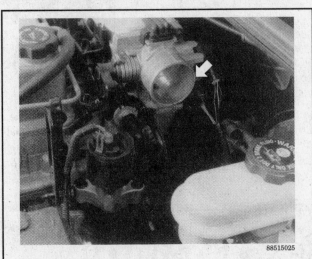

Fig. 56 View of the Throttle body used in a Saturn with 1.9L MFI engine

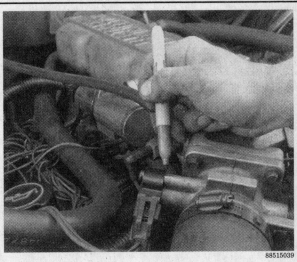

Fig. 58 Marking the position of the TPS Sensor

The MFI throttle body assembly is used primarily as an air metering device and is usually mounted at the front of the intake manifold. It houses several vacuum ports, the throttle position sensor, automatic idle speed control or idle air control valve. On some units, an air flow sensing device is placed inside the throttle body to relay either air flow or air density information to the PCM. Air flow through the throttle body is controlled by a cable operated throttle blade located in the base of the throttle body.

THROTTLE POSITION SENSOR (TPS)

▶ **See Figures 57 and 58**

The Throttle Position Sensor (TPS) may also be called a Throttle Angle Valve, Throttle Potentiometer or a Throttle Valve Switch. It is connected to the throttle shaft and is controlled by the throttle mechanism. A 5 volt reference signal is sent to the TPS from the PCM. As the throttle valve angle is changed

(accelerator pedal moved), the resistance of the TPS also changes. At a closed throttle position, the resistance of the TPS is high, so the output voltage to the PCM will be low (approximately 0.5 volt). As the throttle plate opens, the resistance decreases so that, at wide open throttle, the output voltage should be approximately 5 volts. At closed throttle position, the voltage at the TPS should be less than 1.25 volts.

By monitoring the output voltage from the TPS, the PCM can determine fuel delivery based on throttle valve angle (driver demand). The TPS can either be misadjusted, shorted, open or loose. Misadjustment might result in poor idle or poor wide-open throttle performance. An open TPS signals the PCM that the throttle is always closed, resulting in poor performance. This usually sets a code. A shorted TPS gives the PCM a constant wide-open throttle signal will store a code. A loose TPS indicates to the PCM that the throttle is moving. This causes intermittent bursts of fuel from the injector and an unstable idle. Once the fault code is set, the PCM will use an artificial default value and some vehicle performance will return.

Idle/Full throttle switches are contained within the throttle position sensor on some vehicles. These switches are used to provide specific information to the PCM. When the idle switch is closed, the throttle plates are closed. The switch opens when the throttle plates open approximately 1 degree. The idle switch signal determines the operation of the stabilize valve, deceleration fuel shut-off and operation of a ignition timing map.

The full throttle switch closes at approximately 10 degrees before full throttle. The full throttle switch signal determines the full throttle enrichment and operation of a ignition timing map for full engine load.

TORQUE CONVERTER CLUTCH SOLENOID

The purpose of the torque converter clutch system is designed to eliminate power loss by the converter (slippage) to increase fuel economy. By locking the converter clutch, a more effective coupling to the flywheel is achieved. The converter clutch is operated by the PCM controlled torque converter clutch solenoid.

TRACTION CONTROL SYSTEM (TCS)

The TCS operates to reduce wheel spin during periods of limited traction. The TCS control unit exchanges signals with the engine PCM. When traction control is required, the TCS controller partially closes the throttle plate through the throttle actuator stepper motor. The stepper motor moves the throttle plate into a less open position, reducing engine power. Note that this closing of the throttle plate occurs regardless of the accelerator position; even with the accelerator calling for wide-open throttle the stepper motor will partially close the throttle is sensors indicate wheelspin is present.

TURBOCHARGER CONTROL UNIT

This control unit is used on turbocharged engines only. The turbocharger control unit, controls the operation of the turbocharger system. It usually interfaces with the PCM and other control modules.

VEHICLE SPEED SENSOR (VSS)

▶ **See Figure 59**

The vehicle speed sensor (VSS) is mounted behind the speedometer in the instrument cluster or on the transmission/speedometer drive gear. It provides electrical pulses to the PCM from the speedometer head. The pulses indicate the road speed. The PCM uses this information to operate the IAC, canister purge and TCC.

➡**A vehicle equipped with a speed sensor, should not be driven without a the speed sensor connected, as idle quality may be affected.**

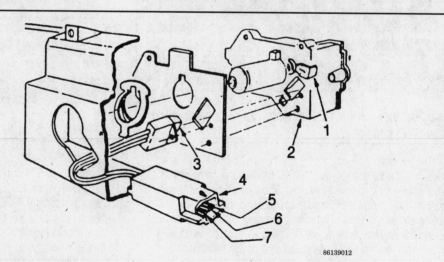

1. Reflector plate
2. Speedometer frame
3. VSS and photo cell
4. Buffer circuit
5. Supplied voltage
6. Ground
7. VSS Output

86139012

Fig. 59 Typical instrument panel mounted Vehicle Speed Sensor (VSS). Many newer models use a sensor in the transaxle.

CARBURETOR SYSTEMS

The Electronic Feedback Carburetor (EFC) system incorporates an oxygen sensor, a 3-way catalytic converter, a feedback carburetor, a solenoid-operated regulator valve, and a combustion computer incorporating Electronic Spark Control.

The feedback carburetor computer is the information processing component of the system, monitoring oxygen sensor voltage (low voltage/lean mixture, high voltage/rich mixture), engine coolant temperature, manifold vacuum, engine speed, and engine operating mode (starting or running). The computer examines the incoming information and then sends a signal to the solenoid-operated regulator which then sends the proper rich or lean signal to the carburetor.

Feedback Carburetor Operations

ELECTRONIC FEEDBACK CONTROL (EFC) SYSTEM

The EFC system is essentially an emissions control system which utilizes an electronic signal, generated by an exhaust gas oxygen sensor to precisely control the air/fuel mixture ratio in the carburetor. This, in turn, allows the engine to produce exhaust gases of the proper composition, permitting the use of a 3-way catalyst. The 3-way catalyst is designed to convert the 3 pollutants (1) hydrocarbons (HC), (2) carbon monoxide (CO), and (3) oxides of Nitrogen (NOx) into harmless substances.

There are 2 operating modes in the EFC system:

1. Open Loop — air/fuel ratio is controlled by information programmed into the computer at manufacture.

2. Closed Loop — air/fuel ratio is varied by the computer based on information supplied by the oxygen sensor.

When the engine is cold, the system will be operating in the open loop mode. During that time, the air/fuel ratio will be fixed at a richer level. This will allow proper engine warm up and driveability. Also, during this period, air injection (from the air injection pump) will be injected upstream in the exhaust manifold.

Both closed loop and open loop operation are possible in the EFC system. Open loop operation occurs under any one of the following conditions: coolant temperature under 150°F, oxygen sensor temperature under 660°F, low manifold vacuum (less than 4.5 in. Hg engine cold, or less than 3.0 in. Hg engine hot), oxygen sensor failure, or hot engine starting. Closed loop operation begins when engine temperature reaches 150°F.

Carburetor Systems

▶ **See Figures 60 and 61**

Principal sub-assemblies on most carburetor models include a bowl cover, carburetor body and throttle body. A thick gasket between the throttle body and main body retards heat transfer to the fuel to resist fuel percolation in warm weather. To correctly identify the carburetor model, always check the part number stamped on the main body or attached tag. The carburetor includes four basic fuel metering systems. The idle system provides a mixture for smooth idle and a transfer sys-

Fig. 60 Typical 4 barrel carburetor GM engine

Fig. 61 Typical feedback carburetor shown being removed from the engine

tem for low speed operation. The main metering system provides an economical mixture for normal cruising conditions and a fuel regulator solenoid responsive to the oxygen sensor. The accelerator system provides additional fuel during acceleration. The power enrichment system provides a richer mixture when high power output is desired.

In addition to these 4 basic systems, there is a fuel inlet system that constantly supplies the fuel to the basic metering systems. A choke system temporarily enriches the mixture to aid in starting and running a cold engine.

FUEL INLET SYSTEM

▶ **See Figure 62**

All fuel enters the fuel bowl through the fuel inlet fitting in the carburetor body. The fuel inlet needle seats directly in the fuel inlet fitting. The needle is retained by a cap that permits the fuel to flow out holes in the side of the cap. The design of

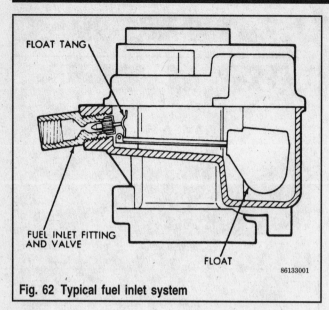

Fig. 62 Typical fuel inlet system

the fuel bowl eliminates the necessity of a fuel baffle. The fuel inlet needle is controlled by a special float (a closed-cell buoyant material which cannot collapse or leak) and a stainless steel float lever which is hinged by a stainless steel float shaft.

The fuel inlet system must constantly maintain the specified level of fuel as the basic fuel metering systems are calibrated to deliver the proper mixture only when the fuel is at this level. When the fuel level in the bowl drops, the float also drops permitting additional fuel to flow past the fuel inlet needle into the bowl. All carburetors with external bowl vents are vented to the vapor canister.

FLOAT CIRCUIT
▶ See Figure 63

The purpose of the float circuit is to maintain an adequate supply of liquid fuel at the proper, predetermined level in the bowl for use by the idle, acceleration pump, power and main metering circuits. One or 2 separate float circuits may be used, each circuit containing a float assembly and needle and seat. All circuits are supplied with fuel from the fuel bowl.

IDLE SYSTEM
▶ See Figure 64

Fuel used during curb idle and low-speed operation flows through the main metering jet into the main well. An angular connecting idle well intersects the main well. An idle tube is installed in the idle well. Fuel travels up the idle well and mixes with air which enters through the idle air bleed located in the bowl cover. At curb idle the fuel and air mixture flows down the idle channel and is further mixed or broken up by air entering the idle channel through the transfer slot above the throttle plate. The idle system is equipped with a restrictor in the idle channel, located between the transfer slot and the idle port, which limits the maximum attainable idle mixture. During low speed operation the throttle plate moves exposing the transfer slot and fuel begins to flow through the transfer slot as well as the idle port. As the throttle plates are opened further and engine speed increases, the air flow through the carburetor also increases. This increased air flow creates a vacuum in the venturi and the main metering system begins to discharge fuel.

MAIN METERING SYSTEM
▶ See Figure 65

As the throttle valves continue opening, the air flow through the carburetor increases and creates a low pressure area in the venturi. This low pressure causes fuel to flow from the fuel bowl through the main jets and into the main wells. In addition to the main jet, fuel also enters the main well through a parallel circuit. Fuel flow in this circuit is regulated by the O_2 feedback solenoid. Air from the main air bleed mixes with the fuel through holes in the sides of main well tube. The mixture is then drawn from the main well tube and discharged through the venturi nozzle. By controlling the amount of fuel released, the solenoid regulates the total air/fuel mixture. The solenoid acts in direct response to the engine demand. As air flow through the carburetor increases, the amount of air/fuel mixture discharged also increases and the idle system tapers off.

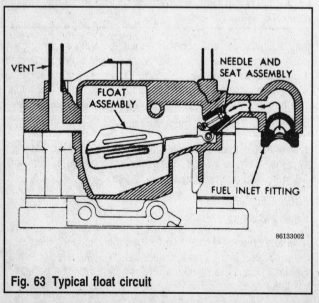

Fig. 63 Typical float circuit

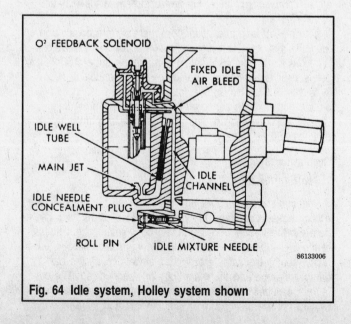

Fig. 64 Idle system, Holley system shown

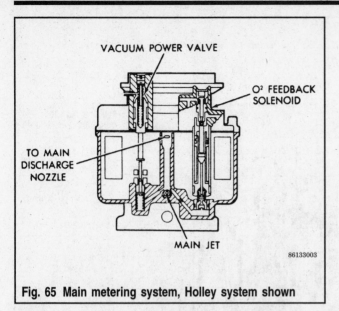

Fig. 65 Main metering system, Holley system shown

POWER ENRICHMENT SYSTEM (MODULATED POWER VALVE)

▶ **See Figure 66**

During high speed (or low manifold vacuum) the carburetor must provide a richer mixture than is needed when the engine is running at cruising speed. Added fuel for power operation is supplied by a vacuum modulated power enrichment system. A vacuum passage in the throttle body transmits manifold vacuum to the vacuum piston chamber in the bowl cover.

Under light throttle and light load conditions, there is sufficient vacuum acting on the vacuum piston to overcome the piston spring tension. When the throttle valves are opened more, vacuum that is acting on the piston is bled to atmosphere and manifold vacuum is closed off, insuring proper mixture for this throttle opening. The vent port is right in line with the throttle shaft, which has a small hole drilled through it. When the throttle valve is opened sufficiently, the hole in the throttle shaft will line up with the port in the base of the carburetor, venting the piston vacuum chamber to atmosphere and allowing the spring loaded piston to open the power valve. As engine power demands are reduced, and the throttle valve begins to close, manifold vacuum increases. The increased vacuum acts on the vacuum piston, overcoming the tension of the piston spring. This closes the power valve and shuts off the added supply of fuel which is no longer required.

ACCELERATING PUMP SYSTEM

▶ **See Figure 67**

When the throttle plates are opened suddenly, the air flow through the carburetor responds almost immediately. However, there is a brief time interval or lag before the additional fuel can move into the system and maintain the desired air/fuel ratio. The accelerating pump provides a measured amount of fuel necessary to insure smooth engine operation upon acceleration at lower vehicle speeds.

When the throttle is closed, the pump plunger moves upward in the pump cylinder and fuel is drawn into the pump cylinder through the intake check, located at the bottom of the cylinder.

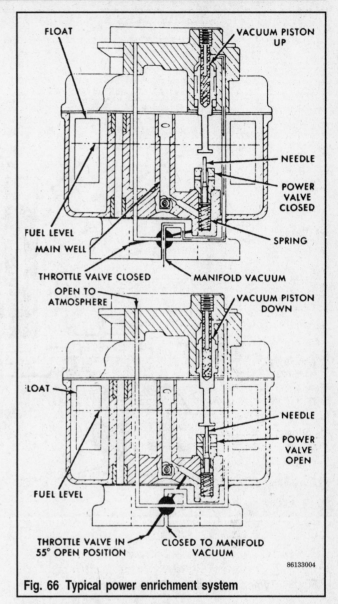

Fig. 66 Typical power enrichment system

The discharge check (needle) is seated at this time to prevent air from being drawn into the pump cylinder.

When the throttle is opened, the pump plunger moves downward closing the intake check and forcing fuel out through the discharge passage, past the check needle and out through the pump jets.

At higher speeds, pump discharge is no longer necessary to insure smooth acceleration. Therefore, in order to prevent unnecessary plunger movement, external pump linkage is so constructed that it travels 'over center' when the throttle is in the higher speeds positions, thus imparting just enough stroke to the plunger to keep all passages filled with liquid fuel.

A plastic tube is used to connect the outlet opening at the bottom of the pump cylinder with passage just below the discharge check. Make sure this tube is not damaged or collapsed when servicing the carburetor.

The spring in the pump cylinder, above the plunger is used to remove all free play from the pump operating linkage and insure an instant fuel discharge the moment the throttle valves are cracked.

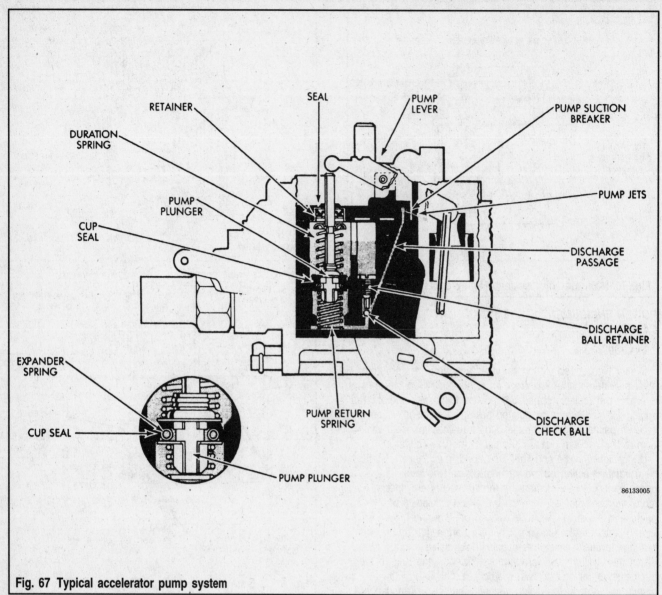

Fig. 67 Typical accelerator pump system

AUTOMATIC CHOKE SYSTEM

▶ See Figure 68

The automatic choke provides the richer air/fuel mixture required for starting and operating a cold engine. A bi-metal spring inside the choke housing pushes the choke valve toward the closed position. When the engine starts, manifold vacuum is applied to the choke diaphragm through a hose from the throttle body. This adjustment of the choke valve opening when the engine starts is called vacuum kick. Manifold vacuum alone is not strong enough to provide the proper degree of choke opening during the entire choking period. The force of air rushing past the partially open choke valve provides the additional opening force. As the engine warms up, manifold heat transmitted to the choke housing relaxes the bi-metal spring until it eventually permits the choke to open fully. An electric heater assists engine heat to open the choke rapidly in summer temperatures.

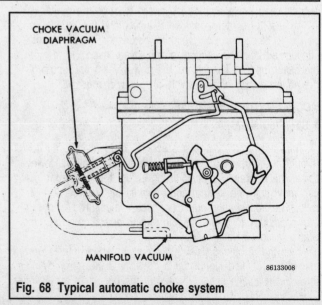

Fig. 68 Typical automatic choke system

IDLE SOLENOID

The solenoid is an electric, position-holding or adjusting solenoid. When the engine is running, the solenoid is extended to hold the throttle at curb idle, i.e. throttle valve(s) almost but not completely closed. When the engine is off, the solenoid retracts, allowing the throttle to close entirely, preventing afterrun (dieseling) by cutting off the air flow. Curb idle is adjusted with a screw on the solenoid. On some models the the stroke is fixed, but different calibrations may have different strokes. On other models models the Idle Speed Control solenoid is a motor that can move to any position in order to obtain the proper idle condition. The solenoid receives its electrical signal from the spark control or engine computer.

LOW SPEED CIRCUIT

▶ See Figure 69

Fuel for idle and early part throttle operation is metered through the low-speed circuit which is located on the primary side only.

Liquid gasoline enters the idle wells through the main metering jets. Each low-speed jet has a calibrated orifice at its lower tip which measures the amount of fuel for idle and early part throttle operation. The air bypass passages, and idle air bleeds are carefully calibrated and serve to break up the liquid fuel, mixing it with air as it moves through the passages to the idle ports and idle adjustment screw ports. Turning the idle mixture screws toward their seats reduces the quantity of fuel mixture supplied by the idle circuit.

The idle system is equipped with a restrictor in the idle channel, located between the transfer slot and the idle port, which limits the maximum attainable idle mixture

HIGH SPEED CIRCUIT

▶ See Figure 70

Fuel for part throttle and full throttle engine operation is supplied through the high-speed circuit, which is divided into the primary high-speed circuit and secondary high-speed circuit. These 2 circuit functions are described separately.

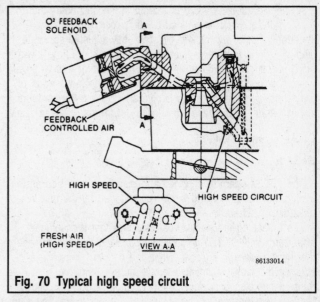

Fig. 70 Typical high speed circuit

Primary Side

In the primary metering section, the 2 metering rods are yoked to a single step-up piston which rides in a cylinder within the bowl cover casting. The primary jets which work with the metering rods are located in the fuel bowl.

In the low and medium-speed range, the cam and lever lift the step-up piston and metering rods in proportion to the primary throttle valve opening. This action provides positive mixture control. The length of the step-up piston rod is factory-adjusted with equipment not available in service. Tampering with the setting will upset performance and emission control.

Secondary Side

▶ See Figure 71

Liquid fuel for the high-speed circuit in the secondary portion of the carburetor is metered at the secondary metering jets. The main bleed tubes in the secondary side with their calibrated perforations and air bleeds, function to provide calibrated air-fuel mixtures in response to engine demands.

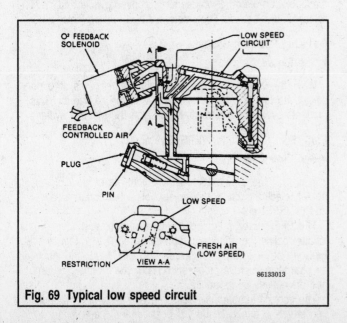

Fig. 69 Typical low speed circuit

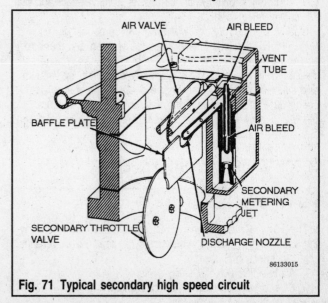

Fig. 71 Typical secondary high speed circuit

A spring-loaded air valve is located in the secondary side of the carburetor which is opened by air velocity through the secondary bores and closed by accurately-adjusted spring tension. A unique feature of this air valve is its shape; the lower edge of the valve is contoured in such a manner that when air velocity through the carburetor is high, and the lower edge of the air valve approaches the secondary nozzles, the contours act as venturi to increase air velocity at the tips of the nozzles.

Choke Opener System

FAST IDLE UNLOADER

The fast idle cam is engaged and disengaged by depressing the accelerator pedal and is also disengaged by the fast idle unloading mechanism.

The unloading mechanism consists of a fast idle unloader and thermovalves. The unloader has 2 diaphragms to release the throttle valve is 2 steps. When the coolant temperature reaches the first thermovalve temperature setting, the thermovalve closes to shut off the vacuum bleed. This allows the inside diaphragm of the unloader to retract to the first step by manifold vacuum. Then, as the coolant temperature further rises and reaches the second thermovalve temperature setting, the second thermovalve closes and manifold vacuum is applied onto the outside diaphragm of the unloader. This allows the unloader to operate on the second step.

CHOKE OPENER

This system is designed to promote easy starting. When starting the engine, manifold vacuum is transmitted to the choke opener; thus, the choke valve is opened a fixed amount.

The first thermovalve works to open the choke valve in response to engine coolant temperature. When the engine coolant temperature is below the set temperature of the thermovalve, it opens and manifold vacuum is bled from the valve. In this situation the choke opener diaphragm is retracted to an intermediate position because of the balance between the vacuum and the spring force of the choke opener.

When the engine coolant temperature exceeds the set temperature of the thermovalve, it closes to shut off the vacuum bleed and this allows the choke opener to fully retract and pull the choke valve open.

On Prelude carburetors, when the engine coolant is below 60°F (15°C), the thermovalve operates to open and manifold vacuum is bled from the choke opener. The choke opener diaphragm is retracted to an intermediate position by vacuum and spring force. When the engine coolant temperature exceeds 60°F (15°C), the thermovalve shuts off the vacuum bleed and allows the choke opener to retract fully and pull the choke valve open.

FEEDBACK (FBC) SYSTEM OPERATION

▶ **See Figure 72**

The Feedback Carburetor (FBC) System includes the following sub-systems. Not all sub-systems are used on all vehicles.
- Air Induction System
- Air Injection Reactor (AIR) System
- Closed Loop Emission Control System
- Coasting Fuel Cut System
- Early Fuel Evaporation System (EFE)
- Evaporative Emission Control System
- Exhaust Gas Recirculation (EGR) System
- High Altitude Emission Control System
- Mixture Control Valve System
- Positive Crankcase Ventilation (PCV) System
- Thermostatically Controlled Air Cleaner System (TCA)
- 3-Way Catalytic Converter System

Air Induction System

▶ **See Figure 73**

This system reduces HC and CO emissions by admitting filtered air through the air induction valves into the exhaust manifold to cool the exhaust gas stream before the gases enter the catalytic converter.

In warm conditions, after the engine is started, the system introduces air into the exhaust manifold for 3 seconds then cuts it off. In cold starts with an engine idle speed greater than 4000 rpm, induction is always cut off.

While the engine is running at normal operating temperature, the air induction system admits cooling air according to rpm, water temperature and throttle position.

Air Injection Reactor (AIR) System

▶ **See Figures 74, 75 and 76**

In order to reduce HC and CO emissions, this system draws air into the exhaust ports to speed up oxidation. The air management valve switches air passage from the air pump through a vacuum management valve which is actuated by an electric signal supplied from the ECM.

Closed Loop Emission Control (CFC) System

The closed loop emission control system precisely controls the air/fuel ratio near the optimum mixture and allows the use of the 3-way catalyst to reduce the oxides of nitrogen and oxidize hydrocarbons and carbon monoxide. The essential components of the closed loop system are the coolant temperature sensor, oxygen sensor, electronic control module (ECM), feedback carburetor, 3-way catalytic converter, idle and WOT switches, MAP sensor, duty solenoid and fuel cut solenoid.

Coasting Fuel Cut System

▶ **See Figure 77**

While the vehicle is decelerating, this system cuts off a portion of the fuel flow in the slow circuit of the carburetor. This prevents overheating and afterburning in the exhaust system.

Early Fuel Evaporation (EFE) System

▶ **See Figure 78**

The early fuel evaporation system consists of the EFE heater, electronic control module, coolant temperature sensor and the EFE relay.

The EFE heater is equipped with a ceramic ring which is located below the primary carburetor bore. The ring is an integral part of the carburetor gasket. The EFE heats the incoming air charge to improve atomization. This offers better cold start and drive-away performance.

The coolant temperature sensor is activated when the ignition switch is turned to the **ON** position and the engine is

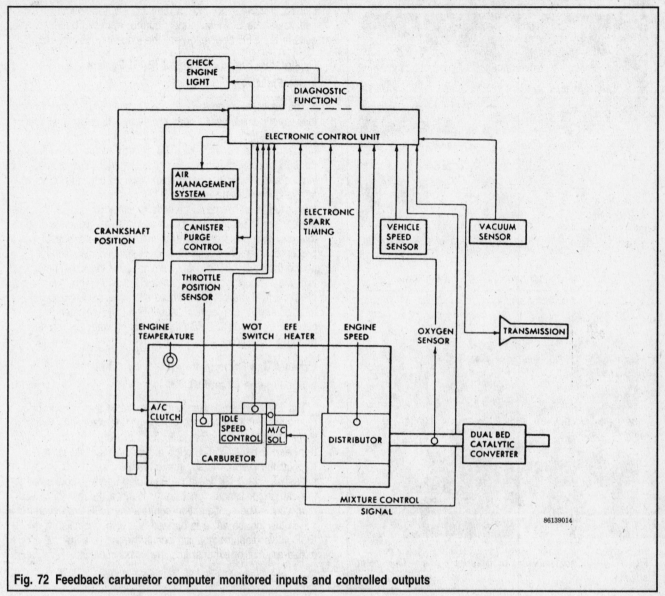

Fig. 72 Feedback carburetor computer monitored inputs and controlled outputs

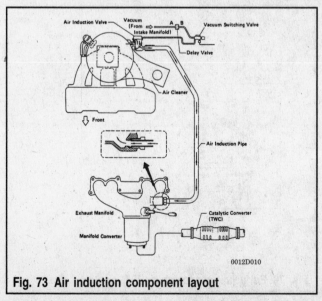

Fig. 73 Air induction component layout

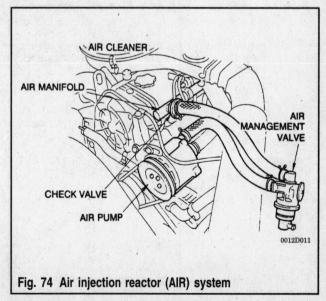

Fig. 74 Air injection reactor (AIR) system

Fig. 75 Air management valve — Chevrolet shown

Fig. 76 Anti-backfire valve or Diverter valve — Chevrolet shown

started. If the engine coolant temperature is below the specified value, the ECM will supply current from the battery to the coils in the EFE heater to heat the incoming fuel/air charge.

Evaporative Emission Control (ECS) System
▶ See Figure 79

The evaporative emission control system is designed to trap fuel vapors which would normally escape from the fuel tank and carburetor. This serves to limit the amount of fuel vapor released to the atmosphere. The system accomplishes the task through the use of a fuel vapor canister that absorbs fuel vapors and stores them until such time as they are removed and re-burned in the engine.

The fuel vapor removal process is accomplished by the carburetor and a solenoid operated bowl vent. The non-vented fuel cap also plays a role in the vapor removal process. The domed fuel tank has a vent which is located high enough above the fuel level to allow the vent pipe to be in contact with the vapor stream at all times. The single vent pipe has a direct path to the canister, where the excess fuel vapor is trapped and stored for future use. From the canister, the vapors are routed to the PCV system where they are burned during combustion.

Exhaust Gas Recirculation (EGR) System
▶ See Figures 80 and 81

The EGR system lowers temperatures in the combustion chamber in order to reduce nitrogen oxide emissions in the exhaust gas stream. Exhaust gases are drawn from the cylinder head exhaust port through the intake manifold riser through the cylinder head, intake manifold and EGR valve passages. The EGR valve vacuum diaphragm is connected to the carburetor flange signal port through a thermal valve vacuum valve. The configuration controls the EGR cold override. When the throttle valve is opened, vacuum is applied to the EGR valve diaphragm which opens the valve, admitting a controlled amount of exhaust into the intake manifold.

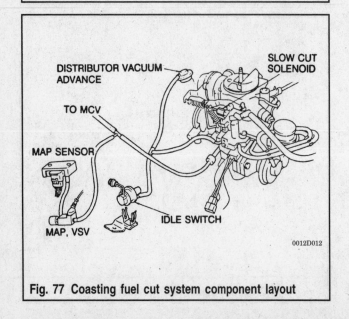

Fig. 77 Coasting fuel cut system component layout

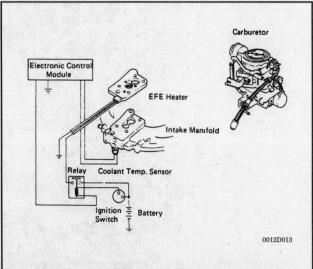

Fig. 78 Early fuel evaporation (EFE) system schematic

Fig. 79 Typical Evaporative Canister

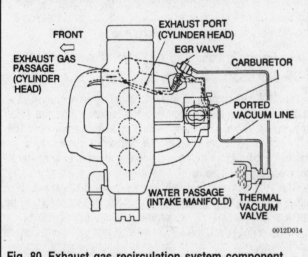

Fig. 80 Exhaust gas recirculation system component layout

Fig. 81 Typical EGR valve without a position sensor — Typical V8 GM engine shown

High Altitude Emission Control System

♦ **See Figures 82 and 83**

To avoid an excessively rich carburetor mixture at high altitudes due to decreased air density, the system functions to supply additional air through the carburetor metering orifices. In addition, the system stabilizes the idle speed during high altitude operation, the system adjusts the fuel/air mixture according to signals from the altitude sensing device.

On earlier vehicles, the altitude sensing switch will close the circuit between the battery and the idle-up solenoid valve. The solenoid valve will open the passage between the air cleaner and the carburetor. Fresh air is then admitted through the 3 metering orifices and is supplied to the idle, off idle, primary and secondary main metering systems. Also, the idle up solenoid valve will open the passage to the port downstream of the throttle valve, providing additional fuel/air mixtures for stable idle speed at high altitude.

On later vehicles, a MAP sensor is used to measure atmospheric pressure though a vacuum switching valve. The system

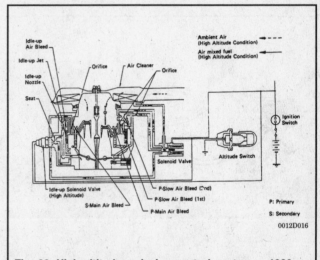

Fig. 82 High altitude emission control system — 1988 and earlier

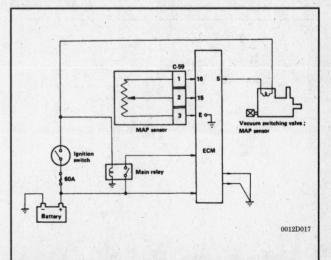

Fig. 83 High altitude emission control system — 1989 and later

prevents the vehicle's self-diagnostic system from generating a false 'Rich Fuel Metering Error' at altitudes higher than the system's set point.

Mixture Control Valve System
▶ See Figure 84

This system functions to reduce HC and CO emissions by allowing air to enter the intake manifold during vehicle deceleration.

Positive Crankcase Ventilation (PCV) System
▶ See Figures 85 and 86

The PCV system admits blow-by gases from the crankcase back into the intake manifold. These gases are re-burned in the combustion chamber with the fuel/air mixture.

The system is a closed type system. It includes the cylinder head cover baffle plate, PCV valve and attendant hoses and connections.

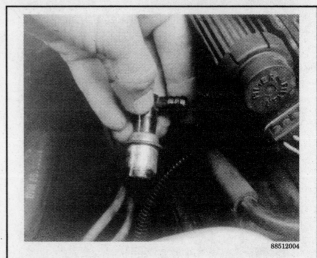
88512004

Fig. 86 Many PCV valves are mounted into the valve cover

The baffle plate functions to separate the oil particles from the blow-by gas and the PCV valve controls the admission of the blow-by into the combustion chamber.

Thermostatically Controlled Air (TCA) Cleaner System
▶ See Figures 87, 88 and 89

The TCA functions to maintain ambient air temperature at an optimum level so that the fuel/air ratio remains constant. This ensures fuel combustion and reduces pollutant emissions. The TCA system is mounted on the air cleaner. It consists of a vacuum motor, hot air control damper and an inlet temperature compensator (ITC) valve.

When the engine is running, there is no vacuum signal at either the vacuum motor or the ITC valve. In this condition the vacuum motor spring closes off the passage from the hot air duct. On a cold start, the ITC valve delivers maximum vacuum to the vacuum motor which moves the hot air control damper to the fully open position. This closes the ambient air passage and opens the hot air duct. If the engine speed increases, the system vacuum level will drop allowing the diaphragm spring to

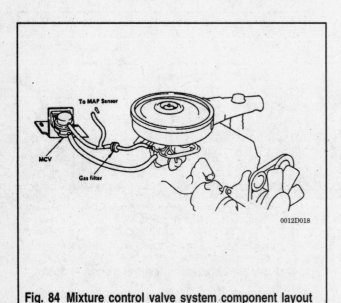
0012D018

Fig. 84 Mixture control valve system component layout

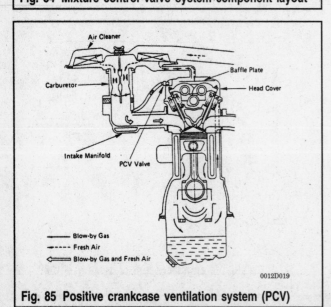
0012D019

Fig. 85 Positive crankcase ventilation system (PCV)

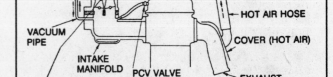
0012D020

Fig. 87 Thermostatically controlled air (TCA) cleaner system

Fig. 88 Evaporative Thermostatic Vacuum Valve (TVV) used in a thermostatically controlled air cleaner — Chevrolet shown

Fig. 89 Typical Inlet Temperature Compensator (ITC) or Thermac sensor used in a thermostatically controlled air cleaner

overcome the vacuum force and push the hot air control damper to the fully closed position.

When the engine is running under normal conditions, the ITC valve closes the passage to the intake manifold and opens the passage to the from the air cleaner to the vacuum motor. As fresh air is fed to the vacuum motor, the diaphragm spring forces the air control valve to close off the hot air duct and open the ambient air passage.

During conditions of extended idling, hill climbing or high speed driving, there is a substantial increase in engine and engine compartment temperatures. This results in an excessive amount of fuel vapor entering the intake manifold, causing an over-rich mixture. The over-rich mixture causes rough idling and increased CO emissions. To prevent this, the ITC valve opens the passage from the air cleaner to the intake manifold. Fresh air is allowed to enter the intake manifold and lean out the mixture.

Carburetor and Computer Monitored Components

▶ **See Figures 90, 91 and 92**

AIR CONDITIONER REQUEST SIGNAL

This signal indicates to the ECM that an air conditioning mode is selected at the switch and that the A/C low pressure switch is closed. The ECM controls the A/C and adjusts the idle speed in response to this signal.

AIR SWITCHING VALVE

The Electronic control module (ECM) provides the signals to actuate the valve via a vacuum switching solenoid valve. The air switching valve is open to allow the injection of the air into the exhaust ports of the engine when (1) the temperature of the coolant is below the specified level or (2) during a given period or time after the acceleration comes up to wide open throttle condition.

AIR VALVE DIAPHRAGM

▶ **See Figure 93**

In addition to the choke functions described, a vacuum diaphragm is used to further control the choke (on some models). The operation of the dashpot plus the control restrictions and passages is as follows:

During primary throttle operating conditions (secondary valves not open), manifold vacuum is transmitted through the passages connecting the choke diaphragm to the underside of the carburetor flange. If the secondary valves are opened from either a closed throttle or part throttle position (of the primary valves), the restrictions 'A', 'B' and 'C' bleed off manifold pressure to the diaphragm, allowing the choke to open at a rate that will provide smooth secondary operation.

Restrictions 'A' and 'C' are series restrictions for controlling rate of pressure bleed-off to the diaphragm with the secondary throttle valves closed. Restriction 'B' has an added function: during steady, extreme high-speed operation (70 mph approximately) it is possible that the secondary valves may be opened very slightly. If the diaphragm was directly connected to manifold vacuum at all times, the diaphragm might pull the choke to a closed position causing an over-rich mixture. Restriction 'B' prevents this. When the secondary is slightly opened, the restriction at 'B' bleeds off a part of the manifold vacuum to the diaphragm. The diaphragm can then properly position the air valve for satisfactory performance.

BAROMETRIC SWITCH

The barometric switch is connected to the ECM and intended to make the System Malfunction indicator lamp inoperative in the case of the 'Rich Oxygen Sensor Error' alone at the

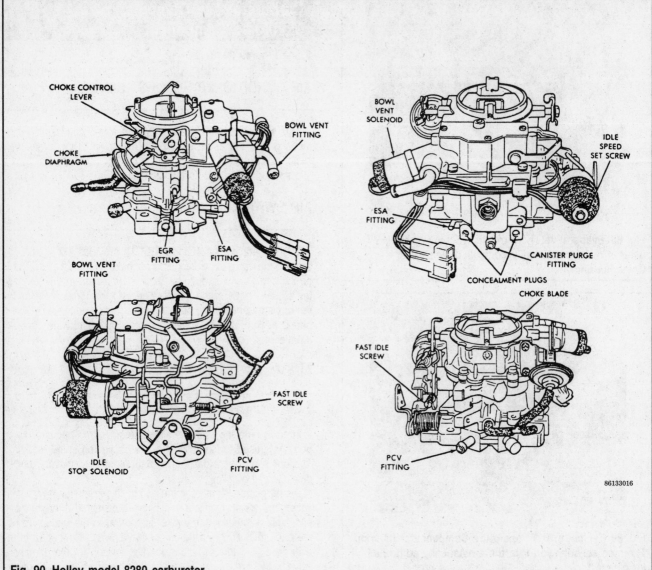

Fig. 90 Holley model 8280 carburetor

prescribed altitude or higher. There is no interaction between the barometric switch and the emission control system.

COOLANT TEMPERATURE SENSOR

▶ **See Figure 94**

This sensor is used by all systems. It is usually located on the engine block, under the intake manifold. It sends the coolant temperature information back to the ECM. The ECM then uses this information to determine the engine temperature for calculating the required air/fuel mixture.

CANISTER PURGE

▶ **See Figure 95**

The canister purge is sometimes called a purge control or cutoff solenoid valve. This solenoid valve, which is controlled

by the PCM controls vacuum to the purge valve in the charcoal canister. In open loop, before a specified time has expired and below a specified rpm, the solenoid valve is energized and blocks vacuum to the purge valve. When the system is in closed loop, after a specified time and above a specified rpm, the solenoid valve is de-energized and vacuum can be applied to the purge valve. This releases the collected vapors into the intake manifold. On systems not using an PCM controlled solenoid, a Thermo Vacuum Valve (TVV) is used to control purge.

CATALYTIC CONVERTER

The 3-way catalytic converter reduces oxides of nitrogen while oxidizing hydro-carbons and carbon monoxide. To maintain high conversion efficiency it is necessary to closely control the air-fuel ratio near stoichiometric.

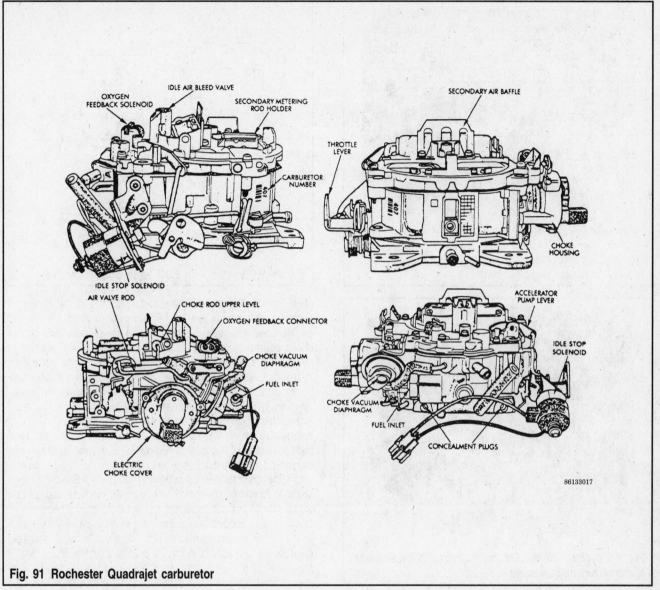

Fig. 91 Rochester Quadrajet carburetor

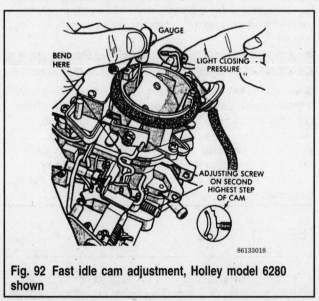

Fig. 92 Fast idle cam adjustment, Holley model 6280 shown

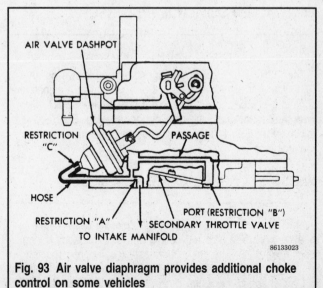

Fig. 93 Air valve diaphragm provides additional choke control on some vehicles

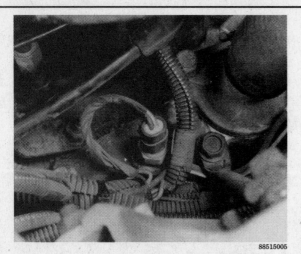

Fig. 94 Engine Coolant Temperature (ECT) sensor — Typical Chevrolet engine shown

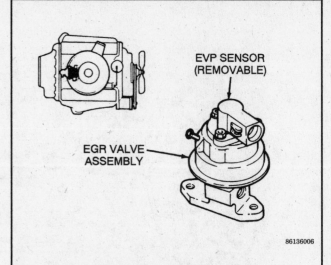

Fig. 96 EGR valve with EGR valve position sensor

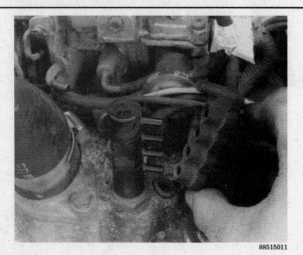

Fig. 95 Typical Thermo Switching Valve (TSV) used with the canister purge system

EGR VALVE POSITION (EVP) SENSOR

▶ See Figure 96

The EGR valve position sensor, sometimes known as an EGR valve lift sensor, is mounted on EGR valve. It signals the computer of EGR opening so that it may subtract EGR flow from total air flow into the manifold. In this way, EGR flow is excluded from air flow information used to determine mixture requirements.

ELECTRIC CHOKE HEATER ASSEMBLY

Most vehicles are equipped with an electric assist choke heating system to help reduce HC and CO emissions during engine warm-up. The choke thermostatic coil spring reacts to engine temperature. An electric heating element located next to a bimetal spring inside the choke well assists engine heat to control choke duration. Power to the heater element is sup-

plied through the choke control switch. Power to the choke control switch is supplied by the oil pressure switch; if the engine does not have a minimum of 4 psi oil pressure, the choke control switch will not engage and the heater will not function. Choke heater wattage is part of the choke calibration.

The dual stage electric assist choke is designed to shorten choke duration above approximately 80°F and stabilize choke duration in the winter. Summer electric assist heat levels are higher than the winter assist levels. Winter heat levels are established by an electric resistor permanently connected to both terminals of the control. Below 55°F, power is reduced by the resistor. Above 80°F, the resistor is bypassed by a switch within the control, thereby supplying full power. Switch temperature is controlled by engine temperature. Engines started in winter conditions will experience 2 levels of choke heating. LOW heat is applied during engine warm up and HIGH heat is applied after engine warm-up. The additional level of heat applied to the choke after warm-up insures that the choke will stay open under all driving conditions. Engines started in summer temperatures will not experience low choke heat levels. Engines restarted hot will only experience the high heat or summer level because the control switch is generally warmer than 80°F.

✳✳CAUTION

Operation of any type, including idling, should be avoided if there is any loss of choke power. Under this condition, any loss of power to the choke will cause the choke to remain fully on during the operation of the vehicle. This will cause a very rich mixture to burn, which may cause damage to the catalyst or to the underbody parts of the vehicle. It is advised that the electric choke power not be disconnected to troubleshoot cold start problems.

FUEL CUT DEVICE

The fuel cutoff system is used by the feedback system and consists principally of a slow cut solenoid valve that is incorporated in the carburetor, an engine speed sensor, a transmission switch, an accelerator switch, and clutch switch. This system is an auxiliary fuel system operated by the slow cut solenoid. When de-energized, the solenoid puts a plunger out to make the slow passage closed.

IDLE SPEED CONTROL (ISC)

▶ See Figure 97

The idle speed control or stepper motor does just what its name implies-it controls the idle. The ISC is used to maintain low engine speeds while at the same time preventing stalling due to engine load changes. The system consists of a motor assembly mounted on the carburetor which moves the throttle lever so as to open or close the throttle blades.

The whole operation is controlled by the ECM. The ECM monitors engine load to determine the proper idle speed. To prevent stalling, it monitors the air conditioning compressor switch, the transmission, the park/neutral switch and the ISC throttle switch. The ECM processes all this information and then uses it to control the ISC motor which in turn will vary the idle speed as necessary.

MANIFOLD ABSOLUTE PRESSURE (MAP) SENSOR

▶ See Figure 98

The Manifold Absolute Pressure (MAP) sensor or Atmospheric Pressure Sensor, measures the changes in the intake manifold pressure which result from engine load and speed changes. The pressure measured by the MAP sensor is the difference between barometric pressure (outside air) and manifold pressure (vacuum). A closed throttle engine coastdown would produce a relatively low MAP value (approximately 20-35 kPa), while wide-open throttle would produce a high value (100 kPa). This high value is produced when the pressure inside the manifold is the same as outside the manifold, and 100% of outside air (or 100 kPa) is being measured. This MAP output is the opposite of what you would measure on a vacuum gauge. The use of this sensor also allows the PCM to adjust automatically for different altitude.

The PCM sends a 5 volt reference signal to the MAP sensor. As the MAP changes, the electrical resistance of the sensor also changes. By monitoring the sensor output voltage the PCM can determine the manifold pressure. A higher pressure, lower vacuum (high voltage) requires more fuel, while a lower pressure, higher vacuum (low voltage) requires less fuel. The PCM uses the MAP sensor to control fuel delivery and ignition timing.

MIXTURE CONTROL SOLENOID (M/C)

▶ See Figure 99

The M/C solenoid and the Oxygen sensor feedback solenoid preform the same function. Different manufacturers refer to them by different terms. The fuel flow through the carburetor idle main metering circuits is controlled by a mixture control (M/C) solenoid located in the carburetor. The M/C solenoid changes the air/fuel mixture to the engine by controlling the fuel flow through the carburetor. The PCM controls the solenoid by providing a ground. When the solenoid is energized, the fuel flow through the carburetor is reduced, providing a leaner mixture. When the PCM removes the ground, the solenoid is de-energized, increasing the fuel flow and providing a richer mixture. The M/C solenoid is energized and de-energized at a rate of 10 times per second.

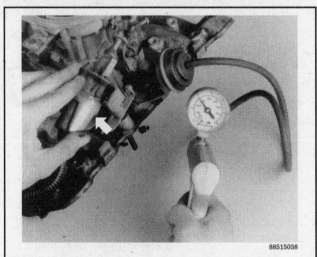

Fig. 97 Typical Idle Speed Control (ISC) Solenoid — Ford V6 engine shown

88515038

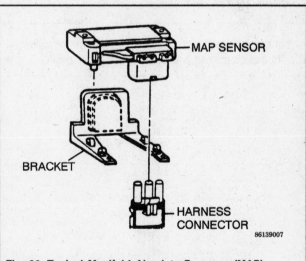

Fig. 98 Typical Manifold Absolute Pressure (MAP) sensor

86139007

OXYGEN (O₂) FEEDBACK SOLENOID

▶ **See Figure 99**

Fuel metering is controlled by specially-shaped metering rods which operate in the main metering jets. The rods are positioned by a plunger in the oxygen feedback solenoid (sometimes called the mixture control solenoid). The solenoid plunger is controlled by an electrical output signal generated by the Engine Control computer. The computer, responding to an electrical signal from the oxygen sensor in the exhaust manifold, alternately energizes and de-energizes the solenoid. When energized, the solenoid moves the metering rods to the lean position and when the solenoid is de-energized, the rods return to the rich position. The up-and-down movement of the solenoid plunger and the rods occurs ten times per second.

OXYGEN SENSOR

▶ **See Figures 101 and 100**

The oxygen sensor is a galvanic battery which produces electrical voltage. The sensor is mounted in the exhaust manifold and must be heated by the exhaust gas before producing a voltage. When there is a large amount of oxygen present (lean mixture) the sensor produces a low voltage. When there is a lesser amount present, it produces a higher voltage. By monitoring the oxygen content and converting it to electrical voltage, the sensor acts as a rich/lean switch. The voltage is transmitted to the Spark Control Computer. The computer sends a signal to the oxygen feedback solenoid mounted on the carburetor to change the air/fuel ratio back to stoichiometric.

PARK/NEUTRAL SWITCH

This switch indicates to the PCM when the transmission is in **P** or **N**. the information is used by the PCM for control on the

Fig. 100 Removing the Oxygen Sensor from the exhaust manifold — Typical GM engine shown

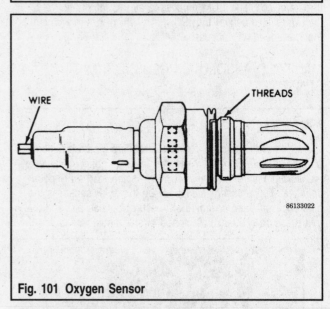

Fig. 101 Oxygen Sensor

torque converter clutch, EGR, and the idle air control valve operation.

➡ **Vehicle should not be driven with the park/neutral switch disconnected as idle quality may be affected in park or neutral and a DTC for the VSS may be set.**

POWER STEERING PRESSURE SWITCH

▶ **See Figure 102**

The power steering pressure switch is used so that the power steering oil pressure pump load will not effect the engine idle. Turning the steering wheel increase the power steering oil pressure and pump load on the engine. The power steering pressure switch will close before the load can cause an idle problem. The PCM will also turn the A/C clutch off when high power steering pressure is detected.

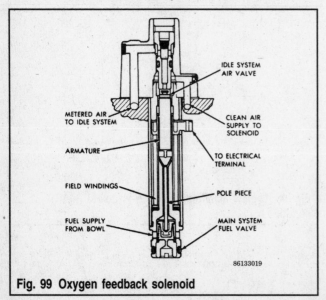

Fig. 99 Oxygen feedback solenoid

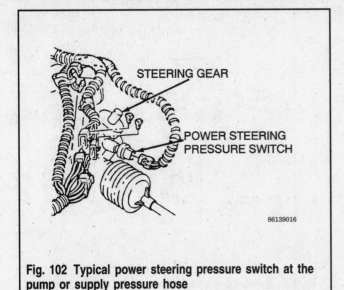

Fig. 102 Typical power steering pressure switch at the pump or supply pressure hose

SECONDARY THROTTLE LOCKOUT

Secondary throttle operation is eliminated during the choke cycle by use of a latch triggered by the fast idle system.

THROTTLE POSITION SENSOR (TPS)

▶ **See Figures 103 and 104**

The Throttle Position Sensor (TPS) may also be called a Throttle Angle Valve, Throttle Potentiometer or a Throttle Valve Switch. It is connected to the throttle shaft and is controlled by the throttle mechanism. A 5 volt reference signal is sent to the TPS from the PCM. As the throttle valve angle is changed (accelerator pedal moved), the resistance of the TPS also changes. At a closed throttle position, the resistance of the TPS is high, so the output voltage to the PCM will be low (approximately 0.5 volt). As the throttle plate opens, the resistance decreases so that, at wide open throttle, the output volt-

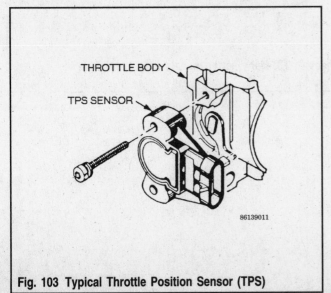

Fig. 103 Typical Throttle Position Sensor (TPS)

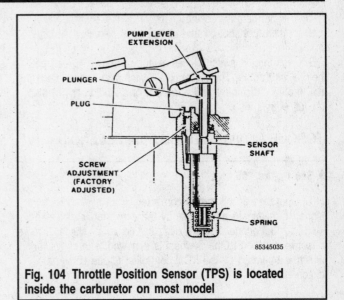

Fig. 104 Throttle Position Sensor (TPS) is located inside the carburetor on most model

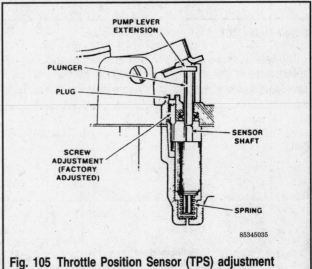

Fig. 105 Throttle Position Sensor (TPS) adjustment screw on a typical General Motors carburetor

age should be approximately 5 volts. At closed throttle position, the voltage at the TPS should be less than 1.25 volts.

By monitoring the output voltage from the TPS, the PCM can determine fuel delivery based on throttle valve angle (driver demand). The TPS can either be misadjusted, shorted, open or loose. Misadjustment might result in poor idle or poor wide-open throttle performance. An open TPS signals the PCM that the throttle is always closed, resulting in poor performance. This usually sets a code. A shorted TPS gives the PCM a constant wide-open throttle signal will store a code. A loose TPS indicates to the PCM that the throttle is moving. This causes intermittent bursts of fuel from the injector and an unstable idle. Once the fault code is set, the PCM will use an artificial default value and some vehicle performance will return.

Idle/Full throttle switches are contained within the throttle position sensor on some vehicles. These switches are used to provide specific information to the PCM. When the idle switch is closed, the throttle plates are closed. The switch opens when the throttle plates open approximately 1 degree. The idle switch signal determines the operation of the stabilize valve, deceleration fuel shut-off and operation of a ignition timing map.

The full throttle switch closes at approximately 10 degrees before full throttle. The full throttle switch signal determines the full throttle enrichment and operation of a ignition timing map for full engine load.

TORQUE CONVERTER CLUTCH SOLENOID

▶ **See Figure 106**

The purpose of the torque converter clutch system is designed to eliminate power loss by the converter (slippage) to increase fuel economy. By locking the converter clutch, a more effective coupling to the flywheel is achieved. The converter clutch is operated by the PCM controlled torque converter clutch solenoid.

VEHICLE SPEED SENSOR (VSS)

▶ **See Figure 107**

The vehicle speed sensor (VSS) is mounted behind the speedometer in the instrument cluster or on the transmission/speedometer drive gear. It provides electrical pulses to the

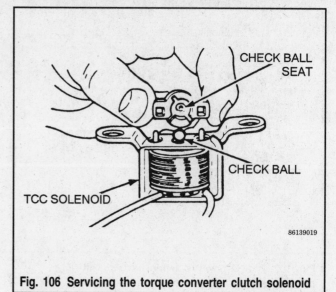

Fig. 106 Servicing the torque converter clutch solenoid

PCM from the speedometer head. The pulses indicate the road speed. The PCM uses this information to operate the IAC, canister purge and TCC.

➡ **A vehicle equipped with a speed sensor, should not be driven without a the speed sensor connected, as idle quality may be affected.**

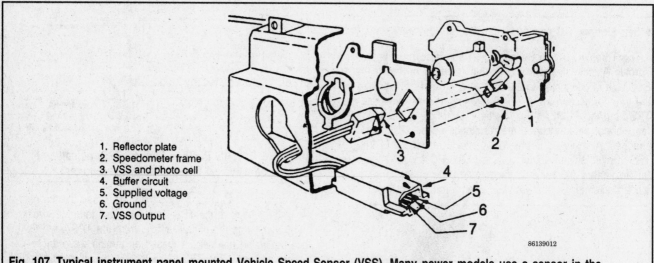

1. Reflector plate
2. Speedometer frame
3. VSS and photo cell
4. Buffer circuit
5. Supplied voltage
6. Ground
7. VSS Output

Fig. 107 Typical instrument panel mounted Vehicle Speed Sensor (VSS). Many newer models use a sensor in the transaxle.

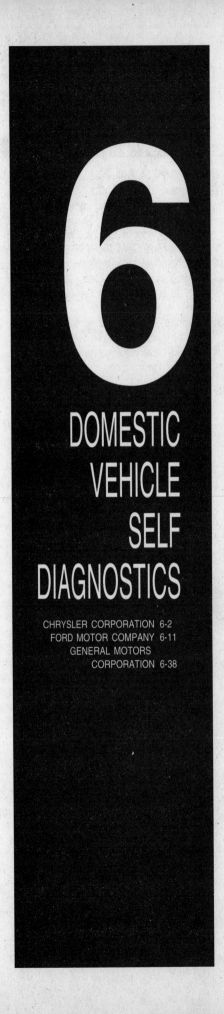

6

DOMESTIC VEHICLE SELF DIAGNOSTICS

CHRYSLER CORPORATION

Self-Diagnostics

The Chrysler fuel injection systems combine electronic spark advance and fuel control. At the center of these systems is a digital, pre-programmed computer, known as an Powertrain Control Module (PCM). The PCM can also be referred to as the Single Module Engine Controller (SMEC) or as the Single Board Engine Controller (SBEC). The PCM regulates ignition timing, air-fuel ratio, emission control devices, cooling fan, charging system idle speed and speed control. It has the ability to update and revise its commands to meet changing operating conditions.

Various sensors provide the input necessary for PCM to correctly regulate fuel flow at the injectors. These include the Manifold Absolute Pressure (MAP), Throttle Position Sensor (TPS), oxygen sensor, coolant temperature sensor, charge temperature sensor, and vehicle speed sensors.

In addition to the sensors, various switches are used to provide important information to the PCM. These include the neutral safety switch, air conditioning clutch switch, brake switch and speed control switch. These signals cause the PCM to change either the fuel flow at the injectors or the ignition timing or both.

The PCM is designed to test it's own input and output circuits, If a fault is found in a major system, this information is stored in the PCM for eventual display to the technician. Information on this fault can be displayed to the technician by means of the instrument panel CHECK ENGINE light or by connecting a diagnostic read-out tester and reading a numbered display code, which directly relates to a general fault. Some inputs and outputs are checked continuously and others are checked under certain conditions. If the problem is repaired or no longer exists, the PCM cancels the fault code after approximately 50 key ON/OFF cycles.

When a fault code is detected, it appears as either a flash of the CHECK ENGINE light on the instrument panel or by watching the Diagnostic Readout Box version II (DRB-II). This indicates that an abnormal signal in the system has been recognized by the PCM. Fault codes do indicate the presence of a failure but they don't identify the failed component directly.

VISUAL INSPECTIONS

This is possibly the most critical step of diagnosis. A detailed examination of connectors, wiring and vacuum hoses can often lead to a repair without further diagnosis. A careful inspector will check the undersides of hoses as well as the integrity of hard-to-reach hoses blocked by the air cleaner or other component. Wiring should be checked carefully for any sign of strain, burning, crimping, or terminals pulled-out from a connector. Checking connectors at components or in harnesses is required; usually, pushing them together will reveal a loose fit.

FAULT CODES

Fault codes are 2 digit numbers that tell the technician which circuit is bad. Fault codes do indicate the presence of a failure but they don't identify the failed component directly. Therefore a fault code a result and not always the reason for the problem.

INDICATOR CODES

Indicator codes are 2 digit numbers that tell the technician if particular sequences or conditions have occurred. Such a condition where the indicator code will be displayed is at the beginning or the end of a diagnostic test. Indicator codes will not generate a CHECK ENGINE light or engine running test code.

ACTUATOR TEST MODE (ATM) CODES

Starting in 1985, ATM test codes are 2 digit numbers that identify the various circuits used by the technician during the diagnosis procedure. In 1989 the PCM and test equipment changed design. The actuator test functions where expanded, but access to these functions may have changed, dependent on vehicle or test equipment being used.

ENGINE RUNNING TEST CODES

Engine running test codes where introduced on fuel injected vehicles. These are 2 digit numbers. The codes are used to access sensor readouts while the engine is running and place the engine in particular operating conditions for diagnosis. Feedback carburetor system does not offer engine running sensor test mode.

CHECK ENGINE (MIL) LIGHT

The CHECK ENGINE or Maintenance Indicator Lamp (MIL) light has 2 modes of operation: diagnostic mode and switch test mode.

If a DRB-II diagnostic tester is not available, the PCM can show the technician fault codes by flashing the CHECK ENGINE light on the instrument panel in the diagnostic mode. In the switch test mode, after all codes are displayed, switch function can be confirmed. The light will turn on and off when a switch is turned **ON** and **OFF**.

Even though the light can be used as a diagnostic tool, it cannot do the following:

Once the light starts to display fault codes, it cannot be stopped. If the technician loses count, he must start the test procedure again.

The light cannot display all of the codes or any blank displays.

The light cannot tell the technician if the oxygen feed-back system is lean or rich and if the idle motor and detonation systems are operational.

The light cannot perform the actuation test mode, sensor test mode or engine running test mode.

➡ **Be advised that the CHECK ENGINE light can only perform a limited amount of functions and is not to be used as a substitute for a diagnostic tester. All diagnostic procedure described herein are intended for use with a Diagnostic Readout Box II (DRB-II) or equivalent tool.**

LIMP-IN MODE

The limp-in mode is the attempt by the PCM to compensate for the failure of certain components by substituting information from other sources. If the PCM senses incorrect data or no data at all from the MAP sensor, throttle position sensor or coolant temperature sensor, the system is placed into limp-in mode and the CHECK ENGINE light on the instrument panel is activated. This mode will keep the vehicle drive able until the customer can get it to a service facility.

TEST MODES

There are 5 modes of testing required for the proper diagnosis of the system. They are as follows:

Diagnostic Test Mode — This mode is used to access the fault codes from the PCM's memory.

Circuit Actuation Test Mode (ATM Test) — This mode is used to turn a certain circuit on and off in order to test it. ATM test codes are used in this mode.

Switch Test Mode — This mode is used to determine if specific switch inputs are being received by the PCM.

Sensor Test Mode — This mode looks at the output signals of certain sensors as they are received by the PCM when the engine is not running. Sensor access codes are read in this mode. Also this mode is used to clear the PCM memory of stored codes.

Engine Running Test Mode — This mode looks at sensor output signals as seen by the PCM when the engine is running. Also this mode is used to determine some specific running conditions necessary for diagnosis.

Reading Codes

OBTAINING TROUBLE CODES

▶ **See Figures 1, 2 and 3**

Entering the Jeep or Eagle self-diagnostic system requires the use of a special adapter that connects with the Diagnostic Readout Box II (DRB-II). These systems require the adapter because all of the system diagnosis is done Off-Board instead of On-Board like most vehicles. The adapter, which is a computer module itself, measures signals at the diagnostic connector and converts the signals into a form which the DRB-II can use to perform tests. On vehicles other than Jeep and

Eagle the following procedures will obtain stored Diagnostic Trouble Codes (DTC).

Using the Dash MIL lamp

Codes display on vehicles built before 1989 are displayed in numerical order, after 1989 codes are displayed in order of occurrence.

1. Connect the readout box to the diagnostic connector located in the engine compartment near PCM.

2. Start the engine, if possible, cycle the transmission selector and the A/C switch if applicable. Shut off the engine.

3. Turn the ignition switch **ON — OFF, ON — OFF, ON — OFF, ON** within 5 seconds.

4. Observe the CHECK ENGINE light on the instrument panel.

5. Just after the last ON cycle, the dash warning (MIL) lamp will begin flashing the stored codes.

6. The codes are transmitted as two digit flashes.

7. Example would be Code 21 will be displayed as a FLASH FLASH pause FLASH.

8. Be ready to write down the codes as they appear; the only way to repeat the codes is to start over at the beginning.

Scan Tool

The scan tool is the preferred choice for fault recovery and system diagnosis. Some hints on using the DRB-II include:

- To use the HELP screen, press and hold F3 at any time.
- To restart the DRB-II at any time, hold the MODE button and press ATM at the same time.
- Pressing the up or down arrows will move forward or backward one item within a menu.
- To select an item, either press the number of the item or move the cursor arrow to the selection, then press ENTER.
- To return to the previous display (screen), press ATM.
- Some test screens display multiple items. To view only one, move the cursor arrow to the desired item, then press ENTER.

To read stored faults with the DRB-II:

1. With the ignition switch **OFF**, connect the tool to the diagnostic connector near the engine controller under the hood. On some 1988 and earlier models cycling the ignition key ON-

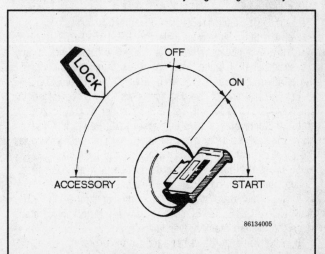

Fig. 1 Turn the ignition switch On and Off three times to enter self-diagnostics

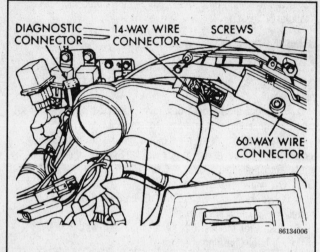

DIAGNOSTIC CONNECTOR — 14-WAY WIRE CONNECTOR — SCREWS

60-WAY WIRE CONNECTOR

86134006

Fig. 2 Typical view of the Powertrain Control Module diagnostic link connector

```
----- FUEL/IGN FAULTS -----
NO FAULTS DETECTED

X STARTS SINCE ERS
```

```
1 OF X FAULTS
[message
appears here]
X STARTS SINCE SET
```

86134007

Fig. 3 Example of DRB-II display screen while reading trouble codes

OFF three times may be necessary to enter diagnostics. On 1989 and newer models, simply turn the ignition switch **ON** to access the read fault code data.

2. Start the engine if possible. Cycle the transmission from **P**ark to a forward gear, then back to **P**ark. Cycle the air conditioning ON and OFF. Turn the ignition switch **OFF**.

3. Turn the ignition switch **ON** but do not start the engine. The DRB-II will begin its power-up sequence; do not touch any keys on the scan tool during this sequence.

4. Reading faults must be selected from the FUEL/IGN MENU. To reach this menu on the DRB-II:

a. When the initial menu is displayed after the power-up sequence, use the down arrow to display choice 4) SELECT SYSTEM and select this choice.

b. Once on the — SELECT SYSTEM — screen, choose 1) ENGINE. This will enter the engine diagnostics section of the program.

c. The screen will momentarily display the engine family and SBEC identification numbers. After a few seconds the screen displays the choices 1) With A/C and 2) Without A/C. Select and enter the correct choice for the vehicle.

d. When the — ENGINE SYSTEM — screen appears, select 1) FUEL/IGNITION from the menu.

e. On the next screen, select 2) READ FAULTS

5. If any faults are stored, the display will show how many are stored (1 of 4 faults, etc.) and issue a text description of the problem, such as COOLANT SENSOR VOLTAGE TOO LOW. The last line of the display shows the number of engine starts since the code was set. If the number displayed is 0 starts, this indicates a hard or current fault. Faults are displayed in reverse order of occurrence; the first fault shown is the most current and the last fault shown is the oldest.

6. Press the down arrow to read each fault after the first. Record the screen data carefully for easy reference.

7. If no faults are stored in the controller, the display will state NO FAULTS DETECTED and show the number of starts since the system memory was last erased.

8. After all faults have been read and recorded, press ATM.

9. Refer to the appropriate diagnostic chart for a diagnostic path. Remember that the fault message identifies a circuit problem, not a component. Use of the charts is required to sequentially test a circuit and identify the fault.

Switch Test

The PCM only recognizes 2 switch input states — HI and LOW. For this reason the PCM cannot tell the difference between a selected switch position and an open circuit, short circuit or an open switch. However, if one of the switches is toggled, the controller does have the ability to respond to the change of state in the switch. If the change is displayed, it can be assumed that entire switch circuit to the PCM is operational.

1988 AND EARLIER

After all codes have been shown and has indicated Code 55 end of message, actuate the following component switches. The digital display must change its numbers between 00 and 88 and the CHECK ENGINE light will blink when the following switches are activated and released:

Brake pedal
Gear shift selector
A/C switch
Electric defogger switch (1984)

1989 AND NEWER

To enter the switch test mode, activate read input states or equivalent function on the readout box for the following switch tests:

Z1 Voltage Sense
Speed Control Set
Speed Control **ON/OFF**
Speed Control Resume
A/C Switch Sense
Brake Switch
Park/neutral Switch

Scan Tool Functions

❈❈CAUTION

Always apply the parking brake and block the wheels before performing any diagnostic procedures with the engine running. Failure to do so may result in personal injury and/or property damage.

After stored faults have been read and recorded, the scan tool may be used to investigate states and functions of various components. This ability compliments but does not replace the use of diagnostic charts. The DRB-II functions are useful in identifying circuits which are or are not operating correctly as well as checking component function or signal.

When diagnosing an emissions-related problem, keep in mind that the SBEC system only enters closed loop mode under certain conditions. The single most important criteria for entry into closed loop operation is that the engine be at normal operating temperature; i.e., fully warmed up. The engine is considered to be at normal operating temperature if any of the following are true: the electric cooling fan cycles on at least once or the upper radiator hose is hot to the touch or the heater is able to deliver hot air.

In open loop operation, the signal from the oxygen sensor is ignored by the engine controller and the fuel injection is controlled by pre-programmed values within the computer. Once closed loop operation is begun, the signal from the oxygen sensor is used by the engine controller to constantly adjust the fuel injection to maintain the proper air/fuel ratio. The system will switch in and out of closed loop operation depending on sensor signals and driver input. In most cases, the system will be in closed loop operation during normal driving, acceleration or deceleration and idle. Wide open throttle will cause the system to momentarily switch to open loop operation. Additionally, some engine control systems will momentarily switch to open loop under hard acceleration or deceleration until the MAP sensor signal stabilizes.

The DRB-II may be operated in the following diagnostic modes from the FUEL/IGN MENU screen.

STATE DISPLAY

The State Display programs allow the operator to view the present conditions in the SBEC system. These choices are displayed on the FUEL/IGN STATE screen and offer the choices of MODULE INFO, SENSORS, INPUTS/OUTPUTS, or MONITORS. Viewing system data through these windows can be helpful in observing the effects of repairs or to compare the problem vehicle to a known-good vehicle.

Module Info

This choice identifies the engine and transmission family and provides the SBEC identification number. It is always wise to check this screen first to insure that the correct controller is installed in the vehicle. The SBEC identification number must be used if the unit is to be replaced.

Sensors

This function displays current data being transmitted from the fuel and ignition sensors to the engine controller. Examples of sensor data available include MAP voltage, throttle position sensor voltage and percentage, RPM, coolant temperature, voltage sensor, total spark advance, and vehicle speed. Many other sensors may be monitored depending on engine/transmission combinations.

Data for each sensor is displayed in the appropriate units, such as volts, mph, in. Hg, degrees F, etc.

1988 AND EARLIER

1. Put the system into the diagnostic test mode and wait for Code 55 to appear on the display screen.

2. Press the ATM button on the diagnostic tool to activate the display. If a specific sensor read test is desired, hold the ATM button down until the desired test code appears.

3. Slide the READ/HOLD switch to the **HOLD** position to display the corresponding sensor output.

Sensor Read Test Display Codes:

Code 01 — Battery temperature sensor; display voltage divided by 10 equals sensor temperature

Code 02 — Oxygen sensor voltage; display number divided by 10 equals sensor voltage

Code 03 — Charge temperature sensor voltage; display number divided by 10 equals sensor voltage

Code 04 — Engine coolant temperature sensor; display number multiplied by 10 equals degrees of engine coolant sensor

Code 05 — Throttle position sensor voltage; display number divided by 10 equals sensor voltage or temperature

Code 06 — Peak knock sensor voltage; display number is sensor voltage

Code 07 — Battery voltage; display number is battery voltage

Code 08 — Map sensor voltage; display number divided by 10 equals sensor voltage

Code 09 — Speed control switches:
   Display is blank — Cruise **OFF**
   Display shows 00 — Cruise **ON**
   Display shows 10 — Cruise **SET**
   Display shows 01 — Cruise **RESUME**

Code 10 — Fault code erase routine; display will flash 0's for 4 seconds

1989 AND NEWER

To enter the sensor test mode, activate read sensor voltage or read sensor values or equivalent functions on the readout box for the following sensor displays:

Read Sensor Voltage
Battery temperature sensor
Oxygen sensor input
Throttle body temperature sensor
Coolant temperature sensor
Throttle position
Minimum throttle
Battery voltage
MAP sensor voltage
Read Sensor Values
Throttle body temperature
Coolant temperature
MAP gauge reading

AIS motor position
Added adaptive fuel
Adaptive fuel factor
Barometric pressure
Engine speed
Module spark advance
Vehicle speed
Oxygen sensor state

ENGINE RUNNING TEST MODE

1988 and Earlier

The Engine Running Test Mode monitors the sensors on the vehicle which check operating conditions while the engine is running. The engine running test mode can be performed with the engine idling in **NEUTRAL** and with parking brake set or under actual driving conditions. With the diagnostic readout box READ/HOLD switch in the **READ** position, the engine running test mode is initiated after the engine is started.

Select a test code by switching the READ/HOLD switch to the **READ** position and pressing the actuator button until the desired code appears. Release actuator button and switch the READ/HOLD switch to the **HOLD** position. The logic module will monitor that system test and results will be displayed.

Only fuel injected engine offer this function. The Feedback carburetor system does not offer engine running sensor test mode.

ENGINE RUNNING TEST DISPLAY CODES

Code 61 — Battery temperature sensor; display number divided by 10 equals voltage

Code 62 — Oxygen sensor; display number divided by 10 equals voltage

Code 63 — Fuel injector temperature sensor; display number divided by 10 equals voltage

Code 64 — Engine coolant temperature sensor; display number multiplied by 10 equals degrees F

Code 65 — Throttle position sensor; display number divided by 10 equals voltage

Code 67 — Battery voltage sensor; display is voltage

Code 68 — Manifold vacuum sensor; display is in. Hg

Code 69 — Minimum throttle position sensor; display number divided by 10 equals voltage

Code 70 — Minimum airflow idle speed sensor; display number multiplied by 10 equals rpm (see minimum air flow check procedure)

Code 71 — Vehicle speed sensor; display is mph

Code 72 — Engine speed sensor; display number multiplied by 10 equals rpm

FUEL/IGNITION INPUT/OUTPUT

The engine controller recognizes only two states of electrical signals, voltage high or low. In some cases this corresponds to a switch or circuit being on or off; in other circuits a voltage signal may change from low voltage to higher voltage as a sensor opens. The controller cannot recognize the difference between a selected switch position and an open or shorted circuit.

In this test mode, the change in the circuit may be viewed as the switch is operated. For example, if the BRAKE SWITCH state is selected, the display should change from Low to High as the brake pedal is pressed. If a change in a circuit is displayed as the switch is used, it may be reasonably assumed that the entire switch circuit into the engine controller is operating correctly.

Depending on the engine/transmission in the vehicle, some of the switch states which may be checked include the air conditioning switch, brake switch, park/neutral switch, fuel flow signal, air conditioning clutch relay, radiator fan relay, CHECK ENGINE lamp, overdrive solenoid(s), lock-up solenoid and the speed control vent or vacuum solenoids. The scan tool will recognize the correct choices for each vehicle and only offer the appropriate systems on the screen.

Monitors

On vehicles built before 1991, this display is called ENGINE PARAMETERS. 1991 and newer vehicles name the screen MONITORS. This display allows close observation of groups of related signals. For example, if RPM is chosen, the screen will display data for many of the factors affecting the rpm such as throttle position sensor, advance, air conditioning status, park/neutral status, AIS status and coolant temperature.

One of the screens within this test is NO START. When this display is selected, the screen shows the initial data sent to the engine controller during cranking. Using this screen to identify missing or unusual signals can shorten diagnostic time.

ACTUATOR TESTS

The purpose of the circuit actuation mode test is to check for proper operation of the output circuits that the PCM cannot internally recognize. The PCM can attempt to activate these outputs and allow the technician to affirm proper operation. Most of the tests performed in this mode issue an audible click or visual indication of component operation (click of relay contacts, injector spray, etc.). Except for intermittent conditions, if a component functions properly when it is tested, it can be assumed that the component, attendant wiring and driving circuit are functioning properly.

1988 and Earlier

The Actuator Test Mode ID Code number was introduced in 1985. In 1983-84 ATM function only provided 3 ignition sparks, 2 AIS motor cycles and 1 injector pulse.

1. Put the system into the diagnostic test mode and wait for Code 55 to appear on the display screen.

2. Press ATM button on the tool to activate the display. If a specific ATM test is desired, hold the ATM button down until the desired test code appears.

3. The computer will continue to turn the selected circuit on and off for as long as 5 minutes or until the ATM button is pressed again or the ignition switch is turned to the **OFF** position.

4. If the ATM button is not pressed again, the computer will continue to cycle the selected circuit for 5 minutes and then shut the system off. Turning the ignition to the **OFF** position will also turn the test mode off.

Actuator Test Display Codes:

Code 01 — Spark activation — once every 2 seconds

Code 02 — Injector activation — once every 2 seconds

Code 03 — AIS activation — one step open, one step closed every 4 seconds

Code 04 — Radiator fan relay — once every 2 seconds

Code 05 — A/C WOT cutout relay — once every 2 seconds

Code 06 — ASD relay activation — once every 2 seconds

Code 07 — Purge solenoid activation — one toggle every 2 seconds (The A/C fan will run continuously and the A/C switch must be in the **ON** position to allow for actuation)

Code 08 — Speed control activation — speed control vent and vacuum every 2 seconds (Speed control switch must be in the **ON** position to allow for activation)

Code 09 — Alternator control field activation — one toggle every 2 seconds

Code 10 — Shift indicator activation — one toggle every 2 seconds

Code 11 — EGR diagnosis solenoid activation — one toggle every 2 seconds

1989 and Newer

This family of tests is chosen from the FUEL/IGN MENU screen. The actuator tests allow the operation of the output circuits not recognized by the engine controller to be checked by energizing them on command. Testing in this fashion is necessary because the controller does not recognize the function of all the external components. If an output to a relay is triggered, and the relay is heard to click, it may be reasonably assumed that both the output circuit and the relay are operating properly. In this mode, most of the tests cause a response that may be seen or heard, although close attention may be necessary to notice the change.

Once selected, the ACTUATOR TEST screen offers a choice of items to be activated. Depending on engine and fuel system, some of the choices include:

- Stop all tests
- Engine rpm
- Ignition coil
- Fuel injector
- Fuel system
- Solenoid/relay

AIS motor

The engine speed may be set to a desired level through the ENGINE RPM screen. Once a system is chosen, related screens will appear allowing detailed selection of which relay, injector or component is to be operated.

EXITING DIAGNOSTIC TEST

By turning the ignition switch to the **OFF** position, the test mode system is exited. With a Diagnostic Readout Box attached to the system and the ATM control button not pressed, the computer will continue to cycle the selected circuits for 5 minutes and then automatically shut the system down.

CLEARING CODES

Stored faults should only be cleared by use of the DRB-II or similar scan tool. Disconnecting the battery will clear codes but is not recommended as doing so will also clear all other memories on the vehicle and may affect drive ability. Disconnecting the PCM connector will also clear codes, but on newer models it may store a power loss code and will affect driveability until the vehicle is driven and the PCM can relearn it's drive ability memory.

The — ERASE — screen will appear when ATM is pressed at the end of the stored faults. Select the desired action from ERASE or DON'T ERASE. If ERASE is chosen, the display asks ARE YOU SURE? Pressing ENTER erases stored faults and displays the message FAULTS ERASED. After the faults are erased, press ATM to return the FUEL/IGN MENU.

Diagnostic Trouble Codes

Chrysler Domestic Built Fuel Injection System

Code 88 — Display used for start of test.

Code 11 — Camshaft signal or Ignition signal — no reference signal detected during engine cranking.

Code 12 — Memory to controller has been cleared within 50-l00 engine starts.

Code 13 — MAP sensor pneumatic signal — no variation in MAP sensor signal is detected or no difference is recognized between the engine MAP reading and the stored barometric pressure reading..

Code 14 — MAP voltage too high or too low.

Code 15 — Vehicle speed sensor signal — no distance sensor signal detected during road load conditions.

Code 16 — Knock sensor circuit — Open or short has been detected in the knock sensor circuit.

Code 16 — Battery input sensor — battery voltage sensor input below 4 volts with engine running.

Code 17 — Low engine temperature — engine coolant temperature remains below normal operating temperature during vehicle travel; possible thermostat problem.

Code 21 — Oxygen sensor signal — neither rich or lean condition is detected from the oxygen sensor input.

Code 22 — Coolant voltage low — coolant temperature sensor input below the minimum acceptable voltage/Coolant voltage high — coolant temperature sensor input above the maximum acceptable voltage.

Code 23 — Air Charge or Throttle Body temperature voltage HIGH/LOW — charge air temperature sensor input is above or below the acceptable voltage limits.

Code 24 — Throttle Position sensor voltage high or low.

Code 25 — Automatic Idle Speed (AIS) motor driver circuit — short or open detected in 1 or more of the AIS control circuits.

Code 26 — Injectors No. 1, 2, or 3 peak current not reached, high resistance in circuit.

Code 27 — Injector control circuit — bank output driver stage does not respond properly to the control signal.

Code 27 — Injectors No. 1, 2, or 3 control circuit and peak current not reached.

Code 31 — Purge solenoid circuit — open or short detected in the purge solenoid circuit.

Code 32 — Exhaust Gas Recirculation (EGR) solenoid circuit — open or short detected in the EGR solenoid circuit/EGR system failure — required change in fuel/air ratio not detected during diagnostic test.

Code 32 — Surge valve solenoid — open or short in turbocharger surge valve circuit — some 1993 vehicles.

Code 33 — Air conditioner clutch relay circuit — open or short detected in the air conditioner clutch relay circuit. If vehicle doesn't have air conditioning ignore this code.

Code 34 — Speed control servo solenoids or MUX speed control circuit HIGH/LOW — open or short detected in the vacuum or vent solenoid circuits or speed control switch input above or below allowable voltage.

Code 35 — Radiator fan control relay circuit — open or short detected in the radiator fan relay circuit.

Code 35 — Idle switch shorted — switch input shorted to ground — some 1993 vehicles.

Code 36 — Wastegate solenoid — open or short detected in the turbocharger wastegate control solenoid circuit.

Code 37 — Part Throttle Unlock (PTU) circuit for torque converter clutch — open or short detected in the torque converter part throttle unlock solenoid circuit.

Code 37 — Baro Reed Solenoid — solenoid does not turn off when it should.

Code 37 — Shift indicator circuit (manual transaxle).

Code 37 — Transaxle temperature out of range — some 1993 models.

Code 41 — Charging system circuit — output driver stage for generator field does not respond properly to the voltage regulator control signal.

Code 42 — Fuel pump or no Autoshut-down (ASDZ) relay voltage sense at controller.

Code 43 — Ignition control circuit — peak primary circuit current not respond properly with maximum dwell time.

Code 43 — Ignition coil #1, 2, or 3 primary circuits — peak primary was not achieved within the maximum allowable dwell time.

Code 44 — Battery temperature voltage — problem exists in the PCM battery temperature circuit or there is an open or short in the engine coolant temperature circuit.

Code 44 — Fused J2 circuit in not present in the logic board; used on the single engine module controller system.

Code 45 — Turbo boost limit exceeded — MAP sensor detects overboost.

Code 44 — Overdrive solenoid circuit — open or short in overdrive solenoid circuit.

Code 46 — Battery voltage too high — battery voltage sense input above target charging voltage during engine operation.

Code 47 — Battery voltage too low — battery voltage sense input below target charging voltage.

Code 51 — Air/fuel at limit — oxygen sensor signal input indicates LEAN air/fuel ratio condition during engine operation.

Code 52 — Air/fuel at limit — oxygen sensor signal input indicates RICH air/fuel ratio condition during engine operation.

Code 52 — Logic module fault — 1984 vehicles.

Code 53 — Internal controller failure — internal engine controller fault condition detected during self test.

Code 54 — Camshaft or (distributor sync.) reference circuit — No camshaft position sensor signal detected during engine rotation.

Code 55 — End of message.

Code 61 — Baro read solenoid — open or short detected in the baro read solenoid circuit.

Code 62 — EMR mileage not stored — unsuccessful attempt to update EMR mileage in the controller EEPROM.

Code 63 — EEPROM write denied — unsuccessful attempt to write to an EEPROM location by the controller.

Code 64 — Flex fuel sensor — Flex fuel sensor signal out of range — (new in 1993) — CNG Temperature voltage out of range — CN gas pressure out of range.

Code 65 — Manifold tuning valve — an open or short has been detected in the manifold tuning valve solenoid circuit (3.3L and 3.5L LH-Platform).

Code 66 — No CCD messages or no BODY CCD messages or no EATX CCD messages — messages from the CCD bus or the BODY CCD or the EATX CCD were not received by the PCM.

Code 76 — Ballast bypass relay — open or short in fuel pump relay circuit.

Code 77 — Speed control relay — an open or short has been detected in the speed control relay.

Code 88 — Display used for start of test.

Code Error — Fault code error — Unrecognized fault ID received by DRBII.

➡ **If more than one definition is listed for a code or the code is not listed here, consult your 'Chilton Total Car Care' manual to obtain the specific meaning for your vehicle. This list is for reference and does not mean that a component is defective. The code identifies the circuit and component that require further testing.**

Chrysler Domestic Built
Feedback Carburetor System

Code 88 — Display used for start of test — must appear or other codes aren't valid.

Code 11 — Carburetor oxygen solenoid.

Code 12 — Transmission unlock relay — 3.7L and 5.2L.

Code 13 — Air switching solenoid — 3.7L and 5.2L.

Code 13 — Vacuum operated secondary control solenoid — 2.2L.

Code 14 — Battery feed to computer disconnected with 20-40 engine starts.

Code 16 — Ignore.

Code 17 — Electronic throttle control solenoid.

Code 18 — EGR or Purge control solenoid.

Code 21 — Distributor pick-up signal.

Code 22 — Oxygen feedback stays rich or lean too long — 3.7L and 5.2L.

Code 22 — Oxygen feedback is LEAN too long — 2.2L.

Code 23 — Oxygen feedback is RICH too long — 2.2L.

Code 24 — Vacuum transducer signal problem.

Code 25 — Charge temperature switch signal — 3.7L and 5.2L engine.

Code 25 — Radiator fan temperature switch signal — 2.2L engine.

Code 26 — Charge temperature sensor signal — 3.7L and 5.2L engine.

Code 26 — Engine temperature sensor signal — 2.2L.

Code 28 — Speed sensor circuit (if equipped).

Code 31 — Battery feed to computer.

Code 32 — Computer can't enter diagnostics.

Code 33 — Computer can't enter diagnostics.

Code 55 — End of message.

Code 88 — Display used for start of test.

Code 00 — Diagnostic readout box is powered up and waiting for codes.

➡ **If more than one definition is listed for a code or the code is not listed here, consult your 'Chilton Total Car Care' manual to obtain the specific meaning for your vehicle. This list is for reference and does not mean that a component is defective. The code identifies the circuit and component that require further testing.**

Chrysler Import Built
Fuel Systems

1984-1988 Colt, Vista, Summit and D50

Code 1 — Oxygen sensor.

Code 2 — Crank angle sensor.

Code 2 — Ignition signal.

Code 3 — Air flow sensor.

Code 4 — Barometric pressure sensor.

Code 5 — Throttle Position Sensor (TPS).

Code 6 — Motor Position Sensor (MPS).

Code 6 — Idle Speed Control (ISC) position sensor.

Code 7 — Engine Coolant Temperature Sensor.

Code 8 — No. 1 cylinder TDC Sensor.

Code 8 — Vehicle speed sensor.

➡ **Some 1988 Multi-Point injected vehicles use 1989 2-digit codes.**

➡ **If more than one definition is listed for a code or the code is not listed here, consult your 'Chilton Total Car Care' manual to obtain the specific meaning for your vehicle. This list is for reference and does not mean that a component is defective. The code identifies the circuit and component that require further testing.**

1988-1993 Colt, Summit, Vista, Laser, Talon, Stealth and D50

Code 11 — Oxygen sensor.

Code 12 — Air flow sensor.

Code 13 — Intake Air Temperature Sensor.

Code 14 — Throttle Position Sensor (TPS).

Code 15 — ISC Motor Position Sensor (MPS).

Code 21 — Engine Coolant Temperature Sensor.

Code 22 — Crank angle sensor.

Code 23 — No. 1 cylinder TDC (Camshaft position) Sensor.

Code 24 — Vehicle speed sensor.

Code 25 — Barometric pressure sensor.

Code 31 — Knock (KS) sensor.

Code 32 — Manifold pressure sensor.

Code 36 — Ignition timing adjustment signal.

Code 39 — Oxygen sensor (rear — turbocharged).

Code 41 — Injector.

Code 42 — Fuel pump.

Code 43 — EGR-California.

Code 44 — Ignition Coil — power transistor unit (No. 1 and No. 4 cylinders) on 3.0L Stealth.

Code 52 — Ignition Coil — power transistor unit (No. 2 and No. 5 cylinders) on 3.0L Stealth.

Code 53 — Ignition coil, power transistor unit (No. 3 and No. 6 cylinders).

Code 55 — IAC valve position sensor.

Code 59 — Heated oxygen sensor.

Code 61 — Transaxle control unit cable (automatic transmission).

Code 62 — Warm up control valve position sensor (non-turbo).

Jeep and Eagle Built
Fuel Systems

1988-90 2.5L, 3.0L and 4.0L Engine

Code 1000 — Ignition line low.
Code 1001 — Ignition line high.
Code 1002 — Oxygen heater line.
Code 1004 — Battery voltage low.
Code 1005 — Sensor ground line out of limits.
Code 1010 — Diagnostic enable line low.
Code 1011 — Diagnostic enable line high.
Code 1012 — MAP line low.
Code 1013 — MAP line high.
Code 1014 — Fuel pump line low.
Code 1015 — Fuel pump line high.
Code 1016 — Charge air temperature sensor low.
Code 1017 — Charge air temperature sensor high.
Code 1018 — No serial data from the ECU.
Code 1021 — Engine failed to start due to mechanical, fuel, or ignition problem.
Code 1022 — Start line low.
Code 1024 — ECU does not see start signal.
Code 1025 — Wide open throttle circuit low.
Code 1027 — ECU sees wide open throttle.
Code 1028 — ECU does not see wide open throttle.
Code 1031 — ECU sees closed throttle.
Code 1032 — ECU does not see closed throttle.
Code 1033 — Idle speed increase line low.
Code 1034 — Idle speed increase line high.
Code 1035 — Idle speed decrease line low.
Code 1036 — Idle speed decrease line high.
Code 1037 — Throttle position sensor reads low.
Code 1038 — Park/Neutral line high.
Code 1040 — Latched B+ line low.
Code 1041 — Latched B+ line high.
Code 1042 — No Latched B+ ½ volt drop.
Code 1047 — Wrong ECU.

Code 1048 — Manual vehicle equipped with automatic ECU.
Code 1049 — Automatic vehicle equipped with manual ECU.
Code 1050 — Idle RPM's less than 500.
Code 1051 — Idle RPM's greater than 2000.
Code 1052 — MAP sensor out of limits.
Code 1053 — Change in MAP reading out of limits.
Code 1054 — Coolant temperature sensor line low.
Code 1055 — Coolant temperature sensor line high.
Code 1056 — Inactive coolant temperature sensor.
Code 1057 — Knock circuit shorted.
Code 1058 — Knock value out of limits.
Code 1059 — A/C request line low.
Code 1060 — A/C request line high.
Code 1061 — A/C select line low.
Code 1062 — A/C select line high.
Code 1063 — A/C clutch line low.
Code 1064 — A/C clutch line high.
Code 1065 — Oxygen reads rich.
Code 1066 — Oxygen reads lean.
Code 1067 — Latch relay line low.
Code 1068 — Latch relay line high.
Code 1070 — A/C cutout line low.
Code 1071 — A/C cutout line high.
Code 1073 — ECU does not see speed sensor signal.
Code 1200 — ECU defective.
Code 1202 — Injector shorted to ground.
Code 1209 — Injector open.
Code 1218 — No voltage at ECU from power latch relay.
Code 1220 — No voltage at ECU from EGR solenoid.
Code 1221 — No injector voltage.
Code 1222 — MAP not grounded.
Code 1223 — No ECU tests run.

➡ Prior to 1988 vehicles used an 0ff-Board Diagnostic system which required special diagnostic equipment to read codes. After 1991 Jeep and Eagle vehicles used the Chrysler Domestic Built Engine Control system. The code list for Chrysler Built Domestic Fuel injection System also covers 1991 and newer Jeep and Eagle vehicles.

FORD MOTOR COMPANY

Introduction To Ford Self-Diagnostics

The engine control systems are used in conjunction with either a throttle body (CFI) injection or multi-point (EFI and SEFI) injection fuel delivery system or feedback carburetor systems depending on the year, model and powertrain. Although the individual system components vary slightly, the electronic control system operation is basically the same. The major difference is the number and type of output devices being controlled by the ECA.

Automotive manufacturers have developed on-board computers to control engines, transmissions and many other components. These on-board computers with dozens of sensors and actuators have become almost impossible to test without the help of electronic test equipment.

One of these electronic test devices has become the on-board computer itself. The Powertrain Control Modules (PCM), sometimes called the Electronic Control Assembly (ECA), used on todays vehicles has a built in self testing system. This self test ability is called self-diagnosis. The self-diagnosis system will test many or all of the sensors and controlled devices for proper function. When a malfunction is detected this system will store a fault code in memory that's related to that specific circuit. You can access the computer to obtain fault codes recorded in memory by using an analog voltmeter or special diagnostic scan tool. This will help narrow down what area to begin testing.

Fault code meanings can vary from year to year even on the same model. It is extremely important after retrieving a fault code to verify its meaning with a proper manual. Servicing a fault code incorrectly will not only lead to the wrong conclusion but could also cause damage if tested or serviced incorrectly. There is a list of general code descriptions provide later in this manual.

WHAT SYSTEM IS ON MY CAR?

There are 3 electronic fuel control systems used by Ford Motor Company. These systems all operate using similar components and on-board computers. Self-Diagnostic on these systems will vary, but, the basic fuel control operation is the same. Ford uses the following systems:

- **EEC-IV and EEC-V** engine control system: used on most domestic built Ford vehicles since 1984.
- **Non-NAAO** EEC engine control system: used on import built Ford vehicles, referred to as Non-NAAO cars.
- **MCU** feedback carburetor system: used on most Ford vehicles before 1984 and some later model vehicles equipped with a V8 engine and feedback carburetor.

Most Ford vehicles made after 1983 except for Capri, Festiva, Probe, Escort and Tracer use the 4th generation Electronic Engine Control system, commonly designated EEC-IV.

If you own a Capri, Festiva, Probe 2.0L, 2.2L, or 2.5L, an Escort or Tracer with a 1.6L or 1.8L engine, then the fuel control system is referred to as NON-NAAO (Not North American Automotive Operations produced vehicles) system. The

fuel system used on these vehicles is called Electronic Engine Control (EEC). This Non-NAAO EEC system components and operation are basically the same as the EEC-IV system. The self-diagnostic function on the EEC system differs from the EEC-VI system and is covered under NON-NAAO vehicle.

Most 1984-94 Ford domestic built vehicles employ the 4th generation Electronic Engine Control system, commonly called EEC-IV, to manage fuel, ignition and emissions on vehicle engines. In 1994 the EEC-V system was introduced on some models. The diagnostic system on EEC-V provides 3 digit codes in place of 2 digit codes, and it is capable of monitoring more inputs and outputs.

If your vehicle was made before 1984, or has a feedback carburetor equipped V8 engine, then it probably uses the Microprocessor Control Unit (MCU). The MCU system was used on most 1981-83 carburetor equipped vehicles, and 1984 and newer V8 engines with feedback carburetors. The MCU system uses a large six sided connector, identical to the one used with EEC-IV systems. The MCU system does NOT use the small single wire connector, like the EEC-IV system. The MCU system is covered in greater detail later in this manual.

EEC-IV and EEC-V Diagnostic System

This system includes all Ford Motor Company vehicles with the exception of imported vehicles like the Capri, Festiva, Probe 2.0L, 2.2L and 2.5L engine and the Escort and Tracer equipped with the 1.8L engine.

Most 1984-94 Ford domestic built vehicles employ the 4th generation Electronic Engine Control system, commonly designated EEC-IV, to manage fuel, ignition and emissions on vehicle engines. In 1994 the EEC-V system was introduced on some models. The diagnostic system on EEC-V provides 3 digit codes in place of 2 digit codes and monitors more components.

ENGINE CONTROL SYSTEM

The Powertrain Control Modules (PCM), usually referred to as the Electronic Control Assembly (ECA) by Ford, is given responsibility for the operation of the emission control devices, cooling fans, ignition and advance and in some cases, automatic transmission functions. Because the EEC-IV oversees both the ignition timing and the fuel injector operation, a precise air/fuel ratio will be maintained under all operating conditions. The ECA is a microprocessor or small computer which receives electrical inputs from several sensors, switches and relays on and around the engine.

Based on combinations of these inputs, the ECA controls outputs to various devices concerned with engine operation and emissions. The engine control assembly relies on the signals to form a correct picture of current vehicle operation. If any of the input signals is incorrect, the ECA reacts to what ever picture is painted for it. For example, if the coolant temperature sensor is inaccurate and reads too low, the ECA may see a picture of the engine never warming up. Consequently, the engine settings will be maintained as if the engine were cold. Because so many inputs can affect one output, correct diagnostic procedures are essential on these systems.

One part of the ECA is devoted to monitoring both input and output functions within the system. This ability forms the core of the self-diagnostic system. If a problem is detected within a circuit, the controller will recognize the fault, assign it an identification code, and store the code in a memory section. Depending on the year and model, the fault code(s) may be represented by two or three digit numbers. The stored code(s) may be retrieved during diagnosis.

➡**When the term Powertrain Control Module (PCM) is used in this manual it will refer to the engine control computer regardless that it may also be called an Electronic Control Assembly (ECA).**

While the EEC-IV system is capable of recognizing many internal faults, certain faults will not be recognized. Because the computer system sees only electrical signals, it cannot sense or react to mechanical or vacuum faults affecting engine operation. Some of these faults may affect another component which will set a code. For example, the ECA monitors the output signal to the fuel injectors, but cannot detect a partially clogged injector. As long as the output driver responds correctly, the computer will read the system as functioning correctly. However, the improper flow of fuel may result in a lean mixture. This would, in turn, be detected by the oxygen sensor and noticed as a constantly lean signal by the ECA. Once the signal falls outside the pre-programmed limits, the engine control assembly would notice the fault and set an identification code.

Additionally, the EEC-IV system employs adaptive fuel logic. This process is used to compensate for normal wear and variability within the fuel system. Once the engine enters steady-state operation, the engine control assembly watches the oxygen sensor signal for a bias or tendency to run slightly rich or lean. If such a bias is detected, the adaptive logic corrects the fuel delivery to bring the air/fuel mixture towards a centered or 14.7:1 ratio. This compensating shift is stored in a non-volatile memory which is retained by battery power even with the ignition switched off. The correction factor is then available the next time the vehicle is operated.

➡**If the battery cable(s) is disconnected for longer than 5 minutes, the adaptive fuel factor will be lost. After repair it will be necessary to drive the car a' least 10 miles to allow the processor to relearn the (orrect factors. The driving period should include stea' -throttle open road driving if possible. During the drive, the vehicle may exhibit driveability symptoms not noticed before. These symptoms should clear as the ECA computes the correction factor. The ECA will also store Code 19 indicating loss of power to the controller.**

Failure Mode Effects Management (FMEM)

The engine controller assembly contains back-up programs which allow the engine to operate if a sensor signal is lost. If a sensor input is seen to be out of range — either high or low — the FMEM program is used. The processor substitutes a fixed value for the missing sensor signal. The engine will continue to operate, although performance and driveability may be noticeably reduced. This function of the controller is sometimes referred to as the limp-in or fail-safe mode. If the missing sensor signal is restored, the FMEM system immediately returns the system to normal operation. The dashboard warning lamp will be lit when FMEM is in effect.

Hardware Limited Operation Strategy (HLOS)

This mode is only used if the fault is too extreme for the FMEM circuit to handle. In this mode, the processor has ceased all computation and control; the entire system is run on fixed values. The vehicle may be operated but performance and driveability will be greatly reduced. The fixed or default settings provide minimal calibration, allowing the vehicle to be carefully driven in for service. The dashboard warning lamp will be lit when HLOS is engaged. Codes cannot be read while the system is operating in this mode.

DASHBOARD WARNING LAMP

The CHECK ENGINE or SERVICE ENGINE SOON dashboard warning lamp is referred to as the Malfunction Indicator Lamp (MIL). The lamp is connected to the engine control assembly and will alert the driver to certain malfunctions within the EEC-IV system. When the lamp is lit, the ECA has detected a fault and stored an identity code in memory. The engine control system will usually enter either FMEM or HLOS mode and driveability will be impaired.

The light will stay on as long as the fault causing it is present. Should the fault self-correct, the MIL will extinguish but the stored code will remain in memory.

Under normal operating conditions, the MIL should light briefly when the ignition key is turned **ON**. As soon as the ECA receives a signal that the engine is cranking, the lamp will be extinguished. The dash warning lamp should remain out during the entire operating cycle.

➡**On Continental, the CHECK ENGINE message is displayed on the message center. When a fault is detected, the message is accompanied by a 1 second tone every 5 seconds. The tone stops after 1 minute. When the Continental system enters HLOS, the additional message CHECK DCL is displayed. DCL refers to the Data Communications Link running between the engine controller and the message center.**

EEC-IV and EEC-V Scan Tool Functions

Although stored codes may be read by using a analog voltmeter, the use of hand-held scan tools such as Ford's Self-Test Automatic Readout (STAR) tester or the second generation SUPER STAR II tester or their equivalent is recommended. There are many manufacturers of these tools; the purchaser must be certain that the tool is proper for the intended use.

Both the STAR and SUPER STAR testers are designed to communicate directly with the EEC-IV system and interpret the electrical signals. The SUPER STAR tester may be used to read either 2 or 3 digit codes; the original STAR tester will not read the 3 digit codes used on many 1990 and newer vehicles.

The scan tool allows any stored faults to be read from the engine controller memory. Use of the scan tool provides additional data during troubleshooting but does not eliminate the use of the charts. The scan tool makes collecting information easier; the data must be correctly interpreted by an operator familiar with the system.

ELECTRICAL TOOLS

The most commonly required electrical diagnostic tool is the Digital Multimeter, allowing voltage, resistance and amperage to be read by one instrument. Many of the diagnostic charts require the use of a volt or ohmmeter during diagnosis.

The multimeter must be a high impedance unit, with 10 megohms of impedance in the voltmeter. This type of meter will not place an additional load on the circuit it is testing; this is extremely important in low voltage circuits. The multimeter must be of high quality in all respects. It should be handled carefully and protected from impact or damage. Replace the batteries frequently in the unit.

Additionally, an analog (needle type) voltmeter may be used to read stored fault codes if the STAR tester is not available. The codes are transmitted as visible needle sweeps on the face of the instrument.

Almost all diagnostic procedures will require the use of the Breakout Box, a device which connects into the EEC-IV harness and provides testing ports for the 60 wires in the harness. Direct testing of the harness connectors at the terminals or by backprobing is not recommended; damage to the wiring and terminals is almost certain to occur.

Other necessary tools include a quality tachometer with inductive (clip-on) pickup, a fuel pressure gauge with system adapters and a vacuum gauge with an auxiliary source of vacuum.

EEC-IV and EEC-V Self-Diagnostics

Diagnosis of a driveability problem requires attention to detail and following the diagnostic procedures in the correct order. Resist the temptation to begin extensive testing before completing the preliminary diagnostic steps. The preliminary or visual inspection must be completed in detail before diagnosis begins. In many cases this will shorten diagnostic time and often cure the problem without electronic testing.

VISUAL INSPECTION

This is possibly the most critical step of diagnosis. A detailed examination of all connectors, wiring and vacuum hoses can often lead to a repair without further diagnosis. Performance of this step relies on the skill of the technician performing it; a careful inspector will check the undersides of hoses as well as the integrity of hard-to-reach hoses blocked by the air cleaner or other components. Wiring should be checked carefully for

any sign of strain , burning, crimping or terminal pull-out from a connector.

Checking connectors at components or in harnesses is required; usually, pushing them together will reveal a loose fit. Pay particular attention to ground circuits, making sure they are not loose or corroded. Remember to inspect connectors and hose fittings at components not mounted on the engine, such as the evaporative canister or relays mounted on the fender aprons. Any component or wiring in the vicinity of a fluid leak or spillage should be given extra attention during inspection.

Additionally, inspect maintenance items such as belt condition and tension, battery charge and condition and the radiator cap carefully. Any of these very simple items may affect the system enough to set a fault.

DIAGNOSTIC CONNECTOR LOCATION

▶ **See Figure 4**

The Diagnostic Link Connectors (DLC) are located a 6 basic locations:
- Near the bulkhead (right or left side of vehicle)
- Near the wheel well (right or left side of vehicle)
- Near the front corner of the engine compartment (right or left side of vehicle)

EEC-IV and EEC-V Reading Codes

The EEC-IV system may be interrogated for stored codes using the Quick Test procedures. These tests will reveal faults immediately present during the test as well as any intermittent codes set within the previous 80 warm up cycles. If a code was set before a problem self-corrected (such as a momentarily loose connector), the code will be erased if the problem does not reoccur within 80 warm-up cycles.

The Quick Test procedure is divided into 2 sections, Key On Engine Off (KOEO) and Key On Engine Running (KOER). These 2 procedures must be performed correctly if the system is to run the internal self-checks and provide accurate fault codes. Codes will be output and displayed as numbers on the hand scan tool, i.e. 23. Code 23 would be displayed as 2 needle sweeps and pause and 3 more needle sweeps. For codes being read on an analog voltmeter, the needle sweeps indicate the code digits in the same manner as the lamp flashes on other systems.

In all cases, the codes 11 or 111 are used to indicate PASS during testing. Note that the PASS code may appear, followed by other stored codes. These are codes from the continuous memory and may indicate intermittent faults, even though the system does not presently contain the fault. The PASS designation only indicates the system passes all internal tests at the moment.

Once the Quick Test has been performed and all fault codes recorded, refer to the code charts. The charts direct the use of

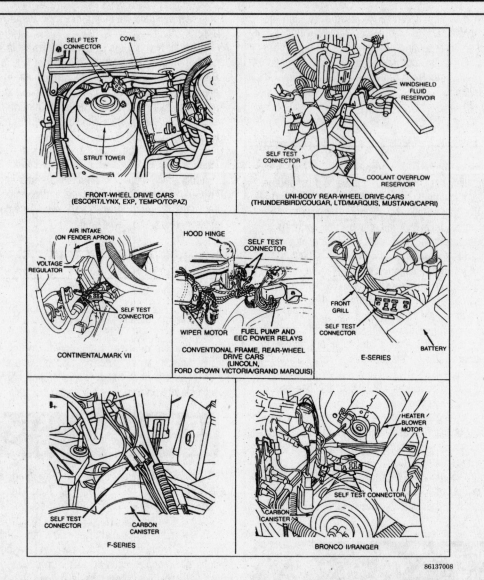

Fig. 4 Typical diagnostic link connector locations. Locations may vary on different years or models and years

specific pinpoint tests for the appropriate circuit and will allow complete circuit testing.

�֍CAUTION

To prevent injury and/or property damage, always block the drive wheels, firmly apply the parking brake, place the transmission in Park or Neutral and turn all electrical loads off before performing the Quick Test procedures.

READING CODES WITH ANALOG VOLTMETER

▶ See Figures 5, 6 and 7

➡There are inexpensive tools available at autoparts stores that make reading and clear Ford engine codes very easy. Reading the voltmeter needle sweeps is sometimes difficult. Always check the code more than once to make certain it was read correctly.

In the absence of a scan tool, an analog voltmeter may be used to retrieve stored fault codes. Set the meter range to read DC 0-15 volts. Connect the + lead of the meter to the battery positive terminal and connect the - lead of the meter to the self-test output pin of the diagnostic connector.

Follow the directions given for performing the KOEO and KOER tests. To activate the tests, use a jumper wire to connect the signal return pin on the diagnostic connector to the self-test input connector. The self-test input line is the separate wire and connector with or near the diagnostic connector.

The codes will be transmitted as groups of needle sweeps. This method may be used to read either 2 or 3 digit codes. The Continuous Memory codes are separated from the KOEO codes by 6 seconds, a single sweep and another 6 second delay.

Key On Engine Off Test

1. Connect the scan tool to the self-test connectors. Make certain the test button is unlatched or up.

2. Start the engine and run it until normal operating temperature is reached.

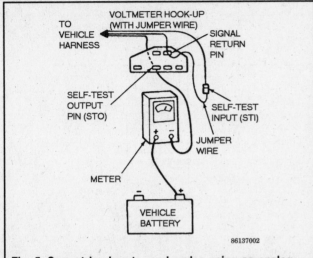

Fig. 5 Correct hookup to read codes using an analog voltmeter

3. Turn the engine **OFF** for 10 seconds.

4. Activate the test button on the STAR tester.

5. Turn the ignition switch **ON** but do not start the engine. For vehicles with 4.9L engines, depress the clutch during the entire test. For vehicles with the 7.3L diesel engine, hold the accelerator to the floor during the test.

6. The KOEO codes will be transmitted. Six to nine seconds after the last KOEO code, a single separator pulse will be transmitted. Six to nine seconds after this pulse, the codes from the Continuous Memory will be transmitted.

7. Record all service codes displayed. Do not depress the throttle on gasoline engines during the test.

Key On Engine Running Test
◆ See Figures 8, 9, 10 and 11

1. Make certain the self-test button is released or de-activated on the STAR tester.

2. Start the engine and run it at 2000 rpm for two minutes. This action warms up the oxygen sensor.

3. Turn the ignition switch **OFF** for 10 seconds.

4. Activate or latch the self-test button on the scan tool.

5. Start the engine. The engine identification code will be transmitted. This is a single digit number representing ½ the number of cylinders in a gasoline engine. On the STAR tester, this number may appear with a zero, i.e., 20 = 2. For 7.3L diesel engines, the ID code is 5. The code is used to confirm that the correct processor is installed and that the self-test has begun.

6. If the vehicle is equipped with a Brake On/Off (BOO) switch, the brake pedal must be depressed and released after the ID code is transmitted.

7. If the vehicle is equipped with a Power Steering Pressure Switch (PSPS), the steering wheel must be turned at least ½ turn and released within 2 seconds after the engine ID code is transmitted.

8. If the vehicle is equipped with the E4OD transmission, the Overdrive Cancel Switch (OCS) must be cycled after the engine ID code is transmitted.

9. Certain Ford vehicles will display a Dynamic Response code 6-20 seconds after the engine ID code. This will appear as one pulse on a meter or as a 10 on the STAR tester. When this code appears, briefly take the engine to wide open throttle. This allows the system to test the throttle position, MAF and MAP sensors.

10. All relevant codes will be displayed and should be recorded. Remember that the codes refer only to faults present during this test cycle. Codes stored in Continuous Memory are not displayed in this test mode.

11. Do not depress the throttle during testing unless a dynamic response code is displayed.

Testing with Continental Message Center
◆ See Figure 12

The stored fault codes may be displayed on the electronic message screen in Continentals so equipped. To perform the KOEO test, press all 3 buttons on the electronic instrument cluster (GAUGE SELECT, ENGLISH/METRIC, SPEED ALARM or SELECT, RESET and SYSTEM CHECK) simultaneously. Turn the ignition switch ON and release the buttons; stored codes will be displayed on the screen.

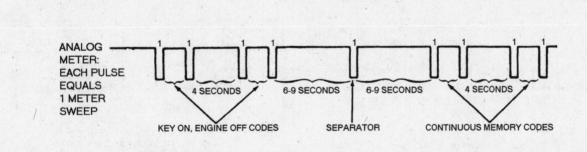

Fig. 6 Code transmission during KOEO test. Note the continuous memory codes are transmitted after a pause and a separator pulse

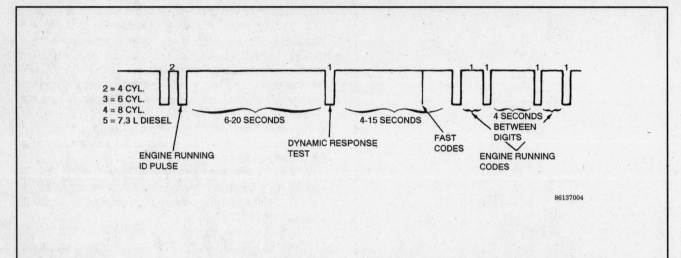

2 = 4 CYL.
3 = 6 CYL.
4 = 8 CYL.
5 = 7.3 L DIESEL

6-20 SECONDS

DYNAMIC RESPONSE TEST

4-15 SECONDS

FAST CODES

4 SECONDS BETWEEN DIGITS

ENGINE RUNNING CODES

ENGINE RUNNING ID PULSE

86137004

Fig. 7 Code transmission during KOER testing begins with the engine identification pulse and may include a dynamic response prompt

86137013

Fig. 8 On some models you must depress the clutch or throttle to the floor for the dynamic portion of the KOER test

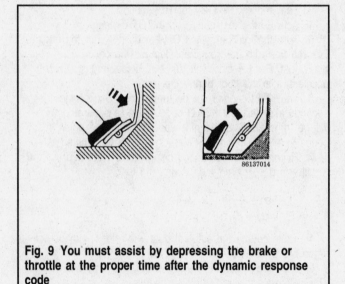

86137014

Fig. 9 You must assist by depressing the brake or throttle at the proper time after the dynamic response code

To perform the KOER test:

1. Hold in all 3 buttons, start the engine and release the buttons.

2. Press the SELECT or GAUGE SELECT button 3 times. The message **dEALEr 4** should appear at the bottom of the message panel.

3. Initiate the test by using a jumper wire to connect the signal return pin on the diagnostic connector to the self-test input connector. The self-test input line is the separate wire and connector with or near the diagnostic connector.

4. The stored codes will be output to the vehicle display.

5. To exit the test, turn the ignition switch **OFF** and disconnect the jumper wire.

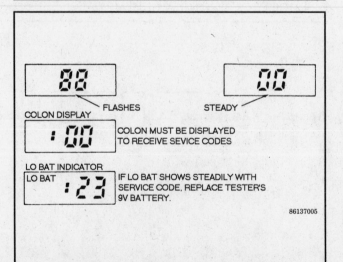

FLASHES STEADY

COLON DISPLAY

COLON MUST BE DISPLAYED TO RECEIVE SEVICE CODES

LO BAT INDICATOR

LO BAT

IF LO BAT SHOWS STEADILY WITH SERVICE CODE, REPLACE TESTER'S 9V BATTERY.

86137005

Fig. 10 Example of STAR tester display screen. The colon must be present before codes can be retrieved

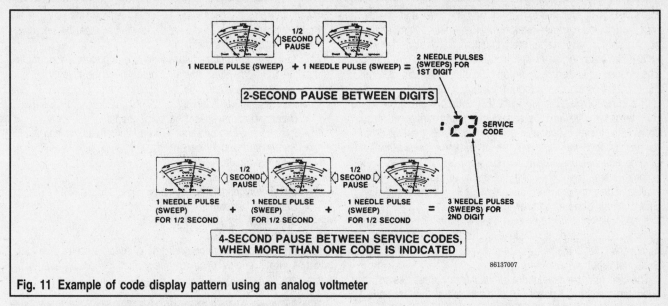

Fig. 11 Example of code display pattern using an analog voltmeter

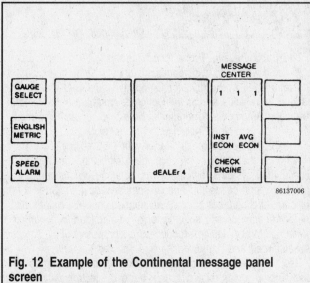

Fig. 12 Example of the Continental message panel screen

ADVANCED TEST MODES

Continuous Monitor or Wiggle Test Mode

Once entered, this mode allows the technician to attempt to recreate intermittent faults by wiggling or tapping components, wiring or connectors. The test may be performed during either KOEO or KOER procedures. The test requires the use of either an analog voltmeter or a hand scan tool.

To enter the continuous monitor mode during KOEO testing, turn the ignition switch **ON**. Activate the test, wait 10 seconds, then deactivate and reactivate the test; the system will enter the continuous monitor mode. Tap, move or wiggle the harness, component or connector suspected of causing the problem; if a fault is detected, the code will store in the memory. When the fault occurs, the dash warning lamp will illuminate, the STAR tester will light a red indicator (and possibly beep) and the analog meter needle will sweep once.

To enter this mode in the KOER test:

1. Start the engine and run it at 2000 rpm for two minutes. This action warms up the oxygen sensor.

2. Turn the ignition switch **OFF** for 10 seconds.

3. Start the engine.

4. Activate the test, wait 10 seconds, then deactivate and reactivate the test; the system will enter the continuous monitor mode.

5. Tap, move or wiggle the harness, component or connector suspected of causing the problem; if a fault is detected, the code will store in the memory.

6. When the fault occurs, the dash warning lamp will illuminate, the STAR tester will light a red indicator (and possibly beep) and the analog meter needle will sweep once.

Output State Check

This testing mode allows the operator to energize and de-energize most of the outputs controlled by the EEC-IV system. Many of the outputs may be checked at the component by listening for a click or feeling the item move or engage by a hand placed on the case. To enter this check:

1. Enter the KOEO test mode.

2. When all codes have been transmitted, depress the accelerator all the way to the floor and release it.

3. The output actuators are now all ON. Depressing the throttle pedal to the floor again switches the all the actuator outputs OFF.

4. This test may be performed as often as necessary, switching between ON and OFF by depressing the throttle.

5. Exit the test by turning the ignition switch **OFF**, disconnecting the jumper at the diagnostic connector or releasing the test button on the scan tool.

Cylinder Balance Test

This test is only for SEFI engines. On SEFI engine the EEC-IV system allows a cylinder balance test to be performed on engines equipped with the Sequential Electronic Fuel Injection system. Cylinder balance testing identifies a weak or non-contributing cylinder.

Enter the cylinder balance test by depressing and releasing the throttle pedal within 2 minutes of the last code output in the KOER test. The idle speed will become fixed and engine rpm is recorded for later reference. The engine control assembly will shut off the fuel to the highest numbered cylinder (4, 6 or 8), allow the engine to stabilize and then record the rpm. The injector is turned back on and the next one shut off and the process continues through cylinder No. 1.

The controller selects the highest rpm drop from all the cylinders tested, multiplies it by a percentage and arrives at an rpm drop value for all cylinders. For example, if the greatest drop for any cylinder was 150 rpm, the processor applies a multiple of 65% and arrives at 98 rpm. The processor then checks the recorded rpm drops, checking that each was at least 98 rpm. If all cylinders meet the criteria, the test is complete and the ECA outputs Code 90 indicating PASS.

If one cylinder did not drop at least this amount, then the cylinder number is output instead of the 90 code. The cylinder number will be followed by a zero, so 30 indicates cylinder No. 3 did not meet the minimum rpm drop.

The test may be repeated a second time by depressing and releasing the throttle pedal within 2 minutes of the last code output. For the second test, the controller uses a lower percentage (and thus a lower rpm) to determine the minimum acceptable rpm drop. Again, either Code 90 or the number of the weak cylinder will be output.

Performing a third test causes the ECA to select an even lower percentage and rpm drop. If a cylinder is shown as weak in the third test, it should be considered non-contributing. The tests may be repeated as often as needed if the throttle is depressed within two minutes of the last code output. Subsequent tests will use the percentage from the third test instead of selecting even lower values.

CONTINUOUS MEMORY CODES

These codes are retained in memory for 80 warm-up cycles. To clear the codes for the purposes of testing or confirming repair, perform the KOEO test. When the fault codes begin to be displayed, de-activate the test by either disconnecting the jumper wire (meter, MIL or message center) or releasing the test button on the hand scanner. Stopping the test during code transmission will erase the Continuous Memory. Do not disconnect the negative battery cable to clear these codes; the Keep Alive memory will be cleared and a new code, 19, will be stored for loss of ECA power.

Keep Alive Memory

The Keep Alive Memory (KAM) contains the adaptive factors used by the processor to compensate for component tolerances and wear. It should not be routinely cleared during diagnosis. If an emissions related part is replaced during repair, the KAM must be cleared. Failure to clear the KAM may cause severe driveability problems since the correction factor for the old component will be applied to the new component.

To clear the Keep Alive Memory, disconnect the negative battery cable for at least 5 minutes. After the memory is cleared and the battery reconnected, the vehicle must be driven at least 10 miles so that the processor may relearn the needed correction factors. The distance to be driven depends on the engine and vehicle, but all drives should include

steady-throttle cruise on open roads. Certain driveability problems may be noted during the drive because the adaptive factors are not yet functioning.

To prevent the replacement of good components, remember that the EEC-IV system has no control over the following items:

- Fuel quantity and quality
- Damaged or faulty ignition components
- Internal engine condition — rings, valves, timing belt, etc.
- Starter and battery circuit
- Dual Hall sensor
- TFI or DIS module
- Distributor condition or function
- Camshaft sensor
- Crankshaft sensor
- Ignition or DIS coil
- Engine governor module   Any of these systems can cause erratic engine behavior easily mistaken for an EEC-IV problem.

Non-NAA0 Diagnostic System

The Capri, Festiva, Probe 2.0L, 2.2L and 2.5L engine, Escort and Tracer with 1.8L engine diagnostic system vehicles are referred to by Ford Motor Company as NON-NAAO, indicating the vehicles and/or their engines originate outside North American Automotive Operations. Note that some of the models also contain North American engines, such as the Probe with 3.0L engine, Escort or Tracer with 1.9L engine.

Although these vehicles share many similarities in their engine control systems, differences must also be considered. While the fault codes are almost standardized (i.e., Code 14 indicates the barometric pressure sensor), not all engines use the same components so a code may be unique to a particular engine or family. These procedures encompass both turbocharged and non-turbocharged engines.

Beside the engine diagnostic function, these procedures will also display codes related to the 4-speed Electronically-controlled Automatic Transaxle (4EAT) used in these vehicles. Note that the 4EAT codes are displayed by these procedures even though retrieving the engine fault codes may require the North American procedures described at the beginning of this section. The Probe with 3.0L engine, Escort and Tracer with 1.9L engine are examples of this situation.

ENGINE CONTROL SYSTEM

These vehicles employ the Electronic Engine Control system, commonly designated EEC, to manage fuel, ignition and emissions on vehicle engines. This system is not EEC-IV, but does share some similarities.

The engine control assembly (ECA) is given responsibility for the operation of the emission control devices, cooling fans, ignition and advance and in some cases, automatic transmission functions. Because the EEC oversees both the ignition timing and the fuel injector operation, a precise air/fuel ratio will be maintained under all operating conditions. The ECA is a microprocessor or small computer which receives electrical inputs from several sensors, switches and relays on and around the engine.

Based on combinations of these inputs, the ECA controls outputs to various devices concerned with engine operation and emissions. The engine control assembly relies on the signals to form a correct picture of current vehicle operation. If any of the input signals is incorrect, the ECA reacts to whatever picture is painted for it. For example, if the coolant temperature sensor is inaccurate and reads too low, the ECA may see a picture of the engine never warming up. Consequently, the engine settings will be maintained as if the engine were cold. Because so many inputs can affect one output, correct diagnostic procedures are essential on these systems.

One part of the ECA is devoted to monitoring both input and output functions within the system. This ability forms the core of the self-diagnostic system. If a problem is detected within a circuit, the controller will recognize the fault, assign it an identification code, and store the code in a memory section. Most NON-NAAO vehicles use two-digit codes for both engine and 4EAT transaxle faults. The stored code(s) may be retrieved during diagnosis.

➡**When the term Powertrain Control Module (PCM) is used in this manual it will refer to the engine control computer regardless that it may also be called an Electronic Control Assembly (ECA).**

While the EEC system is capable of recognizing many internal faults, certain faults will not be recognized. Because the computer system sees only electrical signals, it cannot sense or react to mechanical or vacuum faults affecting engine operation. Some of these faults may affect another component which will set a code. For example, the ECA monitors the output signal to the fuel injectors, but cannot detect a partially clogged injector. As long as the output driver responds correctly, the computer will read the system as functioning correctly. However, the improper flow of fuel may result in a lean mixture. This would, in turn, be detected by the oxygen sensor and noticed as a constantly lean signal by the ECA. Once the signal falls outside the pre-programmed limits, the engine control assembly would notice the fault and set an identification code.

DASHBOARD WARNING LAMP

The CHECK ENGINE dashboard warning lamp is referred to as the Malfunction Indicator Lamp (MIL). The lamp is connected to the engine control assembly and will alert the driver to certain malfunctions within the EEC system. When the lamp is lit, the ECA has detected a fault and stored an identity code in memory.

The light will stay on as long as the fault causing it is present. Should the fault self-correct, the MIL will extinguish but the stored code will remain in memory.

Under normal operating conditions, the MIL should light briefly when the ignition key is turned **ON**. As soon as the ECA receives a signal that the engine is running, the lamp will be extinguished. The dash warning lamp should remain out during the entire operating cycle.

Vehicles with a 4EAT transaxle (except 1.8L and 1.9L engines) also provide a manual shift light, indicating when the transmission is in manual shift mode. On 2.2L turbocharged engines, this lamp will light to advise the driver of certain electronic malfunctions.

Non-NAAO Scan Tool Functions

Although stored codes may be read by using an analog voltmeter by counting the needle sweeps, the use of hand-held scan tools such as Ford's second generation SUPER STAR II tester or equivalent is recommended. There are many manufacturers of these tools; the purchaser must be certain that the tool is proper for the intended use.

➡**The engine and 4EAT fault codes on NON-NAAO vehicles may only be read with the SUPER STAR II or its equivalent. The regular STAR tester or voltmeter may be capable not retrieve the stored codes.**

The SUPER STAR II tester is designed to communicate directly with the EEC system and interpret the electrical signals. The scan tool allows any stored faults to be read from the engine controller memory. Use of the scan tool provides additional data during troubleshooting but does not eliminate the use of the charts. The scan tool makes collecting information easier; the data must be correctly interpreted by an operator familiar with the system.

An adapter cable will be required to connect the scan tool to the vehicle; the adapter(s) may differ depending on the vehicle being tested.

ELECTRICAL TOOLS

The most commonly required electrical diagnostic tool is the Digital Multimeter, allowing voltage, resistance and amperage to be read by one instrument. Many of the diagnostic charts require the use of a voltmeter or ohmmeter during diagnosis.

The multimeter must be a high impedance unit, with 10 megohms of impedance in the voltmeter. This type of meter will not place an additional load on the circuit it is testing; this is extremely important in low voltage circuits. The multimeter must be of high quality in all respects. It should be handled carefully and protected from impact or damage. Replace the batteries frequently in the unit.

Additionally, an analog (needle type) voltmeter may be used to read stored fault codes if the SUPER STAR II tester is not available. The codes are transmitted as visible needle sweeps on the face of the instrument.

Almost all diagnostic procedures will require the use of the Breakout Box, a device which connects into the EEC harness and provides testing ports for the 60 wires in the harness. Direct testing of the harness connectors at the terminals or by backprobing is not recommended; damage to the wiring and terminals is almost certain to occur.

Other necessary tools include a quality tachometer with inductive (clip-on) pickup, a fuel pressure gauge with system adapters and a vacuum gauge with an auxiliary source of vacuum.

Non-NAAO Self-Diagnostics

Diagnosis of a driveability problem requires attention to detail and following the diagnostic procedures in the correct order. Resist the temptation to begin extensive testing before completing the preliminary diagnostic steps. The preliminary or visual inspection must be completed in detail before diagnosis begins. In many cases this will shorten diagnostic time and often cure the problem without electronic testing.

Keep in mind that all the things that previously went wrong with vehicles, before the age of electronics, can still go wrong and are still the cause of the majority of the driveability problems. The best diagnosis starts with a list of symptoms and possible causes, followed by careful checking of those causes in the most likely order. Eliminate all the possible mechanical causes before considering electrical faults.

VISUAL INSPECTION

This is possibly the most critical step of diagnosis. A detailed examination of all connectors, wiring and vacuum hoses can often lead to a repair without further diagnosis. Performance of this step relies on the skill of the technician performing it; a careful inspector will check the undersides of hoses as well as the integrity of hard-to-reach hoses blocked by the air cleaner or other components. Wiring should be checked carefully for any sign of strain , burning, crimping or terminal pull-out from a connector.

Checking connectors at components or in harnesses is required; usually, pushing them together will reveal a loose fit. Pay particular attention to ground circuits, making sure they are not loose or corroded. Remember to inspect connectors and hose fittings at components not mounted on the engine, such as the evaporative canister or relays mounted on the fender aprons. Any component or wiring in the vicinity of a fluid leak or spillage should be given extra attention during inspection.

Additionally, inspect maintenance items such as belt condition and tension, battery charge and condition and the radiator cap carefully. Any of these very simple items may affect the system enough to set a fault.

Non-NAAO Reading Codes

▶ **See Figure 13**

The EEC system may be interrogated for stored codes using the Quick Test procedures. If a code was set before a problem self-corrected (such as a momentarily loose connector), the code will remain in memory until cleared.

The Quick Test procedure is divided into 3 sections, Key On Engine Off (KOEO), Key On Engine Running (KOER) and the Switch Monitor test. These 3 procedures must be performed correctly if the system is to run the internal self-checks and provide accurate fault codes. Codes will be output and displayed as numbers on the hand scan tool, i.e. 23. If the codes are being read by an analog voltmeter, the codes will be displayed as groups of needle sweeps separated by pauses.

Code 23 would be shown as two sweeps, a pause and three more sweeps. A longer pause will occur between codes.

Unlike the EEC-IV system, the EEC system does not broadcast a PASS designator or code. If no fault codes are stored, the display screen of the hand scanner will remain blank. Additionally, the EEC system does not operate switches or sensors during KOEO or KOER testing.

Once the Quick Test has been performed and all fault codes recorded, refer to the service code charts. The charts direct the use of specific pinpoint tests for the appropriate circuit and will allow complete circuit testing.

The EEC diagnostic connector is located at the left rear corner of the engine compartment on most vehicles except when equipped with the 1.6L engine. The 1.6L diagnostic connector is in the right rear corner of the engine compartment. When connecting the test equipment and adaptors, note that the Self-Test Input (STI) connector is separate from the main diagnostic connector on all NON-NAAO engines except for the 1.8L engine. The Self-Test Output (STO) connector is contained within the main diagnostic connector.

✳✳CAUTION

To prevent injury and/or property damage, always block the drive wheels, firmly apply the parking brake, place the transmission in Park or Neutral and turn all electrical loads off before performing the Quick Test procedures.

READING CODES WITH ANALOG VOLTMETER

In the absence of a scan tool, an analog voltmeter may be used to retrieve stored fault codes. Set the meter range to read DC 0-20 volts. Connect the + lead of the meter to the STO pin in the diagnostic connector and connect the - lead of the meter to the negative battery terminal or a good engine ground.

Follow the directions given for performing the KOEO and KOER tests. To activate the tests, use a jumper wire to connect the STI connector to ground. The codes will be transmitted as groups of needle sweeps.

Key On Engine Off (KOEO) Test

1. Make certain the scan tool is OFF; connect it to the self-test connectors. Switch the scan tool to the MECS position. Except on 1.8L engines, make certain the adapter ground cable is connected to the negative battery terminal. On the 1.8L engine, make certain the switch on the adapter is set to EEC or ECA if engine codes are to be retrieved. The other switch position will retrieve codes from the 4EAT.

2. Make certain the scan tool test button is ON or latched down.

3. For all engine or 4EAT codes except 1.8L and 1.9L engines, turn the ignition switch **ON** but do not start the engine, then turn the scan tool ON. On 1.8L and 1.9L engines, turn the scan tool ON first, then turn the ignition switch **ON**.

4. Once energized, the tester should display **888** and beep for 2 seconds. Release the test button; **00** should appear, signifying the tool is ready to read codes.

5. Re-engage the test button.

6. The KOEO codes will be transmitted.

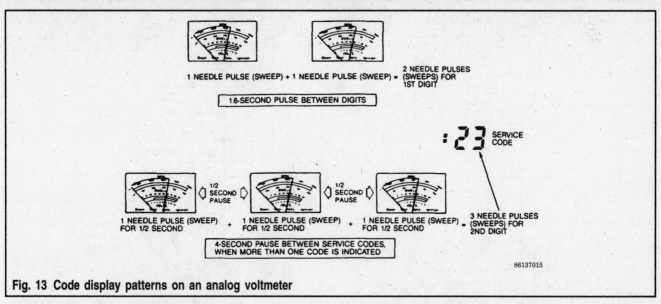

Fig. 13 Code display patterns on an analog voltmeter

7. Record all service codes displayed.

8. After all codes are received, release the test button to review all the codes retained in tester memory.

9. Make sure all codes displayed are recorded. Clear the ECA memory and perform the KOEO test again. This will isolate hard faults from intermittents. Any hard faults will cause the code(s) to be repeated in the 2nd test. An intermittent which is not now present will not set a new code.

10. Record all codes from the 2nd test. After repairs are made on hard fault items, the intermittents must be recreated by tapping suspect sensors, wiggling wires or connectors or reproducing circumstances on a test drive.

➡For both KOEO and KOER tests, the message STO LO always displayed on the screen indicates that the system cannot initiate the Self-Test. The message STI LO displayed with an otherwise blank screen indicates Pass or No Codes Stored.

Key On Engine Running (KOER) Test

1. Make certain the self-test button is released or de-activated on the SUPER STAR II tester and that the tester is properly connected.

2. Start the engine and run it at 2000 rpm for 2 minutes. This action warms up the oxygen sensor.

3. Turn the ignition switch **OFF**.

4. Turn the ignition switch **ON** for 10 seconds but do not start the engine.

5. Start the engine and run it at idle.

6. Activate or latch the self-test button on the scan tool.

7. All relevant codes will be displayed and should be recorded.

Switch Monitor Tests
▶ **See Figures 14 and 15**

This test mode allows the operator to check the input signal from individual switches to the ECA. All switches to be tested must be OFF at the time the test begins; if one switch is on, it will affect the testing of another. The test must begin with the engine cool. The tests may be performed with either the SUPER STAR II tester or an analog voltmeter. When using the

scan tool, the small LED on the adapter cable will light to show that the ECA has received the switch signal. If the voltmeter is used, the voltage will change when the switch is engaged or disengaged.

1. The engine must be off and cooled. Place the transmission in Park or Neutral.

2. Turn all accessories **OFF**.

3. If using the SUPER STAR II, connect it properly. If using an analog voltmeter, use a jumper to ground the STI terminal. Connect the + voltmeter lead to the SML terminal of the diagnostic connector and connect the - lead to a good engine ground.

4. Turn the ignition switch **ON**. Engage the center button on the SUPER STAR II. Most switches can be exercised without starting the engine.

5. Operate each switch according to the test chart and note the response either on the LED or the volt scale. Remember that an improper response means the ECA did not see the switch operation; check circuitry and connectors before assuming the switch is faulty.

6. Turn the ignition switch **OFF** when testing is complete.

CLEARING CODES

Codes stored within the memory must be erased when repairs are completed. Additionally, erasing codes during diagnosis can separate hard faults from intermittents.

To erase stored codes, disconnect the negative battery cable, then depress the brake pedal for at least 10 seconds. Reconnect the battery cable and recheck the system for any remaining or newly-set codes.

MCU Carbureted Diagnostic System

The Microprocessor Control Unit (MCU) system was used on most 1981-83 carburetor equipped vehicles, and 1984 and newer V8 engines with feedback carburetors. The MCU system uses a large six sided connector, identical to the one used

Switch	1.3L	1.8L	2.2L	2.2L Turbo	SUPER STAR II Tester LED or Analog VOM Indications
Clutch engage Switch/ Neutral Gear Switch (CES/NGS) (MTX only)	X	X	X	X	LED on or 12V in gear and clutch pedal released
Manual Lever Position Switch (MLP) (ATX Only)	X	X	X		LED on or 12V in P or N
Idle Switch (IDL)	X	X	X	X	LED on or 12V with accelerator pedal depressed
Brake On-Off Switch (BOO)	X	X MTX	X	X	LED on or 12V with brake pedal depressed
Headlamps Switch (HLDT)	X	X	X	X	LED on or 12V with headlamp switch on
Blower Motor Switch (BLMT)	X	X	X	X	LED on or 12V with blower switch at 2nd or above position
A/C Switch (ACS)	X	X			LED on or 12V with A/C switch on and blower on
Defrost Switch (DEF)	X	X	X	X	LED on or 12V with defrost switch on
Coolant Temperature Switch (CTS)	X	X		X	LED on or 12V with cooling fan on
Wide Open Throttle Switch (WOT)	X	X MTX			LED off or 0V with accelerator pedal fully depressed

86137016

Fig. 14 Switch tests for 1990 and early Ford Non-NAAO vehicles

with EEC-IV systems. The MCU system does NOT use the small single wire connector, like the EEC-IV system.

This system has limited ability to diagnose a malfunction within itself. Through the use of trouble codes, the system will indicate where to test. When an analog voltmeter or special tester is connected to the diagnostic link connector and the system is triggered, the self-test simulates a variety of engine operating conditions and evaluates all the responses received from the various MCU components, so any abnormal operating conditions can be detected.

MCU Carbureted Self-Diagnostics

Diagnosis of a driveability problem requires attention to detail and following the diagnostic procedures in the correct order. Resist the temptation to begin extensive testing before completing the preliminary diagnostic steps. The preliminary or visual inspection must be completed in detail before diagnosis

begins. In many cases this will shorten diagnostic time and often cure the problem without electronic testing.

VISUAL INSPECTION

This is possibly the most critical step of diagnosis. A detailed examination of all connectors, wiring and vacuum hoses can often lead to a repair without further diagnosis. Performance of this step relies on the skill of the technician performing it; a careful inspector will check the undersides of hoses as well as the integrity of hard-to-reach hoses blocked by the air cleaner or other components. Wiring should be checked carefully for any sign of strain , burning, crimping or terminal pull-out from a connector.

Checking connectors at components or in harnesses is required; usually, pushing them together will reveal a loose fit. Pay particular attention to ground circuits, making sure they are not loose or corroded. Remember to inspect connectors and hose fittings at components not mounted on the engine, such as the evaporative canister or relays mounted on the

Switch	1.3L	1.6L	1.8L	2.2L	2.2L Turbo	SUPER STAR II Tester LED or Analog VOM Indications
Clutch engage Switch/ Neutral Gear Switch (CES/NGS) (MTX only)	X	X	X	X	X	LED on or less than 1.5V in gear and clutch pedal released
Manual Lever Position Switch (MLP) (ATX Only)	X	X	X	X	X	LED on or less than 1.5V in P or N
Idle Switch (IDL)	X	X	X	X	X	LED on or less than 1.5V with accelerator pedal depressed
Brake On-Off Switch (BOO)	X	X	X MTX	X	X	LED on or less than 1.5V with brake pedal depressed (not fully)
Headlamps Switch (HLDT)	X	X	X	X	X	LED on or less than 1.5V with headlamp switch on
Blower Motor Switch (BLMT)	X	X	X	X	X	LED on or less than 1.5V with blower switch at 2nd or above position
A/C Switch (ACS)	X	X	X	X	X	LED on or less than 1.5V with A/C switch on and blower on
Defrost Switch (DEF)	X	X	X	X	X	LED on or less than 1.5V with defrost switch on
Coolant Temperature Switch (CTS)	X	X	X	X	X	LED on or less than 1.5V with cooling fan on
Wide Open Throttle Switch (WOT)	X		X			LED off or 0V with accelerator pedal fully depressed
Knock Control (KC)					X	LED on or less than 1.5V while tapping on engine

86137017

Fig. 15 Switch tests for 1991 and newer Ford Non-NAAO vehicles

fender aprons. Any component or wiring in the vicinity of a fluid leak or spillage should be given extra attention during inspection.

Additionally, inspect maintenance items such as belt condition and tension, battery charge and condition and the radiator cap carefully. Any of these very simple items may affect the system enough to set a fault.

MCU Carbureted Reading Codes

▶ See Figure 16

PREPARATION FOR READING CODES

1. Turn OFF all electrical equipment and accessories in vehicle.
2. Follow all safety precautions during testing.
3. Make sure all fluids are at proper levels.

4. Perform 'Visual Inspection' as detailed in EEC-IV system testing, earlier in this section.
5. Start the engine and let it idle, until the engine reaches normal operating temperature. This is when the upper radiator hose is Hot and engine RPM has dropped to its normal warm idle speed.
6. Turn ignition switch OFF.

❋❋CAUTION

Always operate vehicle in well ventilated area. Exhaust gases are very poisonous.

In-line 4 and 6 Cylinder Engines
▶ See Figures 17, 18, 19 and 20

On in-line 4 and 6 cylinder engines with canister control valves, remove the hose that goes to the carbon canister (this simulates a clean carbon canister). Do NOT plug this hose for the remainder of the test procedure. Make certain the throttle linkage is off of the high choke cam setting.

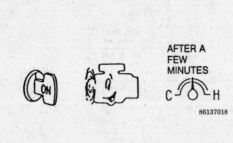

Fig. 16 Let the engine warm up to normal operating temperature before extracting trouble codes

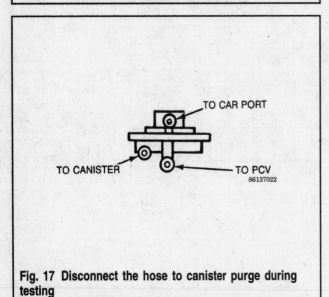

Fig. 17 Disconnect the hose to canister purge during testing

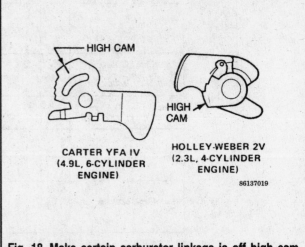

Fig. 18 Make certain carburetor linkage is off high cam and choke is open

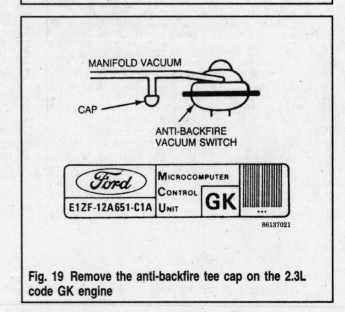

Fig. 19 Remove the anti-backfire tee cap on the 2.3L code GK engine

The 2.3L engines with GK code, you must remove the cap from the anti-backfire vacuum switch tee during testing. The switch is near the rear of the MCU module. On 2.3L engines with an EGR vacuum load control (wide open throttle) valve, you must cover the atmospheric vent holes with a piece of tape.

V6 and V8 Engines
▶ See Figure 21

On V6 and V8 engines, remove the PCV valve from breather cap on valve cover. On the 4.2L and 5.8L engines with vacuum delay valves, uncap the restrictor on the thermactor vacuum control line. On the V6 4.2L engine the vacuum cap is on the TAD line on the 5.8L engine the vacuum cap is on the TAB line.

➡Remember to replace vacuum lines, tee caps and return all components to original condition after testing is complete.

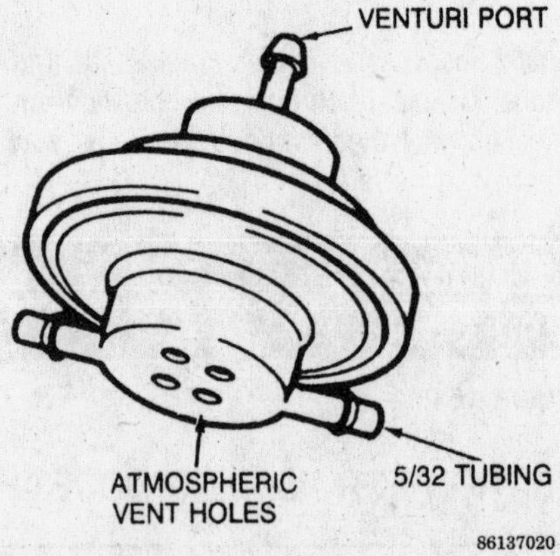

Fig. 20 Cover the EGR control valve vent holes with tape on the 2.3L engine

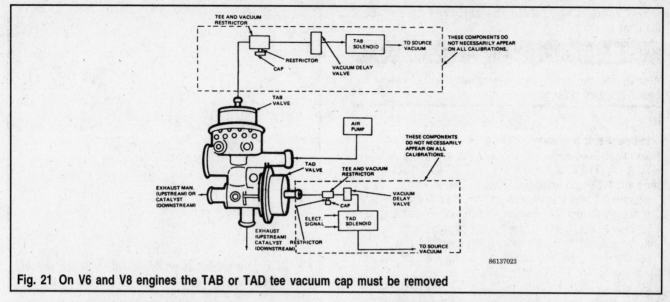

Fig. 21 On V6 and V8 engines the TAB or TAD tee vacuum cap must be removed

After you have performed any special procedures for your vehicle, have a pencil and paper nearby to write down codes. Now you are ready to perform the KOEO test.

USING AN ANALOG VOLTMETER

Key ON Engine OFF Test
▶ See Figure 22

1. With the ignition switch in the **OFF** position, connect a jumper wire between circuits 60 and 201 on the self-test connector.
2. Connect the analog voltmeter from the battery positive post to the self-test output connector.
3. Self the voltmeter scale to 0-15 volt range.
4. Turn the ignition switch ON, but do NOT start the engine. One quick initialization pulse may occur. The output codes will follow in about 5 seconds.
5. Count the voltmeter sweeps, to determine which codes are being transmitted.
6. The MCU system uses 2-digit codes with the pause between each digit being about 2 seconds long. The pause between the two different codes is about 4 seconds long. The code group is sent twice. This allow you to check the accuracy of the codes as you record them.
7. Once this test has been performed and all fault codes recorded, you can refer to the 'Code Descriptions' in this manual for the meaning of the fault code(s). For more detailed code retrieval information and to repair faults refer to your specific vehicle service manual.

Key ON Engine Running (KOER) Test
▶ See Figure 23

1. Turn OFF all electrical equipment and accessories in vehicle.
2. Follow all safety precautions during testing.
3. Make sure all fluids are at the proper levels.

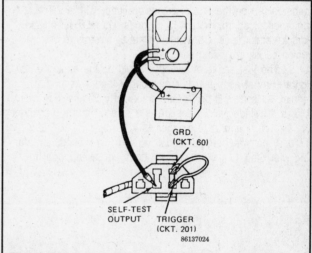

Fig. 22 Connecting the analog voltmeter to the MCU diagnostic link connector

4. Perform 'Visual Inspection' as detailed earlier in this manual.

➡**The following steps involve servicing the engine with the engine running. Observe safety precautions.**

- Apply the parking brake.
- Put the shift lever in **P** (automatic transmission) or NEUTRAL (manual transmission).
- Block the drive wheels.
- Always operate vehicle in well ventilated area. Exhaust gases are very poisonous.
- Stay clear of hot and moving engine parts.

5. The engine should be at normal operating temperature for this test. If not, start the engine and let it idle, until the engine reaches normal operating temperature. This is when the upper radiator hose is Hot and engine RPM has dropped to its normal warm idle speed and repeat Key ON Engine OFF test again.

6. If engine is warm, after codes have been retrieved, Start the engine.

✳✳CAUTION

Always operate vehicle in well ventilated area. Exhaust gases are very poisonous.

7. To extract the fault codes:

In-line 4 and 6 cylinder engines: Start the engine and raise idle to 3000 RPM within 20 seconds of starting vehicle. Hold at 3000 RPM until codes are sent. When codes are sent release throttle and let engine return to idle speed.

V6 and V8 engines: Start engine are raise to 2000 RPM for 2 minutes and turn OFF ignition. Immediately re-start engine and allow to idle. Some engines equipped with throttle kicker will increase idle during the testing, this is normal.

8. If your vehicle is equipped with a knock sensor perform the following test, if not skip to Step 10.

Simulate a spark knock by placing a ³⁄₈ inch socket extension (or similar tool) on the manifold near the base of knock sensor. Tap on the end of extension lightly with a 2-6oz. hammer for approximately 15 seconds. Do NOT hit on the knock sensor itself. Count the voltmeter sweeps to determine which codes are being sent.

9. The first series of sweeps should be the engine ID code, ignore any sweeps that last any longer than 1 second. The engine ID code will be ½ the number of cylinders. For example, a 4 cylinder would appear as 2 sweeps and a 6 cylinder as 3 sweeps and an 8 cylinder as 4 sweeps.

10. If no sweeps occur repeat KOER test procedures, starting with Step 1. If the meter still does not sweep, you have a

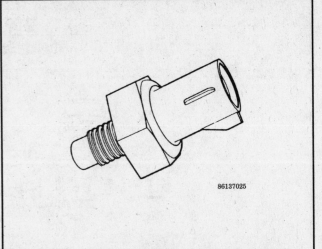

86137025

Fig. 23 If your vehicle is equipped with a knock sensor, you must simulate a spark knock for the self-test

problem which must be repaired before proceeding. Refer to your specific vehicle service manual.

11. Count the sweeps on the meter to find out which codes are being sent. All codes are 2-digits long and will appear the same way as in KOEO Self-Test. Ignore any sweeps lasting more than 1 second. Write codes down on a piece of paper, codes will be sent twice so you can check your list for accuracy. Write codes down in the order they appear. Turn the ignition switch OFF when codes are finished and remove jumper wire.

Diagnostic Trouble Codes

FORD EEC-IV DIAGNOSTIC ENGINE CODES

The code definitions listed general 2-digit codes for Ford Vehicles using the Ford EEC-IV engine control system. In 1991 Ford started introducing vehicles that use 3-digit codes. The code definitions for both the 2 and 3-digit codes are found in this section. For a specific code definition or component test procedure consult your 'Chilton Total Car Care' manual for your vehicle. A diagnostic code does not mean the component is defective. For example a Code 29 is a vehicle speed sensor code. This does not mean the sensor is defective, but to check the sensor and related components. A defective speedometer cable or transmission problem will also set this code.

➡When the term Powertrain Control Module (PCM) is used in this manual it will refer to the engine control computer regardless that it may be a PCM or Electronic Control Module (ECM) or Electronic Control Assembly (ECA).

FORD EEC NON-NAAO VEHICLES

The Capri, Festiva, Probe, Escort and Tracer are referred to as NON-NAAO (Not North American Automotive Operations) produced vehicles. The fuel system used on these vehicles is called Electronic Engine Control (EEC). This EEC system components and operation are basically the same as the EEC-IV system. The self-diagnostic function on the EEC system differs from the EEC-VI system and is covered under NON-NAAO vehicle.

The Non-NAAO EEC system self-diagnostics and code retrieval many be different than domestic built Ford engines. The code descriptions are mostly the same for all of the NON-NAAO vehicles. Take note that not all vehicles use all codes. The transaxle codes were introduced in 1992 some Capri, Escort, Probe and Tracer models. Late model Probe and Escort may be equipped with EEC-IV fuel control system, the diagnostic link connector (DLC) will be of the EEC-IV design.

FORD MCU SYSTEM
DIAGNOSTIC ENGINE CODES

The code definitions listed are general for Ford Vehicles using the Microprocessor Control Unit (MCU) engine control system. Most Ford vehicles up to 1983 and feedback carburetor equipped V8 engines into the 1990's use the MCU engine control system. A diagnostic code does not mean the component is defective. For example a Code 44 is an oxygen sensor code (rich oxygen sensor signal). This code may set if a carburetor is flooding or has a very restricted air cleaner. Replacing the oxygen sensor would not fix the problem. This list is for reference and does not mean a component is defective, consult your 'Chilton Total Car Care' manual for specific component descriptions or testing for your specific vehicle.

Ford EEC-IV System
2-Digit Diagnostic Trouble Codes

1981-94 Passenger Car
1984-94 Light Truck

Code 11 — System Pass.

Code 12 (R) — Idle control fault — RPM Unable To Reach Upper Limit Self-Test.

Code 13 (C) — DC Motor Did Follow Dashpot.

Code 13 (O) — DC Motor Did Not Move.

Code 13 (R) — Idle control fault — Cannot control RPM during Self-Test low RPM check.

Code 14 (C) — Engine RPM signal fault — Profile Ignition Pickup (PIP) circuit failure or RPM sensor.

Code 15 (C) — EEC Processor, power to Keep Alive Memory (KAM) interrupted or test failed.

Code 15 (O) — Power Interrupted To Processor or EEC Processor ROM Test failure.

Code 16 (O,R) — RPM too low to perform Exhaust Gas Oxygen (EGO) sensor test or fuel control error.

Code 17 (O) — CFI Fuel Control System fault — Rich/Lean condition indicated; 3.8L V-6/5.0L V-8 (1984).

Code 17 (R) — RPM Below Self-Test Limit, Set Too Low.

Code 18 (C) — Ignition diagnostic monitor (IDM) circuit failure, loss of RPM signal or SPOUT circuit grounded.

Code 18 (O) — Ignition Diagnostic Monitor (IDM) circuit.

Code 18 (R) — SPOUT or SAW circuit open.

Code 19 (C) — Cylinder Identification (CID) Sensor Input failure.

Code 19 (O) — Failure in EEC Processor internal voltage.

Code 19 (R) — Erratic RPM During EGR Test or RPM Too Low During ISC Off Test.

Code 21 — Engine Coolant Temperature (ECT) out of Self-Test range.

Code 22 (O,R) — Manifold Absolute Pressure (MAP)/Barometric Pressure (BP/BARO) Sensor circuit out of Self-Test range.

Code 23 — Throttle Position (TP) Sensor out of Self-Test range.

Code 24 (O,R) — Air Charge (ACT) or Intake Air (IAT) Temperature out of Self-Test range.

Code 25 (R) — Knock not sensed during dynamic response test.

Code 26 (O,R) — Transmission Fluid Temp (TFT) out of Self-Test range.

Code 26 (O,R) — Vane Air (VAF) or Mass Air (MAF) sensor out of self-test range.

Code 28 (C) — Loss Of Primary Tach, Right Side.

Code 29 (C) — Insufficient input from Vehicle Speed Sensor (VSS) or Programmable Speedometer/Odometer Module (PSOM).

Code 31 — EGR valve position sensor circuit below minimum voltage.

Code 32 — EGR Valve Position (EVP) sensor circuit voltage below closed limit.

Code 33 (C) — Throttle Position (TP) sensor noisy/harsh on line.

Code 33 (R,C) — EGR valve position sensor circuit, EGR valve opening not detected.

Code 34 — EGR valve circuit out of self-test range or valve not closing.

Code 35 — EGR valve circuit above maximum voltage — except 2.3L HSC with Feedback Carburetor System.

— **or** — Throttle Kicker on 2.3L HSC with Feedback Carburetor System.

Code 38 (C) — Idle Track Switch Circuit Open.

Code 39 (C) — AXOD Torque Converter or Bypass Clutch Not Applying Properly.

Code 41 (R,C) — Oxygen Sensor circuit indicates system always lean.

Code 42 (R,C) — Oxygen Sensor circuit indicates system always rich, right side if 2 sensors used.

Code 43 (C) — Oxygen Sensor Out Of Test Range — on 1992 and earlier vehicles.

— **or** — Throttle Position Sensor failure — on 1993 and newer vehicles.

Code 43 (R) — Exhaust Gas Oxygen (EGO) sensor cool down has occurred during testing — 2.3L HSC and 2.8L FBC truck.

Code 44 (R) — Air injection control system failure (right side cylinders, if a split system).

Code 45 (C) — Coil 1 primary circuit failure.

Code 45 (R) — Air injection control system air flow misdirected.

Code 46 (C) — Coil Primary Circuit failure.

Code 46 (R) — Thermactor air not bypassed during Self-Test.

Code 47 (C) — 4x4 switch is closed — on Truck.

Code 47 (R) — Airflow low at idle — on fuel injected engines.

— **or** — 4 x 4 switch is closed — on Truck.

— **or** — Fuel control system/Exhaust Gas Oxygen (EGO) Sensor fault — on 2.3L HSC and 2.8L FBC truck.

Code 48 (C) — Coil Primary Circuit failure; Except 2.3L Truck

— **or** — Loss Of Secondary Tach, Left Side — with 2.3L Truck engine.

Code 48 (R) — Airflow high at base idle.

Code 49 (C) — Electronic Transmission Shift Error — on Truck and 1992 and later cars.

— **or** — SPOUT Signal Defaulted To 10 Degrees BTDC or SPOUT Open — Up to 1991 passenger cars.

Code 51 (O,C) — Engine Coolant Temperature (ECT) circuit open or out of range during self-test.

Code 52 (O) — Power Steering Pressure Switch (PSPS) circuit open.

Code 52 (R) — Power Steering Pressure Switch (PSPS) circuit did not change states.

Code 53 (O,C) — Throttle Position (TP) circuit above maximum voltage.

Code 54 (O,C) — Air Charge (ACT) or Intake Air (IAT) Temperature circuit open.

Code 55 (R) — Key Power Input To Processor — open circuit.

Code 56 (O,C) — Mass Air (MAF) or Vane Air (VAF) Flow circuit above maximum voltage — Port fuel injected engines.

— **or** — Transmission oil temperature (TOT) circuit open — on vehicles with automatic transaxle.

Code 57 (C) — AXOD Circuit failure — on vehicles with automatic overdrive transaxle.

— **or** — Octane Adjust Circuit failure — on some 1992 and newer cars.

Code 58 (R) — Idle Tracking Switch circuit fault.

Code 59 (C) — Automatic Transmission Shift Error — on 1991 and newer.

— **or** — AXOD 4/3 or Neutral Pressure Switch Failed Open — on 3.0L EFI and 3.8L AXOD — vehicles with automatic overdrive transaxle.

Code 59 (O) — AXOD 4/3 Pressure Switch Failed Closed — on 3.8L engine AXOD — vehicles with automatic transaxle.

— **or** — Idle Adjust Service Pin In Use — on 2.9L EFI engine.

— **or** — Low Speed Fuel Pump Circuit failure — on 3.0L SHO engine.

Code 61 (O,C) — Engine Coolant Temperature (ECT) circuit grounded.

Code 62 (C) — Converter clutch error.

Code 62 (O) — Electronic Transmission Shift Error.

Code 63 (O,C) — Throttle Position (TP) circuit below minimum voltage.

Code 64 (O,C) — Air Charge (ACT) or Intake Air (IAT) Temperature circuit grounded.

Code 65 (C) — Fuel System Failed To Enter Closed Loop Mode or key power.

Code 65 (O) — Key Power Check — Possible Charging System overvoltage condition.

Code 65 (R) — Overdrive Cancel Switch (OCS) circuit did not switch.

Code 66 (C) — Mass Air (MAF) or Vane Air (VAF) Flow circuit below minimum voltage — engine with Port fuel injection.

— **or** — Transmission Oil Temperature (TOT) circuit grounded — vehicles with automatic transaxle.

Code 67 (O,C) — Manual Lever Position (MLP) sensor out of range and A/C ON.

Code 67 (O,C) — Neutral/Drive Switch (NDS) circuit open/A/C on during Self-Test.

Code 67 (O,R) — Neutral Drive Circuit Failed or A/C Input High

— **or** — Clutch Switch Circuit failed — on vehicles with manual transaxle

— **or** — Manual Lever Position Sensor out of range — on vehicles with automatic transaxle.

Code 68 (C) — Transmission Fluid Temp (TFT) transmission over temp (over heated).

Code 68 (O) — Idle Tracking Switch circuit — on 2.8L FBC truck only.

— **or** — Air temperature sensor — except FBC truck.

Code 68 (R,C) — Air Temperature Sensor Circuit failure — on 1.9L EFI engine.

— **or** — Idle Tracking Switch Circuit failure — on CFI engine.

— **or** — Transmission Temperature Circuit.

Code 69 (O,C) — Transmission Shift Error.

Code 70 (C) — Data Communications Link Circuit failure.

Code 71 (C) — Software Re-Initialization Detected — on 1.9L EFI and 2.3L Turbo.

— **or** — Idle Tracking Switch failure — on CFI engine.

— **or** — Message Center Control Circuit failure — on vehicles with Message Center Control Center.

— **or** — Power Interrupt Detected — except vehicles with 3.8L AXOD (automatic overdrive transaxle).

Code 72 (R) — Insufficient Manifold Absolute Pressure (MAP) change during Dynamic Response Test.

Code 73 (R) — Insufficient Throttle Position (TP) change during Dynamic Response Test.

Code 74 (R,C) — Brake On/Off (BOO) circuit open/not actuated during Self-Test.

Code 75 (R) — Brake On/Off (BOO) circuit closed/EEC processor input open.

Code 76 (R) — Insufficient Airflow Output Change During Test.

Code 77 (R) — Brief Wide Open Throttle (WOT) not sensed during Self-Test/operator error (Dynamic Response/Cylinder Balance Tests).

Code 78 (C) — Power Interrupt Detected.

Code 79 (O) — A/C on/Defrost on during Self-Test.

Code 81 (C) — MAP Sensor Has Not Changing Normally.

Code 81 (O) — Air Management Circuit failure.

Code 82 (O) — Supercharger Bypass Circuit failure, 3.8L SC engine.

— **or** — Air Management Circuit failure, Except 3.8L SC engine.

— **or** — EGR Solenoid Circuit failure, 2.3L OHC engine.

Code 83 — O/C — Low speed fuel pump relay circuit failure.

Code 83 (O) — High Speed Electro Drive Fan Circuit failure, Except 2.3L OHC and 3.0L SHO engine.

— **or** — Low Speed Fuel Pump Relay Circuit failure, 3.0L SHO engine.

Code 84 (O) — EGR Vacuum Regulator (EVR) circuit failure.

Code 84 (R) — EGR Solenoid Circuit failure.

Code 85 (C) — Adaptive Lean Limit Reached.

Code 85 (O) — Canister Purge (CANP) circuit failure.

Code 86 (C) — Adaptive Rich Limit Reached.

Code 86 (O) — Shift Solenoid (SS) circuit failure.

— **or** — Wide Open Throttle (WOT) A/C Cutoff Solenoid circuit — on Carbureted engine

Code 87 — Fuel Pump circuit fault.

Code 88 (C) — Loss Of Dual Plug Input control.

Code 88 (O) — Electro Drive Fan Circuit failure. — fuel injected engine

— **or** — Throttle Kicker, feedback carburetor system

Code 89 — O — Transmission solenoid circuit failure.

Code 89 (O) — Clutch Converter Override (CCO) circuit failure.

— **or** — Exhaust Heat Control (EHC) Solenoid circuit — 3.8L CFI engine

Code 91 (C) — No Heated Exhaust Gas Oxygen (HEGO) sensor switching detected — left HEGO.

Code 91 (O) — Shift Solenoid 1 (SS1) circuit failure.

Code 91 (R) — Heated Exhaust Gas Oxygen (HEGO) sensor circuit indicates system lean — left HEGO.

Code 92 (O) — Shift Solenoid Circuit failure.

Code 92 (R) — Oxygen Sensor Circuit failure.

Code 93 — O — Throttle Position Sensor (TPS) input low at maximum DC motor extension — OR — Shift solenoid circuit failure.

Code 93 (O) — Coast Clutch Solenoid (CCS) circuit failure.

Code 94 (O) — Torque Converter Clutch (TCC) solenoid circuit failure.

Code 94 (O) — Converter Clutch Control (CCC) Solenoid circuit failure.

Code 94 (R) — Thermactor Air System System inoperative, left side.

Code 95 (O,C) — Fuel Pump secondary circuit failure/Fuel Pump circuit open — EEC processor to motor ground.

Code 96 (O,C) — Fuel Pump secondary circuit failure/Fuel Pump circuit open — battery to EEC processor.

Code 97 (O) — Overdrive Cancel Indicator Light (OCIL) circuit failure.

Code 98 — R — Electronic control assembly failure.

Code 98 (O) — Electronic Pressure Control (EPC) Driver open in EEC processor.

Code 98 (R) — Hard fault is present — FMEM mode.

Code 99 (O,C) — Electronic Pressure Control (EPC) circuit failure.

Code 92 (O) — Shift Solenoid 2 (SS2) circuit failure.

Code 92 (R) — Heated Exhaust Gas Oxygen (HEGO) sensor circuit indicates system rich — left HEGO.

Code 93 (O) — Throttle Position Sensor Input Low At Max DC Motor Extension, CFI engine.

— **or** — Shift Solenoid Circuit failure — Except CFI engine.

Code 94 (O) — Converter Clutch Solenoid Circuit failure.

Code 94 (R) — Thermactor Air System Inoperative.

Code 95 (O,C) — Fuel Pump Circuit failure, ECA To ground.

Code 96 (O,C) — Fuel Pump Circuit failure.

Code 97 (O) — Transmission Indicator Circuit failure.

Code 98 (O) — Electronic Pressure Control Circuit failure.

Code 98 (R) — Electronic Control Assembly failure.

Code 99 (O,C) — Electronic Pressure Control Circuit or Transmission Shift failure.

Code 99 (R) — EEC System Has Not Learned To Control Idle: Ignore Codes 12 & 13.

➡**If more than one definition is listed for a code or the code is not listed here, consult your 'Chilton Total Car Care' manual to get the specific meaning for your vehicle. This list is to be used as a reference for testing and does not mean a specific component is defective.**

(O) — Key On, Engine Off
(R) — Engine running
(C) — Continuous Memory
No Code — Unable to Run Self Test or Output Codes, or list does not apply to vehicle tested, refer to service manual

Ford EEC-IV System
3-Digit Diagnostic Trouble Codes

1991-95 Passenger Car and Light Truck

Code 111 — System pass.

Code 112 — Intake Air Temperature (IAT) Sensor circuit below minimum voltage.

Code 113 — Intake Air Temperature (IAT) Sensor circuit above maximum voltage.

Code 114 — Intake Air Temperature (IAT) higher or lower than expected.

Code 116 — Engine Coolant Temperature (ECT) higher or lower than expected.

Code 117 — Engine Coolant Temperature (ECT) Sensor circuit below minimum voltage.

Code 118 — Engine Coolant Temperature (ECT) Sensor circuit above maximum voltage.

Code 121 — Closed throttle voltage higher or lower than expected.

Code 121 — Indicates Throttle Position voltage inconsistent with Mass Air Flow (MAF) Sensor.

Code 122 — Throttle Position (TP) Sensor circuit below minimum voltage.

Code 123 — Throttle Position (TP) Sensor circuit above maximum voltage.

Code 124 — Throttle Position (TP) Sensor circuit voltage higher than expected.

Code 125 — Throttle Position (TP) Sensor circuit voltage lower than expected.

Code 126 — Manifold Absolute Pressure/Barometric Pressure (MAP/BARO) Sensor higher or lower than expected.

Code 128 — Manifold Absolute Pressure (MAP) Sensor vacuum hose damaged/disconnected.

Code 129 — Insufficient Manifold Absolute Pressure (MAP)/Mass Air Flow (MAF) change during Dynamic Response Test — KOER.

Code 136 — Lack of Heated Oxygen Sensor (HO2S-2) switches during KOER, indicates lean — Bank # 2.

Code 137 — Lack of Heated Oxygen Sensor (HO2S-2) switches during KOER, indicates rich — Bank # 2.

Code 138 — Cold Start Injector (CSI) flow insufficient — KOER.

Code 139 — No Heated Oxygen Sensor (HO2S-2) switches detected — Bank # 2.

Code 141 — Fuel system indicates lean.

Code 144 — No Heated Oxygen Sensor (HO2S-1) switches detected — Bank # 1.

Code 157 — Mass Air Flow (MAF) Sensor circuit below minimum voltage.

Code 158 — Mass Air Flow (MAF) Sensor circuit above maximum voltage.

Code 159 — Mass Air Flow (MAF) higher or lower than expected.

Code 167 — Insufficient Throttle Position (TP) change during Dynamic Response Test — KOER.

Code 171 — Fuel system at adaptive limits, Heated Oxygen Sensor (HO2S-1) unable to switch — Bank # 1.

Code 172 — Lack of Heated Oxygen Sensor (HO2S-1) switches, indicates lean — Bank # 1.

Code 173 — Lack of Heated Oxygen Sensor (HO2S-1) switches, indicates rich — Bank # 1.

Code 174 — Heated Oxygen Sensor (HO2S) switching time is slow — Right side — 1992 vehicles only.

Code 175 — Fuel system at adaptive limits, Heated Oxygen Sensor (HO2S-2) unable to switch — Bank # 2.

Code 176 — Lack of Heated Oxygen Sensor (HO2S-2) switches, indicates lean — Bank # 2.

Code 177 — Lack of Heated Oxygen Sensor (HO2S-2) switches, indicates rich — Bank # 2.

Code 178 — Heated Oxygen Sensor (HO2S) switching time is slow — Left side — 1992 vehicles only.

Code 179 — Fuel system at lean adaptive limit at part throttle, system rich — Bank # 1.

Code 181 — Fuel system at rich adaptive limit at part throttle, system lean — Bank # 1.

Code 182 — Fuel system at lean adaptive limit at idle, system rich — Right side — 1992 vehicles only.

Code 183 — Fuel system at rich adaptive limit at idle, system lean — Right side — 1992 vehicles only.

Code 184 — Mass Air Flow (MAF) higher than expected.

Code 185 — Mass Air Flow (MAF) lower than expected.

Code 186 — Injector pulse width higher or Mass Air Flow (MAF) lower than expected (without BARO Sensor).

Code 187 — Injector pulse width lower than expected (with BARO Sensor.

Code 187 — Injector pulse width lower or Mass Air Flow (MAF) higher than expected (without BARO Sensor).

Code 188 — Fuel system at lean adaptive limit at part throttle, system rich — Bank # 2.

Code 189 — Fuel system at rich adaptive limit at part throttle, system lean — Bank # 2.

Code 191 — Adaptive fuel lean limit is reached at idle — Left side — 1992 vehicles only.

Code 192 — Adaptive fuel rich limit is reached at idle — Left side — 1992 vehicles only.

Code 193 — Flexible Fuel (FF) Sensor circuit failure.

Code 211 — Profile Ignition Pickup (PIP) circuit failure.

Code 212 — Loss of Ignition Diagnostic monitor (IDM) input to Powertrain Control Module (PCM)/SPOUT circuit grounded.

Code 213 — SPOUT circuit open.

Code 214 — Cylinder Identification (CID) circuit failure.

Code 215 — Powertrain Control Module (PCM) detected Coil 1 Primary circuit failure (EI).

Code 216 — Powertrain Control Module (PCM) detected Coil 2 Primary circuit failure (EI).

Code 217 — Powertrain Control Module (PCM) detected Coil 3 Primary circuit failure (EI).

Code 218 — Loss of Ignition Diagnostic Monitor (IDM) signal — left side (dual plug EI).

Code 219 — Spark Timing defaulted to 10 degrees — SPOUT circuit open (EI).

Code 221 — Spark Timing error (EI).

Code 222 Loss of Ignition Diagnostic Monitor (IDM) signal — right side (dual plug EI).

Code 223 — Loss of Dual Plug Inhibit (DPI) control (Dual Plug EI).

Code 224 — Powertrain Control Module (PCM) detected Coil 1,2,3,or 4 Primary circuit failure (Dual Plug EI).

Code 225 — Knock not sensed during Dynamic Response Test — KOER.

Code 226 — Ignition Diagnostic Monitor (IDM) signal not received (EI).

Code 232 — Powertrain Control Module (PCM) detected Coil 1,2,3,or 4 Primary circuit failure (EI).

Code 238 — Powertrain Control Module (PCM) detected Coil 4 Primary circuit failure (EI).

Code 241 — Ignition Control Module (ICM) to Powertrain Control Module (PCM) Ignition Diagnostic Monitor (IDM) Pulse Width Transmission error (EI).

Code 244 — Cylinder Identification (CID) circuit fault present when Cylinder Balance Test requested.

Code 311 — Secondary Air Injection (AIR) system inoperative during KOER — Bank # 1 with dual HO2S.

Code 312 — Secondary Air Injection (AIR) misdirected during KOER.

Code 313 — Secondary Air Injection (AIR) not bypassed during KOER.

Code 314 — Secondary Air Injection (AIR) system inoperative during KOER — Bank # 2 with dual HO2S.

Code 326 — EGR (PFE/DPFE) circuit voltage lower than expected.

Code 327 — EGR (EVP/PFE/DPFE) circuit below minimum voltage.

Code 328 — EGR (EVP) closed valve voltage lower than expected.

Code 332 — Insufficient EGR flow detected/EGR Valve opening not detected (EVP/PFE/DPFE).

Code 334 — EGR (EVP) closed valve voltage higher than expected.

Code 335 — EGR (PFE/DPFE) Sensor voltage higher or lower than expected during KOEO.

Code 336 — Exhaust pressure high/EGR (PFE/DPFE) circuit voltage higher than expected.

Code 337 — EGR (EVP/PFE/DPFE) circuit above maximum voltage.

Code 338 — Engine Coolant Temperature (ECT) lower than expected (thermostat test).

Code 339 — Engine Coolant Temperature (ECT) higher than expected (thermostat test).

Code 341 — Octane Adjust service pin open.

Code 411 — Cannot control RPM during KOER low rpm check.

Code 412 — Cannot control RPM during KOER high rpm check.

Code 415 — Idle Air Control (IAC) system at maximum adaptive lower limit.

Code 416 — Idle Air Control (IAC) system at upper adaptive learning limit.

Code 452 — Insufficient input from Vehicle Speed Sensor (VSS) to PCM.

Code 453 — Servo leaking down (KOER IVSC test).

Code 454 — Servo leaking up (KOER IVSC test).

Code 455 — Insufficient RPM increase (KOER IVSC test).

Code 456 — Insufficient RPM decrease (KOER IVSC test).

Code 457 — Speed Control Command Switch(s) circuit not functioning (KOEO IVSC test).

Code 458 — Speed Control Command Switch(s) stuck/circuit grounded (KOEO IVSC test).

Code 459 — Speed Control ground circuit open (KOEO IVSC test).

Code 511 — Powertrain Control Module (PCM) Read Only Memory (ROM) test failure (KOEO).

Code 512 — Powertrain Control Module (PCM) Keep Alive Memory (KAM) test failure.

Code 513 — Powertrain Control Module (PCM) internal voltage failure (KOEO).

Code 519 — Power Steering Pressure (PSP) Switch circuit open — KOEO.

Code 521 — Power Steering Pressure (PSP) Switch circuit did not change states — KOER.

Code 522 — Vehicle not in park or neutral during KOEO/Park/Neutral Position (PNP) Switch circuit open.

Code 524 — Low speed Fuel Pump circuit open — battery to PCM.

Code 525 — Indicates vehicle in gear/A/C on.

Code 526 — Neutral Pressure Switch (NPS) circuit closed;A/C on — 1992 vehicles only.

Code 527 — Park/Neutral Position (PNP) Switch open — A/C on, KOEO.

Code 528 — Clutch Pedal Position (CPP) switch circuit failure.

Code 529 — Data Communications Link (DCL) or PCM circuit failure.

Code 532 — Cluster Control Assembly (CCA) circuit failure.

Code 533 — Data Communications Link (DCL) or Electronic Instrument Cluster (EIC) circuit failure.

Code 536 — Brake On/Off (BOO) circuit failure/not actuated during KOER.

Code 538 — Insufficient RPM change during KOER Dynamic Response Test.

Code 538 — Invalid Cylinder Balance Test due to throttle movement during test — SFI only.

Code 538 — Invalid Cylinder Balance test due to Cylinder Identification (CID) circuit failure.

Code 539 — A/C on/Defrost on during Self-Test.

Code 542 — Fuel Pump secondary circuit failure.

Code 543 — Fuel Pump secondary circuit failure.

Code 551 — Idle Air Control (IAC) circuit failure — KOEO.

Code 552 — Secondary Air Injection Bypass (AIRB) circuit failure — KOEO.

Code 553 — Secondary Air Injection Diverter (AIRD) circuit failure — KOEO.

Code 554 — Fuel Pressure Regulator Control (FPRC) circuit failure.

Code 556 — Fuel Pump Relay primary circuit failure.

Code 557 — Low speed Fuel Pump primary circuit failure.

Code 558 — EGR Vacuum Regulator (EVR) circuit failure — KOEO.

Code 559 — Air Conditioning On (ACON) Relay circuit failure — KOEO.

Code 563 — High Fan Control (HFC) circuit failure — KOEO.

Code 564 — Fan Control (FC) circuit failure — KOEO.

Code 565 — Canister Purge (CANP) circuit failure — KOEO.

Code 566 — 3-4 Shift Solenoid circuit failure, A4LD transmission — KOEO.

Code 567 — Speed Control Vent (SCVNT) circuit failure — KOEO IVSC test.

Code 568 — Speed Control Vacuum (SCVAC) circuit failure — KOEO IVSC test.

Code 569 — Auxiliary Canister Purge (CANP2) circuit failure — KOEO.

Code 571 — EGRA solenoid circuit failure KOEO.

Code 572 — EGRV solenoid circuit failure KOEO.

Code 578 — A/C Pressure Sensor circuit shorted (VCRM) mode.

Code 579 — Insufficient A/C pressure change (VCRM) mode.

Code 581 — Power to fan circuit over current (VCRM) mode.

Code 582 — Fan circuit open (VCRM) mode.

Code 583 — Power to Fuel Pump over current (VCRM) mode.

Code 584 — Power ground circuit open (Pin 1) (VCRM) mode.

Code 585 — Power to A/C Clutch over current (VCRM) mode.

Code 586 — A/C Clutch circuit open (VCRM) mode.

Code 587 — Variable Control Relay Module (VCRM) communication failure.

Code 593 — Heated Oxygen Sensor Heater (HO2S HTR).

Code 617 — 1-2 Shift error.

Code 618 — 2-3 Shift error.

Code 619 — 3-4 Shift error.

Code 621 — Shift Solenoid 1 (SS1) circuit failure — KOEO.

Code 622 — Shift Solenoid 2 (SS2) circuit failure — KOEO.

Code 623 — Transmission Control Indicator Lamp (TCIL) circuit failure.

Code 624 — Electronic Pressure Control (EPC) circuit failure.

Code 625 — Electronic Pressure Control (EPC) driver open in PCM.

Code 626 — Coast Clutch Solenoid (CCS) circuit failure — KOEO.

Code 627 — Torque Converter Clutch (TCC) solenoid circuit failure.

Code 628 — Excessive Converter Clutch slippage.

Code 629 — Torque Converter Clutch (TCC) solenoid circuit failure.

Code 631 — Transmission Control Indicator Lamp (TCIL) circuit failure — KOEO.

Code 632 — Transmission Control Switch (TCS) circuit did not change states during KOER.

Code 633 — 4 x 4L Switch closed during KOEO.

Code 634 — Manual Lever Position (MLP) voltage higher or lower than expected/ error in Transmission Select Switch (TSS) circuit(s).

Code 636 — Transmission Oil Temperature (TOT) higher or lower than expected.

Code 637 — Transmission Oil Temperature (TOT) Sensor circuit above maximum voltage/circuit open.

Code 638 — Transmission Oil Temperature (TOT) Sensor circuit below minimum voltage/circuit shorted.

Code 639 — Insufficient input from Transmission Speed Sensor (TSS) .

Code 641 — Shift Solenoid 3 (SS3) circuit failure.

Code 643 — Torque Converter Clutch (TCC) circuit failure.

Code 645 — Incorrect gear ratio obtained for first gear.

Code 646 — Incorrect gear ratio obtained for second gear.

Code 647 — Incorrect gear ratio obtained for third gear.

Code 648 — Incorrect gear ratio obtained for fourth gear.

Code 649 — Electronic Pressure Control (EPC) higher or lower than expected.

Code 651 — Electronic Pressure Control (EPC) circuit failure.

Code 652 — Torque Converter Clutch (TCC) Solenoid circuit failure.

Code 654 — Manual Lever Position (MLP) Sensor not indicating park during KOEO.

Code 655 — Manual Lever Position (MLP) Sensor indicating not in neutral during Self-Test.

Code 656 — Torque Converter Clutch (TCC) continuous slip error.

Code 657 — Transmission Over Temperature condition occurred.

Code 659 — High vehicle speed in park indicated.

Code 667 — Transmission Range sensor circuit voltage below minimum voltage.

Code 668 — Transmission Range sensor circuit voltage above maximum voltage.

Code 675 — Transmission Range sensor circuit voltage out of range.

Code 691 — 4x4 Low switch open or short circuit.

Code 692 — Transmission state does not match calculated ratio.

Code 998 — Hard fault present — FMEM Mode.

➡**If specific cylinder banks or sides are referred to in any of the above codes, but the vehicle code is being obtained from has a 4 cylinder engine, or only one Oxygen Sensor, disregard the bank/side reference, but the code definition and components it pertains to is always the same.**

Ford EEC-V System
OBD-II Diagnostic Trouble Codes

1994 Passenger Cars and Light Trucks

- DTC **PO102** — Mass Air Flow (MAF) Sensor circuit low input
- DTC **PO103** — Mass Air Flow (MAF) Sensor circuit high input
- DTC **PO112** — Intake Air Temperature (IAT) Sensor circuit low input
- DTC **PO113** — Intake Air Temperature (IAT) Sensor high input
- DTC **PO117** — Engine Coolant Temperature (ECT) low input
- DTC **PO118** — Engine Coolant Temperature (ECT) Sensor circuit high input
- DTC **PO122** — Throttle Position (TP) Sensor circuit low input
- DTC **PO123** — Throttle Position (TP) Sensor high input
- DTC **PO125** — Insufficient coolant temperature to enter closed loop fuel control
- DTC **PO132** — Upstream Heated Oxygen Sensor (HO$_2$S 11) circuit high voltage (Bank #1)
- DTC **PO135** — Heated Oxygen Sensor Heater (HTR 11) circuit malfunction
- DTC **PO138** — Downstream Heated Oxygen Sensor (HO$_2$S 12) circuit high voltage (Bank #1)
- DTC **PO140** — Heated Oxygen Sensor (HO$_2$S 12) circuit no activity detected (Bank #1)
- DTC **PO141** — Heated Oxygen Sensor Heater (HTR 12) circuit malfunction
- DTC **PO152** — Upstream Heated Oxygen Sensor (HO$_2$S 21) circuit high voltage (Bank #2)
- DTC **PO155** — Heated Oxygen Sensor Heater (HTR 21) circuit malfunction
- DTC **PO158** — Downstream Heated Oxygen Sensor (HO$_2$S 22) circuit high voltage (Bank #2)
- DTC **PO160** — Heated Oxygen Sensor (HO$_2$S 12) circuit no activity detected (Bank #2)
- DTC **PO161** — Heated Oxygen Sensor Heater (HTR 22) circuit malfunction
- DTC **PO171** — System (adaptive fuel) too lean (Bank #1)
- DTC **PO172** — System (adaptive fuel) too lean (Bank #1)
- DTC **PO174** — System (adaptive fuel) too lean (Bank #1)
- DTC **PO175** — System (adaptive fuel) too lean (Bank #1)
- DTC **PO300** — Random misfire detected
- DTC **PO301** — Cylinder #1 misfire detected
- DTC **PO302** — Cylinder #2 misfire detected
- DTC **PO303** — Cylinder #3 misfire detected
- DTC **PO304** — Cylinder #4 misfire detected
- DTC **PO305** — Cylinder #5 misfire detected
- DTC **PO306** — Cylinder #6 misfire detected
- DTC **PO307** — Cylinder #7 misfire detected
- DTC **PO308** — Cylinder #8 misfire detected

- DTC **PO320** — Ignition engine speed (Profile Ignition Pickup) input circuit malfunction
- DTC **PO340** — Camshaft Position (CMP) sensor circuit malfunction (CID)
- DTC **PO402** — Exhaust Gas Recirculation (EGR) excess flow detected (valve open at idle)
- DTC **PO420** — Catalyst system efficiency below threshold (Bank #1)
- DTC **PO430** — Catalyst system efficiency below threshold (Bank #2)
- DTC **PO443** — Evaporative emission control system Canister Purge (CANP) Control Valve circuit malfunction
- DTC **PO500** — Vehicle Speed Sensor (VSS) malfunction
- DTC **PO505** — Idle Air Control (IAC) system malfunction
- DTC **PO605** — Powertrain Control Module (PCM) — Read Only Memory (ROM) test error
- DTC **PO703** — Brake On/Off (BOO) switch input malfunction
- DTC **PO707** — Manual Lever Position (MLP) sensor circuit low input
- DTC **PO708** — Manual Lever Position (MLP) sensor circuit high input
- DTC **PO720** — Output Shaft Speed (OSS) sensor circuit malfunction
- DTC **PO741** — Torque Converter Clutch (TCC) system incorrect mechanical performance
- DTC **PO743** — Torque Converter Clutch (TCC) system electrical failure
- DTC **PO750** — Shift Solenoid #1 (SS1) circuit malfunction
- DTC **PO751** — Shift Solenoid #1 (SS1) performance
- DTC **PO755** — Shift Solenoid #2 (SS2) circuit malfunction
- DTC **PO756** — Shift Solenoid #2 (SS2) performance
- DTC **P1000** — OBD II Monitor Testing not complete
- DTC **P1100** — Mass Air Flow (MAF) sensor intermittent
- DTC **P1101** — Mass Air Flow (MAF) sensor out of Self-Test range
- DTC **P1112** — Intake Air Temperature (IAT) sensor intermittent
- DTC **P1116** — Engine Coolant Temperature (ECT) sensor out of Self-Test range
- DTC **P1117** — Engine Coolant Temperature (ECT) sensor intermittent
- DTC **P1120** — Throttle Position (TP) sensor out of range low
- DTC **P1121** — Throttle Position (TP) sensor inconsistent with MAF sensor
- DTC **P1124** — Throttle Position (TP) sensor out of Self-Test range
- DTC **P1125** — Throttle Position (TP) sensor circuit intermittent
- DTC **P1130** — Lack of HO_2S 11 switch, adaptive fuel at limit
- DTC **P1131** — Lack of HO_2S 11 switch, sensor indicates lean (Bank #1)
- DTC **P1132** — Lack of HO_2S 11 switch, sensor indicates rich (Bank #1)
- DTC **P1137** — Lack of HO_2S 12 switch, sensor indicates lean (Bank #1)
- DTC **P1138** — Lack of HO_2S 12 switch, sensor indicates rich (Bank #1)
- DTC **P1150** — Lack of HO_2S 21 switch, adaptive fuel at limit
- DTC **P1151** — Lack of HO_2S 21 switch, sensor indicates lean (Bank #2)
- DTC **P1152** — Lack of HO_2S 21 switch, sensor indicates rich (Bank #2)
- DTC **P1157** — Lack of HO_2S 22 switch, sensor indicates lean (Bank #2)
- DTC **P1158** — Lack of HO_2S 22 switch, sensor indicates rich (Bank #2)
- DTC **P1351** — Ignition Diagnostic Monitor (IDM) circuit input malfunction
- **P1352** — Ignition coil A primary circuit malfunction
- DTC **P1353** — Ignition coil B primary circuit malfunction
- DTC **P1354** — Ignition coil C primary circuit malfunction
- DTC **P1355** — Ignition coil D primary circuit malfunction
- DTC **P1364** — Ignition coil primary circuit malfunction
- DTC **P1390** — Octane Adjust (OCT ADJ) out of Self-Test range
- DTC **P1400** — Differential Pressure Feedback Electronic (DPFE) sensor circuit low voltage detected
- DTC **P1401** — Differential Pressure Feedback Electronic (DPFE) sensor circuit high voltage detected
- DTC **P1403** — Differential Pressure Feedback Electronic (DPFE) sensor hoses reversed
- DTC **P1405** — Differential Pressure Feedback Electronic (DPFE) sensor upstream hose off or plugged
- DTC **P1406** — Differential Pressure Feedback Electronic (DPFE) sensor downstream hose off or plugged
- DTC **P1407** — Exhaust Gas Recirculation (EGR) no flow detected (valve stuck closed or inoperative)
- DTC **P1408** — Exhaust Gas Recirculation (EGR) flow out of Self-Test range
- DTC **P1473** — Fan Secondary High with fan(s) off
- DTC **P1474** — Low Fan Control primary circuit malfunction
- DTC **P1479** — High Fan Control primary circuit malfunction
- DTC **P1480** — Fan Secondary low with low fan on
- DTC **P1481** — Fan Secondary low with high fan on
- DTC **P1500** — Vehicle Speed Sensor (VSS) circuit intermittent
- DTC **P1505** — Idle Air Control (IAC) system at adaptive clip
- DTC **P1605** — Powertrain Control Module (PCM) — Keep Alive Memory (KAM) test error
- DTC **P1703** — Brake On/Off (BOO) switch out of Self-Test range
- DTC **P1705** — Manual Lever Position (MLP) sensor out of Self-Test range
- DTC **P1711** — Transmission Fluid Temperature (TFT) sensor out of Self-Test range
- DTC **P1742** — Torque Converter Clutch (TCC) solenoid mechanically failed (turns MIL on)
- DTC **P1743** — Torque Converter Clutch (TCC) solenoid mechanically failed (turns TCIL on)
- DTC **P1744** — Torque Converter Clutch (TCC) system mechanically stuck in off position
- DTC **P1746** — Electronic Pressure Control (EPC) solenoid circuit low input (open circuit)
- DTC **P1747** — Electronic Pressure Control (EPC) solenoid circuit high input (short circuit)

- DTC **P1751** — Shift Solenoid #1 (SS1) performance
- DTC **P1756** — Shift Solenoid #2 (SS2) performance
- DTC **P1780** — Transmission Control Switch (TCS) circuit out of Self-Test range

1995 Passenger Cars and Light Trucks

- DTC **PO102** — Mass Air Flow (MAF) Sensor circuit low input
- DTC **PO103** — Mass Air Flow (MAF) Sensor circuit high input
- DTC **PO112** — Intake Air Temperature (IAT) Sensor circuit low input
- DTC **PO113** — Intake Air Temperature (IAT) Sensor high input
- DTC **PO117** — Engine Coolant Temperature (ECT) low input
- DTC **PO118** — Engine Coolant Temperature (ECT) Sensor circuit high input
- DTC **PO121** — In range operating Throttle Position (TP) sensor circuit failure
- DTC **PO122** — Throttle Position (TP) Sensor circuit low input
- DTC **PO123** — Throttle Position (TP) Sensor high input
- DTC **PO125** — Insufficient coolant temperature to enter closed loop fuel control
- DTC **PO126** — Insufficient coolant temperature for stable operation
- DTC **PO131** — Upstream Heated Oxygen Sensor (HO$_2$S 11) circuit out of range low voltage (bank #1)
- DTC **PO132** — Upstream Heated Oxygen Sensor (H0$_2$S 11) circuit high voltage (Bank #1)
- DTC **PO133** — Upstream Heated Oxygen Sensor (HO2S 11) circuit slow response (Bank #1)
- DTC **PO135** — Heated Oxygen Sensor Heater (HTR 11) circuit malfunction
- DTC **PO136** — Downstream Heated Oxygen Sensor (HO$_2$S 12) circuit malfunction (Bank #1
- DTC **PO138** — Downstream Heated Oxygen Sensor (HO$_2$S 12) circuit high voltage (Bank #1)
- DTC **PO140** — Heated Oxygen Sensor (HO$_2$S 12) circuit no activity detected (Bank #1)
- DTC **PO141** — Heated Oxygen Sensor Heater (HTR 12) circuit malfunction
- DTC **PO151** — Upstream Heated Oxygen Sensor (HO$_2$S 21) circuit out of range low voltage (Bank #2)
- DTC **PO152** — Upstream Heated Oxygen Sensor (HO$_2$S 21) circuit high voltage (Bank #2)
- DTC **PO153** — Upstream Heated Oxygen Sensor (HO$_2$S 21) circuit slow response (Bank #2)
- DTC **PO155** — Heated Oxygen Sensor Heater (HTR 21) circuit malfunction
- DTC **PO156** — Downstream Heated Oxygen Sensor (HO$_2$S 22) circuit malfunction (Bank #2)
- DTC **PO158** — Downstream Heated Oxygen Sensor (HO$_2$S 22) circuit high voltage (Bank #2)
- DTC **PO160** — Heated Oxygen Sensor (HO$_2$S 12) circuit no activity detected (Bank #2)
- DTC **PO161** — Heated Oxygen Sensor Heater (HTR 22) circuit malfunction
- DTC **PO171** — System (adaptive fuel) too lean (Bank #1)
- DTC **PO172** — System (adaptive fuel) too rich (Bank #1)
- DTC **PO174** — System (adaptive fuel) too lean (Bank #2)
- DTC **PO175** — System (adaptive fuel) too rich (Bank #2)
- DTC **PO222** — Throttle Position Sensor B (TP-B) circuit low input
- DTC **PO223** — Throttle Position Sensor B (TP-B) circuit high input
- DTC **PO230** — Fuel pump primary circuit malfunction
- DTC **PO231** — Fuel pump secondary circuit low
- DTC **PO232** — Fuel pump secondary circuit high
- DTC **PO300** — Random misfire detected
- DTC **PO301** — Cylinder #1 misfire detected
- DTC **PO302** — Cylinder #2 misfire detected
- DTC **PO303** — Cylinder #3 misfire detected
- DTC **PO304** — Cylinder #4 misfire detected
- DTC **PO305** — Cylinder #5 misfire detected
- DTC **PO306** — Cylinder #6 misfire detected
- DTC **PO307** — Cylinder #7 misfire detected
- DTC **PO308** — Cylinder #8 misfire detected
- DTC **PO320** — Ignition engine speed (Profile Ignition Pickup) input circuit malfunction
- DTC **PO340** — Camshaft Position (CMP) sensor circuit malfunction (CID)
- DTC **PO350** — Ignition Coil primary circuit malfunction
- DTC **PO351** — Ignition Coil A primary circuit malfunction
- DTC **PO352** — Ignition Coil B primary circuit malfunction
- DTC **PO353** — Ignition Coil C primary circuit malfunction
- DTC **PO354** — Ignition Coil D primary circuit malfunction
- DTC **PO400** — Exhaust Gas Recirculation (EGR) flow malfunction
- DTC **PO401** — Exhaust Gas Recirculation (EGR) flow insufficient detected
- DTC **PO402** — Exhaust Gas Recirculation (EGR) excess flow detected (valve open at idle)
- DTC **PO411** — Secondary Air Injection system incorrect flow detected
- DTC **PO412** — Secondary Air Injection system control valve malfunction
- DTC **PO420** — Catalyst system efficiency below threshold (Bank #1)
- DTC **PO430** — Catalyst system efficiency below threshold (Bank #2)
- DTC **PO443** — Evaporative emission control system Canister Purge (CANP) Control Valve circuit malfunction
- DTC **PO500** — Vehicle Speed Sensor (VSS) malfunction
- DTC **PO505** — Idle Air Control (IAC) system malfunction
- DTC **PO603** — Powertrain Control Module (PCM) — Keep Alive Memory (KAM) test error
- DTC **PO605** — Powertrain Control Module (PCM) — Read Only Memory (ROM) test error
- DTC **PO704** — Clutch Pedal Position (CPP) switch input circuit malfunction
- DTC **PO703** — Brake On/Off (BOO) switch input malfunction
- DTC **PO707** — Manual Lever Position (MLP) sensor circuit low input
- DTC **PO708** — Manual Lever Position (MLP) sensor circuit high input
- DTC **PO712** — Transmission Fluid Temperature (TFT) sensor circuit low input
- DTC **PO713** — Transmission Fluid Temperature (TFT) sensor circuit high input

- DTC **PO715** — Turbine Shaft Speed (TSS) sensor circuit malfunction
- DTC **PO720** — Output Shaft Speed (OSS) sensor circuit malfunction
- DTC **PO731** — Incorrect ratio for first gear
- DTC **PO732** — Incorrect ratio for second gear
- DTC **PO733** — Incorrect ratio for third gear
- DTC **PO734** — Incorrect ratio for fourth gear
- DTC **PO736** — Reverse incorrect gear
- DTC **PO741** — Torque Converter Clutch (TCC) system incorrect mechanical performance
- DTC **PO746** — Electronic Pressure Control (EPC) solenoid performance
- DTC **PO743** — Torque Converter Clutch (TCC) system electrical failure
- DTC **PO750** — Shift Solenoid #1 (SS1) circuit malfunction
- DTC **PO751** — Shift Solenoid #1 (SS1) performance
- DTC **PO755** — Shift Solenoid #2 (SS2) circuit malfunction
- DTC **PO756** — Shift Solenoid #2 (SS2) performance
- DTC **PO760** — Shift Solenoid #3 (SS3) circuit malfunction
- DTC **PO761** — Shift Solenoid #3 (SS3) performance
- DTC **PO781** — 1 to 2 shift error
- DTC **PO782** — 2 to 3 shift error
- DTC **PO783** — 3 to 4 shift error
- DTC **PO784** — 4 to 5 shift error
- DTC **P1000** — OBD II Monitor Testing not complete
- DTC **U1039** — OBD II Monitor not complete
- DTC **U1051** — Brake switch signal missing or incorrect
- DTC **P1100** — Mass Air Flow (MAF) sensor intermittent
- DTC **P1101** — Mass Air Flow (MAF) sensor out of Self-Test range
- DTC **P1112** — Intake Air Temperature (IAT) sensor intermittent
- DTC **P1116** — Engine Coolant Temperature (ECT) sensor out of Self-Test range
- DTC **P1117** — Engine Coolant Temperature (ECT) sensor intermittent
- DTC **P1120** — Throttle Position (TP) sensor out of range low
- DTC **P1121** — Throttle Position (TP) sensor inconsistent with MAF sensor
- DTC **P1124** — Throttle Position (TP) sensor out of Self-Test range
- DTC **P1125** — Throttle Position (TP) sensor circuit intermittent
- DTC **P1130** — Lack of HO$_2$S 11 switch, adaptive fuel at limit
- DTC **P1131** — Lack of HO$_2$S 11 switch, sensor indicates lean (Bank #1)
- DTC **P1132** — Lack of HO$_2$S 11 switch, sensor indicates rich (Bank #1)
- DTC **U1135** — Ignition switch signal missing or incorrect
- DTC **P1137** — Lack of HO$_2$S 12 switch, sensor indicates lean (Bank #1)
- DTC **P1138** — Lack of HO$_2$S 12 switch, sensor indicates rich (Bank #1)
- DTC **P1150** — Lack of HO$_2$S 21 switch, adaptive fuel at limit
- DTC **P1151** — Lack of HO$_2$S 21 switch, sensor indicates lean (Bank #2)
- DTC **P1152** — Lack of HO$_2$S 21 switch, sensor indicates rich (Bank #2)
- DTC **P1157** — Lack of HO$_2$S 22 switch, sensor indicates lean (Bank #2)
- DTC **P1158** — Lack of HO$_2$S 22 switch, sensor indicates rich (Bank #2)
- DTC **P1220** — Series Throttle Control malfunction
- DTC **P1224** — Throttle Position Sensor (TP-B) out of Self-test range
- DTC **P1233** — Fuel Pump driver Module offline
- DTC **P1234** — Fuel Pump driver Module offline
- DTC **P1235** — Fuel Pump control out of range
- DTC **P1236** — Fuel Pump control out of range
- DTC **P1237** — Fuel Pump secondary circuit malfunction
- DTC **P1238** — Fuel Pump secondary circuit malfunction
- DTC **P1260** — THEFT detected - engine disabled
- DTC **P1270** — Engine RPM or vehicle speed limiter reached
- DTC **P1351** — Ignition Diagnostic Monitor (IDM) circuit input malfunction
- DTC **P1352** — Ignition coil A primary circuit malfunction
- DTC **P1353** — Ignition coil B primary circuit malfunction
- DTC **P1354** — Ignition coil C primary circuit malfunction
- DTC **P1355** — Ignition coil D primary circuit malfunction
- DTC **P1358** — Ignition Diagnostic Monitor (IDM) signal out of Self-Test range
- DTC **P1359** — Spark output circuit malfunction
- DTC **P1364** — Ignition coil primary circuit malfunction
- DTC **P1390** — Octane Adjust (OCT ADJ) out of Self-Test range
- DTC **P1400** — Differential Pressure Feedback Electronic (DPFE) sensor circuit low voltage detected
- DTC **P1401** — Differential Pressure Feedback Electronic (DPFE) sensor circuit high voltage detected
- DTC **P1403** — Differential Pressure Feedback Electronic (DPFE) sensor hoses reversed
- DTC **P1405** — Differential Pressure Feedback Electronic (DPFE) sensor upstream hose off or plugged
- DTC **P1406** — Differential Pressure Feedback Electronic (DPFE) sensor downstream hose off or plugged
- DTC **P1407** — Exhaust Gas Recirculation (EGR) no flow detected (valve stuck closed or inoperative)
- DTC **P1408** — Exhaust Gas Recirculation (EGR) flow out of Self-Test range
- DTC **P1409** — Electronic Vacuum Regulator (EVR) control circuit malfunction
- DTC **P1414** — Secondary Air Injection system monitor circuit high voltage
- DTC **P1443** — Evaporative emission control system - vacuum system purge control solenoid or purge control valve malfunction
- DTC **P1444** — Purge Flow Sensor (PFS) circuit low input
- DTC **P1445** — Purge Flow Sensor (PFS) circuit high input
- DTC **U1451** — Lack of response from Passive Anti-Theft system (PATS) module - engine disabled
- DTC **P1460** — Wide Open Throttle Air Conditioning Cut-off (WAC) circuit malfunction
- DTC **P1461** — Air Conditioning Pressure (ACP) sensor circuit low input
- DTC **P1462** — Air Conditioning Pressure (ACP) sensor circuit high input
- DTC **P1463** — Air Conditioning Pressure (ACP) sensor insufficient pressure change
- DTC **P1469** — Low air conditioning cycling period

- DTC **P1473** — Fan Secondary High with fan(s) off
- DTC **P1474** — Low Fan Control primary circuit malfunction
- DTC **P1479** — High Fan Control primary circuit malfunction
- DTC **P1480** — Fan Secondary low with low fan on
- DTC **P1481** — Fan Secondary low with high fan on
- DTC **P1500** — Vehicle Speed Sensor (VSS) circuit intermittent
- DTC **P1505** — Idle Air Control (IAC) system at adaptive clip
- DTC **P1506** — Idle Air control (IAC) overspeed error
- DTC **P1518** — Intake Manifold Runner Control (IMRC) malfunction (stuck open)
- DTC **P1519** — Intake Manifold Runner Control (IMRC) malfunction (stuck closed)
- DTC **P1520** — Intake Manifold Runner Control (IMRC) circuit malfunction
- DTC **P1507** — Idle Air control (IAC) underspeed error
- DTC **P1605** — Powertrain Control Module (PCM) — Keep Alive Memory (KAM) test error
- DTC **P1650** — Power steering Pressure (PSP) switch out of Self-Test range
- DTC **P1651** — Power steering Pressure (PSP) switch input malfunction
- DTC **P1701** — Reverse engagement error
- DTC **P1703** — Brake On/Off (BOO) switch out of Self-Test range
- DTC **P1705** — Manual Lever Position (MLP) sensor out of Self-Test range
- DTC **P1709** — Park or Neutral Position (PNP) switch out of Self-test range
- DTC **P1729** — 4X4 Low switch error
- DTC **P1711** — Transmission Fluid Temperature (TFT) sensor out of Self-Test range
- DTC **P1741** — Torque Converter Clutch (TCC) control error
- DTC **P1742** — Torque Converter Clutch (TCC) solenoid mechanically failed (turns MIL on)
- DTC **P1743** — Torque Converter Clutch (TCC) solenoid mechanically failed (turns TCIL on)
- DTC **P1744** — Torque Converter Clutch (TCC) system mechanically stuck in off position
- DTC **P1746** — Electronic Pressure Control (EPC) solenoid circuit low input (open circuit)
- DTC **P1747** — Electronic Pressure Control (EPC) solenoid circuit high input (short circuit)
- DTC **P1749** — Electric Pressure Control (EPC) solenoid failed low
- DTC **P1751** — Shift Solenoid #1 (SS1) performance
- DTC **P1756** — Shift Solenoid #2 (SS2) performance
- DTC **P1780** — Transmission Control Switch (TCS) circuit out of Self-Test range

Ford MCU System
Diagnostic Trouble Codes

The code definitions listed are general for Ford Vehicles using the Microprocessor Control Unit (MCU) engine control system. Most Ford vehicles up to 1983 and feedback carburetor equipped V8 engines into the 1990's use the MCU engine control system. For a specific code definition or component test procedure consult service manual for your vehicle. A diagnostic code does not mean the component is defective. For example a Code 44 is an oxygen sensor code (rich oxygen sensor signal). This code may set if a carburetor is flooding or has a very restricted air cleaner. Replacing the oxygen sensor would not fix the problem. This list is for reference and does not mean a component is defective, consult your 'Chilton Total Car Care' manual for specific component testing for your vehicle.

➡When the term Powertrain Control Module (PCM) is used in this manual it will refer to the engine control computer regardless that it may be a Powertrain Control Module (PCM) or Electronic Control Module (ECM) or Electronic Control Assembly (ECA).

Code 11 — System Pass — Except High Altitude.
— **or** — Altitude (ALT) circuit is open — High Altitude.
Code 12 — RPM out of specification (throttle kicker system).
Code 25 — Knock Sensor (KS) signal is not detected during Key On Engine Running (KOER) Self-Test.
Code 33 — Key On Engine Running (KOER) Self-Test not initiated.
Code 41 — Oxygen sensor voltage signal always Lean (low value) — does not switch.
Code 42 — Oxygen sensor voltage signal always Rich (high value) — does not switch.
Code 44 — Oxygen sensor signal indicates Rich — excessive fuel, restricted air intake.
— **or** — Inoperative Thermactor System.
Code 45 — Thermactor Air flow is always upstream (going into exhaust manifold).
Code 46 — Thermactor Air System unable to bypass air (vent to atmosphere).
Code 51 — Low or Mid Temperature vacuum switch circuit is open when engine is hot — on In-line 4 and 6 cylinder engines.
— **or** — HI or HI/LOW vacuum switch circuit is always open — on V6 or V8 engines.
Code 52 — Idle Tracking Switch (ITS) voltage does not change from closed to open throttle. (Closed throttle checked during KOEO condition. Open throttle checked during KOER conditions) — on 4 cylinder car.
— **or** — Idle/Decel Vacuum switch circuit always open — on 4 cylinder truck.
— **or** — Wide Open Throttle vacuum switch circuit always open — on In-line 6 cylinder engine.
Code 53 — Wide Open Throttle vacuum switch circuit always open — on 4 cylinder engine.
— **or** — Crowd vacuum switch circuit is always open — on In-line 6 cylinder engine.
— **or** — Dual temperature switch circuit is always open — on V6 and V8 engines.
Code 54 — Mid temperature switch circuit is always open.
Code 55 — Road load vacuum switch circuit is always open — on 4 cylinder engine.
— **or** — Mid vacuum switch circuit is always open — on V6 and V8 engines.
Code 56 — Closed throttle vacuum switch circuit is always open.
Code 61 — Hi/Low Vacuum switch circuit is always closed.

Code 62 — Idle Tracking Switch (ITS) circuit is closed at idle.

— **or** — Idle/Decel vacuum switch circuit is always closed — on 4 cylinder car.

— **or** — Wide Open Throttle vacuum switch circuit always closed — on 4 cylinder truck.

— **or** — System Pass — High Altitude; Altitude (ALT) circuit is open — except High Altitude on V6 and V8 engines.

Code 63 — Wide Open Throttle (WOT) vacuum switch circuit is always closed — on 4 cylinder engine.

— **or** — Crowd vacuum switch circuit is always closed — on 6 cylinder engine.

Code 65 — System pass — on 4 cylinder engine (High Altitude).

— **or** — Altitude (ALT) circuit is open — 4 cylinder engine (except High Altitude).

— **or** — Mid vacuum circuit is always closed — V6 and V8 engines.

Code 66 — Closed Throttle Vacuum switch circuit is always closed.

➡ **If more than one definition is listed for a code or the code is not listed here, consult your 'Chilton Total Car Care' manual to get the specific meaning for your vehicle. This list is for reference and does not mean a specific component is defective. NOTE: High Altitude refers to vehicles with computer adjusted for operation at high elevations as in mountain regions.**

Ford Non-NAAO ECC System
Diagnostic Trouble Codes

The code definitions listed general 2-digit codes for Ford Vehicles using the Ford EEC engine control system. For a specific code definition or component test procedure consult a vehicle service manual for your vehicle. A diagnostic code does not mean the component is defective. For example a Code 6 is a vehicle speed sensor code. This does not mean the sensor is defective, but to check the sensor and related components. A defective speedometer cable or transmission problem will also set this code.

➡ **When the term Powertrain Control Module (PCM) is used in this manual it will refer to the engine control computer regardless that it may be a Powertrain Control Module (PCM) or Electronic Control Module (ECM) or Electronic Control Assembly (ECA).**

Code 02 — Crankshaft position sensor.
Code 03 — Cylinder identification sensor #1, 1.6L engine.
Code 06 — Vehicle speed sensor, 1.6L engine.
Code 08 — Air flow signal.
Code 09 — Engine coolant temperature sensor.
Code 10 — Air temperature sensor.
Code 12 — Throttle position sensor, 1.6L engine.
Code 14 — Barometric pressure sensor.
Code 15 — Oxygen sensor, signal LEAN.
Code 16 — EGR position valve, 2.2L engine.
Code 17 — Oxygen sensor, signal RICH.
Code 25 — Fuel pressure regulator solenoid, 1.6L engine.
Code 26 — Canister purge solenoid.
Code 34 — Idle speed control solenoid.
Code 41 — High speed inlet air control solenoid.
Code 55 — Pulse generator, transaxle code.
Code 57 — Down shift signal, transaxle code.
Code 60 — 1-2 Shift solenoid, transaxle code.
Code 61 — 2-3 Shift solenoid, transaxle code.
Code 62 — 3-4 Shift solenoid, transaxle code.
Code 63 — Lock-up control, transaxle code.

➡ **If more than one definition is listed for a code or the code is not listed here, consult your 'Chilton Total Car Care' manual to get the specific meaning for your vehicle. This list is to be used as a reference for testing and does not mean a specific component is defective.**

No Code — Unable to Run Self Test or Output Codes, or list does not apply to vehicle tested, refer to specific vehicle service manual.

GENERAL MOTORS CORPORATION

Self-Diagnostics

Automotive manufacturers have developed on-board computers to control engines, transmissions and many other components. These on-board computers with dozens of sensors and actuators have become almost impossible to test without the help of electronic test equipment.

One of these electronic test devices has become the on-board computer itself. The Powertrain Control Modules (PCM), sometimes called the Electronic Control Module (ECM), used on todays vehicles has a built in self testing system. This self test ability is called self-diagnosis. The self-diagnosis system will test many or all of the sensors and controlled devices for proper function. When a malfunction is detected this system will store a code in memory that's related to that specific circuit. The computer can later be accessed to obtain fault codes recorded in memory using the procedures for Reading Codes. This helps narrow down what area to begin testing.

Fault code meanings can vary from year to year even on the same model. It is extremely important after retrieving a fault code to verify its meaning with a proper manual. Servicing a code incorrectly will not only lead to the wrong conclusion but could also cause damage if tested or serviced incorrectly.

Since the control module is programmed to recognize the presence and value of electrical inputs, it will also note the lack of a signal or a radical change in values. It will, for example, react to the loss of signal from the vehicle speed sensor or note that engine coolant temperature has risen beyond acceptable (programmed) limits. Once a fault is recognized, a numeric code is assigned and held in memory. The dashboard warning lamp — CHECK ENGINE or SERVICE ENGINE SOON — will illuminate to advise the operator that the system has detected a fault.

More than one code may be stored. Although not every engine uses every code and the same code may carry different meanings relative to each engine or engine family. For example, on the 3.3L (VIN N), Code 46 indicates a fault found in the power steering pressure switch circuit. The same code on the 5.7L (VIN F) engine indicates a fault in the VATS anti-theft system. The list of codes and descriptions can be found in the 'Code Descriptions' section of the manual.

In the event of an PCM failure, the system will default to a pre-programmed set of values. These are compromise values which allow the engine to operate, although possibly at reduced efficiency. This is also known as the default, limp-in or back-up mode. Driveability is almost always affected when the PCM enters this mode.

SERVICE PRECAUTIONS

- Protect the on-board solid-state components from rough handling or extremes of temperature.
- Always turn the ignition **OFF** when connecting or disconnecting battery cables, jumper cables, or a battery charger. Failure to do this can result in PCM or other electronic component damage.

- Remove the PCM before any arc welding is performed to the vehicle.
- Electronic components are very susceptible to damage caused by electrostatic discharge (static electricity). To prevent electronic component damage, do not touch the control module connector pins or soldered components on the control module circuit board.

VISUAL INSPECTION

This is possibly the most critical step of diagnosis. A detailed examination of all connectors, wiring and vacuum hoses can often lead to a repair without further diagnosis. Also, take into consideration if the vehicle has been serviced recently? Sometimes things get reconnected in the wrong place, or not at all. A careful inspector will check the undersides of hoses as well as the integrity of hard-to-reach hoses blocked by the air cleaner or other components. Correct routing for vacuum hoses can be obtained from your specific vehicle service manual or Vehicle Emission Control Information (VECI) label in the engine compartment of the vehicle. Wiring should be checked carefully for any sign of strain, burning, crimping or terminals pulled-out from a connector.

Checking connectors at components or in harnesses is required; usually, pushing them together will reveal a loose fit. Also, check electrical connectors for corroded, bent, damaged, improperly seated pins, and bad wire crimps to terminals. Pay particular attention to ground circuits, making sure they are not loose or corroded. Remember to inspect connectors and hose fittings at components not mounted on the engine, such as the evaporative canister or relays mounted on the fender aprons. Any component or wiring in the vicinity of a fluid leak or spillage should be given extra attention during inspection.

➡ **There are many problems with connectors on electronic engine control systems. Due to the low voltage signals that these systems use any dirt, corrosion or damage will affect their operation. Note that some connectors use a special grease on the contacts to prevent corrosion. Do not wipe this grease off, it is a special type for this purpose. You can obtain this grease from your vehicle dealer.**

Additionally, inspect maintenance items such as belt condition and tension, battery charge and condition and the radiator cap carefully. Any of these very simple items may affect the system enough to set a fault.

DASHBOARD WARNING LAMP

▶ See Figure 24

The primary function of the dash warning lamp is to advise the operator that a fault has been detected, and, in most cases, a code stored. Under normal conditions, the dash warning lamp will illuminate when the ignition is turned **ON**. Once the engine is started and running, the PCM will perform a system check and extinguish the warning lamp if no fault is found.

Additionally, the dash warning lamp can be used to retrieve stored codes after the system is placed in the Diagnostic Mode. Codes are transmitted as a series of flashes with short or long pauses. When the system is placed in the Field Service Mode (available on fuel injected model), the dash lamp will indicate open loop or closed loop function.

INTERMITTENT PROBLEMS

If a fault occurs intermittently, such as a loose connector pin breaking contact as the vehicle hits a bump, the PCM will note the fault as it occurs and energize the dash warning lamp. If the problem self-corrects, as with the terminal pin again making contact, the dash lamp will extinguish after 10 seconds but a code will remain stored in the PCM memory. When an unexpected code appears during an intermittent failure that self-corrected; the codes are still useful in diagnosis and should not be discounted.

DIAGNOSTIC CONNECTOR LOCATION

▶ **See Figures 25 and 26**

The Assembly Line Communication Link (ALCL) or Assembly Line Diagnostic Link (ALDL) is a Diagnostic Link Connector (DLC) located in the passenger compartment. It has terminals which are used in the assembly plant to check that the engine is operating properly before it leaves the plant.

This DLC is where you connect you jumper the terminals to place the engine control computer into self-diagnostic mode. The standard term DLC is sometimes referred to as the ALCL or the ALDL in different manuals. Either way it is referred to, they all still perform the same function.

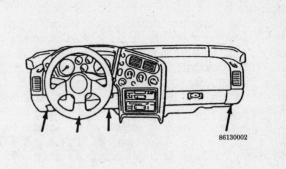

Fig. 25 The diagnostic link connector (DLC) is located under the instrument panel near the steering column on most vehicles

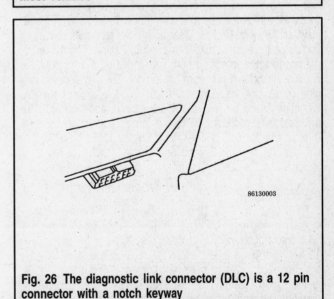

Fig. 26 The diagnostic link connector (DLC) is a 12 pin connector with a notch keyway

Reading Codes

READING CODES (except Cadillac)

▶ **See Figure 27**

Since the inception of electronic engine management systems on General Motors vehicles, there has been a variety of connectors provided to the technician for retrieving Diagnostic Trouble Codes (DTC)s. Additionally, there have been a number of different names given to these connectors over the years; Assembly Line Communication Link (ALCL), Assembly Line Diagnostic Link (ALDL), Data Link Connector (DLC). Actually when the system was initially introduced to the 49 states in 1979, early 1980, there was no connector used at all. On these early vehicles there was a green spade terminal taped to the ECM harness and connected to the diagnostic enable line at the computer. When this terminal was grounded with the key **ON**, the system would flash any stored diagnostic

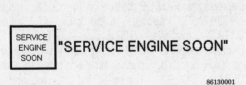

Fig. 24 Check Engine or Service Engine Soon (MIL) lamp is used for reading flash codes

trouble codes. The introduction of the ALCL was found to be a much more convenient way of retrieving fault codes. This connector was located underneath the instrument panel on most GM vehicles, however on some models it will not be found there. On early Corvettes the ALCL is located underneath the ashtray, it can be found in the glove compartment of some early FWD Oldsmobiles, and between the seats in the Pontiac Fiero. The connector was first introduced as a square connector with four terminals, then progressed to a flat five terminal connector, and finally to what is still used in 1993, a 12 terminal double row connector. To access stored Diagnostic Trouble Codes (DTC) from the square connector, turn the ignition **ON** and identify the diagnostic enable terminal (usually a white wire with a black tracer) and ground it. The flat five terminal connector is identified from left to right as A, B, C, D, and E. There is a space between terminal D and E which permits a spade to be inserted for the purposes of diagnostics when the ignition key is **ON**. On this connector terminal D is the diagnostic enable line, and E is a ground. The 12 terminal double row connector has been continually expanded through the years as vehicles acquired more on-board electronic systems such as Anti-lock Brakes. Despite this the terminals used for engine code retrieval have remained the same. The 12 terminal connector is identified from right-to-left on the top row A-F, and on the bottom row from left-to-right, G-L. To access engine codes turn the ignition **ON** and insert a jumper between terminals A and B. Terminal A is a ground, and terminal B is the diagnostic request line. Stored trouble codes can be read through the flashing of the **Check Engine Light** or on later vehicles the **Service Engine Soon** lamp. Trouble codes are identified by the timed flash of the indicator light. When diagnostics are first entered the light will flash once, pause, then two quick flashes.

This reads as Code 12 which indicates that the diagnostic system is working. This code will flash indefinitely if there are no stored trouble codes. If codes are stored in memory, Code 12 will flash three times before the next code appears. Codes are displayed in the next highest numerical sequence. For example, Code 13 would be displayed next if it was stored in memory and would read as follow: flash, pause, flash, flash,

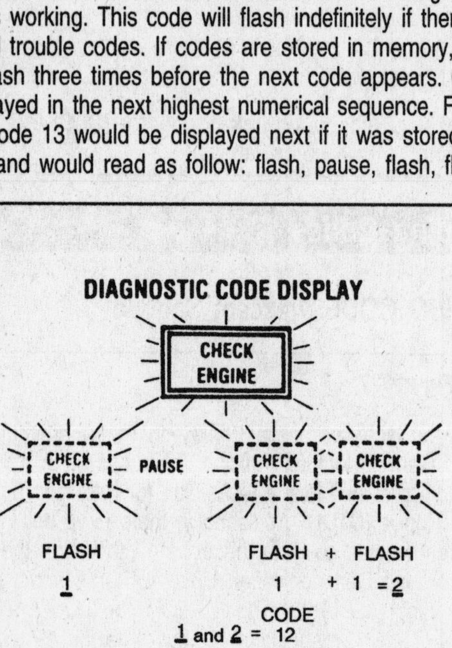

flash, long pause, repeat twice. This sequence will continue until all codes have been displayed, and then start all over again with Code 12.

CLEARING CODES (except Cadillac)

Except Riviera, Toronado and Trofeo

To clear any Diagnostic Trouble Codes (DTCs) from the PCM memory, either to determine if the malfunction will occur again or because repair has been completed, power feed must be disconnected for at least 30 seconds. Depending on how the vehicle is equipped, the system power feed can be disconnected at the positive battery terminal pigtail, the inline fuseholder that originates at the positive connection at the battery, or the ECM/PCM fuse in the fuse block. The negative battery terminal may be disconnected but other on-board memory data such as preset radio tuning will also be lost. To prevent system damage, the ignition switch must be in the **OFF** position when disconnecting or reconnecting power.

When using a Diagnostic Computer such as Tech 1, or equivalent scan tool to read the diagnostic trouble codes, clearing the codes is done in the same manner. On some systems, DTCs may be cleared through the Tech 1, or equivalent scan tool.

On Riviera, Toronado and Trofeo, clearing codes is part of the dashboard display menu or diagnostic routine. Because of the amount of electronic equipment on these vehicles, clearing codes by disconnecting the battery is not recommended.

Riviera, Toronado and Trofeo (Non-CRT/DID Vehicles)

Using the On-Board Diagnostic Display System

First turn the ignition to the **ON** position. On Riviera depress the OFF and TEMP buttons on the ECCP at the same time and hold until all display segments light. This is known as the Segment Check. On Toronado and Trofeo follow the same procedure, however, depress the OFF and WARMER buttons on the ECCP instead. After diagnostics is entered, any DTCs stored in computer memory will be displayed. Codes may be stored for the PCM, BCM, IPC or SIR systems. Following the display of DTCs, the first available system for testing will be displayed. For example, 'EC?' would be displayed on Riviera for ECM testing, while on Toronado and Trofeo the message 'ECM?' will appear. The message is more clear on these vehicles due to increased character space in the IPC display area.

1. Depress the 'FAN UP' button on the ECCP until the message 'DATA EC?' appears on the display for Riviera, or 'ECM DATA?' is displayed on Toronado and Trofeo.

2. Depress the 'FAN DOWN' button on the ECCP until the message 'CLR E CODE' appears on the display for Riviera, or 'ECM CLEAR CODES?' is displayed on Toronado and Trofeo.

3. Depressing the 'FAN UP' button on the ECCP will result in the message 'E CODE CLR' or 'E NOT CLR' on Riviera, 'ECM CODES CLEAR' or 'ECM CODES NOT CLEAR' on Toronado and Trofeo. This message will appear for 3 seconds. After 3 seconds the display will automatically return to the next available test type for the selected system. It is a good idea to either cycle the ignition once or test drive the vehicle to ensure the code(s) do not reset.

DIAGNOSTIC CODE DISPLAY

CHECK ENGINE

CHECK ENGINE PAUSE CHECK ENGINE CHECK ENGINE

FLASH   FLASH + FLASH
  1   1   + 1 = 2
              CODE
         1 and 2 = 12

86130004

Fig. 27 Example of reading Code 12 from the Check Engine lamp

Toronado and Trofeo (CRT/DID Equipped)

Using the On-Board Diagnostic Display System

First turn the ignition switch to the **ON** position. Depress the 'OFF' hardkey and 'WARM' softkey on the CRT/DID at the same time and hold until all display segments light. This is the 'Segment Check.' During diagnostic operation, all information will be displayed on the Driver Information Center (DIC) located in the Instrument Panel Cluster (IPC). Because of the limited space available single letter identifiers are often used for each of the major computer systems. These are: E for ECM, B for BCM, I for IPC and R for SIR. After diagnostics is entered, any DTCs stored in computer memory will be displayed. Codes may be stored for the PCM, BCM, IPC or SIR systems. Following the display of DTCs, the first available system for testing will be displayed. This will be displayed as 'ECM?'.

1. Depress the 'YES' softkey until the display reads 'ECM DATA?'.
2. Depress the 'NO' softkey until the display reads 'ECM CLEAR CODES?'.
3. Depressing the 'YES' softkey will result in either the message 'ECM CODES CLEAR' or 'ECM CODES NOT CLEAR' being displayed, indicating whether or not the codes were successfully cleared. This message will appear for 3 seconds. After 3 seconds the display will automatically return to the next available test type for the selected system. It is a good idea to either cycle the ignition once or test drive the vehicle to ensure the code(s) do not reset.

READING AND CLEARING CADILLAC ENGINE CODES

➡ **The Cadillac Cimmaron used the 12 terminal DLC and codes can be accessed in the conventional manner as all other General Motors vehicles. The rear wheel drive Cadillac equipped with either the 4.1L V6, 5.0L V8, or the 5.7L V8 all can also be accessed in the conventional manner using the DLC.**

1980-1983 DIGITAL FUEL INJECTION

1. Turn the ignition switch **ON**.
2. Depress the **OFF** and **WARMER** buttons on the Electronic Climate Control (ECC) panel simultaneously and hold until .. is displayed.
3. The numerals **88** should then appear indicating that all display segments are functional. Diagnosis should not be attempted unless the entire **88** is displayed or misdiagnosis will result.
4. If trouble codes are present they will appear on the digital ECC panel as follows:
   a. The lowest numbered code will be displayed for approximately two seconds.
   b. Progressively higher numbered codes, if present, will be displayed consecutively for two second intervals until the highest code has been displayed.
   c. **88** is again displayed.
   d. Parts A, B, and C will be repeated a second time.

   e. After the trouble codes have been displayed Code 70 will then appear. **70** indicates that the ECM is prepared for the switch test procedure.
5. If no trouble codes are stored in memory, **88** will appear for a longer time, and then the ECM will display Code 70.

Clearing Codes

While still in the diagnostic mode, press the **OFF** and **HIGH** buttons simultaneously until **00** appears. Trouble codes are now removed from the system memory.

➡**NOTE: The fuel data panel will go blank when the system is displaying in the diagnostic mode.**

1984 DIGITAL FUEL INJECTION

1. Turn the ignition switch **ON**.
2. Depress the **OFF** and **WARMER** buttons on the Electronic Climate Control (ECC) panel simultaneously and hold until .. is displayed.
3. **-1.8.8** should then appear indicating that all display segments are functional. Diagnosis should not be attempted unless the entire **-1.8.8** is displayed or misdiagnosis will result.
4. If trouble codes are present they will appear on the digital ECC panel as follows:
   a. The lowest numbered code will be displayed for approximately two seconds.
   b. Progressively higher numbered codes, if present, will be displayed consecutively for two second intervals until the highest code has been displayed.
   c. **88** is again displayed.
   d. Parts A, B, and C will be repeated a second time.
   e. After the trouble codes have been displayed Code 70 will then appear. **70** indicates that the ECM is prepared for the switch test procedure.
5. If no trouble codes are stored in memory, **-1.8.8** will appear for a longer time, and then the ECM will display Code 70.

Clearing Codes

While still in the diagnostic mode, press the **OFF** and **HIGH** buttons simultaneously until **.0.0** appears. Trouble codes are now removed from the system memory.

➡**NOTE: The fuel data panel will go blank when the system is displaying in the diagnostic mode.**

1985-1986 DIGITAL FUEL INJECTION

1. Turn the ignition switch **ON**.
2. Depress the **OFF** and **WARMER** buttons on the Climate Control Panel (CCP) simultaneously and hold until -188 is displayed.
3. -188 should then appear indicating that all display segments are functional. Diagnosis should not be attempted unless the entire -188 is displayed or misdiagnosis will result.
4. If trouble codes are present they will appear on the Fuel Data Center (FDC) panel as follows:
   a. Display of trouble codes will begin with an 8.8.8 on the FDC panel for approximately one second. ...**E** will then be displayed which indicates beginning of the ECM stored trouble codes. The initial pass of ECM codes includes all the detected malfunctions whether or not they are currently pre-

sent. If no ECM codes are stored the ...E display will be bypassed.

b. Following the display of ...E the lowest numbered ECM code will be displayed for approximately two seconds. All ECM codes will be prefixed with an E (i.e. E12, E13, etc.).

c. Progressively higher numbered codes, if present, will be displayed consecutively for two second intervals until the highest code has been displayed.

d. .E.E is again displayed which indicates the start of the second pass of ECM trouble codes. On the second pass only current faults (hard codes) will be displayed. Codes displayed on the first pass are history failures or (soft codes). If all displayed codes were history codes the .E.E will be bypassed.

e. When all ECM codes have been displayed, BCM codes will appear with the prefix F in the same manner as the ECM did.

5. After the display of all codes, or if no codes were stored, Code .7.0 will appear indicating the start of the switch tests.

Clearing Codes

While still in the diagnostic mode, press the OFF and HIGH buttons simultaneously until E.0.0 appears. Trouble codes are now removed from the ECM memory.

1987-1993 DEVILLE AND FLEETWOOD

1. Turn the ignition switch ON.

2. Depress the OFF and WARMER buttons on the Climate Control Panel (CCP) simultaneously and hold until -188 is displayed.

3. -188 should then appear indicating that all display segments are functional. Diagnosis should not be attempted unless the entire -188 is displayed or misdiagnosis will result.

4. If trouble codes are present they will appear on the Fuel Data Center (FDC) panel as follows:

a. Display of trouble codes will begin with an 8.8.8 on the FDC panel for approximately one second. ...E will then be displayed which indicates beginning of the ECM stored trouble codes. The initial pass of ECM codes includes all the detected malfunctions whether or not they are currently present. If no ECM codes are stored the ...E display will be bypassed.

b. Following the display of ...E the lowest numbered ECM code will be displayed for approximately two seconds. All ECM codes will be prefixed with an E (i.e. E12, E13, etc.).

c. Progressively higher numbered codes, if present, will be displayed consecutively for two second intervals until the highest code has been displayed.

d. .E.E is again displayed which indicates the start of the second pass of ECM trouble codes. On the second pass

only current faults (hard codes) will be displayed. Codes displayed on the first pass are history failures or (soft codes). If all displayed codes were history codes the .E.E will be bypassed.

e. When all ECM codes have been displayed, BCM codes will appear with the prefix F in the same manner as the ECM did.

5. After the display of all codes, or if no codes were stored, Code .7.0 will appear indicating the start of the switch tests.

Clearing Codes

While still in the diagnostic mode, press the OFF and HIGH buttons simultaneously until E.0.0 appears. Trouble codes are now removed from the ECM memory.

1987-1993 ALLANTE, ELDORADO AND SEVILLE

1. Turn the ignition switch ON.

2. Depress the OFF and WARMER buttons on the Climate Control Panel (CCP) simultaneously and hold until the segment check appears on the Instrument Panel Cluster (IPC) and the Climate Control Driver Information Center (CCDIC).

3. Diagnosis should not be attempted unless all of the segments of the vacuum fluorescent display are working as this could lead to misdiagnosis. On the IPC however the turn signal indicators do not light during this check.

4. After the service mode is entered, any trouble codes stored in the computer memory will be displayed, starting with ECM codes prefixed with an E.

5. If no trouble codes are present, the message NO ECM CODES will be displayed. Some later systems will display NO X CODES present, with X representing the system selected such as ECM, BCM, SIR, etc.

Clearing Codes

1. While still in the service mode, and the ECM diagnostic code display has been completed press the HI button on the CCP.

2. This action should cause the display to read 'ECM DATA?'.

3. Press the LO button on the CCP until the display reads 'ECM CLEAR CODES?'.

4. Press the HI button on the CCP and the display should read 'ECM CODES CLEAR'.

5. After approximately 3 seconds, all stored ECM codes will be erased.

➡ NOTE: The Cadillac Cimmaron used the 12 terminal DLC and codes can be accessed in the conventional manner. The rear wheel drive Cadillacs equipped with either the 4.1L V6, 5.0L V8, or the 5.7L V8 all can be accessed in the conventional manner using the DLC.

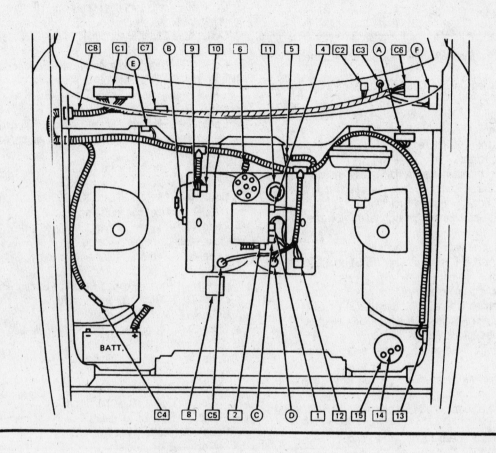

"F" SERIES

2.8L (173 CID) V6   RPO: LC1/LL1 H.O.   V.I.N. CODE: 1/L

COMPUTER SYSTEM

C1	Electronic Control Module (ECM)
C2	ALCL Connector
C3	"CHECK ENGINE" Light
C4	System Power
C5	System Ground
C6	Fuse Panel
C7	Lamp Driver
C8	Computer Control Harness

AIR/FUEL SYSTEM

1	Mixture Control
2	Idle Speed Solenoid
4	Heated Grid EFE

TRANSMISSION CONVERTER CLUTCH CONTROL SYSTEM

5	Trans. Conv. Clutch Connector

IGNITION SYSTEM

6	Electronic Spark Timing Connector

AIR INJECTION SYSTEM

8	Air Injection Pump
9	Air Control Solenoid Valve (Divert)
10	Air Switching Solenoid Valve

EXHAUST GAS RECIRCULATION CONTROL SYSTEM

11	Exhaust Gas Recirculation Valve
12	Exhaust Gas Recirculation Solenoid Valve

FUEL VAPOR CONTROL SYSTEM

13	Canister Purge Solenoid Valve
14	From Fuel Tank
15	Vapor Canister

SEM   S/SWITCHES

A	Differential Pressure Sensor
B	Exhaust Oxygen Sensor
C	Throttle Position Sensor
D	Coolant Sensor
E	Barometric Pressure Sensor
F	Vehicle Speed Sensor

85344084

Fig. 28 Example of the components on a 2.8L Firebird that the on-board computer controls or monitors

Diagnostic Trouble Codes

Except
Front Wheel Drive Cadillac

Code 12 — No engine RPM reference pulses — System Normal.

Code 13 — Oxygen Sensor (O2S) circuit open — left side on 2 sensor system.

Code 14 — Engine Coolant Temperature (ECT) sensor — possible circuit high or shorted sensor.

Code 15 — Engine Coolant Temperature (ECT) sensor — circuit low or open circuit.

Code 16 — Direct ignition system (DIS), fault line circuit.

— or — Distributor ignition system (low resolution pulse).

— or — Missing 2x reference circuit

— or — OPTI-Spark ignition timing system (low resolution pulse).

— or — System voltage out of range.

Code 17 — Camshaft Position Sensor (CPS) or spark reference circuit error.

Code 18 — Crank/Cam error.

Code 19 — Crankshaft Position Sensor (CPS) circuit.

Code 21 — Throttle Position (TP) sensor circuit — signal voltage out of range, probably high.

Code 22 — Throttle Position (TP) sensor circuit — signal voltage low.

Code 23 — Intake Air Temperature (IAT or MAT) sensor circuit — temperature out of range, low.

— or — Open or grounded M/C solenoid — Feedback Carburetor system.

Code 24 — Vehicle Speed Sensor (VSS) circuit.

Code 25 — Intake Air Temperature (IAT or MAT) sensor circuit — temperature out of range, high.

Code 26 — Quad-Driver Module #1 circuit.

— or — Transaxle gear switch circuit.

Code 27 — Quad-Driver Module circuit.

— or — Transaxle gear switch, probably 2nd gear switch circuit.

Code 28 — Quad-Driver Module (QDM) #2 circuit.

— or — Transaxle gear switch, probably 3rd gear switch circuit.

Code 29 — Transaxle gear switch, probably 4th gear switch circuit.

Code 31 — Camshaft sensor circuit fault.

— or — Park/Neutral Position (PNP) switch circuit.

— or — Wastegate circuit signal.

Code 32 — Exhaust Gas Recirculation (EGR) circuit fault.

— or — Barometric Pressure Sensor circuit low — Feedback Carburetor system.

Code 33 — Manifold Absolute Pressure (MAP) sensor — signal voltage out of range, high.

— or — Mass Air Flow (MAF) sensor — signal voltage out of range, probably high.

Code 34 — Manifold Absolute Pressure (MAP) sensor — circuit out of range voltage, low.

— or — Mass Air Flow (MAF) sensor circuit (gm/sec low).

Code 35 — Idle Air Control (IAC) or idle speed error.

— or — Idle Speed Control (ISC) circuit — throttle switch shorted — Feedback Carburetor system.

Code 36 — Ignition system circuit error.

— or — Transaxle shift problem — 4T60E Transaxle.

Code 38 — Brake input circuit fault — Torque converter clutch signal.

Code 39 — Clutch input circuit fault — Torque converter clutch signal.

Code 41 — Cam sensor or cylinder select circuit fault — ignition control (IC) reference pulse system fault.

— or — Electronic Spark Timing (EST) circuit open or shorted.

Code 42 — Electronic Spark Timing (EST) circuit grounded.

— or — Ignition Control (IC) circuit grounded or faulty bypass line.

Code 43 — Knock Sensor (KS) or Electronic Spark Control (ESC) circuit fault.

Code 44 — Oxygen Sensor (O2S), left side on 2 sensor system — lean exhaust indicated.

Code 45 — Oxygen Sensor (O2S), left side on 2 sensor system — rich exhaust indicated.

Code 46 — Personal Automotive Security System (PASS-Key II) circuit.

— or — Power Steering Pressure Switch (PSPS) circuit.

Code 47 — PCM-BCM data circuit.

Code 48 — Misfire diagnosis.

Code 51 — Calibration error, faulty MEM-CAL, ECM or EEPROM failure.

Code 52 — Engine oil temperature sensor circuit, low temperature indicated.

— or — Fuel Calpac missing.

— or — Over voltage condition.

— or — EGR Circuit fault.

Code 53 — Battery voltage error.

— or — EGR problem.

— or — Personal Automotive Security System (PASS-Key) circuit.

Code 54 — EGR #2 problem.

— or — Fuel pump circuit (low voltage).

— or — Shorted mixture control solenoid circuit — Feedback Carburetor system.

Code 55 — A/D Converter error.

— or — PCM error or not grounded.

— or — EGR #3 problem.

— or — Fuel lean monitor.

— or — Grounded voltage reference, faulty oxygen sensor, fuel lean — Feedback Carburetor system.

Code 56 — Quad-Driver Module (QDM) #2 circuit.

— or — Secondary air inlet valve actuator vacuum sensor circuit signal high — 5.7L (VIN J).

Code 57 — Boost control problem.

Code 58 — Vehicle Anti-theft System fuel enable circuit.

Code 61 — A/C system performance.

— or — Cruise vent solenoid circuit fault.

— or — Oxygen Sensor (O2S) — degraded signal.

— or — Secondary port throttle valve system fault — 5.7L (VIN J).

— or — Transaxle gear switch signal.

Code 62 — Cruise vacuum solenoid circuit fault.

— or — Engine oil temperature sensor, high temperature indicated.

— or — Transaxle gear switch signal circuit fault.

Code 63 — Oxygen Sensor (O2S), right side — circuit open.

— **or** — Cruise system problem (speed error).

— **or** — Manifold Absolute Pressure (MAP) sensor — circuit out of range.

Code 64 — Oxygen Sensor (O2S), right side — lean exhaust indicated.

Code 65 — Oxygen Sensor (O2S), right side — rich exhaust indicated.

— **or** — Cruise servo position circuit.

— **or** — Fuel injector circuit low current.

Code 66 — A/C pressure sensor circuit fault, probably low pressure.

— **or** — Engine power switch, voltage high or low or PCM fault — 5.7L (VIN J).

Code 67 — A/C pressure sensor circuit, sensor or A/C clutch circuit failure.

— **or** — Cruise switch circuit fault.

Code 68 — A/C compressor relay (shorted circuit).

— **or** — Cruise system fault.

Code 69 — A/C clutch circuit or head pressure high.

Code 70 — A/C refrigerant pressure sensor circuit (high pressure).

Code 71 — A/C evaporator temperature sensor circuit (low temperature).

Code 72 — Gear selector switch circuit.

Code 73 — A/C evaporator temperature sensor circuit (high temperature).

Code 75 — Digital EGR #1 solenoid error.

Code 76 — Digital EGR #2 solenoid error.

Code 77 — Digital EGR #3 solenoid error.

Code 79 — Vehicle Speed Sensor (VSS) circuit signal high.

Code 80 — Vehicle Speed Sensor (VSS) circuit signal low.

Code 81 — Brake input circuit fault — Torque converter clutch signal.

Code 82 — Ignition Control (IC) 3X signal error.

Code 85 — PROM error.

Code 86 — Analog/Digital ECM error.

Code 87 — EEPROM error.

Code 99 — Power management.

➡**If more than one definition is listed for a code or the code is not listed here, consult your 'Chilton Total Car Care' manual to get the specific meaning for your vehicle. This list is for reference and does not mean a specific component is defective.**

Front Wheel Drive Cadillac

Cadillac Codes may start with an 'E', 'E0', 'P' or 'P0' dependent on model or type of code display. This prefix has been left off the following code description list.

Code 12 — No spark reference from ignition control module or distributor.

Code 13 — Oxygen sensor No.1 not ready.

Code 14 — Engine Coolant Temperature (ECT) sensor circuit shorted.

Code 15 — Engine Coolant Temperature (ECT) sensor circuit open.

Code 16 — System voltage out of range.

Code 17 — Oxygen sensor No.2 not ready.

Code 19 — Fuel pump circuit shorted.

Code 20 — Fuel pump circuit open.

Code 21 — Throttle Position Sensor (TPS) circuit shorted.

Code 22 — Throttle Position Sensor (TPS) circuit open.

Code 23 — Electronic Spark Timing (EST) circuit fault or Ignition Control (IC) circuit problem.

Code 24 — Vehicle Speed Sensor (VSS) circuit problem.

Code 26 — Throttle Position (TP) switch circuit shorted.

Code 27 — Throttle Position (TP) switch circuit open.

Code 28 — Transaxle pressure switch problem.

Code 29 — Transaxle shift 'B' solenoid problem.

Code 30 — Idle Speed Control (ISC) RPM out of range.

Code 31 — Manifold Absolute Pressure (MAP) sensor circuit shorted.

Code 32 — Manifold Absolute Pressure (MAP) sensor circuit open.

Code 33 — Extended travel brake switch input circuit problem.

Code 34 — Manifold Absolute Pressure (MAP) sensor signal too high.

Code 35 — Ignition ground voltage out of range.

Code 36 — EGR valve pintle position out of range.

Code 37 — Intake Air Temperature (IAT) Manifold Air Temperature (MAT) circuit shorted.

Code 38 — Intake Air Temperature (IAT) sensor, Manifold Air Temperature (MAT) circuit open.

Code 39 — Torque Converter Clutch (TCC) engagement problem.

Code 40 — Power Steering Pressure Switch (PSPS) open.

Code 41 — Cam sensor circuit fault.

Code 42 — Oxygen sensor No.1 LEAN exhaust signal.

Code 43 — Oxygen sensor No.1 RICH exhaust signal.

Code 44 — Oxygen sensor No.2 LEAN exhaust signal.

Code 45 — Oxygen sensor No.2 RICH exhaust signal.

Code 46 — Bank-to-bank fueling difference.

Code 47 — ECM — Body Control Module (BCM) or IPC/PCM data fault.

Code 48 — EGR control system fault.

Code 50 — 2nd gear pressure circuit fault.

Code 51 — MEM-CAL error or PROM checksum mismatch.

Code 52 — ECM memory reset indicator or PCM keep alive memory reset.

Code 53 — Spark reference signal interrupt from Ignition Control (IC) module.

Code 55 — Closed throttle angle out of range or Throttle Position Sensor (TPS) misadjusted.

Code 56 — Transaxle input speed sensor circuit problem.

Code 57 — Shorted transaxle temperature sensor circuit.

Code 58 — Personal Automotive Security System (PASS) control fault.

Code 59 — Open transaxle temperature sensor circuit.

Code 60 — Cruise — transaxle not in drive.

Code 61 — Cruise — vent solenoid circuit fault.

Code 62 — Cruise — vacuum solenoid circuit fault.

Code 63 — Cruise — vehicle speed and set speed difference.

Code 64 — Cruise — vehicle acceleration too high.

Code 65 — Cruise — servo position sensor failure.

Code 66 — Cruise — engine RPM too high.

Code 67 — Cruise — set/coast or resume/accel input shorted.

Code 68 — Cruise Control Command (CCC) fault or servo position out of range.

Code 69 — Traction control active in cruise.

Code 70 — Intermittent Throttle Position (TP) sensor signal.

Code 71 — Intermittent Manifold Absolute Pressure (MAP) sensor signal.

Code 73 — Intermittent Engine Coolant Temperature (ECT) sensor signal.

Code 74 — Intermittent Intake Air Temperature (IAT) sensor signal.

Code 75 — Vehicle Speed Sensor (VSS) signal intermittent.

Code 76 — Transaxle pressure control solenoid circuit malfunction.

Code 80 — Fuel system rich or TP Sensor/idle learn not complete.

Code 81 — Cam to 4X reference correlation problem.

Code 83 — 24X Reference signal high.

Code 85 — Idle throttle angle too high, Throttle body service required.

Code 86 — Undefined gear ratio.

Code 88 — Torque Converter Clutch (TCC) not disengaging.

Code 89 — Long shift and maximum adapt.

Code 90 — Viscous Converter Clutch (VCC) brake switch input fault.

Code 91 — Park/neutral switch fault.

Code 92 — Heated windshield fault.

Code 93 — Traction control system PWM link failure.

Code 94 — Transaxle shift 'A' solenoid problem.

Code 95 — Engine stall detected.

Code 96 — Torque converter overstress.

Code 97 — Park/neutral to drive/reverse at high throttle angle.

Code 98 — High RPM P/N to D/R shift under Idle Speed Control (ISC).

Code 99 — Cruise control servo not applied in cruise.

Code P102 — Shorted Brake Booster Vacuum (BBV) sensor.

Code P103 — Open Brake Booster Vacuum (BBV) sensor.

Code P105 — Brake Booster Vacuum (BBV) too low.

Code P106 — Stop lamp switch input circuit problem.

Code P107 — PCM/BCM data link problem.

Code P108 — PROM checksum mismatch.

Code P109 — PCM keep alive memory reset.

Code P110 — Generator L-terminal circuit problem.

Code P112 — Total EEPROM failure.

Code P117 — Shift 'A'/Shift 'B' circuit output open or shorted.

Code P131 — Active Knock Sensor (KS) failure.

Code P132 — Knock Sensor (KS) circuit failure.

Code P137 — Loss of ABS/TCS data.

➡**If more than one definition is listed for a code or the code is not listed here, consult your 'Chilton Total Car Care' manual to get the specific meaning for your vehicle. This list is for reference and does not mean a specific component is defective.**

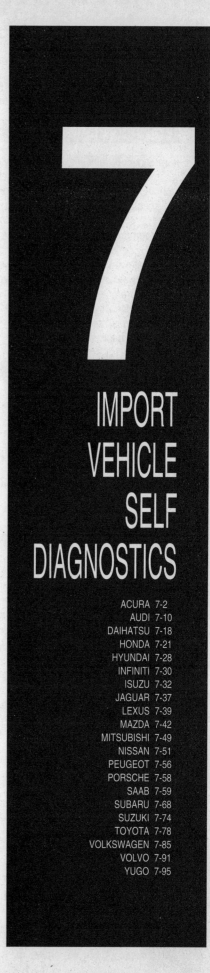

7

IMPORT VEHICLE SELF DIAGNOSTICS

ACURA

General Information

Programmed Fuel Injection (PGM-FI) System is a fully electronic microprocessor based engine management system. The Electronic Control Unit (ECU) is given responsibility for control of injector timing and duration, intake air control, ignition timing, cold start enrichment, fuel pump control, fuel cut-off, A/C compressor operation, alternator control as well as EGR function and canister purge cycles.

The ECU receives electric signals from many sensors and sources on and around the engine. The signals are processed against pre-programmed values; correct output signals from the ECU are determined by these calculations. The ECU contains additional memories, back-up and fail-safe functions as well as self diagnostic capabilities.

Self-Diagnostics

SERVICE PRECAUTIONS

- Do not operate the fuel pump when the fuel lines are empty.
- Do not operate the fuel pump when removed from the fuel tank.
- Do not reuse fuel hose clamps.
- The washer(s) below any fuel system bolt (banjo fittings, service bolt, fuel filter, etc.) must be replaced whenever the bolt is loosened. Do not reuse the washers; a high-pressure fuel leak may result.
- Make sure all ECU harness connectors are fastened securely. A poor connection can cause an extremely high voltage surge and result in damage to integrated circuits.
- Keep all ECU parts and harnesses dry during service. Protect the ECU and all solid-state components from rough handling or extremes of temperature.
- Use extreme care when working around the ECU or other components; the airbag or SRS wiring may be in the vicinity. On these vehicles, the SRS wiring and connectors are yellow; do not cut or test these circuits.
- Before attempting to remove any parts, turn the ignition switch **OFF** and disconnect the battery ground cable.
- Always use a 12 volt battery as a power source for the engine, never a booster or high-voltage charging unit.
- Do not disconnect the battery cables with the engine running.
- Do not disconnect any wiring connector with the engine running or the ignition **ON** unless specifically instructed to do so.
- Do not apply battery power directly to injectors.
- Whenever possible, use a flashlight instead of a drop light.
- Keep all open flame and smoking material out of the area.
- Use a shop cloth or similar to catch fuel when opening a fuel system. Consider the fuel-soaked rag to be a flammable solid and dispose of it in the proper manner.

- Relieve fuel system pressure before servicing any fuel system component.
- Always use eye or full-face protection when working around fuel lines, fittings or components.
- Always keep a dry chemical (class B-C) fire extinguisher near the area.

READING CODES

▶ **See Figures 1, 2, 3, 4 and 5**

1986-90 Legend
1986-91 Integra

When a fault is noted, the ECU stores an identifying code and illuminates the CHECK ENGINE light. The code will remain in memory until cleared; the dashboard warning lamp may not illuminate during the next ignition cycle if the fault is no longer present. Not all faults noted by the ECU will trigger the dashboard warning lamp although the fault code will be set in memory. For this reason, troubleshooting should be based on the presence of stored codes, not the illumination of the warning lamp while the car is operating.

Stored codes are displayed by a flashing LED on the ECU. When the CHECK ENGINE warning lamp has been on or reported on, lift or remove the carpet from the right front passenger footwell. The ECU is below a protective cover; the LED may be viewed through a small window without removing the ECU cover. Turn the ignition switch **ON**; the LED will display any stored codes by rhythmic flashing. Note that 1986-90 Legends have two LEDs on the controller; one is red and one is amber. The red one will flash the fault codes; the amber one is used during idle adjustment and is not related to this procedure. 1986-91 Integra use a single LED which is used to display codes only.

Codes 1-9 are indicated by a series of short flashes; two-digit codes use a number of long flashes for the first digit followed by the appropriate number of short flashes. For example, Code 43 would be indicated by 4 long flashes followed by

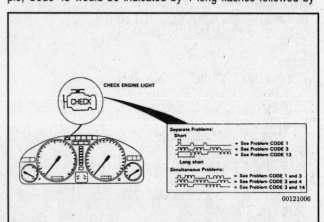

Fig. 1 Fault code display pattern and CHECK ENGINE light location — 1986-95 Acura

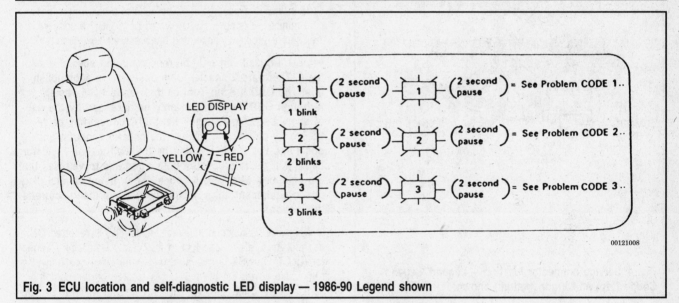

Fig. 2 ECU location and self-diagnostic LED display — 1986-91 Integra shown

Fig. 3 ECU location and self-diagnostic LED display — 1986-90 Legend shown

3 short flashes. Codes are separated by a longer pause between transmissions. The position of the codes during output can be helpful in diagnostic work. Multiple codes transmitted in isolated order indicate unique occurrences; a display of showing 1-1-1-pause-9-9-9 indicates two problems or problems occurring at different times. An alternating display, such as 1-9-1-9-1, indicates simultaneous occurrences of the faults.

When counting flashes to determine codes, a code not valid for the vehicle may be found. In this case, first recount the flashes to confirm an accurate count. If necessary, turn the ignition switch **OFF**, then recycle the system and begin the count again. If the Code is not valid for the vehicle, the ECU must be replaced.

1992-95 Integra
1991-95 Legend, NSX and Vigor
1995 2.5TL

When a fault is noted, the ECU stores an identifying code and illuminates the CHECK ENGINE light. The code will re-main in memory until cleared; the dashboard warning lamp may not illuminate during the next ignition cycle if the fault is no longer present. Not all faults noted by the ECU will trigger the dashboard warning lamp although the fault code will be set in memory. For this reason, troubleshooting should be based on the presence of stored codes, not the illumination of the warning lamp while the car is operating.

Beginning in 1991 on the Legend and in 1992 on Integra, codes are read thorough the use of the CHECK ENGINE light or more commonly know today as the Malfunction Indicator Lamp (MIL). NSX and Vigor are read in the same manner. The 1995 Legend equipped with the 2.7L V6 engine and the 2.5TL utilize OBD II trouble codes. These codes may be read either through the CHECK ENGINE light or by using a special OBD II scan tool.

Additionally, all models are equipped with a service connector in side the cabin of the vehicle. If the service connector is jumped, the CHECK ENGINE lamp will display the stored codes in the same fashion. The 2-pin service connector is located under the extreme right dashboard on Integra, Legend,

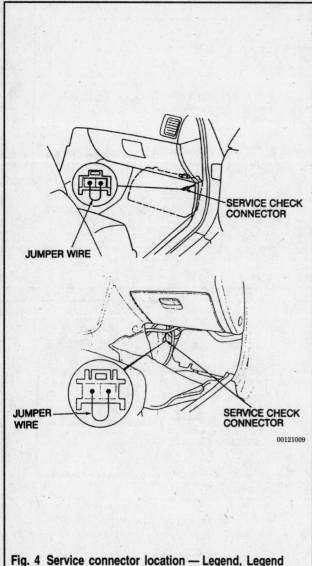

Fig. 4 Service connector location — Legend, Legend Coupe (top) and Vigor (bottom) shown

2.5TL and NSX; on Vigor models, it is found behind the right side of the center console, well under the dashboard.

Codes 1-9 are indicated by a series of short flashes; two-digit codes use a number of long flashes for the first digit followed by the appropriate number of short flashes. For example, Code 43 would be indicated by 4 long flashes followed by 3 short flashes. Codes are separated by a longer pause between transmissions. The position of the codes during output can be helpful in diagnostic work. Multiple codes transmitted in isolated order indicate unique occurrences; a display of showing 1-1-1-pause-9-9-9 indicates two problems or problems occurring at different times. An alternating display, such as 1-9-1-9-1, indicates simultaneous occurrences of the faults.

When counting flashes to determine codes, a code not valid for the vehicle may be found. In this case, first recount the flashes to confirm an accurate count. If necessary, turn the ignition switch **OFF**, then recycle the system and begin the count again. If the Code is not valid for the vehicle, the ECU must be replaced.

➡**On vehicles with automatic transaxles, the S, D or D$_4$ lamp may flash with the CHECK ENGINE lamp if certain codes are stored. For Legend and NSX, this may occur with Codes 6, 7 or 17. On Vigor and Integra it may occur with codes 6, 7 or 13. In addition, the TCS lamp on NSX may flash with codes 3, 5, 6, 13, 15, 16, 17, 35 or 36. In all cases, proceed with the diagnosis based on the engine code shown. After repairs, recheck the lamp. If the additional warning lamp is still lit, proceed with diagnosis for that system.**

1995 OBD II Codes

OBD II codes are the new style of Diagnostic Trouble Code (DTC) being used by manufacturer's today. Some manufacturer's began instituting these codes as of 1994 others as of 1995. The OBD II code differs from the single digit or 2 digit code in that it is accompanied by a letter prefix before a 4 digit number. Example: P0101 would be a OBD II code which indicates a problem concerning the mass air flow circuit.

➡**OBD II codes can only be read by using special scan tools. There are 2 special tools designed to accomplish this. The OBD II Scan Tool or the Honda PGM Tester. Although OBD II codes can only be accessed by the use of special equipment, equivalent DTC codes may be retrieved by connecting the service check connector and observing the codes flashing by the Malfunction Indicator Lamp (MIL). The procedure below pertains to vehicles that are equipped with OBD II codes. When using special diagnostic equipment, always observe the tool manufacturer's instructions.**

When the Malfunction Indicator Light (MIL) is reported **ON**, connect the OBD II scan tool to the 16 pin Data Link Connector (DLC). On NSX it is located under the glove box behind a removable cover. On the 2.5TL it is located on the center console behind the ashtray. Turn the ignition switch to the **ON** position. If using the Honda PGM Tester, use the tool manufacturer's instructions for troubleshooting. Diagnostic charts are not needed with this tool.

If using an OBD II scan tool, check the diagnostic troubles and make a note of each one. Also check and note the freeze fram data. Refer to the Diagnostic Trouble Code Chart and proceed with troubleshooting.

➡**When using either the Honda Tester or scan tool, always refer to the tool manufacturer's specific operating instructions. The scan tool or tester can read the diagnostic trouble codes, freeze frame data, current data, and other ECM data.**

Freeze frame data indicates the engine conditions when the first malfunction, misfire or fuel trim malfunction was detected, It can be useful information when troubleshooting.

CLEARING CODES

1986-95 Vehicles

Stored codes are removed from memory by removing power to the ECU. Disconnecting the power may also clear the memories used for other solid-state equipment such as the clock and radio. For this reason, always make note of the radio presets before clearing the system. Additionally, some radios contain anti-theft programming; obtain the owner's code number before clearing the codes.

While disconnecting the battery will clear the memory, this is not the recommended procedure. The memory should be cleared after the ignition is switched **OFF** by removing the appropriate fuse for at least 10 seconds. The correct fuses and their locations are:

1990 and earlier Legend — ALTERNATOR SENSE, in the underhood fuse and relay panel.

1991 and later Legend — ACG, in the dashboard fuse panel. Removing this fuse also cancels the memory for the power seats.

Integra, U.S. vehicles — BACK UP, in the underhood fuse and relay panel.

Integra, Canadian vehicles — HAZARD/BACK UP in the underhood fuse and relay panel.

Vigor — BACK UP, located in the underhood fuse and relay panel. Removing this fuse will cancel memories for the clock and radio.

1991-94 NSX — CLOCK, located in the main fuse and relay panel in the front luggage compartment, right side. Removing this fuse will cancel memories for the clock and radio.

1995 NSX — CLOCK, located in the main fuse and relay panel in the front luggage compartment, right side. Removing this fuse will cancel memories for the clock and radio. Codes may also be cleared using the OBD II scan tool or an equivalent tool, using the tool manufacturer's directions.

1995 2.5TL — BACK UP, located in the underhood fuse and relay panel. Removing this fuse will cancel memories for the clock and radio. Codes may also be cleared using the OBD II scan tool or an equivalent tool, using the tool manufacturer's directions.

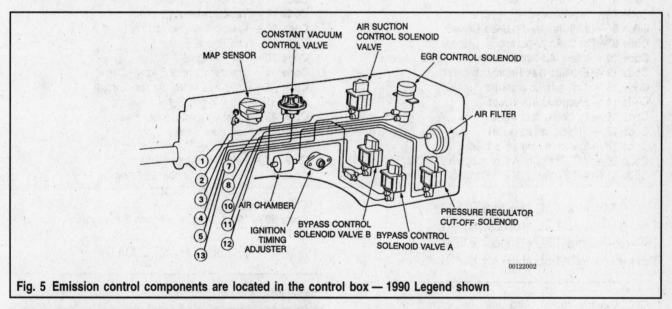

Fig. 5 Emission control components are located in the control box — 1990 Legend shown

Diagnostic Trouble Codes

1986-93 Integra 1.6L (1590cc)

Code 0 — Electronic Control Unit
Code 1 — Oxygen Content
Code 2 — Replace Engine Control Unit with known-good unit
Code 3 — Manifold Absolute Pressure
Code 4 — Replace Engine Control Unit with known-good unit
Code 5 — Manifold Absolute Pressure
Code 6 — Coolant Temperature
Code 7 — Throttle Angle
Code 8 — Crank Angle (TDC)
Code 9 — Crank Angle (Cyl)
Code 10 — Intake Air Temperature
Code 12 — EGR system (if equipped)
Code 13 — Atmospheric Pressure
Code 14 — Electronic Air Control
Code 15 — Ignition output signal
Code 16 — Fuel injector
Code 17 — Vehicle speed sensor
Code 19 — Lock up solenoid valve
Code 20 — Electric load (to 1989)
Code 43 — Fuel supply system

1986-87 Legend 2.5L (2494cc) C25A1

Code 0 — Electronic Control Unit
Code 1 — Oxygen Content
Code 2 — Replace Engine Control Unit with known-good unit
Code 3 — Manifold Absolute Pressure
Code 4 — Replace Engine Control Unit with known-good unit
Code 5 — Manifold Absolute Pressure
Code 6 — Coolant Temperature
Code 7 — Throttle Angle

Code 8 — Crank Angle (TDC)
Code 9 — Crank Angle (Cyl)
Code 10 — Intake Air Temperature
Code 12 — EGR system (if equipped)
Code 13 — Atmospheric Pressure
Code 14 — Electronic Air Control
Code 15 — Ignition output signal
Code 16 — Fuel injector
Code 17 — Vehicle speed sensor
Code 20 — Electric load (to 1989)
Code 43 — Fuel supply system

1987-90 Legend 2.7L (2675cc) C27A1

Code 0 — Electronic Control Unit (ECU)
Code 1 — Front Oxygen Content
Code 2 — Rear Oxygen Content
Code 3 — Manifold Absolute Pressure (MAP)
Code 4 — Crank angle
Code 5 — Manifold Absolute Pressure (MAP)
Code 6 — Coolant Temperature
Code 7 — Throttle angle
Code 8 — Crank Angle-Top Dead Center
Code 9 — Crank Angle-Number 1 Cylinder
Code 10 — Intake Air temperature
Code 12 — Exhaust Gas Recirculation system
Code 13 — Atmospheric pressure
Code 14 — Electronic Idle Control
Code 15 — Ignition output signal
Code 17 — Vehicle speed pulser
Code 18 — Ignition timing adjustment
Code 30 — A/T FI Signal A (if equipped)
Code 31 — A/T FI Signal B (if equipped)

1991-93 Integra 1.8L (1834cc) B18A1
1992-93 Integra 1.7L (1678cc) B17A1
1994-95 Integra 1.8L (1834cc) B18B1
1994-95 Integra 1.8L (1797cc) B18C1

Code 0 — Electronic Control Unit
Code 1 — Oxygen Content
Code 3 — Manifold Absolute Pressure
Code 4 — Crank Angle sensor
Code 5 — Manifold Absolute Pressure
Code 6 — Coolant Temperature
Code 7 — Throttle Angle
Code 8 — TDC Position
Code 9 — No. 1 Cylinder Position
Code 10 — Intake Air Temperature
Code 12 — EGR system
Code 13 — Atmospheric Pressure
Code 14 — Electronic Air Control
Code 15 — Ignition output signal
Code 16 — Fuel injector
Code 17 — Vehicle speed sensor
Code 20 — Electric Load Detector
Code 21 — VTEC Solenoid Valve (1.8L GS-R)
Code 22 — VTEC Oil Pressure Switch (1.8L GS-R)

Code 30 — TCM Signal 'A'
Code 31 — TCM Signal 'B'
Code 41 — HO2S Heater
Code 43 — Fuel supply system

1991-95 Legend 3.2L (3206cc) C32A1

Code 0 — Electronic Control Unit (ECU)
Code 1 — Left Oxygen Sensor
Code 2 — Right Oxygen Sensor
Code 3 — Manifold Absolute Pressure (MAP)
Code 4 — Crank angle 1
Code 5 — Manifold Absolute Pressure (MAP)
Code 6 — Coolant Temperature
Code 7 — Throttle angle
Code 9 — Crank Angle-Number 1 Cylinder
Code 10 — Intake Air temperature
Code 12 — Exhaust Gas Recirculation (EGR) system
Code 13 — Atmospheric pressure
Code 14 — Electronic Air Control (EACV)
Code 15 — Ignition output signal
Code 17 — Vehicle speed pulser
Code 18 — Ignition timing adjustment
Code 23 — Left Knock Sensor
Code 30 — A/T FI Signal A
Code 35 — Traction Control System Circuit
Code 36 — Traction Control System Circuit
Code 41 — Left Oxygen Sensor Heater
Code 42 — Right Oxygen Sensor Heater
Code 43 — Left Fuel Supply System
Code 44 — Right Fuel Supply System
Code 45 — Left Fuel Supply Metering
Code 46 — Right Fuel Supply Metering
Code 53 — Right Knock Sensor
Code 54 — Crank Angle 2
Code 59 — No. 1 Cylinder Position 2 (Cylinder Sensor)

1991-95 NSX 3.0L (2977cc) C30A1

Code 0 — ECU
Code 1 — Front Oxygen Sensor
Code 2 — Rear Oxygen Sensor
Code 3 — Manifold Absolute Pressure (MAP)
Code 4 — Crank angle A
Code 5 — Manifold Absolute Pressure (MAP)
Code 6 — Coolant Temperature
Code 7 — Throttle angle
Code 9 — Crank Angle-Number 1 Cylinder/Position A
Code 10 — Intake Air temperature
Code 12 — Exhaust Gas Recirculation (EGR) system
Code 13 — Atmospheric pressure
Code 14 — Electronic Air Control (EACV)
Code 15 — Ignition output signal
Code 16 — Fuel Injector
Code 17 — Vehicle speed pulser
Code 18 — Ignition timing adjustment
Code 22 — VTEC System; front, bank 2
Code 23 — Front Knock Sensor
Code 30 — A/T FI Signal A

Code 31 — A/T FI Signal B
Code 35 — TC STB signal
Code 36 — TCFC signal
Code 37 — Accelerator Position; Sensors 1, 2 or 1 and 2 circuits
Code 40 — Throttle Position or Throttle Valve Control Motor Circuits 1 or 2
Code 41 — Front Oxygen Sensor Heater; (circuit malfunction; bank 2 sensor 1)
Code 42 — Rear Primary Heated Oxygen Sensor Heater (circuit malfunction)
Code 43 — Front Fuel Supply System
Code 44 — Rear Fuel Supply System
Code 45 — Front Fuel Supply Metering; front bank 2
Code 46 — Rear Fuel Supply Metering; rear bank 1
Code 47 — Fuel Pump
Code 51 — Rear Spool Solenoid Valve
Code 52 — VTEC System; rear, bank 1
Code 53 — Rear Knock Sensor
Code 54 — Crank Angle B
Code 59 — No. 1 Cylinder Position B (Cylinder Sensor)
Code 61 — Front Heated Oxygen Sensor (slow response; bank 2 sensor 1)
Code 62 — Rear Primary Heated Oxygen Sensor (slow response; bank 1 sensor 1)
Code 63 — Front Secondary Oxygen Sensor (slow response or circuit voltage high or low)
Code 65 — Front Secondary Heated Oxygen Sensor (circuit malfunction; bank 2 sensor 2)
Code 64 — Rear Secondary Oxygen Sensor (slow response or circuit voltage high or low)
Code 66 — Rear Secondary Heated Oxygen Sensor (circuit malfunction; bank 1 sensor 2)
Code 67 — Front Catalytic Converter System
Code 68 — Rear Catalytic Converter System
Code 80 — Exhaust Gas Recirculation (EGR) system
Code 86 — Coolant temperature
Code 70 — Automatic Transaxle; the **D** indicator light and MIL may come on simultaneously.
Code 71 — Misfire detected; cylinder No. 1 or random misfire
Code 72 — Misfire detected; cylinder No. 2 or random misfire
Code 73 — Misfire detected; cylinder No. 3 or random misfire
Code 74 — Misfire detected; cylinder No. 4 or random misfire
Code 75 — Misfire detected; cylinder No. 5 or random misfire
Code 76 — Misfire detected; cylinder No. 6 or random misfire
Code 79 — Spark Plug Voltage Detection; circuit malfunction; (Front Bank (Bank 2) or (Rear Bank (Bank 1)
Code 79 — Spark Plug Voltage Detection; circuit malfunction; (Front Bank (Bank 2) or (Rear Bank (Bank 1)
Code 79 — Spark Plug Voltage Detection Module; reset circuit malfunction; (Front Bank (Bank 2)) or (Rear Bank (Bank 1)
Code 92 — Evaporative Emission Control System

1992-94 VIGOR 2.5L (G25A1)

Code 0 — Electronic Control Unit
Code 1 — HO2S circuit
Code 3 — Manifold Absolute Pressure
Code 4 — Crank Angle Sensor
Code 5 — Manifold Absolute Pressure
Code 6 — Coolant Temperature
Code 7 — Throttle Angle
Code 8 — TDC and or Crankshaft Position sensors
Code 9 — No. 1 Cylinder Position
Code 10 — Intake Air Temperature
Code 12 — EGR system
Code 13 — Atmospheric Pressure
Code 14 — Electronic Air Control
Code 15 — Ignition output signal
Code 16 — Fuel injector
Code 17 — Vehicle speed sensor
Code 18 — Ignition Timing Adjuster
Code 20 — Electric Load Detector
Code 30 — A/T FI Signal
Code 31 — A/T FI Signal
Code 41 — HO2S Heater
Code 43 — Fuel supply system
Code 45 — Fuel Supply Metering
Code 50 — Mass Air Flow (MAF) circuit — 2.5TL
Code 53 — Rear Knock Sensor
Code 54 — Crankshaft Speed Fluctuation sensor — 2.5TL
Code 61 — HO2S sensor heater — 2.5TL
Code 65 — Secondary HO2S sensor — 2.5TL
Code 67 — Catalytic Converter System — 2.5TL
Code 70 — Automatic transaxle or A/T FI Data line — 2.5TL
Code 71 — Misfire detected; cylinder No. 1 or random misfire
Code 72 — Misfire detected; cylinder No. 2 or random misfire
Code 73 — Misfire detected; cylinder No. 3 or random misfire
Code 74 — Misfire detected; cylinder No. 4 or random misfire
Code 75 — Misfire detected; cylinder No. 5 or random misfire
Code 76 — Random misfire detected — 2.5TL
Code 80 — EGR system — 2.5TL
Code 86 — Coolant Temperature circuit — 2.5TL
Code 92 — Evaporative Emission Control System — 2.5TL

OBD II CODES
1995 2.5TL and NSX

Code P0101 — Mass Air Flow Circuit; range and performance problem
Code P0102 — Mass Air Flow Circuit; low input
Code P0103 — Mass Air Flow Circuit; high input
Code P0106 — Manifold Absolute Pressure circuit; range and performance problem
Code P0107 — Manifold Absolute Pressure circuit; low input
Code P0108 — Manifold Absolute Pressure circuit; high input
Code P0112 — Intake Air Temperature circuit; low input

Code P0113 — Intake Air Temperature circuit; high input

Code P0116 — Engine Coolant Temperature circuit; range and performance problem

Code P0117 — Engine Coolant Temperature circuit; low input

Code P0118 — Engine Coolant Temperature circuit; high input

Code P0122 — Throttle Position circuit; low input

Code P0123 — Throttle Position circuit; high input

Code P0130 — Primary Heated Oxygen Sensor; circuit malfunction

Code P0131 — Rear Primary Heated Oxygen Sensor circuit; low voltage (on NSX, Bank 1, Sensor 1)

Code P0132 — Rear Primary Heated Oxygen Sensor circuit; high voltage (on NSX, Bank 1, Sensor 1)

Code P0133 — Primary Heated Oxygen Sensor; slow response (on NSX, Rear Bank 1, Sensor 1) .

Code P0135 — Rear Primary Heated Oxygen Sensor Heater; circuit malfunction (on NSX, on NSX, Bank 1, Sensor 1)

Code P0137 — Rear Secondary Heated Oxygen Sensor circuit; low voltage (on NSX, Bank 1, Sensor 2)

Code P0138 — Rear Secondary Heated Oxygen Sensor circuit; high voltage (on NSX, Bank 1, Sensor 2)

Code P0139 — Secondary Heated Oxygen Sensor; slow response (on NSX, Rear Bank 1, Sensor 2)

Code P0141 — Secondary Heated Oxygen Sensor Heater; circuit malfunction (on NSX, Rear Bank 1, Sensor 2)

Code P0151 — Front Primary Heated Oxygen Sensor circuit; low voltage (on NSX, Bank 2, Sensor 1)

Code P0152 — Front Primary Heated Oxygen Sensor circuit; high voltage (on NSX, Bank 2, Sensor 1)

Code P0153 — Front Primary Heated Oxygen Sensor; slow response (on NSX, Bank 2, Sensor 1)

Code P0155 — Front Primary Heated Oxygen Sensor Heater; circuit malfunction (on NSX, Bank 2, Sensor 1)

Code P0157 — Front Secondary Heated Oxygen Sensor circuit low voltage (on NSX, Bank 2, Sensor 2)

Code P0158 — Front Secondary Heated Oxygen Sensor circuit high voltage (on NSX, Bank 2, Sensor 2)

Code P0159 — Front Secondary Heated Oxygen Sensor; slow response (on NSX, Bank 2, Sensor 2)

Code P0161 — Front Secondary Heated Oxygen Sensor Heater; circuit malfunction (on NSX, Bank 2, Sensor 2)

Code P0171 — System Too Lean; (on NSX, Rear Bank (Bank 1))

Code P0172 — System Too Rich; (on NSX, Rear Bank (Bank 1))

Code P0174 — System Too Lean; (on NSX, Front Bank (Bank 2))

Code P0175 — System Too Rich; (on NSX, Front Bank (Bank 2))

Code P0106 — Manifold Absolute Pressure circuit; range and performance problem

Code P0107 — Manifold Absolute Pressure circuit; low input

Code P0108 — Manifold Absolute Pressure circuit; high input

Code P0112 — Intake Air Temperature circuit; low input

Code P0113 — Intake Air Temperature circuit; high input

Code P0116 — Engine Coolant Temperature circuit; range and performance problem

Code P0117 — Engine Coolant Temperature circuit; low input

Code P0118 — Engine Coolant Temperature circuit; high input

Code P0122 — Throttle Position circuit; low input

Code P0123 — Throttle Position circuit; high input

Code P0131 — Rear Primary Heated Oxygen Sensor circuit; low voltage (Bank 1, Sensor 1)

Code P0132 — Rear Primary Heated Oxygen Sensor circuit; high voltage (Bank 1, Sensor 1)

Code P0133 — Rear Primary Heated Oxygen Sensor; slow response (Bank 1, Sensor 1)

Code P0135 — Rear Primary Heated Oxygen Sensor Heater; circuit malfunction (Bank 1, Sensor 1)

Code P0137 — Rear Secondary Heated Oxygen Sensor circuit; low voltage (Bank 1, Sensor 2)

Code P0138 — Rear Secondary Heated Oxygen Sensor circuit; high voltage (Bank 1, Sensor 2)

Code P0139 — Rear Secondary Heated Oxygen Sensor; slow response (Bank 1, Sensor 2)

Code P0141 — Rear Secondary Heated Oxygen Sensor Heater; circuit malfunction (Bank 1, Sensor 2)

Code P0151 — Front Primary Heated Oxygen Sensor circuit; low voltage (Bank 2, Sensor 1)

Code P0152 — Front Primary Heated Oxygen Sensor circuit; high voltage (Bank 2, Sensor 1)

Code P0153 — Front Primary Heated Oxygen Sensor; slow response (Bank 2, Sensor 1)

Code P0155 — Front Primary Heated Oxygen Sensor Heater; circuit malfunction (Bank 2, Sensor 1)

Code P0157 — Front Secondary Heated Oxygen Sensor circuit low voltage (Bank 2, Sensor 2)

Code P0158 — Front Secondary Heated Oxygen Sensor circuit high voltage (Bank 2, Sensor 2)

Code P0159 — Front Secondary Heated Oxygen Sensor; slow response (Bank 2, Sensor 2)

Code P0161 — Front Secondary Heated Oxygen Sensor Heater; circuit malfunction (Bank 2, Sensor 2) .

Code P0171 — System Too Lean; (Rear Bank (Bank 1))

Code P0172 — System Too Rich; (Rear Bank (Bank 1))

Code P0174 — System Too Lean; (Front Bank (Bank 2))

Code P0175 — System Too Rich; (Front Bank (Bank 2))

Code P0300 — Random misfire detected — 2.5TL

Code P0301 — Misfire detected; cylinder No. 1 or random misfire

Code P0302 — Misfire detected; cylinder No. 2 or random misfire

Code P0303 — Misfire detected; cylinder No. 3 or random misfire

Code P0304 — Misfire detected; cylinder No. 4 or random misfire

Code P0305 — Misfire detected; cylinder No. 5 or random misfire

Code P0325 — Rear Knock Sensor (KS1); circuit malfunction

Code P0327 — Front Knock Sensor circuit; low input

Code P0328 — Front Knock Sensor circuit; high input

Code P0330 — Front Knock Sensor (KS2); circuit malfunction

Code P0332 — Rear Knock Sensor circuit; low input

Code P0333 — Rear Knock Sensor circuit; high input

Code P0335 — Crankshaft Position Sensor; low input (on NSX, A circuit)

Code P0336 — Crankshaft Position Sensor; range and performance (on NSX, A circuit)

Code P0401 — Exhaust Gas Recirculation; insufficient flow detected

Code P0420 — Rear Catalyst System; efficiency below threshold

Code P0430 — Front Catalyst System; efficiency below threshold

Code P0441 — Evaporative Emission Control System; incorrect purge flow

Code P0500 — Vehicle Speed Sensor circuit; low input

Code P0505 — Idle Control System; malfunction

Code P0700 — Automatic Transaxle

Code P0715 — Automatic Transaxle

Code P0720 — Automatic Transaxle

Code P0725 — Automatic Transaxle

Code P0730 — Automatic Transaxle

Code P0740 — Automatic Transaxle

Code P0753 — Automatic Transaxle

Code P0758 — Automatic Transaxle

Code P1107 — Barometric Pressure circuit; low input

Code P1108 — Barometric Pressure circuit; high input

Code P1201 — Misfire detected; cylinder 1

Code P1202 — Misfire detected; cylinder 2

Code P1203 — Misfire detected; cylinder 3

Code P1204 — Misfire detected; cylinder 4

Code P1205 — Misfire detected; cylinder 5

Code P1206 — Misfire detected; cylinder 6

Code P1241 — Throttle Valve Control Motor; circuit 1 malfunction

Code P1242 — Throttle Valve Control Motor; circuit 2 malfunction

Code P1243 — Throttle Position insufficient

Code P1244 — Closed Throttle Position insufficient

Code P1246 — Accelerator Position Sensor 1; circuit malfunction

Code P1247 — Accelerator Position Sensor 2; circuit malfunction

Code P1248 — Accelerator Position Sensor 1 and 2; incorrect correlation

Code P1259 — VTEC System malfunction; (Rear Bank (Bank 1))

Code P1279 — VTEC System malfunction; (Front Bank (Bank 2))

Code P1297 — Electric load Detector circuit; low input

Code P1298 — Electric load Detector circuit; high input

Code P1300 — Random Misfire

Code P1301 — Misfire detected; cylinder 1

Code P1302 — Misfire detected; cylinder 2

Code P1303 — Misfire detected; cylinder 3

Code P1304 — Misfire detected; cylinder 4

Code P1305 — Misfire detected; cylinder 5

Code P1306 — Misfire detected; cylinder 6

Code P1316 — Spark Plug Voltage Detection; circuit malfunction; (Front Bank (Bank 2))

Code P1317 — Spark Plug Voltage Detection; circuit malfunction; (Rear Bank (Bank 1))

Code P1318 — Spark Plug Voltage Detection Module; reset circuit malfunction; (Front Bank (Bank 2))

Code P1319 — Spark Plug Voltage Detection Module; reset circuit malfunction; (Rear Bank (Bank 1))

Code P1336 — Crankshaft Position Sensor; range and performance (on NSX, sensor B)

Code P1337 — Crankshaft Position Sensor; low input (on NSX, circuit B)

Code P1359 — Crankshaft Position Sensor and TDC Sensor — 2.5TL

Code P1361 — TDC Sensor; intermittent interruption — 2.5TL

Code P1362 — TDC Sensor; no signal — 2.5TL

Code P1381 — Cylinder Position Sensor; intermittent interruption (on NSX, Sensor A)

Code P1382 — Cylinder Position Sensor; no signal (on NSX, Sensor A)

Code P1386 — Cylinder Position Sensor B; intermittent interruption

Code P1387 — Cylinder Position Sensor B; no signal

Code P1459 — Evaporative Emission Purge Flow Switch malfunction

Code P1491 — EGR Valve; insufficient lift detected

Code P1498 — EGR Valve Lift Sensor; high voltage

Code P1508 — Idle Air Control Valve; circuit failure — 2.5TL

Code P1607 — ECM internal circuit failure A

Code P1608 — ECM internal circuit failure B

Code P1660 — A/T FI Data Line; failure

Code P1671 — A/T FI Data Line; no signal

Code P1672 — A/T FI Data Line; failure

Code P1676 — TCS FI Data Line; no signal

Code P1677 — TCS FI Data Line; failure

Code P1681 — A/T FI Signal A; low input — 2.5TL

Code P1682 — A/T FI Signal A; high input — 2.5TL

Code P1686 — A/T FI Signal B; low input — 2.5TL

Code P1687 — A/T FI Signal B; high input — 2.5TL

Code P1705 — Automatic Transaxle

Code P1706 — Automatic Transaxle

Code P1753 — Automatic Transaxle

Code P1758 — Automatic Transaxle

Code P1768 — Automatic Transaxle

Code P1788 — Automatic Transaxle

Code P1790 — Automatic Transaxle

Code P1791 — Automatic Transaxle

Code P1792 — Automatic Transaxle

Code P1793 — Automatic Transaxle

Code P1795 — Automatic Transaxle

AUDI

General Information

MOTRONIC AND MULTI POINT INJECTION (MPI) SYSTEMS

The Motronic and MPI fuel injection systems are similar and share most components and modes of operation. Audi uses Motronic to describe the fuel injection system on the V8 Quattro, S4, 200 Quattro and the 200 Quattro Wagon. Audi uses MPI to describe the systems used on the 90 Quattro, Coupe Quattro and the 2.8L V6 equipped 100 series vehicles.

The Motronic and MPI fuel injection systems are self-learning adaptive systems. They continuously learn using a sophisticated feedback system that readjusts various control settings. These new values are then stored in the ECU memory. The adaptive capability allows the systems to compensate for changes in the engine's operating conditions, such as intake leaks, altitude changes or any other system malfunction. If the battery or ECU is disconnected, the vehicle must be driven so ECU can 're-learn' its operating conditions.

Operation of the fuel injection system is based on the information received by the various sensors. This keeps the system constantly updated on engine speed, coolant temperature, throttle position and the intake air volume.

On the V8, the power supply to ECU is at terminal 18, through a 5 amp fuse (S27) in the main fuse/relay panel. Power from fuse S27 energizes the power supply relay in the ECU when engine speed reaches 25 rpm. The main fuse/relay panel is located behind the side kick panel cover on the passenger's side.

A Hall effect signal from the right distributor helps the ECU establish a reference point to start the fuel injection process. After the engine is running, the reference sender and speed sensor provide the necessary information to the ECU for ignition and fuel injection.

The ECU has a self-diagnostic feature. Any faults detected by the sensors are sent to the ECU and are recorded in the ECU memory. Fault codes can be displayed using LED tester US 1115 and a jumper wire.

CONTINUOUS INJECTION SYSTEM (CIS-E)

The CIS-E system incorporates 2 control units. An Ignition Control Unit (ICU) or Knock Sensor Control Unit (KSCU, on 5000S only) and a Fuel Injection Control Unit (FICU).

The CIS-E system also has self-diagnosis and troubleshooting capabilities. Input and output signals from various sensors, switches and signaling devices are constantly monitored for faults. These faults are stored in the control unit memory. Faults can be displayed by a flashing 4 digit code sequence from an LED light located on the instrument panel.

CIS-MOTRONIC FUEL INJECTION SYSTEM

The CIS Motronic system used on Audi 80 and 90 models use a single Electronic Control Unit (ECU), located behind the A/C evaporator assembly. The ECU controls the fuel delivery, ignition system and operation of the emission control components. The CIS Motronic system also incorporates self-diagnostic capabilities. The CIS-Motronic system consists of the following components:

- Ignition coil with power stage
- Differential pressure regulator
- Cold start valve
- Idle stabilizer valve
- Ignition distributor with Hall sender
- Knock sensor
- Coolant temperature sensor
- Idle/Full throttle switches
- Air sensor potentiometer
- Oxygen sensor
- Carbon canister frequency valve
- Carbon canister ON/OFF valve
- CIS Motronic control unit

The ECU receives signals from various sensors, switches and signaling components which are constantly monitored for faults. These faults are stored in the ECU memory. Faults can be displayed by using a suitable test light connected between the battery positive terminal and the test lead, located next to the fuel distributor in the engine compartment. Characteristics of the CIS-Motronic system are as follows:

- Fuel injection control
- Oxygen sensor regulation with adaptive learning capability
- MAP type ignition control with individual cylinder knock regulation
- Idle speed control
- Fuel tank ventilation control
- Permanent fault memory for self-diagnosis

Self-Diagnostics

SERVICE PRECAUTIONS

- Do not disconnect the battery or power to the control module before reading the fault codes. On the Motronic SMPI and Audi SMPI systems, fault code memory is erased when power is interrupted.
- Make sure the ignition switch is **OFF** before disconnecting any wiring.
- Before removing or installing a control module, disconnect the negative battery cable. The unit receives power through the main connector at all times and will be permanently damaged if improperly powered up or down.
- Keep all parts and harnesses dry during service. Protect the control module and all solid-state components from rough handling or extremes of temperature.
- Do not apply voltage to engine control module to simulate output signals.

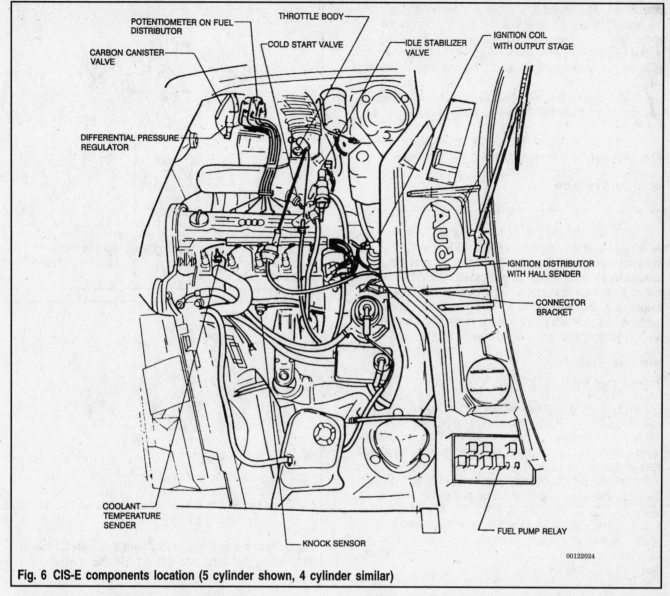

Fig. 6 CIS-E components location (5 cylinder shown, 4 cylinder similar)

- When coil wire, terminal **4**, is disconnected from distributor, always ground using a jumper wire.
- Do not try to start the engine with the fuel injectors removed.
- In emergency starting situations, use a fast charge for cranking up to 15 seconds only and not more than 16.5 volts; allow at least 1 minute between attempts.

GENERATING CODES

Before attempting to read trouble codes, the vehicle must be driven for at least 5 minutes to set codes in the computer's memory. This procedure is referred to as 'generating codes'.

CIS Systems

1. The engine must be running to generate fault codes. Read all the Steps in this procedure before starting.
2. On 1985-88 models, turn the ignition switch **ON** without starting the engine to make sure the engine warning light works, if equipped. If it does not light with the ignition **ON**,

engine not running, but does light when attempting to retrieve fault codes, either the wiring between the control units is faulty or the ignition control unit is faulty.

3. On 1989-92 California models only, turn the ignition switch **ON** without starting the engine to make sure the engine warning light On Board Diagnostics (OBD) works. If it does not light with the ignition **ON**, engine not running, then turn ignition **OFF** and bridge terminals of diagnostic connectors using adapter (cable 357 971 514E) or an equivalent tool. Now turn ignition **ON**, but do not start the engine. The engine warning light OBD will light up, if it does not light the wiring between the control modules is faulty or the ignition control module is faulty. Consult a wiring diagram and complete the necessary repairs before continuing.

4. Fuel pump relay and fuses 13, 19, 24 and 28 on 1985-88 models or 13, 19, 21, 24, 27 and 28 on 1989-92 models, must be good and all ground connections in the engine compartment must be good. Also, make sure the air conditioning is **OFF**.

5. To generate fault codes, the vehicle must be driven with air conditioner **OFF**, for at least 5 minutes at normal operating

temperature. The engine must be kept above 3000 RPM for the majority of the test drive with at least one full throttle application. On turbocharged engines, full boost should be reached during the full throttle acceleration. After the test drive, allow the engine to idle for at least 2 minutes before retrieving codes.

6. Do not turn the ignition switch **OFF** or the temporary memory will be erased. If the engine stalls, do not restart it. The codes will still be in memory.

7. If the engine will not run, operate the starter for at least 6 seconds and leave the ignition switch **ON**.

READING CODES

▶ **See Figures 7, 8, 9 and 10**

➡Vehicles that do not have a CHECK ENGINE light or Malfunction Indicator Lamp (MIL) codes can only be accessed by the use of special equipment. US 1115 LED tester, VAG 1551 diagnostic tester or equivalent special testers can only be used to retrieve diagnostic codes from these vehicles. When using special diagnostic equipment, always observe the tool manufacturer's instructions.

With Flash Tester

1985-94 Vehicles

1. On California models equipped with a engine warning light, an LED tester is not required. On models not equipped with a engine warning light, connect the US 1115 LED tester or equivalent to the test connectors under the left-hand side of dash and above the pedals.

2. On 1985-88 models with a engine warning light, locate the fuel pump relay on the main fuse/relay panel. Insert a spare fuse into the terminals on top of the relay for at least 4 seconds, then remove the fuse to activate the diagnostic program. The engine warning light on the instrument panel or the LED tester will begin to flash the first code. It will continue to flash this code until the fuse is installed.

3. On all models, codes should be retrieved with the engine running at idle. If engine will not start, operate the starter for

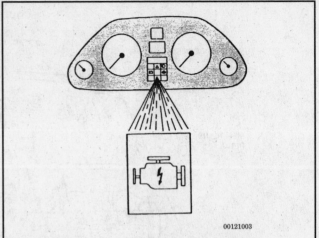

Fig. 8 Location of the fault indicator light in the instrument panel — Vehicles equipped with an ENGINE WARNING light

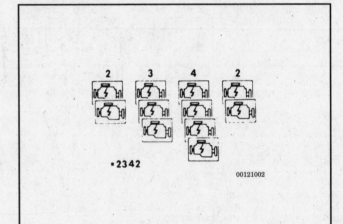

Fig. 9 Example of the indicator light sequence for Code 2342 — vehicles equipped with an ENGINE WARNING LIGHT

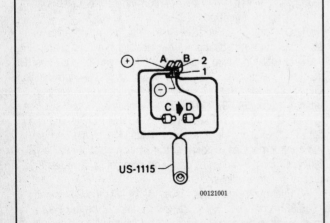

Fig. 7 Activating the diagnostic mode — 1985-86 vehicles

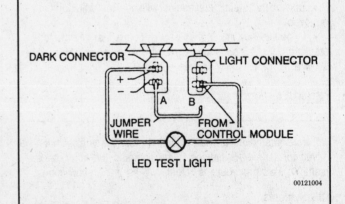

Fig. 10 On 1989-94, connect the LED tester and momentarily connect jumper terminals A and B to read fault codes

approximately 6 seconds and leave the ignition switch **ON**. On CIS systems the engine should be left running after the generating codes procedure.

4. On 1989-94 models, so equipped, locate the test connectors above the pedals and connect the tester. To connect the LED tester, connect the positive terminal of the LED tester to the positive terminal in connector **A**. Connect the negative terminal of the LED tester to the only terminal in connector **B**. Connect one end of a jumper wire to the negative terminal in connector **A**, touch the other end of the jumper wire to the terminal in connector **B** for at least 4 seconds.

5. Fault codes will now be displayed as flashing by the tester or by the engine warning light on California models. Touch the jumper wire to the terminal in connector **B** for another 4 seconds to advance to the next code. Do not leave jumper wire connected for ten seconds or memory will be erased. Engine idle speed may increase slightly when reading injection control module codes.

6. All flash codes are 4 digits, with about 2.5 seconds between digits. Codes are displayed in order of importance, usually beginning with ignition system codes. Count the flashes and write down the code, then proceed onto the next code. Read all codes, before starting any repairs. If the first code is 4444 or 0000 there are no faults present. 0000 is represented by the light ON for 2.5 seconds with 2.5 second intervals between. When all fault codes have been reported (0000 or 4444 displayed), turn the ignition OFF.

➡️**On CIS systems codes are erased when the ignition is turned OFF.**

With Diagnostic Tester

1987-89 Vehicles

1. On all 1987-88 models, the VAG 1551 or equivalent diagnostic tester can be connected to the terminals on top of the fuel pump relay. For power to the tester, a separate power supply wire must be connected to the positive battery terminal. On 1989 models, the tester can be connected to the diagnostic terminals above the pedals. The terminals are shaped so they cannot be connected incorrectly. Power for the tester is supplied through fuse 21.

2. With the tester connected, turn the ignition switch **ON**, but do not start the engine or the codes will be erased.

3. Select menu option 2, Blink Code Output. Press and release, then press and hold the run (arrow) key until the program starts, then release the key. An asterisk (*) will appear and flash the codes, which the tester will count and report on the screen as numbers. If Code 4444 is displayed, no faults are found in memory.

4. Press the run key to advance to the next code. Read all the fault codes before starting repairs.

5. All engine system fault codes will be displayed first. If there are other control units on the vehicle, press the run key again to access those codes.

6. When the End of the Report Code 0000 is displayed and there are no other control units on the vehicle, pressing the run key again may return to the main menu or it may erase the codes. To stop the program without erasing the codes, turn the ignition switch **OFF** and press the clear button once.

1990-91 Vehicles

1. Connect the VAG 1551 or equivalent diagnostic tester to the diagnostic terminals above the pedals or in the passenger side foot well. The terminals are shaped so they cannot be connected incorrectly. Power for the tester is supplied through fuse 21 or 27.

2. On all models, codes should be retrieved with the engine running at idle. If the engine will not start, operate the starter for at least 5 seconds and leave the ignition switch **ON**. On CIS systems, the engine should be left running after the procedure for generating codes.

3. Operate the tester to select menu option 2, Blink Code Output or Fault Memory Recall. An asterisk (*) will appear and flash the codes, which the tester will count and report on the screen as numbers. If Code 4444 is displayed, no faults are found in memory.

4. If the engine is not running, some codes will be displayed. These codes can be ignored if the engine has been intentionally stalled but should be investigated if the engine will not start.

5. Press the run key to advance to the next code. Read all the fault codes before starting repairs.

6. When the End of the Report Code 0000 is displayed and there are no other control units on the vehicle, pressing the run key again may return to the main menu or it may erase the codes. To stop the program without erasing the codes, turn the ignition switch **OFF** and press the clear button once.

1992-94 Vehicles with 2.2L and 2.8L Engines

Diagnostic trouble codes (DTCs) may be accessed using the VAG 1551 scan tool.

1. Turn the ignition switch to the **OFF** position.

2. Connect the VAG1551/1 diagnostic lead to the data link connectors (DLCs) in the underhood relay box.

➡️**Observe the connector shape when connecting diagnostic leads.**

3. Connect the black lead of the VAG1551/1 diagnostic lead to the DLC 1, and the white lead to the DLC 4.

4. Connect the VAG1551/1 diagnostic lead to the VAG 1551 scan tool. The scan tool should read — VAG self diagnosis — 1 Rapid Data Transmission or 2 Flash Code Output.

5. Additional operating instructions may be accessed by pressing the help key on the VAG 1551 scan tool. press the arrow key to continue fault tracing.

1992-94 Vehicles with 4.2L Engine

Diagnostic trouble codes (DTCs) may be accessed using the VAG 1551 scan tool.

1. Turn the ignition switch to the **OFF** position.

2. Connect the VAG1551/1 diagnostic lead to the data link connectors (DLCs) under the passenger side footwell carpet.

➡️**Observe the connector shape when connecting diagnostic leads.**

3. Connect the black lead of the VAG1551/1 diagnostic lead to the DLC 1, and the white lead to the DLC 2 and the blue lead to the DLC 4.

4. Connect the VAG1551/1 diagnostic lead to the VAG 1551 scan tool. The scan tool should read — VAG self diagnosis — Rapid Data Transmission or 2 Flash Code Output.

5. Additional operating instructions may be accessed by pressing the help key on the VAG 1551 scan tool. Press the arrow key to continue fault tracing.

With On Board Diagnostic (OBD) Display

1992-94 Vehicles

▶ See Figure 11

The air conditioning system On-Board Diagnostic (OBD) can be accessed without the need of a scan tool. The air conditioning control head contains a 61 channel OBD display.

1. To start the display, turn the ignition **ON** or start the engine.

2. Press and hold down RECIRCULATION button 1 and press and hold down upper AIR DISTRIBUTION button 2.

3. Release both buttons and '01c' will be displayed, 01c indicates channel **1**, 02c indicates channel **2**, etc.

4. To change to a different channel, press the temperature + button to go to the next higher channel or the temperature - button to go to the next lower channel.

5. To call up information about a particular channel, select the desired channel and press RECIRCULATION button **1**.

➡**Diagnostic channel 1 01c contains the DTC's. There are also graphics channels 1 and 2 in diagnostic channel 52, to aid in diagnosis.**

6. When using channel 52, graphics channels 1 and 2, a segment of an 88.8 display will appear. This appears when there is a compressor off situation. Each segment has an alpha numeric denomination, which can be used to diagnose a particular air conditioning compressor off problem.

7. To leave the memory display, press AUTO button or switch the ignition OFF.

8. The VAG 1551 is needed to erase codes from memory. See clearing codes using diagnostic tester section.

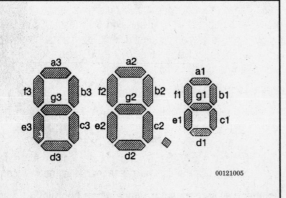

Fig. 11 Vehicles with automatic climate control, codes can also be accessed through the On Board Diagnostic display through graphics channels 1 and 2 display — 1992-94 vehicles

00121005

GENERATING OUTPUT SIGNALS

Without Diagnostic Tester

1985-86 Vehicles

1. Insert the fuse in the opening on top of the fuel pump relay for 4 seconds.

2. Remove the fuse from the fuel pump relay.

3. The fault code will be displayed by observing the indicator light in the instrument cluster and counting the flashes.

4. To display the next code repeat Steps 1 and 2.

5. Each code will repeat until the fuse is inserted into the fuel pump relay.

6. The diagnosis procedure will be cancelled if the engine speed is raised above 2000 rpm or the ignition switch is turned **OFF**.

1987-89 Vehicles

1. With the ignition switch **OFF**, insert the spare fuse in the top of the fuel pump relay or connect the jumper wire to the test connectors.

2. Turn the ignition switch **ON**. The first code will be displayed. If the first code is for the fuel pump relay, or the pump begins to run, remove the fuse or jumper wire quickly to prevent flooding the engine.

3. To go to the next output signal, momentarily remove the fuse from the fuel pump relay or disconnect the jumper wire. The next item on the output code list will be activated when the full throttle switch is closed. Be sure to use the correct output code list, the sequence is not the same on all engines.

4. When the full throttle switch is closed, each solenoid or frequency valve can be checked by listening or touching the valve to detect operation. Cold start valves are operated for only 10 seconds.

5. When the last output test has been completed, Code 0000 will be displayed. At this time, the fault code memory can be erased or the test can be repeated by turning the ignition switch **OFF** and **ON** again.

6. If the starter is operated at any point in the output test, the control unit will switch to reporting input signal codes.

1990-94 Vehicles

1. With the ignition switch **OFF**, connect the LED test light and the jumper wire to the test connectors.

2. Turn the ignition switch **ON**. The first code will be displayed. If the first code is for the fuel pump relay, or the pump begins to run, remove the jumper wire quickly to prevent flooding the engine.

3. To go to the next output signal, momentarily disconnect the jumper wire. The next item on the output code list will be activated when the full throttle switch is closed. Be sure to use the correct output code list, the sequence is not the same on all engines.

4. When the full throttle switch is closed, each solenoid or frequency valve can be checked by listening or touching the valve to detect operation. Cold start valves on CIS systems are operated for only 10 seconds.

5. When the last output test has been completed, Code 0000 will be displayed. At this time, the fault code memory can be erased.

6. If the starter is operated at any point in the output test, the control module will switch to reporting input signal codes.

With Diagnostic Tester

1987-91 Vehicles

1. Follow the procedure for retrieving fault codes. After all codes have been reported, turn the ignition switch **OFF** and press the clear button.

2. Select the Blink Code Output program on the tester. Press and hold the run key until the Continuous Short Circuit message appears on the screen, then turn the ignition switch **ON** without starting the engine.

3. Press and release the run key. The first output code should appear on the display. If the first output signal is for the fuel pump relay, remove the fuse for the fuel pump quickly after that test to avoid flooding the engine.

4. The code for each item in the output signal test will appear in the order listed. Press the run key to change to the next item on the list.

5. Except for the cold start valve, the output signal will be activated, as long as the code appears on the screen. As each item is activated, touch each valve to physically check that it is vibrating or humming.

6. When the test is completed, turn the ignition switch **OFF** to stop the test. The test can be repeated by turning the ignition switch **ON**.

1992-94 Vehicles

1. Go to Step 3, if not using Rapid Data Transfer. Turn the ignition **ON**, but do not start the car.

➡**The engine must not be running when output checks are being performed. The output check mode will not work if the car is running.**

2. After selecting mode 1, Rapid Data Transfer, and the Select Function display appears, enter 01 for engine electronics. Now the control module coding and engine identification numbers will appear. After the coding is deciphered and the information matches your engine, press the Run key to continue. If the Fault In Communication display appears, one of the four displays indicating an open/short wire will appear or possibly the control module may be defective. Pushing the Help button will give you a list of possible causes for this problem. This problem must be corrected before continuing.

3. When the Select Function message appears, select 03 for Output Check Diagnosis. Each output check being tested will be displayed on the VAG 1551. Press the Run key to advance the next output check. The output check displayed on the screen will be performed until the next output check is selected.

➡**When testing the fuel pump, do not run the test too long or the engine could become flooded. When the output checks are finished the Select Function Menu will appear. The output tests can be run again by selecting function 03. Turn the ignition OFF for approximately 20 seconds, before selecting Output Check Diagnosis again.**

4. Follow the procedure for retrieving fault codes. After all codes have been reported, turn the ignition switch **OFF** and press the clear **C** button.

5. Select the Blink Code Output program on the tester, then turn the ignition **ON**, but do not start the engine. Output checks can only be performed with the engine NOT RUNNING. The tests will be stopped if the engine is started or a speed impulse is recognized.

6. Press and release the Run key. The first output code should appear on the display. If the first output signal is for the fuel pump relay, remove the fuse for the fuel pump quickly after that test to avoid flooding the engine.

➡**During output checks diagnosis, the carbon canister solenoid valve, idle stabilizer valve and cold start valve are checked audibly or by touch. Avoid background noise while audibly checking these components.**

7. The code for each item in the output signal test will appear in the order listed for your particular engine. Press the Run key to change to the next item on the list.

8. Except for the cold start valve, the output signal will be activated, as long as the code appears on the screen. As each item is activated, touch each valve to physically check that it is vibrating or humming.

9. When the test is completed, turn the ignition switch **OFF** to stop the test. The test can be repeated by turning the ignition switch **ON**.

CLEARING CODES

Without Diagnostic Tester

1985-88 Vehicles

1. On California vehicles, the output signals must be tested before codes can be erased. Leave the ignition switch **ON**.

2. After the last output signal code is displayed, install the fuse for at least 4 seconds and remove it again. The engine warning light should come **ON** for 2.5 seconds, then go **OFF** for 2.5 seconds, displaying Code 0000.

3. Install the fuse again for at least 10 seconds, then remove it. If the engine warning light stays **ON**, all codes have been erased.

4. On Federal vehicles, after activating the fault code memory, the codes will automatically be erased when the ignition switch is turned **OFF** or when the engine is started.

1989-94 Vehicles

1. The output signals must be tested before codes can be erased. Leave the ignition switch **ON**.

2. After the last output signal code is displayed, connect the test connector jumper wire for at least 4 seconds and remove it again. The engine warning light or flash tester light should come **ON** for 2.5 seconds, then go **OFF** for 2.5 seconds, displaying Code 0000.

3. Connect the jumper wire again for at least 10 seconds, then remove it. If the engine warning light or tester light stays **ON**, all codes have been erased.

With Diagnostic Tester

1985-88 Vehicles

When all control unit memory codes have been retrieved and Code 0000 is displayed, press and hold the run key with the ignition switch **ON** to clear all codes.

1989-91 Vehicles — Except CIS-E III

When all control module memory codes have been retrieved and code 0000 or End of output is displayed, press the run key, now press 05 and the codes will be erased using mode **1** (Rapid Data Transfer). Mode **1** will display a message saying: Fault memory is erased! after erasing the codes. In mode **2** (Blink Code Output), press and hold the run key with the ignition **ON** and all codes will be cleared.

➡**This procedure erases all control module codes, make sure you have checked all control modules for DTC's before performing the erasing codes procedure.**

1992-94 Vehicles — Except CIS-E III

Diagnostic trouble codes (DTCs) may be erased after they are retrieved using the VAG 1551 scan tool.
1. Turn the ignition switch to the **OFF** position.
2. Connect the VAG1551 scan tool as outlined in Generating Output Signals.
3. Press 01 on the VAG scan tool to select VAG address 'Engine Electronics'.
4. Press the arrow button until the display reads 'Select Function XX'.
5. Press the Q on the VAG scan tool and view all DTCs.
6. Press the 05 on the VAG scan tool to select 02 — Cancel Fault Code Memory. Press Q to erase all DTCs.
7. Road test the vehicle and reactivate DTC memory to ensure all faults have been eliminated.

1989-92 Vehicles — CIS-E III

After activating the fault code memory, the codes will automatically be erased when the ignition switch is turned **OFF** or when the engine is started.

➡**CIS-E III California models have permanent memory and will retain the fault codes after the ignition is turned off. This memory can be erased by following the erasure method using the VAG 1551 diagnostic tester. Control module part numbers can be used to identify the control modules and determine whether the CIS-E III system has permanent or temporary memory.**

Diagnostic Trouble Codes

1985-89 Vehicles

2.1L (MC), 2.2L (MC), 2.0L (3A) and 2.3L (NG, NF) Engines

Code 1111 — Ignition control unit or fuel injection control unit
Code 1231 — Transmission speed sensor
Code 2111 — Engine speed sensor
Code 2112 — Ignition reference sensor

Code 2113 — Hall sensor
Code 2121 — Idle switch
Code 2122 — Engine speed/Hall sensor
Code 2123 — Full throttle switch
Code 2132 — No data being transmitted from fuel injection control unit to ignition control unit
Code 2141 — Knock control 1, knock sensor 1 for cylinder 2; knock control 2, knock sensor 2 for cylinder 4
Code 2142 — Knock sensor 1 on cylinder 2; knock sensor 2 on cylinder 4
Code 2143 — Knock control 1, knock sensor 1 for cylinder 2; knock control 2, knock sensor 2 for cylinder 4
Code 2144 — Knock sensor 1 on cylinder 2; knock sensor 2 on cylinder 4
Code 2212 — Throttle valve potentiometer (position sensor)
Code 2221 — Vacuum hose to pressure sensor in control unit
Code 2222 — Pressure sensor in control unit
Code 2223 — Altitude sensor
Code 2232 — Air sensor potentiometer (position sensor)
Code 2233 — Reference (supply) voltage
Code 2234 — MPI control unit supply voltage
Code 2242 — CO potentiometer
Code 2312 — Engine coolant temperature (ECT) sensor
Code 2322 — Intake air temperature (IAT) sensor
Code 2341 — Oxygen sensor control unit is at its limit
Code 2342 — Oxygen sensor (does not control)
Code 4431 — Idle stabilizer valve
Code 4444 — No faults stored in memory
Code 0000 — End of diagnosis

1990-94 Vehicles

2.0L (3A), 2.3L (NG, NF, 7A), 2.2L (MC, 3B, AAN), 2.8L (AAH), 3.6L (PT) and 4.2L (ABH) Engines

Code 00000 or 0000 — No faults in memory (1992-93 all engines except 2.8L and 1992 2.3L)
Code 00000 or 0000 — End of diagnosis (1990-91 all engines; 1992-94 2.8L and 1992 2.3L)
Code 00000 or 4444 — No faults in memory (1990-91 all engines; 1992-94 2.8L and 1992 2.3L)
Code 00281 or 1231 — Vehicle speed sender signal is missing
Code 00513 or 2111 — Engine speed (RPM) sensor has no change in signal
Code 00513 or 2231 — Air mass sensor has open/short in circuit
Code 00514 or 2112 — Crankshaft position (CKP) sensor has no change in signal
Code 00515 or 2113 — Hall sender has fault in basic setting or open/short in circuit
Code 2114 — Hall sender is not on reference point or out of adjustment
Code 00516 or 2121 — Idle switch (closed throttle position switch 4.2L ABH) has open/short in circuit
Code 00517 or 2123 — Full throttle switch
Code 00518 or 2212 — Throttle position (TP) sensor has open/short in circuit
Code 00519 or 2222 — Manifold vacuum sensor signal is out of range

Code 00520 or 2232 — Air mass sensor signal is missing/signal out of limit

Code 00521 or 2242 — CO potentiometer position sensor (2.3L 7A 1990-91)

Code 00522 or 2312 — Engine coolant temperature (ECT) sensor signal is out of range

Code 00523 or 2322 — Intake air temperature (IAT) sensor has open/short in circuit

Code 00524 or 2142 — Knock sensor (KS) 1 has no change in signal, possible open/short between KS and ECM

Code 00525 or 2342 — Oxygen sensor signal is out of range

Code 00528 or 2223 — Pressure sensor (altitude sensor 1990-91) has open/short in circuit

Code 00529 or 2122 — Engine RPM signal missing (2.3L NG,NF)

Code 00531 or 2233 — Air mass sensor reference voltage signal missing; voltage high (2.3L 7A 1990-91)

Code 00532 or 2234 — Supply voltage signal is too high or low

Code 00533 or 2231 — Idle speed regulation, the idle speed is too low or too high

Code 00535 or 2141 — Knock sensor regulation has exceeded its maximum control limit (1992 2.3L NG)

Code 00536 or 2141 — First & second knock regulation, the maximum control limits have been exceeded (4.2L ABH engine)

Code 00536 or 2143 — Second knock control has exceeded its control limits (1992-93 2.8L AAH)

Code 00537 or 2341 — Oxygen sensor signal is out of range

Code 2343 — Air/fuel mixture rich (2.0L engine)

Code 2344 — Air/fuel mixture lean (2.0L engine)

Code 00538 or 2241 — Second knock control (1991 2.2L 3B)

Code 00540 or 2144 — Knock sensor 2 has no change in signal, possible open/short between KS and ECM

Code 00543 or 2214 — Engine speed signal is too high, the RPM exceeds maximum limit

Code 00544 or 2224 — Wastegate frequency valve has exceeded maximum boost pressure (Manifold dump valve 1990-91 2.2L MC)

Code 00545 or 2314 — Engine/Transmission electrical connection has ground between ECM and TCM

Code 00546 or 2132 — Fuel injection/ignition control data link (2.3L NG,NF)

Code 00553 or 2324 — Mass air flow (MAF) sensor signal

Code 00554 or 2331 — Oxygen control for cylinders (4-6) exceeded control limits (1992-93 2.8L AAH)

Code 00555 or 2332 — Oxygen sensor 2 (G108) signal is missing (1992-93 2.8L AAH)

Code 00560 or 2411 — EGR system not working properly

Code 00560 or 2441 — EGR system has false readings (1992-93 2.8L AAH, California)

Code 00561 or 2413 — Fuel mixture too rich

Code 00575 or 2221 — Manifold pressure signal missing (1990-91 2.2L MC)

Code 00577 or 2141 — Knock regulation cylinder 1 has exceeded control limit

Code 00578 or 2141 — Knock regulation cylinder 2 has exceeded control limit

Code 00579 or 2141 — Knock regulation cylinder 3 has exceeded control limit

Code 00580 or 2143 — Knock regulation cylinder 4 has exceeded control limit

Code 00581 or 2143 — Knock regulation cylinder 5 has exceeded control limit

Code 00824 or 3424 — Engine warning light is defective

Code 4312 — EGR frequency valve (2.3L 7A 1990-91)

Code 4331 — Carbon canister solenoid valve 2

Code 01242 or 4332 — Ignition final control circuit problem (1992-93 2.8L AAH)

Code 01247 or 4343 — Carbon canister solenoid has short/open in circuit

Code 01249 or 4411 — Fuel Injector cylinder 1 (& 5 on 3.6/4.2L) open/short injector circuit, fuse 23 open (fuse 13 on 2.8L)

Code 01250 or 4412 — Fuel Injector cylinder 2 (& 7 on 3.6/4.2L) open/short injector circuit, fuse 23 open (fuse 13 on 2.8L)

Code 01251 or 4413 — Fuel Injector cylinder 3 (& 6 on 3.6/4.2L) open/short injector circuit, fuse 23 open (fuse 13 on 2.8L)

Code 01252 or 4414 — Fuel Injector cylinder 4 (& 8 on 3.6/4.2L) open/short injector circuit, fuse 23 open (fuse 13 on 2.8L)

Code 01253 or 4415 — Fuel Injector cylinder 5 (code applies to 2.8L) has open/short in injector circuit, fuse 13 is open, ECM

Code 01253 or 4416 — Fuel Injector cylinder 6 (code applies to 2.8L) has open/short in injector circuit, fuse 13 is open, ECM

Code 01253 or 4421 — Fuel Injector cylinder 5 (code does not apply to 6 & 8 cylinder engines) has open/short in injector circuit, fuse 23 is open

Code 01254 or 4422 — Fuel Injector cylinder 6 has open/short in circuit (1992-93 2.8L AAH)

Code 01257 or 4431 — Idle air control (IAC) has open/short in circuit, fuse 2 is open

Code 01262 or 4442 — Boost pressure limiting valve has open/short in circuit, thermofuse S75 for EVAP frequency valve is blown

Code 01265 or 4312 — EGR valve has open/short in circuit (1992-93 2.8L AAH)

Code 65535 or 1111 — Control module is defective

Code 65535 or 2324 — Engine control module (ECM) is defective (1992-93 4.2L ABH) Ignore this code if displayed as an intermittent

DAIHATSU

General Description

Daihatsu electronic fuel injection system consists of 3 sub-systems: air intake, electronic control and fuel supply. The model G100 Charade is a 3 cylinder 1.0L engine while the G102 model is a 4 cylinder 1.3L engine.

AIR INTAKE SYSTEM

The system supplies air for all engine needs. It consists of the air cleaner, air intake pipe, surge tank, throttle body, auxiliary air valve, fast idle mechanism, and intake manifold.

ENGINE CONTROL SYSTEM

The Electronic Control Unit (ECU) controls the amount of fuel and air mixture, based on engine conditions and running conditions, as determined by signal input by various sensors. The ECU also controls electronic ignition timing, fuel pump operation, idle-up control, a self-diagnosis function and the fail safe and back-up functions.

Ignition Timing Control

Based on sensor input and engine load, the ECU controls the ignition timing. This maintains optimum engine operation.

Idle-up Control

This system controls the idle-up Vacuum Switching Valve (VSV), which is necessary to increase engine idle to compensate for headlight or rear defogger operation.

Exhaust Gas Recirculation (EGR) System

The EGR system lowers temperatures in the combustion chamber in order to reduce nitrogen oxide emissions in the exhaust gas stream. Exhaust gases are drawn from the cylinder head exhaust port through the intake manifold riser through the cylinder head, intake manifold and EGR valve passages.

FUEL DELIVERY SYSTEM

Fuel is supplied to the engine by an in-tank fuel pump. The fuel pump delivers fuel under a pressurized condition. The pressure regulator mounted at the delivery pipe keeps the fuel pressure at 36.7 psi higher than the intake manifold inner pressure. The fuel injection amount for each injector is kept at a constant level by this method. The operation of the electric fuel pump is controlled by the Electronic Control Unit (ECU).

Fuel Pump Control

This system actuates the fuel pump by turning on the fuel pump relay when the ignition switch is turned to **START** or when the ECU detects engine rotation.

Self-Diagnostics

SERVICE PRECAUTIONS

- The Daihatsu self-diagnostic system Diagnostic Trouble Codes (DTCs) are erased when the battery ground cable is disconnected from the battery terminal. For this reason, before starting any repairs, be sure to check to see if any DTCs are stored. Otherwise, the codes will be lost if the battery is disconnected.
- Keep all ECU parts and harnesses dry during service. Protect the ECU and all solid-state components from rough handling or extremes of temperature.
- Before attempting to remove any parts, turn the ignition switch to **OFF** or **LOCK**. Disconnecting the ground cable is also usually a safeguard.
- Guard against electrostatic discharge damage. It is possible for less than 100 volts of static electricity to cause damage to some electronic components. By comparison, it takes as much as 4,000 volts for a person to detect the jolt from a static discharge. Simply sliding across a car seat can develop as much as 25,000 volts. Use care when handling or testing electronic components. Never touch the ECM connector pins or soldered components on the ECM circuit board.
- To prevent ECM damage, the key (ignition switch) must be in the **OFF** or **LOCK** position when disconnecting or reconnecting ECM power.

READING CODES

▶ See Figures 12 and 13

1988-92 Charade and Rocky

A self-diagnosis system is built into the Electronic Fuel Injection (EFI) Electronic Control Unit (ECU). If a problem occurs in the engine management system or the sensors, the ECU sets a Diagnostic Trouble Code (DTC). In some cases, the amber Malfunction Indicator Lamp (MIL), also called the CHECK ENGINE light will illuminate to warn the operator of serious trouble.

To access DTCs, the ECU TEST terminal of the underhood check connector is shorted to ground. Any DTCs will be shown as flash codes of the MIL. The MIL will normally come on when the ignition switch is turned to **ON** as a bulb check, and should go out after the engine starts. Read DTCs with the following procedure:

1. Make sure the battery is fully charged, the throttle is closed and all accessories are turned OFF.
2. Locate the check connector under the hood.
3. On Charade, the check connector is located at the upper section of the transaxle. The connector should have a protective cap.
4. On Rocky, the check connector is located under the hood, at the fender panel right side of the engine compartment, near the battery. Note that there are 2 check connectors side by side. The light green connector is for the engine EFI

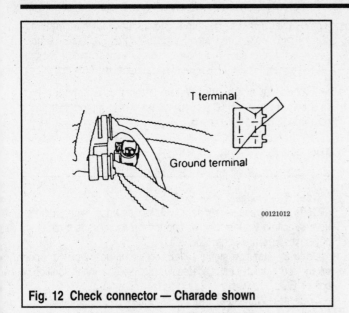

Fig. 12 Check connector — Charade shown

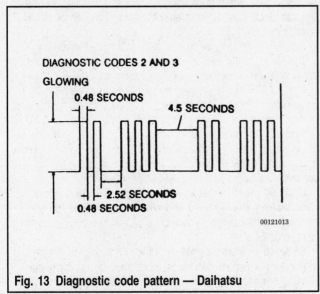

DIAGNOSTIC CODES 2 AND 3

GLOWING

0.48 SECONDS

4.5 SECONDS

2.52 SECONDS

0.48 SECONDS

00121013

Fig. 13 Diagnostic code pattern — Daihatsu

system. The gray connector is for the rear wheel ABS system. There should be a protective cap on the check connectors.

5. Remove the protective cap from the green connector and use a jumper wire to connect the test terminal with the ground terminal. Use care to connect only these terminals.

6. Turn the ignition switch to **ON**. Do not start the engine.

7. The first MIL flash code should appear 4½ seconds after turning the ignition switch to **ON**. Read the flash codes by observing the MIL. If the MIL does not flash, check the connections at the check connector.

8. The MIL should flash ½ second for each DTC. For example, DTC 3 should flash 3 — ½ second flashes in a row, followed by a 4½ second pause, then 3 — ½ second flashes, a 4½ second pause, and so on.

9. If there are more than 1 DTC stored in the ECU memory, the MIL will show these, from the smallest number to the largest. There will be a 2½ second pause between DTC number series, then a 4½ second pause, then the sequence will be repeated.

10. After DTCs have been read, turn the ignition switch to **OFF** and disconnect the jumper wire. Install the protective cap on the check terminal.

CLEARING CODES

1988-92 Charade and Rocky

DTCs should be cleared from the EFI ECU memory after repairs have been made. The codes are erased when the battery ground cable is disconnected from the negative battery terminal. Another way to clear the codes is to remove the Back-Up fuse on G100 models (3-cylinder) or the 15 amp EFI No. 1 fuse on G102 models (4-cylinder) in the underhood relay block assembly located next to the battery. Always make sure the ignition switch is turned to **OFF** before disconnecting the battery negative cable or removing fuses.

Diagnostic Trouble Codes

1988-92 Charade 1.0L (992cc)

Code 1 — Normal

Code 2* — Pressure sensor — Pressure sensor open or shorted; open or shorted pressure sensor circuit, defective pressure sensor or ECU

Code 3* — Ignition signal — Ignition confirmation signal (IGF) not received; open or shorted ignition circuit, defective ignitor or ECU

Code 4* — Water temperature sensor — Water temperature sensor circuit open or shorted; open or shorted water temperature sensor circuit, defective water temperature sensor or ECU

Code 5* — Oxygen sensor signal and/or fuel system — Oxygen sensor circuit open or shorted; open or shorted oxygen sensor circuit, defective oxygen sensor or ECU, malfunction in the fuel system

Code 6* — Revolution signal — Ne and/or G signal not received a few seconds after engine cranking starts or Ne signal of several milliseconds is not received when engine speed is 1000 rpm or faster; open or shorted distributor circuit, defective distributor or ECU

Code 7* — Throttle position sensor signal — Throttle position sensor circuit open or shorted; open or shorted throttle position sensor circuit, defective throttle position sensor or ECU

Code 8* — Intake air temperature sensor signal — Intake air temperature sensor circuit open or shorted; open or shorted intake air temperature sensor circuit, defective intake air temperature sensor or ECU

Code 9* — Vehicle speed sensor signal — Vehicle speed sensor circuit open or shorted; open or shorted vehicle speed sensor circuit, defective vehicle speed sensor or ECU

Code 10 — Starter signal — Starter circuit open or shorted (code may be set by push-starting the vehicle); open or shorted starter signal circuit, defective ECU

Code 11 — Switch signal — Air conditioner switch is turned OFF or the idle switch is turned OFF with terminal T shorted (code will not be memorized); open or shorted air conditioner switch or idle switch circuit, defective air conditioner switch, throttle position sensor or ECU

Code 12* — EGR control system — Abnormal EGR function; defective EGR valve, modulator, EGR Vacuum Switching Valve (EVSV), water temperature sensor or ECU

➡* **When the diagnostic system detects a malfunction in this system, the CHECK ENGINE lamp will go on without terminal T being grounded.**

1990-92 Charade 1.3L (1295cc)

Code 1 — Normal

Code 2* — Pressure sensor — Pressure sensor signal differs from specified value; open or shorted pressure sensor circuit, defective pressure sensor or ECU

Code 3* — Ignition signal — Ignition signal not received; open or shorted ignition circuit, defective distributor, ignitor, ignition coil or ECU

Code 4* — Water temperature sensor — Water temperature sensor signal differs from specified value; water temperature sensor circuit open or shorted, defective water temperature sensor or ECU

Code 5* — Oxygen sensor signal — Oxygen sensor signal not received under certain conditions; oxygen sensor circuit open or shorted, defective oxygen sensor or ECU

Code 7* — Throttle position sensor — Both idle switch and power switch enter ON condition; open or shorted throttle position sensor circuit, defective throttle position sensor or ECU

Code 8* — Intake air temperature sensor signal — Intake air temperature sensor signal differs from specified value; open or shorted intake air temperature sensor circuit, defective intake air temperature sensor or ECU

Code 9 — Vehicle speed sensor signal — Vehicle speed sensor signal not received under certain conditions; open or shorted vehicle speed sensor circuit, defective vehicle speed sensor or ECU

Code 10 — Starter signal — Starter circuit signal not received under certain conditions (code may be set by push-starting the vehicle); open or shorted starter signal circuit, defective ECU

Code 11 — Switch signal — When 1 of the following conditions is met with the test terminal grounded: air conditioner is ON, idle switch is OFF or shift lever is placed in ranges other than N or P on vehicle equipped with automatic transaxle; open or shorted throttle position sensor circuit, malfunctioning air conditioner system, defective throttle position sensor, neutral start switch or ECU

Code 12* — EGR control system — Abnormal EGR function; defective EGR valve, modulator, EGR Vacuum Switching Valve (EVSV) or water temperature sensor

Code 15* — Air/fuel ratio (rich fail) — Feedback function performs reduction compensation above the specified level; injector circuit, water temperature circuit, intake air temperature sensor circuit open or shorted, abnormal fuel pressure, defective injector, pressure regulator, pressure sensor, water temperature sensor, intake air temperature sensor or ECU

Code 16* — Air/fuel ratio (lean fail) — Feedback function performs increased compensation below the specified level; in-

jector circuit, water temperature circuit, intake air temperature sensor circuit open or shorted, abnormal fuel pressure, defective injector, pressure regulator, pressure sensor, water temperature sensor, intake air temperature sensor or ECU

➡* **When the diagnostic system detects a malfunction in this system, the CHECK ENGINE lamp will go on without terminal T being grounded.**

1990-92 Rocky 1.6L (1589cc)

Code 1 — Normal

Code 2 — Pressure sensor — Pressure sensor signal differs from specified value; open or shorted pressure sensor circuit, defective pressure sensor or ECU

Code 3 — Ignition signal — Ignition signal not received; open or shorted ignition circuit, defective distributor, ignitor, ignition coil or ECU

Code 4 — Water temperature sensor — Water temperature sensor signal differs from specified value; water temperature sensor circuit open or shorted, defective water temperature sensor or ECU

Code 5 — Oxygen sensor signal — Oxygen sensor signal not received under certain conditions; oxygen sensor circuit open or shorted, defective oxygen sensor or ECU

Code 7 — Throttle position sensor — Both idle switch and power switch enter ON condition; open or shorted throttle position sensor circuit, defective throttle position sensor or ECU

Code 8 — Intake air temperature sensor signal — Intake air temperature sensor signal differs from specified value; open or shorted intake air temperature sensor circuit, defective intake air temperature sensor or ECU

Code 9 — Vehicle speed sensor signal — Vehicle speed sensor signal not received under certain conditions; open or shorted vehicle speed sensor circuit, defective vehicle speed sensor or ECU

Code 10 — Starter signal — Starter circuit signal not received under certain conditions (code may be set by push-starting the vehicle); open or shorted starter signal circuit, defective ECU

Code 11 — Switch signal — When 1 of the following conditions is met with the test terminal grounded: air conditioner is ON or the idle switch is OFF; open or shorted throttle position sensor circuit, malfunctioning air conditioner system, defective throttle position sensor, or ECU

Code 12 — EGR control system — Abnormal EGR function; defective EGR valve, modulator, EGR Vacuum Switching Valve (EVSV) or water temperature sensor

Code 15 — Air/fuel ratio (rich fail) — Feedback function performs reduction compensation above the specified level; injector circuit, water temperature circuit, intake air temperature sensor circuit open or shorted, abnormal fuel pressure, defective injector, pressure regulator, pressure sensor, water temperature sensor, intake air temperature sensor or ECU

Code 16 — Air/fuel ratio (lean fail) — Feedback function performs increased compensation below the specified level; injector circuit, water temperature circuit, intake air temperature sensor circuit open or shorted, abnormal fuel pressure, defective injector, pressure regulator, pressure sensor, water temperature sensor, intake air temperature sensor or ECU

HONDA

General Information

Honda utilizes 2 types of fuel systems. The first is the feedback carburetor system of which there are 2 types; a 2 barrel down draft-fixed venturi type, and 2 side draft carburetors variable venturi type. The feedback carburetor was in use up to 1991 in Honda vehicles.

The second type fuel system is Programmed Fuel Injection (PGM-FI) system. This system began in 1985 and was available in the Accord and Civic. As of 1992 all Hondas are fuel injected.

Self-Diagnostics

SERVICE PRECAUTIONS

• Make sure all ECM harness connectors are fastened securely. A poor connection can cause an extremely high voltage surge and result in damage to integrated circuits.

• Keep all ECM parts and harnesses dry during service. Protect the ECM and all solid-state components from rough handling or extremes of temperature.

• Use extreme care when working around the ECM or other components. The airbag or SRS wiring may be in the vicinity. On these vehicles, the SRS wiring and connectors are yellow. Do not cut or test these circuits.

• Before attempting to remove any parts, turn the ignition switch **OFF** and disconnect the battery ground cable.

• Always use a 12 volt battery as a power source for the engine, never a booster or high-voltage charging unit.

• Do not disconnect the battery cables with the engine running.

• Do not disconnect any wiring connector with the engine running or the ignition **ON** unless specifically instructed.

• Do not apply battery power directly to injectors.

• Whenever possible, use a flashlight instead of a drop light.

• Relieve fuel system pressure before servicing any fuel system component.

• Always use eye or full-face protection when working around fuel lines, fittings or components.

READING CODES

▶ **See Figures 14, 15, 16 and 17**

1985-89 Vehicles

When a fault is noted, the ECU stores an identifying code and illuminates the **CHECK ENGINE** light. The code will remain in memory until cleared; the dashboard warning lamp may not illuminate during the next ignition cycle if the fault is no longer present. Not all faults noted by the ECU will trigger the dashboard warning lamp although the fault code will be set in memory. For this reason, troubleshooting should be based

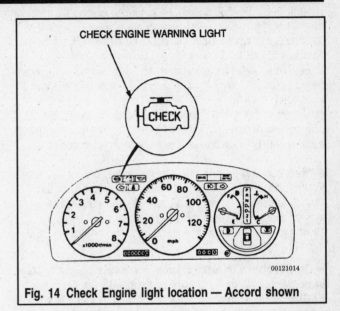

Fig. 14 Check Engine light location — Accord shown

on the presence of stored codes, not the illumination of the warning lamp while the car is operating.

Stored codes are displayed by either a single flashing LED (Light Emitting Diode) light, or an illuminated light pattern of 4 LED lights on the ECU. When the CHECK ENGINE warning lamp has been on or reported on, check the ECU LED for presence of codes.

The location of the malfunction is determined by observing the LED display. Earlier Hondas used 2 types of LED displays: a single LED and a 4 LED display. After 1987 all models use the single LED display.

Systems with a single LED indicate the malfunction with a series of flashes. The number of flashes indicates a code which identifies the location of the component or system malfunction. The code will flash, followed by a 2 second pause, repeat, followed by another 2 second pause, then move to the next code.

On systems with 4 LED's a display pattern identifies the malfunction. The LED's are numbered 1, 2, 4 and 8 as counted from right-to-left. The code is determined by observing which LED's are lit on the display. Each code is displayed once, followed by a 2 second pause, then the next code is displayed.

The LED's are part of the Electronic Control Module (ECM). Depending on the vehicles, the ECU is located in the following places:

1985-89 Accord — Under the driver side front seat

1985-87 Civic and CRX — Under the passenger side seat

1988-89 Civic and CRX — Under the passenger side footwell, below the dashboard

1987 Prelude — Behind driver side rear seat trim panel

1988-89 Prelude — Under the passenger side footwell, below the dash. (The LED may be viewed through a small window without removing the ECU cover).

Turn the ignition switch **ON**; the LED will display any stored codes.

On the 1985 Accord and 1985-87 Civic/CRX having the 4 LED display, codes are indicated by a specific pattern of LED lights illuminated on the ECU.

On 1986-89 Accord, 1988-89 Civic, and Prelude having the single LED display, codes 1-9 are indicated by a series of short flashes; two-digit codes use a number of long flashes for the first digit followed by the appropriate number of short flashes. For example, Code 43 would be indicated by 4 long flashes followed by 3 short flashes. Codes are separated by a longer pause between transmissions. The position of the codes during output can be helpful in diagnostic work. Multiple codes transmitted in isolated order indicate unique occurrences; a display of showing 1-1-1 pause 9-9-9 indicates two problems or problems occurring at different times. An alternating display, such as 1-9-1-9-1, indicates simultaneous occurrences of the faults.

When counting flashes to determine codes, a code not valid for the vehicle may be found. In this case, first recount the flashes to confirm an accurate count. If necessary, turn the ignition switch **OFF**, then recycle the system and begin the count again. If the Code is not valid for the vehicle, the ECU must be replaced.

➡**On vehicles with electronically controlled automatic transaxles, the S, D or D4 lamp may flash with the CHECK ENGINE lamp if certain codes are stored. If this does occur, proceed with the diagnosis based on the engine code shown. After repairs, recheck the lamp. If the additional warning lamp is still lit, proceed with diagnosis for that system.**

1990-95 Vehicles

When a fault is noted, the ECM stores an identifying code and illuminates the **CHECK ENGINE** light. The code will remain in memory until cleared. The dashboard warning lamp may not illuminate during the next ignition cycle if the fault is no longer present. Not all faults noted by the ECM will trigger the dashboard warning lamp although the fault code will be set in memory. For this reason, troubleshooting should be based on the presence of stored codes, not the illumination of the warning lamp while the car is operating.

In 1990, the Accord and Prelude were equipped with a 2-pin service connector in addition to the LED. If the service connector is jumpered, with the ignition key in the **ON** position, the CHECK ENGINE lamp will display the stored codes in a series of flashes. The 2-pin service connector is located under the passenger side of dash on the Accord and behind the center console on the Prelude.

As of 1992, the LED on the ECU was eliminated and all vehicles obtain codes by jumping the 2-pin connector when the ignition switch is **ON**. The CHECK ENGINE light will then flash codes present in the ECU memory.

Diagnostic Codes 1-9 are indicated by a series of short flashes; two-digit codes use a number of long flashes for the first digit followed by the appropriate number of short flashes. For example, Code 43 would be indicated by 4 long flashes followed by 3 short flashes. Codes are separated by a longer pause between transmissions. The position of the codes during output can be helpful in diagnostic work. Multiple codes transmitted in isolated order indicate unique occurrences; a display of showing 1-1-1 pause 9-9-9 indicates two problems or problems occurring at different times. An alternating display, such as 1-9-1-9-1, indicates simultaneous occurrences of the faults.

When counting flashes to determine codes, a code not valid for the vehicle may be found. In this case, first recount the flashes to confirm an accurate count. If necessary, turn the ignition switch **OFF**, then recycle the system and begin the count again. If the code is not valid for the vehicle, the ECM must be replaced.

➡**On vehicles with electronically controlled automatic transaxles, the D4 lamp may flash with the CHECK ENGINE lamp if certain codes are stored. If this does occur, proceed with the diagnosis based on the engine code shown. After repairs, recheck the lamp. If the additional warning lamp is still lit, proceed with diagnosis for that system.**

1995 OBD II Codes

OBD II codes are the new style of Diagnostic Trouble Code (DTC) being used by manufacturer's today. Some manufacturer's began instituting these codes as of 1994 others as of 1995. The OBD II code differs from the single digit or 2 digit code in that it is accompanied by a letter prefix before a 4 digit number. Example: P0101 would be a OBD II code which indicates a problem concerning the mass air flow circuit.

➡**OBD II codes can only be read by using special scan tools. There are 2 special tools designed to accomplish this. The OBD II Scan Tool or the Honda PGM Tester. Although OBD II codes can only be accessed by the use of special equipment, equivalent DTC codes may be retrieved by connecting the service check connector and observing the codes flashing by the Malfunction Indicator Lamp (MIL). The procedure below pertains to vehicles that are equipped with OBD II codes. When using special diagnostic equipment, always observe the tool manufacturer's instructions.**

When the Malfunction Indicator Light (MIL) is reported **ON**, connect the OBD II scan tool to the 16 pin Data Link Connector (DLC). On Accord with 2.7L V6 engine it is located on the center console behind the ashtray. Turn the ignition switch to the **ON** position. If using the Honda PGM Tester, use the tool manufacturer's instructions for troubleshooting. Diagnostic charts are not needed with this tool.

If using an OBD II scan tool, check the diagnostic troubles and make a note of each one. Also check and note the freeze fram data. Refer to the Diagnostic Trouble Code Chart and proceed with troubleshooting.

➡**When using either the Honda Tester or scan tool, always refer to the tool manufacturer's specific operating instructions. The scan tool or tester can read the diagnostic trouble codes, freeze frame data, current data, and other ECM data.**

Freeze frame data indicates the engine conditions when the first malfunction, misfire or fuel trim malfunction was detected, It can be useful information when troubleshooting.

CLEARING CODES

1985-87 Vehicles

The memory for the PGM-FI **CHECK ENGINE** lamp on the dashboard will be erased when the ignition switch is turned

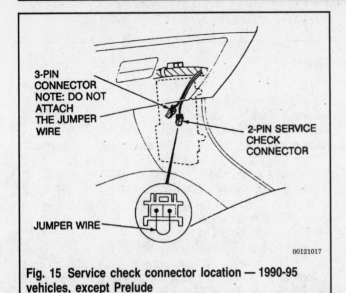

Fig. 15 Service check connector location — 1990-95 vehicles, except Prelude

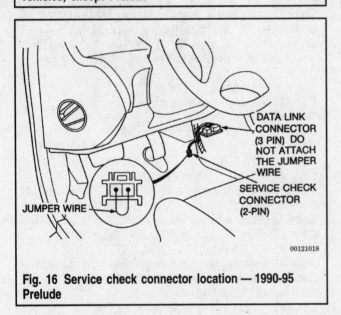

Fig. 16 Service check connector location — 1990-95 Prelude

OFF; however, the memory for the LED display will not be canceled. Thus, the CHECK ENGINE lamp will not come on when the ignition switch is again turned ON unless the trouble is once more detected. Troubleshooting should be done according to the LED display even if the CHECK ENGINE lamp is off.

After making repairs, disconnect the battery negative cable from the battery negative terminal for at least 10 seconds and reset the ECU memory. After reconnecting the cable, check that the LED display is turned off.

Turn the ignition switch ON. The PGM-FI CHECK ENGINE lamp should come on for about 2 seconds. If the CHECK ENGINE lamp won't come on, check for: — Blown CHECK ENGINE lamp bulb — Blown fuse (causing faulty back up light, seat belt alarm, clock, memory function of the car radio) — Open circuit in Yellow wire — Open circuit in wiring and control unit.

After the PGM-FI CHECK ENGINE lamp and self-diagnosis indicators have been turned on, turn the ignition switch OFF. If the LED display fails to come on when the ignition switch is turned ON again, check for: — Blown fuses, especially No. 10 fuse — Open circuit in wire between ECU fuse.

Replace the ECU only after making sure that all couplers and connectors are connected securely.

1988-90 Vehicles

The memory for the PGM-CARB and PGM-FI CHECK ENGINE lamp on the dashboard will be erased when the ignition switch is turned OFF; however, the memory for the LED display will not be canceled. Thus, the CHECK ENGINE lamp will not come on when the ignition switch is again turned ON unless the trouble is once more detected. Troubleshooting should be done according to the LED display even if the CHECK ENGINE lamp is off.

To clear the ECU trouble code memory, remove the ECU memory power fuse for at least 10 seconds. The correct fuse to remove is:

1988 — 89 Accord — CLOCK fuse from the underhood relay box

1988-90 Accord — BACK UP fuse from the underhood relay box

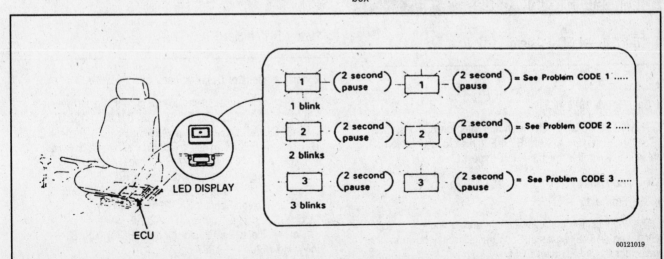

Fig. 17 Electronic Control Module location and Code flash indications — Accord shown

Civic — HAZARD fuse at the main fuse box

Prelude with PGM-CARB — EFI-ECU fuse from the underhood relay box

Prelude with PGM-FI — CLOCK fuse from the underhood relay box

➡️**Removing these fuses will also erase the clock, radio station presets, and the radio anti-theft codes. Make sure you have the anti-theft code and station presets before removing fuse so they may be reset when repairs are complete.**

1990-95 Vehicles

Stored codes are removed from memory by removing power to the ECU. Disconnecting the power may also clear the memories used for other solid-state equipment such as the clock and radio. For this reason, always make note of the radio presets before clearing the system. Additionally, some radios contain anti-theft programming; obtain the owner's code number before clearing the codes.

While disconnecting the battery will clear the memory, this is not the recommended procedure. The memory should be cleared after the ignition is switched **OFF** by removing the appropriate fuse for at least 10 seconds. The correct fuses and their locations are:

Accord — BACK UP fuse from the underhood relay box

Civic — HAZARD fuse at the main fuse box

Civic del Sol — BACK UP fuse from the underhood relay box

Odyssey — BACK UP fuse from the underhood relay box

Prelude with PGM-CARB — EFI-ECU fuse from the underhood relay box

Prelude with PGM-FI — CLOCK fuse from the underhood relay box

➡️**Removing these fuses will also erase the clock, radio station presets, and the radio anti-theft codes. Make sure you have the anti-theft code and station presets before removing fuse so they may be reset when repairs are complete.**

Diagnostic Trouble Codes

1985-87 4 — LED System

Accord
▶ **See Figure 18**

This list includes vehicles with fuel injection engines: 1.5L (EW3), 1.5L (D15A3), 1.8L (ES3) Engine. Code definition as shown in illustration for the 4-LED type ECM.

Civic and CRX
▶ **See Figure 19**

This list includes the following carbureted engines: 1.5L (EW1 and D15A2) engines. Code definition as shown in illustration for the 4-LED type ECM.

1986-93 Single LED System

1988-91 Prelude

This list includes all of the following carbureted engines: 2.0L (B20A5, B20A3) Engines

Code 1 — Oxygen content

Code 2 — Vehicle speed pulser

Code 3 — Manifold Absolute Pressure (MAP)

Code 4 — Vacuum switch signal

Code 5 — Manifold Absolute Pressure (MAP)

Code 6 — Coolant temperature

Code 7 — Coolant switch signal (MT) or Shift position switch signal (AT) (1990-91 engines only)

Code 8 — Ignition coil signal

Code 9 — No. 1 cylinder position sensor

Code 10 — Intake air temperature sensor (IAT sensor)

Code 12 — Exhaust Gas Recirculation (EGR) System (except Del Sol and Civic & CRX 1.6L D16A6)

Code 13 — Barometric pressure sensor (BARO sensor)

Code 14 — Idle air control (IAC valve) except 1987 — A20A3 engine or — 1986 BS, BT and 1987 A20A3 Engines, Code 14 or high is possible faulty Electronic Control Module (ECM)

Code 14 — Electronic Air Control

Code 15 — Ignition output signal

Code 16 — Fuel Injector

Code 17 — Vehicle Speed sensor (VSS)

Code 19 — A/T lock-up control solenoid valve A/B (D15B1, D15B2, D15B6, D15B7, D15B8, D15Z1, D16A6, D16Z6)

Code 20 — Electric load detector (ELD)

Code 21 — V-TEC control solenoid (D15Z1, D16Z6, H22A1)

Code 22 — V-TEC pressure switch (D15Z1, D16Z6, H22A1)

Code 23 — Knock sensor (H22A1-DOHC — VTEC)

Code 30 — A/T FI Signal A (F22A1, F22A4, F22A6)

Code 31 — A/T FI Signal B (F22A1, F22A4, F22A6)

Code 41 — Heated Oxygen Sensor Heater (F22A1, F22A4)

Code 43 — Fuel supply system (except D15B1, D15B2, D15B6, B20A5, B21A, D16A6)

Code 48 — Heated oxygen sensor (D15Z1 engine only, except Calif. emission)

1985-95 Vehicles

Accord, Civic, Del Sol, Odyssey and Prelude

This list includes all of the following fuel injected engines: 1.5L (D15B1, D15B2, D15B6, D15B7, D15B8, D15Z1), 1.6L (B16A3, D16A6, D16Z6), 2.0L (A20A3, BS, BT, B20A5) 2.1L (B21A) 2.2L (F22A1, F22A4, F22A6, F22B1, F22B2, H22A1), 2.3L (H23A1) and 2.7L (C27A4) Engines

Code 0 — Electronic Control Module (ECM)

Code 1 — Heated oxygen sensor (or Oxygen content)

  or — Oxygen content A (A20A3, B20A5)

Code 2 — Oxygen content B (A20A3, B20A5)

  or — Electronic Control Module (ECM) (BS, BT — 1986 only) and (A20A3 — 1987 only)

Code 3 — Manifold Absolute Pressure (MAP)

Code 4 — Crankshaft position sensor

ECM TROUBLE CODES

Code	Explanation
○ ○ ○ ○ (Dash Warning Light ON only)	Loose or poorly connected power line to Electronic Control Unit (ECU). Short circuit in combination meter or warning light wire. Faulty ECU
○ ○ ○ ● (1)	Disconnected oxygen sensor coupler. Spark plug misfire. Short or open circuit in oxygen sensor circuit. Faulty oxygen sensor
○ ○ ● ○ (2)	Faulty Electronic Control Unit (ECU)
○ ○ ● ● (2 1)	Disconnected Manifold Absolute Pressure (MAP) sensor coupler. Short or open circuit in MAP sensor wire. Faulty MAP sensor
○ ● ○ ○ (4)	Faulty Electronic Control Unit (ECU)
○ ● ○ ● (4 1)	Disconnected Manifold Absolute Pressure (MAP) sensor piping
○ ● ● ○ (4 2)	Disconnected coolant temperature sensor coupler. Open circuit in coolant temperature sensor wire. Faulty coolant temperature sensor (thermostat housing)
○ ● ● ● (4 2 1)	Disconnected throttle angle sensor coupler. Open or short circuit in throttle angle sensor wire. Faulty throttle angle sensor
● ○ ○ ○ (8)	Short or open circuit in crank angle sensor wire. Crank angle sensor wire interfering with high tension wire. Crank angle sensor at fault
● ○ ○ ● (8 ... 1)	Short or open circuit in crank angle sensor wire. Crank angle sensor wire interfering with high tension wire. Crank angle sensor at fault
● ○ ● ○ (8 2)	Disconnected intake air temperature sensor. Open circuit in intake air temperature sensor wire. Faulty intake air temperature sensor
● ○ ● ● (8 2 1)	Disconnected idle mixture adjuster sensor coupler. Shorted or disconnected idle mixture adjuster sensor wire. Faulty idle mixture adjuster sensor
● ● ○ ○ (8 4)	Disconnected Exhaust Gas Recirculation (EGR) control system coupler. Shorted or disconnected EGR control wire. Faulty EGR control system
● ● ○ ● (8 4 1)	Disconnected atmospheric pressure sensor coupler. Shorted or disconnected atmospheric pressure sensor wire. Faulty atmospheric pressure sensor
● ● ● ○ (8 4 2)	Faulty Electronic Control Unit (ECU)
● ● ● ● (8 4 2 1)	Faulty Electronic Control Unit (ECU)

0012A002

Fig. 18 4-LED code definition — 1985 Accord 1.8L (ES3), 1985-86 Civic Si 1.5L (EW3), 1987 Civic/CRX Si 1.5L (D15A3) fuel injected engines

ENGINE CODES

Code				Explanation
8 ○	4 ○	2 ○	1 ●	Short circuit in frequency solenoid valve B (brown/black) wire
8 ○	4 ○	2 ●	1 ○	Short circuit in frequency solenoid valve A (green/white) wire
8 ○	4 ○	2 ●	1 ●	Disconnected Manifold Absolute Pressure (MAP) sensor connector. Short or open circuit in MAP sensor (black/white, green/white, yellow/white) wires. Faulty MAP sensor
8 ○	4 ●	2 ○	1 ○	Short circuit in ignition timing control unit (red/white, blue/white) wires. Faulty ignition timing control unit
8 ○	4 ●	2 ●	1 ○	Disconnected Coolant Temperature Sensor (CTS) A connector. Short or open circuit in coolant temperature sensor A (light blue) wire. Faulty coolant temperature sensor A
8 ●	4 ○	2 ○	1 ○	Short or open circuit in ignition coil (blue) wire
8 ●	4 ●	2 ○	1 ○	Disconnected Exhaust Gas Recirculation (EGR) lift sensor connector. Short or open circuit in EGR lift sensor (yellow, green/white, yellow/white) wires. Faulty EGR lift sensor
8 ●	4 ●	2 ○	1 ●	Disconnected atmospheric pressure sensor connector. Short or open circuit in atmospheric pressure sensor (green/black, green/white, yellow/white) wires. Faulty atmospheric pressure sensor
15 +				If the LED display pattern differs from those listed above, the Electronic Control Unit (ECU) is faulty

0012A001

Fig. 19 4-LED code definition — 1985-87 Civic/CRX with feedback carburetor — 1.5L (EW1 and D15A2) Engines

or — Faulty ECU (BS, BT — 1986 only) and (A20A3 — 1987 only, B20A5, B21A1)

Code 5 — Manifold Absolute Pressure (MAP)

Code 6 — Engine coolant temperature (ECT)

Code 7 — Throttle position sensor (TP sensor)

Code 8 — Top dead center sensor (TDC sensor)

Code 9 — No. 1 cylinder position sensor

Code 10 — Intake air temperature sensor (IAT sensor)

Code 11 — Electronic Control Module (ECM) (BS, BT — 1986 only) and (A20A3 — 1987 only)

Code 12 — Exhaust Gas Recirculation (EGR) System (except Del Sol and Civic & CRX 1.6L D16A6)

Code 13 — Barometric pressure sensor (BARO sensor)

Code 14 — Idle air control (IAC valve) except 1987 — A20A3 engine.

or — 1986 BS, BT and 1987 A20A3 Engines, Code 14 or high is possible faulty Electronic Control Module (ECM)

Code 15 — Ignition output signal

Code 16 — Fuel Injector

Code 17 — Vehicle Speed sensor (VSS)

Code 19 — A/T lock-up control solenoid valve A/B (D15B1, D15B2, D15B6, D15B7, D15B8, D15Z1, D16A6, D16Z6)

Code 20 — Electric load detector (ELD)

Code 21 — V-TEC control solenoid (D15Z1, D16Z6, H22A1)

Code 22 — V-TEC pressure switch (D15Z1, D16Z6, H22A1)

Code 23 — Knock sensor (H22A1-DOHC — VTEC)

Code 30 — A/T FI Signal A (F22A1, F22A4, F22A6)

Code 31 — A/T FI Signal B (F22A1, F22A4, F22A6)

Code 41 — Heated Oxygen Sensor Heater (F22A1, F22A4)

Code 43 — Fuel supply system (except D15B1, D15B2, D15B6, B20A5, B21A, D16A6)

Code 45 — Fuel supply metering

Code 48 — Heated oxygen sensor (D15Z1 engine only, except Calif. emission)

Code 61 — Front Heated Oxygen Sensor

Code 63 — Rear Heated Oxygen Sensor

Code 65 — Rear Heated Oxygen Sensor Heater

Code 67 — Catalytic Converter System

Code 70 — Automatic Transaxle or A/F FI Data line

Code 71 — Misfire detected; cylinder No. 1 or random misfire

Code 72 — Misfire detected; cylinder No. 2 or random misfire

Code 73 — Misfire detected; cylinder No. 3 or random misfire

Code 74 — Misfire detected; cylinder No. 4 or random misfire

Code 75 — Misfire detected; cylinder No. 5 or random misfire

Code 76 — Misfire detected; cylinder No. 6 or random misfire

Code 80 — Exhaust Gas Recirculation (EGR) system

Code 86 — Coolant temperature

Code 92 — Evaporative Emission Control System

OBD II CODES
1995 Accord

Code P0106 — Manifold Absolute Pressure circuit; range and performance problem

Code P0107 — Manifold Absolute Pressure circuit; low input

Code P0108 — Manifold Absolute Pressure circuit; high input

Code P0112 — Intake Air Temperature circuit; low input

Code P0113 — Intake Air Temperature circuit; high input

Code P0116 — Engine Coolant Temperature circuit; range and performance problem

Code P0117 — Engine Coolant Temperature circuit; low input

Code P0118 — Engine Coolant Temperature circuit; high input

Code P0122 — Throttle Position circuit; low input

Code P0123 — Throttle Position circuit; high input

Code P0131 — Front Heated Oxygen Sensor circuit; low voltage (Sensor 1)

Code P0133 — Front Heated Oxygen Sensor; slow response (Sensor 1)

Code P0135 — Front Heated Oxygen Sensor Heater; circuit malfunction (Sensor 1)

Code P0137 — Rear Heated Oxygen Sensor circuit; low voltage (Sensor 2)

Code P0138 — Rear Heated Oxygen Sensor circuit; high voltage (Sensor 2)

Code P0139 — Rear Heated Oxygen Sensor; slow response (Sensor 2)

Code P0141 — Rear Heated Oxygen Sensor Heater; circuit malfunction (Sensor 2)

Code P0171 — System Too Lean

Code P0172 — System Too Rich

Code P0174 — System Too Lean

Code P1300 — Random misfire detected

Code P0301 — Misfire detected; cylinder No. 1 or random misfire

Code P0302 — Misfire detected; cylinder No. 2 or random misfire

Code P0303 — Misfire detected; cylinder No. 3 or random misfire

Code P0304 — Misfire detected; cylinder No. 4 or random misfire

Code P0305 — Misfire detected; cylinder No. 5 or random misfire

Code P0306 — Misfire detected; cylinder No. 6 or random misfire

Code P0335 — Crankshaft Position Sensor; low input

Code P0336 — Crankshaft Position Sensor; range and performance

Code P0401 — Exhaust Gas Recirculation; insufficient flow detected

Code P0420 — Catalyst System; efficiency below threshold

Code P0441 — Evaporative Emission Control System; incorrect purge flow

Code P0500 — Vehicle Speed Sensor circuit; low input

Code P0505 — Idle Control System; malfunction

Code P0715 — Automatic Transaxle

Code P0720 — Automatic Transaxle

Code P0725 — Automatic Transaxle

Code P0730 — Automatic Transaxle

Code P0740 — Automatic Transaxle

Code P0753 — Automatic Transaxle

Code P0758 — Automatic Transaxle

Code P1107 — Barometric Pressure circuit; low input

Code P1108 — Barometric Pressure circuit; high input

Code P1297 — Electric load Detector circuit; low input

Code P1298 — Electric load Detector circuit; high input

Code P1361 — TDC Sensor; intermittent interruption

Code P1362 — TDC Sensor; no signal

Code P1381 — Cylinder Position Sensor; intermittent interruption

Code P1382 — Cylinder Position Sensor; no signal

Code P1459 — Evaporative Emission Purge Flow Switch malfunction

Code P1491 — EGR Valve; insufficient lift detected

Code P1498 — EGR Valve Lift Sensor; high voltage

Code P1508 — Idle Air Control Valve; circuit failure

Code P1607 — ECM internal circuit failure A

Code P1660 — A/T FI Data Line; failure

Code P1681 — A/T FI Signal A; low input

Code P1682 — A/T FI Signal A; high input

Code P1686 — A/T FI Signal B; low input

Code P1687 — A/T FI Signal B; high input

Code P1705 — Automatic Transaxle

Code P1706 — Automatic Transaxle

Code P1753 — Automatic Transaxle

Code P1758 — Automatic Transaxle

Code P1768 — Automatic Transaxle

Code P1786 — Automatic Transaxle

Code P1790 — Automatic Transaxle

Code P1791 — Automatic Transaxle

Code P1792 — Automatic Transaxle

Code P1794 — Automatic Transaxle

HYUNDAI

General Information

Hyundai utilizes 2 fuel system types. The first is a feedback carburetor and the second is fuel injection. The feedback carburetor is used on 1986-93 Excel.

Multi-point Fuel Injection (MFI) was introduced in 1989 on the Sonata. In 1990 Excel was available with fuel injection also. Scoupe, Elantra and Accent came only with MFI.

Self-Diagnostics

SERVICE PRECAUTIONS

- Keep the ECU parts and harnesses dry during service. Protect the ECU and all solid-state components from rough handling or temperature extremes.
- Use extreme care when working around the ECU or other components.
- Disconnect the negative battery cable before attempting to disconnect or remove any electronic parts.
- Disconnect the negative battery cable and ECU connector before performing arc welding on the vehicle.
- Disconnect and remove the ECU from the vehicle before subjecting the vehicle to the temperatures experienced in a heated paint booth.

READING CODES

▶ See Figures 20, 21, 22 and 23

➡Hyundai utilized a Feedback carburetor system in the Excel. However, the self-diagnostic system is not used. Self-diagnosis pertains to fuel injected vehicles only. 1993-94 Scoupe and 1995 Accent have the ability to read diagnostic codes through the Malfunction Indicator Lamp (MIL) and therefore special equipment is not required to retrieve codes. All other vehicles however, do not process this ability, therefore either a Multi-Use Tester or and Analog voltmeter must be used to retrieve codes. When using special diagnostic equipment, always observe the tool manufacturer's instructions.

1989-95 Vehicles

Using Multi-Use Tester

1. Turn the ignition switch to the **OFF** position.
2. Connect the multi-use tester to the diagnosis connector in the fuse box.
3. Connect the power-source terminal of the multi-use tester to the cigar lighter.
4. Turn the ignition switch to the **ON** position.
5. Follow the manufacturer's instructions to retrieve the trouble codes. The codes will be displayed in numerical order.

Using Analog Voltmeter

1. Connect the voltmeter to the self-diagnosis connector.

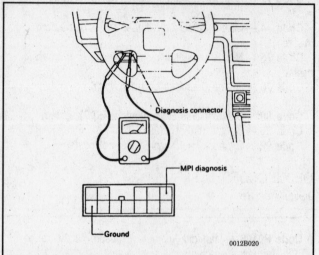

Fig. 20 Connections for reading engine codes using an analog voltmeter — 1989-91 Hyundai

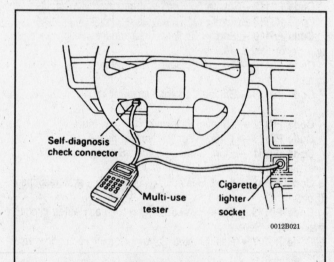

Fig. 21 Connections for reading engine codes using a multi-use tester — 1989-91 Hyundai

2. Turn the ignition switch to the **ON** position.
3. Observe the voltmeter to read the trouble codes. The code is determined by noting the duration of the voltmeter sweeps. A sweep of long duration indicates the multiple of ten digit, while a sweep of short duration indicates the single digit. For example, the code number 12 is indicated by 1 sweep of long duration followed by 2 sweeps of short duration and so on. The trouble codes will be displayed in numerical order.

Using Engine (MIL) Lamp

The 1993-94 Scoupe and 1995 Accent has the ability to read codes by using the Maintenance Indicator Lamp (MIL).

1. Turn the ignition switch **ON** but do not start the vehicle.
2. Ground the L-wire (PIN 10) in the diagnostic terminal for 2 ½ seconds.
3. The first code to flash should be (4444) which will flash until the L-wire is disconnected.

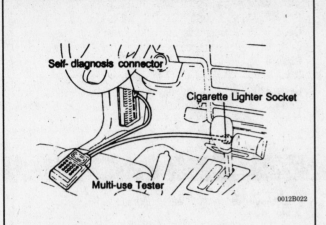

Fig. 22 Connections for reading engine codes using a multi-use tester — 1992-95 Hyundai

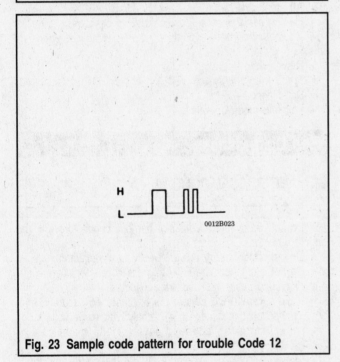

Fig. 23 Sample code pattern for trouble Code 12

4. Ground the L-wire again for 2½ seconds and record flash codes until the end of output code (3333) is flashed.

CLEARING CODES

1989-95 Vehicles

1. Turn the ignition switch to the **OFF** position.
2. Disconnect the negative battery cable for at least 15 seconds.
3. Disconnect the multi-use tester or analog voltmeter.
4. Reconnect the negative battery cable.

Diagnostic Trouble Codes

1989-94 Excel
1992-95 Elantra
1991-92 Scoupe
1989-95 Sonata

Code 11 — Oxygen sensor — check harness and connector, fuel pressure, fuel injectors, oxygen sensor, check for intake air leaks
Code 12 — Air flow sensor — check harness, connector and air flow sensor
Code 13 — Air temperature sensor — check harness, connector and air temperature sensor
Code 14 — Throttle position sensor — check harness and connector, throttle position sensor, idle position switch
Code 15 — Motor position sensor — check harness and connector, motor position sensor
Code 21 — Engine coolant temperature sensor — check harness and connector, engine coolant temperature sensor
Code 22 — Crank angle sensor — check harness, connector and distributor assembly
Code 23 — No. 1 cylinder top dead center sensor — check harness, connector and distributor assembly
Code 24 — Vehicle speed sensor (reed switch) — check harness and connector, and vehicle speed sensor
Code 25 — Barometric pressure sensor — check harness, connector and barometric pressure sensor
Code 41 — Injector — check harness and connector, injector coil resistance
Code 42 — Fuel pump — check harness and connector, control relay
Code 43 — EGR — check harness and connector, EGR temperature sensor, EGR valve, EGR control solenoid valve, EGR valve control vacuum (California)
Code 44 — Ignition coil fault, faulty power transistor
Code 59 — Oxygen (HO2S) sensor fault

1993-95 Scoupe
1995 Accent

Code 1122 — Electronic Control Unit failure-RAM/ROM
Code 1169 — Electronic Control Unit failure
Code 1233 — Electronic Control Unit failure-ROM
Code 1234 — Electronic Control Unit failure-RAM
Code 2121 — Boost sensor control valve
Code 3112 — Injector No.1
Code 3114 — IAC opening failure
Code 3116 — Injector No. 3
Code 3117 — Airflow sensor
Code 3121 — Boost pressure sensor failure
Code 3122 — IAC closing failure
Code 3128 — HO2S sensor
Code 3135 — Evaporative purge control solenoid valve
Code 3137 — Alternator output/low battery
Code 3145 — Coolant temperature sensor
Code 3149 — A/C compressor
Code 3152 — Turbo boost to high

Code 3153 — Throttle position sensor
Code 3159 — Vehicle speed sensor
Code 3211 — Knock sensor
Code 3222 — Phase sensor
Code 3224 — ECM-knock evolution sensor
Code 3232 — Crankshaft position sensor
Code 3233 — ECM-knock evolution sensor
Code 3234 — Injector No. 2
Code 3235 — Injector No. 4
Code 3241 — ECM-injector or purge control valve

Code 3242 — ECM-IAC motor or A/C relay
Code 3243 — Electronic Control Unit failure
Code 4133 — Electronic Control Unit failure
Code 4151 — Air/fuel control
Code 4152 — Air/fuel adaptive failure
Code 4153 — Air/fuel adaptive (multiple) failure
Code 4154 — Air/fuel adaptive (additive) failure
Code 4155 — ECM-a/c relay, IAC motor, injector or PCV
Code 4156 — Boost sensor control deviation failure

INFINITI

General Information

The Infiniti Electronic Concentrated Control System (ECCS) is an air flow controlled, sequential port fuel injection and engine control system. It is used on all models equipped with 2.0L, 3.0L and 4.5L engines. The ECCS electronic control unit consists of a microcomputer, an inspection lamp, a diagnostic mode selector and connectors for signal input and output, powers and grounds.

The safety relay prevents electrical damage to the electronic control unit, or ECU, and the injectors in case the battery terminals are accidentally connected in reverse. The safety relay is built into the fuel pump control circuit.

Ignition timing is controlled in response to engine operating conditions. The optimum ignition timing in each driving condition is pre-programmed in the computer. The signal from the control unit is transmitted to the power transistor and this signal controls when the transistor turns the ignition coil primary circuit on and off (hence, the ignition timing). The idle speed is also controlled according to engine operating conditions, temperature and gear position. On manual transmission models, if battery voltage is less than 12 volts for a few seconds, a higher idle speed will be maintained by the control unit to improve charging function.

There is a fail-safe system built into the ECCS control unit. This system makes engine starting possible if a portion of the ECU's central processing unit circuit fails. Also, if a major component such as the crank angle sensor or the air flow meter were to malfunction, the ECU substitutes or borrows data to compensate for the fault. For example, if the output voltage of the air flow meter is extremely low, the ECU will substitute a pre-programmed value for the air flow meter signal and allows the vehicle to be driven as long as the engine speed is kept below 2000 rpm. Or, if the cylinder head temperature sensor circuit is open, the control unit clamps the warm-up enrichment at a certain amount. This amount is almost the same as that when the cylinder head temperature is between 68-176°F (20-80°C).

If the fuel pump circuit malfunctions, the fuel pump relay comes on until the engine stops. This allows the fuel pump to receive power from the relay.

The electronic control unit controls the following functions:
- Injector pulse width
- Ignition timing
- Intake valve timing control (Q45)
- Air regulator control (G20)
- Exhaust gas recirculation (EGR) solenoid valve operation

- Exhaust gas sensor heater operation
- Idle speed
- FICD solenoid valve operation (G20 and M30)
- Fuel pump relay operation
- Fuel pump voltage (M30 and Q45)
- Fuel pressure regulator control (M30)
- AIV control (G20)
- Carbon canister control solenoid valve operation
- Air conditioner relay operation (During early wide-open throttle)
- Radiator fan operation (G20)
- Traction control system (TCS) operation (Q45, if equipped)
- Self-diagnosis
- Fail-safe mode operation

Self-Diagnostics

SERVICE PRECAUTIONS

- Do not disconnect the injector harness connectors with the engine running.
- Do not apply battery power directly to the injectors.
- Do not disconnect the ECU harness connectors before the battery ground cable has been disconnected.
- Make sure all ECU connectors are fastened securely. A poor connection can cause an extremely high surge voltage in the coil and condenser and result in damage to integrated circuits.
- When testing the ECU with a DVOM make sure that the probes of the tester never touch each other as this will result in damage to a transistor in the ECU.
- Keep the ECCS harness at least 4 in. away from adjacent harnesses to prevent an ECCS system malfunction due to external electronic noise.
- Keep all parts and harnesses dry during service.
- Before attempting to remove any parts, turn **OFF** the ignition switch and disconnect the battery ground cable.
- Always use a 12 volt battery as a power source.
- Do not attempt to disconnect the battery cables with the engine running or the ignition key **ON**.
- Do not clean the air flow meter with any type of detergent.
- Do not attempt to disassemble the ECCS control unit under any circumstances.
- Avoid static electricity build-up by properly grounding yourself prior to handling any ECU or related parts.

READING CODES

▶ **See Figures 24 and 25**

➡Diagnostic codes may be retrieved by observing code flashes through the LED lights located on the Electronic Control Module (ECM). A special Nissan Consult monitor tool can be used, but is not required. When using special diagnostic equipment, always observe the tool manufacturer's instructions.

1990-95 Vehicles

2-Mode Diagnostic System

Infiniti vehicles use a 2-mode diagnostic system incorporated in the ECU which uses inputs from various sensors to determine the correct air/fuel ratio. If any of the sensors malfunction the ECU will store the code in memory.

An Infiniti/Nissan Consult monitor may be used to retrieve these codes by simply connecting the monitor to the diagnosis connector located on the driver's side near the hood release. Turn the ignition switch **ON** and press START, ENGINE and then SELF-DIAG RESULTS, the results will then be output to the monitor.

The conventional CHECK ENGINE or red LED ECU light may be used for self-diagnostics. The conventional 2-mode diagnostic system is broken into 2 separate modes each capable of 2 tests, an ignition switch **ON** or engine running test as outlined below:

Mode 1 — Bulb Check

In this mode the RED indicator light on the ECU and the CHECK ENGINE light should be ON. To enter this mode simply turn the ignition switch **ON** and observe the light.

Mode 1 — Malfunction Warning

In this mode the ECU is acknowledging if there is a malfunction by illuminating the RED indicator light on the ECU and the CHECK ENGINE light. If the light turns OFF, the system is

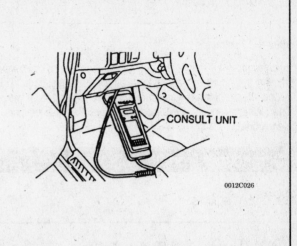

Fig. 25 Reading diagnostic codes using the Consult tester

normal. To enter this mode, simply start the engine and observe the light.

Mode 2 — Self-Diagnostic Codes

In this mode the ECU will output all malfunctions via the CHECK ENGINE light or the red LED on the ECU. The code may be retrieved by counting the number of flashes. The longer flashes indicate the first digit and the shorter flashes indicate the second digit. To enter this mode proceed as follows:

1. Turn the ignition switch **ON**, but do not start the vehicle.
2. Turn the ECU diagnostic mode selector fully clockwise for 2 seconds, then turn it back fully counterclockwise.
3. Observe the red LED on the ECU or CHECK ENGINE light for stored codes.

Mode 2 — Exhaust Gas Sensor Monitor

In this mode the red LED on the ECU or CHECK ENGINE light will display the condition of the fuel mixture and whether the system is in closed loop or open loop. When the light flashes ON, the exhaust gas sensor is indicating a lean mixture. When the light stays OFF, the sensor is indicating a rich mixture. If the light remains ON or OFF, it is indicating an open loop system. If the system is equipped with 2 exhaust gas sensors, the left side will operate first. If already in Mode 2, proceed to Step 3 for exhaust gas sensor monitor.

1. Turn the ignition switch **ON**.
2. Turn the diagnostic switch ON, by turning the switch fully clockwise for 2 seconds and then fully counterclockwise.
3. Start the engine and run until thoroughly warm. Raise the idle to 2,000 rpm and hold for approximately 2 minutes. Ensure the red LED or CHECK ENGINE light flash ON and OFF more than 5 times every 10 seconds with the engine speed at 2,000 rpm.

➡If equipped with 2 exhaust gas sensors, switch to the right sensor by turning the ECU mode selector fully clockwise for 2 seconds and then fully counterclockwise with the engine running.

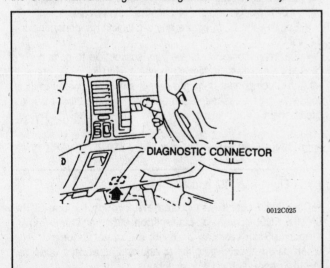

Fig. 24 ECU diagnostic connector for the Consult tester

CLEARING CODES

1990-95 Vehicles

All control unit diagnostic codes may be cleared by disconnecting the negative battery for a period of 15 seconds. The codes will be cleared when mode 1 is re-entered from mode 2. The Nissan Consult Monitor or equivalent can also be used to clear codes.

Diagnostic Trouble Codes

1990-95 Vehicles

Code 11 — Crankshaft position sensor
Code 12 — Mass Air flow sensor
Code 13 — Engine coolant temperature sensor circuit
Code 14 — Vehicle speed sensor

Code 16 — TCS Signal
Code 21 — Ignition signal missing in primary coil
Code 31 — ECM (engine ECCS control unit)
Code 32 — EGR circuit
Code 33 — Heated oxygen sensor circuit
Code 34 — Knock Sensor (KS) circuit
Code 35 — EGR temperature sensor circuit
Code 42 — Fuel temperature sensor circuit
Code 43 — Throttle sensor circuit
Code 45 — Injector leak
Code 46 — Secondary throttle sensor circuit
Code 51 — Injector circuit
Code 53 — Heated oxygen sensor circuit (right bank)
Code 54 — A/T controller circuit
Code 55 — No malfunctioning in the above circuit

ISUZU

General Information

Isuzu vehicles may be fitted with either a Feedback Carburetor (FBC), a Throttle Body Fuel Injection (TBI) system or a Multi-port Fuel Injection System (MFI).

The Feedback Carburetor System (FBC) is primarily used on 1985 and earlier normally aspirated engines, although some engines may use this system up to 1993. The system Electronic Control Module (ECM) constantly monitors and controls engine operation by reading data from various sensors and outputting signals to the carburetor. This helps lower emissions while maintaining the fuel economy, driveability and performance of the vehicle.

The Throttle Body (TBI) fuel injection system was put into production in 1989. It is used on 2.8L and 3.1L engines. The system functions much the same as a multi-port fuel injection system but with one exception — fuel is injected into the intake manifold rather than into each individual cylinder. This system may also control the ignition system.

The I-TEC Multi-port Fuel Injection (MFI) system was first used in 1985 and continues to be used today. The system constantly monitors and controls engine operation through the use of data sensors, an Electronic Control Module (ECM) and other components. Individual fuel injectors are mounted at each cylinder and provide a metered amount of fuel as required by current operating conditions. This system may also control the ignition system and, as equipped, the turbocharger system.

Self-Diagnostics

All vehicles covered in this section have self-diagnostic capabilities. The ECM diagnostics are in the form of trouble codes stored in the system's memory. When a trouble code is detected by the control module, it will turn the malfunction indicator lamp ON until the code is cleared. An intermittent problem will set a code. The lamp will turn OFF if the problem goes away, but the trouble code will stay in memory until ECM power is interrupted.

SERVICE PRECAUTIONS

• Keep all ECM parts and harnesses dry during service. Protect the ECM and all solid-state components from rough handling or extremes of temperature.
• Use extreme care when working around the ECM or other solid-state components. Do not allow any open circuit to short or ground in the ECM circuit. Voltage spikes may cause damage to solid-state components.
• Before attempting to remove any parts, turn the ignition switch **OFF** or disconnect the negative battery cable.
• Remove the ECM before any arc welding is performed to the vehicle.
• Electronic components are very susceptible to damage caused by electrostatic discharge (static electricity). To prevent electronic component damage, do not touch the control module connector pins or soldered components on the control module circuit board.

READING CODES

▶ **See Figures 26, 27 and 28**

➡**Diagnostic codes may be retrieve through the use of the CHECK ENGINE light or Malfunction Indicator Lamp (MIL). A special Scan tool can be used, but is not required. When using special diagnostic equipment, always observe the tool manufacturer's instructions.**

1982-86 Vehicles

The trouble code system is actuated by connecting a diagnostic lead to ground. The location of the diagnostic lead differs from model-to-model and, in some cases from year-to-year within the same model.

I-Mark RWD models for 1982-86; the trouble code test leads are usually taped to the wiring harness under the instrument panel, at the right side of the steering column and just above the accelerator pedal.

I-Mark FWD models for 1985-86; a 3 terminal connector, also known as the Assembly Line Diagnostic Link (ALDL) or Assembly Line Communications Link (ALCL) is located near the ECM connector. Connect a jumper wire between **A** and **C**.

Impulse for 1983-86; connect diagnostic lead terminals together (1 male and 1 female). Terminals are located under dash near the top of the driver's side kick panel.

Trooper II for 1985; connect the diagnostic lead terminals together (1 male and 1 female). The terminals are located under dash, on the passenger's side, behind the radio. The terminal leads for 1986 models are located near the ALDL connector, under dash, on the driver's side behind the cigarette lighter.

Pick-up truck for 1982; connect the diagnostic lead terminals together (1 male and 1 female). The terminals are branched from the harness near the ECM, under the dash on the driver's side behind the hood release.

The trouble code is determined by counting the flashes of the 'Check Engine' lamp. Trouble Code 12 will flash first, indicating that the self-diagnostic system is working. Code 12 consists of 1 flash, short pause, then 2 flashes. There will be a longer pause and Code 12 will repeat 2 more times. Each code flashes 3 times. The cycle will then repeat itself until the engine is started or the ignition switch is turned **OFF**. In most cases, the codes will be checked with the engine running since no codes other than 12 or 51 will be present on initial key **ON**.

1987-94 Vehicles

With Scan Tool

1. Turn the ignition key to the **OFF** position.
2. Connect the scan tool to the Assembly Line Diagnostic Link (ALDL).
3. Turn **ON** the ignition for scan tool to access engine computer.

Without Scan Tool

1987-89 Vehicles

1. With the ignition turned **ON**, and the engine stopped, the CHECK ENGINE lamp should be **ON**. This is a bulb check to indicate the light is working properly.

2. For the I-Mark, connect a jumper wire between the A and C terminals of the Assembly Line Diagnostic Link (ALDL). The connector is located next to the ECM near the heater blower motor.

3. For the Impulse, Trooper and Pickup; connect the trouble code TEST lead (white cable) to the ground lead (black cable). It is located 8 in. from the ECM connector next to the clutch pedal or center console.

4. The CHECK ENGINE light will begin to flash a trouble Code 12. Code 12 consists of 1 flash, short pause and then 2 more flashes. There will be a longer pause and then a Code 12 will repeat 2 more times. The check indicates that the self-diagnostic system is working. This cycle will repeat itself until the engine is started or the ignition switch is turned OFF. If

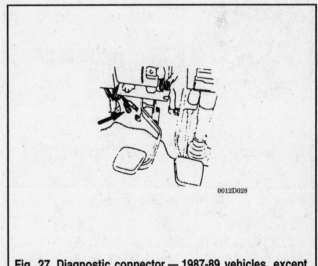

Fig. 27 Diagnostic connector — 1987-89 vehicles, except Trooper

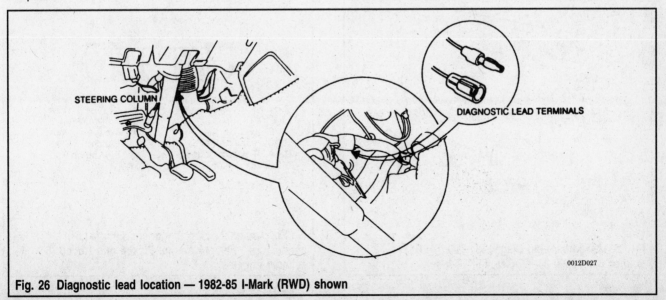

Fig. 26 Diagnostic lead location — 1982-85 I-Mark (RWD) shown

more than a single fault code is stored in the memory, the lowest number code will flash 3 times followed by the next highest code number until all the codes have been flashed. The faults will then repeat in the same order. In most cases, codes will be checked with the engine running since no codes other than Codes 12 and 51 will be present on the initial key ON. Remove the jumper wire from the test terminal before starting the engine.

➡**The fault indicated by trouble Code 15 takes 5 minutes of engine operation before it will display.**

1990-94 Vehicles

◆ **See Figures 29, 30, 31 and 32**

1. With the ignition turned **ON** and the engine stopped, the CHECK ENGINE lamp should be ON. This is a bulb check to indicate the light is working properly.
2. Enter the diagnostic modes as follows:
   a. For the Impulse, Stylus, and Trooper; jumper the 1 and 3 terminals (outer terminals) of the white Assembly Line Di-

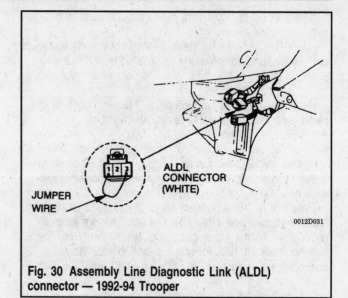

Fig. 30 Assembly Line Diagnostic Link (ALDL) connector — 1992-94 Trooper

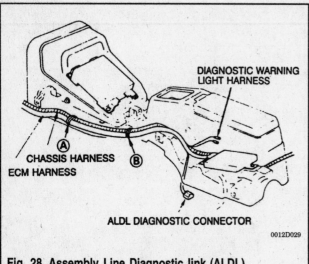

Fig. 28 Assembly Line Diagnostic link (ALDL) connector — 1988-91 Trooper with 2.6L engine

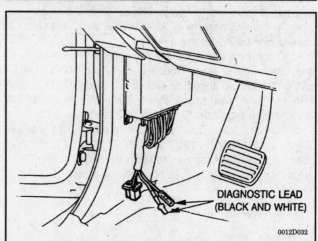

Fig. 31 Assembly Line Diagnostic Link (ALDL) connector — 1990-94 Amigo, Pickup and Rodeo (4 cylinder engines)

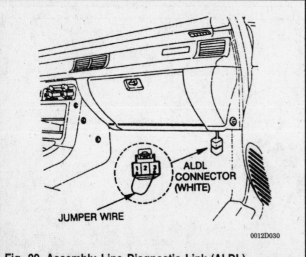

Fig. 29 Assembly Line Diagnostic Link (ALDL) connector — 1990-93 Impulse and Stylus

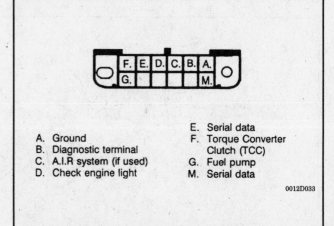

A. Ground
B. Diagnostic terminal
C. A.I.R system (if used)
D. Check engine light
E. Serial data
F. Torque Converter Clutch (TCC)
G. Fuel pump
M. Serial data

Fig. 32 Assembly Line Diagnostic Link (ALDL) connector — 1990-94 Amigo, Pickup and Rodeo (6 cylinder engines)

agnostic Link (ALDL). The connector for Impulse and Stylus is located behind the kick panel on the passenger side of the vehicle. On Trooper, the ALDL connector is located behind the left side of the center console.

b. For the Amigo, Pickup, and Rodeo with 4 cylinder engine; connect the trouble code TEST lead (white cable) and a ground lead (black cable) together. It is located 8 in. from the ECM connector (next to the clutch pedal or brake pedal).

c. For the Amigo, Pickup, and Rodeo with 6 cylinder engine; jumper wire the A and B terminals together of the Assembly Line Diagnostic Link (ALDL). The ALDL is located in the center console and is sometimes covered by a plastic cover labeled DIAGNOSTIC CONNECTOR. Read the trouble codes with the ignition switch **ON** and the engine **OFF**.

3. The CHECK ENGINE light will begin to flash a trouble Code 12. Code 12 consists of 1 flash, a short pause and then 2 more flashes. There will be a longer pause and a Code 12 will repeat 2 more times. Code 12 indicates that the self-diagnostic system is working. If any other faults are present, the faults will be displayed 3 times each in the same fashion. Fault codes are flashed from lowest to highest after the Code 12. Remember to remove the jumper wire from the ALDL connector before starting the engine. After all codes have been displayed, the cycle will repeat itself until the engine is started or the ignition switch is turned **OFF**.

➡**The fault indicated by trouble Code 15 takes 5 minutes of engine operation before it will display (4 cylinder engine only).**

CLEARING CODES

1982-86 Vehicles

The trouble code memory is fed a continuous 12 volts even with the ignition switch in the **OFF** position. After a fault has been corrected, it will be necessary to remove the voltage for 10 seconds to clear any stored codes. Voltage can be removed by disconnecting the 14 pin ECM connector or by removing the fuse marked 'ECM' or fuse No. 4 on some models. Since all memory will be lost when removing the fuse, it will be necessary to reset the clock and other electrical equipment.

1987-94 Vehicles

The trouble code memory is fed a continuous 12 volts even with the ignition switch in the **OFF** position. After a fault has been corrected, it will be necessary to remove the voltage for 30 seconds to clear any stored codes. The quickest way to remove the voltage is to remove the ECM fuse from the fuse block or the MAIN 60A fuse for 10 seconds. The voltage can also be removed by disconnecting the negative battery cable. This will mean electronic instrumentation, such as a clock and radio, would have to be reset.

1987-89 I-Mark; to clear the trouble codes; turn the ignition switch **OFF** and remove the ECM (30 amp) slow blow fuse located in the engine compartment fuse block for 30 seconds.

1987-89 Impulse; turn the ignition switch OFF and disconnect the ECM 13-pin connector or remove the No. 4 fuse from the fuse block for 30 seconds. The electronic functions with memory have to be reset after removing the No. 4 fuse.

1987-89 Pickup and Trooper; turn the ignition switch OFF and disconnect the ECM 13-pin connector or remove the No. 4 fuse from the fuse block for 30 seconds.

The 60 amp slow blow fuse may be removed from the fuse block in the engine compartment. However, the electronic functions with memory have to be reset after removing the No. 4 fuse for 30 seconds.

1990-93 I-Mark, Impulse and Stylus; to clear the trouble codes, turn the ignition switch **OFF** and remove the ECM (30 amp) fusible link (FL 3) located in the engine compartment relay and fuse block for 30 seconds.

1992-94 Amigo, Pickup, Rodeo and Trooper; To clear the trouble codes; turn the ignition switch **OFF** and remove the ECM fuse from the under-dash fuse block for 30 seconds. Removing the number 3 fuse from the under dash fuse panel will result in having to reset all the electronic functions with memory in the vehicle. This applies to trucks with 4-cylinder engines.

Removing the 60 amp slow blow fuse from the fuse block in the engine compartment will also erase codes.

Diagnostic Trouble Codes

1982-94 Vehicles

1982 1.8L FBC Truck Engine
1982-84 1.8L FBC Car Engine

Code 12 — Idle switch is not turned ON
Code 13 — Idle switch is not turned OFF
Code 14 — Wide Open Throttle (WOT) switch is not turned ON
Code 15 — Wide Open Throttle (WOT) switch is not turned ON
Code 21 — Output transistor is not turned ON
Code 22 — Output transistor is not turned OFF
Code 23 — Abnormal oxygen sensor
Code 24 — Abnormal Water Temperature Sensor (WTS) switch
Code 25 — Abnormal Random Access Memory (RAM)
Code 12, 13, 14 and 15'Check Engine' lamp not ON
Code 21, 22, 23, 24 and 25'Check Engine' lamp ON

1985-89 1.5L FBC (Vin 7) Engine
1983 1.8L FBC Truck Engine
1983-86 2.0L FBC (Vin A) Engine
1986-94 2.3L FBC (Vin L) Engine

Code 12 — Normal
Code 13 — Oxygen sensor circuit
Code 14 — Coolant Temperature Sensor (CTS) — circuit shorted
Code 15 — Coolant Temperature Sensor (CTS) — circuit open
Code 21 — Idle switch — circuit open or Wide Open Throttle (WOT) switch — circuit shorted
Code 22 — Fuel Cut Solenoid (FCS) — circuit open or grounded
Code 23 — Mixture Control (M/C) solenoid — circuit open or grounded, or Vacuum Control Solenoid (VCS) — circuit open or

grounded (1983 1.8L Truck, 1983-86 2.0L Truck, 1986-88 2.3L Truck)

Code 24 — Vehicle Speed Sensor (VSS) circuit

Code 25 — Air Switching Solenoid (ASS) — circuit open or grounded

Code 25 — Vacuum Switching Valve (VSV) — circuit open or grounded (1987-89 1.5L Car)

Code 26 — Vacuum Switching Valve (VSV) system for canister purge — circuit open or grounded

Code 27 — Vacuum Switching Valve (VSV)-constant high voltage to ECM

Code 31 — No ignition reference pulses to ECM

Code 32 — EGR temperature sensor — system malfunction

Code 34 — EGR temperature sensor — circuit failure electronic idle control

Code 42 — Fuel Cut Relay and/or circuit shorted

Code 44 — Oxygen Sensor circuit — lean indication

Code 45 — Oxygen Sensor circuit — rich indication

Code 51 — Shorted Fuel Cut Solenoid (FCS) circuit and/or faulty Electronic Control Module (ECM), or faulty calibration unit (PROM) or installation on 1985-89 1.5L I-Mark

Code 52 — Faulty Electronic Control Module (ECM) — Random Access Memory (RAM) problem in ECM

Code 53 — Shorted Air Switching Solenoid (ASS) or Air Injection System and/or faulty Electronic Control Module (ECM)

Code 54 — Shorted Vacuum Control Solenoid (VCS) and/or faulty Electronic Control Module (ECM)

Code 54 — Shorted Mixture Control Solenoid circuit and/or faulty Electronic Control Module (ECM) (1987-89 1.5L I-Mark)

Code 55 — Faulty Electronic Control Module (ECM)

1985-87 2.0L Turbo EFI (Vin F) Engine
1983-89 2.0L EFI (Vin A) Engine
1988-89 2.3L EFI (Vin L) Engine
1988-94 2.6L EFI (Vin E) Engine

Code 12 — Normal

Code 13 — Oxygen sensor circuit

Code 14 — Engine Coolant Temperature (ECT) sensor — grounded

Code 15 — Engine Coolant Temperature (ECT) sensor — incorrect signal (open circuit on 1988-94 2.6L)

Code 16 — Engine Coolant Temperature (ECT) sensor — open circuit

Code 21 — Throttle Valve Switch (TVS) system — idle contact and full contact made simultaneously

Code 22 — Starter — no signal input

Code 23 — Ignition power transistor — output terminal grounded

Code 25 — Vacuum Switching Valve (VSV) — output terminal grounded or open

Code 26 — Canister purge/Vacuum Switching Valve (VSV) — open or grounded

Code 27 — Canister purge/Vacuum Switching Valve (VSV) — faulty transistor or bad ground circuit

Code 32 — EGR temperature sensor — faulty sensor or harness

Code 33 — Fuel injector system — output terminal grounded or open

Code 34 — EGR/Vacuum switching valve — output terminal grounded or open

Code 35 — Ignition power transistor — open circuit

Code 41 — Crank Angle sensor (CAS) — no signal or faulty signal

Code 43 — Throttle Valve Switch — idle contact closed continuously

Code 44 — Fuel metering system — lean signal (Oxygen sensor-low voltage)

Code 45 — Fuel metering system — rich signal (Oxygen sensor-high voltage)

Code 51 — Faulty ECM

Code 52 — Faulty ECM

Code 53 — Vacuum Switching Valve (VSV) — grounded or faulty power transistor

Code 54 — Ignition power transistor — grounded or faulty power transistor

Code 55 — Faulty ECM

Code 61 — Air Flow Sensor (AFS) — grounded, shorted, open or broken HOT wire

Code 62 — Air Flow Sensor (AFS) — broken COLD wire

Code 63 — Vehicle Speed Sensor (VSS) — no signal input

Code 64 — Fuel injector system — grounded or faulty transistor

Code 65 — Throttle Valve Switch (TVS) — full contact closed continuously

Code 66 — Knock sensor — grounded or open circuit

Code 71 — Throttle Position Sensor (TPS) — turbo control system - abnormal signal

Code 72 — EGR/Vacuum switching valve — output terminal grounded or open

Code 73 — EGR/Vacuum switching valve — faulty transistor or grounded system

1987-89 1.5L Turbo EFI (Vin 9) Engine
1989 1.6L EFI (Vin 5) Engine
1991-92 1.6L Turbo EFI (Vin 4) Engine
1989-91 2.8L TBI (Vin R) Engine
1991-94 3.1L TBI (Vin Z) Engine

Code 12 — Normal

Code 13 — Oxygen sensor circuit

Code 14 — Engine Coolant Temperature (ECT) sensor — high temperature indicated

Code 15 — Engine Coolant Temperature (ECT) sensor — low temperature indicated

Code 21 — Throttle Position Sensor (TPS) — voltage high

Code 22 — Throttle Position Sensor (TPS) — voltage low

Code 23 — Intake Air Temperature (IAT) — low temperature indicated

Code 24 — Vehicle Speed Sensor (VSS) — no input signal

Code 25 — Intake Air Temperature (IAT) — high temperature indicated

Code 31 — Turbocharger wastegate control

Code 32 — EGR system fault

Code 33 — Manifold Absolute Pressure (MAP) sensor — voltage high

Code 34 — Manifold Absolute Pressure (MAP) sensor — voltage low

Code 42 — Electronic Spark Timing (EST) circuit fault

Code 43 — Electronic Spark Control (ESC) — knock failure circuit

Code 44 — Oxygen sensor circuit — lean exhaust

Code 45 — Oxygen sensor circuit — rich exhaust

Code 51 — PROM error — faulty or incorrect PROM
Code 52 — CALPAK error — faulty or incorrect CALPAK
Code 54 — Fuel Pump Circuit — low voltage
Code 55 — ECM error

1990-91 1.6L EFI (Vin 5) Engine
1992-94 1.8L EFI (Vin 8) Engine
1991-94 2.3L EFI (Vin 5/6) Engine
1992-94 3.2L EFI (Vin V/W) Engine

Code 13 — Oxygen sensor circuit
Code 14 — Engine Coolant Temperature (ECT) sensor — out of range
Code 21 — Throttle Position Sensor (TPS) — out of range

Code 23 — Intake Air Temperature (IAT) — out of range
Code 24 — Vehicle Speed Sensor (VSS) — no input signal
Code 32 — EGR system fault
Code 33 — Manifold Absolute Pressure (MAP) sensor — out of range
Code 44 — Oxygen sensor circuit — lean exhaust
Code 45 — Oxygen sensor circuit — rich exhaust
Code 51 — ECM failure

JAGUAR

General Information

Fuel metering is controlled by regulating the time that the injectors are open during the engine operating cycle. Constant fuel pressure is maintained within the fuel rail; injector duration or operating time controls the volume of fuel admitt ed to the cylinders.

The injection system is managed by a digital Engine Control Unit (ECU). This micro-processor based unit controls the electrical signals to the injectors, triggering them for the correct time period. The ECU relies primarily on the manifold pressure and rpm signals from the engine. Once these signals, indicating engine speed and load, are received, the controller uses them to choose proper injector operating periods. This basic pulse length will be slightly modified by the signals from other engine sensors. These secondary control factors include engine coolant temperature, inlet air temperature, throttle position and battery condition.

The injectors are triggered 6 times per engine cycle; on V-12 engines, the injectors of both banks are operated 6 times per cycle.

Self-Diagnostics

SERVICE PRECAUTIONS

• Keep all PCME parts and harnesses dry during service. Protect the PCME and all solid-state components from rough handling or extremes of temperature.
• Before attempting to remove any parts, turn the ignition switch **OFF** and disconnect the battery ground cable.
• Make sure all harness connectors are fastened securely. A poor connection can cause an extremely high voltage surge, resulting in damage to integrated circuits.
• Always use a 12 volt battery as a power source.
• Do not disconnect the battery cables with the engine running; never run the engine with battery cables loose or disconnected.
• Do not attempt to disassemble the PCME unit under any circumstances.
• When performing PCME input/output signal diagnosis, remove the water-proofing rubber plug, if equipped, from the connectors to make it easier to insert tester probes into the connector. Always reinstall it after testing.
• When connecting or disconnecting pin connectors from the PCME, take care not to bend or break any pin terminals. Check that there are no bends or breaks on PCME pin terminals before attempting any connections.
• When measuring supply voltage of PCME-controlled components, keep the tester probes separated from each other and from accidental grounding. If the tester probes accidentally make contact with each other during measurement, a short circuit will damage the PCME.
• Use great care when working on or around air bag systems. Due to back-up circuitry, the system may stay armed for a period of time without battery power.
• When working on or around air bag wiring or components, always disarm the system using the correct procedures. Once disarmed, attach a flag or note to the steering wheel. Re-arm the system when repairs are completed and remove the wheel marker.
• Never attempt to measure the resistance of the air bag squib; detonation may occur.

READING CODES

1987-94 Vehicles

For 1987-91 vehicles, only the 6 cylinder engines provide fault codes. For 1992-94 vehicles, all engines will provide fault codes. The codes may be read on the trip computer display on the dashboard. Generally, codes will be held in memory and the dash warning lamp will be lit when a fault is sensed by the PCME.

➡**Not every stored code will cause the warning lamp to light after the first occurrence. Always check for codes during diagnosis, including cases where the dash warning lamp was not reported lit.**

To read the stored codes on the XJ6 models, bring the vehicle to a complete stop. Switch the ignition **OFF** and wait at least 10 seconds. Turn the ignition to the **II** or **ON** position but do not start or crank the engine. Press the trip computer button **(VCM)**. After a short period of time, the stored codes will be displayed graphically on the trip computer panel. The display may include the designation FF, an abbreviation for

FUEL system FAILURE. The codes on XJS models will be displayed 5 seconds after the ignition key is turned to the **II** or **ON** position but do not start or crank the engine.

On both XJ6 and XJS models, the fault codes are displayed in order of priority, one at a time. The next is only displayed when the preceding one is cleared. To retrieve next code, turn the ignition key to the **OFF** position; now repeat the read and clear procedure again for as many times as necessary.

CLEARING

1987-91 Vehicles

Codes will not be cleared from memory until all stored codes have been displayed. Interrupting the display cycle will allow some codes to be retained and the memory will not clear.

To clear stored codes, drive the vehicle in excess of 19 mph (20 km/h); the memories will be cleared electronically. Each system will perform its self-check function and any new codes will be set. If no faults are present in a particular system, the failure memory will remain cleared.

1992-94 Vehicles

To clear engine codes on XJ6 & XJS models find the Diagnostic Trouble Code (DTC) reset connector. On XJ6 models the DTC connector is a red round econo seal connector with a pink/red wire. The connector is located behind the passenger side under dash panel next to the PCME. On XJS models the DTC connector is a purple male PM5 connector with a yellow/green wire. The connector is located behind the passenger side center console footwell panel. To clear the codes use a jumper wire to connect the DTC connector to ground for 3 seconds. This will clear one code at a time so you can proceed to the next trouble code. Repeat this procedure until no more trouble codes are present.

Diagnostic Trouble Codes

1987-89 3.6L Engine

Code 1 — Cranking signal failure — crankshaft signal missing after cranking for 6 seconds or cranking signal line from L12-8 is active above 2000 rpm

Code 2 — Airflow meter circuit — open or shorted to ground

Code 3 — Coolant temperature sensor failure

Code 4 — Feedback failure (where applicable)

Code 5 — Airflow meter/throttle potentiometer failure — low throttle potentiometer voltage with high airflow meter voltage

Code 6 — Airflow meter/throttle potentiometer failure — high throttle potentiometer voltage with low airflow meter voltage

Code 7 — Idle fuel adjustment potentiometer failure

Code 8 — Not allocated — If this code appears, a 6.8 kilo-ohm resistor installed in place of a hot start sensor is faulty

1989-94 4.0L, 1992-94 5.3L Engine

Code 11 — Idle potentiometer TPS out of range

Code 12 — Airflow meter circuit signal out range

Code 13 — PCME pressure sensor loss of vacuum signal, incorrect fuel pressure or faulty PCME

Code 14 — Engine Coolant Temperature (ECT) — sensor signal out of range or static during engine warm-up

Code 16 — Intake Air Temperature (IAT) — sensor resistance out of range or faulty thermistor

Code 17 — Throttle Position Sensor (TPS), open or short

Code 18 — Throttle Position Sensor (TPS)/Mass Air Flow Meter (MAFS) calibration TPS voltage signal is low with high air flow

Code 19 — Throttle Position Sensor (TPS)/Mass Air Flow Meter (MAFS) calibration TPS voltage signal is high with low air flow

Code 22 — PCME output to fuel pump relay

Code 23 — Poor feedback control in rich direction

Code 23 — Fuel supply (rich or lean) — open or short in fuel supply circuit, faulty or restricted fuel line or injectors (5.3L)

Code 24 — Ignition drive — PCME output to ignition amplifier module

Code 26 — Air leak — poor feedback control in lean direction

Code 29 — PCME self check problem

Code 33 — Injector drive fault — PCME output to injectors

Code 34 — Injector drive circuit — injector leakage

Code 34 — Bank A (Right) injectors — open or short circuit / faulty or restricted fuel injectors (5.3L)

Code 36 — Bank B (Left) injectors — open or short circuit / faulty or restricted fuel injectors (5.3L)

Code 37 — EGR drive — PCME output to EGR switch valve

Code 39 — EGR check sensor — checks EGR operation

Code 44 — Oxygen (Lambda) sensor — feedback out of control, fuel mixture rich or lean

Code 44 — Right Oxygen (Lambda) sensor — resistance out of range (5.3L)

Code 45 — Left Oxygen (Lambda) sensor — resistance out of range (5.3L)

Code 46 — Idle speed control coil 1 drive — PCME output to idle speed control stepper motor

Code 47 — Idle speed control coil 2 drive — PCME output to idle speed control stepper motor

Code 48 — Idle speed control motor/valve — stepper motor out of position, temperature less than 86°F (30°C)

Code 49 — Fuel injection ballast resistor — open circuit or faulty resistor (5.3L)

Code 66 — Secondary Air Injection Relay — voltage out of operating range

Code 68 — Road speed sensor — PCME senses vehicle travel at greater than 5 km/h with high engine air flow

Code 69 — Park/Neutral/Park Switch

Code 89 — Purge valve drive

LEXUS

General Information

This system is broken down into 3 major systems: the Fuel System, Air Induction System and the Electronic Control System.

The air induction system provides sufficient clean air for the engine operation. This system includes the throttle body, air intake ducting and cleaner and idle control components. Lexus equips the ES300, SC300 and SC400 with a system of induction tuning that changes the induction path length. The Intake Air Control Valve (IACV) changes the length of the induction path to broaden the power curve by matching the resonance characteristics of the intake charge with the engine speed. When the IACV opens, the effective length of the intake tract is shortened, boosting top end power. With the IACV closed, the intake tract is long, boosting the low end torque.

Lexus engines are equipped with a computer which centrally controls the electronic fuel injection, electronic spark advance and the exhaust gas recirculation valve. The systems can be diagnosed by means of an Electronic Control Unit (ECU).

The ECU receives signals from the various sensors indicating changing engine operations conditions such as:
- Intake air flow
- Intake air temperature
- Coolant temperature sensor
- Engine rpm
- Acceleration/deceleration
- Exhaust oxygen content

These signals are utilized by the ECU to determine the injection duration necessary for an optimum air/fuel ratio.

Self-Diagnostics

SERVICE PRECAUTIONS

- Keep all ECU parts and harnesses dry during service. Protect the ECU and all solid-state components from rough handling or extremes of temperature.
- Before attempting to remove any parts, turn the ignition switch OFF and disconnect the battery ground cable.
- Make sure all harness connectors are fastened securely. A poor connection can cause an extremely high voltage surge, resulting in damage to integrated circuits.
- Always use a 12 volt battery as a power source.
- Do not attempt to disconnect the battery cables with the engine running.
- Do not attempt to disassemble the ECU unit under any circumstances.
- If installing a 2-way or CB radio, mobile phone or other radio equipment, keep the antenna as far as possible away from the electronic control unit. Keep the antenna feeder line at least 8 in. away from the EFI harness and do not run the lines parallel for a long distance. Be sure to ground the radio to the vehicle body.
- When performing ECU input/output signal diagnosis, remove the water-proofing rubber plug, if equipped, from the

connectors to make it easier to insert tester probes into the connector. Always reinstall it after testing.
- Always insert test probes into a connector from the wiring side when checking continuity, amperage or voltage.
- When connecting or disconnecting pin connectors from the ECU, take care not to bend or break any pin terminals. Check that there are no bends or breaks on ECU pin terminals before attempting any connections.
- When measuring supply voltage of ECU-controlled components, keep the tester probes separated from each other and from accidental grounding. If the tester probes accidentally make contact with each other during measurement, a short circuit will damage the ECU.
- Use great care when working on or around air bag systems. Wait at least 20 seconds after turning the ignition switch to LOCK and disconnecting the negative battery cable before performing any other work. The air bag system is equipped with a back-up power system which will keep the system functional for 20 seconds without battery power.
- All air bag connectors are a standard yellow color. The related wiring is encased in standard yellow sheathing. Testing and diagnostic procedures must be followed exactly when performing diagnosis on this system. Improper procedures may cause accidental deployment or disable the system when needed.
- Never attempt to measure the resistance of the air bag squib. Detonation may occur.

READING CODES

▶ See Figure 33

1990-95

All models contain a self-dignostic system. Stored fault codes are transmitted through the blinking of the CHECK ENGINE warning lamp. This occurs when the system is placed in normal diagnostic mode or in test mode. Normal diagnostic mode is used to read stored codes while the vehicle is stopped. The test mode is used after the vehicle is driven under certain conditions. In test mode, while the ECU monitors, the technician will simulate conditions of the suspected fault in an attempt to cause the malfunction. When a malfunction is found, the CHECK ENGINE lamp will illuminate to alert the technician that the fault is presently occurring.

When troubleshooting 1995 ES300 and LS400 models, an OBD II scan tool or LEXUS hand held tester is necessary to access codes and read data output from the ECM. This is special tool, some aftermarket tools may be available from your autoparts store for purchase or rent.

WITHOUT OBD II SYSTEM

To read the fault codes, the following initial conditions must be met:
1. Battery voltage at or above 11 volts.
2. Throttle fully closed.
3. Transmission in N.
4. All electrical systems and accessories OFF.

Normal Diagnostic Mode

1. Turn the ignition **ON** but do not start the engine.

2. Use a jumper wire to connect terminals TE_1 and E_1 of the check connector in the engine compartment or of the TDCL connector below the left side of the dash, if so equipped.

3. Fault codes will be transmitted through the controlled flashing of the CHECK ENGINE warning lamp.

4. If no malfunction was found or no code was stored, the lamp will flash 2 times per second with no other pauses or patterns. This confirms that the diagnostic system is working but has nothing to report. This light pattern may be referred to as the system normal signal. It should be present when no other codes are stored.

5. If faults are present, the CHECK lamp will blink the number of the code(s). All codes are 2 digits; the pulsing of the light represents the digits, not the count. For example, Code 25 is displayed as 2 flashes, a pause and 5 flashes.

6. If more than 1 code is stored, the next will be transmitted after a 2½ second pause.

➡**If multiple codes are stored, they will be transmitted in numerical order from lowest to highest. This does not indicate the order of fault occurrence.**

7. When all codes have been transmitted, the entire pattern will repeat after a 4½ second pause. The cycle will continue as long as the diagnostic terminals are connected.

8. After recording the codes, disconnect the jumper at the diagnostic connector and turn the ignition **OFF**.

Test Mode

1. Turn the ignition switch **OFF**.

2. Use a jumper wire to connect the TE_2 and E_1 terminals of the check connector or TDCL. The test mode cannot be initiated if the connection between TE_2 and E_1 is made with the key in the **ON** position.

3. Turn the ignition switch **ON**, but do not start the engine. The CHECK ENGINE light should flash. If the light does not flash check the TE_1 terminal circuit.

4. Start the engine and simulate the conditions of the problem or malfunction.

5. When the road test is complete, connect the TE_1 and E_1 terminals of the TDCL or check connector and read trouble codes.

6. After the codes are read and noted, disconnect the jumpers from the connector. When the engine is not cranked, a code for starter signal and cam position sensors will be set, but this is not abnormal. If any of the sensed switches are used, the transmission shift lever, throttle or air conditioner, the switch condition code will be set, but this is not abnormal either.

CLEARING CODES

▶ **See Figure 34**

1990-95 Vehicles

Although the CHECK ENGINE lamp will reset itself after a repair is made, the original fault code will still be stored in memory. It is therefore necessary to clear the code after repairs are completed.

1. Turn the ignition **OFF**

2. Remove the 20 amp EFI fuse from junction fuse box No. 2

3. Wait at least 10 seconds before reinstalling the EFI fuse.

4. Road test vehicle and check to see that no fault codes are present.

Diagnostic Trouble Codes

1990-95 Vehicles Without OBD II System

Constant blinking of CHECK ENGINE light: Normal system operation

Code 12 — Rpm NE, G1 or G2 signal to ECU — missing for 2 seconds or more after STA turns ON

Code 13 — Rpm NE signal to ECU — missing for 50 msec. or more with engine speed above 1000 rpm, between 2 pulses of the G signal, NE signal of other than 12 pulses to ECU, or

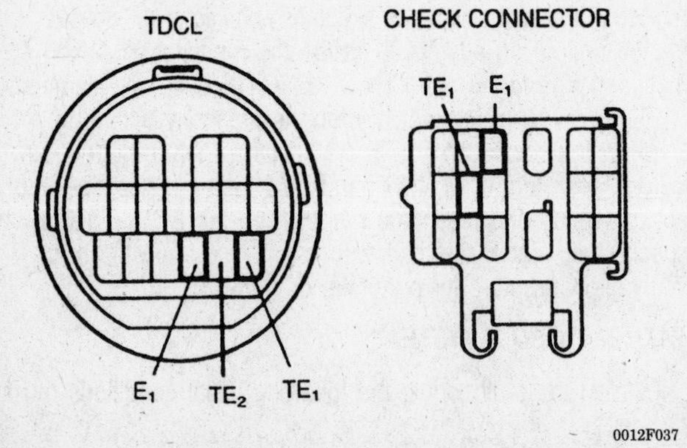

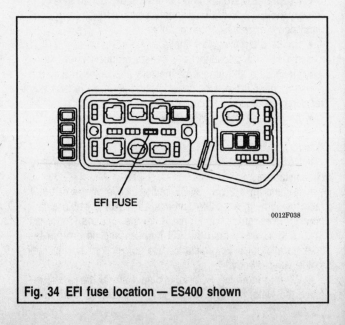

Fig. 33 Jump terminals TE_1 and E1 to enter normal diagnostic mode, Jump terminals TE_2 and E_1 to enter test mode — Lexus

Fig. 34 EFI fuse location — ES400 shown

deviance of G1, G2 and NE signal continues for 1 second with engine warm and idling.

Code 14 — Igniter IGF1 signal to ECU — missing for 8 successive ignitions

Code 15 — Igniter IGF2 signal to ECU — missing for 8 successive ignitions

Code 16 — ECT control signal — normal signal missing from ECT CPU (1990-94)

Code 16 — A/T control system — normal signal missing from between the engine CPU and A/T CPU in the ECM (1995)

Code 17 — No. 1 cam position sensor — G1 signal to ECU missing

Code 18 — No. 2 cam position sensor — G2 signal to ECU — missing

Code 21* — Left bank main oxygen sensor signal — signal voltage is remains between 0.35-0.70 V for 60 seconds or more at driving speed between 40-50 mph, A/C ON and ECT in 4th gear or open/short sensor heater circuit

Code 22 — Engine Coolant Temperature sensor circuit — open/short for 0.5 seconds or more

Code 24 — Intake air temperature sensor circuit — open/short for 0.5 seconds or more

Code 25* — Air/fuel ratio LEAN malfunction — voltage output from oxygen sensor is less than 0.45 V for 90 seconds with engine racing at 2000 rpm, feedback frequency 5 Hz or more with main oxygen sensor signal centered at 0.45 V and idle switch ON, or feedback value of right and left banks differs by more than a certain percentage.

Code 26* — Air/fuel ratio RICH malfunction — feedback frequency 5 Hz or more with main oxygen sensor signal centered at 0.45 V and idle switch ON, or feedback value of right and left banks differs by more than a certain percentage.

Code 27* — Left bank sub-oxygen sensor signal — output of main oxygen sensor is 0.45 V or more and output of sub-oxygen sensor is 0.45 V or less with engine at wide open throttle for 4 seconds or more and sensors warmed.

Code 28* — Right bank main oxygen sensor signal — signal voltage is remains between 0.35-0.70 V for 60 seconds or more at driving speed between 40-50 mph, A/C ON and ECT in 4th gear or open/short sensor heater circuit

Code 29* — Right bank sub-oxygen sensor signal — output of main oxygen sensor is 0.45 V or more and output of sub-oxygen sensor is 0.45 V or less with engine at wide open throttle for 4 seconds or more and sensors warmed.

Code 31 — Air flow meter circuit signal to ECU — missing for 2 seconds when engine speed is above 300 rpm

Code 32 — Air flow meter circuit — E2 circuit open or VC and VS shorted

Code 35 — HAC sensor circuit — open/short for 0.5 seconds or more/Baro sensor

Code 41 — Throttle Position Sensor signal — open or short in the throttle position sensor circuit.

Code 42 — Vehicle speed sensor circuit — engine RPM over 2350, and VSS shows zero miles per hour.

Code 43 — Starter signal to ECU — missing

Code 47 — Sub-throttle position sensor signal (VTA2) — open/short for at least 0.5 seconds or signal outputs exceed 1.45 V with idle contacts ON.

Code 51 — A/C signal ON, IDL contacts off, or shift in R, D, 2 or 1 range — during check mode

Code 52 — No. 1 knock sensor signal — missing from ECU for 3 revolutions when engine speed is between 1600-5200 rpm

Code 53 — Knock control signal — ECU knock control malfunction detected with engine speed between 650-5200 rpm

Code 55 — No. 2 knock sensor signal — missing from ECU for 3 revolutions when engine speed is between 1600-5200 rpm

Code 71* — EGR gas temperature below 149°F (65°C) for 90 seconds or more during EGR control

Code 78* — Fuel pump control signal — open or short in the fuel pump control circuit

➡ ***2 trip detection logic code: A single occurrence of this fault will be temporarily stored in memory. CHECK ENGINE light will NOT illuminate until fault is detected a second time (during a separate ignition cycle).**

1995 Engines With OBD II System

Code P0100 — Mass Air Flow Circuit; open or short

Code P0101 — Mass Air Flow Circuit; range and performance problem

Code P0110 — Intake Air Temperature circuit; open or short

Code P0115 — Engine Coolant Temperature circuit; open or short

Code P0116 — Engine Coolant Temperature circuit; range and performance problem

Code P0120 — Throttle Position circuit; open or short

Code P0121 — Throttle Position circuit; range and performance problem

Code P0125 — Insufficient coolant temperature for closed loop fuel control

Code P0130 — Heated Oxygen Sensor; circuit malfunction

Code P0133 — Heated Oxygen Sensor; slow response on Bank 1, Sensor 1

Code P0135 — Heated Oxygen Sensor Heater; circuit malfunction on Bank 1, Sensor 1

Code P0136 — Heated Oxygen Sensor circuit; low voltage on Bank 1, Sensor 2

Code P0141 — Heated Oxygen Sensor circuit; circuit malfunction on Bank 1, Sensor 1

Code P0150 — Heated Oxygen Sensor circuit; circuit malfunction on Bank 2, Sensor 1

Code P0153 — Heated Oxygen Sensor; slow response on, Bank 2, Sensor 1

Code P0155 — Heated Oxygen Sensor; circuit malfunction on Bank 2, Sensor 1

Code P0156 — Heated Oxygen Sensor circuit low voltage on Bank 2, Sensor 2

Code P0161 — Heated Oxygen Sensor circuit malfunction on Bank 2, Sensor 2

Code P0170 — System Too Lean or Rich

Code P0171 — System Too Lean

Code P0172 — System Too Rich

Code P0300 — Random misfire detected

Code P0301 — Misfire detected; cylinder No. 1 or random misfire

Code P0302 — Misfire detected; cylinder No. 2 or random misfire

Code P0303 — Misfire detected; cylinder No. 3 or random misfire

Code P0304 — Misfire detected; cylinder No. 4 or random misfire

Code P0305 — Misfire detected; cylinder No. 5 or random misfire

Code P0306 — Misfire detected; cylinder No. 6 or random misfire

Code P0307 — Misfire detected; cylinder No. 7 or random misfire

Code P0308 — Misfire detected; cylinder No. 8 or random misfire

Code P0325 — Rear Knock Sensor 1; circuit malfunction

Code P0330 — Front Knock Sensor 2; circuit malfunction

Code P0335 — Crankshaft Position Sensor; circuit malfunction

Code P0336 — Crankshaft Position Sensor; range and performance

Code P0401 — Exhaust Gas Recirculation; insufficient flow detected

Code P0402 — Exhaust Gas Recirculation; excessive flow detected

Code P0403 — Exhaust Gas Recirculation; circuit malfunction

Code P0420 — Catalyst System; efficiency below threshold

Code P0430 — Catalyst System; efficiency below threshold

Code P0440 — Evaporative Emission Control System malfunction

Code P0441 — Evaporative Emission Control System; incorrect purge flow

Code P0446 — Evaporative Emission Control System malfunction

Code P0500 — Vehicle Speed Sensor circuit; low input

Code P0505 — Idle Control System; malfunction

Code P0510 — Closed Throttle Position Switch malfunction

Code P0753 — Automatic Transaxle

Code P0755 — Automatic Transaxle

Code P0758 — Automatic Transaxle

Code P0770 — Automatic Transaxle

Code P0773 — Automatic Transaxle

Code P1100 — Barometric Pressure circuit; open or short

Code P1200 — Fuel Pump relay

Code P1300 — Igniter Circuit malfunction

Code P1305 — Igniter Circuit malfunction

Code P1335 — Crankshaft Position Sensor circuit malfunction

Code P1400 — Sub Throttle Position sensor malfunction

Code P1401 — Sub Throttle Position sensor range/performance problem

Code P1500 — Starter signal circuit malfunction

Code P1600 — ECM battery malfunction

Code P1605 — Knock Control CPU malfunction

Code P1765 — Shift solenoid malfunction

Code P1780 — Park/Neutral position switch malfunction

MAZDA

General Information

Mazda utilizes 2 types of fuel systems between the years 1984-94. The Feedback Carburetor (FBC) system and Electronic Gas Injection (EGI) system, or fuel injection system. The feedback carburetor system was used in the GLC, 323, 626 and RX-7 between years 1984-87.

It was also used in the B2000, B2200 and B2600 pickup trucks between years 1984-92.

Electronic Gas Injection (EGI) was first available in the 1984 RX-7. 626 picked it up in 1986, 323 in 1987. In 1988 all models except B2200 and B2600 pickup trucks came equipped with fuel injection. Mazda uses various variations of EGI. Navajo uses the Ford EEC-IV system. However, the EEC-IV system will not be covered in this section.

Self-Diagnostics

SERVICE PRECAUTIONS

• Before connecting or disconnecting the ECU harness connectors, make sure the ignition switch is **OFF** and the negative battery cable is disconnected to avoid the possibility of damage to the control unit.

• When performing ECU input/output signal diagnosis, remove the pin terminal retainer from the connectors to make it easier to insert tester probes into the connector.

• When connecting or disconnecting pin connectors from the ECU, take care not to bend or break any pin terminals. Check that there are no bends or breaks on ECU pin terminals before attempting any connections.

• Before replacing any ECU, perform the ECU input/output signal diagnosis to make sure the ECU is functioning properly or not.

• After checking through EGI troubleshooting, perform the EFI self-diagnosis and driving test.

• When measuring supply voltage of ECU controlled components with a circuit tester, separate 1 tester probe from another. If the 2 tester probes accidentally make contact with each other during measurement, a short circuit will result and may damage the ECU.

READING CODES

➡**Diagnostic codes may be retrieve through the use of the CHECK ENGINE light or Malfunction Indicator Lamp (MIL). Special System Checker No. 83, Digital Code Checker and a Self-diagnosis Checker are all special diagnostic equipment used to retrieve codes, however these tools are not required. When using special diagnostic equipment, always observe the tool manufacturer's instructions.**

1984-86 VEHICLES
WITH SYSTEM CHECKER TOOL 83

▶ See Figures 35 and 36

On 1984-85 GLC, 626 and RX-7, 1986 323 and 1986 B2000 Pick-up, the System Checker No. 83 (tool No. 49-G030-920), is used to detect and indicate any problems of each sensor, damaged wiring, poor contact or a short circuit between each of the sensor control units. Trouble is indicated by a red lamp and a buzzer. If there are more than 2 problems at a time, the indicator lamp turns **ON** in the numerical order of the code number. Even if the problem is corrected during indication, 1 cycle will be indicated, If after a malfunction has occurred and the ignition key is switched **OFF**, the malfunction indicator for the feedback system will not be displayed on the checker.

Read engine trouble codes using the following procedures:

1984-85 GLC

1. Operate the engine until normal operating temperatures are reached. Allow the engine to run at idle.
2. Connect System Checker tool No. 83 (49-G030-920) to the check connector, located near the ECU.
3. Check whether the trouble indication light turns **ON**.

➡**Trouble is indicated by a red light and a buzzer.**

4. If the light turns **ON**, check for cause of problems.

➡**If the trouble code is code number 3 (feedback system), proceed as follows:**

5. Start the engine, letting it run until it reaches normal operating temperature. Connect a tachometer to the engine.
6. Connect a dwell meter (90 degrees, 4 cylinder) to the yellow wire in the service (check) connector of the air/fuel solenoid valve.
7. Run the engine at idle and note the reading on the dwell meter.
8. If the dwell meter reading is 0° degrees, the probable causes are as follows:
   a. The wiring harness from the IG to the check connector BrY terminal lis open.

b. The wiring harness from the check connector Y terminal to the control unit (F) terminal is grounded.
   c. The transistor in the control unit for the air/fuel solenoid is short circuit.
9. If the dwell meter reading is 27°, check whether the green lamp (feedback signal) illuminates or does not illuminate.
10. If the oxygen sensor signal lamp does not illuminate, proceed as follows:
   a. If the green lamp does not illuminate, the air is sucked from the intake system or the air is sucked from the exhaust manifold.
   b. Carburetor jets are clogged.
   c. The valve of the air/fuel solenoid is stuck to the lower position, giving a lean air/fuel mixture condition.
11. If the oxygen sensor signal lamp illuminates, proceed as follows:
   a. If green lamp turns ON, the mixture is richer than stoichiometric air/fuel ratio.
   b. If the green lamp turns ON and OFF, the O2 sensor signal is fed to the control unit.
   c. If the green lamp turns OFF, the mixture is leaner than stoichiometric.

1984-85 626 and B2200

1. Operate the engine until normal operating temperatures are reached. Allow the engine to run at idle.
2. Connect System Checker tool No. 83 (49-G030-920) to the check connector, located near the ECU.
3. Check whether the trouble indication light turns **ON**.

➡**If there is more than 2 problems at the same time, the indicator lamp lights on in the numerical order of the code number. Even if the problem is corrected during indication, 1 cycle will be indicated. If after a malfunction has occurred the ignition key is switched off, the malfunction indicator for the feedback system will not be displayed on the checker. The control unit has a built in fail-safe mechanism. If a malfunction occurs during driving, the control unit will on its own initiative, send out a command and driving performance will be affected. The commands are as follows:**

   a. Water Thermo-Sensor — the control unit outputs a constant 176°F (80°C) command.
   b. Feed-Back Sensor — the control unit holds air/fuel solenoid to dwell meter reading 18° (duty 0%) for 626 or 27° (duty 30%) for B2200.
   c. Vacuum Sensor — the control unit prevents operation of the EGR valve, and holds the air/fuel solenoid to a duty of 0% .
   d. EGR Position Sensor — the control unit prevents operation of the EGR valve.

➡**If the trouble code is code number 3 (feedback system), proceed as follows:**

4. Start the engine, letting it run until it reaches normal operating temperature. Connect a tachometer to the engine.
5. Connect a dwell meter (90 degrees, 4 cylinder) to the yellow wire in the service (check) connector of the air/fuel solenoid valve.
6. Run the engine at idle and note the reading on the dwell meter.

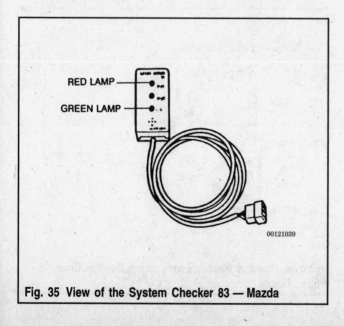

RED LAMP

GREEN LAMP

00121039

Fig. 35 View of the System Checker 83 — Mazda

7. If the dwell meter reading is 0° degrees, the probable causes are as follows:

a. The wiring harness from the IG to the check connector BrY terminal is open.

b. The wiring harness from the check connector Y terminal to the control unit (F) terminal is grounded.

c. The transistor in the control unit for the air/fuel solenoid is open.

8. If the dwell meter reading is 90°, the probable causes are as follows:

a. The wiring harness from the IG to the check connector BrY terminal is open.

b. The wiring harness from the check connector BrY terminal to the control unit (F) terminal is grounded.

c. The transistor in the control unit for the air/fuel solenoid is short circuited.

9. If the dwell meter reading is 18°, check whether the green lamp (feedback signal) illuminates or does not illuminate.

10. If the oxygen sensor signal lamp does not illuminate, proceed as follows:

a. If the green lamp does not illuminate, the air is sucked from the intake system or the air is sucked from the exhaust manifold.

b. Carburetor jets are clogged.

c. The valve of the air/fuel solenoid is stuck to the lower position, giving a lean air/fuel mixture condition.

11. If the oxygen sensor signal lamp illuminates, proceed as follows:

a. If green lamp turns ON, the mixture is richer than stoichiometric air/fuel ratio.

b. If the green lamp turns ON and OFF, the O2 sensor signal is fed to the control unit.

c. If the green lamp turns OFF, the mixture is leaner than stoichiometric.

1984-85 RX-7 and 1986 323

1. Operate the engine until normal temperatures are reached.

2. Allow the engine to run at idle.

3. Check whether the trouble indication light turns **ON**.

➡**Trouble is indicated by a red light and a buzzer.**

4. If the light turns **ON**, check the ECM code problems indicated.

With Digital Code Checker and Self-diagnosis Checker

▶ **See Figures 37 and 38**

The Digital Code Checker tool No. 49-G01829A0 for 1986 or Self-Diagnosis Checker tool No. 49-H018-9A1 are used to retrieve code numbers of malfunctions which have happened and were memorized or are continuing. The malfunction is indicated by the code number and buzzer.

If there is more 1 malfunction, the code numbers will display on the self diagnosis checker 1 by 1 in numerical order. In the case of malfunctions, 09, 13 and 01, the code numbers are displayed in order of 01, 09 and then 13.

The ECU has a built in fail-safe mechanism for the main input sensors. If a malfunction occurs, the emission control unit

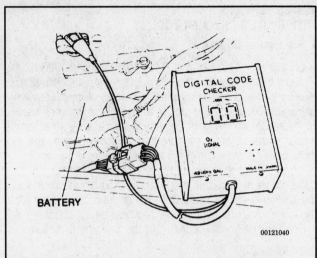

Fig. 37 Reading trouble codes using the Digital Code Checker — Mazda

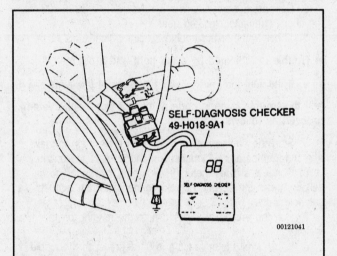

Fig. 38 Reading trouble codes using the Self-Diagnosis Checker — 1986 Mazda

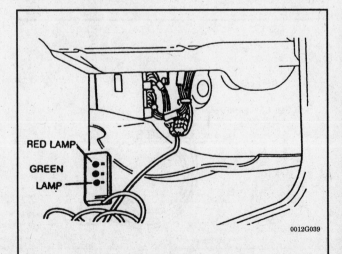

Fig. 36 Reading trouble codes using System Checker 83 — Mazda

will substitute values; this will slightly effect the driving performance but the vehicle may still be driven.

The ECU continuously checks for malfunctions of the input devices within 2 seconds after turning the ignition switch to the **ON** position and the test connector is grounded.

The malfunction indicator light indicates a pattern the same as the buzzer of the self-diagnosis checker when the self-diagnosis check connector is grounded. When the self-diagnosis check connector is not grounded, the lamp illuminates steady while the malfunction recovers. However, the malfunction code is memorized in the emission control unit.

Read engine trouble codes using the following procedures:

1986 Vehicles Except RX-7

1. Warm the engine to normal operating temperatures, by keeping the engine speed below 400 rpm.
2. Connect the Digital Code Checker No.
3. Wait for 3 minutes for the code(s) to register.
4. If the code number flashes, a buzzer will automatically sound, indicating the code number.
5. Note the code number and check the causes, repair as necessary. Be sure to recheck the code numbers by performing the 'After Repair Procedure' after repairing.

1986 RX-7

1. Start the engine and allow it to reach operating temperature.
2. Connect the Digital Code Checker for trouble codes.
3. Check the Digital Code Checker for trouble codes.

➡**After turning the ignition switch to the ON position, the buzzer will sound for 3 seconds.**

After Repair Procedure

➡**This procedure is used on all vehicles 1986 and later.**

1. Clear all trouble codes from the ECU memory.
2. After clearing codes, connect the Digital Code Checker or the Self-Diagnosis Checker to the test connector.
3. If necessary to use a jumper wire, connect it between the test connector (green: pin 1) and a ground.
4. Turn the ignition switch **ON**, but do not start the engine for 6 seconds.
5. Operate the engine until normal operating temperatures are reached, then, run it at 2000 rpm for 2 minutes.
6. Verify that no code numbers are displayed.

1987-94 VEHICLES WITH SELF-DIAGNOSIS CHECKER
▶ **See Figure 39**

The self-diagnosis checker (49-H018-9A1) and System Selector (49-B019-9A0), are used to retrieve code numbers of malfunctions which have happened and were memorized or are continuing. The malfunction is indicated by a code number.

If there is more than 1 malfunction, the code numbers will display on the self-diagnosis checker in numerical order. The ECU has a built in fail-safe mechanism for the main input sensors. If a malfunction occurs, the emission control unit will substitute values. This will affect driving performance, but the vehicle may still be driven.

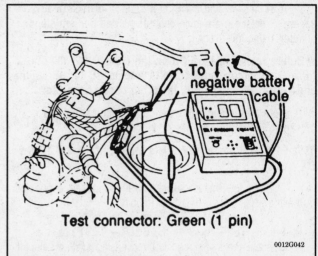

Test connector: Green (1 pin)

0012G042

Fig. 39 Reading trouble codes using the Self-Diagnosis Checker — 1987-94 Mazda

The ECU continuously checks for malfunctions of the input devices. But the ECU checks for malfunctions of the output devices within 3 seconds after the green (1 pin) test connector or TEN terminal of the diagnosis connector is grounded and the ignition switch is turned to the **ON** position.

Read engine trouble codes using the following procedures:

1987-91 323, Miata and Protege

1. Connect the tester to the check connector at the rear of the left side wheel housing and to the negative battery cable.
2. Set the tester select switch to the **A** setting.
3. With a jumper wire, ground the 1-pin test connector.
4. Turn the ignition switch **ON**.
5. Make sure that **88** flashes on the monitor and that the audible buzzer sounds for 3 seconds after turning the ignition switch **ON**.
6. If **88** does not flash, check the main relay, power supply circuit and the check connector wiring.
7. If **88** flashes and the buzzer sounds for more than 20 seconds, replace the engine control unit and repeat Steps 3 and 4.
8. Note any other code numbers that are present and refer to the code chart. Repair if necessary.

1992 626, MX-6, MPV, B2200 and B2600i

The check connector is located at the rear of the left side wheel house on 626/MX-6, front of the left side wheel house on MPV, above the right side wheel house on B2200 and near the fuel filter on B2600i.

1. Connect the tester to the check connector and to ground.
2. Set the tester select switch to the **A** setting.
3. With a jumper wire, ground the 1 pin test connector.
4. Turn the ignition switch **ON**.
5. Make sure that **88** flashes on the monitor and that the audible buzzer sounds for 3 seconds after turning the ignition switch **ON**.
6. If **88** does not flash, check the main relay, power supply circuit and the check connector wiring.

7. If **88** flashes and the buzzer sounds for more than 20 seconds, replace the engine control unit and perform steps number 1 through 6 again.

➡**Before replacing the ECU on the MPV or B2600i, check for a short circuit between ECU terminal 1B for JE engine and 1F for G6 engine and the 6 pin check connector.**

8. Note and record any other code numbers that are present.

1992-94 323, Protege, 929, Miata (MX-5), MX-3 and 1993-94 RX-7

1. Connect the system selector to the diagnosis connector at the rear of the left side wheel housing.
2. Set the SYSTEM SELECT switch to the **1** setting.
3. Set the TEST switch to the **SELF — TEST** position.
4. Connect the self-diagnosis checker, the system selector and ground.
5. Set the self-diagnosis checker SELECT switch to the **A** position.
6. Turn the ignition switch **ON**.
7. Make sure that **88** flashes on the monitor and that the audible buzzer sounds for 3 seconds after turning the ignition switch **ON**.
8. If **88** does not flash, check the main relay, power supply circuit and the diagnosis connector wiring.
9. If **88** flashes and the buzzer sounds for more than 20 seconds, check for a short between ECU terminal 1F and the FEN terminal of the diagnosis connector. Replace the engine control unit if necessary and perform Steps 1 through 7 again.
10. Note and record any other code numbers that are present.

1993-94 626 and MX-6

1. Connect the system selector to the diagnosis connector at the rear of the left side wheel housing.
2. Set the SYSTEM SELECT switch to the **1** setting.
3. Set the TEST switch to the **SELF — TEST** position.
4. Connect the self-diagnosis checker the system selector and ground.
5. Set the self-diagnosis checker SELECT switch to the **A** position.
6. Turn the ignition switch **ON**.
7. Make sure that **88** flashes on the monitor and that the audible buzzer sounds for 3 seconds after turning the ignition switch **ON**.
8. If **88** does not flash, check the main relay, power supply circuit and the diagnosis connector wiring.
9. If **88** flashes and the buzzer sounds for more than 20 seconds, check for a short between PCM terminal 1F (manual trans.), (1G auto trans.) and the FEN terminal of the diagnosis connector. Replace the engine control unit if necessary and perform Steps 1 through 7 again.
10. Note and record any other code numbers that are present.

1984-94 VEHICLES
WITHOUT SELF-DIAGNOSIS CHECKER

The malfunction indicator light indicates a pattern the same as the buzzer of the self-diagnosis checker when the green (1 pin) test connector or FEN terminal of the diagnosis connector is grounded. When the green (1 pin) test connector or FEN terminal of the diagnosis connector is not grounded, the lamp illuminates steady while malfunction of the main input sensor occurs and goes out if the malfunction recovers. However, the malfunction code is memorized in the control unit.

CLEARING CODES

1984-86 Vehicles

All Vehicles

1. Turn the ignition switch **OFF**.
2. Disconnect the negative battery cable.
3. Depress the brake pedal for at least 5 seconds.
4. Reconnect the negative battery cable.

1987-91 Vehicles

All Vehicles

1. Cancel the memory of the malfunction by disconnecting the negative battery cable and depressing the brake pedal for at least 20 seconds, then reconnect the negative battery cable.
2. Except Miata, MX-3, 323 and Protege, connect the Self-Diagnosis Checker 49-H018-9A1 to the check connector. Ground the test connector (green: 1 pin) using a jumper wire.
3. On Miata, MX-3, 323 and Protege, connect Self-Diagnosis Checker (49-B019-9A0) to the diagnosis connector.
4. Turn the ignition switch **ON**, but do not start the engine for approximately 6 seconds.
5. Start the engine and allow it to reach normal operating temperature. Then run the engine at 2000 rpm for 2 minutes. Check that no code numbers are displayed.

1992-94 Vehicles

323, MX-3 (B6 engine), MX-5/Miata

1. Disconnect the negative battery cable.
2. Press the brake pedal for at least 20 seconds.
3. Connect the negative battery cable.
4. Connect the self-diagnosis tester to the diagnosis connector.
5. Turn the ignition switch **ON**.
6. Start and warm-up the engine.
7. Run engine at 2,000 rpm for 3 minutes.
8. Verify that no more codes are stored.

1992 626, MX-6, B2200 (EGI) and B2600i

1. Disconnect the negative battery cable.
2. Press the brake pedal for at least 5 seconds.
3. Connect the negative battery cable.
4. Connect the self-diagnosis tester and ground the test connector.
5. Turn the ignition switch to the **ON** position for 6 seconds.
6. Start and warm-up the engine.
7. Run engine at 2,000 rpm for 2 minutes (3 minutes on truck).
8. Verify that no more codes are stored.

1993-94 626 and MX-6 (FS Engine)

1. Disconnect the negative battery cable.

2. Press the brake pedal for at least 20 seconds.
3. Connect the negative battery cable.
4. Connect the self-diagnosis tester to the diagnosis connector.
5. Turn the ignition switch **ON**.
6. Start and warm-up the engine.
7. Run engine at 2,000 rpm for 2 minutes.
8. Verify that no more codes are stored.

1993-94 626 and MX-6 (KL Engine), MX-3 (K8 engine) and 1993-94 RX-7

1. Disconnect the negative battery cable.
2. Press the brake pedal for at least 20 seconds.
3. Connect the negative battery cable.
4. Connect the self-diagnosis tester to the diagnosis connector.
5. Turn the ignition switch **ON**.
6. Verify that no more codes are stored.

929

1. Turn the ignition switch **OFF**.
2. Disconnect the negative battery cable for 20 seconds.

MPV (JE engine)

1. Disconnect the negative battery cable for at least 20 seconds.
2. Connect the negative battery cable.
3. Connect a jumper wire between the 1 pin test connector and ground.
4. Turn the ignition **ON** and verify that no codes are present.
5. Start the engine and again verify that no codes are present.

MPV (G6 engine)

1. Disconnect the negative battery cable for at least 20 seconds.
2. Connect the negative battery cable.
3. Connect the self-diagnosis tester and ground the test connector.
4. Turn the ignition switch to the **ON** position for 6 seconds.
5. Start and warm-up the engine.
6. Run engine at 2,000 rpm for 3 minutes.
7. Verify that no more codes are stored.

B2200 (FBC engine)

For the pickup with the feedback carburetor fuel system disconnect the negative battery cable for at least 5 seconds.

Diagnostic Trouble Codes

1984-94 Except RX-7

1984-85 Vehicles

2.0L ENGINE (CODE FE)

Code 01 — Engine speed
Code 02 — Water thermosensor
Code 03 — Oxygen sensor
Code 04 — Vacuum sensor
Code 05 — EGR position sensor

1986-87 Vehicles

1.6L, 2.0L AND 2.2L ENGINES

Code 01 — Ignition pulse
Code 02 — Air flow meter
Code 03 — Water thermosensor
Code 04 — Intake air thermo or Temperature sensor
Code 05 — Feedback system
Code 06 — Atmospheric pressure sensor (1986 1.6L)
Code 08 — EGR position sensor
Code 09 — Atmospheric pressure sensor
Code 22 — No. 1 Cylinder sensor (2.2L turbocharged)

1988-94 Vehicles

1.6L, 1.8L, 2.0L, 2.2L, 2.5L, 2.6L AND 3.0L ENGINES

Code 01 — Ignition pulse
Code 02 — Ne signal — distributor
Code 02 — NE 2 signal — crankshaft (1992-93 1.8L V6, 1994 2.0L, 1992-94 3.0L)
Code 03 — G1 signal — distributor (2.2L turbo, 1988-91 3.0L)
Code 03 — G signal — distributor
Code 04 — G2 signal — distributor (2.2L turbo, 1988-91 3.0L);NE 1 signal — distributor (1992-94 1.8L V6, 1994 2.0L, 1992-93 3.0L)
Code 05 — Knock sensor and control unit (Left side on 1992-94 3.0L)
Code 06 — Speed signal
Code 07 — Knock sensor; right side (1992-94 3.0L)
Code 08 — Air flow meter
Code 09 — Engine coolant temperature sensor (CIS)
Code 10 — Intake air temperature sensor
Code 11 — Intake air thermosensor — dynamic chamber (3.0L, 2.6L)
Code 13 — Intake manifold pressure sensor (1.3L)
Code 14 — Atmospheric pressure sensor (in ECU on 2.6L and 1994 2.5L)
Code 15 — Oxygen sensor
Code 15 — Oxygen sensor; left side on 1992-94 1.8L V6, 1994 2.5L, 1990-94 3.0L
Code 16 — EGR position sensor
Code 17 — Closed loop system
Code 17 — Closed loop system; left side on 1992-94 1.8L V6, 1993-94 2.5L 1990-94 3.0L

Code 23 — Heated oxygen sensor; right side on 1992-94 1.8L V6, 1994 2.5L 1990-91 3.0L

Code 24 — Closed loop system; right side on 1992-94 1.8L V6, 1993 2.5L 1990-91 3.0L

Code 25 — Solenoid valve — pressure regulator

Code 26 — Solenoid valve — purge control

Code 26 — Solenoid valve — purge control No. 2 (1988-89 3.0L)

Code 27 — Solenoid valve — purge control No. 1 (1988-89 3.0L)

Code 27 — Solenoid valve — No. 2 purge control (1989 1.6L)

Code 28 — Solenoid valve — EGR vacuum

Code 29 — Solenoid valve — EGR vent

Code 30 — Relay (cold start injector 3.0L)

Code 34 — ISC valve

Code 34 — Idle air control valve (1993-94 2.0L and 2.5L, 1.6L, 1.8L, 2.6L, 3.1L)

Code 36 — Oxygen sensor heater relay (1990 3.0L)

Code 36 — Right side oxygen sensor heater (1992-94 3.0L)

Code 37 — Left side oxygen sensor heater (1992-94 3.0L)

Code 37 — Coolant fan relay

Code 40 — Oxygen sensor heater relay (1991 3.0L)

Code 40 — Solenoid (triple induction system) and oxygen sensor relay (1988-89 3.0L)

Code 41 — Solenoid valve — VRIS (1989-94 MPV 3.0L)

Code 41 — Solenoid valve — VRIS 1 (1992-94 1.8L V6, 1993 2.5L)

Code 41 — Solenoid valve — VICS (3.0L)

Code 42 — Solenoid valve — Waste gate (turbocharged)

Code 46 — Solenoid valve — VRIS 2 (1992-94 1.8L V6, 1993 2.5L)

Code 65 — A/C signal — PCMT (1992-94 3.0L)

Code 67 — Coolant fan relay No. 1 (1993 2.5L)

Code 67 — Coolant fan relay No. 2 (1992-94 1.8L V6)

Code 68 — Coolant fan relay No. 2, No.3 with ATX (1993 2.5L)

Code 69 — Engine coolant temperature sensor — fan (1992-94 1.8L V6, 1993 2.0L and 2.5L)

1984-94 RX-7

1.3L Rotary Engine

Code 01 — Crank angle sensor (1984-87)

Code 01 — Ignition coil — trailing (1988-91)

Code 02 — Air flow meter (1984-87)

Code 02 — Ne signal — crank angle sensor (1988-91)

Code 03 — Water thermosensor (1984-87)

Code 03 — G signal — crank angle sensor (1988-91)

Code 04 — Intake air temperature sensor — in the air flow meter (1984-87)

Code 05 — Oxygen sensor (1984-87)

Code 05 — Knock sensor (1993)

Code 06 — Throttle sensor (1984-87)

Code 06 — Speedometer sensor (1993)

Code 07 — Boost sensor / Pressure sensor (1984-87 turbo)

Code 08 — Air flow meter (1988-91)

Code 09 — Atmospheric pressure sensor (1984-87)

Code 09 — Water thermosensor (1988-94)

Code 10 — Intake air thermosensor — in air flow meter (1988-91)

Code 11 — Intake air thermosensor (1988-93)

Code 12 — Coil with igniter — trailing (1984-87)

Code 12 — Throttle sensor — wide open throttle (1988-94)

Code 13 — Intake manifold pressure sensor (1988-94)

Code 14 — Atmospheric pressure sensor (1988-94, in ECU on 1993)

Code 15 — Intake air temperature sensor — in dynamic chamber (1984-87)

Code 15 — Oxygen sensor (1988-94)

Code 16 — EGR switch (1993 California)

Code 17 — Closed loop system (1988-93)

Code 18 — Throttle sensor — closed or narrow throttle (1988-94)

Code 20 — Metering oil pump position sensor (1988-94)

Code 23 — Fuel thermosensor (1993)

Code 25 — Solenoid valve — pressure regulator control (1993)

Code 26 — Metering oil pump stepping motor (1993)

Code 27 — Step motor — metering oil pump (1988-91)

Code 27 — Metering oil pump (1993)

Code 28 — Solenoid valve — EGR (1993)

Code 30 — Solenoid valve — split air bypass (1988-94)

Code 31 — Solenoid valve — relief No. 1 (1988-94)

Code 32 — Solenoid valve — switching (1988-94)

Code 33 — Solenoid valve — port air bypass (1988-94)

Code 34 — Solenoid valve — bypass air control (1988-91)

Code 34 — Solenoid valve — idle speed control (1993)

Code 37 — Metering oil pump (1988-93)

Code 38 — Solenoid valve — accelerated warm-up system (1988-94)

Code 39 — Solenoid valve — relief No. 2 (1993)

Code 40 — Auxiliary port valve (1988-91)

Code 40 — Solenoid valve — purge control (1993)

Code 41 — Solenoid valve — variable dynamic effect Intake control (1988-91)

Code 42 — Solenoid valve — turbo boost pressure regulator (1988-91)

Code 42 — Solenoid valve — turbo pre-control (1993)

Code 43 — Solenoid valve — wastegate control (1993)

Code 44 — Solenoid valve — turbo control (1993)

Code 45 — Solenoid valve — charge control (1993)

Code 46 — Solenoid valve — charge relief (1993)

Code 50 — Solenoid valve — double throttle control (1993)

Code 51 — Fuel pump relay (1988-94)

Code 54 — Air pump relay (1993)

Code 71 — Injector — front secondary (1988-94)

Code 73 — Injector — rear secondary (1988-94)

Code 76 — Slip lockup off signal — EC-AT CU (1993)

Code 77 — Torque reduced — EC-AT CU (1993)

MITSUBISHI

General Information

Mitsubishi uses 2 types of fuel systems. Feedback carburetor system and fuel injection. The type of fuel injection system is known as Electronic Controlled Injection (ECI).

Mitsubishi uses a conventional downdraft two-barrel compound type carburetor which incorporates an automatic choke, accelerator pump, and enrichment system. In addition, a deceleration device is provided.

The Electronic Fuel Injection (EFI) system, used on Mitsubishi vehicles, is classified as a Multi-Point Injection (MPI) system. The MPI system controls the fuel flow, idle speed, and ignition timing. The basic function of the MPI system is to control the air/fuel ratio in accordance with all engine operating conditions. An Electronic Control Unit (ECU) is the heart of the MPI system. Based on data from various sensors, the ECU computes the desired air/fuel ratio.

Self-Diagnostics

SERVICE PRECAUTIONS

- Before connecting or disconnecting the ECU harness connectors, make sure the ignition switch is **OFF** and the negative battery cable is disconnected to avoid the possibility of damage to the control unit.
- When performing ECU input/output signal diagnosis, remove the pin terminal retainer from the connectors to make it easier to insert tester probes into the connector.
- When connecting or disconnecting pin connectors from the ECU, take care not to bend or break any pin terminals. Check that there are no bends or breaks on ECU pin terminals before attempting any connections.
- Before replacing any ECU, perform the ECU input/output signal diagnosis to make sure the ECU is functioning properly.
- When measuring supply voltage of ECU-controlled components with a circuit tester, separate 1 tester probe from another. If the 2 tester probes accidentally make contact with each other during measurement, a short circuit will result and damage the ECU.

READING CODES

▶ **See Figures 40, 41, 42 and 43**

➥**All though the CHECK ENGINE light or Malfunction Indicator Lamp (MIL) will illuminate when there is trouble detected, diagnostic codes can only be retrieved with the use of either a analog voltmeter or a Multi-use Tester. When using diagnostic equipment, always observe the tool manufacturer's instructions.**

1984-86 Vehicles

With ECI/MPI Tester

Refer to manufacturer's tester manual regarding diagnosis with this tester.

1985-94 Vehicles

With Analog Voltmeter

The voltmeter can be used to retrieve code numbers of malfunctions which have happened and were memorized or are continuing to happen. On the voltmeter, the malfunction is indicated by a sweep of the needle. The voltmeter should be connected to the data link connector located under the driver side dashboard. Connect the voltmeter between the Multi-Point Injection (MPI) terminal and the ground terminal. Turn the ignition switch **ON** if the normal condition exists, the voltmeter pointer will indicate a normal pattern. A normal pattern is indicated by constant needle sweeps. If a problem exists in the system the voltmeter pointer will indicate it in a series of pointer sweeps. For example, a Code 3 would be 3 consecutive short sweeps of the voltmeter needle.

If there is more than 1 malfunction, the low code numbers will first be indicated and after a 2 second pause (no code indication) the higher code will be indicated.

With Multi-Use Tester

To read the trouble codes using the Multi-Use Tester (MB991341 or equivalent) follow the steps below:

1. Turn the ignition switch **OFF**.
2. Insert the power supply terminal to the cigarette lighter socket.
3. Connect the tester connector to the diagnosis connector in the glove compartment, under the hood or under the driver side dashboard.
4. Turn the ignition switch **ON** and push the DIAG key.
5. Observe the trouble code and make the necessary repairs.

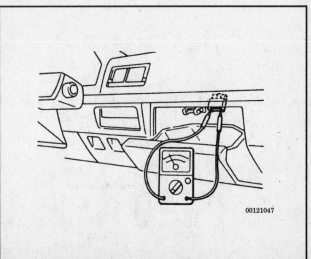

Fig. 40 Diagnosis terminal connector location — Galant, Montero, Sigma, Starion and Van/Wagon

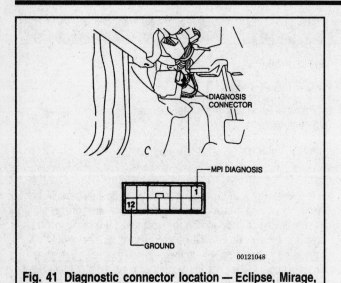

Fig. 41 Diagnostic connector location — Eclipse, Mirage, 3000GT and Precis

On most models the CHECK ENGINE malfunction indicator light will light up and remain illuminated to indicate that there is a problem in the system. After this light has been reported to be ON, the system should be checked for malfunction codes.

CLEARING CODES

Without Multi-Use Tester

1984-86 vehicles; engine codes can be cleared by disconnecting the negative battery terminal or by disconnecting ECU connector for 15 seconds or longer.

1987-94 vehicles; engine codes can be cleared by disconnecting the negative battery terminal for 10 seconds or longer.

With Multi-Use Tester

Engine codes may also be cleared by setting the ignition switch to the **ON** position and using the malfunction code ERASE signal.

Diagnostic Trouble Codes

1984-88 Vehicles

CORDIA, GALANT, MIRAGE, STARION, TREDIA, AND VAN/WAGON

Code 1 — Oxygen sensor
Code 2 — Crank angle sensor
Code 2 — Ignition signal
Code 3 — Air flow sensor
Code 4 — Barometric pressure sensor
Code 5 — Throttle Position Sensor (TPS)
Code 6 — Motor Position Sensor (MPS)
Code 6 — Idle Speed Control (ISC) position sensor
Code 7 — Engine Coolant Temperature Sensor
Code 8 — No. 1 cylinder TDC Sensor
Code 8 — Vehicle speed sensor
* Some 1988 Multi-Port injected vehicles use 1989 2-digit codes

1989-94 Vehicles

DIAMANTE, ECLIPSE, 3000GT, GALANT, MIRAGE, MONTERO, PRECIS, SIGMA, STARION, EXPO, MONTERO, TRUCK AND VAN/WAGON

Code 11 — Oxygen sensor
Code 12 — Air flow sensor
Code 13 — Intake Air Temperature Sensor
Code 14 — Throttle Position Sensor (TPS)
Code 15 — ISC Motor Position Sensor (MPS)
Code 21 — Engine Coolant Temperature Sensor
Code 22 — Crank angle sensor
Code 23 — No. 1 cylinder TDC (Camshaft position) Sensor
Code 24 — Vehicle speed sensor
Code 25 — Barometric pressure sensor

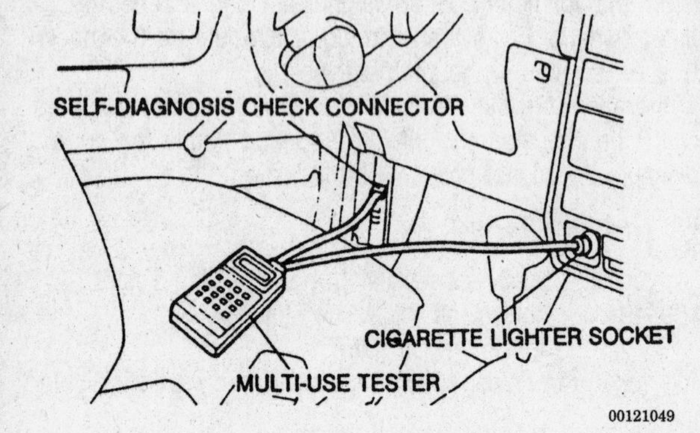

Fig. 42 Connecting the multi-use tester to the self-diagnosis check connector — Eclipse, Mirage, 3000GT and Precis

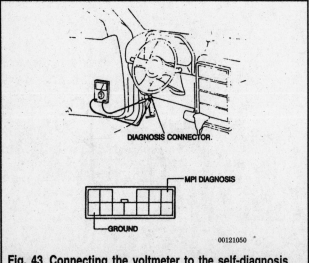

Fig. 43 Connecting the voltmeter to the self-diagnosis check connector — Eclipse, Mirage, 3000GT and Precis

Code 31 — Knock (KS) sensor
Code 32 — Manifold pressure sensor
Code 36 — Ignition timing adjustment signal
Code 39 — Oxygen sensor (rear - turbocharged)
Code 41 — Injector
Code 42 — Fuel pump
Code 43 — EGR-California
Code 44 — Ignition Coil; power transistor unit (No. 1 and No. 4 cylinders) on 3.0L

Code 52 — Ignition Coil; power transistor unit (No. 2 and No. 5 cylinders) on 3.0L
Code 53 — Ignition Coil; power transistor unit (No. 3 and No. 6 cylinders)
Code 55 — IAC valve position sensor
Code 59 — Heated oxygen sensor
Code 61 — Transaxle control unit cable (automatic transmission)
Code 62 — Warmup control valve position sensor (non-turbo)

NISSAN

General Information

Nissan uses 2 types of fuel systems. Electronic Control Carburetor (ECC) system and Electronic Concentrated Control System (ECCS). The ECC system is a Feedback carburetor system. The ECCS is a fuel injected system which may be either throttle body injection or Muti-port injection. Both ECC and ECCS systems were available as of 1984.

Self-Diagnostics

SERVICE PRECAUTIONS

- Do not disconnect the injector harness connectors with the engine running.
- Do not apply battery power directly to the injectors.
- Do not disconnect the ECU harness connectors before the battery ground cable has been disconnected.
- Make sure all ECU connectors are fastened securely. A poor connection can cause an extremely high surge voltage in the coil and condenser and result in damage to integrated circuits.
- When testing the ECU with a DVOM make sure that the probes of the tester never touch each other as this will result in damage to a transistor in the ECU.
- Keep the ECCS harness at least 4 in. away from adjacent harnesses to prevent an ECCS system malfunction due to external electronic noise.
- Keep all parts and harnesses dry during service.
- Before attempting to remove any parts, turn **OFF** the ignition switch and disconnect the battery ground cable.
- Always use a 12 volt battery as a power source.
- Do not attempt to disconnect the battery cables with the engine running or the ignition key **ON**.
- Do not clean the air flow meter with any type of detergent.
- Do not attempt to disassemble the ECCS control unit under any circumstances.
- Avoid static electricity build-up by properly grounding yourself prior to handling any ECU or related parts.

READING CODES

▶ **See Figures 44, 45 and 46**

➡**Diagnostic codes may be retrieved by observing the code flashes through the LED lights located on the Electronic Control Module (ECM). A special Nissan Consult monitor tool can be used, but is not required. When using special diagnostic equipment, always observe the tool manufacturer's instructions.**

Electronic Controlled Carburetor

1987-88 VEHICLES

The 1.6L (E16S) carbureted engine utilizes a duty-controlled solenoid valve for fuel enrichment and an Idle Speed Control (ISC) actuator for basic controls instead of the conventional choke valve plate and fast idle cam. There are several other inputs which further affect the air/fuel ratio. The system is controlled in 2 ways: open or closed loop. To inspect the system for malfunctions, proceed as follows:

1. Position the ECU so the red and green LED's are visible.
2. Run the engine until it is at normal operating temperature.
3. Verify the diagnosis switch on the ECU is **OFF**.
4. Run the engine 2000 rpm for 5 minutes. After 5 minutes, observe the green LED light while maintaining 2000 rpm. The light should be blinking ON and OFF at least 5 times in 10 seconds. If not as specified, inspect the exhaust gas sensor.
5. Turn the engine **OFF** and turn the ECU diagnosis switch **ON**.
6. Turn the ignition switch **ON**. The green LED on the ECU should stay **ON** and the red LED will either flash for a short period indicating a malfunctioning input sensor or for a longer time indicating a malfunctioning output sensor.

Electronic Fuel Injection

1984-94 VEHICLES

Two types of diagnostic systems are used in Nissan vehicles: the 2-mode diagnostic system and the 5-mode diagnostic system. The 2 mode system is used in some vehicles starting in 1990, ultimately, all vehicles used the 2-mode system after 1991 with the exception of 1991-94 Maxima (VG30E engine), Pathfinder and Truck. These vehicles continued to use the 5-mode system. The 5-mode system began in 1984.

5-MODE DIAGNOSTIC SYSTEM

The 5-mode diagnostic system is incorporated in the ECU which uses inputs from various sensors to determine the correct air/fuel ratio. If any of the sensors malfunction the ECU will store the code in memory. The 5-mode diagnostic system is capable of various tests as outlined below. When using these modes, the ECM may have to be removed from its mounting bracket to better access the mode selector switch.

➡Vehicles are equipped with a CHECK ENGINE light on the instrument panel. If any systems are malfunctioning, the light will illuminate the same time as the red lamp while the engine is running and the system is in Mode 1.

Mode 1 — Heated Oxygen Sensor

During closed loop operation the green lamp turns ON when a lean condition is detected and turns OFF under a rich condition. During open loop the green lamp remains ON or OFF. This mode is used to check Heated Oxygen sensor functions for correct operation. To enter Mode 1, proceed as follows:
1. Turn the ignition switch ON.
2. Turn the diagnostic switch located on the side of the ECU ON by either flipping the switch to the ON position or turning the screw switch fully clockwise.
3. Turn the diagnostic switch OFF or fully counterclockwise as soon as the inspection lamps flash 1 time.
4. The self-diagnostic system is now in Mode 1.

Mode 2 — Mixture Ratio Feedback Control Monitor

The green inspection lamp is operating in the same manner as in Mode 1. During closed loop operation the red inspection lamp turns ON and OFF simultaneously with the green lamp when the mixture ratio is controlled within the specified value. During open loop the red lamp remains ON or OFF. Mode 2 is used for checking that optimum control of the fuel mixture is obtained. To enter Mode 2, proceed as follows:
1. Turn the ignition switch ON.
2. Turn the diagnostic switch ON, by either flipping the switch to the ON position or use a screwdriver and turn the switch fully clockwise.

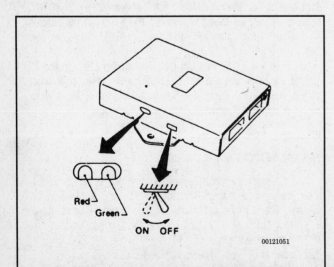

Fig. 44 Entering self-diagnostics using the ON/OFF mode switch

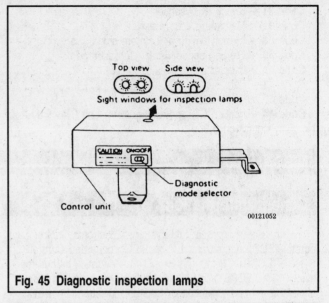

Fig. 45 Diagnostic inspection lamps

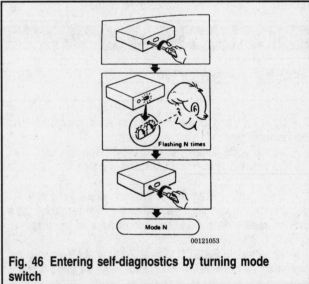

Fig. 46 Entering self-diagnostics by turning mode switch

3. Turn the diagnostic switch OFF or fully counterclockwise as soon as the inspection lamps flash 2 times.
4. The self-diagnostic system is now in Mode 2.

Mode 3 — Self-Diagnosis System

This mode of the self-diagnostics is for stored code retrieval. To enter Mode 3, proceed as follows:
1. Thoroughly warm the engine before proceeding. With the engine OFF, turn the ignition switch ON.
2. Turn the diagnostic switch located on the side of the ECU ON by either flipping the switch to the ON position or using a screwdriver, turn the switch fully clockwise.
3. Turn the diagnostic switch OFF or fully counterclockwise as soon as the inspection lamps flash 3 times.
4. The self-diagnostic system is now in Mode 3.

➡When the battery is disconnected or self-diagnostic Mode 4 is selected after using Mode 3, all stored codes will be cleared. However if the ignition key is turned OFF and then the procedure is followed to enter Mode 4 directly, the stored codes will not be cleared.

5. The codes will now be displayed by the red and green inspection lamps flashing. The red lamp will flash first and the green lamp will follow. The red lamp is the tens and the green lamp is the units, that is, the red lamp flashes 1 time and the green lamp flashes 2 times, this would indicate a Code 12.

Mode 4 — On/Off Switches

This mode checks the operation of the Vehicle Speed Sensor (VSS), Closed Throttle Position (CTP) and starter switches. Entering this mode will also clear all stored codes in the ECU. To enter Mode 4, proceed as follows:

1. Turn the ignition switch **ON**.

2. Turn the diagnostic switch located on the side of the ECU ON by either flipping the switch to the ON position or turning the mode switch fully clockwise.

3. Turn the diagnostic switch OFF or fully counterclockwise as soon as the inspection lamps flash 4 times.

4. The self-diagnostic system is now in Mode 4.

5. Turn the ignition switch to the **START** position and verify the red inspection lamp illuminates. This verifies that the starter switch is working.

6. Depress the accelerator and verify the red inspection lamp goes OFF. This verifies that the CTP switch is working.

7. Raise and properly support the vehicle and verify the lamp goes ON when the vehicle speed is above 12 mph (20 km/h). This verifies that the VSS is working

8. Turn the ignition switch **OFF**.

Mode 5 — Real Time Diagnostics

▶ **See Figures 47 and 48**

In this mode the ECU is capable of detecting and alerting the technician the instant a malfunction in the crank angle sensor, air flow meter, ignition signal or the fuel pump occurs while operating/driving the vehicle. Items which are noted to be malfunctioning are not stored in the ECU's memory. To enter Mode 5, proceed as follows:

1. Turn the ignition switch **ON**.

2. Turn the diagnostic switch located on the side of the ECU ON by either flipping the switch to the ON position or by turning the switch fully clockwise.

3. Turn the diagnostic switch OFF or fully counterclockwise as soon as the inspection lamps flash 5 times.

4. The self-diagnostic system is now in Mode 5.

5. Ensure the inspection lamps are not flashing. If they are, count the number of flashes within a 3.2 second period:
- 1 Flash = Crank angle sensor
- 2 Flashes = Air flow meter
- 3 Flashes = Fuel pump
- 4 Flashes = Ignition signal

2-MODE DIAGNOSTIC SYSTEM

▶ **See Figures 49, 50 and 51**

The 1992-94 300ZX, Stanza, 240SX, Sentra/NX Coupe, Maxima (VE30DE engine), and the 1993-94 Altima and Quest use a 2-mode diagnostic system incorporated in the ECU which uses inputs from various sensors to determine the correct air/fuel ratio. If any of the sensors malfunction the ECU will store the code in memory.

A Nissan Consult monitor, or equivalent may be used to retrieve these codes by simply connecting the monitor to the diagnostic connector located on the driver's side near the hood

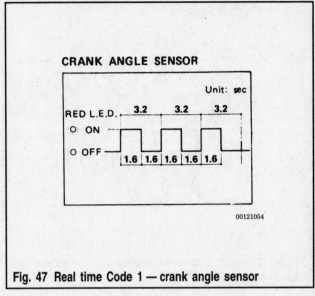

Fig. 47 Real time Code 1 — crank angle sensor

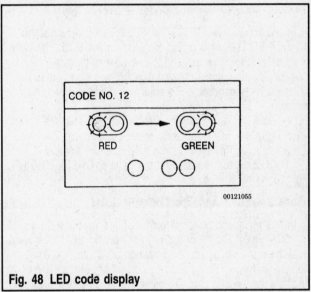

Fig. 48 LED code display

release. Turn the ignition switch to **ON** and press START, ENGINE and then SELF-DIAG RESULTS, the results will then be output to the monitor.

The conventional CHECK ENGINE or red LED ECU light may also be used for self-diagnostics. The conventional 2-Mode diagnostic system is broken into 2 separate modes each capable of 2 tests, an ignition switch **ON** or engine running test as outlined below:

Mode 1 — Bulb Check

In this mode the RED indicator light on the ECU and the CHECK ENGINE light should be ON. To enter this mode simply turn the ignition switch **ON** and observe the light.

Mode 1 — Malfunction Warning

In this mode the ECU is acknowledging if there is a malfunction by illuminating the RED indicator light on the ECU and the CHECK ENGINE light. If the light turns OFF, the system is normal. To enter this mode, simply start the engine and observe the light.

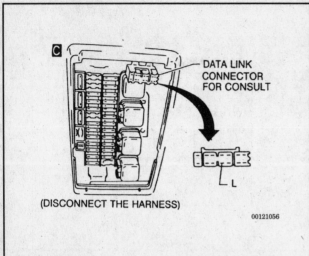

(DISCONNECT THE HARNESS)

00121056

Fig. 49 Data Link connector location-1993-94 Altima and Stanza shown

Mode 2 — Self-Diagnostic Codes — Except Quest

In this mode the ECU will output all malfunctions via the CHECK ENGINE light or the red LED on the ECU. The code may be retrieved by counting the number of flashes. The longer flashes indicate the first digit and the shorter flashes indicate the second digit. To enter this mode proceed as follows:

1. Turn the ignition switch **ON**, but do not start the vehicle.
2. Turn the ECU diagnostic mode selector fully clockwise for 2 seconds, then turn it back fully counterclockwise.
3. Observe the red LED on the ECU or CHECK ENGINE light for stored codes.

Mode 2 — Self-Diagnostic Codes — Quest

In this mode the ECU will output all malfunctions via the CHECK ENGINE light or the red LED on the ECU. The code may be retrieved by counting the number of flashes. The longer flashes indicate the first digit and the shorter flashes indicate the second digit. To enter this mode proceed as follows:

1. Turn the ignition switch **ON**, but do not start the vehicle.
2. Disconnect harness connectors and connect terminals A and B with a jumper wire.
3. Wait 2 seconds, remove the jumper wire and reconnect the harness connector.
4. Observe the CHECK ENGINE light for stored codes.

Mode 2 — Exhaust Gas Sensor Monitor

In this mode the red LED on the ECU or CHECK ENGINE light will display the condition of the fuel mixture and whether the system is in closed loop or open loop. When the light flashes ON, the exhaust gas sensor is indicating a lean mixture. When the light stays OFF, the sensor is indicating a rich mixture. If the light remains ON or OFF, it is indicating an open loop system. If the system is equipped with 2 exhaust gas sensors, the left side will operate first. If already in Mode 2, proceed to Step C to enter the exhaust gas sensor monitor.

1. On all models except Quest, perform the following steps:
a. Turn the ignition switch **ON**.

b. Turn the diagnostic switch ON, by turning the switch fully clockwise for 2 seconds and then fully counterclockwise.
c. Start the engine and run until thoroughly warm. Raise the idle to 2,000 rpm and hold for approximately 2 minutes. Ensure the red LED or CHECK ENGINE light flashes ON and OFF more than 5 times every 10 seconds with the engine speed at 2,000 rpm.

➡**If equipped with 2 exhaust gas sensors, switch to the right sensor by turning the ECU mode selector fully clockwise for 2 seconds and then fully counterclockwise with the engine running.**

2. On Quest models, perform the following steps:
a. Turn the ignition switch **ON**.
b. Disconnect harness connectors and connect terminals A and B with a jumper wire.
c. Wait 2 seconds, remove the jumper wire and reconnect the harness connectors.
d. Start the engine and run until thoroughly warm. Raise the idle to 2,000 rpm and hold for approximately 2 minutes. Ensure the red LED or CHECK ENGINE light flashes ON and OFF more than 5 times every 10 seconds with the engine speed at 2,000 rpm.

CLEARING CODES

ENGINE CODES

Except Mode 5, 3 and 2 Systems

All control unit diagnostic codes may be cleared by disconnecting the negative battery cable for a period of 15 seconds. Entering Mode 4 of the Electronic Fuel Injection system diagnostics will also clear stored ECM engine codes.

Mode 5, 3 and 2 Systems

On 5-mode systems, enter mode 4 immediately after using mode 3 and the codes will be cleared. On 2-mode systems, the codes will be cleared when mode 1 is re-entered from mode 2. The Nissan Consult Monitor or equivalent can also be used to clear codes on 2-mode systems.

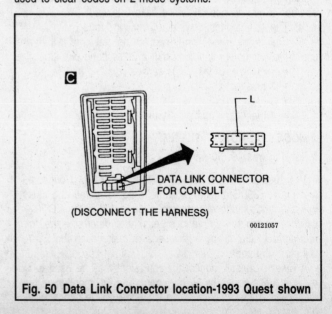

(DISCONNECT THE HARNESS)

00121057

Fig. 50 Data Link Connector location-1993 Quest shown

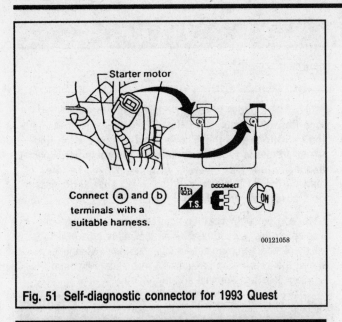

Connect ⓐ and ⓑ terminals with a suitable harness.

00121058

Fig. 51 Self-diagnostic connector for 1993 Quest

Diagnostic Trouble Codes

1984-87 Vehicles

Code 11 — Crankshaft position sensor circuit
Code 12 — Mass Air flow sensor circuit
Code 13 — Engine coolant temperature sensor circuit
Code 21 — Ignition signal circuit
Code 22 — Fuel pump circuit
Code 23 — Idle switch circuit
Code 24 — Transmission switch
Code 31 — AC switch, fast idle control of load signal
Code 32 — Starter signal

Code 33 — EGR gas sensor
Code 34 — Detonation (Knock) sensor
Code 41 — Air or Fuel temperature sensor
Code 42 — Throttle sensor (or BP sensor in Canada)
Code 43 — Mixture feedback control slips out (or low battery in Canada)
Code 44 — No Malfunctioning circuits

1988-94 Vehicles

Code 11 — Crankshaft position sensor circuit
Code 12 — Mass Air flow sensor circuit
Code 13 — Engine coolant temperature sensor circuit
Code 14 — Vehicle speed sensor circuit
Code 15 — Mixture ratio feedback control slips out (1988)
Code 21 — Ignition signal circuit
Code 22 — Fuel pump circuit (to 1991)
Code 23 — Idle switch circuit (to 1991)
Code 24 — Fuel Switch circuit or O.D. switch circuit (to 1990)
Code 25 — AAC valve circuit (to 1991)
Code 31 — Electronic Control Module (ECM) or A/C circuit
Code 32 — Exhaust Gas Recirculation (EGR) function
Code 33 — Oxygen sensor circuit (left side, if two)
Code 34 — Knock sensor circuit
Code 35 — Exhaust gas temperature sensor circuit
Code 41 — Air temperature sensor circuit
Code 42 — Fuel temperature sensor circuit
Code 43 — Throttle position sensor circuit
Code 44 — No malfunctioning circuits
Code 45 — Injector leak
Code 51 — Injector circuit
Code 53 — Heated oxygen sensor circuit (right side)
Code 54 — Signal circuit from A/T control unit to ECM
Code 55 — No malfunctioning in the above circuits

PEUGEOT

General Information

As of 1986 Peugeot employs 3 distinct Bosch fuel injection systems across the model lines. While each system has similarities to the others, each also has significant differences. All fuel systems are computer-controlled but the amount of computer control varies by system. Each Electronic Control Unit (ECU) is unique to its system; the controllers cannot be interchanged.

Peugeot's gasoline engines include a variety of 4-cylinder models as well as a V-6. The 4-cylinder engines appear in SOHC, DOHC and turbocharged form. The V-6 engine did not appear in the 1991 models; only 4-cylinder gasoline engines were available in the US market. Peugeot withdrew from the US market at the end of 1991.

Self-Diagnostics

SERVICE PRECAUTIONS

- Do not disconnect the battery while the engine is running, or allow the engine to run if the battery terminals are not properly tightened.
- Always disconnect the battery for recharging.
- Do not use an auxiliary starting device which has a voltage rating above 12 volts.
- Before conducting any electrical welding on the vehicle be sure to disconnect all ECU's.

Also, do not expose ECU's to temperatures in excess of 176°F (80°C) such as in an infra-red spray booth.

- Do not use a test light or create an arc to check circuit continuity.
- Do not insert the ends of a voltmeter test lead into the receiving end of the component connectors. It is necessary to use the pin-out box or to remove the connector cover and take the test reading where the wires enter the connector.
- Before connecting or disconnecting ECU harness connectors, make sure the ignition switch is **OFF** and the negative battery cable is disconnected to avoid the possibility of damage to the control unit.
- When connecting or disconnecting pin connectors from the ECU, take care not to bend or break any pin terminals. Check that there are no bends or breaks on ECU pin terminals before attempting any connections.
- Before replacing any ECU, perform ECU input/output signal diagnosis to determine if the ECU is functioning properly.
- When measuring supply voltage of ECU controlled components with a circuit tester, separate 1 tester probe from another. If the 2 tester probes accidentally make contact with each other during measurement, a short circuit may result and damage the ECU.

READING CODES

➡**Diagnostic codes may be retrieved by observing the code flashes through the CHECK ENGINE light or Malfunction Indicator Lamp (MIL) however, a jumper switch (momentary type) is required to activate the computer. Special diagnostic tool TAD 99 tester or an equivalent can be used on the M1.3 systems. When using special diagnostic tools always observe the tool manufacturer's instructions.**

You can probably make up your own jumper switch tool. To accomplish this, all you need is a momentary type switch, 2 pieces of wire approximately 2-3 in. long each. Connect each wire to the switch. The un-attached wire ends will connect to the diagnostic test terminal and to ground.

Fuel Injection System

Codes for the M1.3 Motronic system can be read with the aid of a switched jumper, the TAD 99 tester or equivalent. When using a switched jumper, codes are indicated through flashing of CHECK ENGINE light. A code will display by flashing a number of times for the tens digit and then for the units digit. The two sets of flashes will be separated by a pause. The TAD 99 tester is equipped with a display screen to indicate fault codes numerically.

Without Tester

1. Connect jumper switch (momentary contact type) to pin 1 of the 2-pin green connector (wires 4A and 17) found in the underhood relay box on the passenger side and to ground.
2. Turn the ignition **ON**, then depress jumper switch for 3 seconds, CHECK ENGINE indicator will come ON.
3. Release the switch and watch the CHECK ENGINE light. The light will flash 1 time, remain OFF for 1-5 seconds and flash 2 times. This represents Code 12 and indicates the beginning of the test sequence.
4. Wait for the CHECK ENGINE indicator to come ON.
5. Depress the jumper switch for 3 seconds, CHECK ENGINE indicator will come ON.
6. Release the switch and watch the CHECK ENGINE light, a fault code, if present, will display. The tens digit will flash followed by a 1-5 seconds pause and the units digit.
7. Repeat procedure from Step 4 until Code 11 displays indicating the end of the test sequence.

With TAD 99 Tester

1. Connect the tester, or equivalent, to the green 2-pin connector found in the under-hood relay box on the passenger side and to the battery.
2. Set test selector on position 1, then turn the ignition **ON**.
3. Depress the green test button for at least 3 seconds and release. Code 12 will display to identify the start of the test.
4. Wait a few seconds and depress the green test button for at least 3 seconds and release.
5. The next fault code, if present will display.
6. Repeat procedure from Step 4 until Code 11 displays indicating the end of the test sequence.

Ignition System

No diagnostic procedure or scan tool is necessary to extract fault codes from a vehicle with a separate ECU for the ignition. In the event of a fault, the LED indicator in the instrument display will automatically flash the fault code in cycles. The code is a number from 1-6 and will flash constantly until the fault is corrected.

The frequency of the LED flashing is directly proportional to engine rpm, so it is essential that the code is determined by counting the number of blinks at idle. During normal operation the LED may exhibit occasional sporadic flashes; this does not mean that a fault has been detected.

CLEARING CODES

Fuel Injection System

After repairs have been completed, be sure to clear the diagnostic memory.

Without Tester

1. Perform test up to Code 11.
2. Depress the jumper switch for more than 10 seconds, the CHECK ENGINE indicator should be ON.

With TAD 99 Tester

1. Perform test up to Code 11.
2. Depress the RED memory erase button until EF appears on the display and then wait for 00 to display.

Ignition System

After repairs are made the ignition should be switched **OFF** to erase fault codes from memory.

Diagnostic Trouble Codes

1989-91 1.9L Engine

This code list is for the 1.9L engine with Motronic 1.3 fuel system
Code 11 — End of test sequence
Code 12 — Beginning of test sequence
Code 13 — Air temperature sensor
Code 14 — Injection NTC sensor

Code 15 — Fuel pump(s) relay
Code 21 — Throttle switch (idle position)
Code 22 — Electronic Control Unit (ECU)
Code 31 — Self correction richness regulation function; check for air leak at intake
Code 32 — Self correction richness regulation function; check for exhaust leak
Code 33 — Airflow sensor
Code 34 — Canister purge electrovalve
Code 35 — Throttle switch unit (full load position)
Code 41 — Engine rpm sensor
Code 42 — Injectors
Code 43 — Detonation correction regulation (at maximum)
Code 44 — Detonation sensor
Code 51 — Self correction richness regulation function; check lambda sensor and circuit
Code 52 — Self correction richness regulation function; check with new ECU
Code 53 — Battery voltage
Code 54 — Electronic Control Unit (ECU)

1986-91 2.2L Engine

The code list is for the 2.2L(2155cc) engine with LU-Jetronic fuel system
Code 1 — Continued detonation; maximum correction reached
Code 2 — Battery voltage is under 10.5 volts
Code 3 — Detonation correction circuit in the ignition ECU defective
Code 4 — Erroneous signal received from detonation sensor; check for engine speed above 3200 rpm.
Code 5 — Signal from potentiometer is greater than 4.3 volts
Code 6 A: — Connections and wiring between ignition ECU and potentiometer defective
Code 6 B: — No load signal emanating from the injection ECU

1987-89 2.8L Engine

This code list is for the 2.8L (2849cc) engine with LU-Jetronic 2.2 fuel system
Code 2 — NTC temperature sensor
Code 4 — Detonation sensor or ignition ECU
Code 5 — Erroneous load signal from the injection ECU
Code 6 — No. 1 cylinder sensor

PORSCHE

General Information

Except 911 Turbo

Porsche vehicle use 2 forms of electronic fuel injection. The 928 uses LH-Jetronic fuel injection. The 911, 944 and the 968 use Digital Motor Electronics (DME) fuel injection. Both systems are advanced versions of their fuel injection systems and provide excellent control of emissions, fuel economy and performance.

911 Turbo

The Porsche 911 Turbo has always been a specialized vehicle. The latest version is a hybrid of the 911 Carrera 2 body and the proven 3.3L turbocharged engine. While the 3.6L engine of the Carrera 2 uses Digital Motor Electronics as the fuel injection system, the 911 Turbo has used since its introduction the traditional Continuous Injection System (CIS).

Self-Diagnostics

SERVICE PRECAUTIONS

- Do not disconnect the battery or power to the control unit before reading the fault codes. Fault code memory is erased when power is interrupted.
- Make sure the ignition switch is **OFF** before disconnecting any wiring.
- Before removing or installing a control unit, disconnect the negative battery cable. The unit receives power through the main connector at all times and will be permanently damaged if improperly powered up or down.
- Keep all parts and harnesses dry during service. Protect the control unit and all solid-state components from rough handling or extremes of temperature.
- All air bag system wiring is in a yellow harness. Use extreme care when working around this wiring. Do not test these circuits without first disconnecting the air bag units.

READING CODES

➡ **Vehicles prior to 1991 with self diagnostic capability require the use of special tool 9288 Tester or 9268 flash tester to retrieve diagnostics codes. On 1991 and later models, the flash codes can be read on the CHECK ENGINE light on the instrument panel. When using special diagnostic equipment, always observe the tool manufacturer's instructions.**

➡ **1987 vehicles with LH and EZK systems did not have OBD capability.**

1987-93 Vehicles

With 9288 Diagnostic Tester

When the tester is attached to the diagnostic connector, the control units will present country and application codes to the tester for display on the screen. The tester will then provide a menu with instructions for retrieving fault codes from the control unit memory. If the tester display shows fault not present, this indicates the fault is intermittent or the conditions under which the fault occurs do not exist at this time. The necessary conditions will be displayed on the screen. If the display shows signal not plausible, the input or output signal does exist but is out of the correct operating range.

Without 9288 Diagnostic Tester

The control unit is equipped with a self diagnostic program that will detect emissions related malfunctions and turn the CHECK ENGINE light **ON** while the engine is running. Emissions related fault codes stored in the control unit can be read with the 9268 flash tester. On 1991 and later models, the flash codes can be read on the CHECK ENGINE light on the instrument panel. Only faults that may effect exhaust emissions are reported as flash codes. All other codes are only accessible with the 9288 Diagnostic Tester.

1. If required, connect the flash tester to the diagnostic connector using the adapter connector.
2. Turn the ignition switch **ON** without starting the engine.
3. Fully press the accelerator pedal to close the full load switch. After about 3 seconds the CHECK ENGINE light or tester will flash.
4. When the pedal is released, flash codes will be reported. All codes are 4 digits. Each digit will be flashed with about 2.5 seconds between digits. When the whole code has been displayed, the light will stay **ON** or **OFF**. Count the flashes and write the numbers down. If Code 1500 or 2500 is displayed, no codes are stored in memory.
5. Repeat Steps 3 and 4 until Code 1000 appears, indicating all codes have been reported. On 928 models, the EZK unit will display Code 2000 when all codes have been reported.

➡ **On all 928 models, if the first digit is 2, the fault is in the EZK ignition system control unit.**

If the second digit is 1, the detected fault is current. If the second digit is 2, the detected fault has not occurred during the last running of the vehicle but did occur within the last 50 engine starts. The remaining 2 digits indicate which component or circuit is at fault.

CLEARING CODES

1987-93 Vehicles

The fault code memory should be cleared before returning the vehicle to service. All Codes in memory and the idle control adaptation are lost when the control unit or the battery is disconnected. To avoid the loss of the learned idle program, use the instructions on the 9288 tester to clear the memory. If this tester is not available, disconnect the battery or control unit to clear the memory. It will be necessary to drive the vehicle for at least 6 minutes and run the engine at idle for about 10 minutes so the control unit can learn idle speed, timing and mixture parameters. Make sure the engine is at operating temperature and that all accessories are **OFF**. The throttle-at-idle position switch must be closed and functioning or system adaptation will not take place.

Diagnostic Trouble Codes

1221 — Control unit self test
1215 — Air flow sensor
1221 — Oxygen sensor
1222 — Oxygen regulation

1223 — Coolant temperature sensor
1224 — Air temperature sensor
1231 — Battery voltage
1232 — Throttle idle switch
1233 — Throttle full load switch
1251 — Fuel injector group 1, even numbers
1252 — Fuel injector group 2, odd numbers
1261 — Fuel pump relay
1262 — Idle speed control actuator
1263 — Carbon canister purge valve
1264 — Oxygen sensor heater relay

SAAB

General Information

▶ **See Figures 52, 53, 54 and 55**

The LH-Jetronic fuel injection system was introduced in the Saab 900 in 1985. The 9000 picked it up in 1986. The 1990 models and in some markets 1991-94 models are equipped with an LH 2.4 fuel system Electronic Control Unit (ECU). Most 1991-94 models, are equipped with an LH 2.4.2 fuel system ECU, except the 1991 9000 with the B234 engine, which has an LH 2.4.1 fuel system ECU. Turbocharged 900 models are also equipped with an Automatic Performance Control (APC) ECU and 9000 models are equipped with an integrated Direct Ignition-Automatic Performance Control (DI/APC) control unit, which control ignition functions and turbocharger-related functions.

The LH-system ECU has the particular fuel system identification marked on it for identification. Visually, the LH 2.4 fuel system can be differentiated from the LH 2.4.2 fuel system by the pins on the Automatic Idle Control (AIC) valve. The LH 2.4 fuel system AIC valve has 2 pins and the LH 2.4.2 fuel system AIC valve has 3 pins.

The LH 2.4.1 fuel system differs from the LH 2.4 fuel system in that the cold start injector has been discontinued. The direct ignition system has taken over this function. Also, the vehicle speed sensor is used in the control of the AIC function to tell the fuel system ECU whether the car is moving or at a standstill.

The LH 2.4 (some markets) and LH 2.4.2 fuel systems with the Electronic Throttle System (ETS), used on the 1992-94 9000 with traction control, differ from the systems without ETS in the following ways: The electronically controlled throttle eliminates the need for automatic idling and load control throughout the load range, the throttle angle transmitter is located in the actuator motor, which is integrated with the throttle housing and the electronically controlled throttle system carries out compensation for the air conditioning. Vehicles with ETS also have an Automatic Slip Reduction (ASR) control unit that carries out other traction control system functions.

Visually, the throttle housing on engines with ETS is larger, is vacuum operated and has an emergency cable, but in other respects this system operates in the same way as the LH 2.4 and 2.4.2 systems without ETS.

The central component of the LH-Jetronic fuel injection system is the air mass meter that measures the mass of air flow instead of the volume. The microprocessor measures how much electrical energy is used when air flow passes an electrically heated platinum wire in the air mass meter. The higher the rate of air flow, the higher the energy necessary to keep the temperature of the wire constant. At the same time, the microprocessor monitors the engine speed and temperature, calculating the exact amount of fuel needed for optimum performance. The microprocessor also incorporates an rpm limiter that ensures that no opening signals will be transmitted to the injectors at engine speeds above 6000 rpm.

The LH-Jetronic fuel injection system provides the air mass meter with a self-cleaning function. During burn-off the platinum wire in the air mass meter is quickly heated to about 1800°F (1000°C) for a 1 second duration, 4 seconds after the ignition is switched OFF. This burns away any deposits on the wire that would be detrimental to efficient operation.

The APC system on turbocharged vehicles enables the engine to achieve optimum performance and good fuel economy, regardless of the grade of fuel being used. A knock sensor, in conjunction with the pressure transducer and ignition system information, detects knocking in the engine and sends an electrical signal to the microprocessor inside the ECU. The ECU processes these signals and sends electrical pulses to a solenoid valve that controls the charging pressure in the intake manifold. The turbocharger is designed to come into operation at fairly low engine speeds, thereby providing a high torque within the speed range of normal driving. It is water cooled and the coolant for the bearing housing is supplied by a pipe connected to the cooling system.

Charging pressure is regulated by a pressure regulator valve (known as a wastegate). The charging pressure regulator is fitted to the exhaust side of the engine and regulates the flow of exhaust gas to the compressor. The valve remains closed when the engine load is low. As the demand on the engine is increased, the wastegate opens.

The DI/APC system was updated in 1991 to include an air temperature sensor, located upstream of the throttle housing. The boost pressure is governed by the position of the throttle valve, but it is subject to temperature compensation based on information supplied by the new air temperature sensor. The separate pressure-switch function is discontinued, with the

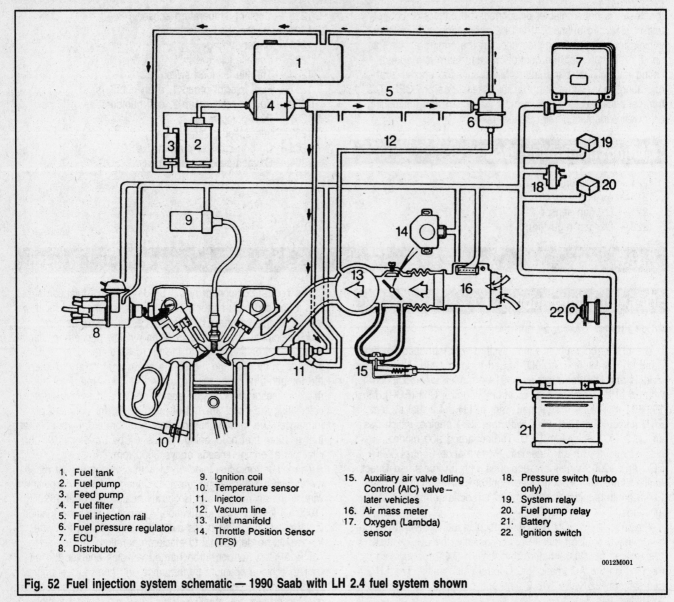

1. Fuel tank
2. Fuel pump
3. Feed pump
4. Fuel filter
5. Fuel injection rail
6. Fuel pressure regulator
7. ECU
8. Distributor

9. Ignition coil
10. Temperature sensor
11. Injector
12. Vacuum line
13. Inlet manifold
14. Throttle Position Sensor (TPS)

15. Auxiliary air valve Idling Control (AIC) valve — later vehicles
16. Air mass meter
17. Oxygen (Lambda) sensor

18. Pressure switch (turbo only)
19. System relay
20. Fuel pump relay
21. Battery
22. Ignition switch

0012M001

Fig. 52 Fuel injection system schematic — 1990 Saab with LH 2.4 fuel system shown

pressure-sensing function now being regulated by the DI/APC-system ECU. The load signal provided by the air mass meter is sent to the LH-system ECU, which will keep the DI/APC system ECU informed of boost status.

Starting in 1991 there is also a spark plug burn-off function that occurs when the engine is stopped. The burn-off function, which operates in all cylinders simultaneously, lasts for 5 seconds at a frequency corresponding to 6000 rpm.

Turbocharged California vehicles, except the 1991-94 9000 Turbo with the B234 engine, are equipped with an electronically controlled EGR system. A modulating valve functions as a 3-way valve as it controls the vacuum to the EGR valve. A vacuum regulator is incorporated in the modulating valve to maintain a constant vacuum to the EGR valve. A vacuum storage tank is connected via a vacuum check valve to the intake manifold. The check valve prevents the loss of vacuum in the tank during acceleration. An EGR temperature sensor provides information to the LH-system ECU. If the temperature deviates from a normal range, a problem is indicated due to improper exhaust gas flow in the EGR pipe and a fault code will be set.

The LH-Jetronic system also incorporates an emergency system known as a limp home function. If a malfunction is detected, the limp home feature of the ECU is actuated, enabling the vehicle to continue its journey, but with somewhat diminished performance. If the vehicle is operated in this mode, the Check Engine Light (CEL) on the display panel will be illuminated. An integrated fault-storing capability enables diagnosis to be carried out efficiently.

Self Diagnostics

SERVICE PRECAUTIONS

• Before connecting or disconnecting ECU harness connectors, make sure the ignition switch is **OFF** and the negative battery cable is disconnected to avoid the possibility of damage to the control unit.

• When connecting or disconnecting pin connectors from the ECU, take care not to bend or break any pin terminals. Check

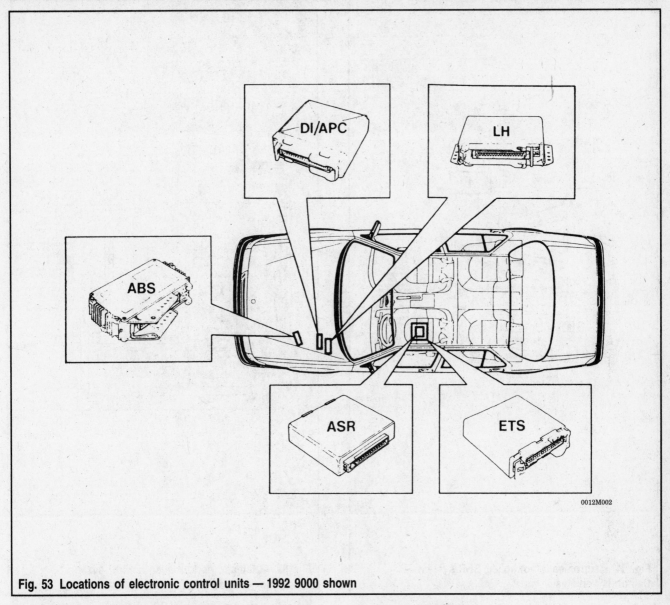

Fig. 53 Locations of electronic control units — 1992 9000 shown

that there are no bends or breaks on ECU pin terminals before attempting any connections.

• Before replacing any ECU, perform ECU input/output signal diagnosis to determine if the ECU is functioning properly.

• When measuring supply voltage of ECU controlled components with a circuit tester, separate 1 tester probe from another. If the 2 tester probes accidentally make contact with each other during measurement, a short circuit may result and damage the ECU.

• Always disarm the airbag (SRS) system when working on the airbag or ABS system.

• Always verify the ignition is switched **OFF** before connecting or disconnecting any electrical connections, especially connections to a control unit.

READING CODES

▶ See Figures 56 and 57

➡Diagnostic codes may be retrieved by observing the code flashes through the CHECK ENGINE light or Malfunction Indicator Lamp (MIL) only on vehicles listed under 'Without Diagnostic Tester' procedure. With this procedure a basic jumper switch (momentary type) is required to activate the computer. Other vehicles would require the use of special diagnostic tools: LH System tester or a ISAT Tester to retrieve codes. Read all procedures before attempting to perform checks. When using special diagnostic tools always observe the tool manufacturer's instructions.

1985-94 Vehicles

With LH System Tester

The Saab LH system tester 8394223 has been developed to simplify service and fault diagnosis work on the LH fuel injec-

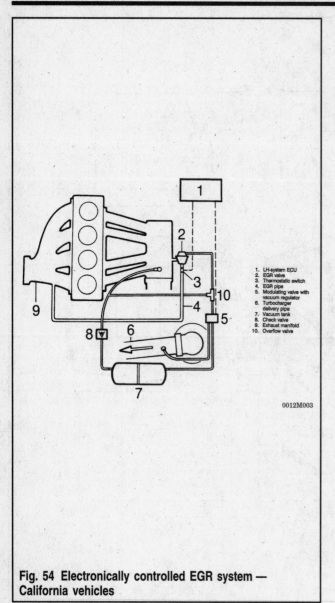

1. LH-system ECU
2. EGR valve
3. Thermostatic switch
4. EGR pipe
5. Modulating valve with vacuum regulator
6. Turbocharger delivery pipe
7. Vacuum tank
8. Check valve
9. Exhaust manifold
10. Overflow valve

0012M003

**Fig. 54 Electronically controlled EGR system —
California vehicles**

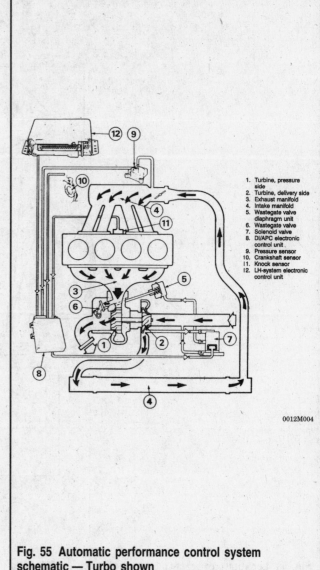

1. Turbine, pressure side
2. Turbine, delivery side
3. Exhaust manifold
4. Intake manifold
5. Wastegate valve diaphragm unit
6. Wastegate valve
7. Solenoid valve
8. DI/APC electronic control unit
9. Pressure sensor
10. Crankshaft sensor
11. Knock sensor
12. LH-system electronic control unit

0012M004

**Fig. 55 Automatic performance control system
schematic — Turbo shown**

tion system. The tester consists of a test unit, power supply lead, test lead incorporating a 2-way 35-pin connector and a pressure sensor with magnetic base.

The tester is equipped with an automatic program for diagnosing faults, both permanent and intermittent, while the vehicle is operating. Faults detected are then stored in memory for recall after the vehicle is road-tested.

Connect the diagnostic tester, or equivalent, as follows:

1. Insert the power supply lead between the door and body where there is a break in the seal, then run it under the back of the hood on the left hand side.

2. Clean the battery terminals to ensure proper contact with lead clips.

3. Connect the power supply lead to the tester first, then connect the lead clips to the battery.

4. Remove the cover on the left side over the space behind the false bulkhead panel.

5. Remove the ABS system ECU and bracket, if equipped.

6. Remove the LH system ECU connector. Connect the test lead between the LH-system ECU and the vehicle's wiring

loom. Fit a couple of ties around the connector and ECU to hold them tightly together.

The tester, designed to perform 3 basic functions, monitor mode, test mode and fuel mode, is now in start mode. If at any time the operation in progress must be interrupted, simultaneously press all 3 control buttons and the tester will revert to the starting point.

Monitor Mode

The monitor mode can be selected either by switching the ignition **ON**, or if the ignition is **OFF**, by pressing the **START TEST** button when MON appears on the tester display.

When in monitor mode, the tester is used to manually control parameter and functional checks.

Test Mode

Test mode can only be selected from the monitor mode. Once the LH system version has been selected, the test mode can be activated. Press the **START TEST** button to select the test mode. TEST will now appear on the display.

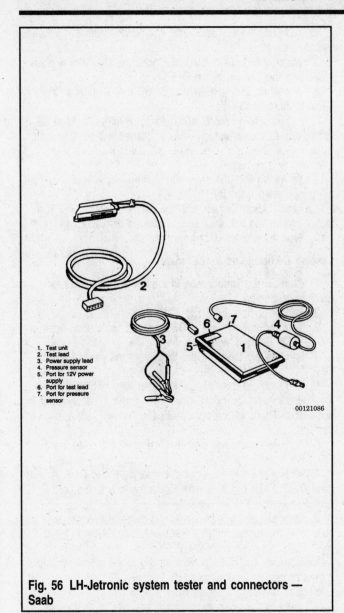

1. Test unit
2. Test lead
3. Power supply lead
4. Pressure sensor
5. Port for 12V power supply
6. Port for test lead
7. Port for pressure sensor

00121086

Fig. 56 LH-Jetronic system tester and connectors — Saab

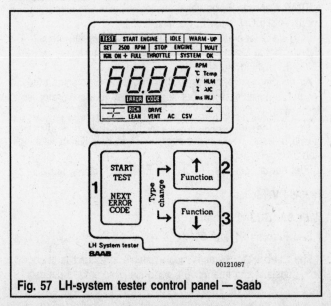

00121087

Fig. 57 LH-system tester control panel — Saab

In the test mode, the program instructs by way of prompts in the upper part of the display.

Fuel Mode

To select the fuel mode, the ignition must be **OFF**. Initially, MON will be displayed on the tester for approximately 5 seconds. During this time, if required, the monitor mode can be selected. If none of the tester buttons are activated, FUEL will appear on the display for approximately 2 seconds. To activate the fuel mode, press the **START** button when FUEL is displayed.

When the tester is in fuel mode the following checks can be performed:

Fuel pump delivery flow
Fuel pressure and fuel-pressure regulator
Residual pressure
Fuel pump delivery pressure
Delivery flow from injectors

Without Diagnostic Tester

▶ See Figures 58, 59 and 60

This method can be used to retrieve fault codes from 1988-94 Saab models equipped with LH 2.4, LH 2.4.1 and LH 2.4.2 fuel injection systems. These systems are capable of an internal self-diagnostic checks and have the ability to store up to 3 intermittent faults at a time. Serious malfunctions are always given priority and must be rectified before the memory can store information on minor faults. The built in diagnosis function also has the capability to manually test the components and signals of the LH system.

The Saab switched jumper lead 8393886, or equivalent, is necessary to conduct these tests.

Connect the switched jumper lead for as follows:

For the Saab 900, Use the switched jumper lead to connect the No. 3 pin in the 3-pin test socket, on the right-hand side in the engine compartment, to the battery ground (negative terminal).

For the Saab 9000, use the switched jumper lead to connect the 3-pin socket, in the test box on the left-hand side of the engine compartment, to the battery ground (negative terminal).

1. Switch the ignition **ON**. The CHECK ENGINE light should now illuminate.

2. Set the jumper switch to ON (grounding ECU pin 16). The CHECK ENGINE light should now be extinguished.

3. Watch the CHECK ENGINE light carefully. After about 2.5 seconds, it will flash briefly, signifying that the first error code is about to display.

4. As soon as the light has flashed, turn the jumper switch OFF.

5. The first of a possible 3 error codes will now be displayed by a series of short flashes. The number 1 is represented by a single flash followed by a long pause. The number 2 is represented by 2 flashes separated from each other by a short pause, but separated from the next number by a long pause. The number 3 would consist of 3 flashes separated by short pauses and followed by a long pause, and so on. For example Code 12112 would consist of: flash-long pause, flash-short pause, flash-long pause, flash-long pause, flash-long pause, flash-short pause, flash-long pause. The code will be displayed repeatedly until the next test step is taken.

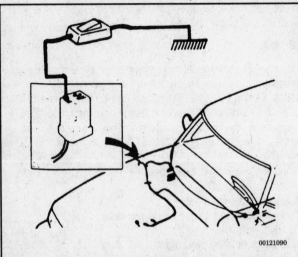

Fig. 58 Switched jumper lead and 3-pin test socket — Saab 900

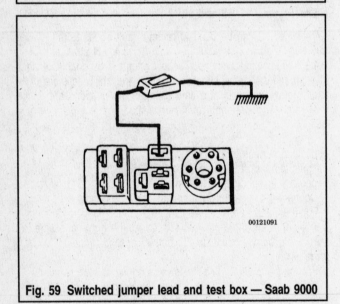

Fig. 59 Switched jumper lead and test box — Saab 9000

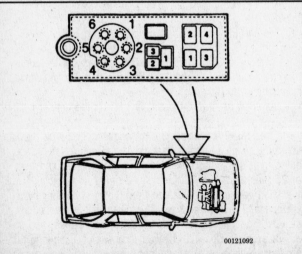

Fig. 60 Test box location for switched jumper — Saab 9000

6. To check for any additional error codes, turn the jumper switch ON.

7. Watch the CHECK ENGINE light carefully. After a short flash, turn the jumper switch OFF.

8. If present, the next error code will now display in the same fashion as the first.

9. If there are no more faults stored or all faults have been remedied, an uninterrupted series of flashes will be displayed.

10. Follow the same procedure until all faults have been identified and corrected.

11. To restart the test procedure (return to the first fault), set the jumper switch to ON.

12. After 2 short flashes, turn the jumper switch OFF. The fault code for the first fault should now be displayed.

13. Proceed with the test from Step 5.

Testing Components and Signals

1. Connect the jumper lead in the same manner as for reading fault codes.

2. Set the jumper switch to ON.

3. Turn the ignition switch **ON** and wait for a short flash of the CHECK ENGINE light.

4. Immediately following the flash, turn the jumper switch OFF.

5. The moment the CHECK ENGINE light begins flashing, the fuel pump should begin running for about 1 second (if it is not faulty). There will be no identification codes sent during this test.

6. To move on to the next test, set the jumper switch to ON.

7. After a short flash, set the jumper switch to OFF. A test code (NOT FAULT CODE) will be displayed and the corresponding component will activate.

8. Continue through the remaining items in the test sequence in the same method — set switch to ON, wait for a short flash, set the switch to OFF:

Components and signals are checked in the following order:

Fuel pump (no code displayed).

Injection valves (1.5 ms-10 Hz).

AIC valve (switches between open and closed positions).

EVAP Canister Purge valve (switches between closed and open) — CHECK ENGINE flashing stops.

EGR valve operates — CHECK ENGINE flashing stops.

Drive signal (changes when shifting from **D** to **N**) — CHECK ENGINE flashing stops.

Air conditioning operates — CHECK ENGINE flashing stops.

Throttle position switch position (changes as accelerator is depressed) — CHECK ENGINE flashing stops.

Throttle position switch W.O.T. position (changes as accelerator is pressed down to the floor) — CHECK ENGINE flashing stops.

Fuel pump operates — CHECK ENGINE flashing stops.

1990-94 Vehicles

With SAAB ISAT Tester

▶ **See Figures 61 and 62**

The Saab ISAT tester is also available to extract fault codes, both constant and intermittent, or to issue command codes.

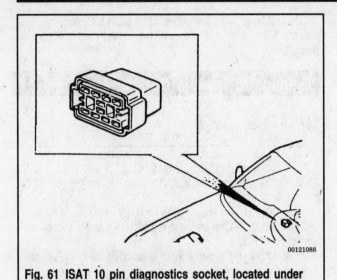

Fig. 61 ISAT 10 pin diagnostics socket, located under RH front seat — Saab

Fig. 62 ISAT tester — Saab

Read codes with the ISAT tester, or equivalent, as follows:

1. Never unplug connector from the ECU or disconnect a battery lead before the fault data stored in the ECU has been transferred to the tester.

2. Connect the diagnostic tester to the diagnostic socket. The diagnosis socket is a black 10-pin connector located under the RH front seat.

3. Turn the ignition to the **ON** position.

4. Press the **No. 1** on the ISAT to identify that you are checking the LH system.

The Trionic system engine fault codes can be read in the same manner, but the Saab adapter # 8611188 must be used with ISAT and current EPROM update.

EZK Ignition Codes

♦ **See Figure 63**

The EZK ignition system is capable of self diagnostics only with the aid of the system tester 8394058, or equivalent. The test should be performed only in the event that a malfunction is suspected or when adjusting ignition timing.

Read fault codes as follows:

1. With the ignition switch **OFF**, connect the tester to the test box on the left-hand side of the engine compartment on the Saab 9000 or to the test socket located forward of the electrical distribution box on the Saab 900.

2. Turn the ignition switch **ON** and start engine. The fault indication LED (green) on the tester should illuminate for about 2 seconds while the starter motor is running.

3. Warm the engine to normal operating temperature, making sure that the engine is briefly run above 2300 rpm at some point during warm-up.

4. Run engine at idling speed and check tester LEDs for flashing. (CHECK ENGINE light will flash at a corresponding rate to any green LED fault indication.) The red LED light indicates spark knocking.

5. The fault code is determined by counting the number of LED flashes.

➡**The EZK ignition fault codes can also be read with the Saab ISAT tester. To pull the ignition codes, follow the procedure for reading LH fuel system codes with ISAT. The EZK codes will be displayed with the fuel system fault codes. The check engine light will illuminate steady if the EZK or fuel system has a fault in memory.**

DI/APC Ignition Codes

The Saab combined Direct Ignition and Automatic Performance Control (DI/APC) system is controlled by the LH fuel injection ECU. The DI/APC system is an adaptive system which compensates for engine wear and other conditions which would adversely affect engine performance. With the aid of the Saab ISAT tester, or equivalent, it is possible to extract fault codes, both constant and intermittent or to issue command codes.

Read codes with the ISAT tester as follows:

1. Never unplug connector from the ECU or disconnect a battery lead before the fault data stored in the ECU has been transferred to the ISAT.

2. The diagnosis socket is a black 10-pin connector located under the RH front seat.

3. Turn the ignition switch to the **ON** position.

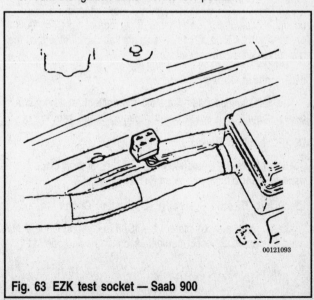

Fig. 63 EZK test socket — Saab 900

4. Press **No. 2** on the ISAT tester to identify the DI/APC system and follow the instructions in the ISAT manual that accompany the tester to read fault codes or issue command codes.

Electronic Throttle Control (ETS) Codes

A Saab ISAT tester must be used to access the fault codes. Make sure to use the correct code chart when diagnosing fault codes, the codes differ for automatic and manual transmissions. Read codes with ISAT tester as follows:

1. Never unplug connector from the ECU or disconnect a battery lead before the fault data stored in the ECU has been transferred to the tester.

2. Connect the diagnostic tester to the diagnostic socket. The diagnosis socket is a black 10-pin diagnostic connector located under the RH front seat.

3. Turn the ignition to the **ON** position.

4. Press the **No. 3** on the ISAT to identify that you are checking the ETS system.

CLEARING CODES

1985-94 Vehicles

With LH System Tester

After completing repairs, reset the tester to the start mode by pressing all 3 control buttons at the same time. If fault codes are still found, disconnect the battery for at least 10 minutes or road test vehicle for 10 minutes or until CHECK ENGINE light extinguishes. The fault code should erase itself after extended operation with the repaired component.

With SAAB ISAT Tester

After repairs are completed, the ISAT command code 900 is used to clear diagnostic memory.

Without System Tester

1. Set the jumper switch to ON.
2. After 3 short flashes, turn the jumper switch OFF.
3. The CHECK ENGINE light will now either flash in a continuous series of long flashes (this represents Code 00000) or display the Code 12444, indicating that the contents of the memory have been erased.

EZK Ignition Codes

The EZK ignition does not store intermittent fault codes. All codes should clear when repair procedures are carried out.

DI/APC Ignition Codes

After repairs are completed, the ISAT command Code 900 is used to clear diagnostic memory.

Electronic Throttle Control (ETS) System Codes

After repairs are completed, the ISAT command Code 900 is used to clear diagnostic memory. A confirmation code '**11111**' will be displayed after the codes have been successfully erased. If this display is not received, repeat the code erasure procedure.

Diagnostic Trouble Codes

1988-94 Flash Codes

Fault codes on 1988-94 vehicles using LH 2.4, 2.4.1 and LH 2.4.2 fuel injected systems may be read without the use of a diagnostic tester.

Code 00000 — No more faults or faults not detected

Code 12111 — Oxygen sensor adaptation fault; air/fuel mixture during idling

Code 12112 — Oxygen sensor adaptation fault; air/fuel mixture with engine running

Code 12113 — Idling control (IAC) adaptation fault; pulse ratio too low

Code 12114 — Idling control (IAC) adaptation fault; pulse ratio too high

Code 12211 — Incorrect battery voltage with engine running (below 10V or over 16V)

Code 12212 — Throttle Position Sensor; faulty idling contacts (grounding when throttle open)

Code 12213 — Throttle Position Sensor; faulty full-throttle contacts (grounding when engine idling)

Code 12214 — Engine Coolant Temperature sensor signal; faulty (signal below -90 degrees or above 160 degrees Centigrade)

Code 12221 — Mass Air Flow (MAF) sensor signal; missing (engine in limp-home mode)

Code 12222 — Idling adjustment (IAC); faulty

Code 12223 — Air/Fuel mixture; lean

Code 12224 — Air/Fuel mixture; rich

Code 12225 — Heated Oxygen sensor; faulty or preheating defective (engine temperature must be 80 degrees Centigrade

Code 12231 — No ignition signal; (always occurs with the engine switched off)

Code 12232 — Memory voltage greater than 1V

Code 12233 — Change made in EPROM (ROM fault 1992 and newer)

Code 12241 — Fuel injector malfunction (1992 and newer)

Code 12242 — Mass Air Flow (MAF) sensor; No filament burn-off (1992 and newer)

Code 12243 — Vehicle Speed Sensor (VSS) signal; missing

Code 12244 — No drive signal to pin 30 in ECM (automatic transmission, 1992 and newer)

Code 12245 — EGR function faulty

Code 12251 — Throttle Position (TP) sensor is faulty (1992 and newer)

Code 12252 — EVAP canister purge valve not working (1992 and newer)

Code 12253 — PRE-Ignition signal lasts more than 20 seconds (1992 and newer)

Code 12254 — Engine RPM signal is missing (1992 and newer)

1985-94 LH-Tester

Fault codes on 1985-94 vehicles using LH 2.2 and LH 2.4 fuel injection systems may be read by using an LH system tester.

Code E001 — No ignition pulse

Code E002 — No signal from Coolant Temperature Sensor (CTS) (LH 2.2) or Throttle Position Sensor (TPS); idling contacts not closing on idling (LH 2.4)

Code E003 — Throttle Position Sensor (TPS); idling contacts not closing on idling (LH 2.2) or Throttle Position Sensor (TPS); full load contacts constantly open (LH 2.4)

Code E004 — Battery voltage to Electronic Control Unit (ECU) memory; missing

Code E005 — Electronic Control Unit (ECU) pin 5 not grounding

Code E006 — Air Mass Meter (AMM) not grounding

Code E007 — No signal from Air Mass Meter (AMM)

Code E008 — Air Mass Meter (AMM); no filament burn-off function

Code E009 — No power to system relay

Code E010 — No signal from Electronic Control Unit (ECU) pin 10 to Automatic Idle Control (AIC) valve

Code E011 — Electronic Control Unit (ECU) pin 11 not grounding

Code E012 — Throttle Position sensor (TPS) — full throttle contacts constantly open

Code E013 — No injection pulse (LH 2.2) or No signal from temperature sensor (LH 2.4)

Code E014 — Air Mass Meter (AMM) — break in CO — adjusting circuit

Code E017 — Fuel pump relay — control circuit faulty (LH 2.2) or break in ground circuit continuity (LH 2.4)

Code E018 — No power at + 15 supply terminal

Code E020 — Faulty signal from Oxygen sensor (LH 2.2) or Fuel pump relay; faulty control circuit (LH 2.4)

Code E021 — System relay; faulty control circuit

Code E023 — No signal from Automatic Idle Control (AIC) valve

Code E024 — No load signal (LH 2.2) or Lambda sensor; faulty signal (LH 2.4)

Code E025 — Electronic Control Unit (ECU) pin 25 not grounding

Code E033 — Signal to Automatic Idle Control (AIC) valve from Electronic Control Unit (ECU); missing

Code E035 — No power at +15 supply terminal

Code E101 — Starter motor revolutions too low

Code E102 — Short in Coolant Temperature Sensor (CTS) circuit (LH 2.2) or Throttle Position Sensor (TPS); idling contacts not opening on increase from idling to 2500 rpm (LH 2.4)

Code E103 — Throttle Position Sensor (TPS); idling contacts not opening on increase from idling to 2500 rpm (LH 2.2) or Throttle Position Sensor (TPS); full load contacts constantly closed (LH 2.4)

Code E107 — Low signal from Air Mass Meter (AMM)

Code E108 — Air Mass Meter (AMM); filament burn-off function constantly actuated

Code E109 — Low voltage from system relay

Code E112 — Throttle Position Sensor (TPS) — full load contacts constantly closed

Code E113 — Erratic or No Injection Pulse

Code E120 — Lambda sensor — signal too low

Code E207 — High signal from Air Mass Meter (AMM)

Code E213 — Continuous pulses to injectors

Code E218 — Continuous pulses from injectors

Code E220 — Lambda sensor — signal too high

Code E320 — DI/APC system Electronic Control Unit (ECU) — pre-ignition signal constantly actuated

Code E328 — Pre-ignition signal constantly grounded

Code AICO — Automatic Idle Control (AIC) valve pulse ratio — faulty

Code GLOU — (Glow) Air Mass Meter (AMM) filament burn-off function operating

Code C1 — Turbo

Code C2 — Turbo with AIC

Code C3 — Turbo with AIC and catalytic converter

Code C4 — Turbo with AIC and Saab DI

Code C5 — Non-Turbo with AIC

Code FPU — Fuel pump relay and system relay operating

Code FUEL — Fuel mode

Code OFF — Starting point for injection valve test

Code FIn — Injection valve open

Code MON — Monitor mode

SUBARU

General Information

Feedback Carburetor

The DFC328 feedback carburetor is a 2 barrel, downdraft type which consists of the following systems:

Float system — Provided with the fuel return system.

Primary side — Which consists of a slow system, main system, accelerating pump system and a choke system.

Secondary side — Which consists of step system and main system.

The primary and secondary side use the same float system. Fuel in the fuel tank is routed through the fuel pump and the needle valve, into the float chamber. Fuel level in the float chamber is maintained constant by the function of the needle and float. Fuel level height is adjusted by adjusting the float seat.

The float system consists of a Float Chamber Ventilation (FCV) system. When the engine is started and the coolant temperature is above 68°F (20°C), the FCV solenoid valve turns on. This allows air from the air filter to flow through the float chamber to the air vent. This ventilates the float chamber.

The choke system consists of a choke valve linked to a bi-metal through a choke lever, so that the choke valve is kept opened at a suitable angle relative to ambient temperature by means of the bi-metal force. When the engine is started, the main vacuum diaphragm is operated by the vacuum sensed in the downstream portion of the secondary throttle valve, so that the choke valve is opened through a vacuum piston and a connecting rod. This allows an appropriate amount of air to be inducted, and the over-choke is prevented.

The auxiliary vacuum diaphragm is also operated by the vacuum, and allows the setting angle of the bi-metal force through a setting piston and a connecting rod. This operation allows the choke valve to be kept open at a moderate position to prevent an over-rich mixture. After the engine is started, the heater warms the bi-metal which adjusts the opening of the choke valve automatically.

A Coasting Fuel Cut (CFC) system is used to activate the anti-dieseling switch on the carburetor during deceleration. This closes the slow system passage for improved fuel economy. The control unit detects deceleration when the following conditions are met:

1. When intake manifold pressure is below -21.65 in. Hg, and the A/C system is **OFF**; or -17.72 in. Hg and the air conditioning system is **ON**

2. When the vehicle is operated at 25 mph

3. Clutch pedal is released

4. When engine reaches 2500 rpm

When the control unit determines that the vehicle is decelerating, current to the anti-dieseling switch is interrupted. This closes the slow system passage so that the fuel flow is shut off. However, when coolant temperature is below 176°F (80°C), the fuel flow will not be shut off.

Single Point Fuel Injection

▶ **See Figure 64**

The SPFI is used on the Loyale 1.8L engine only. The system electronically controls the amount of injection from the fuel injector, and supplies the optimum air/fuel mixture under all operating conditions of the engine. Features of the SPFI system are as follows:

1. Precise control of of the air/fuel mixture is accomplished by an increased number of input signals transmitting engine operating conditions to the control unit.

2. The use of hot wire type air flow meter not only eliminates the need for high altitude compensation, but improves driving performance at high altitudes.

3. The air control valve automatically regulates the idle speed to the set value under all engine operating conditions.

4. Ignition timing is electrically controlled, thereby allowing the use of complicated spark advances characteristics.

5. Wear of the air flow meter and fuel injector is automatically corrected so that they maintain their original performance.

6. Troubleshooting can easily be accomplished by the built-in self-diagnosis function.

Multi-Point Fuel Injection

▶ **See Figure 65**

The MPFI system supplies the optimum air/fuel mixture to the engine under all various operating conditions.

System fuel, which is pressurized at a constant pressure, is injected into the intake air passage of the cylinder head. The amount of fuel injected is controlled by the intermittent injection system where the electro-magnetic injection valve (fuel injector) opens only for a short period of time, depending on the amount of fuel required for 1 cycle of operation. During system operation, the amount of injection is determined by the duration of an electric pulse sent to the fuel injector, which permits precise metering of the fuel.

Each of the operating conditions of the engine are converted into electric signals, resulting in additional features of the system, such as improved adaptability and easier addition of compensating element. The MPFI system also incorporates the following features:

- Reduced emission of exhaust gases
- Reduction in fuel consumption
- Increased engine output
- Superior acceleration and deceleration
- Superior starting and warm-up performance in cold weather since compensation is made for coolant and intake air temperature
- Good performance with turbocharger, if equipped

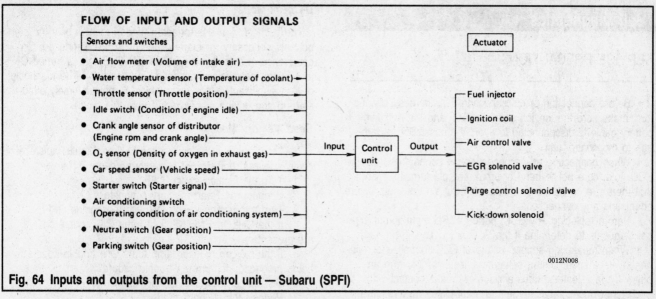

FLOW OF INPUT AND OUTPUT SIGNALS

Sensors and switches

- Air flow meter (Volume of intake air)
- Water temperature sensor (Temperature of coolant)
- Throttle sensor (Throttle position)
- Idle switch (Condition of engine idle)
- Crank angle sensor of distributor
  (Engine rpm and crank angle)
- O_2 sensor (Density of oxygen in exhaust gas)
- Car speed sensor (Vehicle speed)
- Starter switch (Starter signal)
- Air conditioning switch
  (Operating condition of air conditioning system)
- Neutral switch (Gear position)
- Parking switch (Gear position)

Input → **Control unit** → Output

Actuator

- Fuel injector
- Ignition coil
- Air control valve
- EGR solenoid valve
- Purge control solenoid valve
- Kick-down solenoid

0012N008

Fig. 64 Inputs and outputs from the control unit — Subaru (SPFI)

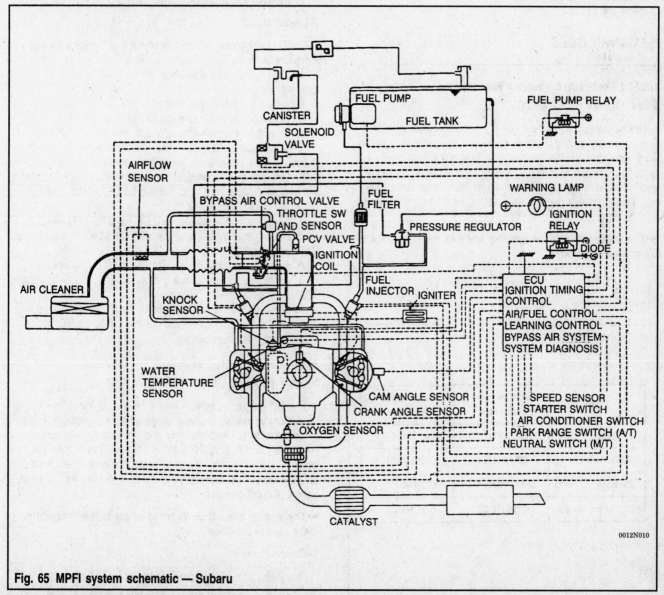

0012N010

Fig. 65 MPFI system schematic — Subaru

Self-Diagnostics

SERVICE PRECAUTIONS

• Before connecting or disconnecting ECU harness connectors, make sure the ignition switch is **OFF** and the negative battery cable is disconnected to avoid the possibility of damage to the control unit.

• When connecting or disconnecting pin connectors from the ECU, take care not to bend or break any pin terminals. Check that there are no bends or breaks on ECU pin terminals before attempting any connections.

• Before replacing any ECU, perform ECU input/output signal diagnosis to determine if the ECU is functioning properly.

• When measuring supply voltage of ECU-controlled components with a circuit tester, separate 1 tester probe from another. If the 2 tester probes accidentally make contact with each other during measurement, a short circuit may result and damage the EC U.

READING CODES

1987-92 Feedback Carburetor Vehicles
▶ See Figures 66, 67 and 68

The self-diagnosis system has 4 modes: U-check mode, Read memory mode, D-check mode and Clear memory mode. Two connectors, Read memory and Test mode, are used. Also, the CHECK ENGINE light is utilized. Connectors are used in various combinations to select the proper test mode and the lamps are used to read codes. No scan tool is necessary to extract codes.

➡ **The engine should be running when in the D-check or clear memory modes.**

Mode	Read memory connector	Test mode connector
U-check	DISCONNECT	DISCONNECT
Read memory	CONNECT	DISCONNECT
D-check	DISCONNECT	CONNECT
(Clear memory)	CONNECT	CONNECT

00121078

Fig. 66 Mode change connectors for different modes

U-Check Mode

The U-check is a user-oriented mode in which only the components necessary for start-up and drive are diagnosed. On occurrence of a fault, the CHECK ENGINE light is turned ON to indicate that system inspection is necessary. The diagnosis of less significant components which do not adversely effect start-up and driving are excluded from this mode.

Read Memory Mode

The Read memory mode is used to detect faults which recently occurred but are not currently present.
1. Turn the ignition switch **OFF**.
2. Connect the Read memory connector.
3. Turn the ignition switch **ON** with the engine **OFF**.
4. If the CHECK ENGINE light turns ON, trouble code(s) are present.
5. If the oxygen monitor lamp turns ON, trouble code(s) are being produced; confirm the trouble code(s).
6. Disconnect the read memory connector.
7. Perform the D-check mode.

D-Check Mode

The D-check mode is used to check the current status of the entire system.
1. Start the engine and warm it to normal operating temperatures.
2. Turn the ignition switch **OFF**.
3. Connect the test mode connector.
4. Turn the ignition switch **ON** with the engine **OFF**.
5. Make sure the CHECK ENGINE light turns ON; there should also be noise from the operation of the fuel pump.
6. Depress the accelerator pedal completely. Return it to 1/2 throttle position and hold it there for 2 seconds, then release the pedal completely.
7. Start the engine: If the CHECK ENGINE light indicates a trouble code, confirm code. If the CHECK ENGINE light turns OFF, continue test.
8. Race the engine briefly with the throttle fully opened.
9. Drive the vehicle above 5 mph, at engine speeds above 1500 rpm, for at least 1 minute.
10. If the CHECK ENGINE light blinks, there are no trouble codes. If the CHECK ENGINE light stays ON, trouble codes are present and must be read.

1987-92 Fuel Injected Vehicles
▶ See Figures 69, 70, 71, 72 and 73

The self-diagnosis system has 4 modes: U-check mode, read memory mode, D-check mode and clear memory mode. Two connectors, Read memory and Test mode, are used. Also, the CHECK ENGINE light is utilized. Connectors are used in various combinations to select the proper test mode and the lamps are used to read codes. No scan tool is necessary to extract codes.

➡ **The engine should be running when in the D-check or clear memory modes.**

U-Check Mode

The U-check is a user-oriented mode in which only the components necessary for start-up and drive are diagnosed. On occurrence of a fault, the CHECK ENGINE light is turned ON

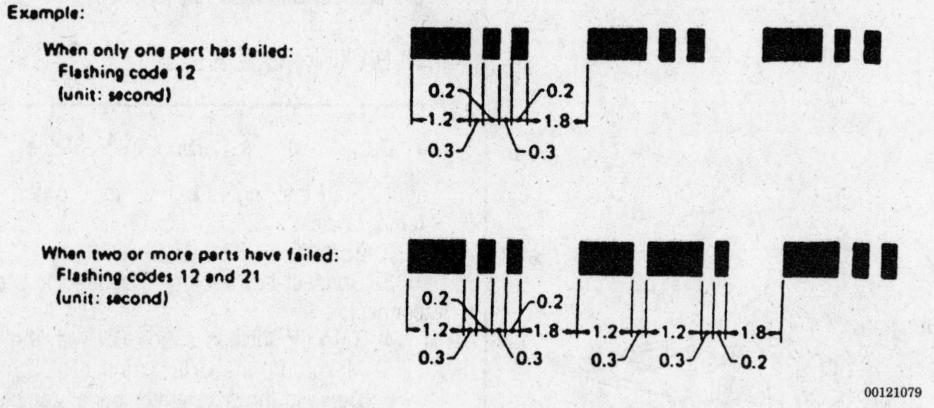

Example:

When only one part has failed:
Flashing code 12
(unit: second)

0.2   0.2
1.2   1.8
0.3   0.3

When two or more parts have failed:
Flashing codes 12 and 21
(unit: second)

0.2   0.2
1.2   1.8   1.2   1.2   1.8
0.3   0.3   0.3   0.3   0.2

00121079

Fig. 67 How to read trouble codes — all models

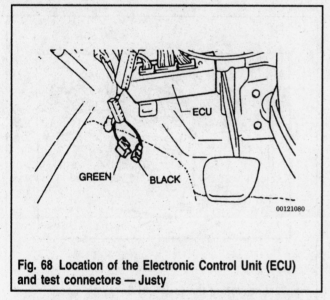

GREEN   BLACK   ECU

00121080

Fig. 68 Location of the Electronic Control Unit (ECU) and test connectors — Justy

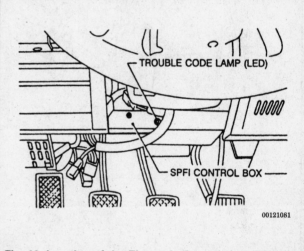

TROUBLE CODE LAMP (LED)

SPFI CONTROL BOX

00121081

Fig. 69 Location of the Electronic Control Unit (ECU) — 1800, Loyale and Legacy

to indicate that system inspection is necessary. The diagnosis of less significant components which do not adversely effect start-up and driving are excluded from this mode.

Read Memory Mode

The Read memory mode is used to detect faults which recently occurred but are not currently present.

1. Turn the ignition switch **OFF**.
2. Connect the Read memory connector.
3. Turn the ignition switch **ON** with the engine **OFF**.
4. If the CHECK ENGINE light turns ON, trouble code(s) are present.
5. If the oxygen monitor lamp turns ON, trouble code(s) are being produced; confirm the trouble code(s).
6. Disconnect the read memory connector.
7. Perform the D-check mode.

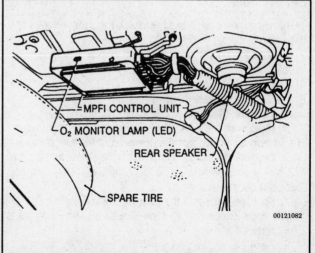

MPFI CONTROL UNIT

O₂ MONITOR LAMP (LED)

REAR SPEAKER

SPARE TIRE

00121082

Fig. 70 Location of the Electronic Control Unit (ECU) — XT

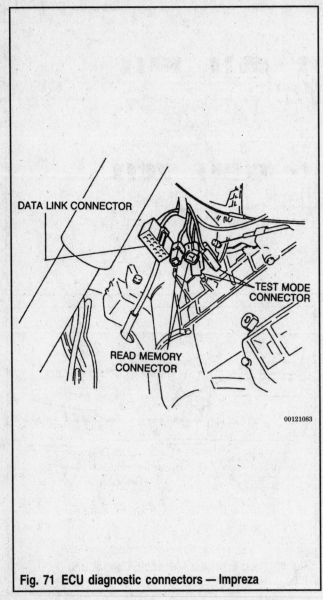

Fig. 71 ECU diagnostic connectors — Impreza

D-Check Mode

The D-check mode is used to check the current status of the entire system.

1. Start the engine and warm it to normal operating temperatures.
2. Turn the ignition switch **OFF**.
3. Connect the test mode connector.
4. Turn the ignition switch **ON** with the engine **OFF**.
5. Make sure the CHECK ENGINE light turns ON; there should also be noise from the operation of the fuel pump.
6. Depress the accelerator pedal completely. Return it to 1/2 throttle position and hold it there for 2 seconds, then release the pedal completely.
7. Start the engine: If the CHECK ENGINE light indicates a trouble code, confirm code. If the CHECK ENGINE light turns OFF, continue test.
8. Race the engine briefly with the throttle fully opened.
9. Drive the vehicle above 5 mph, at engine speeds above 1500 rpm, for at least 1 minute.

10. If the CHECK ENGINE light blinks, there are no trouble codes. If the CHECK ENGINE light stays ON, trouble codes are present and must be read.

CLEARING CODES

1987-92 Feedback Carburetor Vehicles

1. Start the engine and warm it to normal operating temperatures.
2. Turn the ignition switch **OFF**.
3. Connect the test mode connector and the read memory connector.
4. Turn the ignition switch **ON** with the engine OFF.
5. Make sure the CHECK ENGINE light turns ON.
6. Depress the accelerator pedal completely. Return it to 1/2 throttle position and hold it there for 2 seconds, then release the pedal completely.
7. Start the engine; the CHECK ENGINE light should turn OFF.

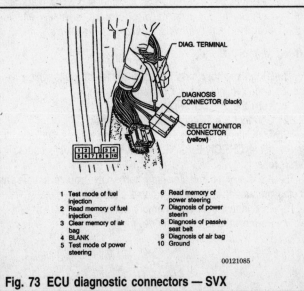

Fig. 72 Location of the ECU — SVX

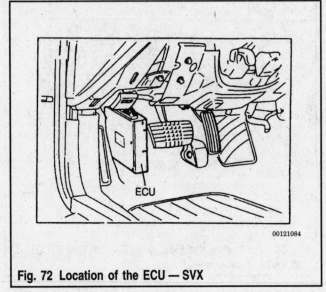

Fig. 73 ECU diagnostic connectors — SVX

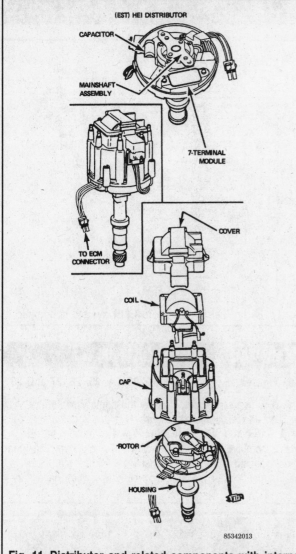

Fig. 11 Distributor and related components with internal ignition coil

Fig. 12 DIS ignition coil pack assembly

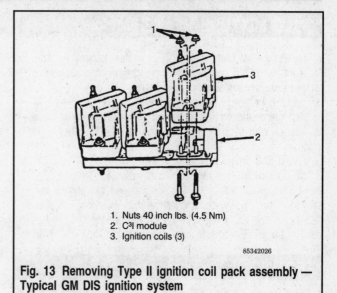

1. Nuts 40 inch lbs. (4.5 Nm)
2. C³I module
3. Ignition coils (3)

Fig. 13 Removing Type II ignition coil pack assembly — Typical GM DIS ignition system

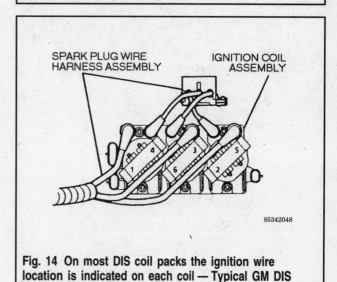

Fig. 14 On most DIS coil packs the ignition wire location is indicated on each coil — Typical GM DIS ignition system shown here

1. Disconnect the negative (-) battery cable.
2. Disconnect the spark plug wires from the coil. Do so by pulling on the boot of the wire while twisting it. You may want to mark a number on each spark plug wire before is disconnecting it from the coil, correct installation is important.
3. Remove the coil mounting screws (2 per coil).
4. Tilt the coil assembly back and disconnect the coil connectors.
5. Remove the coils from the ignition module.
To install:
6. Fit the assembly into position and reconnect the connectors.
7. Install the retaining screws. Torque to specification according to vehicle you are working with.
8. Install the spark plug wires their designated locations as marked during disassembly.
9. Connect the negative battery cable.

COLD MIXTURE HEATER

The Early Fuel Evaporation (EFE) system consists of the (cold mixture) EFE heater, electronic control module, coolant temperature sensor and the EFE relay.

The EFE heater is equipped with a ceramic ring which is located below the primary carburetor bore. The ring is usually an integral part of the carburetor gasket. The EFE heats the incoming air charge to improve atomization. This offers better cold start and drive-away performance.

The coolant temperature sensor is activated when the ignition switch is turned to the **ON** position and the engine is started. If the engine coolant temperature is below the specified value, the ECM will supply current from the battery to the coils in the EFE heater to heat the incoming fuel/air charge.

TESTING

▶ **See Figures 16 and 17**

1. Unplug the wiring connector.
2. Using an ohmmeter, check the resistance between the heater terminals. The resistance is should be around 0.5-2.2Ω. A defective heating element is usually a completely open circuit.
3. With a cold engine (sitting overnight) check for voltage at the EFE connector. If no voltage is present, check the relay or coolant temperature sensor.
4. Reconnect the wiring connector.

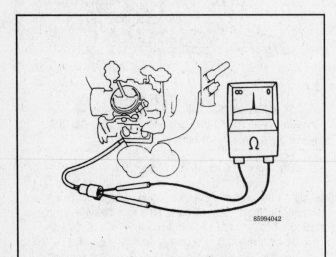

Fig. 16 Checking the resistance of the mixture heater element

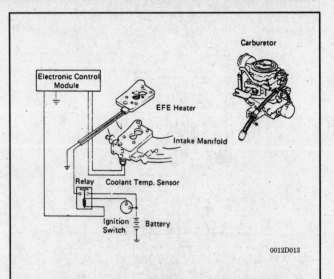

Fig. 17 Early Fuel Evaporation (EFE) system schematic

REMOVAL & INSTALLATION

▶ **See Figures 18, 19, 20, 21, 22, 23, 24, 25, 26, 27 and 28**

The EFE heater is located below the primary carburetor bore. The ring is usually an integral part of the carburetor gasket. The carburetor must be removed to replace the EFE heater assembly. The procedure for removing a carburetor may be very detailed. You should consult a 'Chilton Total Care Care Manual' the for the specific procedures when necessary.

Fig. 18 Remove the air cleaner for access to the carburetor

Fig. 19 Use a back-up wrench when disconnecting fuel lines

Fig. 20 Always tag all the wires and hoses before removing them. This will help during replacement.

Fig. 21 The vacuum modulator line behind the carburetor must also be disconnected, if equipped

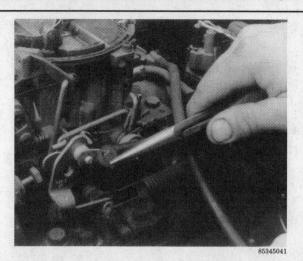

Fig. 22 The accelerator cable retaining clip can be removed using a pair of needle nose pliers

Fig. 23 The return spring and throttle valve cable must also be disconnected from the linkage

Fig. 24 Removing the rear carburetor attaching bolts (Note: a long extension is helpful here)

85345044

Fig. 25 Removing the front carburetor attaching bolts

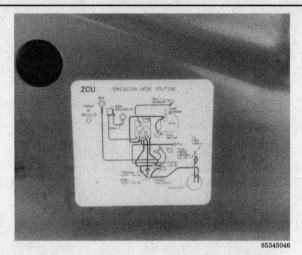

85345046

Fig. 27 The emission hose routing sticker under the hood is helpful when installing the carburetor

85345045

Fig. 26 Always replace this gasket anytime the carburetor is removed

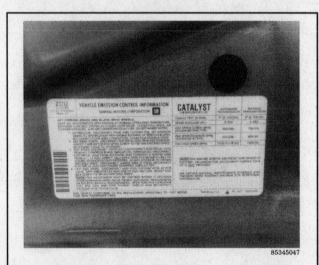

85345047

Fig. 28 The adjustment specifications on the emission control information label must always be followed

COLD START INJECTOR

TESTING

Only a few Multi-Point Fuel Injected (MFI) engines utilize a cold start injector to improve starting ability. The injector only injects fuel for a few minutes and only when the engine is cold. If there is no voltage present at the cold start injector when the engine is cold, the most likely problem is the cold start injector temperature time switch.

1. Check for power to the switch cold start switch with the key ON.
2. With the engine cold you should have power to the injector.
3. Start the engine, you should be able to hear or feel the injector clicking. The injector will should shut off as the engine warms up, or after a minute or two.

REMOVAL & INSTALLATION

1. Relieve the fuel system pressure.
2. With the ignition OFF, unplug the electrical connector to the injector.
3. Using the proper sized wrench, carefully unscrew the injector. Some injectors are held in with clips.

To install:

4. Always use a new O-ring when you replace an injector.
5. Plug the electrical connector.
6. Turn ignition ON with engine COLD and check for proper operation and fuel leaks.

COLD START INJECTOR TIME SWITCH

TESTING

▶ **See Figure 29**

Only a few Multi-Point Fuel Injected (MFI) engines utilize a cold start injector to improve starting ability. This switch controls the length of time the injector will stay on depending on engine temperature. The injector only injects fuel for a few minutes and only when the engine is cold. If there is no voltage present at the cold start injector when the engine is cold, the most likely problem is the cold start injector temperature time switch.

1. Check for power to the switch with the key ON.
2. With the engine cold you should have power on both sides of the switch, if not the switch is probably defective.
3. The switch should shut the power off as the engine warms up, or after a minute or two.
4. The resistance of some switches can also be tested. The switch may function but either too long or not long enough. This test will vary on different engines.

   a. Terminals **STA** and **STJ** — approximately 20-40Ω below 86°F (30°C) or approximately 40-60Ω when above 104°F (40°C)

   b. Terminal **STA** and ground — approximately 20-80Ω

5. If the resistance is not as specified, the switch is probably bad.

REMOVAL & INSTALLATION

➡**Perform this procedure only on a cold engine.**

1. Drain the cooling system as necessary.
2. With the ignition OFF, unplug the electrical connector to the switch.
3. Using the proper sized wrench, carefully unscrew the switch from the engine.

To install:

4. Coat the threads of the switch with a sealant and install it.
5. Plug the electrical connector into the switch.
6. Refill the coolant to the proper level. Road test the vehicle for proper operation.

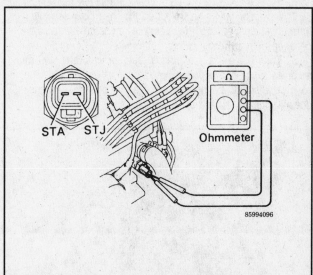

Fig. 29 Testing the cold start injector time switch

COOLANT TEMPERATURE SENSOR

TESTING

▶ **See Figures 30, 31 and 32**

The Coolant Temperature Sensor's (CTS) function is to advise the ECM of changes in engine temperature by monitoring the changes in coolant temperature. The sensor must be handled carefully during removal. It can be damaged (thereby affecting engine performance) by impact.

The chart shown is a good guideline of what most coolant temperature sensor resistances will be. Specific resistance ranges may vary from engine to engine.

The following procedure is a basic guideline on how coolant temperature sensors can be checked. The CTS is a sensor that communicates information to the ECM, therefore there are more extensive diagnostics involved with his circuit. Always consult your 'Chilton Total Car Care' manual for additional information.

1. To test the sensor in the vehicle, with a cold engine, unplug the electrical connector from the sensor.

2. Using an ohmmeter, measure the resistance between both terminals. Refer to the chart for an example resistance reading.

3. Reconnect the sensor, then run the engine until it reaches normal operating temperature.

4. Unplug the electrical connector from the sensor again.

5. Using an ohmmeter, measure the resistance between both terminals. Resistance values should change with temperature. Again, you can refer to the chart for examples of the resistance reading at different temperatures.

6. If the resistance does not change, replace the sensor.

7. A sensor may also be tested that has been removed from an engine. At room temperature, measure the resistance between both terminals with an ohmmeter.

8. Then place the sensor in a glass of ice water and measure the resistance between both terminals as it cools. The resistance should change smoothly as it cools. If resistance doesn't change replace the sensor.

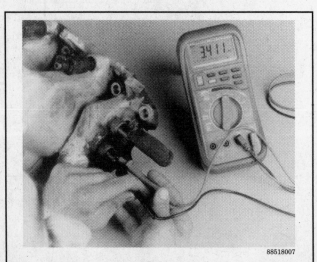

Fig. 30 Measure the resistance between both terminals to test the coolant temperature sensor

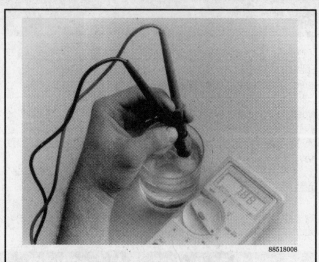

Fig. 31 Testing the coolant temperature sensor in ice water. Resistance values change with temperature.

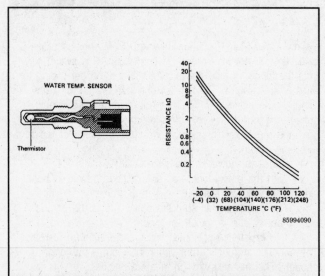

Fig. 32 Coolant temperature sensor resistance chart

REMOVAL & INSTALLATION

▶ **See Figures 33 and 34**

The following procedure is a general procedure. This procedure should be performed on a cold engine.

The sensor must be handled carefully during removal. It can be damaged (thereby affecting engine performance) by impact. The sensor may be located on the intake manifold, on the thermostat housing, on the cylinder head or threaded into the radiator depending on the vehicle you are working with. It is important not to confuse the coolant temperature sensor with the coolant temperature switch. See 'Water temperature Switch' in this section for information concerning the coolant temperature switch. Always consult your 'Chilton Total Car

Care' manual for the specific location on the vehicle you are working with.

> **✳✳CAUTION**
>
> Perform this procedure only on a cold engine. Attempting to remove any component that involves working with engine coolant can result in serious burns.

1. Drain the cooling system part way down.
2. With the ignition OFF, unplug the electrical connector to the sensor.
3. Using the proper sized wrench, carefully unscrew the sensor from the engine coolant passage.

To install:

4. Coat the threads of the sensor with a sealant. Install the sensor.
5. Plug the electrical connector into the sensor.
6. Refill the coolant to the proper level. Road test the vehicle for proper operation and check for leaks.

> **✳✳CAUTION**
>
> When draining the coolant, keep in mind that cats and dogs are attracted by the ethylene glycol antifreeze, and are quite likely to drink any that is left in an uncovered container or in puddles on the ground. This will prove fatal in sufficient quantity. Always drain the coolant into a sealable container. Coolant should be reused unless it is contaminated or several years old.

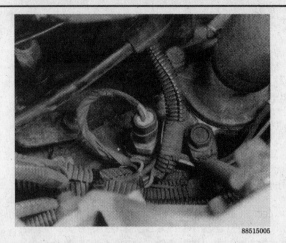

Fig. 33 The coolant temperature sensor is located in a coolant passage, shown here near the thermostat housing

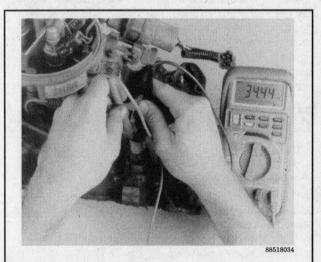

Fig. 34 Example of testing the coolant temperature sensor on a Ford intake manifold

CRANKSHAFT SENSOR

The crankshaft sensor generates a signal to the ignition module, which results in a reference pulse being sent to the ECM. The ECM uses this signal to calculate crankshaft position and engine speed for injector operation.

Essentially there are 2 types of crankshaft sensors. One is a Hall Effect switch and the other is a Magnetic Reluctance sensor. The easiest way to distinguished the switch designs is the Magnetic sensor is a 2 wire sensor and the Hall Effect switch will have a three wire harness.

There is also a Dual Crankshaft sensor or Combination sensor. This design combines 2 sensors together and is normally mounted on a pedestal on the front of the engine, near the harmonic balancer. This type crankshaft sensor is usually a Hall Effect switch. These type sensors usually requires adjustment during replacement.

Magnetic Reluctance type crank sensors are usually mounted on the side of the engine, protruding into the block.

RPM sensors may also be a part of the distributor unit. Replacement of the this type usually requires removing the distributor. However, if a distributor located sensor malfunctions, on some vehicles, the entire distributor unit must be replaced. For more information on Hall switches and Magnetic sensors, see 'Hall Effect Switch and Magnetic Reluctance sensor' in this section.

TESTING

Testing for each type crankshaft sensor is covered briefly under 'Hall Effect Switch' or 'Magnetic Reluctance Sensor' in this section. However, the procedure given is a general procedure and may not apply to the specific vehicle you are working with. If the fuel injectors are spraying fuel, then the crankshaft sensor is working.

When suspecting a crankshaft sensor problem, first perform a visual inspection, most problems can be found in wiring harnesses and connectors.

When diagnosing a suspected faulty crankshaft sensor, remember that a defective ECM or ignition module could also be related. Because of the relationship of these components, proper diagnosing should be accomplished by following the appropriate diagnostic chart(s) found in a 'Chilton Total Car Care' or factory service manual.

REMOVAL & INSTALLATION

MAGNETIC RELUCTANCE SENSOR

▶ See Figures 35 and 38

The following procedure is a example for Magnetic Reluctance type crankshaft sensor. The procedure given here is for a GM MFI 2.3L engine. This particular crankshaft sensor is located on side of the engine, protruding into the block.

On some manufacturers the crankshaft sensor requires an air gap adjustment. In this application no adjustment is required. For more specific information on the vehicle you are

working with, please consult a 'Chilton Total Car Care' or factory service manual.

1. Disconnect the negative battery cable.
2. Disengage the sensor harness connector.
3. Remove the sensor-to-block retaining bolt.
4. Remove the sensor from the engine block.

To install:

5. If equipped, inspect the sensor O-ring for wear, cracks or leakage and replace, if necessary.
6. Lightly coat the O-ring with clean engine oil, then install the sensor to the engine block.
7. Install the sensor-to-block retaining bolt.
8. Engage the sensor wiring harness.
9. Connect the negative battery cable.

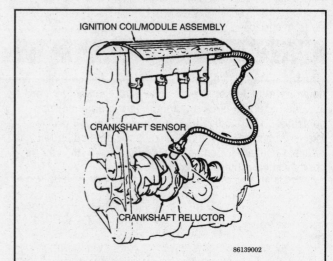

Fig. 35 Reluctance type crankshaft sensor — GM 2.3L MFI engine shown

HALL EFFECT SWITCH

▶ See Figures 36 and 37

The following procedure is a example of a Hall Effect switch type crankshaft sensor. The procedure given here is for a GM MFI 3.3L engine. This particular crankshaft sensor is located on a pedestal on the front of the engine near the harmonic balancer.

1. Disconnect the negative battery cable.
2. Remove the serpentine belt from the crankshaft pulley.
3. Raise and support the vehicle safely.
4. Remove the right front tire and wheel assembly.
5. Remove the right inner fender access cover.
6. Using a correctly sized socket, remove the crankshaft harmonic balancer retaining bolt.
7. Remove the harmonic balancer. Remove crankshaft sensor/pedestal assembly from the engine.
8. Remove the sensor from the pedestal.

To install:

9. Loosely install the crankshaft sensor on the pedestal. Position the sensor/pedestal assembly on the special crankshaft sensor adjustment tool.

10. Position the special tool and pedestal assembly on the block. Install the retaining screws. Torque the mounting screws to specifications.

11. Torque the pedestal pinch bolt to the required torque according to specifications and remove the tool. The special tool will help place the sensor in the correct position.

12. Install the balancer onto the crankshaft and torque the bolt to specifications.

13. Install the inner fender shield. Install the tire and wheel assembly. Lower the vehicle and install the serpentine belt.

14. Connect the negative battery cable.

88515001

Fig. 36 Typical Dual crankshaft sensor/pedestal — GM Hall Effect type sensor

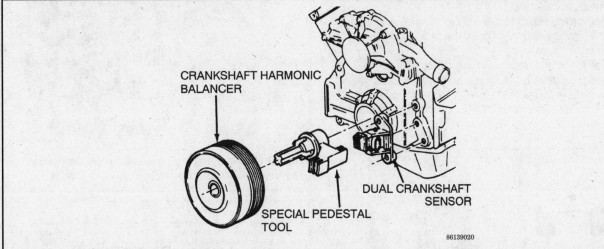

CRANKSHAFT HARMONIC BALANCER

SPECIAL PEDESTAL TOOL

DUAL CRANKSHAFT SENSOR

86139020

Fig. 37 Dual crankshaft sensor and special tool used to adjust the sensor — Hall effect type sensor — GM 3.3L MFI engine shown

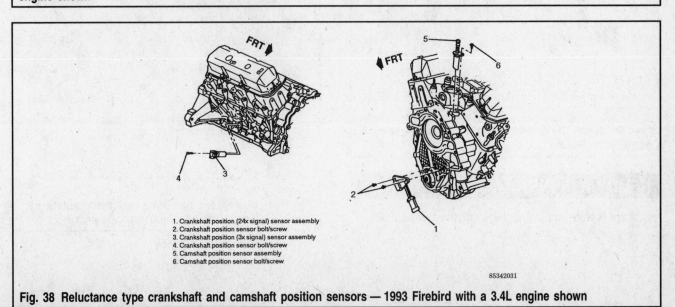

FRT

FRT

1. Crankshaft position (24x signal) sensor assembly
2. Crankshaft position sensor bolt/screw
3. Crankshaft position (3x signal) sensor assembly
4. Crankshaft position sensor bolt/screw
5. Camshaft position sensor assembly
6. Camshaft position sensor bolt/screw

85342031

Fig. 38 Reluctance type crankshaft and camshaft position sensors — 1993 Firebird with a 3.4L engine shown

DISTRIBUTOR CAPS AND ROTORS

TESTING

▶ **See Figures 39, 40 and 41**

Inspect the distributor cap for cracks, wear or damage.

Damaged or worn out distributor caps and rotors can cause a variety of problems such as hard starting, hesitation, lack of power, rough idle, high emissions and poor fuel economy. A good visual inspection is usually all that is required for distributor caps. Always look for the obvious: corrosion build up in the high tension wire terminals, cracks, worn tips under the cap and rotor contacts.

1. Remove the cap. You might have to to unclip or detach some or all of the plug wires to remove the cap. If so, number the wires and the cap before removal.

2. Clean the cap inside and out with a clean rag.

3. Check for carbon paths. A carbon path shows up as a dark powdery trail, usually from one of the cap sockets or inside terminals to a ground.

4. Check for any fine cracks in the cap or rotor. A crack may allow moisture to enter and could cause voltage to arc around the inside of the cap.

5. Check for eroded terminals in the cap or rotor.

6. Check the carbon button in the top center of the distributor cap for damage or wear.

7. If any of the above conditions exist, replace the distributor cap and rotor.

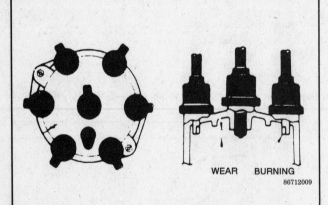

Fig. 39 Inspect the distributor cap for cracks, wear or corrosion build-up

REMOVAL & INSTALLATION

➡ **Always replace the distributor cap and rotor as a set.**

1. Replace the wires one at a time or number the wires and the cap before removal.

2. Most caps are held in place with either spring loaded retaining screws, which have to be pushed down and turned half way to unhook under the distributor, retaining clips which have to be released or retaining screws, which have to be loosened.

3. Depending on the engine, the rotor can either be pulled directly off the shaft or removed by loosening the retaining screw(s). If the rotor is retained with screws, back them out all the way and lift them off with the rotor.

Fig. 40 Mark the spark plug wires on the distributor cap before disconnecting — Typical Ford 6 cylinder engine shown

Fig. 41 Removing the distributor cap, held in place by screws — Typical Ford 6 cylinder engine shown

DISTRIBUTOR PICK-UP COILS

The Distributor pick-up coil is better known as a magnetic pick-coil assembly. There are different designs. On some designs the pick-up contains a permanent magnet, a pole piece with internal teeth and a pick-up coil. A rotating timer core is used with this type. On others, it contains a permanent magnet and a single tooth pick-up coil. A reluctor or armature is used with this type. Some use a photo cell, LED and wheel with slits to provide an rpm signal.

We will discuss the more common magnetic pick-up coil design. When the teeth of the rotating timer core and pole piece align or the reluctor and the single tooth of the pick-up, an induced voltage in the pick-up coil signals the electronic module to open the coil primary circuit. As the primary current decreases, a high voltage is induced in the secondary winding of the ignition coil, directing a spark through the rotor, which in turn fires the spark plugs. The pick-up coil is located inside the ignition distributor.

TESTING

▶ See Figures 42, 43 and 44

➡ Inexpensive ignition module and sensor testers may be available at a local auto parts store for rent or purchase. These special testers are extremely helpful and efficient.

The resistance values given are an average value and may not apply to every vehicle. For specifics, be sure to consult your 'Chilton Total Car Care' manual for the vehicle you are working with. Before you begin, if you have spark, the pick-up assembly isn't the problem.

1. To test the pickup coil, first disconnect pickup coil electrical leads from the module. Set the ohmmeter on the high scale. Connect one lead of the ohmmeter to ground and probe each lead of the pickup coil connector. Any resistance measurement less than infinity requires replacement of the pickup coil.

2. Pickup coil continuity is tested using an ohmmeter (on low range) between the pickup coil connector leads. Normal resistance is 500-1,500Ω. If a vacuum unit is used, move the vacuum advance arm while performing this test. This will detect any break in coil continuity. Such a condition can cause intermittent misfiring. Replace the pickup coil if the reading is outside the specified limits.

3. If no defects have been found at this time, and you still have a problem, then the module will have to be checked. If you do not have access to a module tester, the only possible alternative is a substitution test. If the module fails the substitution test, replace it.

The procedures shown in these diagrams is a general procedure. They apply to typical GM pick-up coils. If your vehicle is a different design it is advisable to obtain a specific 'Chilton Total Car Care' manual for your vehicle.

REMOVAL & INSTALLATION

▶ See Figures 45, 46 and 48

The procedure given below is a general procedure. Procedures differ according to manufacturer. For specific information on the vehicle you are working with, consult your 'Chilton Total Car Care' manual.

1. Disconnect the negative battery cable.
2. Remove the distributor assembly. Prior to removing the distributor, be sure to mark the distributor rotor and housing for installation purposes.
3. Support the distributor assembly in a soft jaw vise. Be careful not to clamp it too tight.
4. Some distributors will require driving the roll pin from the gear and removing the shaft assembly from the distributor housing. On other distributors, the shaft will not have to be removed, but it will be necessary to remove the reluctor or pole piece.
5. Remove the reluctor by carefully prying evenly on both sides of it and sliding it off of the shaft.
6. To remove the pick-up coil, remove the retainer and shield, if applicable.

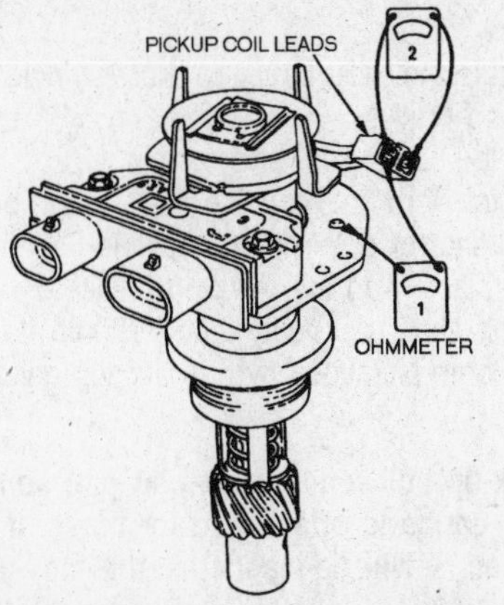

Fig. 42 Testing Pickup coil — Test 1 should read infinite at all times. Test 2 should read a steady value of 500-1500 ohms.

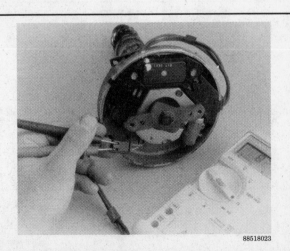

Fig. 43 Measure the resistance between both terminals of the pick-up coil's connector with an ohmmeter set to the low range

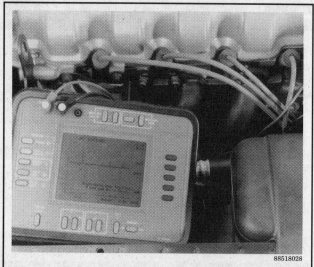
Fig. 44 Testing the ignition system using a oscilloscope

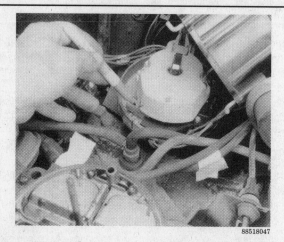
Fig. 45 Prior to removing the distributor from the engine, be sure to mark the rotor and housing for installation purposes — Typical GM HEI ignition shown

Fig. 46 Removing the distributor clamp and bolt — Typical GM ignition

Fig. 47 Removing the distributor from the engine — Typical GM HEI ignition shown

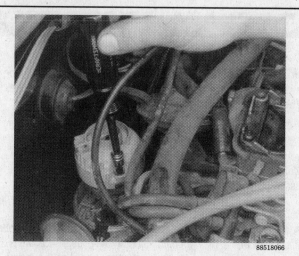
Fig. 48 Removing the distributor rotor — Ford 6 cylinder engine

7. Lift the pick-up coil assembly straight up to remove from the distributor.

To install:

8. Assemble the pick-up coil to the distributor housing. Install shield and retainer, if applicable.

9. Install the shaft, gear and roll pin.

10. On distributors not requiring the shaft to be removed, install the reluctor or pole piece, it should have a roll pin that secures it in place. Tap the roll pin in place.

11. Spin the shaft and verify that the teeth do not touch the pole piece. Some pick-ups have an air gap adjustment. Adjust the air gap.

➡️If the pick-up coil requires and air gap adjustment, a brass feeler gauge is often used for these. If a steel feeler gauge is used, it will de-magnetize the pick-up unit.

12. Install the distributor into the engine according to the installation marks on the rotor and housing.

13. Reconnect the negative battery cable.

ELECTRONIC IDLE SPEED CONTROL SOLENOID

The Electronic Idle Speed Control Solenoid (ICS) may be called different names depending on the manufacturer. It is referred as a Idle Speed Stepper Motor or an Automatic Idle Speed (AIS) Motor etc. In any event, they all perform the same purpose. Earlier solenoids were called Anti-dieseling solenoids or Idle Stop Solenoids. These earlier devices usually functioned whenever current was supplied to them as soon as the ignition switch was turn **ON** or when the air conditioning compressor was engaged. The Electronic Idle Speed Control Solenoid is controlled by the engine computer.

The Idle Speed Control Solenoid function is somewhat self explanatory. It controls engine idle. The electronic idle solenoid is controlled by the PCM. The PCM has a specific idle specification programed in memory. It determines the idle speed by calculating various information bits from engine sensors. It is also aware when the throttle stop is contacting the idle solenoid and when it is not.

By having this information, the PCM is able to the adjust idle solenoid plunger to position the throttle for precise idle rpm conditions. If, for example, the air conditioning is switched **ON**, the extra load from the compressor slows the idle down, the PCM therefore adjusts the idle solenoid to compensate for the added engine load and maintain proper idle speed.

TESTING

▶ See Figure 49

Since this device is controlled by the PCM, complete testing, inspection and checks of the engine control system may be necessary. However, you can make a couple of basic checks to see if the idle speed control solenoid is working.

1. Remove the air cleaner to gain access to the solenoid.
2. Inspect the electrical connector at the idle speed control solenoid. Make sure the connection is clean and making good contact.
3. You will need a tachometer and idle specifications. Connect the tachometer and start the engine.
4. Allow the engine to warm up and allow the fast idle to drop down. Observe the rpm reading at idle.
5. Turn the air conditioning **ON**, the tachometer may respond to the load change but the rpm should remain stable. If the vehicle is not equipped with air conditioning or it is not working, proceed to the next step.
6. Turn the steering from side-to-side or turn the headlights **ON**, the idle should still remain stable.
7. If the vehicle is equipped with automatic transmission, apply the parking brake on, apply the service brake pedal as you place the vehicle in drive position. Make sure no one is standing in front of the vehicle during this test. The tachometer may slightly change but the rpm should remain stable.

8. If the engine idle rpm drops considerably or the engine stalls, further testing of the engine control system is required.

If the Idle Speed Control Solenoid is suspected, shut the engine **OFF**. Further testing of the solenoid will require a wiring chart to identify the proper terminals to test. When battery voltage is applied to the correct terminals the idle solenoid plunger will move out, when the alternated terminals are connected the plunger will move in.

➡ **Do not apply battery voltage to any terminal unless you are sure it is the correct terminal to receive current. Otherwise you could burn out or short the component out. For specific checks and specifications on this device, consult your 'Chilton Total Car Care' manual.**

REMOVAL & INSTALLATION

▶ See Figures 50, 51 and 52

Removal and installation of this device is pretty simple. Here is a general procedure that can be used for most vehicles.

1. Disconnect the negative battery cable.
2. Remove the air cleaner.
3. Disconnect the electrical connector at the ICS.
4. Remove the ICS bracket retaining screws and remove the ICS.

To install:

5. Install the ICS in position and secure it with the mounting screws.
6. Connect the electrical connector.
7. Connect the negative battery cable.
8. Start the engine and test ICS operation.
9. Install the air cleaner.

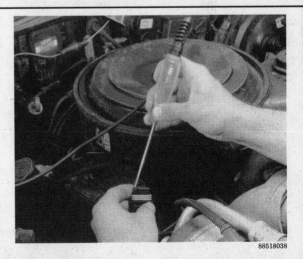

88518038

Fig. 49 Testing for voltage at the idle speed control valve solenoid — Chevrolet 4.3L TBI engine

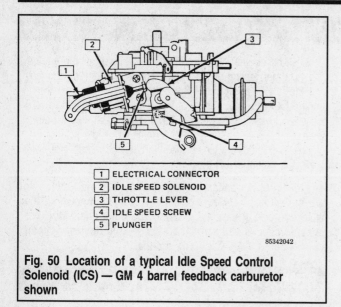

1 ELECTRICAL CONNECTOR
2 IDLE SPEED SOLENOID
3 THROTTLE LEVER
4 IDLE SPEED SCREW
5 PLUNGER

85342042

Fig. 50 Location of a typical Idle Speed Control Solenoid (ICS) — GM 4 barrel feedback carburetor shown

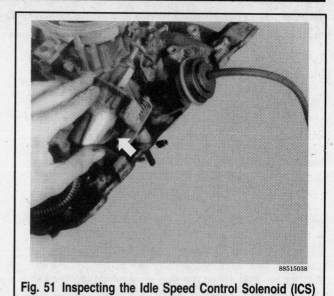

88515038

Fig. 51 Inspecting the Idle Speed Control Solenoid (ICS)

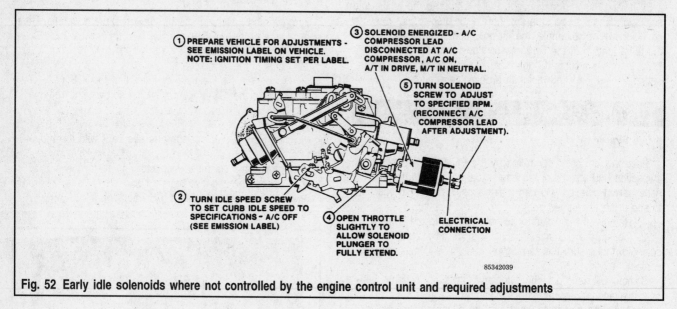

① PREPARE VEHICLE FOR ADJUSTMENTS - SEE EMISSION LABEL ON VEHICLE. NOTE: IGNITION TIMING SET PER LABEL.

③ SOLENOID ENERGIZED - A/C COMPRESSOR LEAD DISCONNECTED AT A/C COMPRESSOR, A/C ON, A/T IN DRIVE, M/T IN NEUTRAL.

⑤ TURN SOLENOID SCREW TO ADJUST TO SPECIFIED RPM. (RECONNECT A/C COMPRESSOR LEAD AFTER ADJUSTMENT).

② TURN IDLE SPEED SCREW TO SET CURB IDLE SPEED TO SPECIFICATIONS - A/C OFF (SEE EMISSION LABEL)

④ OPEN THROTTLE SLIGHTLY TO ALLOW SOLENOID PLUNGER TO FULLY EXTEND.

ELECTRICAL CONNECTION

85342039

Fig. 52 Early idle solenoids where not controlled by the engine control unit and required adjustments

ELECTRONIC IGNITION MODULE

The ignition module fires the ignition coil after the magnetic pick-coil submits an electrical pulse or signal to it. The ignition module interrupts the ignition primary circuit, thus causing the ignition coil to provide spark. This ignition module turns the ignition coil on and off, like the points used to do on older cars. The ignition module turns off the primary circuit to the coil which begins the induction of the magnetic lines of force from the primary side of the coil into the secondary side of the coil. This induction provides spark to the spark plugs. It has assumed the job of the conventional ignition points.

The advantages of the this system are that the transistors in the control unit can make and break the primary ignition circuit much faster than ignition points can, and higher primary voltage can be utilized, since this system is designed to handle higher voltage without adverse effects. On the earlier systems, the ignition module also governs the ignition dwell. On later systems the PCM controls the dwell.

TESTING

Due to the many different styles and configurations of ignition modules, there is no one easy test which will work universally. However, there are several steps you can take to determine if the ignition module is probably defective.

The first check that should be made is for spark at the spark plug wire. This can be done using a spark tester. A spark tester looks like a regular spark plug with a ground clip attached to one side. It allows the ignition system to be checked for spark without damaging the electronics. If the engine is getting spark, the ignition module is probably functioning correctly.

➡Testing the ignition system for spark without the use of a spark tester can damage the ignition module.

If the engine is not getting spark, check the ignition coil, ignition trigger (usually a magnetic reluctance or Hall effect switch) and all associated wiring.

If all other components are functioning properly, the ignition module is probably defective. As a final test, an ignition module tester may be used to check the module circuitry. These testers can be borrowed, rented or purchased at a reasonable price from automotive stores.

A simple test you can do at home involves the use of a test light or logic probe.

1. Locate the ignition coil in the engine compartment. On some ignition systems the coil is located inside the distributor cap.
2. Connect a test light or logic probe between the negative side of the coil and ground. Refer to your 'Chilton Total Car Care' manual for correct wire color and terminal location.
3. Crank the engine using the starter.

✳✳CAUTION

Exercise extreme caution when cranking the engine as it may start.

4. As the engine cranks the test light or logic probe bulb should flicker. This indicates the module is triggering the coil to fire.

If the light does not flicker, chances are the module is at fault.

➡Inexpensive ignition module and sensor testers may be available at a local auto parts store for rent or purchase. These special testers are extremely helpful and efficient.

REMOVAL & INSTALLATION

Removal and installation may vary from manufacturer to manufacturer. Some ignition modules are mounted in the engine compartment on the firewall, inner fender panel, but never on the engine. Others are mounted either in the ignition distributor or on the side of the distributor. Consult your 'Chilton Total Car Care' manual for the specific procedure for the vehicle you are working with. The following procedures are examples of the different types.

EXTERNALLY MOUNTED MODULE

1. Disconnect negative battery cable.
2. Disconnect the harness or harness connectors from the module.
3. Remove the mounting bolts from the module and remove the module.
   To install:
4. Install the module on the mounting surface and install the mounting bolts. Use special dielectric grease between module and housing assembly.
5. Prior to connecting the harness connectors, apply a coating of dielectric grease to the connections. Connect the electrical harnesses to the module.
6. Connect the negative battery cable.

INTERNALLY MOUNTED MODULE

▶ **See Figures 53, 54, 55 and 56**

1. Disconnect negative battery cable.
2. Remove the distributor cap. If the distributor is in a difficult location, it may be necessary to remove it from the engine. On most vehicles, you will be able to perform this job without removing the distributor.
3. Remove the ignition rotor.
4. Remove the mounting screws holding the module in place.
5. Carefully disconnect the electrical connectors at each end of the module and remove the module.
6. Clean the mounting surface of any residue of grease or dirt.
7. Inspect the connectors for signs of deterioration or cracks.

To install:

8. Prior to installing the new module, coat the module mounting surface with a special dielectric grease. Do not attempt to use any other type of grease that is not specified for this purpose.

9. Connect electrical connectors to both ends of the module and place the module in place. Install the retaining screws.

10. Install the distributor if it required removal.

11. Install the distributor rotor and cap.

12. Connect the negative battery cable.

SIDE MOUNTED MODULE

1. Disconnect negative battery cable.

2. Most modules can be removed from the distributor without it having to be removed from the engine.

3. Usually this modules are attached with a torx type screw. You will need to acquire this tool to perform the job. Don't try and use an incorrect tool or you'll damage the screw head.

4. Remove the special screws from the module.

5. Very carefully remove the module by pulling it down and away from the side of the distributor.

To install:

6. Prior to installing the module apply a coating of dielectric grease on the module terminals.

7. Carefully slide the module terminals into the harness of the distributor. Be careful not to bend these terminals.

8. When the module is properly in place, install the special mounting screws.

9. If it was necessary to remove the distributor, install it.

10. Connect the negative battery cable.

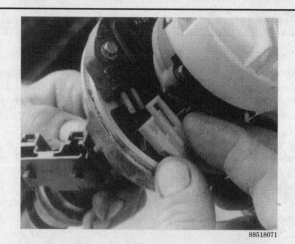

Fig. 54 Carefully disconnect the electrical connectors from the module — GM internally mounted module shown

Fig. 55 Removing the ignition module retaining screws — GM internally mounted module shown

Fig. 53 Apply a coating of the appropriate type of insulation grease prior to installing it. This keeps the module from overheating

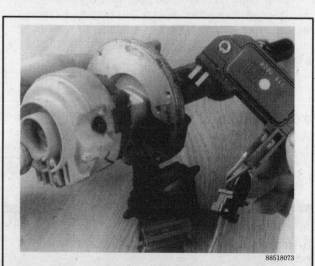

Fig. 56 Remove the ignition module from the distributor — GM internally mounted module shown

EGR VACUUM SWITCHING VALVE

TESTING

▶ **See Figures 57, 58, 59, 60 and 61**

Despite the impressive name, the Exhaust Gas Recircutation Vacuum Switching Valve (EGR-VSV) valve does nothing more than allow vacuum to flow through the system depending on engine coolant temperature. The bi-metallic element within the switch reacts to temperature changes, opening or closing the valve at a pre-determined level. To test the valve:

1. Drain the coolant from the radiator into a suitable container.

✳✳CAUTION

When draining the coolant, keep in mind that cats and dogs are attracted by the ethylene glycol antifreeze, and are quite likely to drink any that is left in an uncovered container or in puddles on the ground. This will prove fatal in sufficient quantity. Always drain the coolant into a sealable container. Coolant should be reused unless it is contaminated or several years old.

2. Label and disconnect the hoses from the VSV.
3. Remove the valve.
4. Using cool water, cool the threaded part of the valve to below 104°F (40°C).
   a. M/T — check that air flows from port M to ports L and N.
   b. A/T — check that air flows through the ports

➡ **The port letter identification is used for illustration only, there are many different designs of vacuum valves. Some vacuum valves will have 2 ports others may have 3 or more ports. The vehicle you are working with may have different port identification letters. Use this as an example, for the specifics on the vehicle you are working with consult your 'Chilton Total Car Care' manual.**

5. Using warm water, heat the threaded part of the valve to above 129°F (54°C) and blow into the ports again. The valve should not allow air to flow.
6. Apply liquid sealer to the threads of the VSV and reinstall it. Connect the vacuum lines.

7. Refill the radiator with coolant.

➡ **The underhood Vehicle Emission Label may help determine which lines should have vacuum. The most common problem is incorrect routing of vacuum lines or broken vacuum lines.**

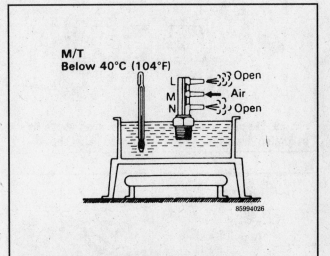

Fig. 57 Example of the VSV air flow when below its calibrated temperature — typical 3 hose valve shown

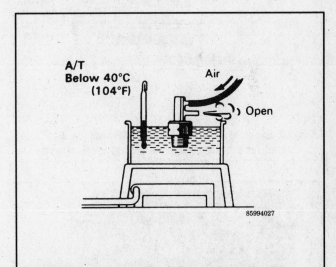

Fig. 58 Example of a VSV air flow when below its calibrated temperature — typical 2 hose valve shown

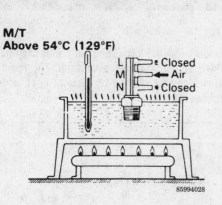

Fig. 59 Example of a the VSV air flow when above its calibrated temperature — typical 3 hose valve shown

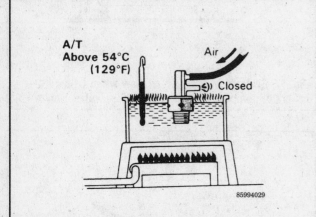

Fig. 60 Example of a VSV air flow when above its calibrated temperature — typical 2 hose valve shown

Fig. 61 Here is a good view of a VSV (left side) and a coolant temperature sensor (right on the thermostat housing)

REMOVAL & INSTALLATION

▶ See Figure 62

The following procedure is a general procedure, consult your 'Chilton Total Car Care' manual on the vehicle you are working with.

✳✳CAUTION

Perform this procedure only on a cold engine. Attempting to remove any component that involves working with engine coolant can result in serious burns.

1. Drain the cooling system as necessary.
2. With the ignition OFF, unplug the electrical connector to the sensor.
3. Using the proper sized wrench, carefully unscrew the sensor from the engine.

To install:

4. Coat the threads of the sensor with a sealant. Install the sensor and tighten to specification.
5. Connect the vacuum hoses to the sensor.
6. Refill the coolant to the proper level. Road test the vehicle for proper operation. Check for leaks.

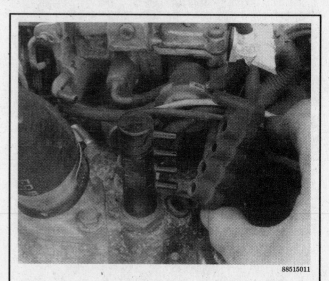

Fig. 62 This EGR VSV has 4 ports — Chevrolet shown

EGR VALVE POSITION SENSOR

The EGR Valve Position (EVP) sensor, sometimes known as an EGR valve lift sensor, is mounted on EGR valve. It signals the computer of EGR opening so that it may subtract EGR flow from total air flow into the manifold. In this way, EGR flow is excluded from air flow information used to determine mixture requirements.

Most EGR position sensors are potentiometers or variable resistance sensors. Their operation is based on resistance changes cased by movement or position of the EGR valve. Electrical resistance within the valve changes as the EGR valve moves. If the EGR valve is fully closed, the resistance reading is at maximum resistance. As the EGR valve begins to open the resistance reading decreases. When the EGR is a maximum open position, the reading is at its lowest specification.

TESTING

▶ **See Figures 63 and 64**

The type of EGR that the vehicle is equipped with will determine how it should be tested. The conventional way of testing the EGR valve does not apply to many of the systems today. On early model vehicles you can use a hand vacuum pump to apply vacuum to the EGR valve. If the valve didn't move it indicated either the valve was stuck or the diaphragm was defective.

Late model vehicles may use positive and negative back-pressure EGR valves and they respond to different types of tests. For example; engines equipped with a negative back-pressure EGR valve, applying vacuum to it with a vacuum pump should cause the EGR valve to open. If the valve fails to move, you know there is a problem with it. On the other hand, engines equipped with a positive backpressure EGR valve, this same test will not move the EGR valve. This is because it is not designed to function without backpressure. In order for a negative backpressure EGR valve to perform it requires a simulation of an exhaust restriction while using the vacuum pump to check movement. To simulate an exhaust restriction you would simply block the tail pipe and have a companion observe any movement of the EGR valve while vacuum was applied to it.

There are various tests required to successfully diagnose an EGR valve problem. To test the position sensor, you will need an ohmmeter and vacuum pump. Again, if the EGR valve is a negative backpressure type, simply disconnect the electrical connector at the position sensor. Check the resistance of the sensor when the EGR valve is closed. Remember, the resistance reading should be at its maximum specification when the valve is closed.

Gradually apply vacuum to the EGR valve and observe the resistance change. As the valve opens the resistance reading should began to decrease until fully open, then it should be at its minimum resistance. Most EGR position sensors have a resistance range of 5000-800 ohms. Depending on the vehicle you are working with the specifications may be different. Because of the variety of different tests, when attempting to test the EGR position valve (EVP) or the EGR system consult your 'Chilton Total Car Care' manual for the vehicle you are working with.

REMOVAL & INSTALLATION

The EGR position sensor is located on the EGR valve. All position sensors are not removable. If found to be defective the EGR valve and sensor might be replace as an assembly. For those that are removable, it is a simple replacement.

Disconnect the electrical connector, remove the bolts attaching the sensor to the EGR valve and remove the sensor. No adjustment is required with the sensor. Simply bolt the new sensor on and connect the connector.

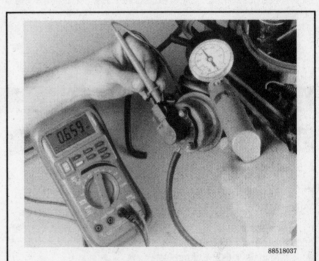

Fig. 63 Testing the EGR position sensor with vacuum applied by a special vacuum tool

Fig. 64 Checking for voltage to the EGR position sensor with self probing type test light

EGR CHECK VALVE

TESTING

▶ **See Figure 65**

Inspect the check valve (one-way valve) by gently blowing air into each end of the valve or hose. Air should flow from the orange or (light colored) pipe to the black pipe but SHOULD NOT flow from the black pipe to the orange or (light colored) pipe.

REMOVAL & INSTALLATION

The EGR check valve may be removed by simply disconnecting the vacuum hoses from either end of the valve. Use care if the hose should stick, excessive force could crack the plastic valve.

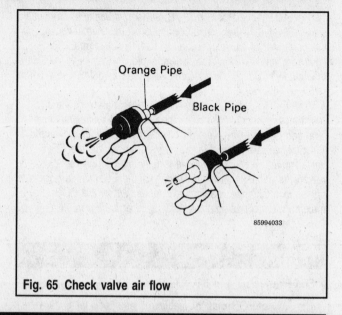

85994033

Fig. 65 Check valve air flow

EGR TEMPERATURE SENSOR

TESTING

▶ **See Figure 66**

➡**The EGR temperature sensor is usually only used on California models.**

1. A sensor may be tested that has been removed from an engine. At room temperature, measure the resistance between both terminals with an ohmmeter.

2. Then place the sensor in a glass of ice water and measure the resistance between both terminals as it cools. The resistance should change smoothly with temperature. If resistance doesn't change replace the sensor.

3. You can use an ohmmeter to measure the resistance between the two terminals. Typical values are as follows:
   a. 69.40-88.50kΩ at 122°F(50°C)
   b. 11.89-14.37kΩ at 212°F(100°C)

4. If the resistance value doesn't change as temperature changes, replace the sensor.

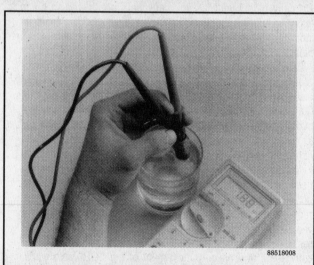

88518008

Fig. 66 Testing an EGR temperature sensor in water. Resistance values change with temperature.

REMOVAL & INSTALLATION

1. With the ignition OFF, unplug the electrical connector to the sensor.

2. Using the proper sized wrench, carefully unscrew the sensor from the engine or EGR valve.

   To install:

3. Install the sensor.

4. Plug the electrical connector into the sensor.

5. Road test the vehicle for proper operation.

EGR SOLENOID VALVE

TESTING

▶ **See Figures 67, 68, 69 and 70**

On some models, the ECM controls the vacuum being supplied to the EGR valve by energizing and de-energizing a solenoid. The ECM uses information from various sensors to determine when EGR is necessary. This device on most vehicles is a simple vacuum valve. No air should pass through the valve when no power is supplied. When power is supplied air should pass. Take note that some newer models do the opposite, shutting off air flow when power is supplied. The basic test is that the valve changes function when voltage is applied. If you check the solenoid with an ohmmeter, you should have some resistance, usually around 40 ohms. If the circuit is open, the solenoid is bad.

REMOVAL & INSTALLATION

▶ **See Figures 67, 68, 69 and 70**

Removing an EGR solenoid is usually a simple matter of disconnecting the electrical connector and vacuum lines at the solenoid and removing the retaining screw(s). On some models it may be necessary to move a component for better access to the solenoid. Some engines, as on some Ford models, install EGR solenoids on the firewall, on others like General Motors, they are simply mounted on a bracket located near the EGR valve.

1. Disconnect the electrical connector at the solenoid.
2. Disconnect the vacuum hoses from the solenoid.
3. Remove the EGR solenoid retaining screw(s).

To install:

4. Install the EGR solenoid and bracket and tighten the retaining screw(s) securely.
5. Connect the vacuum hoses to the solenoid.
6. Connect the electrical connector at the solenoid.

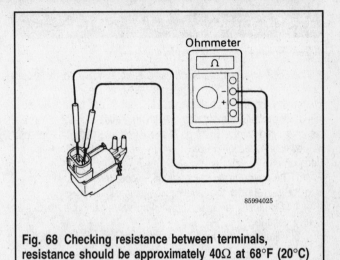

Fig. 68 Checking resistance between terminals, resistance should be approximately 40Ω at 68°F (20°C)

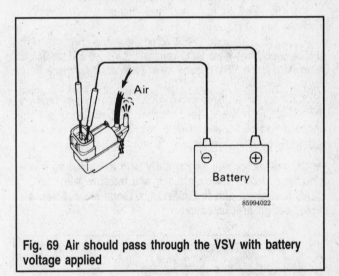

Fig. 69 Air should pass through the VSV with battery voltage applied

Fig. 67 Vacuum control solenoid valves are used to turn components on and off

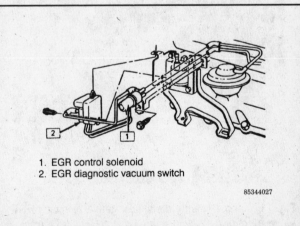

1. EGR control solenoid
2. EGR diagnostic vacuum switch

Fig. 70 Removal and installation of the EGR vacuum solenoid — 2.8L GM engine shown

EGR VACUUM SOLENOID VALVE

TESTING

◆ **See Figures 71, 72, 73 and 74**

The EGR vacuum switching valve is very similar to the vacuum solenoid valve. They are both tested in the same fashion. Depending on the manufacturer, either of the devices may be used. Essentially the vacuum switching valve may not always be controlled by the ECM as is the EGR solenoid. Its source of power may be energized through the activation of another component or system.

1. The vacuum switching circuit is checked by blowing air into the pipe under the following conditions:

  a. Connect the vacuum switching valve terminals to battery voltage.

  b. Blow into the tube and check that the VSV switch is open.

  c. Remove battery voltage from the terminals.

  d. Blow into the tube and check that the VSV switch is closed (no flow).

2. Check for a short circuit within the valve. Using an ohmmeter, check that there is no continuity between the positive terminal and the VSV body. If there is continuity, replace the VSV.

3. Check for an open circuit. Using an ohmmeter, measure the resistance between the 2 terminals of the valve. The resistance should be 38-44Ω at 68°F (20°C). If the resistance is extremely out of range the VSV is probably bad.

➡**The resistance will vary slightly with temperature. It will decrease in cooler temperatures and increase with heat, slight variations due to temperature range are not necessarily a sign of a failed valve.**

Fig. 71 Using a manifold vacuum gauge to check EGR valve function

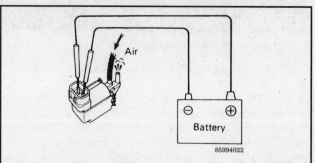

Fig. 72 Air should pass through the VSV with battery voltage applied

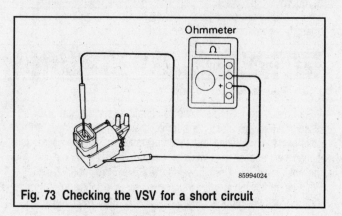

Fig. 73 Checking the VSV for a short circuit

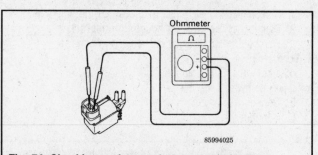

Fig. 74 Checking resistance between terminals, resistance should be approximately 38-44Ω at 68°F (20°C)

REMOVAL & INSTALLATION

Removing a an EGR Vacuum Switching Valve (VSV) is usually a simple matter of disconnecting the electrical connector and vacuum lines at the VSV and removing the retaining screw(s). On some models it may be necessary to move a component for better access to the VSV. The VSV is usually mounted on a bracket located near the EGR valve.

1. Disconnect the electrical connector at the VSV.

2. Disconnect the vacuum hoses from the VSV.

3. Remove the EGR VSV retaining screw(s).

To install:

4. Install the EGR VSV and bracket and tighten the retaining screw(s) securely.

5. Connect the vacuum hoses to the VSV.

6. Connect the electrical connector at the VSV.

EGR (EXHAUST GAS RECIRCUTATION) VALVE

TESTING

▶ **See Figures 75, 76 and 77**

The type of EGR that the vehicle is equipped with will determine how it should be tested. The conventional way of testing the EGR valve does not apply to many of the systems today. On early model vehicles you can use a hand vacuum pump to apply vacuum to the EGR valve. If the valve didn't move it indicated either the valve was stuck or the diaphragm was defective.

Late model vehicles may use positive and negative backpressure EGR valves and they respond to different type tests. For example; engines equipped with a negative backpressure EGR valve, applying vacuum to it with a vacuum pump should cause the EGR valve to open. If the valve fails to move, you know there is a problem with it. On the other hand, engines equipped with a positive backpressure EGR valve, this same test will not move the EGR valve. This is because it is not designed to function without backpressure. In order for a negative backpressure EGR valve to perform it requires a simulation of an exhaust restriction while using the vacuum pump to check movement. To simulate an exhaust restriction you would simply block the tail pipe and have a companion observe any movement of the EGR valve while vacuum was applied to it.

There are various tests required to successfully diagnose an EGR valve problem.

FUNCTIONING TEST

Without special tools

1. Check to see if the EGR valve diaphragm moves freely. Use your finger to reach up under the valve and push on the diaphragm. If it doesn't move freely, the valve should be replaced. The use of a mirror will aid the inspection process.

✳✳CAUTION

If the engine is hot, wear a glove to protect your hand.

2. Install a vacuum gauge into the vacuum line between the EGR valve and the vacuum source. Start the engine and allow it to reach operating temperature.

3. With the vehicle in either **P** or **N**, increase the engine speed until at least 5 in. Hg is showing on the gauge.

4. Remove the vacuum hose from the EGR valve. The diaphragm should move downward (valve closed). The engine speed should increase.

5. Install the vacuum hose and watch for the EGR valve to open (diaphragm moving upward). The engine speed should decrease to its former level, indicating exhaust recirculation.

6. If the diaphragm doesn't move, check engine vacuum; it should be at least 5 in. Hg with the throttle open and engine running.

7. Check to see that the engine is at normal operating temperature.

8. Check for vacuum at the EGR hose. If no vacuum is present, check the hose for leaks, breaks, kinks, improper con-

nections, etc., and repair as necessary. Be aware that on some engines, computer controlled solenoids control the amount of vacuum to the EGR valve, depending on operating conditions.

9. If the diaphragm moves, but the engine speed doesn't change, check the EGR passages in the intake manifold for blockage.

10. Remove the EGR valve and check the valve and passages for damage or blockage.

11. It is a good idea to check the condition of the EGR diaphragm before buying a new valve.

12. Check the valve for sticking and heavy carbon deposits. If a problem is found, clean or replace the valve.

13. Reinstall the EGR valve with a new gasket.

With Vacuum Pump

1. Install a vacuum pump into the vacuum line to the EGR valve. Start the engine and allow it to reach operating temperature.

2. Apply vacuum to the EGR valve.

3. On most vehicles you should be able to see the valve move and you should hear a change in the engine speed.

4. If you can not see the valve more or engine speed is not affected, the EGR valve is probably defective.

5. Remove the EGR valve and attach the vacuum pump to the valve.

6. Apply vacuum to the EGR valve and check that the it functions properly. It should not take more than 10 in. of vacuum to move the valve.

7. If the valve works okay removed from the vehicle, there probably is a blocked or leaking passage and the problem is not the valve itself.

REMOVAL & INSTALLATION

▶ **See Figures 78, 79 and 80**

EGR equipment is generally simple to work on and easy to get to on the engine. On most vehicles, the air cleaner assem-

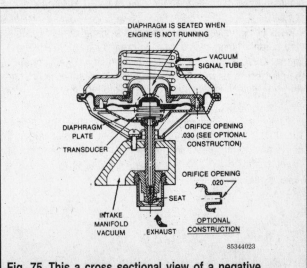

Fig. 75 This a cross sectional view of a negative backpressure EGR valve

Fig. 76 The EGR valve should be cleaned of carbon deposits

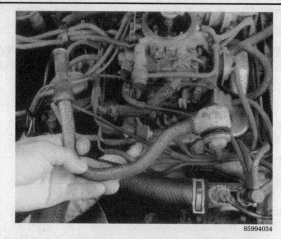

Fig. 78 On some engines, it may be necessary to remove the exhaust gas crossover pipe before removing the EGR valve

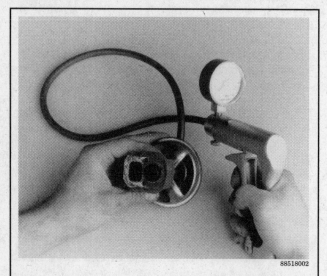

Fig. 77 Testing the condition of the EGR diaphragm

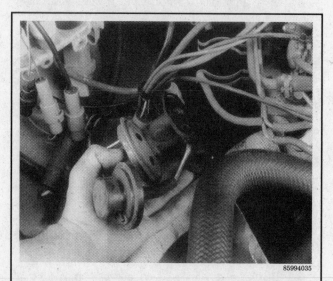

Fig. 79 EGR valves are usually secured with two bolts

bly will need to be removed. Always label each vacuum hose before removing it — they must be replaced in the correct position.

Most of the valves and solenoids are made of plastic. Be very careful during removal not to break or crack the ports; you have NO chance of gluing a broken fitting. Remember that the plastic has been in a hostile environment (heat and vibration); the fittings become brittle and less resistant to abuse or accidental impact.

Most EGR valves are generally held in place by two bolts. The bolts can be difficult to remove due to corrosion. Once the EGR valve is off the engine, clean the bolts and the bolt holes of any rust or debris. Always replace the gasket any time the valve is removed.

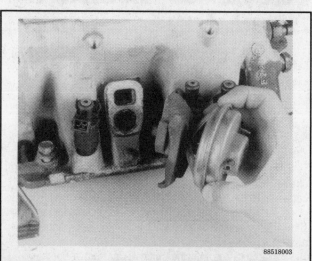

Fig. 80 Most EGR valves are attached to the intake manifold

FUEL INJECTORS (MFI)

TESTING

▶ See Figures 81, 82, 83 and 84

On a multi-port fuel injection systems the injectors can be tested by installing a 'noid light', (headlamp bulb may work) into the injector electrical connector, which confirms voltage when the light flashes.

1. Start the engine and listen to each fuel injector individually for a 'clicking' sound.

2. Turn the engine off and disconnect the electrical connector from the injector(s) that did not have a 'clicking' sound.

3. Check the injector for continuity across the terminals. Compare the resistance value to a known good injector. The

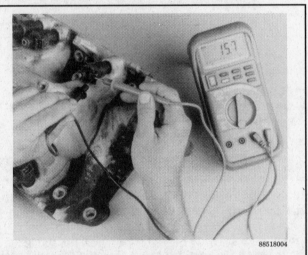

Fig. 81 Testing one of the fuel injectors on a MFI system

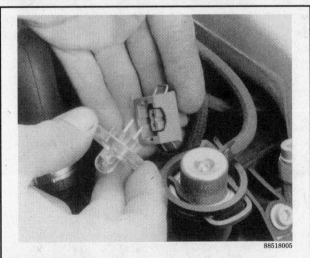

Fig. 82 Plugging a noid light into the fuel injector harness on a MFI system — VW engine shown

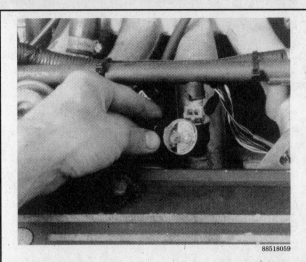

Fig. 83 Using a noid light to check for an injector pulse on a MFI system — Saab engine shown

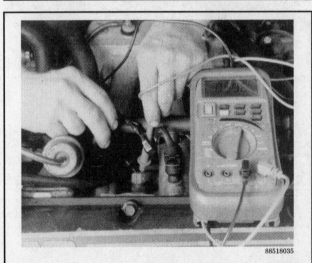

Fig. 84 Testing the fuel injector resistance — Saab MFI engine shown

readings should be similar, if so proceed to the next step. If readings differ greatly, replace the injector.

4. Check between each injector terminal and ground. If continuity exists, replace the injector.

5. Disconnect the fuel injector connector and connect a noid light to the wiring harness connector. Crank the engine, while watching the light. Perform this test on at least two injectors before proceeding. If the light does not flash, check the injector power supply and ground control circuitry. If the light flashes proceed to the next step.

6. If the light flashes, remove the fuel rail from the engine and following the procedure below check the injector operation:

   a. Using mechanic's wire, secure the injector to the fuel rail.

b. Place a clear plastic container around each injector.

❋❋CAUTION

Prior to performing this test, all fuel safety precautions must be followed. Make certain the container is approved to handle fuel and is securely positioned around the injector. Do NOT use a glass container. Glass containers can be easily damaged, resulting in a serious fire hazard.

c. With the help of an assistant or using a remote starter button, crank the engine for 15 seconds while observing the injector operation. The injector should produce a cone shaped spray pattern and all containers should retain equal amounts of fuel.

d. Once the cranking test is complete leave the fuel rail pressurized and observe the injectors for leakage.

7. Replace any injector which is leaking or fails to provide a cone shaped spray pattern when energized.

For more comprehensive diagnosis on your specific fuel injection system, please refer to your 'Chilton Total Car Care' manual.

REMOVAL & INSTALLATION

▶ See Figures 85, 86, 87, 88, 89 and 90

➡Use care in removing injectors to prevent damage to the electrical connector pins and the nozzle. The fuel injector is serviced as a complete assembly only. Since it is an electrical component, DO NOT immerse it in a cleaner.

1. Disconnect the negative battery cable.
2. Relieve the fuel system pressure.
3. You may need to remove the intake plenum and the fuel rail assembly.
4. Rotate the injector retaining clip to the release position.

Fig. 85 Fuel injector shown removed from the intake manifold

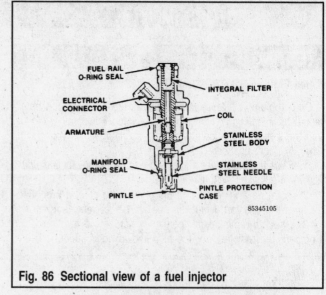

Fig. 86 Sectional view of a fuel injector

5. Remove the fuel injector. Discard the O-rings and the retaining clip.

➡Different injectors are calibrated for different flow rates. When ordering new injectors, be sure to order the identical part number that is inscribed on the old injector.

To install:

❋❋CAUTION

To reduce the risk of fire and personal injury, always install the injector O-rings in the proper position. If the upper and lower O-rings are different colors (black and brown in example), be sure to install the black O-ring in the upper position and the brown O-ring in the lower position. The O-rings are of the same size, but are made of different materials.

➡The fuel injector lower O-ring uses a nylon collar, called the O-ring backup, to properly position the O-ring on the injector. Be sure to install the O-ring backup, or the sealing O-ring may move on the injector when installing the fuel rail. This can result in a vacuum leak and driveability problems will occur.

6. Lubricate the new O-ring seals with clean engine oil and install them on the injector.
7. Assemble a new retainer clip onto the injector.
8. Install the fuel injector into the fuel rail socket with the electrical connections facing outwards.
9. Rotate the injector retaining clip to the lock position.
10. Install the fuel rail assembly.
11. Tighten the fuel filler cap and connect the negative battery cable.
12. With the engine OFF, turn the ignition switch to the ON position for 2 seconds, then turn it to the OFF position for 10 seconds. Again turn it to the ON position and check for fuel leaks.

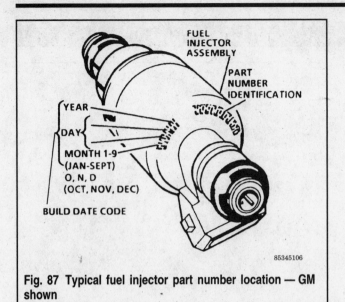

Fig. 87 Typical fuel injector part number location — GM shown

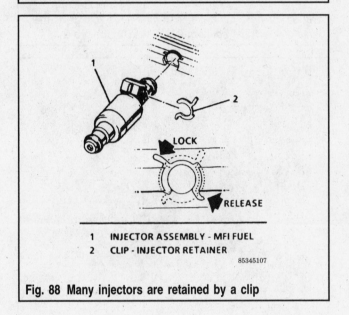

1   INJECTOR ASSEMBLY - MFI FUEL
2   CLIP - INJECTOR RETAINER

Fig. 88 Many injectors are retained by a clip

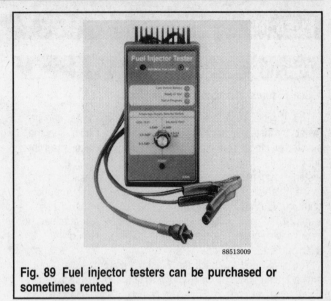

Fig. 89 Fuel injector testers can be purchased or sometimes rented

Fig. 90 Test fuel pressure before replacing injectors, if fuel injectors appear to be working properly

FUEL INJECTORS (TBI)

TESTING

▶ **See Figures 91, 92, 93 and 94**

The Throttle body injection (TBI) system injector(s) can be tested by installing a 'noid light', a small tester bulb, into the injector electrical connector, which confirms voltage when the light flashes. The injector can be checked by using a multi-tester. Disconnect the injector connector and check the resistance. this value is specific for each vehicle usually around 1-3 ohms. If you have more than one injector they should read the same. If not, one of them is defective. When you purchase a new injector check it's resistance to confirm which of the old injectors is out of range.

You also need to check the injector's pattern. A flashlight and a timing light can help you view the fuel injector's operation and spray pattern. For more comprehensive diagnosis on your specific fuel injection system, please refer to your 'Chilton Total Car Care' manual.

REMOVAL & INSTALLATION

▶ **See Figures 95, 96 and 97**

The procedures given here are for a GM engine with TBI. Procedures differ according to manufacturer. For specific information on the vehicle you are working with, consult your 'Chilton Total Car Care' or factory service manual.

➡**Use care in removing injectors to prevent damage to the electrical connector pins on top of the injector, the fuel injector fuel filter and nozzle. The fuel injector is serviced as a complete assembly only and should never be immersed in any type of cleaner.**

1. Relieve the fuel system pressure.
2. Remove the air cleaner.
3. Disconnect the injector connector by squeezing the two tabs together and pulling straight up.

Fig. 91 The throttle body injectors can be seen after removing the air cleaner, as on the General Motors 6 cylinder engine

Fig. 92 Using a multi-tester to check for voltage at the injector electrical connector — GM TBI unit shown

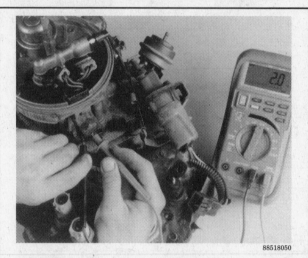

Fig. 93 Testing the fuel injector resistance — Ford TBI engine shown

4. Remove the screws securing the fuel meter cover. Note the location of any short screws for correct placement during reassembly.

✳✳CAUTION

DO NOT remove the four screws securing the pressure regulator to the fuel meter cover. The fuel pressure regulator includes a large spring under heavy tension which could cause personal injury if released.

5. With the old fuel meter gasket in place to prevent damage to the casting, use a screwdriver and fulcrum to pry the injector carefully until it is free from the fuel meter body.
6. Remove the injector.
7. Remove the large O-ring and steel back-up washer at the top of the injector cavity in the fuel meter body.

Fig. 94 You can see the injector operation and spray pattern better with a timing light

8. Remove the small O-ring located at the bottom of the injector cavity.

To Install:

9. Lubricate the new, small O-ring with automatic transmission fluid; then, push the new O-ring on the nozzle end of the injector up against the injector fuel filter.

10. Install the steel backup washer in the recess of the fuel meter body. Lubricate the new large O-ring with automatic transmission fluid, then install the O-ring directly above the backup washer, pressing the O-ring down into the cavity recess. The O-ring is properly installed when it is flush with the casting surface.

✳✳WARNING

Do not attempt to reverse this procedure and install the backup washer and O-ring after the injector is located in the cavity. To do so will prevent proper seating of the O-ring in the cavity recess which could result in a fuel leak and possible fire.

11. Install the injector by using a pushing/twisting motion to center the nozzle O-ring in the bottom of the injector cavity and aligning the raised lug on the injector base with the notch cast into the fuel meter body. Push down on the injector making sure it is fully seated in the cavity. Injector installation is correct when the lug is seated in the notch and the electrical terminals are parallel to the throttle shaft.

12. Using new gaskets on the fuel meter cover and a new dust seal, install the cover to the fuel meter body. The two short screws are located adjacent to the injector.

13. Connect the injector electrical connector by pushing straight down until seated firmly in place.

14. Connect the negative battery cable.

15. With the engine OFF and the ignition ON, check for fuel leaks.

16. Install the air cleaner.

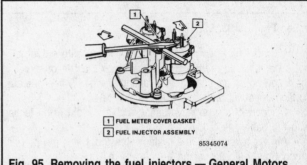

Fig. 95 Removing the fuel injectors — General Motors shown

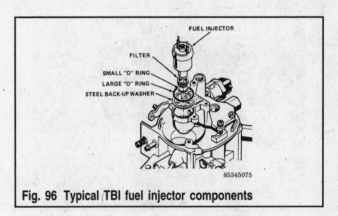

Fig. 96 Typical TBI fuel injector components

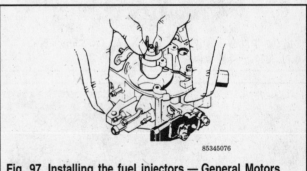

Fig. 97 Installing the fuel injectors — General Motors shown

FUEL PUMP

Electric Fuel Pump

TESTING

◗ See Figures 98, 99, 100 and 101

Testing the fuel pump for operation and pressure output is not a complicated matter. Basically you will want to observe the following precautions before getting started. These precautionary steps will prevent fire and or/explosion.

• Disconnect the negative battery cable, except when testing with the battery is required.

• Always relieve the fuel system pressure, using the proper procedures, before opening a fuel system.

• When possible, use a flashlight instead of a drop light. (Many fires have been started because someone accidentally

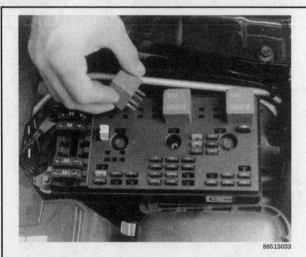

Fig. 98 Removing the fuel pump relay — Saturn with 1.9L MFI engine shown

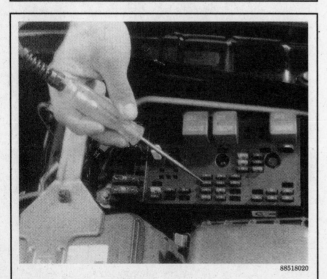

Fig. 99 Testing the fuel pump fuse

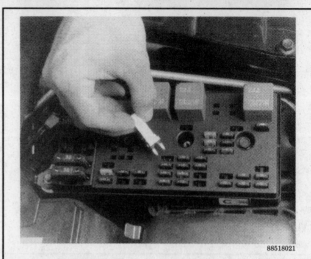

Fig. 100 Removing the fuel pump fuse to check for corrosion — Saturn with 1.9L MFI engine shown

Fig. 101 Bypassing the fuel pump relay and jumping the circuit directly to the fuel pump

dropped a drop light, and the bulb broke igniting a few drips of fuel).

• Use eye protection. When working with high and low pressure fuel systems there is always a possibility of fuel either spraying, dripping or some debris dropping into the eyes.

• Always keep a dry chemical fire extinguisher in the service area.

• Keep all open flame and smoking material out of the area, this is especially important. Keep in mind that fuel vapors can be ignited if the area you are working in is not well ventilated.

• Use a shop cloth to catch fuel when opening the fuel system or relieving fuel system pressure.

If the engine does not start or occasionally stalls and the fuel pump is suspected, preform the following basic checks before condemning the fuel pump. Then proceed to further testing.

Voltage Checks

1. Check to make sure there is adequate fuel in the tank. Many incorrect diagnoses of a bad fuel pump has been made because this first and basic check is overlooked. If you are not certain add a gallon or two just to be sure.

➡ **The procedure given here is a general procedure. For specific information for the vehicle you are working with, consult your 'Chilton Total Car Care'.**

2. If your vehicle has an internal fuel pump make this check. Unscrew the fuel fill cap and have an assistant turn the ignition switch **ON**. Listen to hear if the fuel pump turns on. On most vehicles, the electric fuel pump will energize for a few seconds every time the ignition switch is turned to the **ON** position. On others, it will be necessary to crank the engine a few revolutions. You will know the fuel pump is working by hearing an audible hum or whirling noise form the tank area.

3. If your vehicle is equipped with an external electric fuel pump, make this check. In most cases external fuel pumps are mounted under the vehicle, somewhere in proximity of the fuel tank on the frame of the vehicle. It will be necessary to raise and support the vehicle safely with good jackstands. Locate the fuel pump and have an assistant turn the ignition switch **ON**. Listen to hear if the fuel pump turns on. You should also be able to feel the fuel pump energize for a few seconds every time the ignition switch is turned to the **ON** position. If it does not it may be necessary to crank the engine a few revolutions.

4. If the fuel pump does not respond to the key on and crank test, you must now determine whether or not voltage is getting to the pump.

5. To check voltage supplied to the fuel pump, a systematic check will aid you in a quick and efficient diagnosis.

6. First check the fuel pump fuse. In most cases the fuse is located in the main fuse block either under the dash or in the engine compartment depending on the vehicle. Use a test light to check for voltage on both sides of the fuse. Turn the ignition switch to the **ON** position. Connect the test light to a suitable ground and probe each side of the fuse.

7. If there is voltage on both sides chances are the fuse is okay. But don't take that for granted, remove the fuse anyway and inspect it for corrosion on the contact points. If there is corrosion, clean it and check it again to see if the pump responds.

8. If the fuse is blown, replace it and check the fuel pump operation. If there is voltage supply to the fuse and the fuse checks good, check the fuel pump relay and circuit.

9. Locate the fuel pump relay. The relay may be located in a variety of locations, it may be in the engine compartment mounted on a bracket on the strut tower, on the firewall or near the battery. On some vehicles it will be located under the dash. It will be necessary for you to consult your 'Chilton Total Car Care' manual for the vehicle you are working with. Sometimes the warranty book will give locations of the fuses and relays.

10. Once you have located the relay, remove it and check for voltage at the connector feed terminal. Turn the ignition switch **ON** Using a test light, connect it to a suitable ground and probe the power feed terminal. If voltage exists, use a jumper wire to connect the power feed terminal and the fuel pump terminal circuit. It is best to have a diagram of which

terminals are which. Each vehicle is different. It is important not to jump the wrong circuit and short or burn something out. However, some terminals are labeled to make this test simpler.

11. If you are sure of which terminals to jump, jump the terminals and have an assistant listen for fuel pump operation. If the fuel pump activates, chances are the relay is at fault. If fuel pump still does not activate, go directly to the fuel pump.

12. If you vehicle has a internal pump, locate the harness connection at the pump. Connect a 12 volt lead to the positive side of the pump and listen for the pump to activate. If the pump still does not activate, check the ground wire for a good clean connection. Clean the ground and connection and try to activate the pump again, if the pump still does not come on, chances are the pump is defective.

Pressure Checks

Proper fuel pressure is very important in the engine management system. Insufficient or excessive fuel pressure can cause many problems. Low fuel pressure can cause hard starting, stalling or engine surge problems, while excessive fuel pressure can cause flooding, poor gas mileage or poor performance, etc.

1. Connect a suitable fuel pressure gauge to the fuel tap line. This tap is located at different locations depending on the vehicle you are working with.

2. Turn ignition switch to the ON position, but do not start the engine. If the gauge registers fuel pressure, start the engine and observe the fuel pressure. You will need to check the specifications for the vehicle and system you are working with.

3. If pressure is within specifications, then the test is over. If fuel pressure is low, perform a fuel flow test.

4. If you find the fuel pressure is above specifications, check the fuel pressure regulator for proper operation, and check for a restriction in the return line to the gas tank.

5. If no fuel pressure was evident, when the switch was turned ON, check the operation of the fuel pump as mentioned earlier.

REMOVAL AND INSTALLATION

▶ **See Figures 102, 103, 104 and 105**

The internal fuel pump is a part of the fuel sender assembly located inside the fuel tank.

1. Release the fuel system pressure and disconnect the negative battery cable.

2. Drain the fuel tank, then raise and safely support the vehicle.

3. Remove the fuel tank from the vehicle.

4. Clean the areas surrounding the sender assembly to prevent contamination of the fuel system.

5. Remove the fuel sender from the tank as follows:

6. Use a special tool to remove the sender unit retaining cam. Remove the fuel sender and O-rings from the tank. Discard the O-rings

7. If necessary, separate the fuel pump from the sending unit assembly.

To Install:

8. If removed, install the fuel pump to the sending unit. If the strainer was removed, it must be replaced with a new one.

9. Inspect and clean the O-ring mating surfaces.

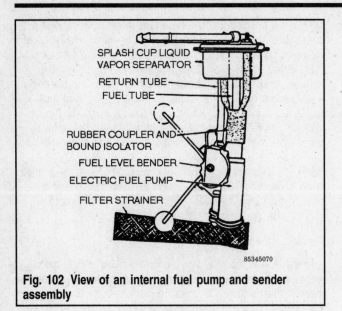

Fig. 102 View of an internal fuel pump and sender assembly

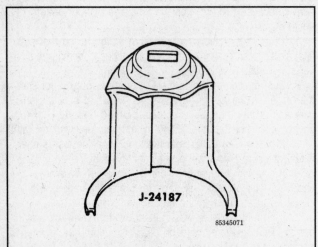

Fig. 103 A special tool used to remove and install the fuel pump locking cam

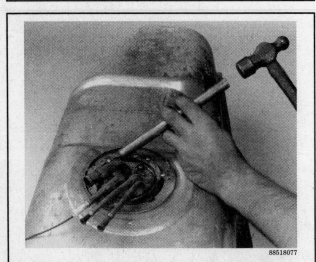

Fig. 104 Using a brass drift to loosen a fuel pump assembly from a fuel tank

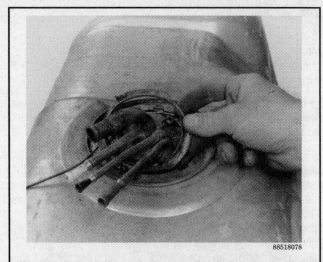

Fig. 105 Fuel pump and sender assembly removed from a fuel tank

10. Install a new O-ring in the groove around the tank opening. If applicable, install a new O-ring on the fuel sender feed tube.

11. Install the fuel sender as follows:

a. The fuel pump strainer must be in a horizontal position, and when installed, must not block the travel of the float arm. Gently fold the strainer over itself and slowly position the sending assembly in the tank so the strainer is not damaged or trapped by the sump walls.

12. Install the fuel tank assembly.

13. Lower the vehicle.

14. Fill the fuel tank, tighten the fuel filler cap and connect the negative battery cable.

15. Start the engine and check for leaks.

FUSES AND CIRCUIT BREAKERS

▶ **See Figures 106, 107, 108, 109, 110, 111, 112 and 113**

Protection devices are fuses, fusible links or circuit breakers. They are designed to open or break the circuit quickly whenever an overload, such as a short circuit, occurs. By opening the circuit quickly, the circuit protection device prevents damage to the wiring, battery and other circuit components. Fuses and fusible links are designed to carry a preset maximum amount of current and to melt when that maximum is exceeded, while circuit breakers merely break the connection and may be manually reset. The maximum amperage rating of each fuse is marked on the fuse body and all contain a see-through portion that shows the break in the fuse element when blown. Fusible link maximum amperage rating is indicated by the gauge or thickness of the wire. Never replace a blown fuse or fusible link with one of a higher amperage rating.

➡ **Resistance wires, like fusible links, are also spliced into conductors in some areas. Do not make the mistake of replacing a fusible link with a resistance wire. Resistance wires are longer than fusible links and are stamped 'RESISTOR-DO NOT CUT OR SPLICE.'**

Circuit breakers consist of 2 strips of metal which have different coefficients of expansion. As an overload of current flows through the bi-metallic strip, the high-expansion metal will elongate due to heat and break the contact. With the circuit open, the bi-metal strip cools and shrinks, drawing the strip down until contact is re-established and current flows once again. In actual operation, the contact is broken very quickly if the overload is continuous and the circuit will be repeatedly broken and re-made until the source of the overload is corrected.

The self-resetting type of circuit breaker is the one most generally used in automotive electrical systems. On manually reset circuit breakers, a button will pop up on the circuit breaker case. This button must be pushed in to reset the circuit breaker and restore power to the circuit. Always repair the source of the overload before resetting a circuit breaker or replacing a fuse or fusible link. When searching for overloads, keep in mind that the circuit protection devices protect only against overloads between the protection device and ground.

TESTING

Testing fuses and circuit breakers is an easy task with a test light or voltmeter.
1. Connect a test light to a good ground.
2. Touch the test light to known good power source to make certain it lights.
3. Then touch the test light each side of the fuse or circuit breaker you want to test.
4. The test light should light up on both sides of the fuse or circuit breaker. If it only lights on one side, then the fuse or breaker is blown. If it doesn't light on either side there is a problem with power before the protection device.

For a problem where there is no power to the protection device you need to find the path that the circuit takes. Most circuits to fuses either come directly from a main fusible link connected to the battery. Remember many circuits are turned OFF when the ignition is turned OFF. For 'IGN' hot circuits, make certain the ignition switch is ON. If there is still no power at the fuse box check the main breakers or fusible links near the battery. You may need to consult a 'Chilton Total Car Care' manual for wiring diagrams.

REMOVAL & INSTALLATION

Replacing fuses and circuit breakers is usually easy. Simply pull the fuse or breaker from its contacts. Many newer vehicles have the fuse box in a location difficult to access. The fuses sometimes fit so flat against the fuse box you can't get your fingers on them. Most auto parts stores have fuse pullers that make this task a snap. A pair of needlenose pliers will also work, but if the fuse is the glass tube type you have to take care not to crush it.

88518054

Fig. 106 Typical fuse and relay block located in the engine compartment-Saturn shown

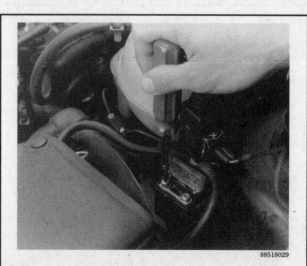

88518029

Fig. 107 Removing a fusible link — Volkswagen 2.0L Motronic engine shown

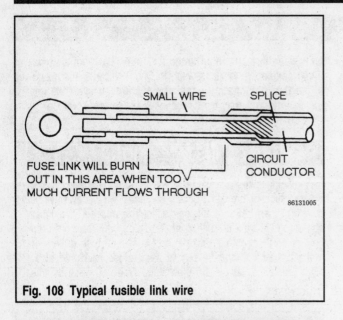

Fig. 108 Typical fusible link wire

Fig. 109 Testing the fusible link for voltage drop

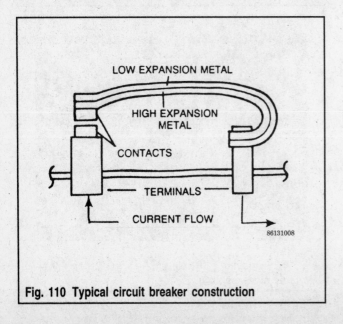

Fig. 110 Typical circuit breaker construction

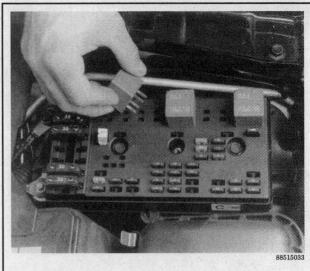

Fig. 111 Most relays simply plug in to a relay box

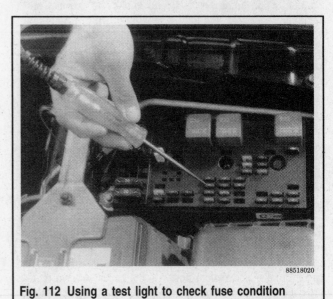

Fig. 112 Using a test light to check fuse condition

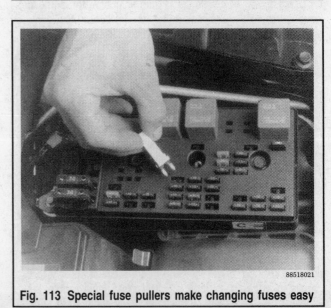

Fig. 113 Special fuse pullers make changing fuses easy

HALL EFFECT SWITCH

▶ **See Figures 114, 115 and 116**

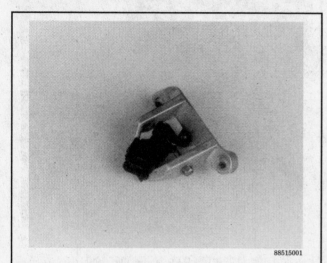

Fig. 116 Typical Dual crankshaft sensor/pedestal — GM Hall Effect type sensor

Hall effect sensors are used on some systems to determine speed and position of a rotating object. They can be distinguished from magnetic sensors by their three wire harness. The most common applications are as engine speed sensors mounted near the camshaft and crankshaft. On some engines, a Hall effect switch is located inside the distributor. These sensors can be tested using a digital multimeter. Common names of these sensors are camshaft sensor, crankshaft sensor and rpm sensors.

TESTING

1. Perform a visual inspection.

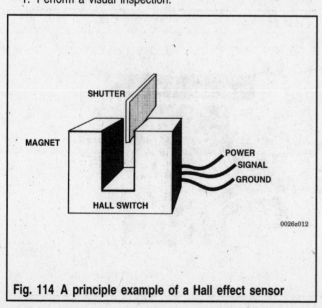

Fig. 114 A principle example of a Hall effect sensor

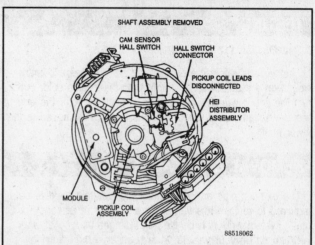

Fig. 115 This TDC sensor is located inside the distributor — Hall effect type shown in a GM 4.9L MFI engine

2. Disconnect the sensor connector and install jumper wires from the power and ground terminals of the sensor connector to the wiring harness. This permits the sensor to receive power and ground without signaling the ignition system during inspection.

➡**Do not connect a jumper wire to the signal terminal on the Hall sensor. This will cause the engine to start. Use extreme caution while performing this test.**

3. Using a multimeter set to the volts setting, check the voltage between the power and ground wires. This voltage may be either 4, 6, 8 or 12 volts depending on the system. Take note of this voltage reading. Refer to your 'Chiton Total Car Care' manual for correct wire color, terminal location and recommended specifications.

4. Connect the multimeter between the signal terminal and the ground wire. Rotate the engine by (tapping the ignition key) with the starter motor. When the engine is rotated, the signal should fluctuate between 0 volts and the system voltage noted in earlier step.

5. While rotating the engine, check for damaged shutter blades or any indication that the shutter blades are hitting the magnet.

REMOVAL & INSTALLATION

Depending on location, these sensors can be removed without too much difficulty. Removal usually involves disconnecting the electrical connector and unbolting the sensor. In some cases, the sensor must be aligned during installation. Refer to your vehicle service manual for proper adjustment procedure. Some manufacturers may have this sensor mounted behind the ignition module or inside the distributor. You may need to refer to a 'Chilton Total Car Care' manual, if the this sensor is difficult to locate or is behind other components.

HEAT CONTROL VALVE

TESTING

▶ **See Figures 117 and 118**

The valve is within the exhaust system and has a counter-weight on the outside of the pipe. With the engine cold, check that the counterweight is in the upper position. After the engine has been warmed up, check that the weight has moved to the lower position.

REMOVAL & INSTALLATION

The exhaust pipe and sometimes the manifold need to be removed to replace this valve. For a number of reasons, exhaust system work can be the most dangerous type of work you can do on your vehicle. Always observe the following precautions:

• Support the vehicle safely. Not only will you often be working directly under it, but you'll frequently be using a lot of force, such as heavy hammer blows, to dislodge rusted parts. This can cause a vehicle that's improperly supported to shift and possibly fall.

• Wear goggles. Exhaust system parts are always rusty. Metal chips can be dislodged, even when you're only turning rusted bolts. Attempting to pry pipes apart with a chisel makes the chips fly even more frequently.

• If you're using a cutting torch, keep it a safe distance from either the fuel tank or lines. Stop what you're doing and feel the temperature of the fuel pipes and tank frequently. Even slight heat can expand and/or vaporize fuel, resulting in accumulated vapor, or even a liquid leak, near your torch.

• Watch where you are hammering and make sure you hit squarely. You could easily tap a brake or fuel line if you hit an exhaust system part with a glancing blow. Inspect all lines and hoses in the area where you've been working.

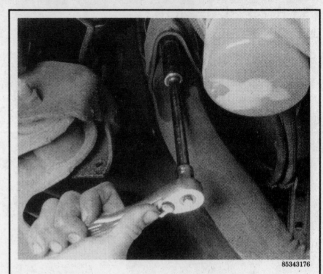

85343176

Fig. 118 Removing the pipe at the manifold

A number of special exhaust system tools can be rented from auto supply houses or local stores that rent special equipment. A common one is a tail pipe expander, designed to enable you to join pipes of identical diameter.

It may also be quite helpful to use solvents designed to loosen rusted bolts or flanges. Soaking rusted parts the night before you do the job can speed the work of freeing rusted parts considerably. Remember that these solvents are often flammable. Apply only to parts after they are cool! If this job looks difficult on your vehicle, it is advised to obtain a 'Chilton Total Car Care' manual for the specific procedures and bolt tightening instructions.

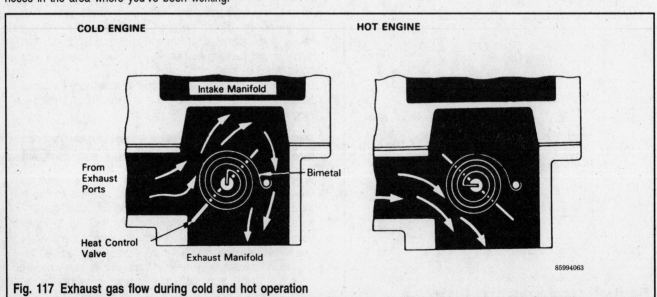

COLD ENGINE   **HOT ENGINE**

Intake Manifold

From Exhaust Ports — Bimetal

Heat Control Valve

Exhaust Manifold

85994063

Fig. 117 Exhaust gas flow during cold and hot operation

HOT AIR INTAKE

▶ **See Figures 119, 120 and 121**

The Hot Air Intake (HAI) system is commonly know as a Thermostatic Air Cleaner (THERMAC).

This system is designed to warm the air entering the carburetor when underhood temperatures are low, and to maintain a controlled air temperature into the carburetor or throttle body at all times. By allowing preheated air to enter, the amount of time the choke is on is reduced, resulting in better fuel economy and lower emissions. Engine warm up time is also reduced.

The THERMAC system is composed of the air cleaner body, a filter, sensor unit, vacuum diaphragm, damper door, associated hoses and connections. Heat radiating from the exhaust manifold is trapped by a heat stove and is ducted to the air cleaner to supply heated air to the carburetor or throttle body. A movable door in the air cleaner case snorkel allows air to be drawn in from the heat stove (cold operation). The door position is controlled by the vacuum motor, which receives intake manifold vacuum as modulated by the temperature sensor.

➡ **A vacuum door which remains open can cause carburetor icing or poor cold driveability. A door which remains closed during normal engine operating temperatures can cause sluggishness, engine knocking and overheating.**

TESTING

▶ **See Figure 122**

This is a basic procedure that will work for most vehicles. For specific information consult your 'Chilton Total Car Care' manual for the vehicle you are working with.

1. Check the vacuum hoses for leaks, kinks, breaks, or improper connections and correct any defects.

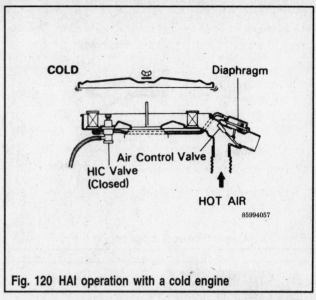

Fig. 120 HAI operation with a cold engine

2. With the engine OFF, check the position of the damper door within the snorkel. A mirror can be used to make this job easier. The damper door should be open to admit outside air.

3. Apply at least 7 in. Hg of vacuum to the damper diaphragm unit. The door should close. If it doesn't, check the diaphragm linkage for binding and correct hookup.

4. With the vacuum still applied and the door closed, clamp the tube to trap the vacuum. If the door doesn't remain closed, there is a leak in the diaphragm assembly.

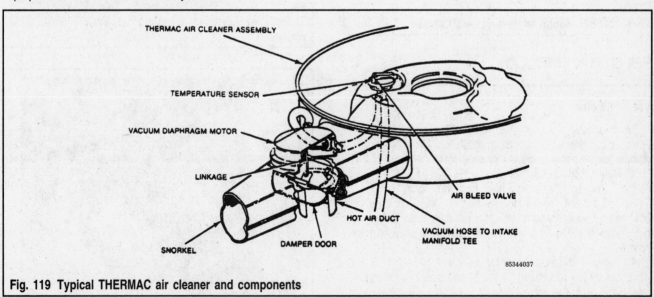

Fig. 119 Typical THERMAC air cleaner and components

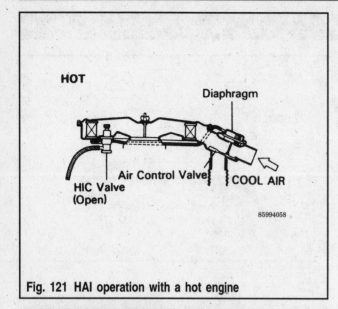

Fig. 121 HAI operation with a hot engine

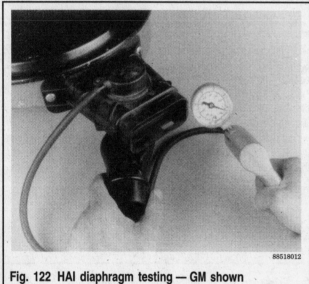

Fig. 122 HAI diaphragm testing — GM shown

REMOVAL & INSTALLATION

Vacuum Motor

This is a basic procedure that will work for most vehicles. For specific information consult your 'Chilton Total Car Care' manual for the vehicle you are working with.

1. Remove the air cleaner.
2. Disconnect the vacuum hose from the motor.
3. Drill out the spot welds with a ⅛ in. (3mm) bit, then enlarge as necessary to remove the retaining strap. Drilling is not always required as some vacuum motor are retained with screws.
4. Remove the retaining strap.
5. Lift up the motor and cock it to one side to unhook the motor linkage at the control damper assembly.

To install:

6. In order to install the new vacuum motor, drill a ⁷⁄₆₄ in. (2.8mm) hole in the snorkel tube at the center of the vacuum motor retaining strap.

7. Insert the vacuum motor linkage into the control damper assembly.

8. Use the motor retaining strap and a sheet metal screw to secure the retaining strap and motor to the snorkel tube.

➡**Make sure the screw does not interfere with the operation of the damper assembly. Shorten the screw if necessary.**

Temperature Sensor

▶ **See Figures 123 and 124**

1. Remove the air cleaner.
2. Disconnect and tag the hoses at the air cleaner.
3. Pry up the tabs on the sensor retaining clip and remove the clip and sensor from the air cleaner.

To install:

4. Position sensor into air cleaner.
5. Install retaining clip.
6. Connect the hoses to the air cleaner.
7. Install the air cleaner.

Fig. 123 Typical Inlet Temperature Compensator (ITC) Thermac sensor used in thermostatically controlled air cleaner

Fig. 124 It's helpful to tag all hoses as you remove them

IGNITION CONTROL MODULE

▶ **See Figures 125 and 126**

The ignition module fires the ignition coil after the magnetic pick-coil submits an electrical pulse or signal to it. The ignition module interrupts the ignition primary circuit, thus causing the ignition coil to provide spark. This ignition module turns the ignition coil on and off, like the points used to do on older cars. The ignition module turns off the primary circuit to the coil which begins the induction of the magnetic lines of force from the primary side of the coil into the secondary side of the coil. This induction provides spark to the spark plugs. It has assumed the job of the conventional ignition points.

The advantages of the this system are that the transistors in the control unit can make and break the primary ignition circuit much faster than ignition points can, and higher primary voltage can be utilized, since this system is designed to handle higher voltage without adverse effects. On the earlier systems, the ignition module also governs the ignition dwell. On later systems the PCM controls the dwell.

TESTING

Due to the many different styles and configurations of ignition modules, there is no one easy test which will work universally. However, there are several steps you can take to determine if the ignition module is probably defective.

The first check that should be made is for spark at the spark plug wire. This can be done using a spark tester. A spark tester looks like a regular spark plug with a ground clip attached to one side. It allows the ignition system to be checked for spark without damaging the electronics. If the engine is getting spark, the ignition module is probably functioning correctly.

➡**Testing the ignition system for spark without the use of a spark tester can damage the ignition module.**

If the engine is not getting spark, check the ignition coil, ignition trigger (usually a magnetic reluctance or Hall effect switch) and all associated wiring.

If all other components are functioning properly, the ignition module is probably defective. As a final test, an ignition module tester may be used to check the module circuitry. These testers can be borrowed, rented or purchased at a reasonable price from automotive stores.

A simple test you can do at home involves the use of a test light or logic probe.

1. Locate the ignition coil in the engine compartment. On some ignition systems the coil is located inside the distributor cap.

2. Connect a test light or logic probe between the negative side of the coil and ground. Refer to your 'Chilton Total Car Care' service manual for correct wire color and terminal location.

3. Crank the engine using the starter.

✳✳CAUTION

Exercise extreme caution when cranking the engine as it may start.

4. As the engine cranks the test light or logic probe bulb should flicker. This indicates the module is triggering the coil to fire.

If the light does not flicker, chances are the module is at fault. For a specific diagnostic test consult your 'Chilton Total Car Care manual'.

➡**Inexpensive ignition module and sensor testers may be available at a local auto parts store for rent or purchase. These special testers are extremely helpful and efficient.**

REMOVAL & INSTALLATION

Removal and installation may vary from manufacturer to manufacturer. Some ignition modules are mounted in the engine compartment on the firewall, inner fender panel, but never

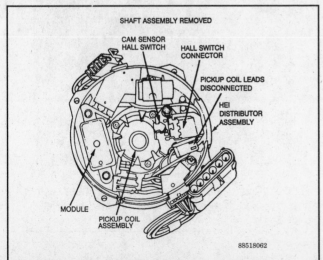

Fig. 125 Many Ignition Modules are located underneath the distributor cap, like the GM car

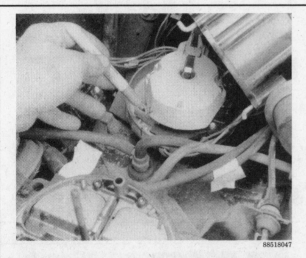

SHAFT ASSEMBLY REMOVED

CAM SENSOR HALL SWITCH

HALL SWITCH CONNECTOR

PICKUP COIL LEADS DISCONNECTED

HEI DISTRIBUTOR ASSEMBLY

MODULE

PICKUP COIL ASSEMBLY

88518062

Fig. 126 General Motors HEI ignition modules are located in the distributor

on the engine. Others are mounted either in the ignition distributor or on the side of the distributor. Consult your 'Chilton Total Car Care manual' for the specific procedure for the vehicle you are working with. The following procedures are examples of the different types.

EXTERNALLY MOUNTED MODULE

1. Disconnect negative battery cable.
2. Disconnect the harness or harness connectors from the module.
3. Remove the mounting bolts from the module and remove the module.
   To install:
4. Install the module on the mounting surface and install the mounting bolts. Use special dielectric grease between module and housing assembly.
5. Prior to connecting the harness connectors, apply a coating of dielectric grease to the connections. Connect the electrical harnesses to the module.
6. Connect the negative battery cable.

INTERNALLY MOUNTED MODULE

▶ **See Figures 127, 128, 129, 130, 131, 132, 133 and 134**

1. Disconnect negative battery cable.
2. Remove the distributor cap. If the distributor is in a difficult location, it may be necessary to remove it from the engine. On most vehicles you will be able to perform this job without removing the distributor.
3. Remove the ignition rotor.
4. Remove the mounting screws holding the module in place.
5. Carefully disconnect the electrical connectors at each end of the module and remove the module.
6. Clean the mounting surface of any residue of grease or dirt.
7. Inspect the connectors for signs of deterioration or cracks.
   To install:
8. Prior to installing the new module, coat the module mounting surface with a special dielectric grease. Do not attempt to use any other type of grease that is not specifically designed for this purpose.
9. Connect electrical connectors to both ends of the module and place the module in place. Install the retaining screws.
10. Install the distributor if it required removal.
11. Install the distributor rotor and cap.
12. Connect the negative battery cable.

SIDE MOUNTED MODULE

1. Disconnect negative battery cable.
2. Most modules can be removed from the distributor without it having to be removed from the engine.

3. Usually this modules are attached with a torx type screw. You will need to acquire this tool to perform the job. Don't try to use an incorrect tool or you'll damage the screw head.
4. Remove the special screws from the module.
5. Very carefully remove the module by pulling it down and away from the side of the distributor.
   To install:
6. Prior to installing the module apply a coating of dielectric grease on the module terminals.
7. Carefully slide the module terminals into the harness of the distributor. Be careful not to bend these terminals.
8. When the module is properly in place, install the special mounting screws.
9. If it was necessary to remove the distributor, install it.
10. Connect the negative battery cable.

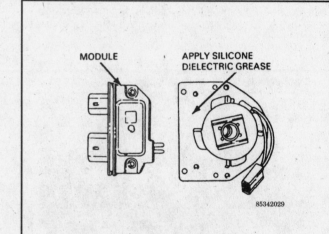

Fig. 127 Ignition module mounting — always coat the module mounting base with dielectric grease

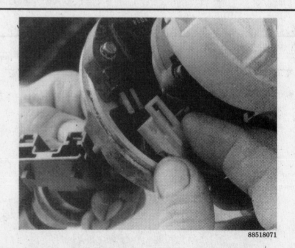

Fig. 128 Carefully disconnect the electrical connectors from the module — GM internally mounted module shown

Fig. 129 Removing the ignition module retaining screws — GM internally mounted module shown

Fig. 130 Remove the ignition module from the distributor — GM internally mounted module shown

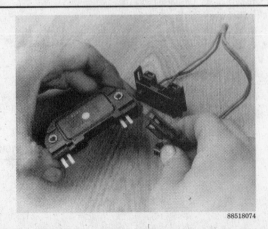

Fig. 131 Inspect the connectors and module terminals, make sure the terminals are not bent or the wiring cracked or severed. — GM internally mounted module shown

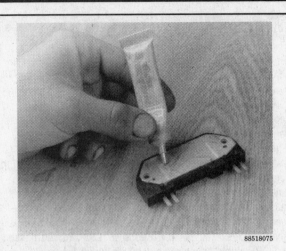

Fig. 132 Apply a coating of the appropriate type of insulation grease prior to installing it. This keeps the module from overheating

Fig. 133 Connect the electrical connectors and secure the module with the retaining screws — GM internally mounted module shown

Fig. 134 Spark timing is also effected and controlled by Spark Control modules mounted on fenders or firewalls

IDLE AIR CONTROL (IAC) VALVE

On fuel injected engines, engine idle speeds are controlled by the ECM through the IAC valve. On most engines, the IAC valve is mounted on the throttle body, others may be mounted on the engine near the throttle body. IAC valves that are located on the throttle body operate as follows, this example given is for a typical GM type IAC valve.

The ECM sends voltage pulses to the IAC motor windings causing the IAC motor shaft and pintle to move **IN** or **OUT** a given distance (number of steps) for each pulse (called counts). The movement of the pintle controls the airflow around the throttle plate, which in turn, controls engine idle speed. IAC valve pintle position counts can be observed using a scan tool. Zero counts correspond to a fully closed passage, while 140 counts or more corresponds to full flow.

IAC valves that are mounted separately from the throttle body operate this way. Based on information the ECM receives from the coolant temperature sensor, intake air temperature sensor and throttle position sensor, it adjusts the opening of the IAC valve accordingly. When the engine is first started it opens the IAC valve to its full amount. This causes the engine to run at a fast idle. As the engine temperature warms up the ECM signals the IAC valve to close and open as increased air is needed. This maintains the idle speed at proper specification.

TESTING

▶ **See Figures 135, 136, 137, 138 and 139**

When suspecting a IAC valve problem, first perform a visual inspection. Most problems can be found in wiring harnesses and connectors. An unstable idle or stalling condition could be caused by a vacuum leak or faulty PCV valve. In some cases, just dirty electrical connections at the IAC valve can cause a problem. Proper diagnosing can only be accomplished by systematic testing procedures. For specific information on the vehicle you are working with consult your 'Chilton Total Car Care' or factory service manual. The following procedure is a general procedure and may not apply to the vehicle you are working with.

For the following test you will need a digital volt/ohmmeter.

1. Start with a cold engine.
2. Start the engine. Using a voltmeter check the volt reading by probing the feed circuit to the IAC valve.
3. Allow the engine to warm up while observing the voltmeter reading.
4. The initial reading should be high close to battery voltage. As the engine warms up the volt reading should gradually decrease to almost 0 volts.

Depending on the vehicle you are working with this voltage specification will vary. You will need to consult your 'Chilton Total Car Care' or factory service manual for exact specifications. Another test that you can make is checking the resistance between the terminals of the IAC valve for an open circuit or checking the positive feed terminal to ground to see if the valve is shorted. These resistance values may vary, but should never be an open circuit.

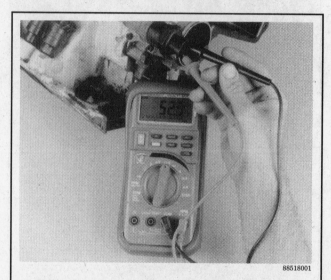

Fig. 135 Testing a typical screw-in type IAC valve

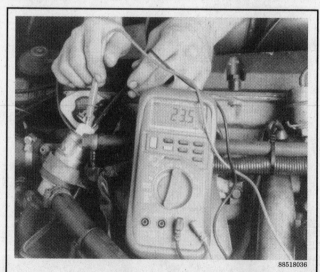

Fig. 136 Testing a IAC valve — Saab MFI engine shown

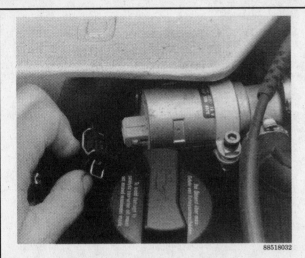

Fig. 137 Inspecting the electrical connector of the Idle stabilizer valve — Volkswagen Jetta engine shown

Fig. 138 Testing an Idle stabilizer valve — Volkswagen Jetta engine shown

Fig. 139 Testing an IAC valve — Chevrolet 4.3L TBI engine shown

REMOVAL & INSTALLATION

▶ **See Figures 140, 141, 142, 143, 144 and 145**

The procedures given here are for various GM engines. Most valves simply unbolt or screw out.

➡ **On some models it may be necessary to remove the air inlet assembly.**

1. Disconnect the negative battery cable. Disconnect the IAC valve electrical connector.
2. Remove the IAC valve by performing the following:
    a. On thread-mounted units, use a 1¼ in. (32mm) wrench.
    b. On flange-mounted units, remove the mounting screw assemblies.
3. Remove the IAC valve gasket or O-ring and discard.
To install:
4. Clean the mounting surfaces by performing the following:
    a. If servicing a thread-mounted valve, remove the old gasket material from the surface of the throttle body to ensure proper sealing of the new gasket.
    b. If servicing a flange-mounted valve, clean the IAC valve surfaces on the throttle body to assure proper seal of the new O-ring and contact of the IAC valve flange.
5. If installing a new IAC valve, measure the distance between the tip of the IAC valve pintle and the mounting flange. If the distance is greater than 1.102 in. (28mm), use finger pressure to slowly retract the pintle. The force required to retract the pintle of a new valve will not cause damage to the valve. If reinstalling the original IAC valve, do not attempt to adjust the pintle in this manner.
6. Install the IAC valve into the throttle body by performing the following:
    a. With thread-mounted valves, install with a new gasket.
    b. With flange-mounted valves, lubricate a new O-ring with transmission fluid and install on the IAC valve. Install the IAC valve to the throttle body. Install the mounting screws using a suitable thread locking compound and tighten.
7. Connect the IAC valve electrical connector.
8. Connect the negative battery cable.
9. No physical adjustment of the IAC valve assembly is required after installation. Reset the IAC valve pintle position by performing the following:
    a. Depress the accelerator pedal slightly.
    b. Start the engine and run for 5 seconds.
    c. Turn the ignition switch to the **OFF** position for 10 seconds.
    d. Restart the engine and check for proper idle operation.

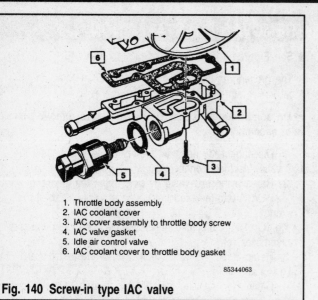

1. Throttle body assembly
2. IAC coolant cover
3. IAC cover assembly to throttle body screw
4. IAC valve gasket
5. Idle air control valve
6. IAC coolant cover to throttle body gasket

85344063

Fig. 140 Screw-in type IAC valve

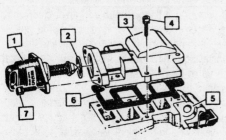

1. Idle air control (IAC) valve assembly
2. Idle air control valve O-ring
3. Idle air/vacuum signal housing assembly
4. Idle air/vacuum signal assembly screw
5. Throttle body assembly
6. Idle air/vacuum signal assembly gasket
7. Idle air control valve screw

85344064

Fig. 141 Flange-mounted IAC valves are retained by a screw

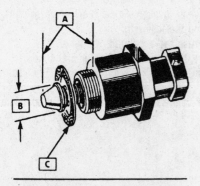

A. Distance of pintle extension
B. Diameter and shape of pintle
C. IAC valve gasket

85344065

Fig. 142 Measure the distance of pintle extension when installing a new IAC valve

88518027

Fig. 143 Removal and installation of the IAC valve — Typical MFI engine

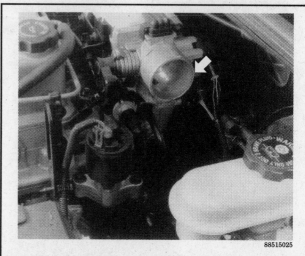

88515025

Fig. 144 Out of range idle may be a dirty IAC valve, or a dirty throttle body, as shown

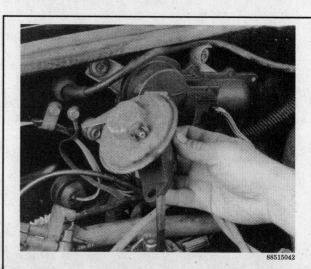

88515042

Fig. 145 Check for a dirty or leaking EGR valve. Out of range idle may be caused by this component, too.

INTAKE AIR TEMPERATURE (IAT) SENSOR

TESTING

▶ See Figures 146, 147, 148 and 149

The IAT sensor advises the ECM of changes in intake air temperature (and therefore air density). As intake air temperature varies, the ECM, by monitoring the voltage change, adjusts the amount of fuel injection according to the air temperature.

1. Unplug the electrical connector from the IAT sensor.

2. Using an ohmmeter, measure the resistance between both terminals. The resistance should be approximately 3,000 ohms at room temperature (70°F). Refer to the chart for sample resistance readings.

3. The intake air temperature sensor and coolant temperature sensor resistance values are usually the same. Because of this, an easy test is, on a cold engine (sitting overnight), to compare the resistance values of the two sensors. If the engine is cold, and both sensors are the same temperature, the resistances values should be about the same.

4. You can start the engine, and as it warms up check that the values change smoothly.

5. You can also heat the sensor using a hair dryer to see if the values change smoothly.

6. If the resistance value doesn't change, the sensor is probably defective. Some manufacturers built the intake air temperature sensor into the air flow sensor. In this case they are usually replaced as a unit. Since this type of sensor is expensive, you should perform air flow sensor testing to make certain it is defective.

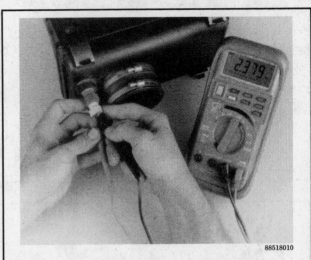

Fig. 146 Testing the Intake Air Temperature (IAT) sensor

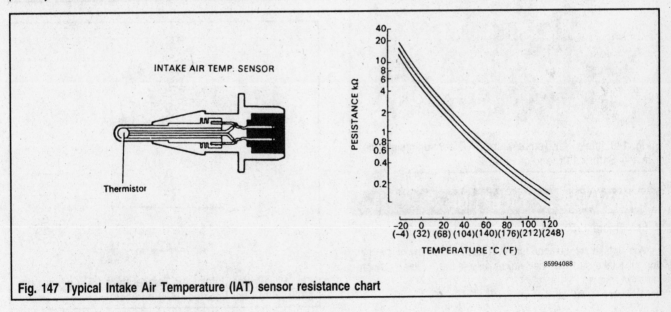

Fig. 147 Typical Intake Air Temperature (IAT) sensor resistance chart

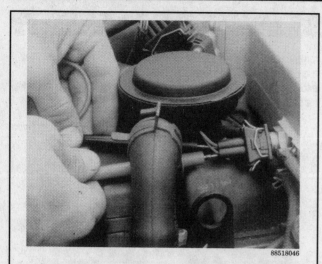

Fig. 148 Intake Air Temperature (IAT) sensor resistance test-Volkswagen Motronic engine shown

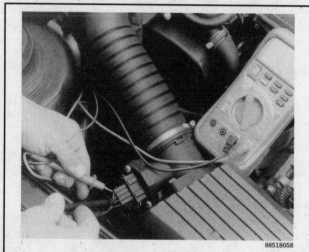

Fig. 149 Intake Air Temperature (IAT) sensor resistance test — Saturn 1.9L engine shown

REMOVAL & INSTALLATION

▶ **See Figures 150 and 151**

Most Intake Air Temperature (IAT) sensors screw or clip into the air intake stream. They are usually at the throttle body or air flow sensor.

1. Remove the air cleaner cover.

2. With the ignition OFF, unplug the electrical connector.

3. Remove the IAT sensor from inside the air cleaner housing or intake plenum.

To install:

4. Install the sensor, making sure it is properly positioned and secure.

5. Connect the wiring harness, and install the air cleaner cover.

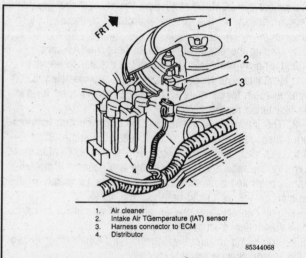

1. Air cleaner
2. Intake Air TGemperature (IAT) sensor
3. Harness connector to ECM
4. Distributor

Fig. 150 Typical Intake Air Temperature (IAT) sensor on Throttle Body Injected (TBI) engines

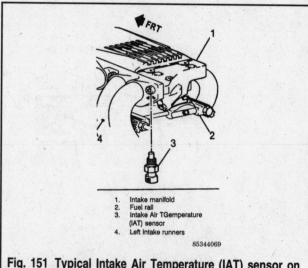

1. Intake manifold
2. Fuel rail
3. Intake Air TGemperature (IAT) sensor
4. Left intake runners

Fig. 151 Typical Intake Air Temperature (IAT) sensor on Multi-point Fuel Injected (MFI) engines

KNOCK SENSOR

TESTING

▶ **See Figures 153 and 152**

The knock sensor is mounted to the engine block or manifold. When spark knock or pinging is present, the sensor produces a voltage signal which is sent to the ECM. The ECM will then retard the ignition timing based on these signals.

When suspecting a knock sensor problem, first perform a visual inspection. Most problems can be found in wiring harnesses and connectors.

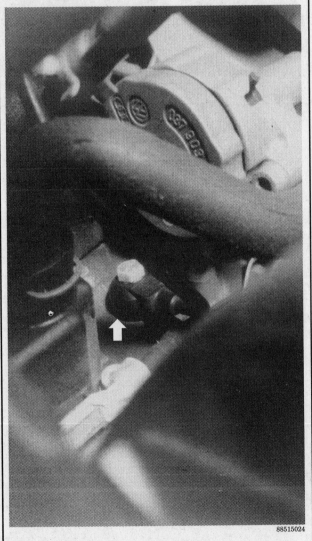

Fig. 152 View of the Knock sensor used in a Saturn with 1.9L MFI engine shown

Perform a basic knock sensor test as follows. To make this test you will need a timing light.

1. Connect a timing light to the engine.
2. Start the engine and allowing warm up sufficiently.
3. Position the timing light toward the timing marks on the harmonic balancer.
4. Locate the knock sensor, some engines may be equipped with 2 knock sensors.
5. Using a suitable metallic tool, tap on the intake manifold or side of the engine block which ever is closest to the knock sensor. Do not strike hard or hit the sensor directly, light tapping should cause the knock sensor to react.
6. If the knock sensor is working the ignition timing will begin to retard as you tap.

If the timing does not change, you will need to check voltage at the knock sensor harness connector. Also make sure the connector is clean and making good connection. For specific testing for the vehicle you are working with, consult your 'Chilton Total Car Care' or factory service manual.

REMOVAL & INSTALLATION

1. Disconnect the negative battery cable.
2. Drain the engine coolant.
3. Raise and properly support the vehicle.
4. Disconnect the knock sensor wiring harness.
5. Remove the knock sensor from the engine block.

✳✳CAUTION

If the knock sensor is mounted in the engine block cooling passage, engine coolant will drain when the sensor is removed.

6. Installation is the reverse of removal.

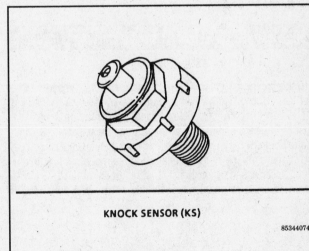

KNOCK SENSOR (KS)

85344074

Fig. 153 Typical knock sensor

MAGNETIC RELUCTANCE SENSOR

Magnetic reluctance sensors are used to determine either position or speed. These sensors are commonly found on or near the camshaft and/or crankshaft. Some sensors may be located inside the distributor. They consist of a magnet assembly and a toothed ring commonly referred to as a reluctor. They can be tested by using a digital multimeter.

Testing

1. Perform a visual inspection.
2. Disconnect the sensor connector.

➡**Never disconnect any connector with the ignition switch ON.**

3. Using a digital multimeter set to the ohms setting, check resistance across the sensor terminals. The resistance should be approximately 500-1200 ohms at 70°F. Resistance will vary with temperature.

➡**This test should be performed with the ignition ON and engine OFF.**

4. Using a thin piece of steel, check the tip of the sensor to see if it is magnetized.
5. Using a digital multimeter set to the millivolts AC scale, connect the test probes to the sensor.
6. Rotate reluctor ring to activate the sensor signal. On camshaft or crankshaft sensors, use the starter to crank the engine. Refer to your 'Chilton Total Car Care' manual for correct wire color, terminal location and recommended specifications.
7. Voltage should be seen as the reluctor ring is rotated. If the reluctor is rotated quickly, a signal of at least 200 millivolts AC should be seen.

REMOVAL & INSTALLATION

▶ **See Figures 154, 155 and 156**

Depending on location, these sensors can be removed without too much difficulty. Removal usually involves disconnecting the electrical connector and unbolting the sensor. In some cases, the sensor must be adjusted during installation. Some manufacturers may mount these sensors behind other components, an example is that General Motors mounts the crankshaft position sensor on the 2.5L engine behind the DIS ignition module. If you can not locate this sensor you may need to refer to your 'Chilton Total Car Care' manual. Some sensor may require a specific spacing adjustment. If necessary this procedure is also provided in the 'Chilton Total Car Care' manual.

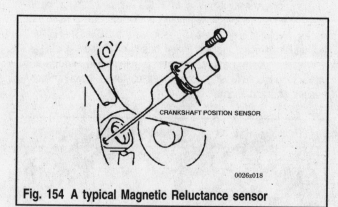

Fig. 154 A typical Magnetic Reluctance sensor

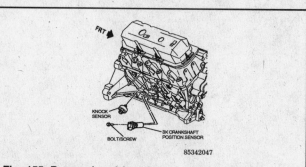

Fig. 155 Removal and location of a typical Magnetic Reluctance sensor — crankshaft sensor

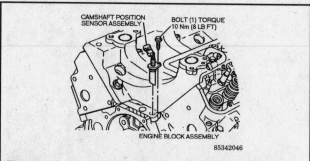

Fig. 156 Removal and location of a typical Magnetic Reluctance sensor — camshaft sensor

MANIFOLD ABSOLUTE PRESSURE (MAP) SENSOR

TESTING

▶ See Figures 157, 158, 159 and 160

There are two types of Manifold Absolute Pressure (MAP) sensors. The analog signal type, which is tested with a voltmeter, is used on most General Motors, Chrysler and import vehicles. The frequency signal type, which is tested with a Hertz meter or digital tachometer is used on most Ford vehicles. If you're not certain which type you have, check the reference voltage which is usually around 5 volts. Then check the signal voltage. If the signal voltage never changes from 2.5 volts, it is most likely a frequency type.

Fig. 159 Connecting a hand operated vacuum pump to the vacuum port on the MAP sensor

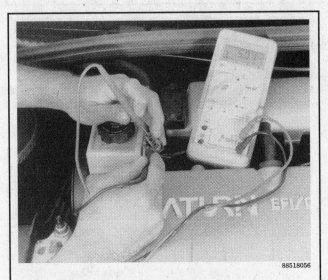

Fig. 157 MAP sensor test — Saturn shown

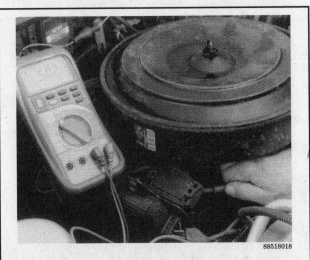

Fig. 158 Reference voltage of 5.02 volts is found on this Chevrolet 4.3L MAP sensor

Fig. 160 Voltage reading should change smoothly as vacuum is applied — Chevrolet 4.3L TBI engine shown

ANALOG SIGNAL TYPE

▶ See Figure 161

➡The analog signal type MAP sensor is used most on General Motors, Chrysler and import vehicles.

These sensors are usually located in the engine compartment near the air cleaner, mounted on the inner fender or firewall. They can be checked using a digital voltmeter and a hand vacuum pump.

1. Disconnect the MAP sensor's electrical connector.
2. Connect one jumper wire from the connector to the MAP sensor's terminal A.
3. Connect the other wire from the connector to terminal C.
4. Connect the positive lead of a digital voltmeter to terminal B and the negative voltmeter lead to ground.

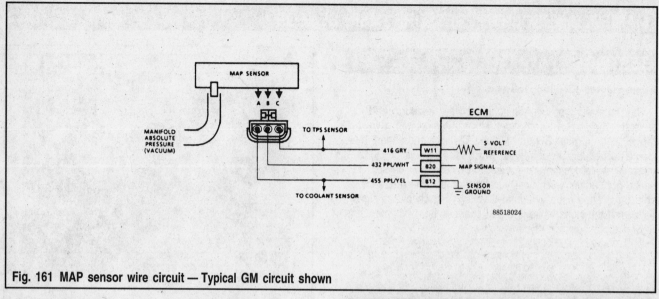

Fig. 161 MAP sensor wire circuit — Typical GM circuit shown

5. Turn the ignition key **ON**. If the reading falls in the voltage range of 4.6 to 5.0, the sensor is functioning properly, at this point.

6. Start the engine and let it idle. An idling engine will produce a large amount of intake manifold vacuum, which should pull the MAP sensor's voltage down to a low reading of approximately 1-2 volts (reading will vary with altitude). This test indicates that the MAP sensor is responding to vacuum.

FREQUENCY SIGNAL TYPE

▶ See Figure 162

➡The frequency signal type MAP sensor is used on most Ford vehicles.

1. Set your digital tachometer on the 4 cyl. scale.
2. Start the engine and let it idle.
3. Connect the tachometer between the sensor's middle terminal and ground.
4. Take a reading and use the conversion chart to convert the tachometer reading to a frequency reading.

MAP sensor frequency can be measured with a digital tachometer. Never use an analog tachometer. A tachometer is a frequency counter. It measures pulses received per second (Hz) and converts them to revolutions per minute. We are going to use the RPM reading to measure the frequency. The following chart converts revolutions per minute into pulses per second.

REMOVAL & INSTALLATION

Replacing the MAP sensor simply requires unplugging the vacuum and electrical connections, then unbolting the sensor. Inspect the vacuum hose over its entire length for any signs of cracking or splitting. The slightest leak can cause false messages to be send to the ECM.

	Tachometer 4-cyl. scale	Equivalent Frequency
0-in. vac	454-464	152-155 HZ
5-in. vac	411-420	138-140 HZ
10-in. vac	370-380	124-127 HZ
15-in. vac	331-339	111-114 HZ
20-in. vac	294-301	93- 98 HZ.

88518025

Fig. 162 Tachometer reading-to-frequency reading conversion chart

MASS AIR FLOW (MAF) SENSOR

TESTING

▶ **See Figure 163**

The Mass Air Flow (MAF) sensor, found on some fuel injected engines, measures the amount of air passing through it. The ECM uses this information to determine the operating conditions of the engine to control fuel delivery. A large quantity of air indicates acceleration, while a small quantity indicates deceleration or idle.

Most MAF sensors require special testing equipment or scan tools to help diagnose a problem. The MAF sensors used on most vehicles are some of the more complicated and expensive components. One method of checking a MAF sensor is to measure the pulse width of the fuel injector. Pulse width is measurement of how long the fuel injector is open, or how much fuel is being delivered by the fuel injector. You can then restrict the air intake and look for a change in fuel control. If a change in fuel delivery is noticed, the MAF sensor is most likely working properly. Some General Motors MAF sensors were sensitive to vibration. You can gently tap on the MAF, if the engine idle changes the MAF sensor is defective.

➠**For specific information and recommended specifications on the vehicle you are working with, consult your 'Chilton Total Car Care' or factory service manual.**

REMOVAL & INSTALLATION

▶ **See Figures 164, 165 and 166**

1. Disconnect the negative battery cable.

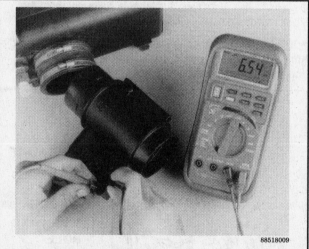

Fig. 163 Checking the resistance of a General Motors design MAF sensor

2. Disconnect the sensor electrical connection.

3. Loosen the clamps and remove the air intake hoses from the MAF sensor.

4. Remove the sensor from the vehicle. On some models it will be necessary to remove the sensor-to-bracket attaching bolts.

5. Installation is the reverse of removal.

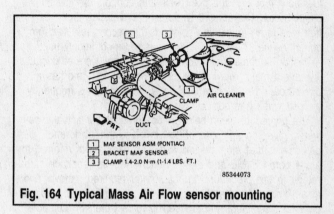

1	MAF SENSOR ASM (PONTIAC)
2	BRACKET MAF SENSOR
3	CLAMP 1.4-2.0 N·m (1-1.4 LBS. FT.)

Fig. 164 Typical Mass Air Flow sensor mounting

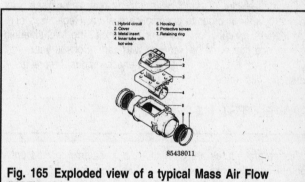

Fig. 165 Exploded view of a typical Mass Air Flow (MAF) sensor

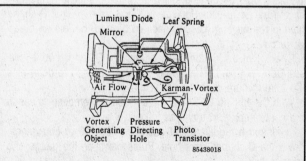

Fig. 166 A Karmen Vortex design MAF sensor uses photo cells to product the air volume signal

MIXTURE CONTROL (M/C) SOLENOID

TESTING

▶ **See Figures 167, 168, 169 and 170**

The Mixture Control (M/C) solenoid valve is used on feedback carburetors. On some vehicles it may be known as a duty cycle solenoid. Basically it controls the fuel flow from the fuel bowl thorough the main well, and controls the idle air bleed circuit. There are 2 types used in vehicles today. The first type is an air pulsing solenoid, the second is a vacuum control valve. The air pulsing type is more commonly used.

Testing is somewhat involved for this small device. Because is plays a major role in how the engine will idle and has a direct bearing on air/fuel emissions. This device is frequently blamed when it is not actually at fault.

The procedure given below is not intended for actual repair, just to give you and idea of how involved the job is and procedures that must be followed. The carburetors referred to are 4 barrel E4ME and E4MC General Motors feedback carburetors. In this procedure, the carburetor required removal and disassembly. We are starting with the carburetor removed, partially disassembled, and proceeding to test the M/C solenoid. On some vehicles, it is not necessary to remove or dissemble the carburetor in order to accomplish this job. Regardless of the level of difficulty for your specific vehicle, the M/C solenoid is a device that must be serviced with care. Consult your 'Chilton Total Car Care' or factory service manual before attempting this repair.

TRAVEL TEST

These procedures are performed on four barrel models only. Before checking the mixture control solenoid travel, it may be necessary to modify the float gauge J-9789-130 or equivalent (used to externally check the float level).

This should be done by filing or grinding sufficient material off the gauge to allow for insertion down the vertical D-shaped hole in the air horn casting (located next to the idle air bleed valve cover).

Check that the gauge freely enters the D-shaped vent hole and does not bind. The gauge will also be used to determine the total mixture control solenoid travel.

With the engine OFF and the air cleaner removed, measure the control solenoid travel as follows:

1. Insert a modified float gauge J-9789-130 or equivalent down the D-shaped vent hole. Press down on the gauge and release it.

2. Observe that the gauge moves freely and does not bind. With the gauge released (solenoid in the up position), be sure to read it at eye level and record the mark on the gauge (in inches/millimeters) that lines up with the top of the air horn casting (upper edge).

3. Lightly press down on the gauge until bottomed (solenoid in the down position). Record (in inches/millimeters) the mark on the gauge that lines up with the top of the air horn casting.

4. Subtract the gauge up dimension from gauge dimension. Record the difference (in inches/millimeters). This difference is total solenoid travel.

5. If total solenoid travel is not within $3/32$-$5/32$ in. (2.4-3.9mm), perform the mixture control solenoid adjustments. If the difference is within specifications, proceed to the idle air bleed valve adjustment.

➡**If adjustment is required, it will be necessary to remove the air horn and drive out the mixture control solenoid screw plug from the underside of the air horn.**

Adjustments

Before making adjustment to mixture control solenoid, verify that the plunger travel is not correct.

1. Remove air horn, mixture control solenoid plunger, air horn gasket and plastic filler block, using normal service procedures.

2. Check carburetor for cause of incorrect mixture:
   a. M/C solenoid bore or plunger worn or sticking
   b. Metering rods for incorrect part number, sticking or rods or springs not installed properly
   c. Foreign material in jets

3. Remove throttle side metering rod. Install mixture control solenoid gauging tool, J-33815-1, BT-8253-A, or equivalent, over the throttle side metering jet rod guide and temporarily reinstall the solenoid plunger into the solenoid body.

4. Holding the solenoid plunger in the **DOWN** position, use tool J-28696-10, BT-7928, or equivalent, to turn lean mixture solenoid screw counterclockwise until the plunger breaks contact with the gauging tool. Turn slowly clockwise until the plunger makes contact with the gauging tool. The adjustment is correct when the solenoid plunger is contacting both the solenoid stop and the gauging tool.

➡**If the total difference in adjustment required less than $3/4$ turn of the lean mixture solenoid screw, the original setting was within the manufacturer's specifications.**

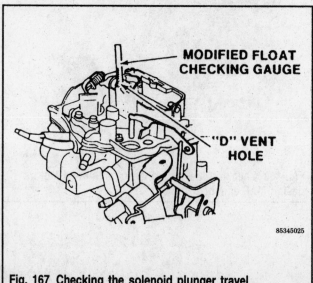

MODIFIED FLOAT CHECKING GAUGE

"D" VENT HOLE

85345025

Fig. 167 Checking the solenoid plunger travel

5. Remove solenoid plunger and gauging tool and reinstall metering rod and plastic filler block.

6. Invert air horn and remove rich mixture stop screw from bottom side of air horn, using tool J-28696-4, BT-7967-A, or equivalent.

7. Remove lean mixture screw plug and the rich mixture stop screw plug from air horn, using a punch.

8. Reinstall rich mixture stop screw in air horn and bottom lightly, then back screw out ¼ turn.

9. Reinstall air horn gasket, mixture control solenoid plunger and air horn to carburetor.

10. Adjust the M/C solenoid plunger travel as follows:

a. Insert float gauge down D-shaped vent hole. Press down on gauge and release, observing that the gauge moves freely and does not bind. With gauge released, (plunger UP position), read at eye level and record the reading of the gauge mark (in inches/millimeters) that lines up with the top of air horn casting, (upper edge).

b. Lightly press down on gauge until bottomed, (plunger DOWN position). Read and record (in inches/millimeters) the reading of the gauge mark that lines up with top of air horn casting.

c. Subtract gauge **UP** position from the gauge **DOWN** position and record the difference. This difference is the total plunger travel. Insert external float gauge in vent hole and, with tool J-28696-10, BT-7928, or equivalent, adjust rich mixture stop screw to obtain ⁵/₃₂ in. (3.9mm) total plunger travel.

11. With solenoid plunger travel correctly set, install plugs (supplied in service kits) in the air horn, as follows:

a. Install plug, hollow end down, into the access hole for the lean mixture (solenoid) screw. Use suitably sized punch to drive plug into the air horn until the top of plug is even with the lower. Plug must be installed to retain the screw setting and to prevent fuel vapor loss.

b. Install plug, with hollow end down, over the rich mixture stop screw access hole and drive plug into place so that the top of the plug is ³/₁₆ in. (4.7mm) below the surface of the air horn casting.

➡**Plug must be installed to retain screw setting.**

12. To check the M/C solenoid dwell, first disconnect vacuum line to the canister purge valve and plug it. Ground diagnostic TEST terminal and run engine until it is at normal operation temperature (upper radiator hose hot) and in closed loop.

13. Check M/C dwell at 3000 rpm. If within 10-50 degrees, calibration is complete. If higher than 50 degrees, check the carburetor for a cause of rich condition. If below 10 degrees, look for a cause of lean engine condition such as vacuum leaks. If none are found, check for the cause of a lean carburetor.

Idle Air Valve
▶ **See Figures 171 and 172**

A cover is in place over the idle air bleed valve. Also, the access holes to the idle mixture needles are sealed with hardened plugs. This is done to seal the factory settings, during original equipment production. These items are NOT to be removed unless required for cleaning, part replacement, improper dwell readings or if a system Performance Check indicated the carburetor was the cause of the trouble.

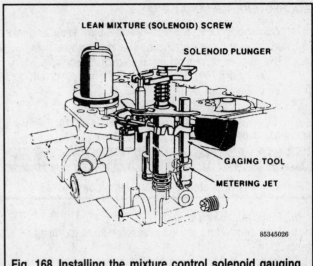

Fig. 168 Installing the mixture control solenoid gauging tool

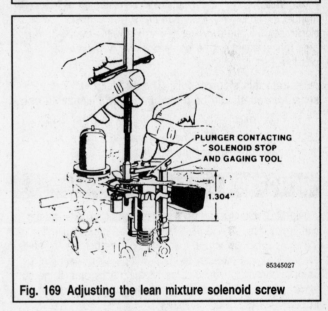

Fig. 169 Adjusting the lean mixture solenoid screw

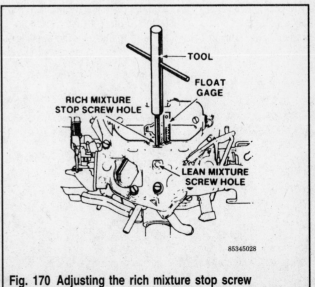

Fig. 170 Adjusting the rich mixture stop screw

ROCHESTER E4ME AND E4MC

1. With engine **OFF**, cover the internal bowl vents and inlet to bleed valve and the carburetor air intakes with masking tape. This is done to prevent metal chips from entering.

2. Carefully drill rivet head of idle air bleed cover, with 0.110 in. (2.8mm) drill bit.

3. Remove rivet head and all pieces of rivet.

4. Lift cover off air bleed valve and blow out any metal shavings, or use a magnet to remove excess metal.

✳✳CAUTION

Always wear eye protection when using compressed air.

5. Remove masking tape.

6. Start engine and allow it to reach normal operating temperature.

7. Disconnect the vacuum hose from the canister purge valve and plug it.

8. While idling in **D** for automatic transmission or **N** for manual transmission, slowly turn the valve counterclockwise or clockwise, until the dwell reading varies within the 25-35 degree range, attempting to be as close to 30 degrees as possible.

➡**Perform this step carefully. The air bleed valve is very sensitive and should be turned in ⅛ turn increments only.**

9. If the dwell reading does not vary and is not within the 25-35 degree range, it will be necessary to remove the plugs and to adjust the idle mixture needles.

REMOVAL & INSTALLATION

The M/C solenoid can be a simple bolt on or may require carburetor removal and disassembly procedures, depending on the type carburetor you are working on. The bolt on solenoids are for the most part simple to do. Simply disconnect the harness connector. Remove the retaining bolts and lift the solenoid off the carburetor. When installing it you would first inspect it for dirt or contamination.

M/C solenoids that require carburetor removal and disassembly also require critical adjustments. For either type solenoid, consult your 'Chilton Total Car Care' manual for the specific

information before attempting to replace the mixture control solenoid.

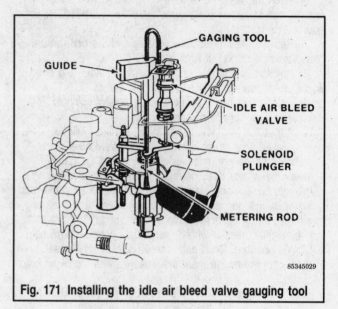

Fig. 171 Installing the idle air bleed valve gauging tool

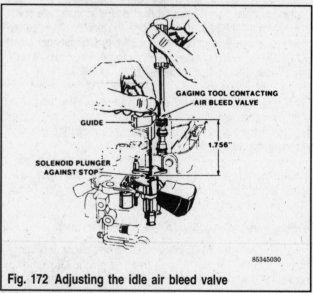

Fig. 172 Adjusting the idle air bleed valve

OXYGEN SENSOR

TESTING

◗ **See Figures 173, 174, 175 and 176**

The oxygen (O_2) sensor is located in the exhaust stream, ahead of the catalytic converter. usually on the exhaust manifold. Some vehicles use more than one sensor. Its function is to detect the concentration of oxygen in the exhaust gas. Using highly refined metals (zirconia and platinum), the sensor uses changes in the oxygen content to generate an electrical signal which is transmitted to the ECM. The computer in turn reacts to the signal by adjusting the fuel metering at the injectors or at the carburetor. More or less fuel is delivered into the cylinders and the correct oxygen level is maintained. The O_2 sensor can be checked using a multimeter set to the millivolt setting.

1. Perform a visual inspection. Black sooty deposits on the O_2 sensor tip may indicate a rich air/fuel mixture. White gritty deposits could be an internal antifreeze leak. Brown deposits indicate oil consumption.

➡**All of these containments will destroy a sensor, if problem is not repaired the new sensor will be destroyed too.**

2. Disconnect the O_2 sensor connector and install jumper wires from the sensor connector to the wiring harness. This permits the engine to operate normally while you check the engine.

✳✳WARNING

Never disconnect any connector with the ignition switch ON.

3. Start the engine and allow it to reach operating temperature. This should take about ten minutes. Turn the engine **OFF**.

4. Connect the positive lead of a multimeter to the O_2 sensor signal wire and the negative lead to the engine ground. Re-start the engine.

➡**For specific information on wire color and terminal identification, it will be necessary to consult your 'Chilton Total Car Care' manual.**

5. The voltage reading should be fluctuating as the O_2 sensor detects varying levels of oxygen in the exhaust stream.

6. If the O_2 sensor voltage does not fluctuate, the sensor may be defective or mixture could be extremely out of range.

7. If the O_2 sensor reads above 550 millivolts constantly, the fuel mixture is probably too rich. If the (O_2) sensor voltage reads below 350 millivolts constantly, the fuel mixture may be too lean or you may have an exhaust leak near the sensor.

8. Under normal conditions the O_2 sensor should fluctuate high and low. Prior to condemning the O_2 sensor, try forcing the system rich by restricting the air intake or lean by removing a vacuum line. If this causes the oxygen sensor to momentarily respond, look for problems in other areas of the system.

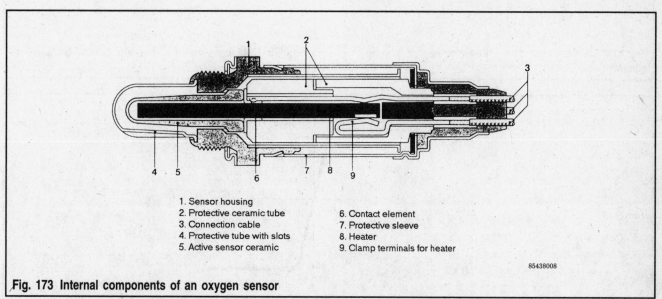

1. Sensor housing
2. Protective ceramic tube
3. Connection cable
4. Protective tube with slots
5. Active sensor ceramic
6. Contact element
7. Protective sleeve
8. Heater
9. Clamp terminals for heater

85438008

Fig. 173 Internal components of an oxygen sensor

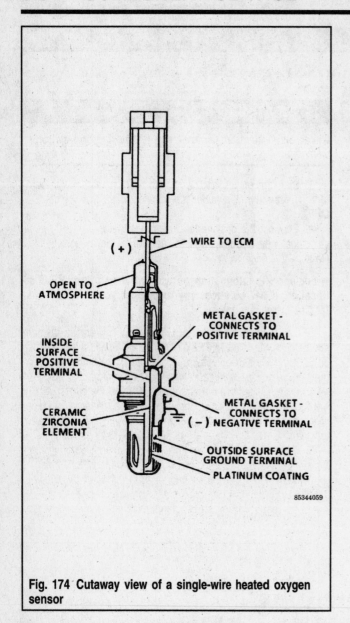

INSIDE SURFACE POSITIVE TERMINAL

OPEN TO ATMOSPHERE

(+)

WIRE TO ECM

METAL GASKET - CONNECTS TO POSITIVE TERMINAL

CERAMIC ZIRCONIA ELEMENT

METAL GASKET - CONNECTS TO (–) NEGATIVE TERMINAL

OUTSIDE SURFACE GROUND TERMINAL

PLATINUM COATING

85344059

Fig. 174 Cutaway view of a single-wire heated oxygen sensor

HEATER TERMINATION

GRIPPER

CLIP RING

INSULATOR

FOUR WIRE IN-LINE CONNECTOR

ZIRCONIA ELEMENT

INNER ELECTRODE

ROD HEATER

WATER SHIELD ASSEMBLY

SENSOR LEAD

FLAT SEAT SHELL

SEAT GASKET

OUTER ELECTRODE & PROTECTIVE COATING

85344060

Fig. 175 Cutaway view of a four-wire heated oxygen sensor

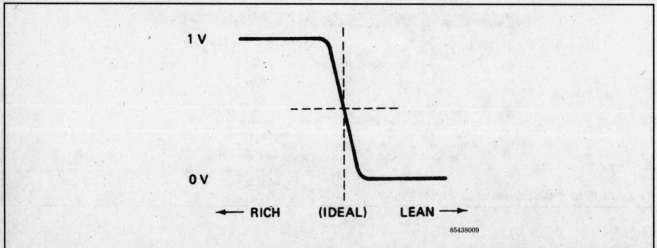

1 V

0 V

◄— RICH   (IDEAL)   LEAN —►

85438009

Fig. 176 The oxygen's function is to provide a varying voltage from 0.1 to 0.9 voltage. This signal is used to keep the fuel mixture ideal

REMOVAL & INSTALLATION

▶ See Figures 177, 178 and 179

✳✳WARNING

Care should be used during the removal of the oxygen sensor. Both the sensor and its wire can be easily damaged.

1. The best condition in which to remove the sensor is when the engine is moderately warm. This is generally achieved after two to five minutes (depending on outside temperature) of running after a cold start. The exhaust manifold has developed enough heat to expand and make the removal easier but is not so hot that it has become untouchable. Wearing heat resistant gloves is highly recommended during this repair.

➡Special wrenches, either socket or open-end, are available from reputable retail outlets for removing the oxygen sensor. These tools make the job much easier and often prevent unnecessary damage.

2. With the ignition OFF, unplug the connector for the sensor.
3. Unscrew the sensor or remove the two sensor attaching bolts.
4. Remove the oxygen sensor from the manifold.
To install:
5. During and after the removal, use great care to protect the tip of the sensor if it is to be reused. Do not allow it to come in contact with fluids or dirt. Do not attempt to clean it or wash it.
6. Apply a coat of anti-seize compound to the bolt threads but DO NOT allow any to get on the tip of the sensor.
7. Install the sensor in the manifold.
8. Reconnect the electrical connector and ensure a clean, tight connection.

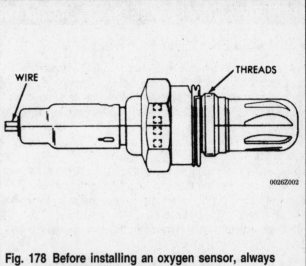

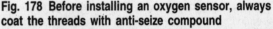

Fig. 178 Before installing an oxygen sensor, always coat the threads with anti-seize compound

Fig. 179 A droplight or flashlight is required to locate many oxygen sensors, like the one on this Saturn

Fig. 177 Removing the Oxygen Sensor from the exhaust manifold

POSITIVE CRANKCASE VENTILATION (PCV)

♦ **See Figures 180, 181, 182, 183 and 184**

A closed Positive Crankcase Ventilation (PCV) system is used on most vehicles. This system cycles incompletely burned fuel which works its way past the piston rings back into the intake manifold for reburning with the fuel/air mixture. The oil filler cap is sealed and the air is drawn from the top of the crankcase into the intake manifold through a valve with a variable orifice.

This valve (commonly known as the PCV valve) regulates the flow of air into the manifold according to the amount of manifold vacuum. When the throttle plates are open fairly wide, the valve is fully open. However, at idle speed, when the manifold vacuum is at maximum, the PCV valve reduces the flow.

A plugged valve or hose may cause a rough idle, stalling or low idle speed, oil leaks in the engine and/or sludging and oil deposits within the engine and air cleaner. A leaking valve or hose could cause an erratic idle or stalling.

TESTING

The PCV valve is easily checked with the engine running at normal idle speed (warmed up). Remove the PCV valve from the valve cover or intake manifold, but leave it connected to its hose. Place your thumb over the end of the valve to check for vacuum. If there is no vacuum, check for plugged hoses or ports. If these are open, the valve is faulty. With the engine off, remove the PCV valve completely. Shake it end to end, listening for the rattle of the needle inside the valve. If no rattle is heard, the needle is jammed (probably with oil sludge) and the valve should be replaced.

An engine which is operated without crankcase ventilation can be damaged very quickly. It is important to check and change the PCV valve at regular maintenance intervals.

REMOVAL & INSTALLATION

➡The procedure given here is a general procedure. For specific information on the vehicle you are working with, consult your 'Chilton Total Car Care' or factory service manual.

Remove the PCV valve from the cylinder head cover or intake manifold. Remove the hose from the valve. Take note of which end of the valve was in the manifold. This one-way valve must be reinstalled correctly or it will not function. While the valve is removed, the hoses should be checked for splits,

kinks and blockages. Check the vacuum port (that the hoses connects to) for any clogging.

Remember that the correct function of the PCV system is based on a sealed engine. An air leak at the oil filler cap and/or around the oil pan can defeat the design of the system.

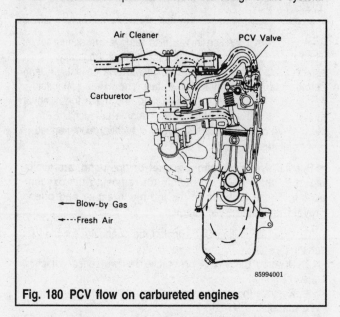

Fig. 180 PCV flow on carbureted engines

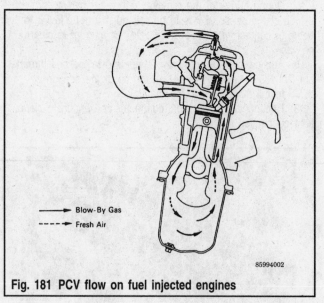

Fig. 181 PCV flow on fuel injected engines

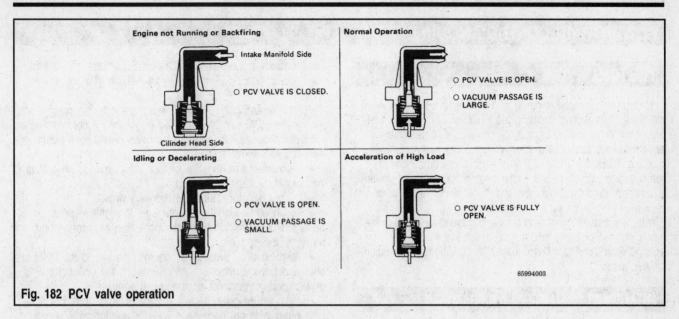

Engine not Running or Backfiring

Intake Manifold Side

○ PCV VALVE IS CLOSED.

Cilinder Head Side

Normal Operation

○ PCV VALVE IS OPEN.

○ VACUUM PASSAGE IS LARGE.

Idling or Decelerating

○ PCV VALVE IS OPEN.

○ VACUUM PASSAGE IS SMALL.

Acceleration of High Load

○ PCV VALVE IS FULLY OPEN.

85994003

Fig. 182 PCV valve operation

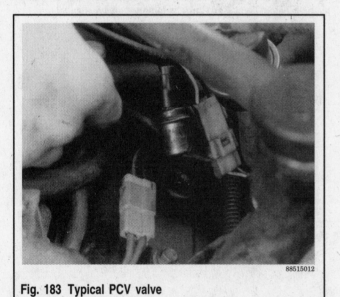

88515012

Fig. 183 Typical PCV valve

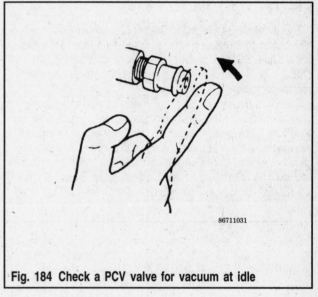

86711031

Fig. 184 Check a PCV valve for vacuum at idle

POWERTRAIN CONTROL MODULE (PCM)

TESTING

There are no methods currently available to test the PCM in the field. Most testing involving the PCM usually involves testing of the components associated with the PCM, and if all appears okay, substituting a known good unit is the common practice. Since the PCM is a very expensive component to replace, accurate diagnosis of the engine management system is advised. Before condemning the PCM, always perform extensive testing to be sure it is defective.

It is rare that PCM is defective, and if found defective, usually a shorted or faulty actuator caused it to go bad. Consult your 'Chilton Total Car Care' manual for additional information on this subject.

REMOVAL & INSTALLATION

▶ **See Figures 185, 186, 187 and 188**

The terminology 'Electronic Control Module' was changed in 1994. Manufacturers are now using the term Powertrain Control Module (PCM). However, whenever term ECM, ECA, SMEC, SBEC or PCM is used, it is referring to the engine control computer.

The PCM may be located in different locations depending on the manufacturer. The most common locations are: on the right or left side kick panels under the dash, under the driver's or passenger seat, or in the trunk area. On some Chrysler vehicles it is located in the engine compartment, near the firewall and may be referred to as an 'Single Module Engine Controller' (SMEC) or 'Single Board Engine Controller' (SBEC). It will

be necessary to consult your 'Chilton Total Care' manual for the specific location pertaining to the vehicle you are working with.

Before removing the PCM, always adhere to the precautions given. The PCM can be damaged very easily if not handled or removed properly. Observe the following precautions before attempting to remove any PCM.

• Disconnect the negative battery cable, except when testing with battery voltage is required.

• Do not puncture the PCM harness wires.

• To prevent internal PCM damage, the ignition switch must be in the **OFF** position when disconnecting or reconnecting power to the computer.

• To prevent electrostatic discharge damage to the PCM or other electronic components, do not touch the connector pins or soldered components on the circuit board.

The procedure given here is a general procedure. For specific information on the vehicle you are working with, consult your 'Chilton Total Car Care' or factory service manual.

1. Disconnect the negative battery cable.
2. Locate the PCM and remove the protective covering.
3. Remove the mounting bolts and carefully pull the PCM from its mounting location.
4. Carefully disconnect the harness connectors and remove the PCM from the vehicle.

To install:

5. Carefully connect the harness connectors to the PCM being very careful not to distort the prongs.
6. Position the PCM its mounting location and secure it in place with the mounting bolts.
7. Install the protective cover.
8. Connect the negative battery cable.

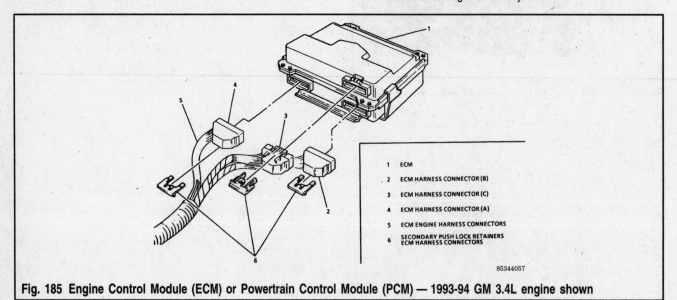

1	ECM
2	ECM HARNESS CONNECTOR (B)
3	ECM HARNESS CONNECTOR (C)
4	ECM HARNESS CONNECTOR (A)
5	ECM ENGINE HARNESS CONNECTORS
6	SECONDARY PUSH LOCK RETAINERS ECM HARNESS CONNECTORS

85344057

Fig. 185 Engine Control Module (ECM) or Powertrain Control Module (PCM) — 1993-94 GM 3.4L engine shown

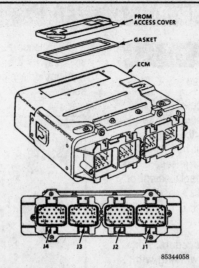

PROM
ACCESS COVER

GASKET

ECM

J4 J3 J2 J1

85344058

Fig. 186 Engine Control Module (ECM)/Powertrain Control Module (PCM) — 1993-94 GM 5.7L LT1 engine shown

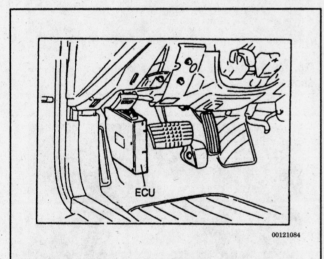

ECU

00121084

Fig. 187 Powertrain Control Module location — Subaru SVX shown

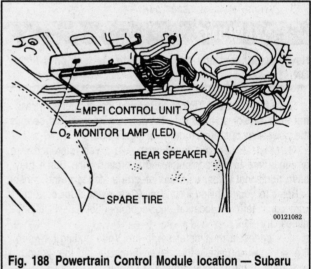

MPFI CONTROL UNIT

O₂ MONITOR LAMP (LED)

REAR SPEAKER

SPARE TIRE

00121082

Fig. 188 Powertrain Control Module location — Subaru XT shown

THROTTLE POSITION (TP) SENSOR

TESTING

▶ **See Figures 189, 190, 191, 192, 193 and 194**

Throttle Position (TP) sensors are usually located on the side of the carburetor or fuel injection throttle body. TP sensors can be checked using a multimeter set to the **Volts** setting. TP sensor failure is common because it has parts that move each time the accelerator is depressed or released. This is one of the more common parts that require replacement or adjustment, due to the amount of movement this sensor endures every time a vehicle is driven. However, it is one of the easiest components to test and replace.

➡**The procedure given here is a general procedure. For specific information on the vehicle you are working with, consult your 'Chilton Total Car Care' or factory service manual.**

1. Perform a visual inspection.

✳✳WARNING

Never disconnect any connector with the ignition switch ON.

2. Disconnect the TP connector and install jumper wires from the sensor connector to the wiring harness. This permits the sensor to operate properly during testing.
3. Most TP sensors use 3 wires — a 5 volt reference wire, a signal wire to the computer and a ground wire. Some may have additional wires, used for integral switches in the sensor.
Refer to your 'Chilton Total Car Care' manual for correct wire color, terminal location and recommended specification, if necessary.
4. Connect a multimeter set to the **Volts** setting between the signal wire (usually the center terminal) and the ground wire (one of the outside terminals) on the TP sensor.

➡**This test should be performed with the ignition ON and the engine OFF.**

5. Check the voltage reading with the throttle in the idle position. Usual voltage readings are approximately 0.45 volts.
Refer to your 'Chilton Total Car Care' or factory service repair manual for specific voltages.
6. Open the throttle slowly. The voltage increase smoothly as the throttle is moved to the Wide Open Throttle (WOT) position. Usual voltage at the WOT position is approximately 4.5 volts.

7. Release the throttle slowly. The voltage should decrease smoothly as the throttle is moved to the idle position. Erratic readings or a momentary infinite reading indicate a defective sensor.

Fig. 189 Testing the throttle position sensor — Saturn shown

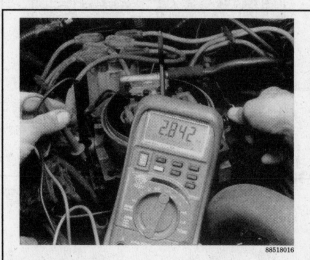

Fig. 190 Testing the throttle position sensor — GM TBI unit shown

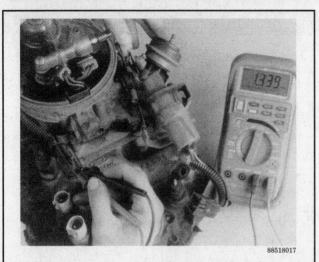

Fig. 191 Testing the throttle position sensor — Ford TBI unit shown

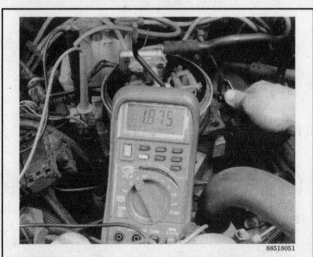

Fig. 192 Testing the throttle position sensor — Ford TBI unit shown

Fig. 193 A close look at backprobing the throttle position sensor wire connection — Chevrolet shown

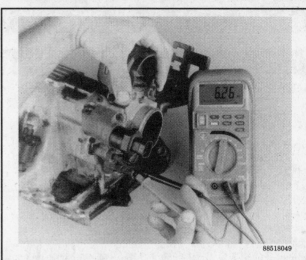

Fig. 194 A ohmmeter can test a TP sensor, if sensor is disconnected from circuit

REMOVAL & INSTALLATION

▶ **See Figure 195**

TP sensors are usually removed by disconnecting the electrical connector and unscrewing the mounting screws. If the screw holes are slotted, the sensor is adjustable. Please refer to your 'Chilton Total Car Care' or factory service manual for the adjustment procedures. The specification is usually around 0.45 volts at closed throttle.

Fig. 195 Removing and installing the throttle position sensor — MFI engine shown

RELAYS

TESTING

▶ **See Figures 196 and 197**

These electrical protection devices are sometimes located in the convenience center, which is a swing down unit located under the instrument panel or under the hood along a fenderwell. The relays are generally serviced by plug-in replacements.

Relay testing may vary depending on the vehicle you are working with and the type of relay being used. On average, there are 2 common types of relays used today. There is the Mechanical relay and the Solid state relay. Mechanical relays used on most cars come under 3 categories. There is the 3 terminal relay, 4 terminal relay and the multiple circuit relay.

Testing procedures will differ depending on what type of relay you are working with. Before trying to test a relay by supplying it with battery voltage to see if it will click, make sure you know if the type of relay you are testing will not be damaged by this. Solid state relays are not always 12 volts and can be damaged easily.

Usually mechanical relays can be tested in this fashion, but specific terminals must be energized to make these tests. If for an example; if you are working with a 4 terminal mechanical relay, 1 of the terminals is designated for power feed (voltage from the battery or ignition switch). The load terminal provides power to the component. One terminal comes from the control switch and one terminal is the ground. A basic test for this type of relay would be as follows:

First test to see if the relay is receiving voltage by using a 12 volt test light or voltmeter, and the grounded terminal has a good ground. Turn the component on and off to see if the relay clicks. If yes, check that voltage is applied to the component load terminal. If voltage is applied, the relay is okay. If no voltage was applied the relay is most likely defective. If the relay didn't click, and you have power and ground at the relay, check for a signal from the switch terminal of the relay. If you don't have a switch signal the problem is before the relay and may involve detailed electrical testing. You can also test some relays by removing the relay. Using a fused jumper wire, connect one end to the positive side of the battery and provide ground to the relay's ground terminal. Most relay terminals are marked. The relay should click. Connect another wire to the negative side of the battery and quickly ground the other component terminal. If it does not click reverse the wires and it should click. If there is still no response from the relay, chances are it is defective.

The other types of relays may require resistance or continuity checks between terminals when voltage is applied or when voltage is not applied. Resistance specifications are very important because although the relay may be working, it may have to much or not enough resistance. This could cause a specific problem with another unit that is dependent on the relay. This could result in the relay or the controlled unit failing prematurely.

Solid state relays should be tested only with special equipment as any other type of testing may damage this relay or a related circuit. Due to the wide variety of relay tests, consult your 'Chilton Total Car Care' manual for the specific relay testing for the vehicle you are working with.

REMOVAL & INSTALLATION

Removal of a relay is pretty simple. Some relays are mounted on a bracket with 1 or 2 screws, just remove the screws and disconnect the connector. Others simply plug in. Care should be taken when disconnecting the connector as not to damage the relay terminals.

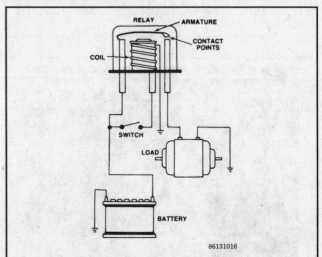

86131016

Fig. 196 Typical 4-pin relay, has power, ground, load and switched terminals

88518057

Fig. 197 Location of externally mounted relays — Chervolet 4.3L engine shown

SPARK PLUG WIRES

TESTING

▶ **See Figures 198, 199, 200, 201, 202, 203, 204 and 205**

Every 15,000 miles (24,100km), inspect the spark plug wires for burns, cuts, or breaks in the insulation. Check the boots and the nipples on the distributor cap. Replace any damaged wiring.

Every 45,000 miles (72,400km) or so, the resistance of the wires should be checked with an ohmmeter. Wires with excessive resistance will cause misfiring, and may make the engine difficult to start in damp weather. Generally, the useful life of the cables is 45,000-60,000 miles (72,400-96,500km),

On vehicles equipped with a distributor, check resistance by removing the distributor cap, leaving the wires in place. Connect one lead of an ohmmeter to an electrode within the cap; connect the other lead to the corresponding spark plug terminal (remove it from the spark plug for this test). On vehicles without a distributor, the other end of the spark plug wires are connected to a coil pack. Remove, test and replace each wire one at a time. Connect one lead of the ohmmeter to the spark plug end of the wire and the other lead of the ohmmeter to the coil pack end of the spark plug wire. Replace any wire which shows a resistance over 30,000 ohms. The following chart gives resistance values as a function of length. Generally speaking, however, resistance should not be considered the outer limit of acceptability.

- 0-15 in. (0-38mm): 3,000-10,000 ohm
- 15-25 in. (38-64mm): 4,000-15,000ohm
- 25-35 in. (64-89mm): 6,000-20,000 ohm
- Over 35 in. (89mm): 25,000 ohm

It should be remembered that resistance is also a function of length; the longer the wire, the greater the resistance. Thus, if the wires on your vehicle are longer than the factory originals, resistance will be higher, quite possibly outside these limits.

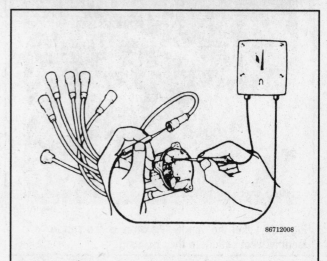

Fig. 199 Checking plug wire resistance through the distributor cap with an ohmmeter

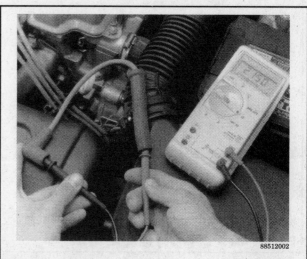

Fig. 200 Checking individual plug wire resistance with an digital ohmmeter

REMOVAL & INSTALLATION

When installing new wires, replace them one at a time to avoid mix-ups. If it becomes necessary to remove all of the wires from the distributor cap or coil packs at one time, take the time to label the distributor cap/coil pack towers to denote the cylinder number of the wire for that position.

Start by replacing the longest one first. Install the boot firmly over the spark plug. Route the wire over the same path as the original. Insert the nipple firmly onto the tower on the distributor cap or coil pack. Another good practice is to apply a little dielectric grease inside each boot. This cuts down of the formation of corrosion due to moisture, helps the flow of voltage, and will ease removal for the next time.

Fig. 198 Checking spark voltage during cranking or while the engine is running — Saturn with 1.9L MFI engine shown

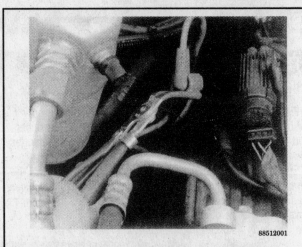

Fig. 201 Label the spark plug wires at the cap to identify what cylinders they go to

Fig. 202 This handy tool makes it easy and safe to disconnect the spark plug wires. Always pull on the boot, not the wire.

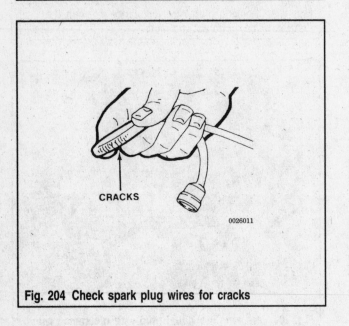

CRACKS

Fig. 204 Check spark plug wires for cracks

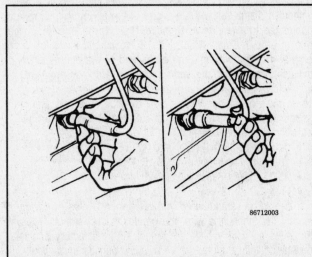

Fig. 203 Pull spark plug off by the boot (left); Never pull on spark plug wire (right)

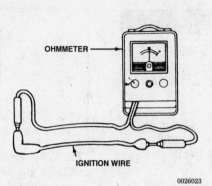

Fig. 205 Use a ohmmeter to check spark plug wires for proper resistance range

TORQUE CONVERTER CLUTCH (TCC) SOLENOID

TESTING

Most late model vehicles with an automatic transmission use a Torque Converter Clutch (TCC) system. The Powertrain Control Module (PCM) controls the torque converter by means of a solenoid mounted in the output drive housing of the transmission. When the vehicle speed reaches a certain point, the PCM sends a signal to the TCC solenoid, (energizing it), and allows the torque converter to mechanically couple the transmission to the engine. When the operating conditions, (according to various sensors), indicate that the transmission should operate as a normal fluid coupled transmission, the PCM will de-energize the solenoid. Depressing the brake pedal will also return the transmission to normal automatic operation.

Testing TCC system and solenoid may vary depending on the manufacturer. Here is a basic check that can be made to see it the TCC is functioning on or not. TCC diagnosis usually involves the use of special testing equipment.

1. Connect a tachometer or special scan tool.

2. Drive the vehicle until the transmission is warmed up sufficiently.

3. Accelerate to 50-55 mph under light load.

4. Maintaining the throttle, lightly touch the brake pedal and check for release of the TCC. You will know if the torque converter clutch disengaged if the engine rpm increases.

5. Release the brake, slowly accelerate and check for a re-application of the TCC. You will know it has engaged by a slight decrease in rpm.

As indicated, this test merely tells you if the torque converter clutch system is functioning, further diagnosis and testing may be involved. Consult your 'Chilton Total Car Care' manual for additional information.

REMOVAL & INSTALLATION

Removal and installation procedures may vary depending on the vehicle you are working with. Some TCC solenoids require transmission removal, some require removing the transmission pan or it may be a simple 'unbolt and pull out' removal. In many cases this can be an involved service routine.

VACUUM SWITCH

TESTING

1 WIRE DESIGN

▶ **See Figures 206 and 207**

1. Using an ohmmeter, check for continuity between the switch terminal and body with the engine OFF and cold.
2. Start the engine and warm it to normal operating temperature.
3. Check that there is no continuity between the switch terminal and body, if continuity didn't change continue test.
4. Disconnect switch and apply a vacuum of 5 in. hg (12mm H_2O) or greater to the port on the switch.
5. Check that there is a continuity change at switch, if not the switch is defective.

2 WIRE DESIGN

▶ **See Figures 208 and 209**

1. Using an ohmmeter, check for no continuity between the switch terminals.
2. Apply a vacuum of 5 in. hg (12mm H_2O) or greater to the port on the switch.
3. Using an ohmmeter, check that there is continuity between the switch terminals.

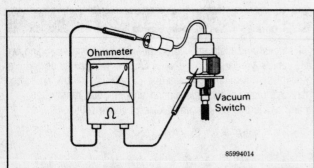

Fig. 206 With the engine off and cold, vacuum switch should have continuity — 1 wire design vacuum switch

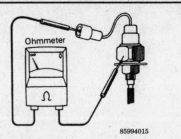

Fig. 207 Vacuum switch should not have continuity with the engine warm and running — 1 wire design vacuum switch

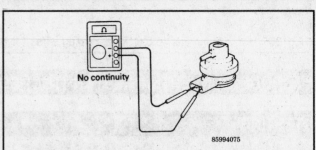

Fig. 208 The switch should not have continuity between the terminals without vacuum applied — 2 wire design vacuum switch

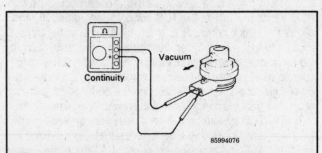

Fig. 209 There should be continuity between the terminals with vacuum applied — 2 wire design vacuum switch

REMOVAL & INSTALLATION

Vacuum switches are relatively easy to replace. Usually it is a simple procedure of disconnecting the vacuum hose and unbolting or unscrewing the switch from a bracket.

VACUUM SWITCHING VALVE

TESTING

◗ **See Figures 210, 211, 212 and 213**

The Vacuum Switching Valve (VSV) is used to provide vacuum to another component, either by command from the PCM or it may energized through the activation of another component or system.

1. The vacuum switching circuit is checked by blowing air into the pipe under the following conditions:

    a. Connect the vacuum switching valve terminals to battery voltage.

    b. Blow into the tube and check that the VSV switch is open.

    c. Remove battery voltage from the terminals.

    d. Blow into the tube and check that the VSV switch is closed (no flow).

2. Check for a short circuit within the valve. Using an ohmmeter, check that there is no continuity between the positive terminal and the VSV body. If there is continuity, replace the VSV.

3. Check for an open circuit. Using an ohmmeter, measure the resistance (ohms) between the two terminals of the valve. The resistance should be 38-44Ω at 68°F (20°C). If the resistance is not within specifications, replace the VSV.

➡**The resistance will vary slightly with temperature. It will decrease in cooler temperatures and increase with heat, slight variations due to temperature range are not necessarily a sign of a failed valve.**

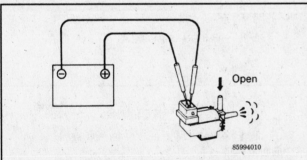

Fig. 210 The VSV should be open with battery voltage applied to the terminals

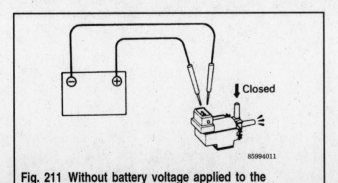

Fig. 211 Without battery voltage applied to the terminals, the VSV should be closed

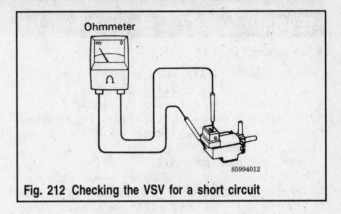

Fig. 212 Checking the VSV for a short circuit

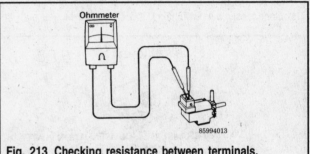

Fig. 213 Checking resistance between terminals, resistance should be approximately 38-44Ω at 68°F (20°C)

REMOVAL & INSTALLATION

Removing a Vacuum Switching Valve (VSV) is usually a simple matter of disconnecting the electrical connector and vacuum lines at the VSV and removing the retaining screw(s). On some models it may be necessary to move a component for better access to the VSV. Vacuum switching valves are usually mounted on a bracket located on the fenderwell or near the component they control.

1. Disconnect the electrical connector at the VSV.

2. Disconnect and tag the vacuum hoses.

3. Remove the EGR VSV retaining screw(s).

To install:

4. Install the EGR VSV and bracket and tighten the retaining screw(s) securely.

5. Connect the vacuum hoses to the VSV.

6. Connect the electrical connector at the VSV.

VANE AIR FLOW METER

TESTING

▶ **See Figure 214**

The Vane Air Flow (VAF) meter senses the incoming volume of air before it enters the throttle body. Essentially, it is a spring loaded air flap with a potentiometer attached to it. As the incoming air forces the flap to open wider, the potentiometer changes resistance values, informing the PCM how far the air flap is open. With this information the PCM decides what the air/fuel ratio requirement should be.

Testing the VAF should first began with a visual inspection for dirt or contamination build-up on the air flap. This is critical to a VAF meter, and perhaps one of the most likely causes of malfunction. Inspect the air flap for movement, it should open and close freely without binding. If it binds, the hinges may be dirty causing it to stick. Spray some carburetor cleaner on the hinges and move it open and closed until it operates freely.

Disconnect the electrical connector from the VAF meter and check the resistance between the sensor terminals. As the flap is gradually moved open to closed, the resistance reading should change without fluctuation. If it the ohmmeter reading is not smooth and steady replace the VAF meter. Some VAF meters may be a frequency design. In this case the ohmmeter reading will not change at all. Check with a 'Chilton Total Care Car' or service manual if you suspect a frequency design meter.

The Vane Air Flow Meter (VAF) is used by early multiport fuel injected Import and some Domestic vehicles. The Mass Air Flow (MAF) sensor is also common on today's fuel injected engines.

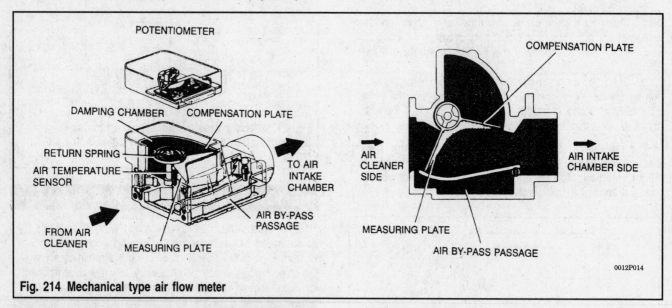

Fig. 214 Mechanical type air flow meter

REMOVAL & INSTALLATION

The VAF is located between the throttle body and air cleaner. It's usually easy to replace.
1. Disconnect the negative battery cable.
2. Disconnect the electrical connector from the VAF sensor.
3. Remove the air hose between the VAF and throttle body.

4. Remove the bolts attaching VAF to the air cleaner.
To install:
5. Position the VAF to the air cleaner and secure it with the retaining bolts.
6. Connect the air hose between the throttle body and VAF and secure it with the retaining strap.
7. Connect the electrical connect to the VAF sensor.
8. Connect the negative battery cable.

VEHICLE SPEED SENSOR (VSS)

▶ **See Figure 215**

The are two types of Vehicle Speed Sensors (VSS). One type is a magnetic pickup that sends and small AC voltage signal, which is proportional to vehicle speed, to the PCM to determine the transmission shift schedule. It also assists supplying information to the PCM required by the Torque Converter Clutch (TCC) system. The other type is a reed switch design, which simply opens and closes a circuit as it is rotated. A defective or disconnect VSS will cause a tremendous decrease in fuel mileage.

TESTING

✴✴CAUTION

The following test will require the vehicle to be raised off the ground, with the engine running and the transmission in D Extreme caution must be used when raising and supporting the vehicle, otherwise personal and/ or vehicle damage may occur.

A basic test for the switch type is to rotate the speedometer cable or wheel and with a ohmmeter see if the circuit opens and closes. A basic test you can make on the AC generator design is as follows:

1. Raise and and safely support the vehicle.
2. Disconnect the VSS wire connector located on the transmission housing.
3. Connect an ohmmeter between the terminals of the speed sensor. Most sensors will usually be between 190-250 ohms.
4. Place the vehicle in drive and allow the wheels to rotate. The ohmmeter should fluctuate. If it does not or the ohmmeter reading is not within specification, replace the sensor.
5. Apply the brake, place the vehicle in park and shut the engine off.
6. Connect the harness connector to the VSS.
7. Lower the vehicle.

Be sure to consult your 'Chilton Total Car Care' manual for the vehicle you are working with.

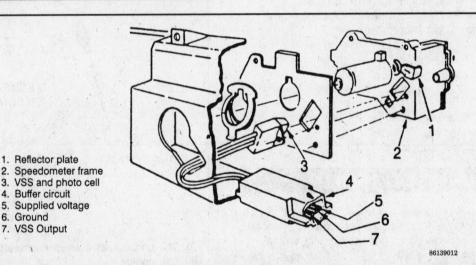

1. Reflector plate
2. Speedometer frame
3. VSS and photo cell
4. Buffer circuit
5. Supplied voltage
6. Ground
7. VSS Output

86139012

Fig. 215 Most older model had a VSS mounted with the speedometer, while newer models use a electronic sender in the transmission

REMOVAL & INSTALLATION

Removal and installation procedures may vary depending on the vehicle you are working with. Most are a simple 'unbolt and pull out' removal. In any event be sure to consult your 'Chilton Tool Car Care' manual for the vehicle you are working with.

WATER TEMPERATURE SWITCH

TESTING

▶ **See Figures 216 and 217**

The water temperature switch is a one or two wire switch that opens or closes a circuit based on water temperature. In a sense, it is considered to be a coolant temperature sensor, but its function and purpose is slightly different. The water temperature functions like a switch. Current is usually supplied to a coolant temperature relay. When the engine is cold, it will not allow current to flow through it. When the engine reaches the a desired temperature (in degrees) it will allow current to flow through it and to the component it is designated to activate.

The water temperature switch may activate a radiator fan, A/C condenser fan, or it may be a sender for the dash warning light or gauge. It is important not to confuse the water (coolant) temperature switch with the coolant temperature sensor. Some vehicles will use more than one coolant temperature switch.

Always consult your 'Chilton Total Car Care' manual for further information on the vehicle you are working with.

1. To test the switch in the vehicle, with a cold engine, unplug the electrical connector from the switch.

2. Using an ohmmeter, check for continuity between the terminals on a 2 wire switch or between the terminal and ground on a one wire switch.

3. Then run the engine until it reaches normal operating temperature.

4. Using an ohmmeter, check that the continuity changed as the engine warmed up.

5. If there was no change, replace the switch.

REMOVAL & INSTALLATION

The switch must be handled carefully during removal. It can be damaged (thereby affecting engine performance) by impact. The switch may be located on the intake manifold, on the thermostat housing, on the cylinder head or threaded into the radiator depending on the vehicle you are working with. You will need to consult your 'Chilton Total Car Care' manual for the specific location on the vehicle you are working with.

✳✳CAUTION

Perform this procedure only on a cold engine. Attempting to remove any component that involves working with engine coolant can result in serious burns.

1. Drain the cooling system part way down.

2. With the ignition OFF, unplug the electrical connector to the switch.

3. Using the proper sized wrench, carefully unscrew the switch from the engine coolant passage.

To install:

4. Coat the threads of the switch with a sealant and install it.

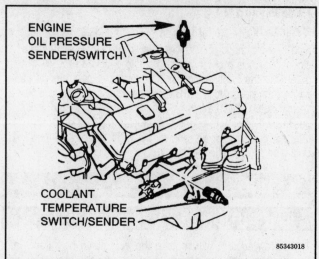

Fig. 216 The water temperature switch is always in a coolant passage, sometimes in the cylinder head

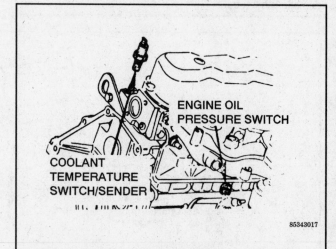

Fig. 217 Location of a water temperature switch on a GM 2.5L engine

5. Plug the electrical connector into the switch.

6. Refill the coolant to the proper level. Road test the vehicle for proper operation. Check for coolant leaks.

✳✳CAUTION

When draining the coolant, keep in mind that cats and dogs are attracted by the ethylene glycol antifreeze, and are quite likely to drink any that is left in an uncovered container or in puddles on the ground. This will prove fatal in sufficient quantity. Always drain the coolant into a sealable container. Coolant should be reused unless it is contaminated or several years old.

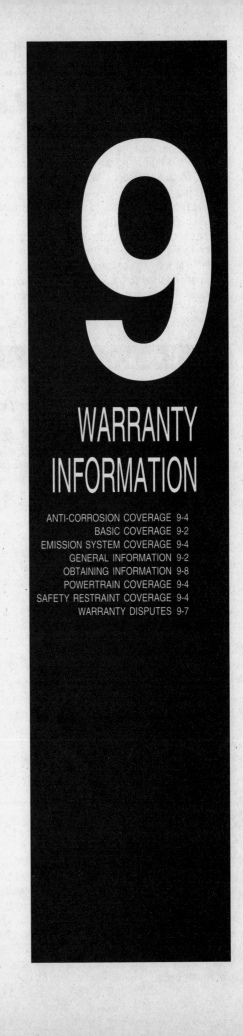

9

WARRANTY
INFORMATION

General Information

This section will familiarize you with the different types of warranties that apply to today's vehicles. You will learn what the vehicle owner must do to maintain warranty coverage as well as some suggestions for resolving a warranty dispute if one should arise.

The days of the 12 month / 12 thousand mile warranty for cars and light trucks appear to be over. The ever increasing complexity of vehicles, better materials, high tech electronics, and on-board computers have improved the quality and durability of today's vehicles. Manufacturer's competition for customers has led to longer and more specialized warranty coverage. This is also the case on many smaller cars and trucks, not just expensive luxury models.

Typical warranty coverage may provide:
- Basic or 'Whole Car' Coverage
- Powertrain Coverage
- Anti-Corrosion Coverage
- Safety Restraint System Coverage
- Emission System Warranty Coverage
- Emission Defects Coverage
- Emission Performance Coverage

Related Topics:
- IM 240 Programs
- Obtaining Warranty Information

The rest of this section will explore each of these coverages and how they work for you, and what to do if you misplace your vehicle's warranty information.

Basic Coverage

Basic warranty, sometimes referred to as 'Whole Car Coverage', covers just about everything on the car, except for the items which have their own coverage under some other part of the vehicle's warranty plan. This used to be the 12 month / 12 thousand mile coverage plan, but is now usually 24, 36 or even 50 months or thousand miles. It often includes the powertrain coverage. When the basic warranty ends, the specific powertrain warranty coverage begins. If your power window stops working, power steering pump fails or the ignition switch breaks, this basic coverage is the warranty that covers you.

The basic warranty is generally the shortest warranty on the vehicle. Parts and labor are usually covered by this plan. This warranty, (and any others that do not start upon the expiration of a preceding warranty), begin on the delivery date of the vehicle to the customer. In the case of vehicles such as dealer demonstrators the warranty begins on the vehicle's actual 'in-service' date. The buyer of a used vehicle is entitled to any remaining warranty coverage when the vehicle is purchased. Any authorized dealer can perform warranty repairs, but if you have your vehicle outside the country in which you bought it, you may have to pay for the repairs and submit the receipt for reimbursement in your own country. If you need to have warranty work performed by someone other than an authorized dealer, be sure to obtain the failed part(s) and keep all receipts. You will need these things, and possibly a letter that explains the circumstances in order to request reimbursement from an authorized dealer.

Towing to the nearest authorized dealer may be covered if the vehicle cannot be driven due to the failure of a covered part. Vehicle owners may be responsible for taxes on warranty work in some states.

Other items to discuss about basic warranty are tires and batteries. Tires that fail are generally replaced by the tire manufacturer, not the vehicle manufacturer. Batteries that fail are most often covered by the vehicle's manufacturer. These items are replaced on a pro-rated basis. During the first part of the warranty period, replacement is often free of charge. As more time passes the items fall into a pro-rated coverage plan, where the vehicle manufacturer and the owner share the replacement costs.

You may also have some implied warranties, such as an implied warranty of merchantability that the car or light truck is reasonably fit for the purpose for which it was sold, or an implied warranty of fitness for a particular purpose that the car or light truck is suitable for your special purposes. If the vehicle is to be covered as to whether it is fit for special purposes, these may have to be disclosed to the manufacturer (not merely to the dealer) prior to purchase.

These implied warranties are limited, to the extent allowed by law, to the time period covered by the written warranties, or to the applicable period provided by state law, whichever period is shorter. Vehicles used primarily for business or commercial purposes may not be covered by these implied warranties, and are completely disclaimed to the extent allowed by law.

Some states do not allow limitations on how long an implied warranty lasts, so the above limitations may not apply to you.

In order to keep warranties in effect, the vehicle owner may have to meet certain obligations. Some maintenance may need to be performed as specified for the vehicle. If the failure of a warranted part can be attributed to improper maintenance or lack of maintenance, the warranty claim may be denied. Damages caused by using improper or contaminated fuel, oil, or other lubricants are not covered. Any tampering involving the odometer or Vehicle Identification Number (VIN) may result in denial of all warranty coverage to the vehicle.

However, it should be stated that the vehicle does not need to serviced by a dealer or have factory parts installed. An example would be that you do not need to use the vehicle manufacturer's oil filter, you can buy an aftermarket oil filter and change the oil yourself. Quality replacement parts that meet manufacturer's specification must be used. You are strongly advised to keep all service records and parts receipts so that proper maintenance can be verified. The manufacturer cannot deny warranty coverage solely on the lack of service records, but it is much more difficult to obtain any type of warranty work if a lack of maintenance is suspected and the owner has no way to show that the maintenance has actually been performed. If you purchase a used vehicle, try to obtain all service records from the previous owner.

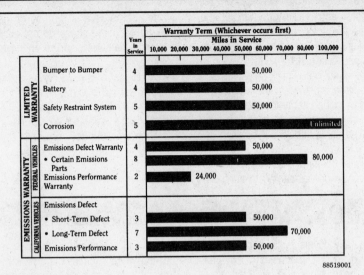

Fig. 1 Typical warranty summary bar graph

88519001

Abbreviations: R = Replace   I = Inspect. Correct or replace if necessary.

MAINTENANCE OPERATION		MAINTENANCE INTERVAL															
Perform at number of miles,	Miles x 1,000	3.75	7.5	11.25	15	18.75	22.5	26.25	30	33.75	37.5	41.25	45	48.75	52.5	56.25	60
kilometers or months,	(km x 1,000)	(6)	(12)	(18)	(24)	(30)	(36)	(42)	(48)	(54)	(60)	(66)	(72)	(78)	(84)	(90)	(96)
whichever comes first.	Months	3	6	9	12	15	18	21	24	27	30	33	36	39	42	45	48
Emission control system maintenance																	
Drive belts									I*								I*
Air cleaner filter	See NOTE (1)								[R]								[R]
Positive crankcase ventilation (P.C.V.) filter (KA24E engine only)	See NOTE (3)								[R]								[R]
Air induction valve filter (KA24E engine only)	See NOTE (2)																
Vapor lines									I*								I*
Fuel lines									I*								I*
Fuel filter	See NOTE (3)*																
Engine coolant	See NOTE (4)																R*
Engine oil		R	R	R	R	R	R	R	R	R	R	R	R	R	R	R	R
Engine oil filter (Use Nissan PREMIUM type or equivalent.)		R	R	R	R	R	R	R	R	R	R	R	R	R	R	R	R
Spark plugs									[R]								[R]
Timing belt (VG30E engine only)																	[R]
Chassis and body maintenance																	
Brake lines & cables									I				I				I
Brake pads, discs, drums & linings			I		I		I		I		I		I		I		I
Manual and automatic transmission, transfer & differential gear oil (exc. L.S.D.)	See NOTE (5)				I				I				I				I
Limited-slip differential (L.S.D.) gear oil	See NOTE (5)				I				R								R
Steering gear (box) & linkage, (steering damper [4x4]), axle & suspension parts			I		I		I		I		I		I		I		I
Drive shaft boots & propeller shaft ([4x4])			I		I		I		I		I		I		I		I
Steering linkage ball joints & front suspension ball joints			I		I		I		I		I		I		I		I
Front wheel bearing grease (4x2)									I								I
Front wheel bearing grease & free-running hub grease ([4x4])	See NOTE (6)				I				R				I				R
Exhaust system			I		I		I		I		I		I		I		I

NOTE: (1) If operating mainly in dusty conditions, more frequent maintenance may be required.
       (2) If operating mainly in dusty conditions, replace every 30,000 miles (48,000 km).
       (3) If vehicle is operated under extremely adverse weather conditions or in areas where ambient temperatures are either extremely low or extremely high, the filters might become clogged. In such an event, replace them immediately.
       (4) After 60,000 miles (96,000 km) or 48 months, replace every 30,000 miles (48,000 km) or 24 months.
       (5) If towing a trailer, using a camper or a car-top carrier, or driving on rough or muddy roads, change (not just inspect) oil at every 30,000 miles (48,000 km) or 24 months except for L.S.D. Change L.S.D. gear oil every 15,000 miles (24,000 km) or 12 months.
       (6) If operating frequently in water, replace grease every 3,750 miles (6,000 km) or 3 months.
       (7) Maintenance items and intervals with "*" are recommended by NISSAN for reliable vehicle operation. The owner need not perform such maintenance in order to maintain the emission warranty or manufacturer recall liability. Other maintenance items and intervals are required.

86711110

Fig. 2 Typical maintenance schedule for severe service

Any damage from modifications, abuse, racing, collisions and other similar misuse or mishaps are not covered by warranties and may void existing warranties. Glass breakage is for the most part not covered, unless a defect can be shown.

Traditionally, maintenance items such as spark plugs, belts, hoses, adjustments, and filters were replaced at the owner's expense. Some vehicles now have such items included at no charge or a reduced charge during the warranty period. In any case, as mentioned before, these items should be replaced at the proper intervals.

Also, remember these additional points of interest. In general, warranties do not cover consequential damages; such as loss of time, loss of the use of the vehicle, or lost wages. However, some states do not allow the exclusion of consequential damages, so the above exclusions may not apply to you.

Additionally, manufacturers sometimes offer special programs which will cover some or all of the expense of certain repairs beyond the warranty period. Review your own warranty information to see if your vehicle manufacturer has this type of program, or call your dealer to find out if such a program is in effect.

Powertrain Coverage

The powertrain warranty generally covers major parts of the engine, transmission, and final drive unit. Examples of covered parts would be engine cylinder head, block and gaskets; any engine mechanical parts like valves and pistons; transmission parts and components that transmit the power from the engine to the wheels. There may be exceptions on some plans, an example is that the clutch and flywheel are usually not covered on a manual transmission.

Anti-Corrosion Coverage

Anti-corrosion warranties differ quite a bit from manufacturer to manufacturer, but they generally cover rust-through of outer-body sheet metal panels. In a few cases, other sheet metal is covered, but this is not a common practice at this time. Only factory sheet metal is covered. Damage caused to factory sheet metal because non-factory parts were used is not covered. Any collision damage must be properly repaired with factory parts to keep the warranty valid. Non-factory bodies, such as the utility bodies commonly seen on trucks, are not covered by the vehicle manufacturer. In some cases, outer body surface rust is covered if it is the result of a defect in factory-supplied material and workmanship. Surface rust caused by a scratch, for example, is not covered.

Some manufacturers also cover paint damage due to industrial fallout when no defect is involved. This is a type of 'goodwill' policy which typically would last no longer than 12 months or 12 thousand miles, whichever comes first.

Also in regards to anti-corrosion warranties, be aware that having the vehicle rust proofed is NOT advised, until after checking your specific warranty. Rust proofing applied by a trained professional can extend your vehicle's life. However, incorrect procedures can damage the vehicle. For that reason, anything that disturbs the factory integrity of the body work and/or paint may void a warranty.

The length of the anti-corrosion warranties will usually vary, with the outer-body coverage being the longest, and any other coverages, if applicable, being shorter in duration.

Safety Restraint Coverage

This warranty covers items such as seat belts and airbags against defects in factory-supplied materials and workmanship. Some manufacturers offer it, check your own warranty information to see if your vehicle has this type of coverage. This warranty is generally longer in duration than the basic warranty on the entire vehicle; one example would be 3\36 coverage on the basic warranty and 5\50 coverage on the restraint system(s).

Emission System Coverage

There are two types of emission system warranties we will discuss. Both are required by U.S. law, and have changed somewhat through the years.

In addition to the usual warranty stipulations, you must be sure that leaded fuel is never used in a vehicle designed to run on unleaded fuel, damages resulting from this would not be covered.

Emissions Defect Coverage

We will discuss this coverage as it applies to passenger cars and light trucks. There are essentially two versions of this warranty, the Federal version and the California version. The Federal version, from 1981 through 1994 covered a period of five years or fifty thousand miles, whichever came first.

The Federal version, beginning in 1995, has a coverage period of 2 years or 24 thousand miles, whichever comes first. Some manufacturers may extend this coverage for a longer period. All parts and labor needed to bring the vehicle into compliance should be covered. In summary, the warranty states that the vehicle:

• is designed, built, and equipped to conform, at the time of sale, with the emissions regulations of the Environmental Protection Agency (EPA), and

• is free from defects in factory-supplied materials and workmanship that could cause it to fail to conform with applicable EPA regulations

Abbreviations: R = Replace   I = Inspect. Correct or replace if necessary.

MAINTENANCE OPERATION Perform at number of miles, kilometers or months, whichever comes first.		MAINTENANCE INTERVAL							
	Miles x 1,000	7.5	15	22.5	30	37.5	45	52.5	60
	(km x 1,000)	(12)	(24)	(36)	(48)	(60)	(72)	(84)	(96)
	Months	6	12	18	24	30	36	42	48
Emission control system maintenance									
Drive belts					I*				I*
Air cleaner filter					[R]				[R]
Positive crankcase ventilation (P.C.V.) filter (KA24E engine only)	See NOTE (1)				[R]				[R]
Vapor lines					I*				I*
Fuel lines					I*				I*
Fuel filter	See NOTE (1)*								
Engine coolant	See NOTE (2)								R*
Engine oil		R	R	R	R	R	R	R	R
Engine oil filter (Use Nissan PREMIUM type or equivalent.)		R		R		R		R	
Spark plugs					[R]				[R]
Timing belt (VG30E engine only)							-		[R]
Chassis and body maintenance									
Brake lines & cables			I		I		I		I
Brake pads, discs, drums & linings			I		I		I		I
Manual and automatic transmission, transfer & differential gear oil (exc. L.S.D.)			I		I		I		I
Limited-slip differential (L.S.D.) gear oil			I		R		I		R
Steering gear (box) & linkage, (steering damper 4x4), axle & suspension parts					I				I
Drive shaft boots (4x4)			I		I		I		I
Steering linkage ball joints & front suspension ball joints									
Front wheel bearing grease (4x2)					I				I
Front wheel bearing grease & free-running hub grease (4x4)			I		R		I		R
Exhaust system			I		I		I		I

NOTE: (1) If vehicle is operated under extremely adverse weather conditions or in areas where ambient temperatures are either extremely low or extremely high, the filters might become clogged. In such an event, replace them immediately.

(2) After 60,000 miles (96,000 km) or 48 months, replace every 30,000 miles (48,000 km) or 24 months.

(3) Maintenance items and intervals with "*" are recommended by NISSAN for reliable vehicle operation. The owner need not perform such maintenance in order to maintain the emission warranty or manufacturer recall liability. Other maintenance items and intervals are required.

86711111

Fig. 3 Typical maintenance schedule for normal service

Here is a sample listing of covered parts:
- Air/Fuel Feedback Control System and Sensors
- Altitude Compensation System
- Catalytic Converter
- Intercooler Assembly-Engine Charger
- Cold Start Enrichment System
- Cold Start Fuel Injector (1)
- Deceleration Controls
- Ignition Distributor
- Electronic Ignition System
- Exhaust Pipe (from exhaust manifold to catalyst)
- Electronic Engine Control Sensors and Switches
- Exhaust Gas Recirculation (EGR) Valve, Spacer, Plate, and related parts
- Exhaust Heat Control Valve
- Exhaust Manifold(s)
- Fuel Filler Cap and Neck Restrictor
- Fuel Injection System
- Fuel Injector Supply Manifold
- Fuel Sensor (1)
- Fuel Tank (gasoline powered vehicles)
- Fuel Tank Pressure Control Valve (1)
- Fuel Vapor Storage Canister, Liquid Separator, and associated Controls
- Ignition Coil and/or Control Module
- Intake Manifold
- Malfunction Indicator Light (MIL)
- PCV System and Oil Filler Cap
- Secondary Air Injection System and related parts
- Spark Control Components
- Spark Plugs and Ignition Wires
- Supercharger Assembly
- Synchronizer Assembly
- Throttle Air Control Bypass Valve
- Throttle Body Assembly
- Turbocharger Assembly
- Three-Way Catalyst (TWC) Air Control Valve
- Volume Air Flow Sensor

(1) Flex-Fuel vehicle only

Remember that this list is a sample. Due to differences in vehicle and engine design, the covered components on your vehicle may vary somewhat from those listed. Items such as related hoses, clamps and gaskets are also covered. Items that require periodic replacement, as shown on the vehicle maintenance schedule, are typically covered only until the end of the first maintenance interval for the specific item in question.

Additionally, there are a few other major emissions components that may be covered by the Emissions Defect Warranty for a longer period of time, such as eight years/eighty thousand miles for the 1995 Federal version of the warranty. A sample list of these items is as follows:

- Catalytic Converter
- Engine Control Module
- On-Board Diagnostic Device

For California cars and light trucks from 1981 through 1989, the Emissions Defect Warranty provided coverage for five years or fifty thousand miles, whichever came first. From 1990 through 1995, Emissions Defect Warranty remains in effect for three years or fifty thousand miles, whichever comes first. Vehicles that are equipped with California certified emissions systems in other areas which have adopted California emissions standards AND California warranty regulations are also covered under the California version of the warranty.

The covered parts are essentially the same as those shown in the preceding sample lists. This is the short-term Emissions Defect Warranty. The California regulations also require a long-term Emissions Defect Warranty. From 1990 through 1995, the long term warranty lasts for seven years or seventy thousand miles, whichever comes first. Here is a sample list of the covered components:

- Catalytic Converter
- Ignition Distributor
- Exhaust Manifold(s)
- Fuel Injection Rail Assembly
- Fuel Injector
- Fuel Injector Supply Manifold
- Fuel Sensor(1)
- Fuel Tank
- Idle Air Control Valve
- Injector Driver Module
- Intake Manifold
- Intercooler
- Powertrain Control Module(PCM)
- Supercharger
- Synchronizer Assembly
- Throttle Body Assembly
- Transducer Assembly
- Turbocharger Assembly
- Three-Way Catalyst (TWC) Air Control Valve
- Volume Air Flow Sensor

(1) Flex-Fuel vehicle only

Again, keep in mind that this is a sample listing. Check the warranty information for your own vehicle to see which specific items are eligible for coverage.

Emissions Performance Coverage

This warranty applies to vehicles which are registered in areas that require periodic emissions testing. The warranty states that the manufacturer will adjust or repair the vehicle's emission system and/or related parts so that it will pass the emissions test. From 1981 through 1994, Federal vehicles were covered for five years or fifty thousand miles, whichever came first, except for 'primary' emissions parts, which were covered for 2 years or 24 thousand miles. Primary emissions parts are defined as those which were not in general use prior to the 1968 model year, and have been added to vehicles for the primary purpose of reducing emissions. This stipulation does not really reduce the number of covered parts by too many; keep in mind that vehicles made before 1968 had very little in the way of emission control devices. Until 1989, California vehicles had the same coverage period. Beginning in 1995, Federal vehicles are covered for 2 years or 24 thousand miles, whichever comes first. California vehicles, from 1990 through 1995 have a coverage term of three years or fifty thousand miles, whichever comes first. All of the usual warranty stipulations apply.

There are two other important points in regard to this warranty. In order to make a claim under this warranty, you must be subject to a real penalty, such as a fine or denial of the use of the vehicle because the vehicle failed the emissions test. Also, a vehicle certified for use at sea level will not qualify under this warranty if it fails an emissions test intended for high altitude certified vehicles. The reason for this is that the high altitude emissions standards are more stringent.

To actually make a warranty claim under this warranty, take the vehicle to an authorized dealer or other factory-authorized shop. Take the paperwork that shows that the vehicle failed the emissions test, and tell them that you are seeking a repair under the Emissions Performance Warranty. Having the vehicle's warranty information on hand may also be helpful. The manufacturer has thirty days, or the period specified by your Inspection/Maintenance Program, whichever is shorter, to either fix the vehicle or deny the claim. Written notification must be given if the claim is denied, and you should have a written record of the date when the vehicle was presented for repair.

If there are problems involved in getting the vehicle evaluated or repaired, you may agree to extend the deadline, and if there are problems beyond the control of the manufacturer or dealer, the deadline may be automatically extended. Should a deadline be missed for reasons other than these, you are entitled to have the repairs made at the shop of your choice, at the manufacturer's expense.

IM 240 Programs

The topic of emissions testing must also include a few words about IM 240 programs. The abbreviation stands for Inspection/Maintenance 240 Seconds.

Some states require this type of emissions testing. It was mandated to begin on January 1, 1995, but there have been delays in some cases, and earlier program starting dates in others.

There are two types of IM 240 tests, Basic and Enhanced. Factors such as population and pollution levels in a given area are used to determine which test will be utilized. Major metropolitan areas would be more apt to require the Enhanced test, while lightly populated rural areas may not use any type of IM240 testing at all.

The Basic test is similar to some current IM programs. The Enhanced test, which takes 240 seconds to perform, is designed to provide a more accurate picture of a vehicle's emissions during an actual operating cycle, not just at idle. This is done by testing the vehicle on a chassis dynamometer. Emissions are constantly monitored as the vehicle idles, accelerates, cruises at two different road speeds, and decelerates.

A vehicle which fails the Enhanced test will not be eligible for a waiver until a minimum of $450.00 has been spent to bring the vehicle into compliance. Any repairs performed under warranty do not count towards the minimum. The Basic test has much lower minimum repair limits; generally around $75.00 for pre-1981 vehicles or about $200.00 for 1981 and later models. The requirements and cost vary from state to state, and sometimes even county to county. Additional information on air pollution, vehicle emissions, emission inspections and the IM240 program can be found in Chapter Four.

Fig. 4 The vehicle emission information is provided on the VECI Vehicle Emission Control Information label located in the engine compartment

Warranty Disputes

If a warranty issue is not resolved to your satisfaction, there are some steps you can take to try to resolve the problem. The first is always to discuss the complaint with the salespeople or service manager of the dealership where you purchased the vehicle. If no solution is reached, speak with the general manager or the owner of the dealership. In most cases, the general manager or owner does not want an unhappy customer, and should help find a solution or compromise. In cases where coverage is denied, it is a good idea to ask for the reason (in writing) why the claim was denied, and who denied it. Also find out who you can appeal the decision to. If the dealership can't help, contact the district or zone office. These are generally listed at the end of the vehicle's warranty information. The zone office may have you try a different dealership repair shop. Remember, the person working on your vehicle may be less knowledgeable about your vehicle's problem than someone at a different location.

If the previous steps weren't satisfactory, you may need to use the customer arbitrations board, which serves as an impartial third party in cases of disputes that can't be resolved through the process described above. Always keep all receipts for service, even those performed for no charge. These re-

ceipts help prove dates and the number of times you've taken your vehicle for service. Invoking a 'lemon law' or taking legal action is usually not necessary. Honest and complete communication of what you feel the problem is and what you expect to be done about it is the best approach. Detailed receipts will help you obtain the best service from the dealership or any other repair shop.

In the case of disputes which involve the Federal or California emissions warranties, you may contact the EPA or the California Air Resources Board (CARB) if you follow the manufacturer's claim procedure through, but you feel that their final decision is unfair. You may write to:

Warranty Complaint
Field Operations and Support Division (6406J)
U.S. Environmental Protection Agency
401 M Street SW
Washington, D.C. 20460
or for emission related information you can contact:
California Air Resources Board
9528 Telstar Avenue
El Monte, CA 91731

Obtaining Information

Warranty information is usually found in a separate booklet in the vehicle's glove compartment. Unfortunately, this information, along with the owner's manual, often becomes misplaced. You may contact a dealer to inquire about obtaining replacement information, or you may write to the appropriate supplier if your vehicle make is listed below.

Be sure to include such information as the year, make, model, and engine size to be certain that you will receive the correct information for your vehicle. In many cases, you will be sent an order form to fill out and return. You may be charged for the items that you request. Should the warranty identification card become lost, contact the dealer.

You can obtain warranty information for some vehicles by writing to the following addresses:

Audi and Chrysler Corporation

Dyment Distribution Services
20770 Westwood Road
Strongsville, OH 44136

Ford Motor Company

Helm Incorporated
14310 Hamilton Avenue
Highland Park, MI 48203

Mazda

Helm Incorporated
14310 Hamilton Avenue
Highland Park, MI 48203

Saab

Customer Assistance Center
Saab Cars U.S.A., Incorporated
4405-A International Boulevard
Norcross, GA 30091

Volkswagen

Dyment Distribution Services
20770 Westwood Road
Strongsville, OH 44136

Volvo

Literature Distribution Center
Volvo Cars of North America, Incorporated
P.O. Box 25577
Milwaukee, WI 53225

➡**You can always contact a dealer to inquire about obtaining replacement information if your vehicle is not listed above, or the information is not readily available.**

10

GLOSSARY

ABBREVIATIONS AND
DEFINITIONS 10-2

ABBREVIATIONS AND DEFINITIONS

4EAT — Electronic automatic 4 speed transaxle.

4X4L — 4x4 Low input switch.

AC DV — Air Cleaner Duct and Valve motor.

A/C P — Air Conditioning Pressure cut-out switch.

A/C — Air Conditioning.

A/F — Air/Fuel Ratio.

A/T — Automatic Transmission.

A4LD — Ford automatic 4 speed lock-up converter drive.

AAC — Auxiliary Air Control Valve.

AAV — Anti-Afterburning Valve.

ABS — Anti-Lock Brake system.

ABSOLUTE PRESSURE — Pressure measured from the point of total vacuum. For instance, absolute atmospheric pressure at sea level is 14.7 psi (100 kPa, or 29.92 in. hg) at a temperature of 80° F (26.7° C).

ACC — Air Conditioning Clutch compressor signal input to the computer relating status of the air conditioning clutch.

ACCS — Air Conditioning Cycling Switch.

ACD — Air Conditioner Demand switch.

ACP — Air Conditioning Pressure sensor.

ACT — Air Charge Temperature sensor or its signal circuit.

ACTUATOR — One name for any computer-controlled output device, such as a fuel injector, an EGR solenoid valve, and EVAP solenoid purge valve, etc. The term also refers to a specific component, the pressure actuator, used on Bosch KE-Jetronic and KE-Motronic continuous injection systems. See Pressure actuator.

ACV — Air Control Valve or Thermactor Air Control Valve.

ADAPTIVE CONTROL — The ability of a control unit to adapt its closed-loop operation to changing operating conditions - such as engine wear, fuel quality or altitude - to maintain proper air-fuel mixture control, ignition timing or idle rpm. Also referred to as self-learning.

ADAPTIVE MEMORY — A feature of computer memory that allows the microprocessor to adjust its memory for computing open-loop operation, based on changes in engine operation.

AFC — Air Flow Controlled fuel injection.

AFS — Air Flow Sensor.

AHFSS — Air conditioning and Heater Function Selection Switch input to the computer.

AI — Air Injection.

AIC — Automatic Idling Control valve.

A.I.R. — Air Injection Reaction system. Injects air into the exhaust system to burn any remaining unburned fuel.

AISC — Air Induction System Control. Injects air into the exhaust system to burn any remaining unburned fuel.

AIR BPV — Thermactor Air Bypass Valve.

AIR FUEL RATIO — The amount of air compared to the amount of fuel in the air-fuel mixture, almost always expressed in terms of mass.

AIRFLOW METER — In Bosch systems, any device that measures the amount of air being used by the engine. The control unit uses this information to determine the load on the engine. The two most common examples of airflow meters are the airflow sensor used in the Bosch L-Jetronic and the air mass sensor used in the Bosch LH-Jetronic systems.

AIR GAP — The distance or space between the reluctor tooth and pick up coil.

AIR INJECTION — A way of reducing exhaust emissions by injecting air into each of the exhaust ports of an engine. The air mixes with the hot exhaust gasses and oxidizes the HC and CO to form H_2O and CO_2.

AIR MASS SENSOR — An airflow meter that uses the changing resistance of a heated wire in the intake air stream to measure the mass of the air being drawn into the engine. Also referred to as a hot-wire sensor.

AIR SENSOR — An air cone with a floating plate which measures air flow and determines plunger position on K-Jetronic type systems.

AIR VANE — The pivoting flap inside an L-Jetronic or Motronic airflow sensor that swings open in relation to the amount of air flowing through the airflow sensor.

AIS — Air Injection System or Automatic Idle Speed circuit and/or motor.

AIV — Air Injection Valve.

ALTERNATING CURRENT (A.C.) — An electric current that is constantly changing polarity from positive to negative and back again.

AMBIENT TEMPERATURE — Temperature of the air surrounding the vehicle being serviced.

AMMETER — An electrical meter used to measure current flow (amperes) in an electrical circuit. An ammeter should be connected in series and current flowing in the circuit to be checked.

AMPERE (AMP) — The unit current flow is measured in. Amperage equals the voltage divided by the resistance.

AMPLITUDE — The maximum rise (or fall) of a voltage signal from 0 volts.

ANALOG — A voltage signal or processing action that is continuously variable relative to the operation being measured or controlled.

ANALOG VOLT-OHMMETER (VOM) — A multi-function meter which measures voltage and resistance. Measurements are made with a D'arsenval meter movement (needle) instead of a digital display.

ANTI-BFV — Anti-Backfire Valve.

ANTI-KNOCK VALUE — The characteristic of gasoline that helps prevent detonation or knocking.

AOD — Automatic Over Drive transmission.

APC — Automatic Performance Control.

APS — Atmospheric Pressure Sensor. Sends information to the computer about pressure in the atmosphere to make correct fuel mixture calculations.

ASCD — Automatic Speed Control Device, often referred to as cruise control.

ASD — Automatic Shut-Down relay driver circuit, fuel pump relay.

ATDC — After Top Dead Center.

ATM — Actuator Test Mode.

ATMOSPHERIC PRESSURE — Normal pressure in the surrounding atmosphere, generated by the weight of the air pressing down from above. At sea level, atmospheric pressure is about 14.7 psi, above zero absolute pressure (100 kPa or 29.92 in hg.) at a temperature of 80°F (26.7°C).

ATS — Air Temperature Sensor.

AUTOMOTIVE EMISSIONS — Gaseous and particulate compounds (hydrocarbons, nitrogen oxides and carbon monoxide) that are emitted from a vehicle's crankcase, exhaust, carburetor and fuel tank.

AUXILIARY AIR REGULATOR — A rotary gate valve which stabilizes idle speed during engine warm-up.

AVOM — Analog Volt/Ohm Meter.

AWG — American Wire Gauge system.

AXOD-E — Electronic Automatic Overdrive transaxle.

AXOD — Automatic Overdrive transaxle.

BAC — Bypass Air Control system.

BACKFIRE — The accidental combustion of gasses in an engine's intake or exhaust manifold.

BACKPRESSURE — The resistance, caused by turbulence and friction, that is created as a gas or liquid is forced through a passage.

BAR — Unit of pressure measurement (1 bar is approximately 14.5 psi).

BARO — Barometric Pressure Sensor. Sends information to the computer about barometric pressure in the atmosphere.

BASE IDLE — Idle rpm determined by throttle switch with idle speed control fully retracted.

BATTERY-HOT — Refers to a circuit that is fed directly from battery voltage circuit. (eg. the starter relay terminal).

BATTERY VOLTAGE — Voltage measured between the two terminals of a battery, usually referring to 12-13 volts.

BCS — Boost Control Solenoid. Receives a voltage signal from the computer to adjust the amount of boost from the turbocharger.

BID — Breakerless Inductive Discharge ignition system.

BOB — Ford Breakout Box. Device which connects in series with the computer and the EEC-IV harness and permits measurements of the processor inputs and outputs. Also used on Mazda Navajo.

BOO — Brake On-Off input to the computer.

BOOST — Turbo charger boost solenoid or its control circuit.

BOTTOM DEAD CENTER (BDC) — The exact bottom of a piston stroke.

BP — Barometric Pressure sensor used to compensate for altitude variations.

BPA — Bypass Air Valve.

BPCSV — Bypass Control Solenoid Valve.

BREAKOUT BOX — A device sometimes call pinout box, which connects in series with the computer and the harness and permits measurements of the processor inputs and outputs.

BTS — Battery Temperature Sensor sends information to the computer about the temperature of the battery.

BTDC — Before Top Dead Center.

BV — Bowl Vent (carburetor).

BVT — Back-pressure Variable Transducer.

BYPASS — A passage inside a throttle body casting that allows air to go around a closed throttle valve.

CALIBRATE — To adjust the scale of any instrument given quantitative measurements.

CAMSHAFT OVERLAP — The period of camshaft rotation in degrees during which both the intake and the exhaust valve are open.

CANISTER PURGE SOLENOID — Electrical solenoid or its control line. Solenoid opens a valve from the fuel vapor canister line to the intake manifold when energized. This controls the flow of vapors between the carburetor bowl vent and the carbon canister.

CANISTER — A container, in a evaporative emission system, that contains charcoal to trap fuel vapors from the fuel system.

CANP — Canister Purge solenoid.

CAPACITANCE — The ability of a condenser (capacitor) to receive and hold an electrical charge.

CAPACITOR — A device which stores an electrical charge.

CAPACITY — The quantity of electricity that can be delivered under specified conditions, as from a battery at a given rate of discharge in amp hours.

CARBON DIOXIDE (CO_2) — One of the many by products of combustion.

CARBON MONOXIDE (CO) — A colorless, odorless gas that is a by product of incomplete combustion of carbon. This gas is poisonous. **NEVER** run any vehicle in a confined space; breathing this gas can quickly prove to be fatal.

CAS — Crank Angle Sensor. Sends information to the computer about the angle of location of the crankshaft.

CATALYST — Special metals (i.e. platinum or palladium) within the catalytic converter that contact the hot exhaust gases and promote more complete combustion of the unburned hydrocarbons and reduction of carbon monoxide.

CATALYTIC CONVERTER — Muffler like assembly placed in the exhaust system that contains a catalyst to change

hydrocarbons and carbon monoxide into water vapor and carbon dioxide.

CBD — Closed Bowl Distributor.

CC — Catalytic Converter.

CCC — Converter Clutch Control solenoid or its circuit.

CCD — Computer Controlled Dwell, used on Ford vehicles.

CCO — Converter Clutch Override output from the computer processor to the transmission.

CCS — Coast Clutch Solenoid or its circuit.

CEC — Computerized Emission Control.

CENTIGRADE — Unit of measuring temperature where water boils at 100° and freezes at 0° at sea level altitude (boiling points will decrease as altitude increases).

CER — Cold Enrichment Rod.

CES — Clutch Engage Switch.

CFC — Coasting Fuel Cut.

CFI — Central Fuel Injection. Another name for throttle body fuel injection.

CHARGE — Any condition where electricity is available. To restore the active materials in a battery cell by electrically reversing the chemical action.

CHECK ENGINE LIGHT — A dash panel light used either to aid in the identification and diagnosis of system problems or to indicate that maintenance is required.

CHECK VALVE — A one way valve which allows a vacuum or gas to flow in one direction only, preventing backflow.

CID — Cylinder Identification sensor or its circuit.

CIRCUIT — The path that electricity travels in route to component and back to power source.

CIS — Continuous Injection System, Bosch K-Jetronic type system.

CKP — Crankshaft Position Sensor.

CLEARANCE VOLUME — The volume of a combustion chamber when the piston is at top dead center.

CLC — Converter Lock-up Clutch.

CLOSED CIRCUIT — A circuit which is uninterrupted from the current source and back to the current source.

CLOSED LOOP — The mode of operation that a system with an oxygen sensor goes into once the engine is sufficiently warmed up. When the system is in closed loop operation, an oxygen sensor monitors the oxygen content of the exhaust gas and sends a varying voltage signal to the control unit, which alters the air/ fuel mixture ratio accordingly.

CMH — Cold Mixture Heater.

CO — Carbon monoxide.

COC — Conventional Oxidation Catalyst.

COLD START INJECTOR — A solenoid type injector installed in the intake plenum that injects extra fuel during cold engine starts. Also referred to as a cold start valve.

COLD START VALVE — See cold start injector.

COMBUSTION CHAMBER — Space left between the cylinder head and the top of the piston at TDC where combustion of the air fuel mixture takes place.

COMPRESSION RATIO — The ratio of maximum engine cylinder volume (when the piston is at the bottom of its stroke) to minimum engine cylinder volume (with the piston at TDC). Thus, the theoretical amount that the air fuel mixture is compressed in the cylinder.

COMPUTER TIMING — The total spark advance in degrees before top dead center. Calculated by the Ford EEC-IV processor, based on sensor input.

COMPUTER — Any device capable of accepting information, comparing, adding, subtracting, multiplying, dividing and integrating this information and then supplying the results of these processes in proper form.

CONDENSER — A device for holding or storing an electric charge.

CONDUCTOR — Any material through which an electrical current can be transmitted easily.

CONTINUITY — Continuous or complete circuit. The type of circuit that can be checked with an ohmmeter.

CONTINUOUS INJECTION SYSTEM (CIS) — A Bosch-developed fuel injection system that injects fuel continuously. Unlike an electronic injection system, which uses a computer to control the pulse width of electronic solenoid injectors, CIS uses hydraulic controls to alter the amount of fuel injected. There are four basic types of CIS: K-Jetronic, K-Jetronic with Lambda (oxygen sensor), KE-Jetronic and KE Motronic.

CONTINUOUS SELF-TEST — A continuous test of the Ford EEC-IV system conducted whenever the vehicle is in operation.

CONTROL MODULE — A transistorized device that processes electrical inputs and produces output signals to control various engine functions. One of several names for a solid state micro computer.

CONTROL PLUNGER — In Bosch CIS, the component inside the fuel distributor that rises and falls with the airflow sensor plate lever, which controls fuel flow to the injectors.

CONTROL PRESSURE REGULATOR — In Bosch CIS, the control pressure regulator is a thermal hydraulic device that alters the control pressure by returning the excess fuel from the control pressure circuit to the fuel tank. The control pressure regulator controls the counter force pressure on top of the control plunger. Also referred to as the warm up regulator.

CONTROL UNIT — An electronic computer that processes electrical inputs and produces electrical outputs to control a series of actuators which alter engine operating conditions. Also referred to as an Electronic Control Assembly (ECA), Electronic Control Module (ECM), Electronic Control Unit (ECU), logic module, or simply, the computer.

CONVENTIONAL THEORY — The flow of current in an electrical circuit in which the direction is from positive to negative.

CORE — The center conductor part or wire of the iron magnetic material or a solenoid magnet.

COUNTERFORCE — The force of the fuel pressure applied to the top of the control plunger to balance the force of the airflow pushing against the sensor plate.

CPS — Crankshaft Position Sensor. Provides the ECU with engine speed and crankshaft angle (position).

CPU — Central Processing Unit.

CTS — Coolant Temperature Sensor.

CURB IDLE — Computer controlled idle rpm.

CURRENT — Amount or intensity of flow of electricity. Measured in amperes.

CURRENT FLOW — The current flow theory which says electricity flows from positive to negative. Also called positive current flow theory.

CVR — Control Vacuum Regulator.

CWM — Cold Weather Modulator.

CYCLE — A complete alternation in an alternating current.

CYL SENSOR — Crankshaft Angle Sensor.

CYLINDER IDENTIFICATION SIGNAL (CID) — A signal generated by the crankshaft timing sensor, that is used to synchronize the ignition coils, due to the fact that some models use a 2 ignition coil pack DIS system.

DAMPENER — A device, sometimes called an accumulator, installed in-line between the fuel pump and the fuel filter on many fuel injection systems, which dampens the pulsations of the fuel pump. The accumulator also maintains residual pressure in the fuel delivery system, even after the engine has been turned off, to prevent vapor lock.

DCL — Data Communications Link is a terminal used to access the computer codes.

DFS — Decel Fuel Shut-off.

DI — Direct Ignition system, each spark plug has its own ignition coil.

DIAGNOSTIC MODE — This operation mode is used by the Engine Control Computer (ECU) and provides historical data to the technician that indicates any malfunctions or discrepancies that have been stored in memory.

DIAPHRAGM — A component which moves a control lever accordingly when supplied with a vacuum signal.

DIELECTRIC SILICONE COMPOUND — Non-conducting silicone grease applied to spark plug wire boots, rotors and connectors to prevent arcing and moisture from entering a connector.

DIESELING — A condition in a gasoline engine in which extreme heat in the combustion chamber continues to ignite fuel after the ignition has been turned off.

DIFFERENTIAL PRESSURE — In Bosch KE-Jetronic systems, the difference between actuator fuel pressure in the lower chambers of the differential pressure valves and the system pressure entering the pressure actuator.

DIGIFANT — Volkswagen collaborated with Bosch to develop this electronic injection system. Digifant is similar to a Motronic system, except that its timing control map is less complicated than the Motronic map. Also, a knock sensor is not used.

DIGIFANT II — A refined version of Volkswagen's Digifant. This system has some control improvements and uses a knock sensor for improved timing control.

DIGITAL — A two level voltage signal or processing function that is either **ON/OFF** or **HIGH/LOW**.

DIGITAL CONTROL — Circuits which handle information by switching the current **ON** and **OFF**.

DIGITAL FUEL INJECTION (DFI) — A General Motors system, similar to earlier electronic fuel injection systems, but with digital microprocessors. Analog inputs from various engine sensors are converted to digital signals before processing. The system is self monitoring and self diagnosing. It also has the capabilities of compensating for failed components and remembering intermittent failures.

DIODE — An electrical device that will allow current to flow in one direction only.

DISPLACEMENT — A measurement of the volume of air displaced by a piston as it moves from the bottom to the top of its stroke. Engine displacement is the piston displacement multiplied by the number of pistons in an engine.

DIRECT CURRENT (D.C.) — An electrical current which flows in only one direction.

DIS — Distributorless Ignition System.

DLC — Data Link Connector.

DOL — Data Output Link. Fuel calculation data from the EEC IV processor to the trip computer.

DRB II — Diagnostic Readout Box tester, for Chrysler system testing. Determines sensor voltage, degrees F, vacuum, rpm and mileage reading with vehicle's engine both on and off.

DRIVEABILITY — The operating characteristics of a vehicle.

DSV — Deceleration Solenoid Valve.

DTC — Diagnostic Trouble Code.

DUAL CATALYTIC CONVERTER — Combines two converters in one shell. Controls NOx, HC and CO. Also called TWC.

DUAL-POINT INJECTION SYSTEM — A computer regulated system, that provides precise air/fuel ratio under all driving conditions. Same as throttle body with 2 injectors.

DUTY CYCLE — Many solenoid-operated metering devices cycle on and off. The duty cycle is a measurement of the amount of time a device is energized or turned on expressed as a percentage of the complete on-off cycle of that device. In other words, the duty cycle is the ratio of the pulse width to the complete cycle width.

DV TW — Delay Valve, 2 Way.

DV — Delay Valve.

DVOM — Digital Volt/Ohm Meter.

DWELL — The amount of time that primary voltage is applied to the ignition coil to energize it. Dwell is also a measurement of the duration of time a component is on, relative to the time it's off. Dwell measurements are expressed in degrees (degrees of crankshaft rotation, for example).

DWELL METER — Measures the amount of time, recorded in degrees, that current passes through a closed switch.

E/L — Electrical Load control unit.

E4OD — Ford Electronic 4 speed Overdrive transmission.

EACV — Electronic Air Control Valve.

ECA — Electronic Control Assembly. Ford's engine controlling computer.

ECCENTRIC — Off center. A shaft lobe which has a center different from that of the shaft.

ECCS — Electronic Concentrated Control System.

ECI — Electronic Control Injection.

ECIT — Electronic Control Ignition Timing.

ECM — Electronic Control Module.

ECS — Emission Control System.

ECT — Engine Coolant Temperature sensor or its circuit, could also be Electronic Control Transmission.

ECU — Electronic Control Unit or Engine Control Unit. Processes input information to trigger the ignition control module.

EDF — Electro-Drive Fan relay or its circuit.

EEC-IV — Electronic Engine Control design 4. A computer controlled system of engine control used on Ford and some Mazda.

EEC — Evaporative Emission Control.

EEGR — Electronic Exhaust Gas Recirculation valve (Sonic).

EET — Electronic Exhaust Gas Recirculation Transducer.

EFC — Electronic Feedback Carburetor. Utilizes an electronic signal, generated by an exhaust gas oxygen sensor to precisely control the air/fuel mixture ratio in the carburetor.

EFC — Electronic Fuel Control.

EFE — Early Fuel Evaporation.

EFI — Electronic Fuel Injection. A computer controlled fuel injection system. On Ford, EFI uses injectors in each intake port and CFI uses an injector in the throttle body.

EGI — Electronic Gasoline Injection.

EGO — Exhaust Gas Oxygen sensor.

EGOG — Exhaust Gas Oxygen Ground.

EGR S/O — Exhaust Gas Recirculation Shut-Off.

EGR — Exhaust Gas Recirculation. System is designed to allow the flow of inert exhaust gases into the combustion chamber to cool combustion and thus reduce nitrous oxides in the exhaust.

EGRC — Exhaust Gas Recirculation Control vacuum solenoid valve or its control circuit.

EGRV — Exhaust Gas Recirculation Vent solenoid valve or its circuit.

EHC — Exhaust Heat Control vacuum solenoid or its circuit.

EICV — Electronic Idle Control Valve.

EIS — Electronic Ignition System which uses a reluctor and a pick up coil along with a module to replace the ignition points and condenser.

ELCD — Evaporative Loss Control Device.

ELECTRON THEORY OF CURRENT FLOW — The current flow theory which says electricity flows from negative to positive.

ELECTRONIC CONTROL UNIT (ECU) — On board computer module, used to control ignition, fuel or other engine function.

ELECTROMAGNETIC — Refers to a device which incorporates both electronic and magnetic principles together in its operation.

EMISSIONS — Unburned parts of the air fuel mixture released in the exhaust. Refers mostly to carbon monoxide (CO), hydrocarbons (HC), and nitrous oxide (NOx).

EMR — Emissions Maintenance Reminder.

EMW — Emission Maintenance Warning.

ENGINE MAPPING — Vehicle operation simulation procedure used to tailor the on-board computer program to a specific engine/ powertrain combination. This program is stored in a PROM or calibration assembly.

ENVIRONMENTAL PROTECTION AGENCY — Federal agency having responsibility for administering congressional programs relating to the protection of the environment.

EPA — Environmental Protection Agency.

EPROM — Erasable Programmable Read Only Memory.

EPS — Engine Position Sensor. Sends information to the computer about the crankshaft's angle of location.

ER — Engine Running. Mode used on some Ford system tests.

ERS — Engine RPM Sensor.

ESA — Electronic Spark Advance.

ESC — Electronic Spark Control.

ESS — Engine Speed Sensor.

EST — Electronic Spark Timing.

ETS — Exhaust Temperature Sensor.

EVAP — Evaporative Emission system.

EVAPORATIVE EMISSION CONTROL (EEC) — A way of controlling HC emissions by collecting fuel vapors from the fuel tank and carburetor fuel bowl vents and directing them through an engines's intake system.

EVP — EGR Valve Position sensor or its circuit.

EVR — EGR Vacuum Regulator or its circuit.

EXHAUST GAS OXYGEN SENSOR — Sensor that changes its voltage output as exhaust gas oxygen content changes as compared to the oxygen content of the atmosphere. The constantly changing electrical signal is used to control fuel mixture.

EXHAUST GAS RECIRCULATION — A procedure where a small amount of exhaust gas is readmitted to the combustion chamber to reduce peak combustion temperatures, thus reducing NOx.

FAHRENHEIT — Unit of measuring temperature where water boils at 212° and freezes at 32° at sea level altitude (boiling points decrease as altitude increases).

FAULT CODES — A series of numbers representing the results of On Board Diagnostic or Vehicle Diagnostics. The computer communicates this service information via the diagnostic connector as a series of timed pulses read either on a scan tool or as flashes of the 'Power Loss or Check Engine' light.

FBC — FeedBack Carburetor — A system of fuel control employing a computer controlled solenoid that varies the carburetor's air/fuel mixture.

FBCA — FeedBack Carburetor Actuator — The computer controlled stepper motor used on Ford feedback carburetors, that varies the air/fuel mixture.

FCS — Fuel Control Solenoid.

FCV — Float Chamber Ventilation system.

FEED CIRCUIT — The power supply or hot wire.

FICB — Fast Idle Cam Breaker.

FIPL — Fuel Injection Pump Lever sensor or its circuit.

FIRING ORDER — The order in which combustion occurs in the cylinders of an engine.

FMEM — Failure Mode Effects Management. Sometimes referred to limp-in mode.

FOM — Fix Operating Mode, limp-in mode.

FOS — Front Oxygen Sensor. Sends information to the computer about the amount of oxygen in the front exhaust manifold.

FPM — Fuel Pump Monitor. A circuit in the Ford EEC system used to monitor fuel pump operation.

FREQUENCY — The number of cycles (complete alterations) of an alternating current per second.

FREQUENCY VALVE — On Bosch CIS, a device that regulates pressure in the lower chamber of the differential-pressure valve, in response to a signal from the Lambda (oxygen) sensor. Also referred to as a Lambda valve or a timing valve.

FTO — Filter Tach Output. An output from the Ford DIS TFI IV module which provides a filtered ignition signal to the processor in order to control dwell.

FTS — Fuel Temperature Sensor.

FUEL ACCUMULATOR — Diaphragm unit which helps maintain residual fuel pressure for hot starting on CIS type fuel system.

FUEL DISTRIBUTOR — The component which feeds fuel to the individual engine cylinders corresponding to the air flow rate metered by the air flow sensor on CIS systems.

FUEL METERING — Control of the amount of fuel that is mixed with engine intake air to form a combustible mixture.

FUEL RAIL — The hollow pipe, tube or manifold that delivers fuel at system pressure to the injectors. The fuel rail also serves as the mounting point for the upper ends of the injectors, and for the damper (if equipped) and the pressure regulator.

FULL LOAD — The load condition of the engine when the throttle is wide open. Full load can occur at any rpm.

FULL LOAD ENRICHMENT — The extra fuel injected during acceleration to enrich the mixture when the throttle is wide open. On some systems, the computer goes open loop during full load enrichment.

FUSIBLE LINK — A device that protects a circuit from damage if a short to ground occurs or if the polarity of the battery or charger is reversed.

GND, GRD or GRND — Ground. Common line leading to the negative side of the battery.

GULP VALVE — A valve used in an air injection system to prevent backfire. During deceleration it redirects air from the air pump to the intake manifold where the air leans out the rich air fuel mixture.

GVW — Gross Vehicle Weight.

HAC — High Altitude Compensation sensor.

HACV — High Altitude Compensation Valve.

HAI — Hot Air Intake.

HALL EFFECT PICK-UP ASSEMBLY — Used to input a signal to the electronic control unit. The system operates on the Hall Effect principle whereby a magnetic field is blocked from the pick-up by a rotating shutter assembly.

HALL EFFECT — A process where current is passed through a small slice of semi-conductor material at the same time as a magnetic field to produce a small voltage in the semi-conductor.

HBV — Heater Blower Voltage input to the ECC-IV processor reflecting heater blower voltage demand.

HC — Hydrocarbons. Any compound composed of hydrogen and carbon, such as petroleum products, that is considered a pollutant.

HCV — Exhaust Heat Control Valve.

HEDF — High-speed Electro-Drive Fan relay or its circuit.

HEGO — Heat Exhaust Gas Oxygen sensor or its circuit.

HERTZ (Hz) — The term meaning the cycles per second.

HIC — Hot Idle Compensator.

HICAS — High Capacity Active Controlled Suspension.

HIGH SPEED SURGE — A sudden increase in engine speed caused by high manifold vacuum pulling in an excess air fuel mixture.

HIGH SWIRL COMBUSTION (HSC) CHAMBER — A combustion chamber in which the intake valve is shrouded or masked to direct the incoming air/fuel charge and create turbulence they will circulate the mixture more evenly and rapidly.

Hg (MERCURY) — A calibration material used as a standard for vacuum measurement.

HLOS — Hardware Limited Operation Strategy. Certain types of computer malfunctions will place the EEC-IV system into HLOS mode. Output commands are replaced with fixed values. Sometimes referred to as limp-in mode.

HT — High Tension.

HYDROCARBON — Any compound composed of carbon and hydrogen, such as petroleum products. Excess amounts are considered undesirable contaminants.

I/O — Input/Output, for computer data transmission.

IAC — Idle Air Control solenoid.

IAS — Inlet Air Solenoid valve or its circuit.

IAT — Intake Air Temperature sensor.

IBP — Integral Back Pressure.

IC — Integrated Circuit.

ICM — Ignition Control Module. Used by Chrysler to supply voltage for spark plug firing.

ICV — Induction Control Valve. Receives a voltage signal from the computer to adjust the air induction into the engine.

IDLE AIR STABILIZATION VALVE — Electronically controlled valve used to maintain idle speed at a predetermined level.

IDLE LIMITER — A device to control minimum and maximum idle fuel richness. The idle limiter is intended to prevent unauthorized persons from making mixture adjustments.

IDLE SPEED STABILIZER — An electronically controlled air bypass around the throttle. Also referred to as an idle speed actuator or a constant idle system.

IDLE TRACKING SWITCH — An input device that sends a signal to the computer to indicate a closed throttle condition.

IDM — Ignition Diagnostics Monitor. A continuous monitor of the ignition input to the EEC-IV processor used to detect intermittent ignition faults.

IG — Ignition.

IGNITER — Term used by Japanese automotive and ignition manufacturers for the electronic control unit or module.

IGNITION COIL — Step-up transformer consisting of a primary and a secondary winding with an iron core. As the current flow in the primary winding stops, the magnetic field collapses across the secondary winding inducing the high secondary voltage. The coil may be oil filled or of an epoxy type design.

ILC — Idle Load Compensation solenoid receives a voltage signal from the computer to adjust the engine idle when the engine is under load.

IMA Sensor — Idle Mixture Adjuster Sensor.

IMPEDANCE — The total opposition a circuit offers to the flow of current. It includes resistance and reactance and is measured in ohms (i.e. 20 megohms.)

IMPELLER — A rotor or rotor blade (vane) used to force a gas or liquid in a certain direction under pressure.

IMS — Inferred Milage Sensor — A circuit using a E-cell which deflates its state with the application of a current. As the vehicle ages, the EEC-IV processor compensates for aging by changing calibration parameters.

INDUCTION — A means of transferring electrical energy in the form of a magnetic field. Principle used in the ignition coil to increase voltage.

INDUCTIVE DISCHARGE IGNITION — A method of igniting the air fuel mixture in an engine cylinder. It is based on the induction of a high voltage in the secondary winding of a coil.

INFINITE READING — A reading on an ohmmeter that indicates an open circuit or infinite reading.

INFINITY — An ohmmeter reading which indicates an open circuit in which no current will flow.

INJECTION VALVE — Same as an injector.

INJECTOR — A solenoid or pressure-operated fuel delivery valve used for fuel injection systems.

INTERCOOLER — An air to air or air to liquid heat exchanger used to lower the temperature of the air/fuel mixture by removing heat from the intake air charge.

INTEGRATED CIRCUIT (IC) — Electronic micro-circuit consisting of a semi-conductor components or elements made using thick-flim or thin-flim technology. Elements are located on a small chip made of a semi-conducting material, greatly reducing the size of the electronic control unit and allowing it to be incorporated within the distributor.

INTERMITTENT — Occurs now and then (not continuously). In electrical circuits, it refers to an occasional open, short, or ground.

IRCM — Integrated Relay Control Module, used on some Ford systems.

ISA — Idle Speed Actuator. Extends or retracts to control engine idle speed and to set throttle stop angle during deceleration.

ISAV — Idle Speed Air Valve

ISC — Idle Speed Control, this could be a computer controlled motor, air bypass valve, or any device used to control idle rpm.

ITS — Idle Tracking Switch. An input device that sends a signal to the control module to indicate throttle position.

JSV — Jet Mixture Solenoid Valve.

JUMPER WIRE — Is used to bypass sections of a circuit. The simplest type is a length of electrical wire with an alligator clip at each end.

KAM — Keep Alive Memory. Battery power memory locations in the computer used to store failure codes and some diagnostic itemmeters.

KAPWR — Keep Alive Power, used to power the KAM circuit of the processor.

KDLH — Kick-Down Low Hold.

KNOCK — A sudden increase in cylinder pressure caused by preignition of some of the air/fuel mixture as the flame front moves out from the spark plug ignition point. Pressure waves in the combustion chamber crash into the piston or cylinder walls. The result is a sound known as knock or pinging. Knock can be caused by using fuel with an octane rating that's too low, overheating, by excessively advanced ignition timing, or by a compression ratio that's been raised by hot carbon deposits on the piston or cylinder head.

KNOCK SENSOR — An input device that responds to spark knock, caused by over advanced ignition timing.

KOEO — Key On/Engine Off.

KOER — Key On/Engine Running.

KS — Knock Sensor. An input device that responds to spark knock caused by excessively advanced ignition timing.

LAMBDA (I) — Expresses the air/fuel ratio in terms of the stoichiometric ratio compared to the oxygen content of the exhaust. At the stoichiometric ratio, when all of the fuel is burned with all of the air in the combustion chamber, the oxygen content of the exhaust is said to be at lambda = 1. If there's an excess of fuel in the exhaust (a shortage of air - rich mixture), then lambda is less than 1.

LEAN MIXTURE — An air/fuel mixture that has excessive oxygen left after all the fuel in the combustion chamber has burned, 1 part fuel to 15 or more parts air.

LEAN SURGE — A change in rpm caused by an extremely lean fuel mixture.

LED — Light Emitting Diode.

LIMP-IN MODE — Is the attempt by the SMEC/SBEC to compensate for the failure of certain components by substituting information from other sources. Used in the Chrysler self diagnostic system.

LOAD — Any electrical device that provides resistance to current flow.

LOBES — The rounded protrusions on a camshaft that force, and govern, the opening of the intake and exhaust valves.

LOGIC PROBE — A simple hand held device used to confirm the operational characteristics of a logic (On/Off) circuit.

LOS — Limited Operation Strategy.

LUS — Lock-Up Solenoid.

M/C — Mixture Control.

M/T — Manual Transmission.

MAF — Mass Airflow sensor. A device used to measure the amount of intake air entering the engine on some fuel injection systems.

MAGNETIC FIELD — The area in which magnetic lines of force exist.

MAGNETIC PICK UP COIL — Coil used in the electronic distributor ignition system to determine exactly when to switch off the coil secondary.

MAP — Manifold Absolute Pressure sensor or its circuit.

MAS — Mixture Adjust Screw.

MAT — Manifold Air Temperature.

MCS — Mixture Control Solenoid. Receives a voltage signal from the computer to adjust the air to fuel mixture (air/fuel ratio).

MCT — Manifold Charge Temperature sensor.

MCV — Mixture Control Valve.

MFI — Multiport Fuel Injection.

MICRON — A unit of length equal to one millionth of a meter, one one-thousandth of a millimeter.

MICROPROCESSOR — A miniature computer on a silicone chip.

MIL — Malfunction Indicator Light. Check engine light.

MILLIAMPERE (mA) — One one-thousandth of one ampere. The current flow to the pressure actuator in KE systems is measured in milliamps.

MLP — Manual (shift) Lever Position sensor or its circuit.

MODE — An operating state i.e. closed loop vs open loop.

MODULE — Electronic control unit, amplifier or igniter of solid state or integrated design which controls the current flow

in the ignition primary circuit based on input from the pick-up coil. When the module opens the primary circuit, the high secondary voltage is induced in the coil.

MONITOR BOX — An optional Ford EEC-IV test device which connects in series with the EEC-IV processor and its harness, and permits measurements in various units of the processor inputs and output.

MPC — Manifold Pressure Controlled.

MPFI — Multi-Point Fuel Injection.

MPS — Motor Position Sensor.

MRL — Maintenance Reminder Light.

MS — Millisecond.

MSD — Multiple Spark Discharge.

NDS — Neutral/Drive Switch.

NGS — Neutral Gear Switch or its circuit.

NITROUS OXIDES (NOx) — A compound formed during the engine's combustion process above 2500° F, when the oxygen combines with nitrogen to form nitrous oxides. This contributes to photochemical smog.

NPS — Neutral Pressure Switch or its circuit.

NTS — Negative Temperature Coefficient Resistor.

OBD — On Board Diagnostics

OCC — Output Cycling Check.

OCT ADJ — Octane Adjust device which modifies ignition spark.

OCT — Octane Switch.

OCTANE RATING — The measurement of the anti-knock value of gasoline.

OHM — The standard unit for measuring the resistance to current flow.

OHMMETER — The electrical meter used to measure the resistance in ohms. Self-powered and must be connected to a voltage free circuit or damage to the ohmmeter will result.

OPEN CIRCUIT — A circuit which does not provide a complete path for the flow of current.

ORIFICE — The calibrated fuel delivery hole at the nozzle end of the fuel injector.

OSC — Output State Check.

OSCILLATING — Moving back and forth with a steady rhythm.

OSCILLOSCOPE — An electric testing device that shows a pattern wave form of an electrical occurrence. Used to test ignition, fuel injection, alternator and other electrical devices.

OVCV — Outer Vent Control Valve.

OVERLAY CARD — A plastic card used for the Ford Breakout or Monitor box to identify connections for each engine tested.

OXYGEN (O₂) SENSOR — Used with the feedback system to sense the presence of oxygen in the exhaust gas and signal the computer which can reference the voltage signal to an air/fuel ratio.

PAIR — Pulsed Air Injection system.

PARALLEL CIRCUIT — A circuit with more than one path for the current to follow.

PART LOAD ENRICHMENT — Extra fuel injected during throttle opening to enrich the mixture during transition. Usually occurs during closed loop operation.

PA SENSOR — Atmospheric Pressure Sensor.

PCV — Positive Crankcase Ventilation. A system that controls the flow of crankshaft vapors into the engine intake manifold where they are burned in combustion rather then being discharged into the atmosphere.

PFE — Pressure Feedback EGR sensor or its circuit.

PGM-FI — Programmed Fuel Injection system.

PGM-IG — Programmed Ignition system.

PHENOMENA — Basis of symptoms; a significant occurrence.

PICK-UP COIL — Inputs signal to the electronic control unit to open the primary circuit. Consists of a fine wire coil mounted around a permanent magnet. As the reluctor's ferrous tooth passes through the magnetic field an alternating current is produced, signaling the electronic control unit. Can operate on the principle of metal detecting, magnetic induction or Hall Effect. Is also referred to as a stator or sensor.

PIP — Profile Ignition Pickup.

PLENUM — A chamber that stabilizes the air/fuel mixture and allows it to rise to a pressure slightly above atmospheric pressure.

PORT INJECTION — A fuel injection system in which the fuel is sprayed by individual injectors into each intake port, upstream of the intake valve.

PORTED VACUUM — The low pressure area (vacuum) just above the throttle in a carburetor.

PORTED VACUUM SWITCH — A temperature actuated switch that changes vacuum connections when the coolant temperature changes.

POSITIVE POLARITY — Also called reverse polarity. An incorrect polarity of the ignition coil connections. Coil voltage is delivered to the spark plugs so that the center electrode of the spark plugs is positively charged and the grounded electrode is negatively charged.

POTENTIOMETER — A variable resistor used to change a voltage signal.

PRC — Pressure Regulator Control solenoid.

PRE-PUMP — In-tank fuel pump.

PRESSURE REGULATOR — A spring loaded diaphragm type pressure relief valve which controls the pressure of fuel delivered to the fuel injector(s) by returning excess fuel to the tank.

PRIMARY CIRCUIT — Is the low voltage side of the ignition system which consists of the ignition switch, ballast resistor or resistance wire, bypass, coil, electronic control unit and pick-up coil as well as the connecting wires and harnesses.

PROFILE IGNITION PICKUP — A hall effect vane switch that furnishes crankshaft position data to the EEC-IV processor.

PROM — Programmable Read Only Memory.

PSP — Power Steering Pressure Switch. The signal is used by a computer to compensate for power steering loads.

PTC HEATER — Positive Temperature Coefficient Heater.

PULSED INJECTION — A system that delivers fuel in intermittent pulses by the opening and closing of solenoid controlled injectors. Also referred to as electronic fuel injection (EFI).

PULSE GENERATOR — Also called a pulse signal generator. Term used by Japanese and German automotive and ignition manufacturers to describe the pick-up and reluctor assembly. Generates an electrical pulse which triggers the electronic control unit or igniter.

PULSE WIDTH — The amount of time the control unit energizes the fuel injectors to spray fuel into the intake manifold, usually measured in milliseconds.

PURGE VALVE — A vacuum operated valve used to draw fuel vapors from a vapor canister.

PVS — Ported Vacuum Switch. A temperature-activated switch that changes vacuum connections when the coolant temperature changes.

QUICK TEST — A functional diagnostic test for Ford EEC-IV system, consisting of test hookup, key on engine off, engine running and continuous self test modes.

RAD — Radiator Temperature Switch.

RAM — Random Access Memory.

RATIO — The proportion of one value divided by another.

RECORDER — A device used to record the electronic signals sent to and from the engine computer. Sometimes referred to as a flight recorder, because it works similar to aircraft recording device; to store what the last functions of the engine computer that where preformed over a 1 minute or some other time period.

REFERENCE VOLTAGE — A constant voltage signal (below battery voltage) applied to a sensor by the computer. The sensor alters the voltage according to engine operating conditions and returns it as a variable input signal to the computer which adjusts the system operation accordingly.

RELAY — A switching device operated by a low current circuit, which controls the opening and closing of another higher current circuit.

RELIEF VALVE — A pressure limiting valve located in the exhaust chamber of the thermactor air pump. Its function is to relieve part of exhaust airflow if pressure exceeds a calibrated value.

RELUCTOR — Also called an armature or trigger wheel. Ferrous metal piece attached to the distributor shaft. Made up of teeth of which the number are the same as the number of engine cylinders. As the reluctor teeth pass through the pick-up magnetic field, an alternating current is generated in the pick-up coil.

RESIDUAL PRESSURE — Pressure remaining in the fuel system after the engine has been shut off.

RESISTOR — Any electrical circuit element that provides resistance in a circuit.

RESISTANCE — The opposition to the flow of current through a circuit or electrical device, and is measured in ohms. Resistance is equal to the voltage divided by the amperage.

RICH MIXTURE — An air/fuel mixture that has more fuel than can burn completely, 1 part fuel to 14 or less parts air.

RMS — Root Mean Square (effective) — The square root average of the squares of the instantaneous amplitudes taken over the duration of the pulse. Example; the wave pattern on a 110vac house receptacle would be 300vac peak-to-peak 300vac divided by 2 times 0.70 equals 105vac RMS.

ROM — Read Only Memory.

RPM — Revolution Per-Minute.

RXD — Receive data line.

SAE — Society of Automotive Engineers.

SAS — Speed Adjusting Screw.

SATURATION — The state of a coil when current flow has reached the design maximum and the magnetic field has reached its maximum strength.

SBEC/SMEC — Single Board Engine Controller/Single Module Engine Controller used on Chrysler vehicles. Both regulate ignition timing, air-fuel ratio, emission control devices, cooling fan, charging system idle speed and speed control.

SBS — Supercharger Bypass Solenoid or its circuit.

SCC — Spark Control Computer.

SCS — Speed Control Solenoid receives a voltage signal from the computer to control the engine idle speed.

SCSV — Slow Cut Solenoid Valve.

SDS — Service Data and Specifications.

SDV — Spark Delay Valve.

SECONDARY — The high voltage side of the ignition system, usually above 20,000 volts. The secondary includes the ignition coil, coil wire, distributor cap and rotor, spark plug wires and spark plugs.

SEFI — Sequential Electronic Fuel Injection. Injectors located in intake ports that inject fuel triggered by ignition timing.

SELF-TEST — One of the 3 subsets of the Ford EEC-IV Quick Test modes.

SENSOR PLATE — A round plate bolted to the air flow sensor lever which floats in the stream of intake air on the CIS type systems.

SENSOR — Also called the pick-up coil or stator. See pick-up coil for definition.

SENSOR TEST MODE — This mode of diagnosis used to read the output signal of a specific sensor when the engine is not running. Specific codes are used to select a specific sensor on the scan tool. The output of this mode is actual output of the selected sensor (temperature, voltage, speed, etc.).

SHORT CIRCUIT — An undesirable connection between a circuit and any other point.

SHUTTER — Also called the vane. Used in a Hall Effect distributor to block the magnetic field from the Hall Effect pickup. The shutter is attached to the rotor and is grounded to the distributor shaft.

SIG RTN — Signal Return circuit for all sensors except HEGO.

SIL — Shift Indicator Light. Indicates to driver optimum time to shift gears.

SIS — Solenoid Idle Stop.

SM — Stepper Motor. Receives a voltage signal from the computer to control engine idle speed.

SMJ — Super Multiple Junction, the main harness connector through the bulkhead for the engine controller circuits.

SOLENOID — A wire coil with a movable core which changes position by means of electromagnetism when current flows through the coil.

SOS — Sub Oxygen Sensor.

SPARK ADVANCE — Causing spark to occur earlier.

SPARK DURATION — The length of time measured in milliseconds the spark is established across the spark plug gap.

SPARK RETARD — Causing less spark advance to be added, resulting in a spark which is introduced later.

SPARK VOLTAGE — The inductive portion of a spark that maintains the spark in the air gap between a spark plug's electrodes. Usually about one quarter of the firing voltage level.

SPFI — Single Point Fuel Injection.

SPI — Single-Point Injection system, same as throttle body injection.

SPOUT — SPark OUTput signal from the EEC-IV processor to the TFI-IV module, used to control amount of timing retard.

SQUARE WAVE — An essentially square or rectangular shaped wave. A wave that alternately assumes 1 to 2 fixed values with a negligible transition time between the 2 values.

SRI — Service Reminder Indicator. The SRI light is used to inform the driver that the vehicle is due for service. Prior to 1993 it was commonly called the Maintenance Reminder Light.

SSI — Solid State Ignition system.

SST — Special Service Tool, or special test equipment to be used for testing or repairs.

STAR — Self Test Automatic Readout (Ford), used to access codes from the EEC-IV processor.

STARTER SAFETY SWITCH — A neutral start switch. It keeps the starting system from operating when a car's transmission is in gear.

STATOR — Another name for a pick-coil. See pick-up coil for definition.

STEPPER MOTOR — Are digital devices actuators, (motors that work with DC current), that move in a fixed amount of increments from the off position.

STI — Self Test Input (Ford) circuit in the EEC-IV systems. Used to place the computer into testing mode.

STO — Self Test Output (Ford) circuit in the EEC-IV systems. Used by the computer to send testing and fault codes to tester.

STOICHIOMETRIC — in general, the precise mixture for the most efficient process of conversion. In automotive use, a ratio of 14.7 parts air to 1 part fuel. This ratio yields the highest combustion efficiency and therefore, the lowest emissions.

STROKE — One complete top to bottom or bottom to top movement of an engine piston.

SUB OXYGEN SENSOR — The second oxygen sensor, (after the catalytic converter), which monitors catalytic converter efficiency.

SWITCHING TRANSISTOR — Used in some electronic ignition systems, it acts as a switch for high current in response to a low voltage signal applied to the base terminal.

T.V. — Throttle Valve.

TA SENSOR — Intake Air Temperature Sensor.

TAB — Thermactor Air Bypass solenoid.

TACH INPUT — An engine rpm signal sent to the computer from the ignition coil primary circuit.

TAD — Thermactor Air Diverter solenoid.

TAS — Throttle Adjust Screw.

TBI — Throttle Body Injection (Fuel).

TCA — Thermostat Controlled Air Cleaner.

TCM — Throttle Control Module.

TCP — Temperature Compensated Accelerator Pump.

TCS — Traction Control System.

TDC — Top Dead Center.

TERMINAL — A connecting point in a electrical circuit, where the circuit can be disconnected or tested.

TES — Thermal Electric Switch.

TEMPERATURE SENSOR — A special type of solid state resistor, known as a thermistor. Used to sense coolant and, on some systems, air temperature also.

TFI — Thick Film Ignition module. Controls the coil and ignition operation on most Ford vehicles.

THERMACTOR AIR CONTROL VALVE — Combines the function of a normally closed air bypass valve and an air diverter valve in one integral valve.

THERMACTOR AIR SYSTEM — The efficiency of the catalytic converter is dependent upon temperature and the chemical makeup of the exhaust gases. These requirements are met by the thermactor air injection system.

THERMISTOR — A device that changes its resistance with temperature.

THERMOSTATIC — Referring to a device that automatically responds to temperature changes in order to activate a switch.

THERMO-TIME SWITCH — A switch which interrupts the electrical circuit of the cold start injector based on temperature and time.

THREE-WAY CATALYST (TWC) — Combines two converters in one shell. Controls NOx, HC and CO. Also called dual catalytic converter.

THROTTLE BODY — The carburetor-like aluminum casting that houses the throttle valve, the idle air bypass (if equipped), the throttle position sensor (TPS), the idle air control (IAC) motor, the throttle linkage and on TBI systems, one or two injectors.

TIMING — Relationship between the spark plug firing and the piston position.

TK or TKS — Throttle Kicker Solenoid. An actuator that moves the throttle linkage to increase idle rpm.

TKS — Throttle Kicker Solenoid. When energized, it supplies manifold vacuum to the throttle kicker actuator, as directed by the computer, to compensate for engine loads. Also called the idle-up system.

TOT — Transmission Oil Temperature sensor.

TP or TPS — Throttle Position Sensor or its circuit. Used to signal computer the position of the throttle plates.

TPI — Tuned Port Injection.

TRANSDUCER — A transducer converts or transduces a form of energy to another. All of the sensors or actuators are transducers.

TRANSFER PUMP — Fuel pump located in the fuel tank, usually used with a 2 pump system.

TRANSISTOR — A semiconductor device that can control an electrical current by varying a smaller base current. This device acts like a mechanical relay with a variable resistor at the points.

TRIGGER WHEEL — See Reluctor for definition.

TTS — Transmission Temperature Switch.

TVS — Temperature Vacuum Switch.

TVSV — Thermostatic Vacuum Switching Valve.

TVV — Thermal Vent Valve.

TW SENSOR — Coolant Temperature Sensor.

TWC — Three-way catalyst, sometimes referred to as a dual catalytic converter. Combines two catalytic converters in one shell to control emissions of NOx, HC and CO.

TWSV — Three Way Solenoid Valve.

TXD — Transmitted data line.

UIM — Universal control unit.

VACUUM ADVANCE — Advances the ignition timing with relation to engine load or computer signals.

VACUUM — A term side to describe a pressure that is less than atmospheric pressure.

VAF — Vane Air-Flow sensor or its circuit.

VAPOR LOCK — A condition which occurs when the fuel becomes so hot that it vaporizes, slowing or stopping fuel flow in the fuel lines.

VARIABLE DWELL — The ignition dwell period varies in distributor degrees at different engine speeds, but remains relatively constant in duration or actual time.

VAT — Vane Air-flow Temperature sensor.

VB VOLTAGE — Battery Voltage.

VBAT — Vehicle Battery voltage.

VCM — Vehicle Condition Monitor.

VCV — Vacuum Control Valve.

VECI LABEL — Vehicle Emission Control Information label, located under the hood.

VENTURI — A restriction in an airflow, such as in a carburetor or TBI, that speeds the airflow and creates a vacuum.

VF VOLTAGE — Battery Voltage.

VIS — Variable Induction System.

VISCOSITY — The tendency of a liquid, such as oil, to resist flowing.

VLC — Vacuum Sensor and Vacuum Line Charging solenoid valve.

VM — Vane Meter.

VOLT — The unit of electrical pressure or electromotive force.

VOLTAGE DROP — The difference in voltage between one point in a circuit and another, usually across a resistance. Voltage drop is measured in parallel with current flowing in the circuit.

VOLTMETER — An electrical meter used to measure voltage in a circuit. Voltmeters must be connected in parallel across the load or circuit.

VOM — Volt/Ohm Meter. Used to measure voltage and resistance.

VOTM — Vacuum Operated Throttle Modulator. Also referred to as throttle kicker or idle-up system.

VPWR — Vehicle Power supply voltage. 10-14 volts DC.

VREF — The reference voltage or power supplied by the computer control unit to some sensors regulated at a specific voltage.

VRS — Variable Reluctance Sensor.

VSC — Vehicle Speed Control sensor or its circuit.

VSS — Vehicle Speed Sensor.

VSV — Vacuum Switching Valve.

VTV — Vacuum Transmitting Valve.

VVC — Variable Voltage Choke.

WARM UP REGULATOR — On Bosch CIS, the original name for the control pressure regulator.

WAC — Wide open throttle Air Conditioning cut-off.

WOT — Wide Open Throttle or Wide Open Throttle switch.